Law and Identity in Colonial South Asia
Parsi Legal Culture, 1772–1947

This book explores the legal culture of the Parsis, or Zoroastrians, an ethnoreligious community unusually invested in the colonial legal system of British India and Burma. Rather than trying to maintain collective autonomy and integrity by avoiding interaction with the state, the Parsis sank deep into the colonial legal system itself. From the late eighteenth century until India's independence in 1947, they became heavy users of colonial law, acting as lawyers, judges, litigants, lobbyists, and legislators. They de-Anglicized the law that governed them and enshrined in law their own distinctive models of the family and community by two routes: frequent intragroup litigation often managed by Parsi legal professionals in the areas of marriage, inheritance, religious trusts, and libel, and the creation of legislation that would become Parsi personal law. Other South Asian communities also turned to law, but none seems to have done so earlier or in more pronounced ways than the Parsis.

Mitra Sharafi is an assistant professor of Law and Legal Studies at the University of Wisconsin – Madison, with an affiliation appointment in History. Her work has appeared in a variety of scholarly journals and has been recognized by the Andrew W. Mellon Foundation, the National Science Foundation, and the Social Science Research Council.

Studies in Legal History

Editors

SARAH BARRINGER GORDON University of Pennsylvania
HOLLY BREWER University of Maryland, College Park
MICHAEL LOBBAN University of London

Michael A. Livingston, *The Fascists and the Jews of Italy: Mussolini's Race Laws, 1938–1943*
Mitra Sharafi, *Law and Identity in Colonial South Asia: Parsi Legal Culture, 1772–1947*

In memory of Douglas W. Buchanan (1951–2007)

Law and Identity in Colonial South Asia
Parsi Legal Culture, 1772–1947

MITRA SHARAFI
University of Wisconsin – Madison

CAMBRIDGE
UNIVERSITY PRESS

32 Avenue of the Americas, New York NY 10013-2473, USA

Cambridge University Press is part of the University of Cambridge.

It furthers the University's mission by disseminating knowledge in the pursuit of education, learning and research at the highest international levels of excellence.

www.cambridge.org
Information on this title: www.cambridge.org/9781107047976

© Mitra Sharafi 2014

This publication is in copyright. Subject to statutory exception and to the provisions of relevant collective licensing agreements, no reproduction of any part may take place without the written permission of Cambridge University Press.

First published 2014

A catalogue record for this publication is available from the British Library

Library of Congress Cataloguing in Publication data
Sharafi, Mitra June, 1974– author.
Law and identity in colonial South Asia : Parsi legal culture,
1772–1947 / Mitra Sharafi, University of Wisconsin – Madison.
pages cm. – (Studies in legal history)
Includes bibliographical references and index.
ISBN 978-1-107-04797-6 (hardback)
1. Parsees – Legal status, laws, etc. – India. – History.   I. Title.
KNS2107.M56.S52 2014
342.5408'73–dc23   2013043748

ISBN 978-1-107-04797-6 Hardback

Cambridge University Press has no responsibility for the persistence or accuracy of URLs for external or third-party internet websites referred to in this publication, and does not guarantee that any content on such websites is, or will remain, accurate or appropriate.

Contents

List of Figures and Map		*page* ix
Acknowledgments		xi
Table of Cases		xvii
A Note on Transliteration, Citation, and Abbreviation		xix
Introduction		1
PART 1. PARSI LEGAL CULTURE		
1	Using Law: Colonial Parsis Go to Court	37
2	Making Law: Two Patterns	84
PART 2. THE CREATION OF PARSI PERSONAL LAW		
3	The Limits of English Law: The Inheritance Acts	127
4	Reconfiguring Male Privilege: The Matrimonial Acts	165
5	The Jury and Intragroup Control: The Parsi Chief Matrimonial Court	193
PART 3. BEYOND PERSONAL LAW		
6	Entrusting the Faith: Religious Trusts and the Parsi Legal Profession	239
7	Pure Parsi: Libel, Race, and Group Membership	274
Conclusion: Law and Identity		313

vii

Appendix: Legislation	317
Glossary	321
Selective Bibliography	325
Index	333

Figures and Map

FIGURES

I.1	Watts's fresco at Lincoln's Inn	*page* 2
I.2	The prophet Zarathustra in Watts's fresco	3
I.3	Crest of D. F. Mulla at Lincoln's Inn	4
I.4	Depiction of Zarathustra, 1912	13
1.1	Mistry family in Burma c.1911	64
1.2	Scene from the *Shah Nameh*, 1912	73
1.3	Independent dastur, 1914	74
2.1	Draft text of 1865 Parsi Acts	92
2.2	Milch-Cow scene with lawyers, 1916	100
2.3	Geese with Gold Mohurs, 1908	101
2.4	Portrait of J. B. Kanga	112
3.1	Advertisement for diamond jewelry in Bombay c.1940s	155
4.1	Portrait of a Parsi woman	169
4.2	Title page from Mansukh's book, 1888	175
4.3	Portrait of a Parsi girl	185
4.4	Portrait of a Parsi boy	186
5.1	Parsi Chief Matrimonial Court (PCMC), 1888	194
5.2	PCMC candidates as dogs with bone, 1916	208
6.1	Parsi Panchayat case as train, 1908	255
6.2	Portrait of D. D. Davar, 1908	256
6.3	Ruling in Parsi General Hospital case, 1907	263
6.4	Muktad ceremonies, 1909	265
6.5	Lawyers as vultures, 1908	271
7.1	P. B. Vachha and two associates c.1909	280
7.2	Parsi woman with *mathabana*, 1910	282

x   *Figures and Map*

7.3   Bella, 1914   286
7.4   "An Inky Sport," 1914   290
7.5   Sir Jamsetjee Jejeebhoy as Shah of Persia, 1925   309

MAP

South Asia and the Indian Ocean littoral in the early
twentieth century, with enlargement of western India   xxiv

Acknowledgments

It has been a great pleasure to have worked with two exceptional editors in writing this book: Michael Lobban, an editor of Cambridge University Press's new "Studies in Legal History" series, and Thomas Green, the outgoing editor of the same series. I feel especially lucky to have caught Tom at the end of his long and illustrious editing career. I thank Lewis Bateman and his colleagues at Cambridge for their professionalism throughout. I owe a huge debt to those who read entire drafts of this book at various stages of its gestation, particularly Hendrik Hartog, Christopher Tomlins, Donald R. Davis Jr., Marc Galanter, Rohit De, H. William Warner, and Lesley Skousen. Thanks are also due to the participants in my 2011 Mellon-sponsored "First Book" workshop at the University of Wisconsin Center for the Humanities, including James C. Oldham, and in my 2010 "Legal History and Religion" workshop, sponsored by the Institute for Legal Studies at the University of Wisconsin Law School. Richard Marshall designed the book's cover and Derek Gottlieb prepared the index. I am fortunate to have worked with both.

I am grateful for the financial support of Sidney Sussex College Cambridge (2005–7); the University of Wisconsin's Law School, Graduate School, Institute for Legal Studies, and Center for the Humanities (2007–13); the National Science Foundation Law and Social Science program (research grant SES-0850581, 2009–11); and the Andrew W. Mellon Foundation Fellowship for Assistant Professors at the Institute for Advanced Study (2011–12).

My research on Parsi legal history began during my doctoral studies in Princeton's History department. I thank my advisers Gyan Prakash and Hendrik Hartog, as well as my committee members Colin Dayan, Robert Tignor, and Michael Laffan. I am especially grateful to Dirk Hartog for his superb mentorship over the past decade. His advice and help have been invaluable not only for me, but also for a rising new generation of legal historians of South Asia. I also thank my teachers and mentors from before and beyond

xi

xii   *Acknowledgments*

Princeton. In addition to my high school debate coach Douglas W. Buchanan (to whose memory this book is dedicated), I am grateful to my other former teachers in my native Canada, particularly John Hannah and D. B. J. Snyder in Penticton; and Faith Wallis and Elizabeth Elbourne in Montreal.

The University of Wisconsin provided me with a most welcoming and stimulating home as an assistant professor. For their ideas and collegiality while they were at UW, I thank Sana Aiyar, Richard Bilder, Nancy Buenger, Preeti Chopra, Shubha Ghosh, Pam Hollenhorst, Phyllis Holman Weisbard, Alexandra Huneeus, Irene Katele, Miranda Johnson, Leonard Kaplan, Kelly Kennington, Karen Koethe, Ada Kuskowski, David Macdonald, Lauren McCarthy, Elizabeth Mertz, Mary Rader, Mark Sidel, Brad Snyder, Susannah Tahk, Stephanie Tai, Felicity Turner, Alan Weisbard, and André Wink. Sumudu Atapattu, Donald R. Davis Jr., James A. Jaffe, and Marc Galanter were especially wonderful colleagues and intellectual kindred spirits who came together to create the UW South Asia Legal Studies Working Group. Howard Erlanger, Kathryn Hendley, and Stewart Macaulay were devoted mentors. I thank them, along with Alta Charo, Meg Gaines, Heinz Klug, Margaret Raymond, and Margaret Speier for their support during difficult times. At UW, I also had the privilege of working with wonderful research assistants. I thank Anita Arenson, Elizabeth Lhost, Amy McGann, Renu Paul, and Lesley Skousen. I have also benefited on a daily basis from the cheerful efficiency of the UW Law Librarians, particularly Lilly Li, Cheryl O'Connor, and Sunil Rao. I could not have produced this book without their help and patience. Thanks are also due to the UW Law School's IT department, especially Darryl Berney. I am grateful to fellow UW South Asianists for help with the transliteration of languages I do not read. For his transliteration of Sanskrit terms in this book, I thank Don Davis. For Punjabi, I thank Izhaarbir Singh Bains. For designing the map in this book, I thank Brian D. Davidson of UW's Cartography Lab.

I am fortunate to have a wonderful group of academic correspondents spread across the globe, many of whom have become dear friends. For their references, insights, and company, I thank Orit Bashkin, Binyamin Blum, Devika Bordia, Nathan Brun, Kathryn Burns-Howard, Arudra Burra, Leia Castañeda, Indrani Chatterjee, Jamsheed Choksy, Raymond Cocks, John Cort, Patricia Crone, Catherine Evans, Mitch Fraas, Sumit Guha, Will Hanley, Kathryn Hansen, Ron Harris, Almut Hintze, Adam Hofri-Winogradow, Anil Kalhan, Sean Killen, Elizabeth Kolsky, Prabha Kotiswaran, Riyad Koya, Jayanth Krishnan, Assaf Likhovski, Maria Macuch, Chandra Mallampalli, Renisa Mawani, Abigail McGowan, Paul McHugh, John McLeod, Rob McQueen, Mary Jane Mossman, Eleanor Newbigin, Mitch Numark, Alexis Pang, Ketaki Pant, Pooja Parmar, Dinyar Patel, Simin and Jehangir Patel, W. Wesley Pue, Kalyani Ramnath, Jeff Redding, Cyrus Schayegh, Kim Lane Scheppele, David Schorr, J. Barton Scott, Prods Oktor Skjærvø, Donald Stadtner, Michael Stausberg, Julie Stephens, Rachel Sturman, Narendra Subramanian, Shabnum Tejani, Stelios Tofaris, Sylvia Vatuk, Yuhan and Leilah Vevaina, and Nurfadzilah Yahaya.

Acknowledgments

xiii

I would especially like to thank Rohit De and Daniel Sheffield for many wonderful exchanges over the years, and for their scholarly generosity. Talking with Rohit has informed most things I have written since 2006, when we first met at Sidney Sussex College. I thank Dan for his transliteration of terms from archaic Persian languages like Avestan and Pahlavi. I owe a special debt of gratitude to John R. Hinnells for his generous mentorship over the past decade. I also thank Daphne Barak-Erez, Ritu Birla, Sarah Barringer Gordon, David Ibbetson, Shai Levy, Oliver Mendelsohn, Werner Menski, John Pincince, and Marika Vicziany for particular insights and research mantras at various stages.

Enormous thanks are due to the staff of the Bombay High Court, particularly U. G. Mukadam and S. P. Mathkar, Additional Prothonotaries and Senior Masters (Original Side), who graciously gave me office space for months at a time; the staff of the Asia, Pacific, and Africa Collections at the British Library; the Privy Council Office, particularly Jackie Lindsey, former head clerk; the Lincoln's Inn Library, especially Frances Bellis; Ursula Sims-Williams at the Ancient India and Iran Trust in Cambridge; and the Highland Council Archives in Inverness, particularly Robert Steward (now retired). I owe special thanks to Ramji Shukla for attending to my research needs with such care and devotion over the past decade at the Bombay High Court.

I presented parts of this book at numerous scholarly meetings and at the invitation of many organizations. These included the American Society for Legal History conferences; the American Bar Foundation; the Ancient India and Iran Trust (Cambridge, UK); the Annual Conference on South Asia (Madison, Wisconsin); the Karachi Zarthosti Banu Mandal; the K. R. Cama Oriental Institute (Mumbai); the Buchmann Faculty of Law, Tel Aviv University; Cambridge University's Centre of South Asian Studies; Duke University; the Law and Social Science Network (LASSNet) conference (Delhi); the Law and Society Association meetings; the Newberry Library; the Princeton Law and Public Affairs program; the Princeton History Department's graduate legal history seminar; the School of Oriental and African Studies; Stanford University; the University of Louisville; the UW Center for South Asia; the UW Law School's Junior Faculty Workshop and Institute for Legal Studies; the Zoroastrian Association of North Texas (ZANT) in Dallas; and the Zoroastrian Association of Houston (ZAH). I am grateful to the organizers and participants at these events for their interest and feedback.

Studying the history of a community as fascinating as the Parsis has been a highlight of my scholarly life to date. Most of all, I thank my hosts in Mumbai, Rustom P. Vachha and Erin R. Broacha. I learned an immense amount from them and their friends while I was staying in their homes. I also thank the many Parsis in Mumbai who shared with me their knowledge of history, law, and religion, including Shirin Bharucha, Muncherji Cama, Roshan Dalvi, Khorshed Gandhy, Pestonji P. Ginwala (now deceased), Pheroza Godrej, Ervad Ramiyar Karanjia, Dara Mehta, Khojeste Mistree and Firoza Punthakey

Mistree, Jehangir Mistry, Nadir Modi, Nawaz Mody, Sohrab E. Morris, Frenie J. Pacca, Homi D. Patel and everyone at the K. R. Cama Oriental Institute, Jehangir and Veera Patel and everyone at *Parsiana*, G. N. Rattansha, Jehangir Sabavala (now deceased), Feroza Seervai (now deceased), Noshir Sethna and everyone at Wadia Ghandy and Co., Jimmy Sidhva, Jerestin and Manek Sidhwa, Soonoo Taraporevala, Darius Udwadia, and Cowas Warden. Beyond Bombay (as Parsis continue to call it), I thank Percy and Pari Kavina, Jamshed Pardivala, Minnie Patel, and Jehangir Vakil in Ahmedabad; Shireen Mahudawala in Bharuch; Fali S. Nariman and Rustom Gae in Delhi; Homi E. Eduljee (now deceased) in Ootacamund; Hutoxy Cowasjee and everyone at the Zarthosti Banu Mandal in Karachi; the Choksy family in Colombo; Jamshed Jee Jee Bhoy in Yangon; Sarosh Zaiwalla, Rusi Dalal, Malcolm Deboo, Sammy Bhiwandiwalla, Rohinten Dady Mazda, Cyrus Todiwala, Blair Southerden, and everyone at the World Zoroastrian Organization and Zoroastrian Trust Funds of Europe in London; Bella Tata in Vancouver; Dolly Dastoor in Montreal; Ratan Vakil, Poras and Pearl Balsara and everyone at ZANT in Dallas; and Aban Rustomji and everyone at ZAH in Houston.

I thank friends who made India feel like a second home: Dinesh and Namrata Singh in Delhi; Tushna Thapliyal in Mumbai; and Rakesh and Angika Basant, as well as Jeemol Unni in Ahmedabad (and, for a time, Mumbai). In Ahmedabad, I also thank my hosts J. V. and Surekhaben Shah; Saloniben Joshi; Nilotpala Gandhi; and everyone else at the AIIS Gujarati program. In Mumbai, I thank Flavia Agnes. In Mahim, James Stevenson and Deepak Sharma rescued me when I found myself in an IT pickle.

For their friendship over the years, I thank Kutlu Akalin, Nicole Albas, Rachel Berger, Nigel DeSouza, Biliana Draganova, Kaveri Gill, Karsten Jedlitschka, Ryan Jordan, Aditi Khanna, Sven Koopmans, Matthew McKernan, Jean Meiring, Volker Menze, Mark Meulenbeld, Clara Oberle, Okeoghene Odudu, Ishita Pande, Lalita du Perron, Shahrzad Pourriahi, Tamara Relis, Hengameh Saberi, Chris Selenta, Debra Shushan, Gibran van Ert, Klaus Veigel, and Farzin Vejdani.

For being such wonderful cousins, I am grateful to the Sixters, namely Shiva, Shireen, Anahita, and Roxanna Guide, as well as Ali and Mohammad Ghaed, Sayed Jovkar, Rod Jowkar and Forough Jokar-Shirazi, Afsun and Mansour Sarai-Moghaddam, and Donna Burrell. In Norway, I thank my sister Pari, Geir Bjarne, my nieces Sunniva and Stella and the entire Listhaug family. I am grateful to my parents in Canada, Ali Ghaed Sharafi and Sylvia Furman, for propelling me toward the scholarly life in ways large and small.

In Madison, I owe a huge debt to my medical team for their superb care during difficult times: Drs. Ahmed Al-Niaimi, Vinai Gondi, Charles Heise, Mark Ritter, and William R. Schelman. I am also grateful to Dr. Kevin Skole in Princeton; and to Liz Allen and Charlie, Kathleen Rothering, Kirsten Norslien and fellow travelers Heidi Jabber, Bridget McCullough, and Peggy Remm for their insights and encouragement.

Acknowledgments

Finally, I thank the incomparable Jean-Luc Thiffeault. I am glad to be married to him for many reasons, but most of all for his kindness, delightful company, sunny disposition, and a sense of humor that is relentless even in the face of adversity.

Core ideas and several images in this book appeared in Mitra Sharafi, *Colonial Parsis and Law: A Cultural History. Government Research Fellowship Lectures, 2009–10* (Mumbai: K. R. Cama Oriental Institute, 2010). I thank the K. R. Cama Oriental Institute for its permission to reproduce these ideas and images here.

Table of Cases

This list covers prominent reported suits between Parsis during the colonial period. It is selective. Cases are listed in order of the first plaintiff's family name. Where the first plaintiff had a Parsi name predating the nineteenth-century adoption of European-style surnames, the case is listed under the first plaintiff's patronymic (i.e., father's first name), which followed the plaintiff's first name. Where the first plaintiff was a Parsi woman, the case appears under her first name if no other name was provided.

Bánáji, Limji Nowroji v. Bápuji Ruttonji Limbuwállá and others ILR 11 Bom 441 (1887)   *page* 58, 62, 258, 264–70

Capadia, Kaikushru Bezonji Nanabhoy v. Shirinbai Bezonji Capadia and others ILR 43 Bom 88 (1919)   58, 105, 144, 170

Cowasji, M. and others v. Bella and another AIR 1919 Lower Burma 56   22–3, 285–9

Cursetjee, Ardaseer v. Perozeboye 6 MIA 348 (1854–7)   172–3

Darukhanawala, Mancherji Hormusji v. Motibai, wife of Mancherji Hormusji Darukhanawala BHC PJ 1894 109   210, 229

Dustoor, Peshotam Hormasji v. Meherba'i ILR 13 Bom 302 (1889)   139, 180, 183–4

Ghandy, Jiwaji Dinshaw and others v. Bomanji Ardeshir Wadia and others 5 Bom LR 655 (1903)   83, 269

Hormusjee, Modee Kaikhooscrow v. Cooverbhaee and others 19 Eng. Rep. 168 (1809–65), reproducing 6 MIA 448 (1854–7)   56, 79, 142–4, 146

Kaikhasru, Era'sha' alias Kharsedji, Minor, by the Guardian Kaikha'sru alias Kha'rsedji Dosa'bhai v. Jerba'i, wife of Ratanji Rastomji ILR 4 Bom 537 (1880)   38, 219

Karkaria, Dinshaw Edalji v. Jehangir Cowasji Mistri ILR 47 Bom 15 (1923)   279–80

xviii   *Table of Cases*

Manekbai, formerly wife of Nadirshaw Jamshedji Vachha and at
  present wife of Rustomji M. Kapadia v. Nadirshaw Jamshedji
  Vachha ILR 60 Bom 868 (1936)   211, 229
Manik-jee, Khoorshed-jee v. Mehrwan-jee Khoorshed-jee and
  Dada-bhaee Khoorshed-jee 18 Eng. Rep. 173 (1809–1865),
  reproducing 1 MIA 431 (1836–7)   143–4
Mistry, Hirabai Jehangir v. Dinshaw Edulji Karkaria ILR 51
  Bom 167 (1927)   280
Mithiba'i v. Limji Nowroji Bana'ji and others; Harrivullubhda's
  Callia'nda's v. Ardasar Fra'mji Moos ILR 5 Bom 506 (1881)   136, 146, 157
Motiwalla, Shapurji Bezonjee v. Dossabhoy Bezonjee
  Motiwalla ILR 30 Bom 359 (1906)   156–7, 242
Petit, Sir Dinsha Manekji, Bart. and others v. Sir Jamsetji
  Jijibhai, Bart., and others ILR 33 Bom. 509
  (1909)   22–3, 31, 33–4, 83, 99, 183, 218, 241–2, 245, 247,
                                    254, 260, 263–4, 268–71, 276, 288–9, 304, 314–15
Ruttunjee, Mihirwanjee v. his brothers Poonjeea Bhaee and Dada
  Bhaee, sons of Ruttunjee Manukjee Paruk 1 Borradaile's
  Reports 141 (1800–20)   144–5
S. (the wife) v. B. (the husband) ILR 16 Bom 639 (1892)   226
Saklat, D. R., A. B. Mehta and others v. J. Hormasjee ILR 7
  Rang 561 (1929)   23, 289
Saklat, D. R. and others v. Bella and another AIR 1920 Lower
  Burma 151   22–3, 285–9
Saklat, D. R. and others v. Bella and one ILR 2 Rang 91
  (1924) or 3 Burma LJ 30 (1924)   22–3, 285–9
Saklat and others v. Bella LR 53 IA 42 (1925–6) or 28
  Bom LR 161 (1926)   22–3, 285–9
Shirinbai, Bai v. Kharshedji Nasarvanji Masalavala ILR
  22 Bom 430 (1898)   139, 184, 209
Tarachand, Jamshedji Cursetjee v. Soonabai and others
  ILR 33 Bom 122 (1909)   58, 62, 170, 250, 260, 264, 266–8, 270
Toddiwala, Erachshaw Dosabhai v. Dinbai, wife of
  Erachshaw Dosabhai Toddiwala ILR 45 Bom 318 (1921)   43, 227–32
Wadia, Navroji Manekji and others v. Dastur Kharsedji
  Mancherji and others ILR 28 Bom 20 (1904)   57, 245–6

A Note on Transliteration, Citation, and Abbreviation

In deciding how to spell Parsi words in English, I have felt torn between a duty of fidelity to the Gujarati, on the one hand, and to the Anglicized usage of the colonial period, on the other. Colonial Parsi elites lived in a bilingual world that cycled constantly between English and Gujarati. Accordingly, I include the proper transliteration of Parsi Gujarati terms the first time they appear, but subsequently use the colonial Anglicized spelling. Where multiple spellings of the same name existed in English (in Roman script), I use the version that most closely reflected the Gujarati (for example, Dinshah rather than Dinsha or Dinshaw). I have adapted a version of the Modern Standard Gujarati transliteration system for Gujarati, representing an anusvar over a nonterminal vowel not as a tilde over the transliterated vowel (e.g., *bãdobast*), but as *ñ* or *m̃* after the vowel (e.g., *bañdobast*). For Persian, I have used the *International Journal of Middle East Studies* transliteration system. Although there is no capitalization in the Indo-Iranian languages transliterated here, I have capitalized transliterated terms to parallel the English. I have relied on the work of other scholars for transliteration of languages I do not read. Translations are my own (Patel and Paymaster included), except where otherwise indicated.

The date following case citation information is the date of the law report volume, not of the filing of the case (reflected in the case number) or of judgment. However, a date preceding citation information reflects the date of judgment. On citation conventions for case law, see my online "Research Guide to Case Law" (accessed on 17 February 2013): http://hosted.law.wisc.edu/wordpress/sharafi/research-guide-to-colonial-south-asian-case-law/

Records from the Bombay High Court (BHC) pertain to Original Side suits, except for Parsi Chief Matrimonial Court (PCMC) suits and where otherwise indicated. Suits fell under the court's Original Civil Jurisdiction (OCJ) when they originated in the city of Bombay, rather than in the *mofussil*. I refer to PCMC suits by giving suit number and year, notebook title, and page reference. Roman numeral references to PCMC notebooks describe separately paginated (or

xix

xx *A Note on Transliteration, Citation, and Abbreviation*

unpaginated) sections within each volume. I have not given the names of the parties to PCMC suits (many held *in camera*) because of my terms of access to these records. Where a PCMC case was reported in the press, however, I have referred to the parties by name. India Office Records, which are held at the British Library, are identifiable by shelfmarks beginning with "IOR/." At the time this research was done, the case records of the Judicial Committee of the Privy Council (JCPC) were housed at the Privy Council Office in London.

In general, I have used colonial spellings of place names in India (e.g., Naosari rather than Navsari). When speaking of postcolonial Bombay, I use the name "Mumbai" in references to the city after its official 1995 name change.

Abbreviations for law reports, journals, legislation, courts, and archives are as follows:

AHR – *American Historical Review*
AI – *Advocate of India*
AIR Lower Burma – *All India Reports Lower Burma*
AIR Oudh – *All India Reports Oudh*
AIR PC – *All India Reports Privy Council*
AIR Rang – *All India Reports Rangoon*
All LJ – *Allahabad Law Journal*
Am. J. Comp. L. – *American Journal of Comparative Law*
Am. J. Leg. Hist. – *American Journal of Legal History*
Am. Jurist Law Mag. – *American Jurist and Law Magazine*
APAC – Asia, Pacific, and Africa Collections [formerly Oriental and India Office Collections (OIOC)], British Library
Austral. J. Asian L.– *Australian Journal of Asian Law*
Beng. LR – *Bengal Law Reports*
BHC – Bombay High Court (Original Side), Mumbai
BHC PJ – Bombay High Court Printed Judgments
Bom. HCt Rep. – *Bombay High Court Reports*
Bom LJ – *Bombay Law Journal*
Bom LR – *Bombay Law Reporter*
BL – British Library
BTJC – *Bombay Times and Journal of Commerce*
Bull. Sch. Orient. Afr. Stud. – *Bulletin of the School of Oriental and African Studies*
Burma LJ – *Burma Law Journal*
Cal LJ – *Calcutta Law Journal*
Cam LJ – *Cambridge Law Journal*
Colum. JL & Soc. Probs. – *Columbia Journal of Law and Social Problems*
Crim. LJ of India – *Criminal Law Journal of India*
CSSH – *Comparative Studies in Society and History*
Eng. Rep. – *English Reports* (England)
EPW – *Economic and Political Weekly* (India)

A Note on Transliteration, Citation, and Abbreviation   xxi

Getty Res. J. – *Getty Research Journal* (US)
HCA – Highland Council Archives (Inverness, Scotland)
Hist. J. – *The Historical Journal*
Hist. Worksh. J – *History Workshop Journal*
HP – *Hindi Punch* (India)
IAQROCR – *Imperial and Asiatic Quarterly Review & Oriental and Colonial Record, new series*
IC – Indian Cases
ICLQ – *International and Comparative Law Quarterly*
IESHR – *Indian Economic and Social History Review*
ILR All – *Indian Law Reports Allahabad series*
ILR Bom – *Indian Law Reports Bombay series*
ILR Cal – *Indian Law Reports Calcutta series*
ILR Mad – *Indian Law Reports Madras series*
ILR Rang – *Indian Law Reports Rangoon series*
Ind. Med. Gaz. – *Indian Medical Gazette*
Indlaw Mum – Indlaw Mumbai
Int. J. Jaina Studies – *International Journal of Jaina Studies*
IOR – India Office Records (British Library)
IPC – Indian Penal Code
IR – *Irish Reports*
IS(A)A – Intestate Succession (Amendment) Act of 1939
JAAS – *Journal of Asian and African Studies*
J. Afr. L. – *Journal of African Law*
J. Anthropol. Soc. Bombay – *Journal of the Anthropological Society of Bombay*
JAOS – *Journal of the American Oriental Society*
JAS – *Journal of Asian Studies*
JBBRAS – *Journal of the Bombay Branch of the Royal Asiatic Society*
J. Brit. Stud.– *Journal of British Studies*
J. Burma Stud. – *Journal of Burma Studies*
JCLIL – *Journal of Comparative Legislation and International Law*
J. Conflict Res. – *Journal of Conflict Research*
JCPC – Judicial Committee of the Privy Council
JIA – *Journal of the Iranian Association*
J. Imperial Commonwealth Hist. – *Journal of Imperial and Commonwealth History*
J. Internat. Assoc. Buddhist Stud. – *Journal of the International Association of Buddhist Studies*
JKRCOI – *Journal of the K. R. Cama Oriental Institute*
J. Law Religion– *Journal of Law and Religion*
J. Legal Stud. – *Journal of Legal Studies*
JLH – *Journal of Legal History*
J. Mod. Hist. – *Journal of Modern History*

J. R. Asiatic Soc. GB Ireland – *Journal of the Royal Asiatic Society of Great Britain and Ireland*
JRAI GB Ireland – *Journal of the Royal Anthropolical Society of Great Britain and Ireland*
J. Royal Asiatic Soc. – *Journal of the Royal Asiatic Society*
JSCL – *Journal of the Society of Comparative* Legislation
J. South Asian Stud. – *Journal of South Asian Studies*
Jura Gentium: J. Philos. Internat. L. Glob. Pol. – *Jura Gentium: Journal of Philosophy of International Law and Global Politics*
J. World Hist. – *Journal of World History*
JAH – *Journal of Asian History*
KH – *Kaiser-i-Hind* (Bombay)
Law Cont. Prob. – *Law and Contemporary Problems*
LQR – *Law Quarterly Review* (England)
LHR – *Law and History Review*
LR – *The Law Reports* (England)
LR IA – *Law Reports Indian Appeals*
LR PC – *Law Reports Privy Council*
LSI – *Law and Social Inquiry*
LSR – *Law and Society Review*
Mad LJ – *Madras Law Journal*
Mad. Rev. – *The Madras Review*
Mah LJ – *Maharashtra Law Journal*
MAS – *Modern Asian Studies*
MG – Musée Guimet (Paris)
MIA – *Moore's Indian Appeals*
MLR – *Modern Law Review* (England)
MSA – Maharashtra State Archives (Mumbai)
N.Y.U. J. Int'l L. & Pol. – *New York University Journal of International Law and Politics*
NYT – *New York Times*
PCMC – Parsi Chief Matrimonial Court of Bombay
PCO – Privy Council Office (London)
PMD(A)A – Parsi Marriage and Divorce (Amendment) Act of 1940
PMDA – Parsi Marriage and Divorce Act of 1865 or 1936
PISA – Parsi Intestate Succession Act of 1865
SAR – *South Asia Research*
S. Cal. Rev. L. Women's Stud. – *Southern California Review of Law and Women's Studies*
SDA – Sudder Dewanny Adawlut
South Asia: J. South Asian Stud. – *South Asia: Journal of South Asian Studies*
Suth. WR – *Sutherland's Weekly Reporter*
TI – *Times of India* (Bombay)
TL – *Times of London*

A Note on Transliteration, Citation, and Abbreviation xxiii

Trav. LJ – *Travancore Law Journal*
U. Toronto LJ – *University of Toronto Law Journal*
Vict. U. Wellington LR – *Victoria University Wellington Law Review*
Virg. LR – *Virginia Law Review*
Wisc. LR – *Wisconsin Law Review*
Wisc. Women's LJ– *Wisconsin Women's Law Journal*
WRTOS – *Weekly Rangoon Times and Overland Summary*
Yale J.L. & Feminism – *Yale Journal of Law and Feminism*
Yale LJ – *Yale Law Journal*

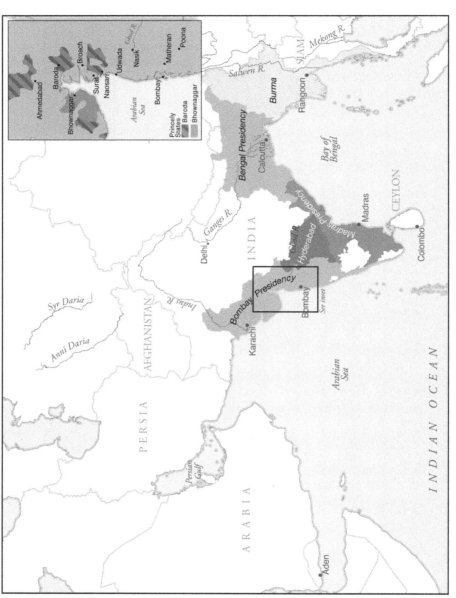

South Asia and the Indian Ocean littoral in the early twentieth century, with enlargement of western India.

Introduction

Between 1852 and 1859, a British artist named George Frederic Watts painted a fresco of world lawgivers in the Great Hall of Lincoln's Inn in London. Watts's idea was to create a semicircle of religious and political figures who had helped create the world's great bodies of law. The diners of Lincoln's Inn – lawmakers of the present and future – would form the other half, closing the circle. Watts's fresco included Justinian, Confucius, Mohammed, Manu, Moses, and the authors of the Magna Carta. With them was a lesser known figure. The ancient Persian prophet Zarathustra sat in a patch of light, swathed in white cloth while leaning against a golden pillar (Figures I.1 and I.2).[1] Watts may have included the Persian prophet as an allusion to Raphael's famous Vatican fresco, *The School of Athens*, which also featured Zarathustra in white and holding a glittering globe. Equally, the prophet may have appeared as part of an all-inclusive survey of world religions. In the same way that one ridge of the Grand Canyon was named the "Zoroaster Temple" (using the Greek version of the prophet's name), Zarathustra's presence may have satisfied the Western comparativist's taste for the exotic.

Watts's inclusion of the figure could not have reflected a careful inquiry into the law-related aspects of the Zoroastrian religion. Had he consulted officials at the India Office circa 1850, he would have been told that Zoroastrianism lacked a real legal tradition. More precisely, colonial administrators would have said that the religion's followers in India, a population of Persian origin called the Parsis, seemed to have no knowledge of any religious law.[2] The fresco was painted at a time when English law governed Parsis in

---

[1] Warwick H. Draper, "The Watts Fresco in Lincoln's Inn," *The Burlington Magazine for Connoisseurs* 9:37 (1906), 8–15; Mark Ockleton, "A Hemicycle of Lawgivers by George Frederic Watts (1817–1904)," in *A Portrait of Lincoln's Inn*, ed. Angela Holdsworth (London: Third Millennium, 2007), 129.

[2] See Chapter 3.

I

FIGURE 1.1. G. F. Watts's "Justice; a Hemi-cycle of Lawgivers" at Lincoln's Inn. Source: Lincoln's Inn photograph. Reproduced with kind permission of the Masters of the Bench of the Honourable Society of Lincoln's Inn.

British India. In this way, Parsis differed from Hindus and Muslims, to whom the colonial courts applied Anglo-Hindu and -Islamic family law, known as personal law. In the words of one British lawyer arguing in court in 1839, "My Lord, *what is Parsi law?* Since I have been in Bombay, I have never been able to discover it; and I have never met any man who had ... I think I may insist, that the Parsis have no law."[3]

Watts was probably familiar with Zarathustra through his friend Henry Thoby Prinseps, a retired East India Company official who had been the Persian secretary to government.[4] For a quarter century, Watts was a guest or lodger at Holland House, the home of Mr. and Mrs. Prinseps. The Kensington property was a favorite meeting place for artists and intellectuals in mid-century

---

[3] "I. Conversion of Two Parsis, and Prosecution of the Rev. John Wilson, D. D., on a Writ of *Habeas Corpus*, before the Supreme Court of Judicature at Bombay. Crown Side," *Oriental Christian Spectator* (June 1839), 255–6; cited in Jesse S. Palsetia, *The Parsis of India: Preservation of Identity in Bombay City* (Leiden: Brill, 2001), 118.

[4] Alexander J. Arbuthnot, "Prinsep, Henry Thoby (1792–1878)," in *Dictionary of National Biography*, ed. Sidney Lee (New York: Macmillan and Co., 1896), XLVI: 392–4.

Introduction

FIGURE I.2. Enlargement of the prophet Zarathustra (in white) from upper right-hand side of Watts's fresco.
Source: Photograph by the author. Reproduced with kind permission of the Masters of the Bench of the Honourable Society of Lincoln's Inn.

London.[5] And although the Parsi legal tradition would have looked thin to most observers in the 1850s, the inclusion of Zarathustra on the fresco was uncannily prescient. Parsis would become some of the British Empire's greatest lawyers and judges. In the century following Watts's creation of the painting, a shifting coterie of Parsi law students dined beneath his fresco at Lincoln's Inn.[6] By the early twentieth century, the Parsi lawyer had become a familiar figure in Bombay and Rangoon, Colombo and Singapore, Aden and Zanzibar, and in London.[7] Soon, there were other signs of the Parsi legal tradition in the Great Hall. Hanging at right angles to the fresco was the crest of Parsi treatise writer and Privy Council judge Dinshah F. Mulla. It bore the words "Vohu Manah," a reference to the Zoroastrian concept of the good mind (meaning good purpose or thinking) in the ancient Persian language of Avestan. It also featured the winged *fravahar* figure (Pahl. *frawahr*), the unofficial symbol of Zoroastrianism (Figure I.3).

---

[5] Allen Staley, *The New Painting of the 1860s: Between the Pre-Raphaelites and the Aesthetic Movement* (New Haven, CT: Yale University Press, 2011), 261.
[6] The Lincoln's Inn admission registers include the names of approximately eighty Parsi students between 1864 and 1947. [*The Records of the Honorable Society of Lincoln's Inn. Vol. II: Admissions from AD 1800 to AD 1893 and Chapel Registers* (London: Lincoln's Inn, 1896); *Vol. III: Admissions from AD 1894 to AD 1956* (London: Lincoln's Inn, 1981).]
[7] For example, see "Parsi Receiver in London," *TI* (19 July 1911), 8; letter from P. B. Mehta (12–13 July 1937) in "File 3/29. Acts and Regulations: The Parsi Marriage and Divorce Ordinance" (30 June 1937–19 May 1939), 10 (IOR/R/20/B/44). See also Chapter 2 at note 201.

FIGURE 1.3. Crest of D. F. Mulla in the Great Hall of Lincoln's Inn.
Source: Photograph by the author. Reproduced with kind permission of the Masters of the Bench of the Honourable Society of Lincoln's Inn.

Study at the Inns of Court was an important pathway for the production of Anglicized elites from across the empire. Arguably, Parsi lawyers were exactly the type of population that Macaulay aspired to create in 1835 – a class South Asian "in blood and color, but English in taste, in opinions, in morals, and in intellect."[8] One could equally assume that the Parsis lost something of

---

[8] Thomas Babington Macaulay, "Minute on Indian Education," in *Archives of Empire. Vol. I: From the East India Company to the Suez Canal*, eds. Mia Carter with Barbara Harlow (Durham, NC: Duke University Press, 2003), 237. See John R. Hinnells, "Parsi Attitudes to Religious Pluralism," in *Modern Indian Responses to Religious Pluralism*, ed. Harold G. Coward (Albany: State University of New York Press, 1987), 205.

Introduction

themselves in assimilating to the ways of the colonizer.[9] Writing on mimicry, Homi Bhabha (himself Parsi) suggests that what colonized mimickers retained was a psychological edge. There was satisfaction in Anglicizing to such a degree that the British were unsettled by it.[10] But there were other rewards, too, including collective institutional ones. In addition to the ironic smiles of colonized subjects who had mastered the colonizers' own game, Parsis gained the tools to de-Anglicize colonial law by working through it. And although a certain degree of Anglicization was a prerequisite for becoming a lawyer in the colonies, fluency in English and a legal education did not necessarily bolster loyalty to British rule. The colonial administration learned this lesson in India through nationalist leaders like Gandhi, Tilak, Jinnah, and Nehru. All were barristers trained at the Inns of Court.[11] Parsi lawyers, too, did not forget their cultural interests simply because they were speaking English and wearing barristers' gowns. On the contrary, their mastery of the form of Anglo legalism enabled them to evacuate its contents.

Scholars like Jerold Auerbach and Mari Matsuda have suggested that adopting common-law legalism eroded the cultural and religious integrity of minorities like Jews and indigenous Hawaiians in the United States.[12] The Parsis were an example to the contrary. Parsi lobbyists, legislators, lawyers, judges, jurists, and litigants de-Anglicized the law that controlled them *by sinking deep into the colonial legal system itself.* Not only did they work in the colonial courts, they also sued each other there. Litigation between Parsis constituted roughly a third of reported lawsuits involving Parsis. It was arguably the most striking type: there was something counterintuitive about taking intragroup disputes to the state courts. Inevitably, these lawsuits produced heartbreak and social loss. But although the microprocess may have been destructive at the personal level, it was part of a macroprocess that was collectively productive: the acquisition of skill in the colonizers' law ways. Through the steady consumption of colonial law, the Parsis built up a knowledge of how legislation and litigation worked. This legal know-how enabled them to create pockets of autonomy right at the heart of state legal institutions. By the end of British rule in 1947, Parsi law consisted of distinctive legal institutions and substantive law, all of which came about

---

[9] See Tanya Luhrmann, *The Good Parsi: The Fate of a Colonial Elite in a Postcolonial Society* (Cambridge, MA: Harvard University Press, 1996), 1–2, 110–16; Dinyar Patel, "Gandhi and the Parsis: A Minority Community's Involvement in the Constructive Program for Swaraj," 4, 6–18, 31, 33 (unpublished paper).

[10] Homi Bhabha, *The Location of Culture* (New York: Routledge, 1994), 85–92.

[11] See Mitra Sharafi, "A New History of Colonial Lawyering: Likhovski and Legal Identities in the British Empire," *LSI* 32:4 (2007), 1060. The same phenomenon occurred elsewhere in the empire. See Assaf Likhovski, *Law and Identity in Mandate Palestine* (Chapel Hill: University of North Carolina Press, 2006), 106.

[12] Jerold Auerbach, *Rabbis and Lawyers: The Journey from Torah to Constitution* (Bloomington: Indiana University Press, 1990); Mari J. Matsuda, "Law and Culture in the District Court of Honolulu, 1844–1845: A Case Study of the Rise of Legal Consciousness," *Am. J. Leg. Hist.* 32 (1988), 16–41.

through Parsi-led initiatives or new professional opportunities exploited by Parsis. The Parsi world of law included special marriage and inheritance legislation applicable to Parsis alone; a jury system of co-religionists for matrimonial cases, a privilege granted to no other population in British India; and a corps of Parsi lawyers and judges who came to manage much of the litigation among Parsis in the colonial courts. In short, the Parsis worked from within and through the colonial state, rather than from outside or against it.

Here was a community unusually invested in colonial law. Through the creation of legislation and litigation in the fields of marriage, inheritance, religious trusts, and libel, Parsi values made their imprint on law. Factions vying for the power to represent their community promoted competing models of Parsi identity. The vision that ultimately captured the power of state law entailed not only a particular picture of the Parsi family, but also a notion of Persianness legitimated through eugenics-inspired claims to racial purity. Law also circled back to shape Parsi identity: being legalistic and litigious became a stereotype of the colonial Parsi. Thus, influence between law and identity flowed in both directions.

This was the Parsi story in a nutshell. The longer version unfolded through three overlapping revelations. The first emerged in answer to the question with which my research began: why did Parsis sue each other so frequently in the colonial courts? The Parsi population of India hovered around 100,000 in the early twentieth century and was most concentrated in Bombay.[13] Even there, they were only 6 percent of the city's population.[14] But they were almost a fifth of the parties in the reported case law.[15] Equally important was the fact that suits between Parsis constituted 5 percent of all reported cases, a rate much higher than one would expect, given their small population.[16] The phenomenon is only interesting if legal pluralism is taken as a basic condition of social life. *Legal pluralism* is the idea that law does not emanate solely from the state, but that a multiplicity of normative orders – of the clan, tribe, religious or ethnic group, club, school, profession, commercial community, and corporation – produce their own rules, enforcement mechanisms, and bodies for dispute resolution among group members.[17] It is only when these non-state legal orders cannot resolve a conflict that most people turn to state law. The Parsis, however, turned to the courts rather than to their own religious or community authorities with striking frequency in disputes among themselves, particularly in religious

---

[13] According to the 1901 census, there were 94,190 Parsis in India. By 1941, the census total was 114,890. [Sapur Faredun Desai, *History of the Bombay Parsi Punchayet, 1860–1960* (Bombay: Trustees of the Bombay Parsi Panchayat, [1977]), 235.]

[14] See Chapter 1 at note 8.

[15] See Chapter 1 at note 9.

[16] See Chapter 1 at 40.

[17] See Sally Engle Merry, "Legal Pluralism," *LSR* 2 (1988), 869–96; Mitra Sharafi, "Justice in Many Rooms since Galanter: De-romanticizing Legal Pluralism through the Cultural Defense," *Law Cont. Prob.* 71 (2008), 139–46.

Introduction

conflicts. Why so? The phenomenon was especially perplexing in South Asia, where community boundaries were tightly sealed and adjudication by religious authorities or *panchayats* (caste or community councils, Guj. *pañcayāt*) was well developed.[18]

The question became even more intriguing because the Parsis were living in a colonized society, British India. Arguably, the conditions of colonial rule made some populations cling to their own internal dispute resolution processes.[19] The Parsis prospered under colonialism; they acted as mercantile middlemen between Indian and British traders during the East India Company's rule and migrated from the Gujarati-speaking hinterland to the new city of Bombay as it morphed from a fishing village into the subcontinent's commercial capital.[20] Could the relative Anglicization of the Parsis have removed any qualms they may have had about taking their intragroup disputes to an outside forum like the colonial courts? There were other similarly placed groups in western India at the time, but the Bohras, Khojas, Marwaris, Jews, and Jains did not exhibit the same litigation pattern as the Parsis.[21]

Taking a step back from the courts brought a second realization. Even before litigation between Parsis began jumping out of every volume of the Bombay law reports, Parsis were organizing themselves into lobby groups. In the 1850s–60s and again in the 1920s–30s, bodies like the Parsi Law Association and the Parsi Central Association drafted legislation that would govern marriage and inheritance among Parsis. They aspired to create a body of personal law for Parsis – community-specific laws governing marriage and inheritance – that would put them on an equal footing with Hindus and Muslims, to whom Anglo-Hindu and -Islamic law had applied since the early period of Company rule. They pushed to have these bills made law, and their campaigns usually succeeded. The reconfiguration of law around a selectively blended amalgam of customary

---

[18] For example, see Amrita Shodhan, *A Question of Community: Religious Groups and Colonial Law* (Calcutta: Samya, 2001), 29–33.

[19] See, for instance, Werner Menski, "Jaina Law as an Unofficial Legal System," in *Studies in Jaina History and Culture: Disputes and Dialogues*, ed. Peter Flügel (London: Routledge, 2006), 428–31.

[20] See Nile Green, *Bombay Islam: The Religious Economy of the Western Indian Ocean, 1840–1915* (Cambridge: Cambridge University Press, 2011), 5.

[21] Ibid. See also Chapter 1 at note 233. There was a handful of intragroup cases among the Jews and Khojas, but they did not compare to the much larger volume of intragroup suits among Parsis. For a sample, see *Advocate General of Bombay, at the relation of Arran Jacob Awaskar and others v. Davi Haim Devaker and two others* ILR 11 Bom. 185 (1887); *Haji Bibi v. His Highness Sir Sultan Mahomed Shah, the Aga Khan* 11 Bom. LR 409 (1909). See also Teena Purohit, *The Aga Khan Case: Religion and Law in Colonial India* (Cambridge, MA: Harvard University Press, 2012); J. C. Masselos, "The Khojas of Bombay: the defining of formal membership criteria during the nineteenth century," in *Caste and Social Stratification among the Muslims*, ed. Imtiaz Ahmad (Delhi: Manohar, 1973), 1–19; Shodhan, *Question*, 82–116. On intragroup litigation among Jains, contrast Menski, "Jaina Law," with John E. Cort, "Jain Identity and the Public Sphere in Nineteenth-Century India," in *Multiplicity and Monoliths: Religious Interactions in India, 18th–20th Centuries*, eds. Vasudha Dalmia and Martin Fuchs (Delhi: Oxford University Press, in press).

8   *Law and Identity in Colonial South Asia: Parsi Legal Culture*

norms and aspirational visions of community life affected everything from the privileges of patriarchs to the intergenerational distribution of wealth. It reflected a readiness to connect law with Parsi social life. Even in a colonial world where political power was anything but representative, the Parsi affinity for colonial legalism reached into legislative processes. Indeed, the absence of representative democracy may have helped. It was by no means clear that minorities fared better under majoritarianism than under colonial rule, particularly when their elites enjoyed close relations with the colonizers.

Another step back revealed a third insight. There was an important account to be written of Parsis in the legal profession. Like Jews in the German-speaking world of the 1930s, Parsis populated the colonial legal professions of western India at disproportionately high rates. In the early twentieth century, between a third and half of Bombay's lawyers and a sixth of its High Court judges were Parsi, even though Parsis constituted just 6 percent of the city's population.[22] Even before the upper ranks of the legal profession were opened up to South Asians from the 1860s on, Parsis were there – as lower ranking legal agents or *vakils* (Pers. *vakīl*) and officials in the colonial courts.[23] These key figures led the earliest efforts to draft legislation for the Parsis and lobbied for its passage. They were also some of the first to send their sons to London to become barristers. These sons returned to Bombay and became advocates in the courts. Eventually, some Parsi lawyers became judges, not only at the Bombay High Court, the highest court in western India, but even in the Judicial Committee of the Privy Council, the final court of appeal for the British Empire. Parsis were also central players in the production of legal texts. They authored treatises on British Indian law and edited law reports and journals, the tools that knitted the far corners of the Anglosphere into an empire of common law.

Together, these pieces of the Parsi law picture – litigation, legislation, and the legal profession – created a rich and fascinating portrait of a minority community that internalized colonial legalism to an extreme degree. The extent to which Parsis turned to the colonial legal system allowed them to make the methods of state law their own. This was particularly so in Bombay, where the Parsi population was concentrated. By the early twentieth century, it was common enough for Parsi solicitors and advocates to represent Parsi litigants suing each other before Parsi judges, all in the mainstream courts of Bombay.[24] These judges were often applying Parsi-drafted legislation or case law from earlier suits between Parsi litigants. The phenomenon of Parsi legalism was an unusual instance of both colonized and minority legal culture. Whereas many colonized and minority populations attempted to protect themselves by avoiding

---

[22] See Chapter 2 at notes 70 and 169.
[23] On *vakils*, see J. D. M. Derrett, "The Administration of Hindu Law by the British," *CSSH* 4:1 (1961), 23 at note 42 and accompanying text.
[24] See Chapter 6 at note 62.

Introduction

interaction with the state, the Parsis did the opposite.[25] Simply by creating the possibility of deciding intragroup disputes in court, the colonial state interfered in South Asian life, altering the power dynamics within families and communities in fundamental ways. The Parsi approach gave a twist to the all-encompassing logic of colonial law. Even within the constraints of Anglo legalism, it was possible to protect community interests to a significant degree by embracing the methods of colonial law and infiltrating its institutions.

LEGAL HISTORY, SOUTH ASIA, AND THE BRITISH EMPIRE

These three revelations about Parsi legal history mirror three areas of research that have remained relatively discrete in South Asian legal history: the history of case law, of legislation, and of the legal profession.[26] In contrast to Anglo-American legal history with its heavy focus on case law, the history of law in South Asia has been dominated by studies of legislation.[27] As the legacy of J. D. M. Derrett has faded, case law has become the neglected stepchild in South Asian legal history.[28] The phenomenon reflects the bifurcated structure of the colonial archive. Records pertaining to the executive and legislative branches of the state are housed in state archives. Comprehensive bodies of court records remain in the law courts. Most historians of South Asia rely on state archives for their staple diet of unpublished materials. These repositories contain the best documentation of the life cycle of bills as they became statutes. But state archives are

---

[25] For example, see Menski, "Jaina Law"; Harold Dick, "Cultural Chasm: 'Mennonite' Lawyers in Western Canada 1900–1939," in *Lawyers and Vampires: Cultural Histories of Legal Professions*, eds. W. Wesley Pue and David Sugarman (Oxford: Hart, 2003), 329–66. See also Werner F. Menski, "Muslim Law in Britain," *JAAS* 62 (2001), 127–63; Latif Taş, "Kurds in the UK: Legal Pluralism and Alternative Dispute Resolution," PhD dissertation (Law), Queen Mary, University of London, 2012; Alvin Esau, "Mennonites and Litigation," unpublished paper (accessed on 8 January 2008): http://www.umanitoba.ca/law/Courses/esau/litigation/mennolitigation.htm.

[26] For a survey of the field until 1990, see Michael R. Anderson, "Classifications and Coercions: Themes in South Asian Legal Studies in the 1980s," *SAR* 10:2 (1990), 158–77.

[27] See R. H. Helmholz and Thomas A. Green, eds., *Juries, Libel and Justice: The Role of English Juries in Seventeenth- and Eighteenth-Century Trials for Libel and Slander: Papers read at a Clark Library Seminar, 28 Feb. 1981* (Los Angeles: William Andrews Clark Memorial Library, 1984), v; Mitra Sharafi, "The Semi-Autonomous Judge in Colonial India: Chivalric Imperialism meets Anglo-Islamic Dower and Divorce Law," *IESHR* 46:1 (2009), 59 at note 7; Rochona Majumdar, *Marriage and Modernity: Family Values in Colonial Bengal* (Durham, NC: Duke University Press, 2009), 168–237. For work that is explicit in its legislative focus, see Perveez Mody, "Love and the Law: Love-Marriage in Delhi," *MAS* 36:1 (2002), 223–56; Elizabeth Kolsky, "Codification and the Rule of Colonial Difference: Criminal Procedure in British India," *LHR* 23:3 (2005), 631–83.

[28] See especially J. D. M. Derrett, *Religion, Law and the State in India* (Delhi: Oxford University Press, 1999). For exceptions, see Rachel Sturman, *The Government of Social Life in Colonial India: Liberalism, Religious Law, and Women's Rights* (Cambridge: Cambridge University Press, 2012); Ashwini Tambe, *Codes of Misconduct: Regulating Prostitution in Law Colonial Bombay* (Minneapolis: University of Minnesota Press, 2009), 79–99; references in Sharafi, "Semi-Autonomous Judge," 59 at note 6.

thin on case law, holding the records of only a tiny fraction of all the cases heard. With few exceptions, these archives only include records of lawsuits that had special relevance to the state – whether because the government was a party to the suit, because the government was approached with reference to a case, or because a case had important political ramifications. To get at case law in all its archival richness, historians of South Asia must look beyond state archives. A galaxy of published case law exists in the libraries of law faculties, the Inns of Court, law firms, and courts. Even more precious are the unpublished case records and judgment notebooks stored in current-day courts themselves. These records are only rarely replicated in state archives and are generally absent from South Asian legal histories.[29] Even the towering figure J. D. M. Derrett failed to use unpublished case records, instead making published law reports the building blocks for his portraits of case law.[30]

Histories of the British Empire often fall prey to what may be called the "codification fallacy" – the idea that where there was no legislation, there was no state law governing a domain of social life.[31] In fact, courts decided many cases on subjects for which legislation was never passed. Their rulings could be just as binding and invasive as statutes would have been. Through the process of reasoning by analogy, lawyers and judges applied principles from cases on related issues – often from jurisdictions across the British Empire.[32] Case law came *before* legislation and *in its absence*. It also came *after* legislation. On occasion, colonial courts pulled against the spirit of a statute, pretending to apply provisions of a colonial statute while quietly unraveling the work of legislators.[33] Yet scholars with a blind spot for the courts imply that areas of social life ungoverned by statute were somehow shielded from interference by the state. In short, case law and its archives deserve a greater role in histories of the British Empire and South Asia. Accordingly, this account of Parsi legal history marries legislation with case law, combining legislative papers from state archives with case records and judgment notebooks from the Judicial Committee of the Privy Council, Bombay High Court, and Parsi Chief Matrimonial Court of Bombay, all of which continue to function as courts today.

---

[29] For an exception, see Arjun Appadurai, *Worship and Conflict under Colonial Rule: A South Indian Case* (Cambridge: Cambridge University Press, 1981), 176–7 at note 41. On locating and using records at Indian courts, see Mitra Sharafi, "Research Guide to Case Law" (accessed on 7 April 2013), available at http://hosted.law.wisc.edu/wordpress/sharafi/research-guide-to-colonial-south-asian-case-law/.

[30] See Derrett, *Religion*.

[31] For example, see Nair, 180–1; Shodhan, *Question*, 73–4; Jon E. Wilson, "Anxieties of Distance: Codification in Early Colonial Bengal," in *An Intellectual History for India*, ed. Shruti Kapila (Cambridge: Cambridge University Press, 2010), 15–16. See also Elsa Goveia, *The West Indian Slave Laws of the Eighteenth Century* (Barbados: Caribbean Universities Press, 1970), 30.

[32] See Mitra Sharafi, "Bella's Case: Parsi Identity and the Law in Colonial Rangoon, Bombay and London, 1887–1925" (PhD Dissertation, Princeton University, 2006), 355–95.

[33] See Sharafi, "Semi-Autonomous Judge."

Introduction   11

The history of the legal profession also deserves greater attention. Like case law, the history of lawyers and judges has been unfortunately neglected in the field of South Asian history. There are histories of the Indian legal profession, but they tend to be inwardly focused examinations of the development of bar councils and professionalization.[34] By contrast, works on the history of substantive law typically pay far too little attention to the lawyers and judges involved in particular areas of law and the ways in which these figures' cultural and religious affiliations informed their legal work. Of special interest is the history of non-European lawyers. A rich body of work exists on the history of lawyers of Anglo stock across the British Empire, mainly in the white settler colonies.[35] But only a handful of studies have linked the work of legal professionals who were neither European nor Protestant to these figures' ethnocultural worlds.[36] As Partha Chatterjee has noted all too briefly, the rise of non-Europeans in the colonial legal professions changed everything.[37]

Much has been written – often with a hagiographical slant – about the role of South Asian lawyers as leaders of the Indian independence movement.[38] A different approach invites us to revisit the colonial experience through the legal work of colonized people. What may be called the "new history of colonial lawyering" sees legal professionals from colonized populations as cultural intermediaries trading in colonial forms of knowledge.[39] These professionals acted as intellectual middlemen and ethnographic translators, reconfiguring colonized cultures for common-law use. Their role in the legal ethnographic project – the production of judicially recognized accounts of the history and value systems of colonized peoples – was an exercise in identity formation.[40] From West Africa to Southeast Asia, lawyers and judges from colonized populations learned the language of imperial law and forged historical and ethnographic accounts of their own and "cousin" communities. African barristers John Mensah Sarbah and Joseph Buaki Danquah worked for the recognition of customary norms of

---

[34] See, for instance, John Paul, *The Legal Profession in Colonial South India* (Bombay: Oxford University Press, 1991).

[35] See Rob McQueen and W. Wesley Pue, eds., *Misplaced Traditions: British Lawyers, Colonial Peoples* (Annandale, Australia: Federation Press, 1999); W. Wesley Pue and David Sugarman, eds., *Lawyers and Vampires: Cultural Histories of Legal Professions* (Oxford: Hart, 2003); Bruce Kercher, *An Unruly Child: A History of Law in Australia* (St Leonards, Australia: Allen and Unwin, 1995), 82–102.

[36] See note 44; along with Pamela Price, "Ideology and Ethnicity under British Imperial Rule: 'Brahmans,' Lawyers and Kin-Caste Rules in Madras Presidency," *MAS* 23:1 (1989), 151–77; Sukanya Banerjee, *Becoming Imperial Citizens: Indians in Late-Victorian Empire* (Durham, NC: Duke University Press, 2010), 116–49.

[37] Partha Chatterjee, *A Princely Impostor? The Strange and University History of the Kumar of Bhawal* (Princeton, NJ: Princeton University Press, 2002), 375–9.

[38] See Sharafi, "A New History," 1060.

[39] See Bernard S. Cohn, *Colonialism and Its Forms of Knowledge: The British in India* (Princeton, NJ: Princeton University Press, 1996).

[40] See Sharafi, "A New History."

the Fanti and Akan of West Africa. Arab lawyer 'Arif al-'Arif packaged Bedouin customary law in a form cognizable to the courts in mandate Palestine. In the Straits Settlements, the Muslim lawyer Bashir Ahmad Mallal reconfigured the tenets of the Ahmadiyya sect for common-law use.[41] And in India, judges such as the orthodox Parsi Dinshah D. Davar and reformist Hindu Narayan G. Chandavarkar handed down judgments in intracommunity religious controversies, discouraging the acceptance of ethnic outsiders into the Parsi community and promoting the cause of Hindu widows, respectively.[42] It is worth tracing connections between the religious and cultural identities of colonized legal professionals and the content of their work. Davar's influence on Parsi litigation is only one example of the type of case studies that abound. From Badruddin Tyabji to Mahadev Govind Ranade, Syed Ameer Ali to Jagmander Lal Jaini, Mohammad Ali Jinnah to Kasinath Trimbak Telang, there are scores of judges and lawyers from South Asia (and elsewhere in the empire) whose lives and work as cultural intermediaries await analysis by legal historians.[43] Scholars such as Rachel Sturman, Alan Guenther, Assaf Likhovski, and Mary Jane Mossman have already begun this valuable work.[44]

ZOROASTRIANISM AND PARSI HISTORY

The Parsis of British India were followers of the ancient Persian religion of Zoroastrianism, a faith over three thousand years old that was structured around the teachings of Zarathustra Spitama (Figure I.4). Zarathustra was also known by the Greek name Zoroaster and by the more Persian name, Zartosht, such that his followers were also known as Zartoshtis. The religion itself was also called *Mazdaism*, a reference to the name of the central deity, Ahura Mazda (Av. *Ahura Mazdā*). At different times, Zarathustra was understood as a reformist poet, priest, philosopher, king, and prophet. He probably lived some time between the late first and mid-second millennium BCE.[45] The earliest Zoroastrians were tribal peoples in central Asia who migrated south into

---

[41] Ibid., 1069, 1073–5.

[42] On Davar, see Chapter 6. On Chandavarkar, see ibid., 1071–2.

[43] See Raymond West, "Mr. Justice Telang," *J. R. Asiatic Soc. GB Ireland* (1894), 105–9; Derrett, *Religion*, 304–5; Alan M. Guenther, "A Colonial Court defines a Muslim," in *Islam in South Asia*, ed. Barbara D. Metcalf (Princeton, NJ: Princeton University Press, 2009), 295; Green, 35; Peter Flügel, "A Short History of Jaina Law," *Int. J. Jaina Studies*, 3:4 (2007), 1–15.

[44] See Sturman, 146–95; Likhovski. By Alan M. Guenther, see "Syed Mahmood and the Transformation of Muslim Law in British India" (PhD dissertation, McGill University, 2004); "A Colonial Court"; "Justice Mahmood and English Education in India," *SAR* 31:1 (2011), 45–67. By Mary Jane Mossman, see *The First Women Lawyers: A Comparative Study of Gender, Law and the Legal Profession* (Oxford: Hart, 2006), 191–237; "Gender and Professionalism in Law: The Challenge of (Women's) Biography," *Windsor Yearbook of Access to Justice* 27 (2009), 19–34.

[45] On the life of Zarathustra, see Stausberg, *Zarathustra*, 20–1.

FIGURE I.4. An early twentieth-century depiction of Zarathustra.
Source: *HP* (8 September 1912), 20. Courtesy of the British Library SV576.

14 *Law and Identity in Colonial South Asia: Parsi Legal Culture*

what is today Iran.[46] The collection of Zoroastrian scriptures known as the *Avesta* (Pahl. *Abestāg*) was first put into writing between the fifth and the tenth centuries CE, after being transmitted orally for as long as two thousand years. These texts were written in the Indo-Iranian languages of Old and Young Avestan, as well as in Old Persian and Middle Persian (or Pahlavi).[47] Zoroastrianism arose during roughly the same period as Judaism, and scholars have suggested that certain tenets of Zoroastrianism had lasting influence on the Judeo-Christian tradition. These doctrines included the concepts of the Day of Judgment, Heaven and Hell, angels and demons, the universal resurrection of the dead, the Apocalypse, and the moralization of light and darkness.[48]

Zoroastrians understood the universe to be the site of a cosmic struggle between Ahura Mazda (also Pahl. *Ohrmazd*), the spirit of order, goodness, truth, fertility, life, and light, and Angra Manyu (Av. *Aŋra Mainiiu*, Pahl. *Ahrimen*), the spirit of evil, deception, darkness, disorder, disease, death, and decay.[49] Lesser deities, as well as teams of angels and demons, allied themselves with these two forces.[50] Ultimately, the forces of good would triumph. The foundation of Zoroastrian ethics was the idea that each human being had a choice in deciding which side to support. Each person therefore bore responsibility for the consequences of his or her actions.[51] Good Zoroastrians had a duty to further the work of Ahura Mazda and his helpers through their good thoughts, good words, and good deeds. Running like a thread between these three ideals was an implied principle of consistency. Good Zoroastrians had a

---

[46] For a general introduction by Prods Oktor Skjærvø, see his *The Spirit of Zoroastrianism* (New Haven, CT: Yale University Press, 2011). For more detailed accounts, see J. Duchesne-Guillemin, *La religion de l'Iran ancien* (Paris: Presses Universitaires de France, 1962); Michael Stausberg, *Die Religion Zarathustras. Geschichte-Gegenwart-Rituale* (Stuttgart: Verlag W. Kohlhammer, 2002). See also Prods Oktor Skjærvø, "Introduction to Zoroastrianism" (2005), 1–68 (accessed on 7 February 2011): http://www.fas.harvard.edu/~iranian/Zoroastrianism/Zoroastrianism1_Intro.pdf.

[47] See Skjærvø, *Spirit of Zoroastrianism*, 2–7; Stausberg, *Zarathustra*, 14–20.

[48] See Mary Boyce, *A History of Zoroastrianism. Vol. 2: Under the Achaemenians* (Leiden: Brill, 1982), 190–5; Mary Boyce and Frantz Grenet, *A History of Zoroastrianism. Vol. 3: Zoroastrianism under Macedonian and Roman Rule* (Leiden: E. J. Brill, 1991), 361–7, 389–95, 401–36; Shaul Shaked, "Zoroastrianism and Judaism," in *A Zoroastrian Tapestry: Art, Religion and Culture*, eds. Pheroza J. Godrej and Firoza Punthakey Mistree (Ahmedabad: Mapin, 2002), 199–209; and Anders Hultgård, "Zoroastrian Influences on Judaism, Christianity and Islam," 101–12 in Michael Stausberg, *Zarathustra and Zoroastrianism* trans. Margret Preisler-Weller (London: Equinox, 2008). By John R. Hinnells, see "Zoroastrian Savior Imagery and its Influence on the New Testament," 45–72; "Zoroastrian Influence on Judaism and Christianity: Some Further Reflections," 73–92; both in John R. Hinnells, *Zoroastrian and Parsi Studies: Selected Works by John R. Hinnells* (Aldershot, UK: Ashgate, 2000). See also Rose, *Zoroastrianism: A Guide*, 60–1.

[49] See Boyce and Grenet, 363–4; Hinnells, "Parsi Attitudes," 198–9.

[50] See Skjærvø, *Spirit of Zoroastrianism*, 14–21; Stausberg, *Zarathustra*, 28–32; Rose, *Zoroastrianism: A Guide*, 28–9.

[51] See Rose, *Zoroastrianism: A Guide*, 35–7, 43.

Introduction

duty to align their thoughts, words, and actions – to be honest and not to dissemble, to have integrity and to keep their promises. Zoroastrian ethics also encouraged moderation and charity, and rejected asceticism.[52] Whether Zoroastrianism was best understood as a dualist or monotheistic religion was a subject of controversy during the colonial period and after.[53] Under Muslim rule in Persia and Christian rule in colonial India, many Zoroastrians favored the view that their religion was monotheistic, appealing to the Abrahamic sensibilities of their rulers.[54]

Religious life centered on ritual, and Zoroastrian priests' main role was to perform religious ceremonies. Zoroastrians were obliged to say daily prayers, to wear the *sudreh* (a ritual undershirt of thin muslin, Guj. *sudreh*) and *kusti* (a cord tied around the waist over the shirt, Guj. *kustī*), to visit the temple and provide priests with offerings of sandalwood for the consecrated fire, and to observe proper religious rites surrounding life-punctuating events like childbirth, initiation into the religion, marriage, and death.[55] They were also obliged to adhere to an elaborate set of purity laws, many of which focused on the avoidance of polluting substances associated with death.[56] Dead matter attracted evil spirits and included not only animal and human corpses, but also saliva, blood, semen, urine, feces, and hair and nails once detached from the body.[57] The purity laws also prohibited the pollution of the elements: fire, water, earth, and air. It was particularly important not to bring fire into contact with polluting substances, including human breath (through smoking or blowing out a flame) or dead bodies (through cremation).[58] Zoroastrian temples were known as "fire temples" because they housed various grades of sacred fire, to be kept burning perpetually.[59] Non-Zoroastrians were prohibited from entering the fire temples, and temple architecture was designed to prevent accidental viewing of the sacred

---

[52] Skjærvø, *Spirit of Zoroastrianism*, 33–4; Rose, *Zoroastrianism: A Guide*, 44, 47.

[53] See Delphine Menant, "Zoroastrianism and the Parsis," *North American Review* (January 1901) in *American Periodicals*, 142–3; Palsetia, *Parsis*, 157–67; Stausberg, *Zarathustra*, 9–10; Rose, *Zoroastrianism: A Guide*, 40–3; Monica M. Ringer, *Pious Citizens: Reforming Zoroastrianism in India and Iran* (Syracuse, NY: Syracuse University Press, 2011), 16–17.

[54] See Mary Boyce, *Zoroastrians: Their Religious Beliefs and Practices* (London: Routledge, 2001), 219–20; Hinnells, "Parsi Attitudes," 206–7; Jenny Rose, *Zoroastrianism: An Introduction* (London: I. B. Tauris, 2011), 220; Ringer, *Pious Citizens*, 113–14.

[55] See J. J. Modi, *The Religious Ceremonies and Customs of the Parsees* (Bombay: Society for the Promotion of Zoroastrian Religious Knowledge and Education, Union Press, 1937); Stausberg, *Zarathustra*, 90. By Rose, see also *Zoroastrianism: An Introduction*, 3–4; *Zoroastrianism: A Guide*, 139, 148.

[56] See Rose, *Zoroastrianism: A Guide*, 128–30; Stausberg, *Zarathustra*, 54–6. Note the absence of major dietary restrictions akin to the concepts of *halāl* or kosher food.

[57] See Modi, *Religious Ceremonies*,49–82, 70–1, 158–68; Jamsheed K. Choksy, *Purity and Pollution in Zoroastrianism: Triumph over Evil* (Austin: University of Texas Press, 1989); Rose, *Zoroastrianism: A Guide*, 38.

[58] See Rose, *Zoroastrianism: A Guide*, 29–32.

[59] See generally ibid., 130–9; Stausberg, *Zarathustra*, 84–5.

fire by outsiders.[60] Traditional death rites consisted of exposing corpses to vultures in the "Towers of Silence" or *dakhmas* (Guj. *dakhmā*), a mode of disposal that held morbid fascination for Western commentators.[61]

Zoroastrianism was the state religion of three dynasties that ruled over the ancient Persian empire: the Achaemenids (550–330 BCE), the Arsacids or Parthians (247 BCE–224 CE), and the Sasanians (224–651 CE).[62] Between the first and second dynasties came conquest by Alexander of Macedon, known among Zoroastrians as Alexander the Destroyer, around 330 BCE.[63] In the seventh century CE, the spread of Islam through Asia ended Sasanian rule. Arab Muslim invaders took advantage of in-fighting within the Persian Empire and effectively defeated the Sasanians during the period between 628 and 642 CE.[64] A huge part of the corpus of Zoroastrian scriptures – as much as 75 percent of Avestan texts – was lost or destroyed following the two invasions of Alexander and the Muslims.[65] In the tenth century, a group of Zoroastrians migrated from Persia to western India.[66] Others followed, particularly in the thirteenth and fourteenth centuries, during the late Abbasid rulers' persecution of Zoroastrians and the Mongol invasions of Persia.[67] The movement of Zoroastrians to India was roughly coeval with the growing conversion of Persians to Islam, a gradual process that took place over centuries.[68] By the fourteenth century, Islam had

---

[60] See Sarosh Wadia, *A Study of Zoroastrian Fire Temples* (Ahmedabad: School of Architecture, Center for Environmental Planning and Technology, 1990), 60, 114.

[61] For example, Charles Dickens, Jr., "A Day at Bombay," *All the Year Round: A Weekly Journal* New Series, 5 (20 May 1871), 585–6; Mark Twain, *Following the Equator: A Journey around the World* (Hartford, CT: American Publishing Company, 1897), 371–7; "A Peep into a Tower of Silence," *The Graphic* (25 August 1923), 278. See generally Rose, *Zoroastrianism: A Guide*, 154–6; Jehangir Barjorji Sanjana, *Ancient Persia and the Parsis. A Comprehensive History of the Parsis and Their Religion from Primeval Times to Present Age* (Bombay: Hosang T. Anklesaria at the Fort Printing Press, 1935), 618–23; Desai, *History*, 217–18. See also 247–8, 316.

[62] See Rose, *Zoroastrianism: An Introduction*, 31–134; Touraj Daryaee, *Sasanian Persia: The Rise and Fall of an Empire* (London: I. B. Tauris, 2008).

[63] See Dosabhai Framji Karaka, *History of the Parsis including their Manners, Customs, Religion and present position* (London: Macmillan, 1884), II: 159; C. Janssen, "At the Banquet of Cultures: Mesopotamia's Heritage in Arabic Times," in *Ideologies as Intercultural Phenomena*, eds. A. Panaino and G. Pettinato (Milan: Univerità di Bologna and IsIAO, 2002), 123–4; Albert de Jong, "Zoroastrianism and the Greeks," in Godrej and Punthakey Mistree, 68–9. Compare Boyce and Grenet, 16–17.

[64] Parvaneh Pourshariati, *Decline and Fall of the Sasanian Empire; The Sasanian-Parthian Confederacy and the Arab Conquest of Iran* (London: I. B. Tauris, 2008), 4–10. For a colonial Parsi account, see Sanjana, *Ancient Persia*, 540–50.

[65] See Karaka, II: 157–64; Desai, *History*, 33; Yuhan Sohrab-Dinshaw Vevaina, "'Enumerating the *Dēn*': Textual Taxonomies, *Cosmological Deixis*, and Numerological Speculations in Zoroastrianism," *History of Religions* 50:2 (2010), 112.

[66] See Boyce, *Zoroastrians*, 166; Rose, *Zoroastrianism: An Introduction*, 190.

[67] Rose, *Zoroastrianism: An Introduction*, 192.

[68] On the persistence of Iranian religious beliefs in the few centuries after the Arab conquest, see Patricia Crone, *The Nativist Prophets of Early Islamic Iran: Rural Revolt and Local Zoroastrianism* (Cambridge: Cambridge University Press, 2012).

Introduction

become the dominant religion in Persia.[69] In the Parsi tradition, the migration to India was a flight from religious persecution. According to archaeological evidence, there had been trade between Persia and Gujarat for centuries before. Zoroastrians may have come to western India in part because they were already familiar with the region through earlier commerce.[70]

A famous anecdote about the Parsis' arrival in India became a founding legend. As the story went, the Parsis received a messenger from the local Hindu ruler, Jadi Rana, shortly after landing in Sanjan on the coast of Gujarat. The messenger handed them a full cup of milk. The raja's message was that his kingdom was already full. The Parsis' representative carefully mixed a spoonful of sugar into the milk, taking care not to make it overflow. His response was that Parsis would not occupy much space or disturb the raja's kingdom. They would only sweeten it.[71] According to popular lore, the Parsis came to an agreement with the raja. He granted them permission to stay if they would adopt certain local customs. Among other things, Parsi women would dress like local women and Parsi men would go unarmed. Parsis were to adopt the local language and hold their weddings at night, as was the local custom.[72] In popular memory, the Parsis also promised not to proselytize. This condition was later held up by orthodox Parsis in defense of their view that converts ought not to be admitted into the community.[73]

In the centuries between their arrival in India and British rule, the Parsi population settled in the part of western India that is today southeast Gujarat. The towns of Surat and Naosari were major Parsi centers, and the village of Udwada was home to the most sacred fire temple in India. During the precolonial period, most Parsis were agriculturalists, artisans (including weavers), and merchants.[74] Parsis developed a dialect of the Gujarati language and ceased to use Persian as a spoken language, although many Persian words were absorbed into Parsi Gujarati.[75] Parsi priests maintained some familiarity with the archaic

---

[69] Rose, *Zoroastrianism: An Introduction*, 162.

[70] Ibid., 191; Rukshana Nanji and Homi Dhalla, "The landing of the Zoroastrians at Sanjan: The archaeological evidence," in *Parsis in India and the Diaspora*, eds. John R. Hinnells and Alan Williams (London: Routledge, 2008), 53; André Wink, *Al-Hind: The Making of the Indo-Islamic World* (Leiden: Brill, 2002), 104–8.

[71] Rose, *Zoroastrianism: A Guide*, 85.

[72] Karaka, I: 34; S. H. Hodivala, "The Kissah-i-Sanjan" in his *Studies in Parsi History* (Bombay: the author, 1920), 102–3.

[73] Witness No. 2 for the Defence: Dastur Dorab Peshotan Sanjana, "Hon. Justice Sir Frank Beaman: Notes in Parsi Panchayat Case Suit No. 689–06 from 7 February 1908 to 13 April 1908," 54 (BHC). See also Desai, *History*, 12; Hodivala, "The Kissah-i-Sanjan," 105.

[74] See Rose, *Zoroastrianism: An Introduction*, 190–7; Sanjana, *Ancient Persia*, 570–3, 575.

[75] See Desai, *History*, 64; Rose, *Zoroastrianism: An Introduction*, 196–7. For dictionaries that include Parsi Gujarati terms from the colonial period, see J. M. Jamasp-Asana and K. E. Kanga, *Pahlavi, Gujarati and English Dictionary* (London: Truebner and Co., 1877–82); L. M. Bengali and H. G. Merchant, *A New Pocket Gujarati into English Dictionary* (Bombay: N. M. Tripathi

Persian languages in which the religious rituals were performed, but most could simply recite prayers without comprehension.[76]

As the British presence gained strength in the eighteenth century, so did the Parsi focus on trade. The Parsis became a community of mercantile middlemen, acting as intermediaries between European and Indian traders.[77] Initially, Surat was the East India Company's leading port in western India. When the Company began to transform Bombay from a fishing village into an even larger port than Surat, Parsis who had worked with the British in Gujarat began migrating south to Bombay, where their prospects soared. In the late eighteenth and early nineteenth centuries, families like the Wadias became famous as shipbuilders for European merchants and the British navy.[78] The Jeejeebhoys and others in the "China trade" made huge fortunes shipping opium from India to China, a trade that was legal at the time in the British Empire and for which the British fought two wars against imperial China.[79] From the later nineteenth century on, these early Parsi fortunes were invested in the industrial development of India. Like the opium trade, textile mills in western India brought huge profits to Parsi "merchant princes."[80] Many of these tycoons built crucial parts of Bombay's infrastructure through philanthropic projects.[81] Companies like Tata and Godrej became leading producers of steel and manufacturers of safes, locks, soap, and

---

and Co., 1899); N.R. Ranina, *A Manual of English-Gujarati Dictionary* (Delhi: Asian Educational Services, 2003; originally published in 1910). See also Daniel Sheffield's guide and cumulative glossary of Parsi Gujarati terms with occasional Persian equivalents (accessed on 13 March 2012): http://www.dansheffield.com/parsi-gujarati-reader/.

[76] Dadabhai Naoroji, *The Parsee Religion* (London: Pearson and Son, 1862), 1–2.

[77] Menant, "Zoroastrianism and the Parsis," 134–5; Sanjana, *Ancient Persia*, 573–6.

[78] Sanjana, *Ancient Persia*, 581–3.

[79] Karaka, II: 245; Thomas Strangman, *Indian Courts and Characters* (London: William Heinemann, 1931), 28; H.D. Darukhanawala, *Parsi Lustre on Indian Soil* (Bombay: G. Claridge and Co., 1939), I: 508–10. See also John R. Hinnells, "Anglo-Parsi Commercial Relations in Bombay Prior to 1847," in his *Zoroastrian and Parsi Studies*, 101–16; John R. Hinnells, *The Zoroastrian Diaspora: Religion and Migration* (Oxford: Oxford University Press, 2005), 159–65; Jesse S. Palsetia, "Merchant Charity and Public Identity Formation in Colonial India: The Case of Jamsetjee Jeejeebhoy," *JAAS* 40:3 (2005), 201; Madhavi Thampi and Shalini Saksena, *China and the Making of Bombay* (Mumbai: K.R. Cama Institute, 2009), 9–68; Rusheed R. Wadia, "Colonial Trade and Parsi Entrepreneurs," in Godrej and Punthakey Mistree, 435–55; David L. White, *Competition and Collaboration: Parsi Merchants and the English East India Company in 18th Century India*. Delhi: Munshiram Manoharlal, 1995. For a fictionalized account, see Amitav Ghosh, *River of Smoke* (New York: Farrar, Straus and Giroux, 2011).

[80] See Sanjana, *Ancient Persia*, 588–9; film, "Merchant Princes of Bombay" (Mumbai: Cinerad Communications, 2004).

[81] See Strangman, 30; Palsetia, "Merchant Charity," 202–3. By John R. Hinnells, see "The Flowering of Zoroastrian Benevolence: Parsi Charities in the 19th and 20th Centuries," 209–40 and "War and Medicine in Zoroastrianism," 280–4, both in his *Zoroastrian and Parsi Studies*. See also Maria Macuch, John R. Hinnells, Mary Boyce, and Shahrokh Shahrokh, "Charitable Foundations," in *Encyclopedia Iranica*, ed. Ehsan Yarshater (London: Routledge and Kegan Paul, 1982–).

Introduction

later, automobiles.[82] Parsis also excelled in the professions, including law and medicine, from the later nineteenth century on.[83] They were key players in the world of Bombay journalism, too, running Gujarati-language newspapers like the *Bombay Samachar* (Guj. *Mumbaī Samācār*) and the *Jam-e-Jamshed* (Guj. *Jāme-Jamśed*) and producing bilingual Anglo-Gujarati publications like the *Kaiser-i-Hind* (Guj. *Kaysare Hind*) and *Hindi Punch* (Guj. *Hiṅdī Pañc*).[84] Western India was home to a large number of small independent states, and Parsis lived and moved between British India and independent princely states like Baroda and Bhownaggar.[85] Some held high government positions in the princely states, including Chief Justice and Prime Minister or *Diwan* (Pers. *Dīvān*).[86]

Most Parsis were staunchly loyal to British rule in the early twentieth century, but a handful of prominent members of the community sided with the nationalist movement. The exiled Bhikhaiji R. Cama (known as Madame Cama) was a leader of the radical extremist strand of the independence movement.[87] Dadabhai Naoroji, Dinshah Wacha, and Pherozeshah Mehta were leaders of the Congress Party in its early constitutional phase (1885–1915), and certain Parsi industrialists allied their commercial enterprises with the Congress movement.[88]

---

[82] See "Memorandum of Sir Shapoorji B. Billimoria" (3 April 1947) in Desai, *History*, 325; Aman Nath and Jay Vithalani, *Horizons: The Tata-India Century 1904–2004* (Mumbai: India Book House, 2004). See in Nawaz B. Mody, ed., *Enduring Legacy: Parsis of the Twentieth Century* (Mumbai: Nawaz B. Mody, 2005), II: R. M. Lala, "Jehangir [J.R.D.] Tata: Global Achiever," 256–65 and B. K. Karanjia, "The Godrej Dynasty: A Household Name," 276–95. See also Chapter 5 at note 131.

[83] See Hinnells, "War and Medicine," 286–8; Mody, *Enduring Legacy*, II.

[84] See Chapter 7 at 278–9.

[85] See Desai, *History*, 159–60; Mitra Sharafi, "The Marital Patchwork of Colonial South Asia: Forum Shopping from Britain to Baroda," *LHR* 28:4 (2010), 979–1009. See map at xxvi.

[86] Dadabhai Naoroji became *Diwan* of Baroda in 1874. See also John R. Hinnells, "Muncherji Bhownagree: Politician and Zoroastrian" in his *Zoroastrian and Parsi Studies*, 309; Darukhanawala, *Parsi Lustre*, I: 310–1, 331.

[87] See Rozina Visram, *Asians in Britain: 400 Years of History* (London: Pluto, 2002), 359; B. D. Yadav and S. R. Bakshi, *Indian Freedom Fighters (Series 31) Struggle for Independence: Madam Bhikhaiji Cama* (Delhi: Anmol Publications, 1991). Several of Madame Cama's letters appear among the papers of Delphine Menant at the Musée Guimet, Paris.

[88] See John R. McLane, *Indian Nationalism and the Early Congress* (Princeton, NJ: Princeton University Press, 1977); Palsetia, *Parsis*, 299–317; Adi H. Doctor, "Parsis and the Spirit of Indian Nationalism," in Godrej and Punthakey Mistree, 493–507. For writings, see Dadabhai Naoroji, *Poverty and Un-British Rule in India* (London: Swan Sonnenshein, 1901); C. L. Parekh, ed., *Essays, Speeches, Addresses and Writings (on Indian Politics) of the Honorable Dadabhai Naoroji* (Bombay: Caxton Printing Works, 1887); R. P. Patwardhan, ed., *Dadabhai Naoroji Correspondence* (Bombay: Allied Publishers, 1977); *Speeches and Writings of Dadabhai Naoroji* (Madras: Natesan, [1917]); C. Y. Chintamini, ed., *Speeches and Writings of the Hon. Sir Pherozeshah M. Mehta* (Allahabad: The Indian Press, 1905); D. E. Wacha, *Shells from the Sands of Bombay, being my Recollections and Reminiscences – 1860–1875* (Bombay: Anklesaria, 1920); *Speeches and Writings of Sir Dinshaw Edulji Wacha* (Madras: Natesan, 1920). For

20   *Law and Identity in Colonial South Asia: Parsi Legal Culture*

British-Parsi interaction changed the way Parsis thought about their religion. From the eighteenth until the mid-nineteenth century, a wave of European Orientalist scholars took an interest in Zoroastrianism. Adding to a handful of earlier European travel accounts on Zoroastrianism in Persia and India, figures such as Abraham-Hyacinthe Anquetil-Duperron, Martin Haug, James Darmesteter, Friedrich Spiegel, J. H. Moulton, A. V. Williams Jackson, and others acquainted Western audiences with Zoroastrianism through their translations of religious texts, dictionaries of archaic Persian languages, and studies of the religion.[89] European missionaries started coming to India after the East India Company's ban on missionary activity was lifted in 1813. They, too, took an interest in the religious traditions of western India, although with a different purpose: to discredit South Asian belief systems in order to win converts to Christianity. A Scottish minister named John Wilson published scathing attacks on a number of the religious traditions in Bombay, including Jainism and Zoroastrianism.[90] In 1839, two Parsi boys attending a school he ran became Christian, causing outrage among Parsis.[91] In reaction to this episode, Parsi philanthropists started funding charitable efforts to better educate Zoroastrians, including priests, in their own religious traditions. The Wilson episode gave rise to new efforts among Parsis to defend Zoroastrianism using the tools of Western scholarship.[92] Parsis had a highly developed notion of religious privacy, restricting physical access to rituals and temples. But there was little sense of informational secrecy, particularly by the late nineteenth century. One necessary precondition for religious litigation was the willingness of Parsis to describe and discuss Zoroastrian rites with non-Parsis. The intellectual history of Western writings on Zoroastrianism and Parsi rejoinders facilitated these courtroom discussions.[93]

---

biographies, see R. P. Masani, *Dadabhai Naoroji: The Grand Old Man of India* (London: George Allen and Unwin, 1939); Omar Ralph, *Naoroji: The First Asian MP* (St. John's, Antigua: Hansib, 1977); Thrity D. Patel, "Sir Pherozeshah Mehta: India's Legendary Legal Luminary," in *Pherozeshah Mehta: Maker of Modern India*, ed. Nawaz Mody (Bombay: Allied, 1997), 185–206; Homi Mody, *Pherozeshah Mehta* (Delhi: Ministry of Information and Broadcasting, 1967); Govind Talwalkar, "Sir Dinshaw Edulji Wacha: Gentleman Politician," 60–75 in Mody, *Enduring Legacy*, I. See also the short biographies published by the Madras-based publisher, Natesan: *Sir Pherozeshah Mehta: A Sketch of His Life and Career* [1916]; *Dadabhai Naoroji: A Sketch of his Life and Career* [1920]; *Dinshaw Edulji Wacha: His Life and Labors* [1920].

[89] See Mary Boyce, *Zoroastrians: Their Religious Beliefs and Practices* (London: Routledge and Kegan Paul, 1987), 194–5, 202–4; Nora Kathleen Firby, *European Travellers and their Perceptions of Zoroastrians in the Seventeenth and Eighteenth Centuries* (Berlin: Verlag von Dietrich Reimer, 1988); John R. Hinnells, "British Accounts of Parsi Religion" in his *Zoroastrian and Parsi Studies*, 117–40; Hinnells, "Parsi Attitudes," 205–7; Stausberg, *Die Religion*, II: 99–104; Rose, *Zoroastrianism: An Introduction*, 175–80, 207–8; Ringer, *Pious Citizens*, 92–109.

[90] See Rose, *Zoroastrianism: An Introduction*, 204–7; Green, 27–8; Mitch Numark, "Scottish Missionaries, 'Jainism,' and the Jains of Colonial Bombay," 40th Annual Conference on South Asia (Madison, 21 October 2011).

[91] Karaka, II: 291–5; Palsetia, *Parsis*, 105–27; Boyce, *Zoroastrians*, 197–9; Ringer, *Pious Citizens*, 52–70.

[92] Hinnells, "Parsi Attitudes," 204–9; Boyce, *Zoroastrians*, 201–2; Green, 32–3.

[93] See Ringer, *Pious Citizens*, 47–141.

Introduction

The Parsis who shaped their community's legal history in the colonial era came from a particular subset of the population. They were almost exclusively affluent senior men who claimed to represent the group as a whole, but whose special interests and visions for the Parsi community dominated.[94] The Parsi heartland remained in the *mofussil* (Pers. *mafaṣal*), the region of Bombay Presidency outside of Bombay City. Even so, the rise of Parsi economic might in Bombay enabled Parsi elites in the city to dominate their *mofussil* counterparts on community issues, particularly from the mid-nineteenth century on. For the century preceding that point, the contest for intracommunity control had been a tug-of-war between Bombay and the *mofussil*. The *mofussil* was generally the home of greater conservatism, and conflicts between orthodox and reformist Parsis typically divided Bombay and the *mofussil*, often on gender issues such as women's education and inheritance rights.[95]

From the later nineteenth century on, Bombay became the clear seat of control within the Parsi community. The key power struggles were now among Bombay Parsis, and these turned on religious controversies rather than explicitly gender-based ones. Orthodox Parsis wanted adherence to strict and elaborate versions of Zoroastrian ritual and a more exclusive principle of group membership. Reformists, by contrast, favored a more flexible approach that accommodated the conditions of late colonial modernity. They ridiculed the orthodox in the pages of *Hindi Punch* through the figure of "Mr. Best-Orthodox," a backward and bigoted figure with a hooked nose who delighted in causing conflict.[96] These self-declared factions clashed on a large array of issues, including the reform of the Zoroastrian calendar (affecting the date of the Zoroastrian New Year); the simplification of funeral and death commemoration ceremonies; the relaxation of rules pertaining to *barashnum* (Pah. *baršnūm*), the highest state of ritual purity that made priestly travel difficult; the curtailment of expenditure on collective religious feasts or *ghambars* (Guj. *ghāhaṁbār*) and on ritual offerings of sandalwood to the consecrated fire; the translation of Avestan prayer books into Gujarati; and the possibility of allowing cremation as an alternative to consignment of the dead to the *dakhmas*.[97] Most hotly contested was the question of whether ethnic outsiders or *juddins* (Guj. *juddīn*) could be admitted into the Parsi Zoroastrian community. Reformists were in favor, wanting *juddins* – often the European wives of wealthy Parsi men – to be allowed to undergo the initiation ceremony known as the *navjote* (Guj. *navjot*) and to

---

[94] On the intracommunity influence of elite Parsi families in Surat, see Douglas E. Haynes, *Rhetoric and Ritual in Colonial India: The Shaping of a Public Culture in Surat City, 1852–1928* (Berkeley: University of California Press, 1991), 79.

[95] Naoroji, *Parsee Religion*, 2.

[96] For example, see in *HP*: "Lecturing Antics" (8 September 1912), 29; "Open Incendiarism" (12 April 1914), 10; "Well-a Done!' (1 November 1925), 12. See also Figure 7.4.

[97] In the *TI*, see "'Jame' Defamation Case" (26 April 1915), 12; (27 April 1915), 9; (29 April 1915), 5; (16 June 1915), 5. See untitled, *HP* (24 November 1918), 23; Desai, *History*, 91–5; Boyce, *Zoroastrians*, 212–14, 221–2. See also Ringer, *Pious Citizens*, 71–90.

become Zoroastrian religiously. They also wanted converts to be entitled to benefit from the properties and funds of Parsi community organizations, including the Bombay Parsi Panchayat. Orthodox Parsis were adamantly opposed to both ideas on economic and racial grounds. If ethnic outsiders were allowed to convert and receive Parsi charitable funds, the orthodox camp predicted that large numbers of India's lower castes would do so, depleting the community's wealth. Furthermore, converts of any ethnicity would dilute Parsi racial purity if they married Parsis, an idea that gained traction with the rise of Parsi eugenics in the early twentieth century.

Two cases brought the *juddin* controversy into the colonial courtroom. *Petit v. Jijibhai* was the single most famous Parsi lawsuit of the colonial period.[98] In 1903, a French woman named Suzanne Brière married R. D. Tata of the Tata corporate dynasty in a Zoroastrian marriage ceremony. She had allegedly been initiated into the Zoroastrian religion shortly before her wedding. Orthodox Parsis opposed the French Mrs. Tata's ability to benefit from the Parsi Panchayat's funds or properties, claiming that whether or not she could become Zoroastrian, she could not become a Parsi, and that Parsi trusts were established for the benefit of people who were ethnically Parsi *and* religiously Zoroastrian. The first Parsi judge of the Bombay High Court, the orthodox Parsi D. D. Davar, ruled against the French Mrs. Tata. Davar made a new semantic distinction between terms previously used interchangeably: *Parsi* and *Zoroastrian*. For him, *Zoroastrian* was a religious label; *Parsi* was an ethnic or racial one. Because most community trusts were endowed for the benefit of Parsis, Davar asserted that they were created for the benefit of an ethnically distinct group. Being Parsi, in other words, was very much about race – and not just about following the Zoroastrian religion.

In the wake of this case came a sequel a decade later from the tiny Parsi community of Rangoon in Burma. In *Saklat v. Bella*, an allegedly Indian orphan named Bella was taken in at birth and raised as a Zoroastrian by a Parsi

---

[98] *Sir Dinsha Manekji Petit, Bart. and others v. Sir Jamsetji Jijibhai, Bart., and others* ILR 33 Bom. 509 (1909) and case papers: Suit No. 689 of 1906 (BHC); also reproduced in unabridged form in *The Parsi Panchayat Case in the High Court of Judicature at Bombay (Suit No.689 of 1906). Sir Dinsha Manockji Petit and others, plaintiffs v. Sir Jamsetjee Jeejeebhoy and others, defendants. Judgment of the Honourable Mr. Justice Davar delivered Friday, 27 November 1908; and Judgment of the Honourable Mr. Justice Beaman delivered Friday, 27 November 1908* (Bombay: n.p., n.d.) and in *Judgments*: Petit v. Jeejeebhoy 1908 and *Saklat v. Bella* 1925 (Mumbai: Parsiana Publications, 2005). See also "Hon. Justice F. C. O. Beaman. Notes in Parsi Panchayat Case Suit No. 698–06 (7 February 1908–13 April 1908)" (BHC). For scholarly accounts, see Mitra Sharafi, "Judging Conversion to Zoroastrianism: Behind the Scenes of the Parsi Panchayat Case (1908)," in *Parsis in India and the Diaspora*, eds. John R. Hinnells and Alan Williams (London: Routledge Curzon, 2007), 159–80; Desai, *History*, 17–28; Hinnells, *Zoroastrian Diaspora*, 118–20; Palsetia; *Parsis of India*, 228–51; Michael Stausberg, *Die Religion*, II: 53–7; Rashna Writer, *Contemporary Zoroastrianism: An Unstructured Nation* (Lanham, MD: University Press of America, 1994), 129–48.

Introduction

couple.[99] Against the protests of orthodox Parsis from across South Asia, Bella's adoptive parents had her initiated into the religion and taken into the Rangoon fire temple as a young teenager. Orthodox Parsis claimed that Bella's entry desecrated the temple, which they claimed was open only to people who were religiously Zoroastrian and ethnically Parsi. They went to court asking for an injunction to bar Bella from the temple. Ultimately, Bella's case was appealed to the Privy Council in London. The Privy Councillors relied on Davar's ethnicized definition of Parsi in *Petit v. Jijibhai*, giving the trustees of the Rangoon fire temple a discretionary power to allow Bella into the temple, but denying her the right to enter. Together, these two rulings gave the question, *who is a Parsi?* a decisively exclusive and racialized answer.

PARSI LEGAL HISTORY

A study of this kind prompts queries about emphasis. First, one could ask whether focusing on a single ethnoreligious community understates the degree of social mixing that went on in British India. What of South Asia's "fluid social fabric," its "built-in cosmopolitanism," and its "public men" whose writings and philanthropy transcended the boundaries of community?[100] At work and in play, people from British India's many communities intermingled in ways that suggested greater social interaction than was often declared. Nonetheless, the community remained a meaningful unit. For Parsis, cosmopolitan mixing was common enough in commercial, professional, and labor relations. Among Parsi elites in Bombay especially, socializing with other wealthy Indians and Europeans led to material gains and imperial honors. For many Parsis, though, large swathes of life were populated exclusively by other Parsis. This was so especially in housing and social settings and in the realm of religious life. The orthodox desire to confine group membership to ethnic Parsis suggested that there were normative limits to acceptable mixing – inspired, perhaps, by precisely the ready intermingling that occurred outside of the home, housing colony, and fire temple. Interaction with co-religionists, in other words, was a central part of many Parsi lives, both descriptively and prescriptively. The fact that these

---

[99] *Dorabjee Rustomjee Saklat, Sheriar Khodabux Irani and Jamsetji Burjorjee Sootaria v. Bella and Sapoorjee Cowasjee (since deceased)* JCPC Suit No. 57 of 1924, 1925: vol. 24, judgment 88 (PCO). For published law reports, see *Saklat and others v. Bella* LR 53 IA 42 (1925–6) or 28 Bom. LR 161 (1926); *M. Cowasji and others v. Bella and another* AIR 1919 Lower Burma 56; *D. R. Saklat and others v. Bella and another* AIR 1920 Lower Burma 151; *D. R. Saklat and others v. Bella and one* ILR 2 Rang 91 (1924) or 3 Burma LJ 30 (1924). See also *D. R. Saklat, A. B. Mehta and others v. J. Hormasjee* ILR 7 Rang 561 (1929).

[100] Chandra Mallampalli, *Race, Religion and Law in Colonial India: Trials of an Interracial Family* (Cambridge: Cambridge University Press, 2011), 244; C. A. Bayly, "Afterword: Bombay's 'intertwined modernities,' 1780–1880," in *Trans-Colonial Modernities in South Asia*, eds. Michael S. Dodson and Brian A. Hatcher (London: Routledge, 2012), 241–2. See also Chandra Mallampalli, "Cosmopolitanism in the Hinterland? Bellary District through Fresh Lenses, 1800–1840," *IESHR* 46 (2009), 183–210.

relationships were so often mediated by law justifies a study like this one, framed as it is around a single community and its internal conflicts.

A second question about emphasis relates not to the relationship between Parsis and other South Asian communities, but between Parsis and the British. The portrait of Parsi elites exercising collective agency through law arguably underemphasizes the inherent restrictions built into the legal setting. Particularly at its upper levels, the colonial legal system was modeled on English law. It operated in English, requiring its participants to follow English legal conventions of dress, etiquette, and record keeping. Was it the Parsis who succeeded by embracing the mechanics and language of this system, or was it the system that won by forcing them into its arena in the first place? The answer must be both, but at different points. For certain South Asian populations, the acceptance of the jurisdiction of the courts was itself a kind of defeat, an acknowledgment – much resented – that the colonial state exercised authority over them. Few Parsis seem to have found the courts' jurisdiction problematic, lacking as they did a robust alternative forum. But conceding the state's authority at the point of entry, Parsi elites then went to work. Moving within the bounds of the colonizers' institutions, Parsis were able to shape the rules to reflect and reproduce their desired models of the family and community, as will become central matters of this study. They did so as major players in the colonial legal system.

The adoption of colonial law's mechanics created a Parsi *habitus* that was first visible in the 1830s and that reproduced itself in increasingly concentrated form until the end of colonial rule in 1947.[101] Because there was more continuity than change in this history, we may speak of a continuing set of patterns or social structures that became entrenched across the space of some five generations.[102] Going to law became common sense within this subculture. It became the seemingly natural way to settle serious disputes with co-religionists. Legalism became a default setting – what Bourdieu would call "strongly interiorized principles" within the Parsi tradition.[103] It became a favorite way of legitimating particular visions of Parsi community life, cloaking them in the mantle of the state's coercive powers.[104]

---

[101] By Pierre Bourdieu, see "Marriage Strategies as Strategies of Social Reproduction," in *Family and Society: Selections from the Annales, Économies, Sociétés, Civilisations*, eds. Robert Forster and Orest Ranum, trans. Elborg Forster and Patricia M. Ranum (Baltimore, MD: Johns Hopkins University Press, 1976), 121, 140–1; *The Logic of Practice* trans. Richard Nice (Stanford: Stanford University Press, 1980), 54–6.

[102] I adopt Hodivala's average figure of twenty-three years per generation (Hodivala, "The Sack of Sanjan" in his *Studies in Parsi History*, 87).

[103] Bourdieu, "Marriage Strategies," 120.

[104] See Robert Cover, "Violence and the Word," in *Narrative, Violence and the Law: The Essays of Robert Cover*, eds. Martha Minow, Michael Ryan, and Austin Sarat (Ann Arbor: University of Michigan Press, 1992), 203–38.

Introduction

Arguably, the 1830s were the inaugural decade for Parsi legal culture. They marked the first major Parsi lobbying effort that led to the passage of legislation: the Succession to Parsees Immovable Property Act of 1837. However, Parsis had been suing each other in the colonial courts for at least a half-century before. In 1786, a Bombay committee hearing a dispute over intermarriage between Zoroastrian priests and laity noted that many disputes arose among Parsis because of the lack of clear knowledge about their own laws.[105] Henry Borradaile, a colonial official with a great interest in customary law, commented in 1828 that because the Parsis had "no regular Code of laws to which all men of their nation pay obedience, great litigation has risen amongst them."[106] If a code of law and customs was not written down, he predicted disaster for the Parsis of Bombay and Surat: "there will be no end to disputes and litigation among the body of your nation."[107] In the long century that followed, Parsis created their own laws, but the volume of intragroup litigation did not abate. Early British observers believed that litigation among Parsis resulted from a lack of clear, written rules, but the precision created by the Parsi codification projects of the nineteenth and twentieth centuries only increased the flow.[108] More law stimulated rather than sated the appetite of Parsi disputants.

Other communities developed strategies of legal mobilization under colonial rule. But the Parsis did so earliest and in response to different stimuli. Being concentrated in Bombay, they also did so in a geographically focused way that made the phenomenon particularly visible and well coordinated. Muslim lobbying for reform of the law of religious trusts and Anglo-Islamic personal law began in the 1870s and continued into the 1930s. The Hindu movement for broad personal law reform gained force in the 1920s–30s, culminating in the passage of several statutes in the 1950s. In both cases, the possibility of Indian independence and rising communal identities stimulated efforts to define what it meant to be Muslim or Hindu through the law of marriage, inheritance, and religious endowments. Parsi legislative lobbying started four decades before the Muslim movement and almost a century before the Hindu one. It had nothing to do with the prospect of independence. On the contrary, it was not the promise of breaking away from British rule but the likely continuation of colonialism that

---

[105] "Report of the Committee appointed for the examination of disputes amongst the Parsees dated 1 May 1786," 2635 (14 September–21 December 1790) (IOR/P/1/148/1). I am grateful to James Jaffe for this reference.

[106] See Harry Borradaile and Mangaldass Nathoobhoy, ed., *Borradaile's Gujarat Caste Rules* (Bombay: Nirnaya-Sagara Press, 1884–7); Amrita Shodhan, "Caste in the Judicial Courts of Gujarat, 1800–60," in *The Idea of Gujarat: History, Ethnography and Text*, eds. Edward Simpson and Aparna Kapadia (Delhi: Orient Black Swan, 2010), 40–1.

[107] "Report into the usages recognized as laws by the Parsee Community of India, and into the necessity of special legislation in connection with them," 2 in "1862–3 Government of India Bill to amend law for Parsees, with supporting papers, copies for further supporting papers dating from 1798" (IOR/L/PJ/5/400).

[108] See Chapter 5 at 215.

pushed Parsis to assert greater control over law. Under the East India Company, the colonial courts applied Hindu and Islamic law to Hindu and Muslim family cases, respectively. Although the colonial courts' understanding of Hindu and Islamic personal law was distorted through the selective and imperfect translation of texts and the Anglicized assumptions of European judges, there was some attempt nonetheless to avoid the wholesale application of English law. By contrast, English law was applied to Parsis because of the view that Zoroastrianism, unlike Hinduism or Islam, lacked a body of religious law.

Here was the crucial background condition against which Parsi legal culture emerged. Parsis first organized themselves into lobby groups in the 1830s to oppose the application of primogeniture in inheritance suits. As Parsi merchants amassed colossal fortunes, they also invested in the creation of infrastructure through joint ventures with the colonial state. Whether building wells, hospitals, or schools through philanthropy or developing the machinery for legislative lobbying, the mentality was the same: Parsi elites sought influence over colonial civic life by becoming deeply involved with the state.[109] By the 1850s–60s, Parsi lobbyists were drafting and campaigning for the passage of the matrimonial and inheritance legislation that would create Parsi personal law. In the 1920s–30s, they revised these statutes. By then, there were not only highly skilled legal professionals within the community, but also Parsi legislators who could shepherd the statutes through the legislative process. Since the 1860s, the upper ranks of the legal profession had also been opening up to South Asians, and Parsis became top lawyers and judges in Bombay especially. They came to manage much of the litigation among Parsis, in turn producing rulings that reflected their values and visions for the community. Similar professional patterns may have existed among particular Hindu or Muslim communities; the Parsi phenomenon was pioneering and pronounced.[110]

With the division of British India into independent India and Pakistan in 1947, some 12 million Hindus, Muslims, Sikhs, and others moved across new borders to the state where they felt their interests would be best protected. Between half and one million people lost their lives in the process.[111] Since the early twentieth century, there had been disagreement among Parsis as to their best collective strategy when India gained independence. Should they assert special protection for their group, as other small minorities like the Anglo-Indians would do, or should they resist the urge?[112] Against the backdrop of Partition's violence, Parsi

---

[109] See Jesse Palsetia, "Partner in Empire: Jamsetjee Jejeebhoy and the public culture of nineteenth-century Bombay" in Hinnells and Williams, 81–99.

[110] On the Muslim context, see the work of Alan Guenther at notes 43–4.

[111] Yasmin Khan, *The Great Partition: The Making of India and Pakistan* (New Haven, CT: Yale University Press, 2007), 6.

[112] See Desai, *History*, 122–8, 324–8; Eckehard Kulke, *The Parsees of India: A Minority as Agent of Social Change* (Delhi: Vikas Publishing House, 1974), 193–9, 214–5. In this context, "Anglo-Indian" described the Christian population of mixed British and Indian descent, rather than Europeans living in India.

Introduction

lobbyists ultimately made efforts not to emphasize their separate community status. During the Constituent Assembly debates that forged the Indian Constitution, they refused the opportunity to reserve seats for Parsis in the future national legislature.[113] In part, this decision reflected a desire not to feed communal conflict. In the words of Rustom K. Sidhwa in the Constituent Assembly, "we have seen with our own eyes how mischief is played by the British by dividing one community against another. Parsis have been asked many a time to demand separate electorates. We have refused and replied, 'We are quite safe with our majority community.' See the goodness of the majority community in this very Assembly. We have all been ... elected by their votes."[114]

Equally, though, Parsi leaders may have had continuing confidence in the formula that had served them well under British rule: the Parsi community would continue to produce elite, legally trained individuals who could safeguard the community's interests at the highest levels. Observing the Parsi community from the outside, Vallabhbhai Patel commented that the Parsis

have themselves voluntarily abandoned any concessions that may be given to them and wisely they have done so. Besides, it is well-known that though small, it is a very powerful community and perhaps very wise. They know that any concessions that they may get would perhaps do more harm to them than any good, *because they can make their way anywhere, and make their way in such a manner that they would get more than they would get by any reservation or by any separate process of elections.* Either in the legislature or in the services, they stand so high in the general standard of the nation that they have disclaimed any concessions and I congratulate them on their decision.[115]

Indeed, some of independent India's most eminent lawyers, judges, and legal officials have been Parsi.[116] Legislative activity pertaining to Parsi law has also continued in the postcolonial period. Parsi matrimonial and

---

[113] See "Status of Parsis in New India. Sir Homi Mody's Stand," *TI* (29 August 1947), 3; comments by R. K. Sidhwa (C. P. and Berar: General) in Constituent Assembly of India Debates, vol. I (18 December 1946) and VII (6 November 1948) (accessed on 24 January 2012), http://viveks.info/search-engine-for-constituent-assembly-debates-in-india.

[114] R. K. Sidhwa in Constituent Assembly Debates, I (18 December 1946). See also Nergish P. Charna, "Parsis in Politics: A Declining Breed," 165–6 in Mody, *Enduring Legacy*, I; "Sidhwa, Rustom K. (1882–1957)," in *Dictionary of National Biography*, ed. S. P. Sen (Calcutta: Institute of Historical Studies, 1974), IV: 199–200.

[115] Vallabhbhai J. Patel (Bombay: General) in Constituent Assembly Debates, V (27 August 1947). Italics added. Similarly, see Desai, *History*, 126–7. By contrast, ten seats in Pakistan's National Assembly are reserved for non-Muslim minorities generally [Constitution of Pakistan, Art.51(4)]. Parsis are entitled to run for these positions and to vote for these candidates, but no particular seat is designated for the Parsi community alone.

[116] H. M. Seervai, Nani Palikhivalla, Fali S. and Rohinton F. Nariman, Soli Sorabjee, S. H. Kapadia, S. K. Vazifdar, and Roshan S. Dalvi are examples. See H. M. Seervai, *The Seervai Legacy* (Delhi: Universal, 2000); Feroza H. Seervai, ed., *Evoking H. M. Seervai: Jurist and Authority on the Indian Constitution 1906–1996* (Delhi: Universal, 2005); Fali S. Nariman, *Before Memory Fades ... An Autobiography* (Delhi: Hay House, 2010); John R. Hinnells, "Parsis in India and the Diaspora in the Twentieth Century and beyond" in Hinnells and Williams, 259.

28 *Law and Identity in Colonial South Asia: Parsi Legal Culture*

inheritance legislation was revised in 1988 and 1991, respectively.[117] And there is still litigation among Parsis in Mumbai and Gujarat, particularly on religious trusts.[118]

Nevertheless, Parsi legal culture in India today is a shadow of what it was during the colonial period. The volume and visibility of Parsi legal patterns have diminished since 1947, a product of larger demographic trends such as the fall in India's Parsi population caused by low birth and high emigration rates. At the turn of the twenty-first century, the number of Parsis in India was estimated to be 60,000–70,000, having dropped from the late colonial population of about 110,000.[119] Legal activity both in India and across the diaspora has not operated in the geographically concentrated way that enabled such synergy and control in colonial Bombay. There are still remarkable Parsi lawyers and well-publicized lawsuits among Parsis in India, but not enough to produce the cumulative effect of the colonial phenomenon.[120] In parts of Asia and Africa, the Parsis are a small but familiar minority. Elsewhere, though, they are a community whose history and religion are utterly unknown to most of the surrounding population. Their numbers are simply too low and diffuse for intragroup litigation or legislative lobbying to be common. Furthermore, common-law jurisdictions outside of Asia and Africa do not recognize the personal law principle, thus excluding the possibility that a body of family law could govern one religious minority alone. This, too, has unraveled the logic of lobbying in the diaspora for a small minority like the Parsis.

CHAPTER OVERVIEW

Only textbooks are comprehensive, and this book leaves out much. Because its focus is the use of law among members of one community, it is heavily skewed in

---

[117] See Mohammad Shabbir and S. C. Manchanda, *Parsi Law in India (as amended by Act of 1988)* (Allahabad: Law Book Company, 1991). By Flavia Agnes, see *Law and Gender Inequality: The Politics of Women's Rights in India*, 135–7 in *Women and Law in India* (Oxford: Oxford University Press, 2004); *Family Law. Vol. I: Family Laws and Constitutional Claims* (Delhi: Oxford University Press, 2011), 82–4.

[118] See Mitra Sharafi, "Law and Modern Zoroastrians," in *Blackwell Companion to the Study of Zoroastrianism*, eds. Michael Stausberg and Yuhan Vevaina (Malden, MA: Blackwell, in press); *Goolrokh M. Gupta v. Burjor Pardiwala and others* Special Civil Application No. 449 of 2010 (unreported judgment, Gujarat High Court, 23 March 2012). I thank Percy Kavina for sharing his insights on this case.

[119] Jenny Rose, *Zoroastrianism: A Guide for the Perplexed* (London: Continuum, 2011), 11. By John R. Hinnells, see "Parsi Attitudes to Religious Pluralism," 196–7; *The Zoroastrian Diaspora*, 44–54, 136, 721; "Parsis in India and the Diaspora," 272–3. See also Stausberg, *Zarathustra and Zoroastrianism*, 3–5.

[120] For example, see *Khojeste Mistree et al v. Minoo Rustomji Shroff et al* 2008 Indlaw Mum. 197; *Jamsheed Kanga and another v. Parsi Panchayat Funds and Properties, and others* 2011 Indlaw Mum. 208. See also Sharafi, "Law and Modern Zoroastrians"; Rose, *Zoroastrianism: A Guide*, 16.

Introduction

favor of civil law. In common-law jurisdictions, civil law governs disputes between private parties. In criminal law, the state represents the victim, the logic being that a crime is an act so serious that it is deemed an act against the public. Even so, Parsis were involved with each other in the domain of criminal law, particularly through the use of private prosecutions. As a device, private prosecutions side-stepped the general rationale of criminal law by allowing private parties, instead of the state, to launch criminal suits. Causes of action like criminal defamation could only be pursued through private prosecutions (with court approval) in late British India. The fact remained, however, that the bulk of intragroup litigation – like legislative lobbying – happened in the domain of civil law. More precisely, the bulk of well-documented activity concerned civil law. Criminal judgments from the upper courts made up only a small fraction of all the decisions published in the law reports of British India. Similarly, the judgment notebooks of Bombay High Court justices indicated that civil cases constituted most of their caseload. The press did cover criminal trials in the Bombay magistrates' courts (also known as the Police Courts) but not always in great detail. And if the unpublished records of these lower courts have survived, they have yet to be unearthed by scholars. The focus on the intragroup role of law also means that several major controversies between Parsis and non-Parsis involving law have been omitted. These include the De Ga case (1873), the Towers of Silence case (1874), the Arthur Crawford case (1889), the Rajabai Tower case (1891), the George Edalji case (1903–7), the Buck Ruxton case (1936), and legal activity surrounding riots in which Parsis were involved or targeted, like the Bombay Dog riots (1832), the Muslim–Parsi riots (1851, 1857, and 1874), and the anti-Parsi Prince of Wales riots (1921).[121]

---

[121] On the De Ga case, see P. B. Vachha, *Famous Judges, Lawyers and Cases of Bombay: A Judicial History of Bombay during the British Period* (Delhi: Universal, 2011), 242–6. On the Towers of Silence case, see Vachha, 247–52; Desai, *History*, 50–61. On the Crawford case, see Desai, *History*, 218–19, 354. On the Rajabai Tower case, see letters by D. Wacha to D. Naoroji (22 May 1891–4 September 1891) in Patwardhan, 244–5, 247, 249, 252, 260–2; "The Rajabai Tower case; as to the cause of death of two Parsi ladies" (14 August 1891), file 1432 (IOR/L/PJ/6/304); *Hansard's Parliamentary Papers* 3rd series, vol. 356, 1890–1 (54 & 55 Victoria), 754–5 (30 July 1891); Palsetia, *Parsis*, 182–3, 188–9; Thrity D. Patel, "Sir Pherozeshah Mehta: India's Legendary Legal Luminary," in *Pherozeshah Mehta: Maker of Modern India*, ed. Nawaz Mody (Bombay: Allied, 1997), 189–93. On the Britain-based Edalji and Ruxton cases, see "The Edalji Case," *Mad. LJ* 17 (1907) 19–20; "Early Life of Dr. B. Ruxton in Bombay," *TI* (16 March 1936), 12; John Glaister and James Couper Brash, *Medico-Legal Aspects of the Ruxton Case* (Baltimore: William Wood and Co., 1937). On the riots, see untitled article, *TI* (26 November 1851), 770; Bomanjee Byramjee Patel and Rustam Barjorji Paymaster, eds., *Pārsī Prakāś (Parsi Prakash being a Record of Important Events in the Growth of the Parsee Community in Western India: chronologically arranged)* (Bombay: Bombay Parsi Panchayat, 1878–1942), II: 485–94 (Guj.); Desai, *History*, 61–3, 265–77; Palsetia, *Parsis*, 124, 188–9; Palsetia, "Mad Dogs and Parsis: The Bombay Dog Riots of 1832," *J. Royal Asiatic Soc.*, third series, 11:1 (2001), 13–30; Hinnells, "Changing Perceptions," 114; Simin Patel, "A Cosmopolitan Crisis: The Bombay Riots of 1874," 39th Annual Conference on South Asia (Madison, 16 October 2010); Dinyar Patel, "Like the Countless Leaves of One Tree: Gandhi and the Parsis, the Prince of Wales Riots, and the Rights of Minorities," 23–33 (unpublished paper).

This portrait of Parsi legal history is divided into three parts. "Part 1: Legal Culture" is a general examination of Parsi law-related activity in British India. The first chapter, "Using Law: Colonial Parsis Go to Court" follows Parsis across the range of non-state and state-based venues for dispute resolution, particularly in their disputes with each other. It links legal pluralism and legal consciousness, asking when and why Parsis decided to go to state-run courts to settle their intragroup conflicts. It draws heavily on matrimonial disputes among Parsis because the testimony recorded in the notebooks of the Parsi Chief Matrimonial Court of Bombay contain the richest descriptions of Parsi views on going to court. Senior relatives played a crucial role in these cases. As guardians of family reputation, senior family members were the main force that kept junior relatives out of court if litigation threatened to sully the family name. Once the secret was out, though, senior relatives were often the prime force pushing younger family members into court. This chapter also lays important groundwork for the rest of the book, introducing the reader to a number of features that predisposed Parsis to using state courts in their intragroup disputes. These included the absence of strong internal adjudicatory bodies and of prohibitions on taking internal disputes out.

Chapter 2, "Making Law: Two Patterns," approaches Parsi legal culture from the other side: production, rather than consumption. Parsis made law in British India as lobbyists, draftsmen, and, ultimately, legislators. In the early phase, Parsi lobbyists pushed for exemptions from existing law. Later, they designed statutes that would create a whole separate body of law for Parsis alone: Parsi personal law. A second way in which they made law was as legal professionals and officials, particularly lawyers and judges. These figures came to manage many of the suits involving their co-religionists. This path was less a deliberate, organized strategy than a pattern that emerged almost incidentally. Many Parsis who became lawyers sought the status and income that came with a successful legal career. But with the repetition of this pathway came another, more haphazard type of collective semiautonomy: professional involvement in suits between Parsis. In tracing the history of the Parsi legal profession, this chapter examines the two branches of the lawyerly profession in colonial Bombay – advocates and solicitors – as well as the judiciary and world of legal publishing. Parsis maintained a strong presence at each of these levels.

Parsi legal culture gave special shape to two social institutions that are the subjects of Parts 2 and 3: the family and the ethnoreligious community. Through the formulation of Parsi personal law, lobbyists delineated the powers and duties of the family patriarch. Through his estate, the senior male had an obligation to provide for his wife and children, but equally, for his parents, widows of his descendants, and a wide circle of other relatives. Through matrimonial law, he had the power to arrange child marriages for his offspring (until 1929) and to beat his wife to a "moderate" degree. He did not enjoy the right to be polygamous (after 1865) or to have sex with prostitutes (after 1936). The Parsi family as reinforced by law looked different from its Hindu, Muslim, or

Introduction

English counterparts. It lacked the joint family, the highly elaborated institution that structured property, inheritance, and tax law for many Hindu families. Parsi husbands, unlike their Muslim equivalents, could not take multiple wives or divorce extrajudicially. And, unlike English property holders who died without a valid will, Parsi intestates' property would be distributed to a wide array of relatives, rather than concentrated in a single heir or small group of heirs.

Parsis used law to give force to a particular vision of community, too. The interlocked debates over conversion, intermarriage, and racial intermixing blurred the line between family and community. From 1871, the census heightened awareness of Parsis' minority status and small numbers.[122] From the early twentieth century, religiously orthodox Parsis adopted a newly restrictive notion of Persian racial purity, asserting that ethnic outsiders (including half-Parsis) were not part of the Parsi community and that they had no right to benefit from Parsi religious trust funds or properties. Sharing in their anxieties over collective extinction through racial dilution, D. D. Davar ruled against the admission of ethnic outsiders in *Petit v. Jijibhai*. Subsequent case law replicated his reasoning. At a time when Christian and Muslim religious bodies welcomed converts, orthodox Parsis like Davar used their legal skills and position to reinforce an exclusive ideal of group membership, further restricting their numbers. The last two parts of the book trace these evolving visions of the family and community by examining fields within personal law (Part 2) and territorial law (Part 3).

"Part 2: The Creation of Parsi Personal Law" consists of three chapters examining the law of marriage and inheritance that applied to Parsis alone. Chapter 3, "The Limits of English Law: The Inheritance Acts" and Chapter 4, "Reconfiguring Male Privilege: The Matrimonial Acts" dissect the elite lobbying efforts that produced the inheritance and marriage-related legislation of 1837–1940. Chapter 3 describes the de-Anglicization of an important area of inheritance law affecting Parsis. The rules governing Parsi wills were entirely English, but Parsis regained control over the law of intestacy, the set of default rules that applied when there was no valid will. The chapter documents the successful Parsi rejection of English doctrines like primogeniture and coverture. The Parsi law of intestacy acquired a distinctive character because of a fundamental difference in values between Parsis and English law. The English law of intestate succession concentrated the property of the deceased in a single person (such as the eldest son) or in a narrow cluster of relatives. By contrast, Parsi customary norms distributed the wealth in smaller pieces to a larger group of relatives. All sons received an equal share, and the estate provided for a wide range of family members. It was this principle of spreading the wealth that made Parsi intestacy law look so different from the English law that governed Parsis until the mid-nineteenth century.

---

[122] For a useful discussion of community identity and the late colonial "enumerative" state, see Purohit, 136–7.

32 Law and Identity in Colonial South Asia: Parsi Legal Culture

Chapters 4 and 5 turn to marriage. Both focus on the history of gender in colonial Parsi life, a topic that has received too little scholarly attention. Chapter 4, "Reconfiguring Male Privilege: The Matrimonial Acts," follows the creation and revision of the Parsi Marriage and Divorce Acts of 1865 and 1936. Elite male Parsis pointed to these statutes as evidence of Parsi enlightenment. The first Act abolished polygamy among Parsis. The second made the grounds of divorce identical for husbands and wives. However, the matrimonial statutes did not consistently prioritize gender equality. Rather, they represented the simultaneous relinquishment of certain patriarchal privileges and retention of others. Parsi husbands surrendered their access to sexual diversity (first their right to polygamy, later their right to have sex with prostitutes), but not their power to control their children (through the right to contract child marriages) and wives (through the right to physically discipline them).

Chapter 5 continues with the theme of marriage, but shifts from legislation to the case law of the unusual court system created by Parsi lobbyists in 1865. "The Jury and Intragroup Control: The Parsi Chief Matrimonial Court" examines the Parsi divorce court of Bombay and its unique jury system of co-religionists. It draws on the case records of this court between 1893 and 1947. The Parsi matrimonial jury was an anomaly. No other population in British India (Europeans included) had the right to a jury in matrimonial cases. The institution was also colonial India's only civil jury. The chapter illuminates the history of the jury in colonial India generally and explores the demographic dynamic at play in the Parsi matrimonial court. First, the Parsi jury was populated by elite senior men. Unlike their Hindu and Muslim counterparts, these men exercised a state-backed power to decide the outcome of matrimonial disputes within their own community. In Hindu and Muslim matrimonial cases, it was colonial judges – typically Europeans until the late nineteenth century – who made these decisions. The courts thus disempowered the senior South Asian men who would have resolved these disputes otherwise, as heads of non-state courts applying religious or customary law. Whereas the colonial legal system had an emasculating effect on senior men from colonized populations, the Parsi matrimonial jury system had an opposite effect on elite Parsi men. Second, the Parsi Chief Matrimonial Court decided cases brought by Parsi plaintiffs who were disproportionately female and working class. These plaintiffs usually won. Rather than reflecting a feminist agenda on the part of delegates, this pattern may have been a means of maintaining the power asymmetries within "standard" Parsi marriages, shoring up the powers of average husbands by removing aberrant ones from the system.[123] In cases of arranged marriage induced by fraud, the Parsi jury's tendency to side with female plaintiffs was especially clear. The Parsi matrimonial jury allowed elite men to discipline nonelite males, exerting their intragroup influence as legal power.

---

[123] For a similar argument, see Hendrik Hartog, *Man and Wife in America: A History* (Cambridge, MA: Harvard University Press, 2000), 5, 160, 165.

Introduction

Part 3, "Beyond Personal Law" moves from the family to the community, and from the religiously focused system of personal law to the territorial law of India that applied equally to everyone. It examines lawsuits that fell under the law of trusts and libel and that featured competing models of Parsi identity. These suits flowed from disagreements about the role of religious and racial criteria in determining membership within the group. Chapter 6, "Entrusting the Faith: Religious Trusts and the Parsi Legal Profession," charts the ways in which religious controversies among Parsis entered the courtroom in the shape of charitable trust suits. It takes us into the mainstream colonial courts, notably the Bombay High Court, which dealt in a heavy traffic of suits among Parsis. More than any other area of law, trust-related litigation highlighted the social damage done by in-fighting in court. But it also illuminated the collectively productive process that developed as suits between Parsis came to be handled by a rising body of Parsi lawyers and judges. More than any other part of the book, this chapter integrates the history of the legal profession with the history of case law. Contributing to the new history of colonial lawyering just described, this chapter shows how non-Europeans in the legal profession were cultural intermediaries who played a critical role in the production of judicial ethnography. Whereas Chapter 2 offers a general portrait of the Parsi legal profession, Chapter 6 focuses on the example of a single judge and his influence on Parsi religious disputes. The orthodox values of D. D. Davar shaped the outcome of the major Parsi trust suits of his day.

Chapter 7, "Pure Parsi: Libel, Race, and Group Membership," returns to a theme begun in Chapter 1: reputation. It examines the law of defamation, a tool employed to rehabilitate one's good name. Libel suits, in which plaintiffs sued for defamation in its written form, were occasionally connected with religious trust suits. In the 1910s, multiple libel suits were launched in response to press coverage of the Rangoon case of *Saklat v. Bella*. While reporting on the main proceedings in the Bella case, Parsi newspapers in Bombay insinuated that certain members of the Parsi community in Rangoon were not of pure Parsi racial stock, but of mixed Asian lineage. Since 1910, the orthodox Parsi solicitor J. J. Vimadalal had published writings adapting Euro-American race theory to the Parsi context. Opposing the French Mrs. Tata's attempt to gain admission into the Parsi community in *Petit v. Jijibhai*, Vimadalal used eugenics to argue that the Parsis were a superior race that ought not to intermarry with non-Parsis. With the rising influence of Parsi eugenics, the Rangoon libel trials reflected the consolidation of a newly restrictive model of collective identity. According to the older, patrilineal model, a person would be eligible for initiation into the religion if he or she had a Parsi father. The new, racialized model required that both of the initiate's parents be ethnically Parsi. It was no longer the male seed alone that mattered, but the purity of blood on both sides. The libel trials also signaled a shift in notions of purity – from ritual to racial – accompanied by a new nostalgia for Persia as it was imagined by a community that had left a millennium before.

F. C. O. Beaman, the second and junior judge in *Petit v. Jijibhai*, described the Parsi community in his concurring opinion. Beaman likened Parsis to Jews, an intriguing comparison given the judge's own Jewish ancestry.[124] Beaman described the Parsis as "a peculiar people, with no country of their own, no separate national life of their own, [owing] allegiance to no Parsi or Zoroastrian temporal sovereign, guests on sufferance of races, of peoples, who had nothing whatever in common with their religious organization."[125] Beaman emphasized the vulnerability of both ethnoreligious diasporic minorities. When he wrote these words in 1908, though, Parsi legal culture reflected anything but a lack of control. From the central legislature in Delhi to Beaman's own Bombay courtroom, the subcultural tendency to use law exhibited itself. And although Parsi elites worked within the structures and strictures of colonial law, they created a meaningful semiautonomy in so doing.

[124] Beaman's mother was a member of the Gompertz family of Jewish converts to Anglicanism. The family included the inventor Lewis Gompertz (d. 1861) and the mathematician Benjamin Gompertz (d. 1865). I am grateful to Roland Hulme-Beaman of Dublin for sharing his family's history with me (4 January 2004). For another implied likening of Parsis to Jews, see Q. in the Corner [Manekjee Cursetjee], *The Parsee Panchayet: its rise, its fall, and the causes that led to the same, being a series of letters in the Bombay Times of 1844–45* (Bombay: L. M.[D'Souza's] Press, 1860), II: 16. I thank Daniel Sheffield and Ursula Sims-Williams for helping me obtain access to this source.

[125] *Petit v. Jijibhai*, 582.

PART I

PARSI LEGAL CULTURE

I

Using Law

Colonial Parsis Go to Court

In 1942, the Parsi Chief Matrimonial Court (PCMC) of Bombay encountered an example of pathological litigiousness.[1] A Parsi woman wanted a divorce on the grounds of desertion. According to Parsi law, one spouse must have abandoned the other at least three years before. The husband acknowledged that he had moved out of the marital home four and a half years before. He had taken his belongings and some furniture. Two years later, he spent three months in jail for disorderly conduct. He was then confined in a mental asylum for almost two years, probably for paranoia. He told the court that he had wanted to be reunited with his wife during that time but that he could not for obvious reasons. His lawyer pushed to have the desertion clock stopped during these periods of institutionalization. The judge refused. The delegates, a jury of Parsis, granted the divorce.[2]

The husband was a man of quarrelsome disposition. He fought with everyone around him, and he fought in a particular way: by turning to law. His wife told the court that they moved constantly between *chawls* (Guj. *cāl*) – poor tenement blocks – because her husband clashed with neighbors and landlords. He initiated court proceedings against them. At least one was a criminal suit heard in the Bombay Police Court. His imprisonment for disorderly conduct was triggered by a related confrontation with fellow tenants. The man's family life, too, was colored by litigation. After his father's death, he had sued his mother over the estate. The case was referred to arbitration, out of which the husband-defendant was awarded Rs 15,000. Developing suspicions about his wife's close friendship with a young Parsi neighbor couple, the man threatened to sue the neighbor husband in police court for having "immoral purposes." And, ultimately, his

---

[1] Suit No. 12 of 1942, "PCMC Judge's Notebook (4 March 1941–3 August 1948)," I: 346–64 (BHC). This chapter's title borrows from Jane Burbank, *Russian Peasants Go to Court: Legal Culture in the Countryside, 1905–1917* (Bloomington: Indiana University Press, 2004).

[2] Suit No. 12 of 1942, 346–7, 359–60, 362.

38   *Law and Identity in Colonial South Asia: Parsi Legal Culture*

wife sued him successfully for divorce in the PCMC. She was funded and encouraged by her brother, who baldly told the court: "I wanted my sister to get rid of him."[3] Tellingly, the husband-defendant had worked as a solicitor's clerk.[4] Many clerks at Parsi-owned law firms were Parsi themselves. Legal knowledge would have surrounded the defendant in that earlier job, explaining perhaps his willingness to criticize his lawyer on technical grounds during the divorce proceedings.[5] His earlier exposure to law may have also sown the seed of the mania that would undo him.

The slide of this man's legal impulses into mental illness was unusual and extreme. But his legal life differed in degree, not kind, from that of many co-religionists. Thirteen years earlier, in 1929, a letter to the *Times of India* had suggested that the "shocking reports of cases in civil and criminal courts" involving Parsis reflected the mental and racial degeneration of the group, a phenomenon some attributed to a millennium of endogamy.[6] Many Parsis who came to court had previous experience with the legal system. Over the course of an adult life, it was not unknown for a Parsi to have resolved debt, housing, inheritance, marital, and low-level criminal disputes with other Parsis through litigation.[7] The numbers were striking. Parsis constituted just 6 percent of the population of Bombay city at the turn of the twentieth century,[8] but they were almost a fifth of the parties listed in the official law reports from 1876 (when these law reports began) until Indian independence in 1947.[9]

Parsis found themselves in court against non-Parsis – usually Hindus, Muslims, or Britons – in about two-thirds of the cases in which they were involved. These cases were generally of two types. First, there were cases between Parsis and other South Asians. These suits most often related to commercial disputes or conflicts over property.[10] In trade, Parsis typically ran businesses with other Parsis, but there were exceptions. They also had

---

[3] Ibid., 346–7, 354–7, 359, 362.
[4] Ibid., 352. For another PCMC suit featuring a former clerk from a Parsi law firm (this time as plaintiff), see Suit No. 18 of 1941, 1941–8 PCMC Notebook, I: 278.
[5] Suit No. 12 of 1942, 1941–8 PCMC Notebook, I: 360.
[6] "To the Editor of the *Times of India*," *TI* (7 December 1929), 26.
[7] In the PCMC notebooks, see Suit No. 5 of 1893, 1893–1903 Notebook, I: 37–61; Suit No. 4 of 1899, 1893–1903 Notebook, II: 59, 96–105; Suit No. 11 of 1935, "PCMC Judge's Notebook (26 March 1935–7 April 1937)," I: 274–97; Suit No. 23 of 1938, "PCMC Judge's Notebook (11 June 1937–4 March 1941)," III: 44–51. See also *Era'sha Kaikhasru alias Kharsedji, Minor, by the Guardian Kaikha'sru alias Kha'rsedji Dosa'bhai v. Jerba'i, wife of Ratanji Rastomji* ILR 4 Bom 537 (1880) at 541; "The Parsee Chief Matrimonial Court. A Case of Divorce. Goolbai v. Dossabhai Dorabjee Gordhan and Bhikhaijee," *TI* (5 March 1888), 3; Suit No. 66 of 1933 in "J. D. Davar's Long Causes 1934," 197–273 especially at 207, 213 (BHC).
[8] Parsis were 46,231 of Bombay's 776,006 people in 1901. [*Gazetteer of Bombay City and Island* (Bombay: Times Press, 1909), I: 273.]
[9] Of the Bombay High Court (Original Side) and Privy Council cases reported in the ILR Bombay series (1876–1947), approximately 19 percent involved one or more Parsi parties.
[10] For example, see *Bhagwandas Parasram v. B. R. Bomanji* ILR 42 Bom 373 (1918).

Using Law: Parsis Go to Court

frequent business dealings with other Gujarati speakers.[11] Like the Parsis of Bombay City, Gujarati-speaking Hindus, Muslims, and Jains had migrated to the city from farther north and west in the Bombay Presidency. Although the local language in the city of Bombay was Marathi, these communities led many of the major business enterprises in Bombay, making Gujarati an important language in the city. Debt cases, usually involving mortgaged property, were a common flavor of litigation between Parsis and other South Asians. Although Parsis usually turned to relatives and then community members to borrow money, the more desperate they became – and ostracized within their own community – the more likely they were to borrow from non-Parsis. Here was the cosmopolitanism of the excluded.[12] In court, down-and-out Parsi husbands described taking loans from Marwari and Pathan moneylenders and being pursued for payment in aggressive ways. One couple told the court that a Pathan creditor threatened to break the Parsi husband's bones if he did not pay. Alternatively, the creditor would accept sex with the wife in discharge of the debt.[13] Equally, the money could travel in the opposite direction: Parsis sometimes loaned money to non-Parsis. When any of these dealings went seriously awry, the parties might find themselves in court.[14]

The second type of litigation across community lines was legal action taken by Parsis against the colonial state. Until the early twentieth century, these disputes were typically about licensing. Parsis challenged the state's attempts to increase the costs of Parsi business activities, from the liquor business to the running of "eating houses."[15] From the early twentieth century, Parsi suits against the state shifted to eminent domain: the confiscation of private land for state purposes, with compensation.[16] It was not usually the taking itself that was the focus of these suits, but the method of calculating compensation.[17] In the later colonial period, taxation was another area over which Parsis clashed with the state, particularly with the introduction of major income tax legislation from the

---

[11] For example, see Christine Dobbin, *Asian Entrepreneurial Minorities: Conjoint Communities in the Making of the World-Economy 1570–1940* (Richmond, UK: Curzon, 1996), 88.

[12] For example, see Suit No. 5 of 1893, "PCMC Judge's Notebook (17 November 1893–24 December 1903)," I: 50–3 (BHC).

[13] Suit No. 6 of 1937, 1937–41 PCMC Notebook, II: 63–4.

[14] For a sample, see *Fatmabai v. D. R. Umrigar* ILR 34 Bom 638 (1910); *S. H. Harver v. Monosseh Jacob Monosseh* ILR 34 Bom 374 (1910).

[15] For a sample, see *Ardeshir J. F. Banaji v. Secretary of State* ILR 6 Bom 398 (1882); *Irani v. Hartley Kennedy* ILR 26 Bom 396 (1902).

[16] On eminent domain affecting properties owned by the Bombay Parsi Panchayat, see Desai, *History*, 162–70.

[17] For example, see the joined cases of *Hamabai Framjee Petit v. Secretary of State for India in Council; and Moosa Hajee Hassam v. Secretary of State for India in Council* ILR 39 Bom 279 (1915); JCPC Suit No. 139 of 1913, 1914: Vol. 33, Judgment No. 93 (PCO); *Secretary of State for India in Council v. Hamabai Framji Petit* (Appeal No. 24 of 1910), Legal Department Records (Suits), vol. B-11/4 of 1908–10 (MSA).

1920s on.[18] Parsi plaintiffs usually lost when they sued the state.[19] But, intriguingly, they continued to initiate these suits. The pattern may have reflected the degree to which Parsis had internalized rule of law values: these plaintiffs seemed eternally optimistic that law would check the power of state officials.[20] Or perhaps the "legal lottery" mechanism was at work: even when potential litigants realized that statistically they were likely to lose, they may still have been willing to try, hoping to get lucky.[21]

Cosmopolitan litigation in colonial India is a rich and fascinating subject, but one for another book. In one sense, its logic was obvious. The colonial legal system was the natural default venue for disputes in which neither side was inclined to accept adjudication from the other side's community. By contrast, it was not at all obvious why members of the *same* community would take their disputes to the colonial courts. The Parsis did just that, suing each other with striking frequency and vigor. Why was it that this population turned to state law – rather than to their own religious or community bodies – to settle their disputes, particularly those of a sensitive religious or personal nature? Between 1876 and 1947, 6 percent of the civil cases in the *Indian Law Reports Bombay series* were suits between Parsi parties.[22] Given their relative size in Bombay, this incidence was again high. At 6 percent of the population, one would expect something twenty times lower to be suits between Parsis.[23] Of course, many

---

[18] For example, see *Commissioner of Income Tax, Bombay v. F. E. Dinshaw* 34 BLR 1235 (1932); Privy Council appeal papers relating to *Dinshaw v. Commissioner of Income Tax* (18 November 1932–16 August 1934; IOR/L/PJ/7/463). See also Chapter 3 at note 88.

[19] For example, see note 17.

[20] On the rule of law, see A. V. Dicey, *Introduction to the Study of the Law of the Constitution* (London: Macmillan, 1889), 189–90; Nasser Hussain, *The Jurisprudence of Emergency: Colonialism and the Rule of Law* (Ann Arbor: University of Michigan Press, 2003), 8–16.

[21] See Sharafi, "Marital Patchwork," 982, 1009; Derrett, "Administration," 18.

[22] Approximately 98 of 1,542 Bombay High Court civil cases in the ILR Bombay series (1876–1947) were suits between Parsis.

[23] I calculate the baseline figure of 0.3 percent in the following way. There were approximately 250,606 males aged over twenty in Bombay City according to the 1901 census. If each man sued every other man once (and did not sue himself), the total number of suits between Bombay men would be: 250,606 × 250,605. The census figures suggest that there were roughly 12,677 Parsi males over the age of twenty in Bombay City in 1901. In the scenario described, the total number of suits in which a Parsi man could find himself matched with another Parsi would be 12,677 × 12,676. This number of Parsi–Parsi suits, as a fraction of the total number of suits, would therefore be: (12,677 × 12,676) ÷ (250,606 × 250,605) × 100 = 0.26% This calculation leaves out males under the age of twenty years and all females. Although people from both excluded groups were sometimes parties to litigation, most Parsi litigants appearing in the reported case law were adult males. This calculation is also skewed by the process of law reporting. It is only possible to tally the total number of Parsi–Parsi suits from the reported case law, not from the complete roster of suits heard by the Bombay courts, which is unavailable. Population figures from *Gazetteer of Bombay City and Island*, I: 273; *Statistical Abstract Relating to British India from 1894–95 to 1903–4* (London: HMSO, 1905), "No. 5: Main Statistics for Cities" and "No. 13: Age, Sex and Civil Condition" (accessed on 1 March 2010): http://dsal.uchicago.edu/statistics/1894_excel/index.html

Using Law: Parsis Go to Court

Parsis were affluent, a factor one would expect to increase the number of Parsi litigants. Similarly, the high density of dealings within the community would elevate the likelihood of disputes among Parsis. At the same time, one would assume that two people from the same community would have more non-state mechanisms for settling their dispute than would two people from different ones. The phenomenon of frequent litigation between Parsis raised intriguing questions. How did Parsis approach conflict within the community? How did they think about audience, privacy, and reputation? What did it mean socially to go to court?

LEGAL PLURALISM

Going to court was not unusual among Parsis, but it was still a final resort. In 1927, *Hindi Punch* commented that the number of Parsi "petty domestic or neighborly squabbles" in the courts was large, although "showing an appreciable decline, thanks to the efforts of worthy peace-makers."[24] Legal pluralism – the existence of multiple normative orders governing the same dispute – existed among colonial Parsis, as it does in any group.[25] At the most informal level, senior or male family members or friends acted as adjudicators or emissaries. Writing of the early nineteenth century, the female Parsi memorialist Dosebai Cowasjee Jessawalla described her grandfather sitting "in judgment on family feuds."[26] A century later in 1914, one husband told the Parsi matrimonial court that during his marital troubles, he stopped his wife's mother and brother from coming to his house: "They used to act as Go-betweens."[27] In the same year, another wife reported that she returned to live with her husband "at the intercession of mutual friends."[28]

Parsis were deeply involved in the personal conflicts of their relatives, friends, and neighbors. The view that such interference was illegitimate was rarely voiced. The only declarations of a right to privacy seem to have come from abusive husbands on the verge of assaulting their wives. In 1913, one wife recounted an angry exchange between her husband and her father after the husband had beaten her. Her father demanded to know why the husband had been violent. The reply reflected the son-in-law's belief in a twinned right to spousal absolutism and privacy: "She is my wife. If I kill her even you have no right to complain or interfere."[29] In another suit of the same year, a female neighbor was complaining about the "constant quarrels and disturbances" involving the couple in question: "I said it was a most inhuman proceeding

---

[24] "1297," *HP* (11 September 1927), 16.
[25] See Sally Engle Merry, "Legal Pluralism," *LSR* 22 (1988), 869–96.
[26] Dosebai Cowasjee Jessawalla, *The Story of My Life* (Bombay: Times Press, 1911), 66.
[27] Suit No. 3 of 1914, "PCMC Judge's Notebook (8 April 1913–24 March 1920)," I: 102.
[28] Suit No. 5 of 1914, 1913–20 PCMC Notebook, I: 91.
[29] Suit No. 5 of 1913, 1913–20 PCMC Notebook, I: 42.

42   *Law and Identity in Colonial South Asia: Parsi Legal Culture*

whereupon the man ... told me to mind my own business."[30] Two decades later in 1937, a woman told her son-in-law not to beat his wife, the speaker's daughter: "He said he as husband had a right to beat his wife and keep her under his control and I should not interfere."[31] Interference from kin and friends signaled that they cared. Resistance to neighborly interference implied that one had something to hide. In a 1903 case, a Parsi wife told the matrimonial court that her husband "was in the habit of taking me where there were no Parsi neighbors" to beat her, even though he did so behind closed doors.[32] There were even situations in which intervening neighbors determined the presentation of facts to an outside audience. Having observed the Muslim driver of a married woman's father sneak into the woman's bedroom while she was alone in the house, a group of Parsi neighbors became convinced that the two were having an affair. Their suspicions were confirmed when they entered the house and pulled the man out from under the marital bed. Rather than expose the guilty pair, the neighbors made a split-second decision to give the woman (and her marriage) a second chance: "We decided to keep the marital relations intact between husband and wife but hammer the co-defendant as if he were a thief." The neighbors chased the man out of the building and down the road on that pretext.[33]

When the intervention of neighbors, friends, and family failed to resolve a situation, the process became somewhat more formal. In these situations, people would "get four or five people together" to try to resolve their conflicts.[34] These mediators were typically senior males from the families of the disputants. But they could also be men who were respected members of the Parsi housing colony, or *baug* (Guj. *bāg*), or who were prominent members of the wider Parsi community.[35] (Parsi housing colonies were walled clusters of subsidized apartment complexes created by wealthy Parsi philanthropists for Parsi residents.[36]) These negotiations could be strikingly formal. Mediators would draw up a written agreement and ask both sides to sign.[37] In one such reconciliation, for instance, the parties agreed to four conditions in writing. A wife accused her husband of being physically and mentally abusive toward her; flashing his genitals at strangers; committing adultery with men and women in Bombay, Aden, and Zanzibar; and misappropriating funds from the family and its business, in part to buy the silence of a male servant with whom he had probably had sex.[38] The husband agreed, in writing, to (1) stop assaulting his wife, (2) cease engaging in financial

---

[30] Suit No. 4 of 1913, 1913–20 PCMC Notebook, I: 13.

[31] Suit No. 19 of 1937, 1937–41 PCMC Notebook, 144–7. See also Suit No. 21 of 1938 in 1937–41 PCMC Notebook, II: 193.

[32] Suit No. 4 of 1903, "PCMC Judge's Notebook (24 September 1903–17 March 1913)," I: 7.

[33] Suit No. 1 of 1927, "PCMC Judge's Notebook (2 November 1924–31 January 1928)," III: 75–7.

[34] Suit No. 4 of 1893, 1893–1903 PCMC Notebook, I: 23.

[35] See Suit No. 21 of 1938, 1937–41 PCMC Notebook, III: 2–3.

[36] See Stausberg, *Die Religion*, II: 48–51.

[37] See, for example, Suit No. 21 of 1938, 1937–41 PCMC Notebook, III: 2–3.

[38] Suit No. 14 of 1939, 1937–41 PCMC Notebook, III: 117–55.

Using Law: Parsis Go to Court

speculation, (3) return some money he had extracted from his wife and children on false pretenses, and (4) undergo treatment at the famous psychiatric hospital in Ranchi "for his perverse sex mentality."[39]

A range of more structured formats akin to arbitration also existed. Formal arbitration bodies run by groups like the Parsi League of Honor, the Grant Road Parsi Association, and the Irani Anjuman arose late in the colonial period – around the 1930s.[40] They specialized in marital disputes and followed on earlier and less successful attempts to create Parsi arbitration bodies.[41] We know little about the operation of these institutions, only catching oblique references to them through the testimony of litigants in the matrimonial court. One man testified in 1936 that he had advised a couple in his family to go to the Grant Road Parsi Association for help with their disagreements.[42] In the early 1940s, a woman turned to the Irani Anjuman with her marital problems "in the hope that they might bring about a reconciliation."[43]

We know more about the workings of solo arbitrators such as Framroz Rustomji Joshi, a former superintendent of the Government Central Press who was also a delegate of the PCMC, a Justice of the Peace, and probably a magistrate. In his retirement, he took on the job of privately arbitrating marital disputes like that of Dinbai and Erachshaw Toddyvala in 1916. Before the Toddyvalas came to court, they went to Joshi. Prior to the arbitration, he knew the husband but not the wife or her side. Joshi met separately with husband and wife, along with their relatives, half a dozen times. He took notes but relied on his memory for the most important part of his testimony in the matrimonial court. He claimed to have pried from the husband's mother the admission that she knew from early on that her future daughter-in-law was of mixed racial background. The husband and his side had claimed that the wife's lineage had been kept from them until after the wedding, thus invalidating the marriage. Mr. Joshi sided with the wife, despite his prior acquaintance with the husband.

Enforcement was a common problem for arbitrators. When Joshi's award was not respected, the couple came to the PCMC, where Joshi became a witness. Cases moved from arbitration to court.[44] They also moved in the opposite direction.[45] The courts often sent a case (or a particular issue) to a court-appointed arbitrator like the Parsi magistrate Hormuzdiar P. Dastur,

---

[39] Ibid., 126.

[40] On the Parsi League of Honor, see Suit No. 9 of 1936, 1935–7 PCMC Notebook, II: 3.

[41] See "Obituary: Jehangir J. Vimadalal" in Patel and Paymaster, VII: 19–20, trans.Homi D. Patel; J.P. Wadia, "The Proposed Arbitration Board," *JIA*, V: 1 (April 1916), 32–6 and V: 3 (June 1916), 115–21.

[42] Suit No. 13 of 1936, 1935–7 PCMC Notebook, II: 144–5.

[43] Suit No. 9 of 1942, 1941–8 PCMC Notebook, I: 335

[44] See Suit No. 3 of 1916 in 1913–20 PCMC Notebook, III: 38–9.

[45] For a suit challenging arbitration related to an inheritance dispute between two brothers, see *Fardunji Edalji v. Jamsedji Edalji* ILR 28 Bom 1 (1904).

44 Law and Identity in Colonial South Asia: Parsi Legal Culture

acting in a separate capacity from his formal judicial role.[46] It was not unusual for divorce suits in the Parsi matrimonial court to fizzle out before judgment because they reached an out of court settlement. With the help of arbitrators, the parties in these cases usually agreed in writing to stay married but live separately and for the husband to make maintenance payments to the wife.[47]

THE COURTS

Parsi legal pluralism had multiple layers. Even so, Parsi disputing behavior was heavily oriented toward state law. Experts in state law took the reins in alternative dispute resolution, even though these forums operated outside of the courts. Parsi lawyers and judges mediated for free during the evenings and on weekends, often at their homes, as friends or senior community members. In a sense, then, colonial law was always there, hovering in the background and suggesting itself as the eventual alternative if negotiations failed. The legal professional managing the meeting must have told people what legal outcome would be most likely, providing information that would significantly affect the bargaining endowments of the participants. In the later nineteenth century, the Parsi pleader Jehangir Merwanji was brought into "many unhappy family quarrels."[48] In the 1920s and 1930s, the barrister (and later judge) J. D. Davar and the solicitor J. B. Boman Behram acted as informal mediators upon request.[49] In the 1940s, Kaikhushru Seervai took on the role. As one husband told the matrimonial court, "We ... first went to the house of Kaikhushru Seervai, Solicitor. Mr. Seervai is a close friend of the defendant's mother's family. We went to him to place all the facts before him and to ask him to intervene if he could."[50] Given the day jobs of figures like these, colonial Parsis were bargaining in the shadow of the law even before a dispute entered the realm of the courts.[51] The state legal system was also full of Parsi personnel. By having Parsi *lawyers* so involved in non-state dispute resolution, the influence of state law reached deep inside Parsi community forums. At the same time, having so many *Parsi* lawyers

---

[46] See *I. H. Gheewalla v. Kamdar Ltd* (Suit A61 of 1942), "Hon. Mr. Justice N. H. C. Coyajee. Judgments 2 March 1943–20 December 1944," 169–70 (BHC); Darukhanawala, *Parsi Lustre*, I: 153; K. D. Umrīgar and M. J. Pāṭhak, eds., *Jāṇītī Pārsī Vyaktio* (*Parsi "Who's Who"*) (Jamnagar: Gujarati Who's Who Publishing Company, [194-]), 189. On other Parsi court-appointed arbitrators, see Suit No. 6 of 1929, "PCMC Judge's Notebook (14 June 1929–26 March 1935)," III: 16–17; Suit No. 17 of 1938, 1937–41 PCMC Notebook, II: 199–20; Suit No. 26 of 1941, 1941–8 PCMC Notebook, IA: 1. See also *K. P. Dalal v. Rustomji S. Jamadar*, ILR 1945 Bom 744.

[47] See *Erachshaw Dosabhai Toddiwala v. Dinbai, wife of Erachshaw Doabhai Toddiwala* ILR 45 Bom 318 (1921) at 322.

[48] "Death of Mr. Jehangeer Merwanjee, Pleader," *TI* (14 December 1883), 3.

[49] See, for instance, Suit No. 3 of 1927, "PCMC Judge's Notebook (31 January 1928–8 April 1929)," II: 45, 79, 120, 175; Suit No. 1 of 1938, 1937–41 PCMC Notebook, II: 80.

[50] Suit No. 27 of 1941, "PCMC Judge's Notebook (6 April 1942–6 November 1944)," I: 8.

[51] See Robert H. Mnookin and Lewis Kornhauser, "Bargaining in the Shadow of the Law: The Case of Divorce," 88 *Yale L J* 950–97 (1978–9).

Using Law: Parsis Go to Court

in the state courts must have made the "outside" forum of the courts feel more like an "inside" setting for many Parsis. Parsi disputing culture blurred the distinction between inside and outside: the inside was constantly looking to the outside, and the outside was full of insiders.

Parsis had ways to resolve their disputes without turning to law, but these were ad hoc and voluntary, neither mandatory nor binding. All that was required to get to court was one party who wanted it – and the loser from the last round of negotiations occasionally did. What did the legal system of British India look like for disputes that had moved out of the social domain? Most of British India fell within three main provinces, known as presidencies. The oldest of the three, Bengal, covered the eastern region of India and much of the north. Its capital was Calcutta, where the East India Company first gained a foothold by the eighteenth century. Madras Presidency extended across the southern third of the Indian subcontinent, with Madras, on the southeasterly Coromandel coast, as its capital. Bombay Presidency occupied western India. The city of Bombay, on the west coast of India facing the Arabian Sea, was its urban center. During the Raj, a High Court sat in each of the three presidency capitals and in several other cities.[52] The High Courts were created in 1862, replacing the East India Company's system of courts.[53] The Company had separate courts and systems of law for those in the presidency capital centers and those outside.[54] From 1773 until 1862, its Supreme Courts operated in the presidency capitals for a mixed European and Indian population. These courts were manned by Company servants and applied Company regulations, supplemented by English law.[55] Outside of the presidency capitals, the Company's Adawlut court system (Pers. 'Adālat) rendered justice, according to legislator Thomas Babington Macaulay, not as much through law as through "a kind of crude and capricious equity" that relied on the vague formula of "justice, equity and good conscience" as its ultimate source of law.[56]

---

[52] High Courts were established in Calcutta, Bombay, and Madras in 1861. Others were added in Agra (1866) then shifted to Allahabad (1875) and in Patna (1916), Lahore (1919), and Nagpur (1936).

[53] See Herbert Cowell, *The History and Constitution of the Courts and Legislative Authorities in India (Tagore Law Lectures 1872)* (Calcutta: Thacker, Spink and Co., 1872), 230–5.

[54] See ibid., 224–6; Elizabeth Kolsky, *Colonial Justice in British India: White Violence and the Rule of Law* (Cambridge: Cambridge University Press, 2010), 11.

[55] Cowell, 224–5; M. P. Jain, *Outlines of Indian Legal History* (Nagpur: Wadhwa, 2001), 110–17. On the history of Company-era courts including the Supreme Court and its predecessors, the Mayors' and Recorders' Courts, see Vachha, 7–34; Jain, *Outlines*, 35–54; Mattison Mines, "Courts of Law and Styles of Self in Eighteenth-Century Madras: From Hybrid to Colonial Self," *MAS* 35: 1 (2001), 33–74; Niels Brimnes, "Beyond Colonial Law: Indigenous Litigation and the Contestation of Property in the Mayor's Court in Late Eighteenth-Century Madras," *MAS* 37: 3 (2003), 513–50; Robert Travers, *Ideology and Empire in Eighteenth-Century India* (Cambridge: Cambridge University Press, 2007), 181–206; Arthur Mitchell Fraas, "'They Have Travailed into a Wrong Latitude': The Laws of England, Indian Settlements, and the British Imperial Constitution 1726–1773" (PhD dissertation, Duke University, 2011).

[56] See Vachha, 7–42; Jain, *Outlines*, 454–60. According to Frederick Pollock, "justice, equity and good conscience" meant the principles of English law. See Frederick Pollock, *The Law of Fraud, Misrepresentation and Mistake in British India* (Calcutta: Thacker, Spink and Co., 1894), 7–11.

46 *Law and Identity in Colonial South Asia: Parsi Legal Culture*

After the creation of the High Courts in 1862, there continued to be a distinction between those living in the presidency capitals and those outside, but it was only an institutional difference that existed at the lower levels; the law that applied in Bombay City and in the presidency was now the same. Populations living in the presidencies outside of the capital cities of Calcutta, Madras, and Bombay were in the *mofussil*. Litigants from these provincial regions were almost always South Asian. They took their cases initially to their local and district courts.[57] Only on appeal would their cases come to the High Courts in the presidency capitals, where proceedings and evidence were translated into English.[58] As a result, the Bombay High Court was divided into two parts. The Appellate Side dealt with cases coming on appeal from the *mofussil*. The Original Side heard cases that originated in the city of Bombay itself, whether as the court of first instance or on appeal. In practice, the new High Courts on their Original Side inherited the personnel and culture of the Company's old Supreme Courts.[59]

Legislation and case law were the two major sources of law for the High Courts. The colonial administration prioritized the codification of areas it cared about most – such as criminal and contract law – passing comprehensive legislation that superseded the preexisting case law.[60] Legislation in British India reflected a mix of influences. Sometimes, a statute was modeled on legislation passed in Britain. Other times, it departed from British models. Colonial codifiers like Macaulay regarded India as a laboratory for utilitarian experiments.[61] The case law that was cited in British Indian courts was increasingly the product of Indian courts as the number of Indian judgments increased and became accessible through the circulation of official published law reports following the passage of the Indian Law Reports Act 1875 (II of 1875).[62] Even then, Indian courts continued to draw on English case law, as well as on precedent from across the empire. In this way, the precedent system did important on-the-ground work for the imperial project. Through this organic, incremental method of legal reasoning, adjudication in the colonial courts connected disparate corners of the globe. The cross-fertilization produced by the use of precedent helped homogenize the Indian subcontinent and the imperial world through law.

Contrast J. D. M. Derrett, "Justice, Equity and Good Conscience," in *Changing Law in Developing Countries*, ed. J. N. D. Anderson (New York: F. A. Praeger, 1963), 151.

[57] Cowell, 250–3. See also Gregory C. Kozlowski, *Muslim Endowments and Society in British India* (Cambridge: Cambridge University Press, 1985), 110.

[58] Kozlowski, 111.

[59] Cowell, 235.

[60] For example, see Frederick Pollock and Dinshah Fardunji Mulla, *The Indian Contract Act* (London: Sweet and Maxwell, 1909); Ratanlal Ranchhoddas and Dhirajlal Keshavlel Thakore, *The Indian Penal Code* (Bombay: Bombay Law Reporter Office, 1926).

[61] See Vachha, 37; Eric Stokes, *The English Utilitarians and India* (Oxford: Oxford University Press, 1989).

[62] Jain, *Outlines*, 659–62.

Using Law: Parsis Go to Court

By the late colonial period, most disputes that came to court fell under the uniform, territorial law that applied to everyone in British India. Family law was different. The personal law system applied to marriage and inheritance. When the parties to a dispute shared the same religion, their religious law governed.[63] Personal law meant Hindu law for Hindus, Islamic law for Muslims, and so on. It was the colonial courts, not community or religious authorities, that applied personal law.[64] With the exception of the Parsi matrimonial court system, community-specific family courts did not operate within the colonial legal system. In general, personal law cases came before the civil courts of India and were decided by the same judges who decided all other types of civil litigation. The personal law system's existence directly undercut the colonial state's promise of non-interference in religious or community affairs, made in 1858 and after. As Rina Verma Williams and Subhasri Ghosh have suggested, these statements of non-interference were more rhetorical than applied. After the handover of British India from the East India Company to the Crown in 1858, the courts of the Raj continued to decide cases on personal law. Equally, legislation on family and religious matters continued to be produced, despite Queen Victoria's 1858 promise that the state would avoid such sensitive matters.[65]

The Bombay High Court heard civil and criminal cases, particularly those involving major crimes, significant property values, and cases on appeal. Suits between Parsis on everything from personal injury to employment were decided there.[66] Below the High Court, a voluminous traffic swirled through an array of specialty courts. The Court of Small Causes dealt with low-level civil disputes and was meant to serve as a fast and inexpensive alternative to the High Court.[67] Its docket was dominated by cases on landlord–tenant and debtor–creditor relations. Writing in 1906, one disillusioned anonymous author described its caseload as "a ceaseless flow" of "misery and indigence, fraud and chicanery, falsehood and mendacity" and its courtrooms as "ill ventilated, stuffy, the reverse of silent, reeking with humanity, and constructed on the most wretched

---

[63] See Pollock, 1–4.

[64] This is a point of some confusion in the literature. For example, see Tambe, 5; Eric Lewis Beverley, "Property, Authority and Personal Law: Waqf in Colonial South Asia," *SAR* 31 (2011), 155–6, 159–60, 174.

[65] See Rina Verma Williams, *Postcolonial Politics and Personal Laws: Colonial Legal Legacies and the Indian State* (Delhi: Oxford University Press, 2006), 66–95; Subhasri Ghosh, "Nineteenth-Century Colonial Ideology and Socio-Legal Reforms: Continuity or Break?" *Institute of Development Studies Kolkata Occasional Paper* (June 2011), 1–50.

[66] See Suit No. 195 of 1941: *Framroze Edulji Tawaria v. 1 Def. and Miss Meherhomji, 2 def.* (24 February 1944), 1–22, "Hon. Mr. Justice N. H. C. Coyajee. Typed Notes of Evidence 3 January 1944–8 January 1945"; Suit No. 21 of 1944: *Kaikusroo Pallonji Mistry v. Karanji and Company* (10 August 1944), "Hon. Mr. Justice N. H. C. Coyajee. Judgments 2 March 1943–20 December 1944," 416–18 (BHC).

[67] See Cowell, 258–63.

acoustic principles."[68] The court represented "all classes and shades of society," from "the bejewelled millionaire to the begrimed millhand, the spruce Parsi and the dirty Marwadi, the smirking Bora, and the stalwart Bhaiya, the shrewd, busy Bhatia trader, and the indifferent, happy-go-lucky Mussalman," as well as British customs officers and police constables, railway guards, and engine drivers, "arbitrary and dictatorial when on duty," mixing cheek by jowl in this sea of humanity.[69] Property seized in discharge of debts included "[p]ots, pans, utensils, bedding and the dirtiest of articles." Such items were regularly hauled into court, a particularly unsavory phenomenon when the bubonic plague swept through the city.[70] Parsis referred to matters in the Court of Small Causes while giving testimony in the Parsi matrimonial court. One husband, accusing his wife of adultery, knew her alleged lover: "we used to lend each other money." The husband had not paid back the money he owed, and the other man had won a decree for Rs 150 in the Court of Small Causes. The husband seemed to be perpetually in debt. His wife's uncle, a man named Dinsha Angra, had also given him a loan. When the husband did not repay it, the uncle had taken him to the same court and obtained a decree for Rs 1,000.[71]

The Court for the Relief of Insolvent Debtors also did a bustling business, one that overlapped with that of the Small Causes Court. Desperate debtors tried to get insolvency status in the Insolvency Court before creditors could press for repayment (or worse) in the Court of Small Causes.[72] The Insolvency Court was technically a special division of the High Court.[73] A judge known as the Commissioner of Insolvency oversaw the court, while another figure called the Official Assignee represented and coordinated the interests of the creditors. Being declared insolvent meant that the total sum owed by the debtor would shrink to the pool of assets actually possessed by him or her. Most creditors would then receive a proportion relative to the size of the debt owed to them. The distribution of assets by *composition*, an out of court agreement under which creditors accepted part payment in discharge of the debt, did occur, but was regarded as clandestine and illegitimate by lawyers. Creditors were so desperate to avoid insolvency proceedings that their interests suffered in these

---

[68] "How Bombay Lives," *Bom LR* (journal) 8 (1906), 3–4. Similarly, see Norman C. Macleod, "Reminiscences from 1894 to 1914," 18 (HRA/D63/A5) in Private Papers of Norman Cranstoun Macleod, Macleod of Cadboll Papers (HCA).

[69] "How Bombay Lives," 3.

[70] Ibid., 8. For a more positive view of the Court of Small Causes, see "The Reminiscences of a Solicitor," *Bom LJ* 13 (1935–6), 22.

[71] Suit No. 12 of 1920, 1920–3 Notebook, IV: 15.

[72] "How Bombay Lives," 4–6; "The Working of the Insolvency Laws in India," *Bom LR* (journal) 11 (1907) 164.

[73] See generally Cowell, 238–9.

Using Law: Parsis Go to Court

agreements.[74] If the Commissioner granted insolvency status with a protection order, the debtor would enjoy legal immunity for all debt-related proceedings for eighteen months. This often kept the insolvent out of debtors' jail. Critics commented that the insolvency system operated in favor of debtors and that a strategic debtor could walk the streets of Bombay "freely snapping his fingers at his creditors" by seeking insolvency status at the right time.[75] One commentator wrote of the "complete and overpowering sense of hopelessness and helplessness among creditors the moment it is known that their debtor is adjudged insolvent."[76] Others complained that aspiring insolvents often hid their assets from the court.[77] Occasionally, though, one got caught. The insolvency court had the power to impose prison sentences in such situations. In one well publicized case from 1892, a Parsi debtor named Hormarji A. Hormarji initiated the insolvency process but was ultimately imprisoned for reckless speculation and concealment of Rs 29,000.[78]

The exposure of sensitive personal information was particularly pronounced in insolvency proceedings because publicity was not mere prurience on the part of the press, but an essential part of the legal process. Public announcements appeared in the papers both to inform creditors that they had a limited time in which to identify themselves if they wanted a share of the shrunken spoils and to announce the public auctioning of insolvents' property.[79] One series of ads in 1924 listed jewelry belonging to an insolvent Parsi businessman named Rustomji Framji Davar. Readers were promised that the long list of items, including emerald-and-pearl collars and diamond-and-ruby roses, were "specially made-to-order by the Insolvent by well-known makers" and that he had imported some of the gems through his own business.[80] Parsi female insolvents were rare but not unknown. Their jewelry, too, was put toward payment of their debts.[81]

Parsis were occasionally creditors in insolvency suits.[82] More often, though, they were the debtors. Parsi names abounded on the lists of insolvents published in the Bombay newspapers every week.[83] In particular, spikes occurred after the

---

[74] V. M. Patel, "An Obnoxious Provision in the Insolvency Law," *Bom LJ* 6 (1928–9) 380.

[75] "The Working of the Insolvency Laws," 163.

[76] "The Lot of Creditors under Insolvency Law," *Bom LJ* 3 (1925–6) 43. See also Patel, "Obnoxious Provision," 371–83.

[77] "The Presidency Small Cause Court and Arrest of Insolvents," *Bom LJ* 5 (1927–8), 112. See also Patel, "Obnoxious Provision," 381.

[78] *In the Matter of Hormarji Ardesir Hormarji, an insolvent* ILR 17 Bom 334 (1893) and ILR 19 Bom 297 (1895); "Re Hormarjee Ardeshir Hormarjee, Insolvent," *TI* (30 August 1892), 3; Patel and Paymaster, III: 846.

[79] "Notice of Intention to Declare Dividends," *TI* (6 February 1939), 2.

[80] "Bona Fide Sale," *TI* (9 June 1924), 4; and (11 June 1924), 4.

[81] "Parsi Lady Adjudged Insolvent," *TI* (17 February 1932), 3.

[82] For instance, see *In re Kalidas Keshowji* ILR 26 Bom 623 (1902); "The Insolvency Law: Its use and abuse," *Bom LJ* 6 (1928–9) 111–25.

[83] See, for instance, "Bombay Insolvency Court, *TI* (4 March 1910), 11; "List of Insolvents," *TI* (12 July 1935), 15; *Bai Jaiji v. N. C. Macleod* 8 Bom LR 122 (1906).

50   *Law and Identity in Colonial South Asia: Parsi Legal Culture*

1865 collapse of the cotton markets that ruined a generation of Bombay merchants and with the strengthening of the Gandhian prohibition campaign that put many Parsi alcohol merchants out of business in the 1930s.[84] For our purposes, the most interesting cases were insolvency suits in which both debtor *and* creditor were Parsi. In the 1914 case of Curverjee Nowrojee Gamadia, the son of a Parsi millionaire defaulted on debts to Parsi creditors and wanted to be declared insolvent. The judge, a Parsi like all of the lawyers, highlighted the intracommunity aspect of the case: the creditors had lent money to Gamadia not because he provided any security for the loan, but because they assumed his father would repay them, if necessary. "They were Parsis and it would be a hollow pretense to say that they did not know the position of the insolvent and his father." But the father refused to get involved. The judge considered the son's behavior as poor as the creditors': "He was in a respectable walk of life assisting his father in his many businesses when suddenly he launched into a life of extravagance and gambl[ing] and its accompanying vices. He borrowed all he could and without any compunction he now came to the Court and applied for his discharge." The judge's solution was a compromise. Gamadia was declared insolvent, but he would only receive a protection order a few months later, leaving him legally unprotected in the interim. This would give the young man's creditors the opportunity to put him in jail for debt.[85]

A 1924 case among Parsis had a similar outcome. Sorabji Framji Kalyanwalla was "an eminently respectable member of the Parsi community and a trustee for several charitable institutions" who speculated during the boom period when "champagne and whisky were the order of the day on the financial market." The debtor's lawyer, none other than Mohammad Ali Jinnah, argued that his client was to be pitied, not punished. Losing money in the share market was "a commonplace occurrence, an everyday affair." But the creditors' lawyer painted a less charitable picture. By his account, Kalyanwalla deserved "no mercy at all as he frittered away his creditors' monies in gambling." The debtor claimed implausibly to keep no written records of his finances and tried to hide assets by transferring them to his wife. The judge granted insolvency status, but with a delayed protection order, such that Kalyanwalla would be under no legal protection for six months.[86]

Finally, the Courts of the Presidency Magistrates (also known as the Police Courts) handled most of the criminal matters of Bombay, from petty theft and

---

[84] On the crash of 1865, see *In re Pestanji Cursetji Shroff* 2 Bom H Ct Reps 42 (1864–6); *In re Manekji Framji, an insolvent* 3 Bom H Ct Reps 167 (1865–7); *In re Mancharji Hirji Readymoney* 5 Bom H Ct Reps 55 (1868–9); *In re Manikji Shapurji Kaka* 5 Bom H Ct Reps 61 (1868–9); *In Re Cawasji Ookerji* ILR 13 Bom 114 (1889); Jessawalla, 117–19. On prohibition, see "List of Insolvents" in *TI*:(6 August 1930), 4; (4 October 1930), 7; (1 July 1932), 10; (5 July 1935), 5; (7 September 1935), 11; (8 January 1937), 2. See also Desai, *History*, 104–12, 305–13.

[85] "A Parsi Millionaire's Son," *TI* (27 November 1914), 5.

[86] "An Insolvent's Plea. Discharge Suspended. *Sorabji Framji Kalyanwalla, Insolvent v. Cursetji M. Bharucha and others,*" *TI* (20 November 1924), 8.

Using Law: Parsis Go to Court

minor assault to seditious libel and kidnapping.[87] As one Indian solicitor described them, these courts were generally "either dark, damp, dirty or draughty," and inspired "a feeling not of awe but of nausea and repugnance." The spirit of the place made "even a law-abiding citizen feel rebellious, let alone a criminal."[88] The memoirs of Thomas Strangman, a leading litigator and Chief Magistrate of Bombay in the 1920s, did little to inspire greater confidence in this court. Strangman remarked that deciding cases in the Police Court was "as simple as falling off a tree" compared to practicing as an advocate in civil suits. "I soon discovered that the vast majority of police cases were true, the vast majority of private complaints were false," and the only hard cases were alleged violations of health and safety legislation. With breathtaking confidence, Strangman declared that "[o]nce these general lines were understood, the arrears vanished and the day's work was often finished by lunch-time."[89]

Parsis experienced criminal law through assault- and adultery-related private prosecutions in the Police Courts. It was not unusual for parties in the PCMC to refer to criminal suits in which they had been involved. In 1898, one wife told the court that she had prosecuted her husband for criminal intimidation after he threatened her with a butcher's knife.[90] In a 1903 case, there were references to a husband's prosecution of his wife's alleged lover for assault. The same husband had prosecuted his wife and her alleged lover for criminal insult and intimidation. In turn, his mother-in-law had pursued him in the Police Court for criminal trespass.[91] The failure to pay maintenance owed by a husband to a wife was also considered a criminal matter. As a result, many Parsi matrimonial cases straddled the lower criminal courts and the PCMC.[92]

If there was a dead body in a criminal case, the Coroner's Court stepped in, although not always exclusively.[93] Much confusion resulted from the overlap between the criminal jurisdictions of the Coroner's Court, the Police Courts, and the Criminal Sessions of the Bombay High Court. Every year, up to twenty cases were tried twice or even three times among these separate courts, occasionally with different outcomes. (The High Court had ultimate authority.[94]) The Coroner of Bombay was a physician with the status of magistrate who carried out inquests. On the basis of his report, a special Coroner's jury produced a verdict. The Coroner's Court held official inquiries into all murders,

---

[87] See, generally, Cowell, 271–3.

[88] "The Reminiscences of a Solicitor," 21.

[89] Strangman, 20.

[90] Suit No. 2 of 1898, 1893–1903 PCMC Notebook, II: 8.

[91] Suit No. 3 of 1903, 1893–1903 PCMC Notebook, III: 69, 74–5

[92] For example, see Suit No. 6 of 1893, I: 65; and 1 of 1897, I: 235, 237; both in 1893–1903 PCMC Notebook.

[93] Cowell, 282–3; I. B. Lyon and L. A. Waddell, *Medical Jurisprudence for India, with illustrative cases* (Calcutta: Thacker, Spink and Co., 1909), 5–6.

[94] "The Question of Double Jurisdiction of the Coroner and a Magistrate" (11 November 1892), 3; untitled editorial (15 November 1892), 4; both in the *TI*.

manslaughter cases, and suicides, including poisonings, drownings, prison deaths, and "crushings by machinery."[95] Work-related accidents were a major cause of death in late colonial Bombay. One coroner in the late 1880s complained of the needless loss of life caused by "the want of overhauling the machinery daily, death from dealing with cargo, or from entering the bilges of ships in the midst of mephitic gas, from cleaning drains, and so on."[96] Poisoning cases, particularly by opium, arsenic, and the seeds of the *dhatura* plant were also not unusual.[97] It was, in fact, because of poisoning that Parsi leaders overcame their own initial resistance in the 1840s to the idea of non-Parsis doing postmortem examinations on Parsi corpses. The purity laws dictated that only Parsis could touch Parsi bodies after death. However, the Parsi Panchayat accepted that only coroners would have the expertise to detect the use of poison.[98] In the nineteenth and early twentieth centuries, poisoning was not an unusual cause of death among Parsis, particularly for suicides.[99]

Criminal cases involving Parsis were usually for nonviolent crimes.[100] As one would expect of any population with clerical, professional, and mercantile expertise, there were cases of alleged white-collar crimes like forgery, fraud, cheating, misappropriation of funds, and criminal breach of trust.[101] In 1927, *Hindi Punch* noted the large number of Parsi cases in the Police Court for cheating and breach of trust, a phenomenon said to besmirch the "once proud name of Parsis."[102] More cases, though, pertained to violations of government licensing and regulatory schemes. In the last two decades of the nineteenth century, especially, Parsis who

[95] Untitled editorial, *TI* (30 May 1889), 4.

[96] Ibid.

[97] See, for instance, "Poisoning in Bombay," *TI* (19 March 1881), 3; "Dhatura Poisoning in Bombay," *TI* (5 June 1893), 5.

[98] Delphine Menant, *Les Parsis: histoire des communautés zoroastriennes de l'Inde. Première partie* (Paris: Ernest Leroux, 1898), 260–3.

[99] See Bomanjee Byramjee Patell, "Suicide amongst the Parsees of Bombay during the Last Twelve Years," *J. Anthropol. Soc. Bombay* 4: 1 (1895), 17, 21. For particular cases, see in the *TI*: "Suicide by Poison" (22 August 1865), 3; "Suicide of a Parsee" (5 January 1885); "Suicide of a Parsee" (13 June 1888), 3; "Sad Suicide of a Parsee Girl" (24 August 1891), 3; "The Suspicious Death of a Parsee Lady" (16 March 1892), 3; "Suicide of a Parsee Doctor" (21 September 1900), 5; "A Parsi's Suicide: Worried by Unemployment" (28 February 1924), 5; "Peculiar Case of Opium Poisoning: Parsi Woman's Death" (10 August 1929), 15; "Parsi Found Dead on Malabar Hill. Opium Poisoning" (1 September 1933), 12.

[100] For violent exceptions, see Menant, *Les Parsis*, 258–60.

[101] For examples, see *Emperor v. Byramji Jamsetji Chaewalla* ILR 52 Bom 280 (1928); *Shapurji Sorabji v. Emperor* ILR 60 Bom 148 (1936); A. J. C. Mistry, *Reminiscences of the Office of Messrs Wadia Ghandy and Co.* (Bombay: Commercial Reporter's Press and the "Echo" Press, [1911]), 73; Jessawalla, 65–6; "Parsi Priest Sentenced," *TI* (5 July 1947), 9. On the notorious solicitor Pestonjee Dinsha, see "A Solicitor Censured," *TI* (12 July 1871), 4; "Action on Two Promissory Notes," *TI* (1 July 1876), 2; "Charge against a Late Solicitor of Extorting Money," *TI* (17 February 1886), 3; Vachha, 242–6. For another example, see *R v. Archibald Duncan Hunter and Jehanger Framgee Moola Fearoz* (1892), Old Bailey Proceedings Online (accessed on 21 May 2012): www.oldbaileyonline.org.

[102] "1297," *HP* (11 September 1927), 16.

Using Law: Parsis Go to Court

were found selling unauthorized amounts of toddy (a locally made liquor) and medicinal forms of cocaine, or who were in possession of unlicensed distilling equipment, were tried under the Bombay *A'bkári* Act (V of 1878), a statute that regulated the production and distribution of alcohol and other intoxicating substances.[103] During the first three decades of the twentieth century, prosecutors' attention seemed to shift from intoxicants to water sanitation. Parsi property owners were convicted for refusing to build the kinds of drains and water storage facilities required by the City of Bombay Municipal Act (III of 1888) and the District Municipalities Act (III of 1901).[104] The early twentieth century was also the period when worker safety received some attention from the state. Parsi supervisors and industrialists were tried for overworking their factory workers, creating unsafe working conditions that caused loss of life, and even for beating their workers to death.[105] Interestingly, it was not unknown for a worker's sudden death to be blamed on his enlarged spleen and not on the employer's violence, echoing a common excuse made for white employers who had beaten their Indian laborers to death.[106]

This was the world up to and including the Bombay High Court. There was equally a world above it. With permission, cases appealed from the Bombay High Court went to the Judicial Committee of the Privy Council, the highest court of appeal for the British Empire.[107] The JCPC, known as the Privy Council for short, consisted of mostly British judges who sat in groups of five at Downing Street in London to hear cases from the colonies.[108] Only lawyers and case

[103] For example, see *Queen-Empress v. Pestanji Barjorji* ILR 9 Bom 456 (1885); *Queen-Empress v. Gustadji Barjorji* ILR 10 Bom 181 (1886); *Queen-Empress v. Byramji Kharsedji* ILR 14 Bom 93 (1890); *Queen-Empress v. Framji Bamanji Kelawala* 2 Bom LR 663 (1900); *Emperor v. Jamsetji C. Cama* ILR 27 Bom 551 (1903); "Bombay Police Courts," *TI* (11 January 1919), 11. See generally Indra Munshi Saldanha, "On Drinking and 'Drunkenness': History of Liquor in Colonial India," *EPW* 30: 37 (16 September 1995), 2323–31.

[104] For example, see *Emperor v. Nadirsha H. E. Sukhia* 6 Bom LR 667 (1904); *In re Dinbai Jijibhai Khambatta* ILR 43 Bom 864 (1919); *Emperor v. Dorabsha Bomanji Dubash* ILR 50 Bom 250 (1926); *Emperor v. Merwanji M. Mistry* ILR 52 Bom 250 (1928).

[105] See *Imperatrix v. Navroji Manakji Parviz* in "Charges brought by Mr. N.M. Parviz, a Parsi railway contractor against Mr. T.S. Greenaway, an Assistant Superintendent of Police (21 June 1900, file 1239 (IOR/L/PJ/6/543); *Emperor v. Byram Nowroji Gamadia* ILR 50 Bom 34 (1926); *Emperor v. Jamshedji Nasserwanji Modi* ILR 55 Bom 866 (1931).

[106] *Imperatrix v. Parviz*. See also H. W. V. Cox, *Medico-Legal Court Companion* (Calcutta: Eastern Law House, 1927), 26, 454; Jordanna Bailkin, "The Boot and the Spleen: When was Murder Possible in British India?" *CSSH* 48: 2 (2006), 462–93; Kolsky, *Colonial Justice*, 135–40.

[107] See L. P. Delves Broughton, *The Code of Civil Procedure, being Act VIII of 1859 and the Acts Amending and Extending It*, ed. C. J. Wilkinson (Calcutta; Thacker Spink and Co., 1871), 753–82; Vachha, 48–9; Kozlowski, 96–7; P. A. Howell, *The Judicial Committee of the Privy Council 1833–1876: Its Origins, Structure and Development* (Cambridge: Cambridge University Press, 1979); David B. Swinfen, *Imperial Appeal: The Debate on the Appeal to the Privy Council, 1833–1986* (Manchester: Manchester University Press, 1987).

[108] Although the JCPC was commonly referred to as the Privy Council, it was not to be confused with the larger nonjudicial body whose full name was the Privy Council. The JCPC's rulings were read out before the full Privy Council during the process of making recommendations to the

records from earlier proceedings, rather than witnesses and new evidence, appeared before this court. The Privy Council served as the final court of appeal for more than a quarter of the world's population and exercised a jurisdiction "more extensive, whether measured by area, population, variety of nations, creeds, languages, laws or customs than that hitherto enjoyed by any court known to civilization."[109] One judge of the Privy Council named Viscount Haldane of Clone reveled in the court's exoticism during a 1921 speech to the University Law Society. Upon entering into the Privy Council Office, his audience members would find themselves "in company with white men, some of whom look as if they had come from the far West, and may be of American appearance; yellow men, some of whom come from Hong Kong; Burmese, who come from Burma, Hindus and Mohammedans from India; Dutch from South Africa; a mixed race from Ceylon – all sorts of people may be straying in there, and you will feel yourself in good Imperial company."[110] The judges administered Roman-Dutch law from South Africa and Ceylon, French law from Quebec, and "curious mixtures of law which prevail in various colonies, sometimes Italian law, sometimes Roman." Haldane was not deaf to the accusation that the judges were dilettantes in most of these areas. "We sit there and we do our best. We are only human beings and I daresay we make mistakes."[111]

Australian and Canadian litigants began sending their own lawyers to London to oversee their Privy Council appeals in the 1890s. Previously, they had hired London barristers. By the 1920s, Indians were doing the same, and nationalist leaders were arguing for the court's abolition as India's final court of appeal. Ill-conceived Privy Council rulings on Indian appeals occasionally caused "confusion and consternation" back in India.[112] As H. S. Gour pointed out in the late 1920s, "[b]eing an absentee Court they cannot make local inspection; living as they do in a foreign land they are without local knowledge and being essentially English Judges they can never become familiar with the Indian systems of personal law and the growing bulk and complexity of its Statute law."[113]

M. K. Gandhi agreed, writing in 1926 that the Privy Council "sitting six thousand miles away" ought to be replaced with a Supreme Court in Delhi. "Our self-respect demands it." Privy Council decisions were at times politically biased. Their rulings on points of custom were "often distortions of the reality,

---

emperor or empress about a given case. See Lord Haldane, "The Work for the Empire of the Judicial Committee of the Privy Council," *Cam LJ* 1 (1923), 145.

[109] Norman Bentwich, *The Practice of the Privy Council in Judicial Matters in its appeals from Courts of Civil, Criminal and Admiralty Jurisdiction and in Appeals from Ecclesiastical and Prize Courts with the Statutes, Rules and Forms of Procedure* (London: Sweet and Maxwell, 1912), viii.

[110] Haldane, 144. Similarly, see 1928 comments of Lord Brougham in Cowell, 212–13.

[111] Haldane,154. See also Ludo Rocher, "Indian Response to Anglo-Hindu Law," *JAOS* 92: 3 (1972), 419.

[112] Vachha, 48. See also Derrett, "Administration," 42, at note 149.

[113] H. S. Gour, "The Privy Council – and After," *Bom LJ* 5 (1927–8), 16.

Using Law: Parsis Go to Court

55

not because they are perverse, but because it is not possible for mortals to know everything."[114] Yet it was not until several years after independence that the Privy Council was abolished as the final court of appeal for India. A Federal Court operated in Delhi between 1937 and 1950. Until 1948, it focused on disputes of a constitutional nature between the various provinces or between a province and the central government. However, its decisions could be appealed to the Privy Council.[115] The Indian Supreme Court was established in 1950, when it became the final court of appeal for all Indian cases.

It was not only for the colonies that the Privy Council was the final court of appeal. It was also the apex court for an eclectic jumble of British jurisdictions. The court decided ecclesiastical and admiralty suits. Prior to 1912, it heard cases pertaining to copyright, patents, lunacy, and Oxford and Cambridge Universities.[116] The fact that judges of the Privy Council occasionally came up through these other court systems, particularly the ecclesiastical ones, explained perhaps why they were so comfortable ruling on religion for the empire. Privy Council judges, like father-and-son duo the Lords Phillimore, had been hearing disputes over Church of England rituals for decades before they joined the Judicial Committee. They were soon deciding cases about Catholic cemeteries in Montreal and Zoroastrian fire temples in Rangoon.[117]

There was another intriguing fact about the Privy Council and the relationship it created between colony and metropole. There was a significant overlap in personnel between the judges of the Privy Council and the judicial House of Lords, the final court of appeal for cases from Britain. At least one rule, however, distinguished the two courts' mode of operation. As Law Lords, the judges could issue dissenting or concurring judgments. Such opinions documented alternative lines of legal reasoning that were put into circulation, potentially having

---

[114] M. K. Gandhi, *The Law and the Lawyers*, ed. B. G. Kher (Ahmedabad: Navajivan Publishing House, 2004), 235-7.

[115] See "A Federal Court," *Mad LJ* 64 (1933), 159-60; "Inauguration of the Federal Court," *Cal LJ* 66 (1937), 11n-18n; "The Federal Court," *Bom LJ* 15 (1937-8), 142-4; Rohit De, "Emasculating the Executive: The Federal Court and Civil Liberties in Late Colonial India, 1942-1944," in *Fates of Political Liberalism in the British Post-Colony: The Politics of the Legal Complex*, eds. T. Halliday, L. Karpik, and M. Feeley (Cambridge: Cambridge University Press, 2012), 59-90.

[116] Bentwich, 15; Cowell, 206.

[117] See *Dame Henriette Brown v. Les Curé et Marguilliers de L'Oeuvre et Fabrique de Notre Dame de Montréal* LR 6 PC (1874-5) 157; *Saklat v. Bella*. Sir Robert Joseph Phillimore (1810-85) wrote the 2,466-page monolith, *The Ecclesiastical Law of the Church of England* (London: Sweet, 1873). He ruled on the lawfulness of numerous points of Anglican ritual, including the use of incense, the elevation of the consecrated elements, the addition of water to wine during consecration, the singing of the *Agnus Dei* between consecration and reception of communion, and the making of the sign of the cross and adoption of excessive prostration by priests. Walter George Frank Phillimore (first Baron Phillimore, 1845-1929) delivered judgments on the use of lighted candles at the communion table, sculptural representations of the transfiguration and ascension, the use of Catholic-style ceremonial dress, and the proper geographic location to be adopted during consecration prayers.

56   *Law and Identity in Colonial South Asia: Parsi Legal Culture*

persuasive power in future cases. These tools were made unavailable to Privy Council judges, making it harder to produce judgments of equal nuance and complexity. The Privy Council issued one single, unanimous opinion per case.[118] The imperial state would only undermine its own authority by speaking in multiple voices. The implication was that, like political "children" or those stuck in the "waiting room of history," colonial subjects needed a clear and unified message.[119]

The Privy Council's judgments had huge influence in India.[120] There was even the story, apocryphal perhaps, that the Privy Council was being worshipped as a deity on the Rajputana plateau.[121] The bulk of the Privy Council's cases came from South Asia while India was a colony. From 1909, an Indian member was appointed to help decide these appeals.[122] Privy Council appeals from India were extremely costly and complicated to push to fruition, given the distance and stringent documentary requirements. At certain points, up to a third of Indian appeals failed for nonprosecution.[123] Even so, the Privy Council produced 2,500 rulings on Indian appeals before its Indian jurisdiction ended in 1949.[124] Of all the appeals from the Bombay High Court that resulted in reported Privy Council judgments, Parsis were parties to a tenth.[125] Among them were suits about trusts, inheritance, eminent domain, taxation, and (less commonly) insolvency.[126] Parsi appeals also came from elsewhere in South Asia, the most famous being religious trust suits from Rangoon and Secunderabad.[127] Indeed, the pursuit of litigation in London held a special place in the history of Parsi–British relations. When the first Parsis went to Britain in 1723, they were traveling to have their case adjudicated by the East India Company's Court of Directors.[128]

---

[118] Bentwich, 341; Haldane, 144; Barnett Hollander, *Colonial Justice: The Unique Achievement of the Privy Council's Committee of Judges* (London: Bowes and Bowes, 1961), 29–30.

[119] Uday Singh Mehta, *Liberalism and Empire: A Study in Nineteenth-Century British Liberal Thought* (Chicago: Chicago University Press, 1999), 31–3; Dipesh Chakrabarty, *Provincializing Europe: Postcolonial Thought and Historical Difference* (Princeton: Princeton University Press, 2002), 8–10.

[120] See Jain, *Outlines*, 339–43.

[121] Haldane, 153; Howell, 1.

[122] Haldane, 148; "India and the Privy Council: Personnel of the Judicial Committee," *TI* (26 February 1926), 8.

[123] Jain, *Outlines*, 320.

[124] Ibid., 342.

[125] In the *ILR Bombay* series, approximately 29 of 271 Privy Council appeals from Bombay High Court judgments (10.7 percent) had at least one Parsi party.

[126] For a sample, see *Modee Kaikhooscrow Hormusjee v. Cooverbhaee* 19 Eng. Rep. 168 (1809–65), reproducing 6 MIA 448 (1846–9); *Phirozshaw Bomanjee Petit v. Bai Goolbai* ILR 47 Bom 790 (1923); *Nowroji Rustomji Wadia v. Government of Bombay* ILR 49 Bom 700 (1925); *Sir Jamshedjee Jeejibhoy v. Sorabji Byramji Warden* 66–7 IA 270 (1939–40); *Dr. Navroji Ardeshir Cooper v. Official Assignee of Bombay* ILR 1942 Bom 740; *Province of Bombay v. Hormusji Manekji* ILR 1947 Bom 495. See also note 17.

[127] See Chapter 7 on *Saklat v. Bella* and Chapter 6 on *Pestonji Jeevanji v. Chinoy*.

[128] Darukhanawala, *Parsi Lustre*, I: 335.

Using Law: Parsis Go to Court

A few patterns emerged across the array of lawsuits between Parsis. Insolvency and matrimonial suits were common and routine, rarely rising to the upper levels of court. By contrast, inheritance and trust suits were often protracted, attracting press coverage and going on appeal to the highest levels. Commercial suits between Parsis were rare. Some did exist, but they were usually settled out of court, precluding judgment.[129] Similarly, libel suits began but usually ended with a public apology and withdrawal of charges.

Why did litigation between Parsis fall along these lines? First, litigants in certain types of suits wanted to change their legal status. These changes could only be granted by the courts. Divorce and insolvency, for instance, were states that existed only in law. If a person wanted the state-backed financial consequences of either, he or she could only get them by going to court. Second, when a dispute had a binary outcome, rather than an incrementally divisible one, there was less likelihood of negotiating a compromise. In trust suits, in particular, each side usually wanted exclusive control over trust properties or funds. Either one side had the right to decide when to close an internal door in the fire temple, or it did not.[130] Either one party could build a second tower of silence, or it could not.[131] Either a particular individual was entitled to enter the temple, or she was not.[132] There was no face-saving middle ground. In commercial suits, by contrast, litigants were usually suing over money. A sum of money could be adjusted until both sides could accept it, thus facilitating a settlement. This was not to say that Parsis never sued each other in commercial matters, but simply that it may explain why these suits were less common than other types of reported cases. Simply put, it was easier to reach a compromise in disputes about money than about power.[133] And the longer a suit continued, the more discrediting it became for either side to give in. A third factor was the role of family. Up to a point, intrafamily disputes may have stayed out of court due to shared concern for the family reputation and the use of relatives as peacemakers. When an intrafamily dispute degenerated, though, the depth of feeling – whole lifetimes of social interaction – probably increased the animosity and longevity of the suit.

---

[129] See, for instance, Suit No. 1927 of 1928: *[Bharucha v. Dubash]*, "Hon. Mr. Justice Davar. Long Causes 5 June 1928 to 10 April 1929," 91–100 (BHC).

[130] See *Navroji Manekji Wadia and others v. Dastur Kharsedji Mancherji and others* ILR 28 Bom 20 (1904); *Udvāḍā Īrānshāh Ātaśbeherām Kesno Cukādo* (Rangoon: Bombay Burma Press, 1933), unpublished trans. Homi D. Patel.

[131] See *Pestonji Jeevanji and others v. Shapurji Edulji Chinoy and others* case papers, JCPC Suit No. 10 of 1907, 1908: vol. 3, judgment 9 (PCO).

[132] See Introduction at note 99.

[133] For a commercial exception, see *Pestonjee Dadabhai v. Hormasji Manekjee* 5 Bom LR 387 (1903). For an exception that proved the rule, see the Privy Council appeal of *Burjorjee D. Contractor v. J. K. Irani* ILR 40 Bom 289 (1916), in which the plaintiff sought specific performance of a contract. For a rare trust suit that ended in compromise, see "Trustees to Manage Fire Temple. Dispute Ends. Compromise in High Court Suit," *TI* (19 July 1939), 14.

58 Law and Identity in Colonial South Asia: Parsi Legal Culture

Inheritance suits especially reflected this dynamic.[134] Finally, there were fights over principle – what Vilhelm Aubert would call conflicts of value, in contrast to conflicts of interest.[135] Parsi trust suits occasionally involved large numbers of community leaders opposing each other on points of religious doctrine and practice. Fighting for a principle meant fighting to the end. It meant not compromising. This litigation-perpetuating impulse lurked in many trust suits.

LEGAL CONSCIOUSNESS

How did colonial Parsis think about going to court? When and why did they decide that they had a legal rather than a social problem? What made them turn to law when they did or hold back when they did not? If legal consciousness – the ways individuals interpret and mobilize legal processes – has been elusive for social scientists conducting interviews with their subjects, historians have found it even harder to recover from archival sources.[136] Parsi litigants must have revealed their attitudes toward law in many different settings and types of disputes, but it was in the PCMC that they answered most explicitly the question: "when and why should I go to court?" In the same way that Parsi personal law came to reflect the particular values and features of Parsi family life, so Parsi disputants' mental calculations vis-à-vis the matrimonial court had a lot to do with family. Concern for family reputation was often the dominant consideration in deciding whether to go to court, and senior family members were the ultimate guardians of that reputation. Reputation was a key concern in cases about sexual behavior, in particular – like the matrimonial suits of Chapter 5 or the libel cases of Chapter 7. More than this, though, it was the unusually rich crop of court records from the matrimonial court that made marital cases the

---

[134] See, for instance, *Bapuji Nusserwanji Vatchagandy and another v. Sorabji Ardeshir Vatchagandy* (Testamentary Suit No. 17 of 1909), "Hon. Justice D. D. Davar. Judgments (22 July 1910–24 December 1910)," 1–152; *Dhanjishaw H. Gorakpurwalla v. Pirojbai H. Gorakpurwalla* (Suit No. 1483 of 1927), "Hon. Justice J. D. Davar. Judgments (10 August 1927–5 April 1928)," 302–3 (both BHC). Famous Parsi inheritance suits included *Limji Nowroji Bánáji v. Bápuji Ruttonji Limbuwállá* ILR 11 Bom 441 (1887); *In the matter of the Trustees' and Mortgagees' Powers Act and In the matter of Hormusji Framji Warden (deceased), Hirjibhai Bomanji Warden and another* ILR 32 Bom 214 (1908); *Dossibai Framji Marker v. Cooverbai Hormusji Marker* ILR 32 Bom 575 (1908); *Jamshedji Cursetjee Tarachand v. Soonabai and others* ILR 33 Bom 122 (1909) and case papers (Suit No. 341 of 1907) (BHC); *Kaikushru Bezonji Nanabhoy Capadia v. Shirinbai Bezonji Capadia and others* ILR 43 Bom 88 (1919).

[135] Vilhelm Aubert, "Competition and Dissensus: Two Types of Conflict and of Conflict Resolution," *J. Conflict Res.* 7: 1 (1963), 26–42. See also William L. F. Felstiner, "The Logic of Mediation," in *Toward a General Theory of Social Control*, ed. Donald Black (New York: Academic Press, 1984), I.

[136] S. S. Silbey, "Legal Culture and Legal Consciousness," *International Encyclopedia of Social and Behavioral Sciences* (New York: Elsevier, Pergamon Press, 2001), 8624. See also Sally Engle Merry, *Getting Justice and Getting Even: Legal Consciousness among Working-Class Americans* (Chicago: University of Chicago Press, 1990), 4.

Using Law: Parsis Go to Court

ideal hunting ground for attitudes about the legal system. Other types of civil litigation were certainly colored by reputational concerns, too, but their records did not illuminate the decision to go to court in the same way.

Fault-based divorce schemes were standard across the English-speaking world in the nineteenth and early twentieth centuries. People could only get divorced if they could prove that their spouses had done something wrong.[137] The Parsi Marriage and Divorce Acts of 1865 and 1936 created such a system for Parsis and were administered through the Parsi matrimonial courts. The largest of these courts sat in the Bombay High Court building and was overseen by a judge of the Bombay High Court, himself often Parsi. Findings on the issues in question were delivered by eleven Parsi delegates who functioned as a jury. A very particular list specified acts that would constitute fault.[138] As in all fault-based schemes, parties who simply wanted a divorce on the basis of mutual consent sometimes fabricated a fault-based narrative that would satisfy the legal tests.[139] If the court spotted any of the three Cs – collusion, connivance, or condonation – it would refuse to grant a divorce. Connivance and collusion referred to a secret agreement made between spouses for fraudulent purposes; namely, to obtain a divorce even though fault was absent. One judge explained the difference to delegates: "connivance refers to what occurred before the [alleged] adultery and collusion to what occurred after in reference to the case."[140] If the plaintiff had delayed in bringing the suit, the court also grew suspicious. Delay hinted at condonation – one spouse's forgiveness of the other after a transgression. Taking back a spouse at fault nullified the offending act for the purposes of divorce law. Ever vigilant, the Parsi Marriage and Divorce Act required that there be "no unnecessary or improper delay in instituting the suit."[141] As a result, many litigants were asked the question: "why did you delay?"

Their answers created a varied portrait of Parsi legal consciousness. Some plaintiffs offered a pragmatic explanation that revealed a good awareness of evidential requirements: they delayed because they were busy collecting

---

[137] See Hartog, *Man*; Lawrence M. Friedman, "A Dead Language: Divorce Law and Practice before No-Fault," *Virg. LR* 86: 7 (2000), 1497–1536; Stephen Michael Cretney, *Family Law in the Twentieth Century: A History* (Oxford: Oxford University Press, 2003), 161–273, 319–91.

[138] See Chapter 5 at 216.

[139] For example, see Suit No. 5 of 1898, 1893–1903 PCMC Notebook, II: 46–7. Compare Henry Maine, "Divorce" (21 January 1863) in M. E. Grant Duff, *Sir Henry Maine: A Brief Memoir of his Life with some of his Indian Speeches and Minutes selected and edited by Whitley Stokes* (London: John Murray, 1892), 96–7; Friedman, "Dead Language."

[140] Suit No. 5 of 1898, 1893–1903 PCMC Notebook, II: 48.

[141] PMDA 1865, s. 32 and PMDA 1936, s. 35(d) in C. N. Wadia and S. B. Katpitia, *The Parsi Marriage and Divorce Act (India Act III of 1936)* (Surat: Jashvantsinh Gulabsinh Thakor at "Surat City" Printing Press, 1939), 95, 103–5. See also Framjee A. Rana, *Parsi Law embodying the Law of Marriage and Divorce and Inheritance and Succession applicable to Parsis in British India* (Bombay: A. B. Dubash at the "Jam-e Jamshed" Printing Works, 1934), 69–70.

evidence.[142] "Making enquiries" was the term used for extracting information from social networks within the community.[143] Through it, wives discovered that their husbands had entered into bigamous marriages or had admitted to being impotent.[144] In one case from 1941, a wife made enquiries and learned not only that her husband had a mistress, but that the pearls the husband had given the wife to wear at her own wedding belonged to the other woman.[145] By asking around, husbands claimed to learn that their wives were having affairs or working as prostitutes.[146] In a case from 1893, one husband told the court that he had learned that his wife had become his own brother's mistress.[147] In a 1903 case, a husband reported that a tip led him to a maternity hospital, where he found his estranged wife with a newborn baby that could not have been his.[148]

Making enquiries occasionally meant getting help from professionals. Suspicious wives sometimes hired detectives like the Irish private eye, Charles Edward Ring. Ring followed more than one Parsi husband to clandestine meetings with other women in private apartments and hotel rooms.[149] He and his assistants engineered confrontations as part of their efforts to gather evidence. In one case, Ring's assistant tried to start a fight with a husband as the latter emerged from a brothel in the red-light district of Kamathipura. As intended, a crowd of bystanders gathered around the two men. According to one policeman who was called to the scene, the husband said that "as he was coming out of a prostitute's *chawl* the Christian youth bumped against him and abused him." The set-up was an attempt to create witnesses other than Ring and his associates who could attest to the husband's probable philandering.[150]

Husbands, by contrast, harnessed the late colonial obsession with registration to collect evidence against their wives, particularly when alleging extramarital pregnancy.[151] In court, they produced birth certificates of the children in question and cross-examined the keepers of death registers from the *dakhmas*, where the bodies of stillborn babies were exposed to vultures.[152] In 1896, one surgeon from Bai Motibai's Lying-In Hospital was put on the witness stand: "This is my register of labor cases. Here she is – aged about 20, male child which

---

[142] Suit No. 3 of 1914, 1913–20 PCMC Notebook, I: 104.

[143] See Suit No. 7 of 1914, 1913–20 PCMC Notebook, II: 101.

[144] See Suit No. 6 of 1919, I: 17; Suit No. 3 of 1919, I: 7; both in 1913–20 PCMC Notebook. See also Sharafi, "Marital Patchwork," 1005.

[145] Suit No. 26 of 1941, 1941–8 PCMC Notebook, IA: 4–5, 14.

[146] For instance, see Suit No. 4 of 1895, 1893–1903 PCMC Notebook, I: 202.

[147] Suit No. 5 of 1893, 1893–1903 PCMC Notebook, I: 37–61.

[148] Suit No. 4 of 1903, 1903–13 PCMC Notebook, I: 33.

[149] For example, see Suit No. 27 of 1941, "Notes of Evidence in PCMC Cases (6 April 1942–6 November 1944)," I: 53–7.

[150] Suit No. 26 of 1941, 1941–8 PCMC Notebook, IA: 1.

[151] On the law of registration across the British Empire, see Sharafi, "Marital Patchwork," 1005 at note 130.

[152] See Suit No. 5 of 1893, I: 38; Suit No. 1 of 1895, I: 162; both in 1893–1903 PCMC Notebook.

Using Law: Parsis Go to Court

lived."[153] The challenge was proving that conception had occurred after the husband's last date of access to his wife. In an age before medicalized paternity tests, cases often turned on timing. In an 1893 case, a plaintiff-husband claimed that he had not had access to his wife in Bombay while away in the princely state of Hyderabad on long-term business. She had given birth to three children during his absence. He convinced the jury that his brother was the father.[154] In another case from 1914, a man estranged from his wife accused her of tricking him into a brief reconciliation during which they had sex three times. He claimed that she was already pregnant and was trying to make her extramarital pregnancy look marital.[155]

How did Parsi plaintiffs gain their knowledge of the legal system? Some told the court that they had relatives or family friends in the legal profession. A lawyer in an 1896 religious trust suit considered one litigant his client on account of their previous friendship, even though they were not formally linked: "I have all along considered Mr. Shapurji as my client, although I hold no power from him. He also considers me as one of his legal advisers. . . . He has also consulted me whenever he casually met me" outside of formal meetings relating to the case.[156] In the 1910s, one couple sought marital advice from J. J. Vimadalal, the eugenicist solicitor, because he was an old friend.[157] Vimadalal described the type of informal legal interactions one would expect in a community so saturated with lawyers: "I charged [the wife] no [f]ees. I gave friendly advice. I acted for the benefit of both who were my friends."[158] In a 1941 case, a hereditary corpse bearer or *nasasalar* (Guj. *nasāsālār*) had been tricked into marrying a woman without knowing that she was pregnant by someone else. The *nasasalar* learned about pauper suits through a lawyer friend: "I am a poor man. . . . Mr. Daji who is a friend of mine advised me to take legal proceedings. . . . Till I saw him I did not know that I could sue as a pauper."[159] One wife appearing in the matrimonial court had a maternal uncle who was a lawyer, while another was the niece of one of the most prominent Parsi judges of the period.[160] A female plaintiff told the court that her brother was a barrister with a doctorate in law from the University of London.[161] Another woman sought a divorce from her husband, an official at the Court of Small Causes, with the support of her brother, an

---

[153] Suit No. 4 of 1896, 1893–1903 PCMC Notebook; I: 229.

[154] Suit No. 5 of 1893, 1893–1903 PCMC Notebook, I: 37–61.

[155] Suit No. 3 of 1914, 1913–20 PCMC Notebook, I: 96–100.

[156] "Evidence of Bezonji Aderji (21–11–1896), Record. No. 14. Proceedings of the Court from 27–2–1896 to 19–6–1897," 26 in *Pestonji Jeevanji v. Chinoy* JCPC case papers.

[157] See Chapter 7 at 297–300.

[158] Suit No. 3 of 1914, 1913–20 PCMC Notebook, I: 109.

[159] Suit No. 3 of 1941, 1941–8 PCMC Notebook, I: 264. On K. N. Daji, see Umrīgar and Pāṭhak, 61.

[160] Suit No. 1 of 1901, 1893–1903 PCMC Notebook, II: 141; 9 of 1920, "PCMC Judge's Notebook (14 June 1920–25 March 1923)," III: 16.

[161] Suit No. 4 of 1914, 1913–20 PCMC Notebook, I: 82.

advocate.[162] In the general civil courts, a Parsi teenager launched a libel suit in the 1930s to protect her sexual reputation. She did so with the professional help of her family's subtenant, a Parsi lawyer.[163] Parsi lawyers gave legal advice both socially and professionally as boarders, friends, and family. There were also cases in which Parsi litigants were themselves lawyers. The plaintiffs in the two most important cases on death commemoration trusts were themselves Parsi barristers.[164]

It was also crucial to consider the effect of domestic service on the flow of information in South Asian society. Many underprivileged people lived and worked in the homes of the more affluent in British India. The matrimonial court records included the testimony of Parsi servants, cooks, and drivers who worked in Parsi homes.[165] In some of these cases, the employer was a Parsi in the legal profession. One Parsi legal official told the matrimonial court in 1895, "I am Clerk to a Judge of the Small Causes Court ... the first defendant has been off and on in my service as a cook."[166] When the first defendant testified, she revealed that she had an inheritance claim to her deceased grandfather's land. She had "heard that [she] was time-barred" and had made several petitions to the Collector.[167] One wonders whether this Parsi cook learned about limitation periods through a casual chat with her boss or perhaps by overhearing law talk in his home. Domestic employment may have been an important conduit for the transmission of legal knowledge between rich and poor Parsis.

Whether it emanated from Parsi lawyers or not, general awareness of the law affecting Parsis was impressive. Some of the best illustrations emerged after the passage of the Parsi Marriage and Divorce Act (III of 1936). The 1936 Act significantly changed the rules, creating new grounds for divorce that could be used by husbands and wives equally.[168] Immediately after the Act came into force, the average annual number of suits in the matrimonial court increased significantly – from about six or seven per year to about thirty.[169] It continued at

---

[162] Suit No. 9 of 1939, 1937–41 PCMC Notebook, III: 85–6, 94–6.

[163] "Girl's Complaint of Defamation," *TI* (12 January 1934), 4. See Chapter 7 at 282–3.

[164] Limji Naoroji Banaji was one of the earliest Parsis admitted to Lincoln's Inn (21 January 1867) and the English Bar (17 November 1869). [*The Records of the Honorable Society of Lincoln's Inn* (London: Lincoln's Inn, 1896), II: 324; Ronald Roxburgh, ed., *The Records of the Honorable Society of Lincoln's Inn. The Black Books* (London: Lincoln's Inn, 1968), V: 411.] He would become Prothonotary of the Bombay High Court (1898–1910), and was the plaintiff in *Bánáji v. Limbuwállá*. Barrister J. C. Tarachand (sometimes transliterated J. K. Tarachand) was the plaintiff in *Tarachand v. Soonabai*; see especially 211–12. See Chapter 6 at 264–70 on both cases.

[165] For example, Suit No. 1 of 1901, 1893–1903 PCMC Notebook, II: 143, 145; Suit No. 2 of 1903, 1893–1903 PCMC Notebook, III: 55; Suit No. 18 of 1941, 1941–8 PCMC Notebook, I: 278.

[166] Suit No. 1 of 1895, 1893–1903 PCMC Notebook, I: 182.

[167] Ibid., I: 183.

[168] See Chapter 4.

[169] These figures were cited in "Unprecedented Rush for Divorce," *TI* (8 February 1937), 12. See also Desai, *History*, 37.

Using Law: Parsis Go to Court

the higher rate for the rest of the colonial period.[170] Popular knowledge about the new regime was widespread. "I filed the suit as soon as the Act came into force," declared one wife in 1936.[171] In another suit initiated on the heels of the Act's entry into force, a wife sued for divorce on the basis of one of the new grounds: a spouse's "profession" of a religion other than Zoroastrianism. The wife asserted that her husband had secretly converted to Islam and that he prayed, studied with a Muslim holy man or *fakir* (Pers. *faqīr*), wore a silver locket with a Quranic inscription, and no longer wore the Zoroastrian *sudreh* and *kusti*.[172] The husband protested that he had merely read about Sufism, not converted to Islam.[173] As the husband told the court, "I do not know that Sufism is Mahomedanism."[174] He said his wife wanted a divorce so she could marry her Parsi lover. The husband lost. Lawyers for both sides noted that the case was the first of its kind, testing the new conversion provisions.[175] In another suit filed in the same year, the sister of the plaintiff-husband urged her brother to fabricate grounds for divorce, using her knowledge of the new statutory provisions. The defendant-wife's Parsi solicitor told the court that the husband's sister "appeared to me to know more about it than the defendant. She told me that under the new Act, the plaintiff could abstain for three years from intercourse, and get a divorce." The sister and the solicitor clashed sharply over her interpretation of the new legislation. As the lawyer told the court, "I said that I refused to be a party to divorce proceedings and that marriage ... could not be dissolved by an arrangement like this."[176] Such debates over legal interpretation – between lawyers and legal laypeople – could only have occurred in a setting in which laypeople had a certain familiarity with state law.

FAMILY REPUTATION

Sometimes Parsis delayed coming to the matrimonial court because they were making enquiries and collecting evidence. At other times, their explanation had to do with concern for the family (Figure 1.1). It was not simply that going to court compromised the family name. Litigants both went to court *and* avoided it to protect the family reputation. When information pertaining to the potential case was not known socially, people were likely to avoid going to court in order to protect their family name. Once the secret was out, reputational concerns

---

[170] According to my figures, the average number of suits per year for the 1893–1935 period was 5.7 (241 cases over 42 years). From 1936 until independence, the average rose to 27 (316 cases over 11.66 years).

[171] Suit No. 2 of 1936, 1935–7 PCMC Notebook, I: 368.

[172] For a similar case, see Suit No. 10 of 1938, 1937–41 PCMC Notebook, II: 126–7, III: 21–5.

[173] South Asian Sufism had followers from multiple religious traditions. See, for instance, Nile Green, *Indian Sufism since the Seventeenth Century* (London: Routledge, 2006), 139–41.

[174] Suit No. 6 of 1936, 1935–7 PCMC Notebook, II: 200.

[175] Suit No. 6 of 1936, 1935–7 PCMC Notebook, II: 97, 209.

[176] Suit No. 5 of 1936, 1935–7 PCMC Notebook, II: 96.

64 *Law and Identity in Colonial South Asia: Parsi Legal Culture*

FIGURE 1.1. A portrait of the Mistry family of Mandalay, Burma circa 1911.
Source: Private collection. Courtesy of Jehangir B. Mistry.

Using Law: Parsis Go to Court

acted as a spur to litigation, rather than a brake. Parsis said that they went to court for the purpose of rehabilitating their family reputation or because any further potential damage was inconsequential.

What did the Parsi notion of reputation look like? People spoke of *ābrū*, a Gujarati term borrowed from Persian that could mean reputation, credit, honor, or the good name of one's family. Witnesses and delegates in the Parsi matrimonial court spoke of the "blackening" of or a stain upon one's character.[177] Scholarship on honor-focused cultures has emphasized a willingness to turn to private violence in response to damage to reputation. In many such value systems, the duel was the correct response to attacks on personal honor, and the feud was the result of attacks on the honor of one's family or clan.[178] Malavika Kasturi has suggested that nineteenth-century Rajput notions of honor or *izzat* may have contributed to a rise in litigation among Rajputs in North India.[179] Despite the colonial state's best efforts, litigation did not replace violence. Rather, Rajputs combined the two, using them as complementary tools in intragroup conflicts. "Feuding factions, especially richer groups pushing litigation in civil courts, took to violence, indulging in 'affrays' when matters were not resolved to their satisfaction. . . . Many members of Rajput lineages of our region died fighting, trying to assert their power over each other."[180] The Parsi approach was different. There were occasional outbreaks of intracommunity violence, but they more often took the form of egg-throwing at meetings than of retaliatory killings.[181] The libel suit was a more common response than private violence, and a public apology was the outcome plaintiffs desired most.

---

[177] Suit No. 9 of 1920, 1920–3 PCMC Notebook, III: 46, 57.

[178] On dueling, see Robert A. Nye, *Masculinity and Male Codes of Honor in Modern France* (Oxford: Oxford University Press, 1993), 172–215; Ute Frevert, *Men of Honor: A Social and Cultural History of the Duel* (Cambridge: Polity Press, 1995); Pieter Spierenburg, ed., *Men and Violence: Gender, Honor, and Rituals in Modern Europe and America* (Columbus: Ohio State University Press, 1998); David S. Parker, "Law, Honor and Impunity in Spanish America: The Debate over Dueling, 1870–1920," *LHR* 19: 2 (2001), 311–41; Steven C. Hughes, *Politics of the Sword: Dueling, Honor, and Masculinity in Modern Italy* (Columbus: Ohio State University Press, 2007); Scott K. Taylor, *Honor and Violence in Golden Age Spain* (New Haven: Yale University Press, 2008); Lisa Fetheringill Zwicker, *Dueling Students: Conflict, Masculinity, and Politics in German Universities, 1890–1914* (Ann Arbor: University of Michigan Press, 2011). On the feud, see Keith M. Brown, *Bloodfeud in Scotland, 1573–1625: Violence, Justice and Politics in an Early Modern Society* (Edinburgh: J. Donald, 1986); Christopher Boehm, *Blood Revenge: The Enactment and Management of Conflict in Montenegro and other tribal societies* (Philadelphia: University of Pennsylvania Press, 1987); William Ian Miller, *Bloodtaking and Peacemaking: Feud, Law and Society in Saga Iceland* (Chicago: University of Chicago Press, 1990).

[179] Malavika Kasturi, *Embattled Identities: Rajput Lineages and the Colonial State in Nineteenth-Century North India* (Oxford: Oxford University Press, 2002), 137–48.

[180] Ibid., 171.

[181] Rotten eggs were hurled at Dr. Nadirshaw Hormusji Sukhia, a veterinary surgeon active in Parsi and municipal politics, when he compared his own suffering to the martyrdom of the prophet Zarathustra. ["Dr. Sukhia's Appeal," *TI* (11 January 1913), 10.]

Parsi conceptions of reputation were thus more closely aligned with notions of credit, inspiring trust and integrity, than with honor and its associates, physical courage and violence.

There were rare flashes of the view that litigiousness damaged one's reputation. Speaking of one witness, another told the court: "He is not a respectable man. He has often been in court in connection with civil litigation."[182] But such comments were striking for their rarity. More commonly, Parsis seem to have avoided court in order to keep information at the heart of a dispute from becoming socially known. "There are so many secrets one must sometimes keep quiet," confided one witness on the stand.[183] Potential plaintiffs often avoided the courts if their action would break the story socially. Whether husbands were violent or wives were cheating, their spouses were often advised not to spread the news – for the sake of preserving the family reputation. In one 1920 case, the mother of one plaintiff-husband advised him to keep quiet when he heard that his wife was being unfaithful: "She said that I should only expose myself by exposing my wife."[184] In another case from the same year, the parents of a woman with an abusive husband tolerated his behavior: "we allowed him to live in the house for the sake of our reputation."[185] In a third case from 1933, the parents of a woman whose husband was impotent opposed the idea of getting an annulment. They wanted "to avoid scandal."[186]

Reputational sanctions existed across multiple domains of social life. People deemed socially disreputable were driven out of their rented housing or business properties. Landlords, building managers, rent collectors, and neighbors watched, listened, and forced fellow residents to leave when scandals arose. The matrimonial court proceedings were full of descriptions of housing-related mechanisms for the enforcement of social mores. In one case, a Parsi husband had brought his brother's wife to live in the marital home. When other residents of the building recognized that the two were having an affair, they approached the husband's own wife. This woman told the court that the residents asked her to send the adulterous couple away "as my reputation suffered."[187] Another Parsi wife told the court that she and her husband moved three times in two months "because his treatment of me caused scandal and other tenants objected."[188] Even the owner of one restaurant came under social pressure when one husband-defendant was seen kissing another woman in the restaurant: "Other tenants complained ... and asked whether I had opened a brothel instead of a restaurant." The owner threw the man out.[189] Most common of all were

---

[182] Suit No. 7 of 1920, 1920–3 PCMC Notebook, II: 25.
[183] Suit No. 3 of 1903, 1893–1903 PCMC Notebook, I: 26.
[184] Suit No. 7 of 1920, 1920–3 PCMC Notebook, I: 46.
[185] Suit No. 9 of 1920, 1920–3 PCMC Notebook, III: 57.
[186] Suit No. 6 of 1933, 1929–35 PCMC Notebook, IV: 122.
[187] Suit No. 2 of 1903, 1893–1903 PCMC Notebook, III: 55.
[188] Suit No. 1 of 1915, 1913–20 PCMC Notebook, II: 88–9.
[189] Suit No. 7 of 1924, 1924–8 PCMC Notebook, I: 13.

Using Law: Parsis Go to Court

landlords who forced tenants to leave on the basis of rumor. The caretaker of one *chawl* told the court, "I ejected a Parsee woman, because I heard she was a bad person."[190]

Parsis who saw themselves as respectable stopped socializing with those they considered not to be. In one 1914 libel suit, a married man in Rangoon named J. D. Contractor sued a Parsi newspaper in Bombay over the allegation that his son was the product of an extramarital affair with a Burmese woman. With a racialized definition of Parsi identity on the rise, Contractor argued that the damage to his reputation was as much due to the insinuation of racial intermixing as to the allegation of an affair.[191] His lawyer described the social mechanics at issue: "The article, if it was true, would mean that he would not be allowed to mix with the Parsi community. The Parsi community would not even allow his children to associate with other Parsi children, and similarly with regard to his wife. He would even find it very difficult to attend religious ceremonies."[192]

Perhaps the most feared social sanction was the damage that a scandal could do to family members' marital prospects. As one father told the court in an 1893 case, "I was afraid my daughter would not get married if I brought a suit."[193] This father did come to court before his daughter was betrothed, probably because the scandal at the heart of the case had been leaked. Said another in a 1941 suit, "I was anxious about my child, and did not want to institute proceedings lest it wreck my daughter's future." This father did come to court eventually, but after his daughter's wedding.[194] Bella's adoptive father and uncle Bomanji fought so long and hard in *Saklat v. Bella* in part for the sake of her marriage prospects. Although she ultimately married a Parsi before the case ended, her father and uncle Bomanji initially felt that it would be hard for her to marry a Parsi if her status as a Zoroastrian remained unclear.[195] Here again was the threshold dynamic at work: breaking news of a scandal through litigation could damage one's daughter's marriageability, but once the scandal was revealed, going to court could be the best way of restoring her chances.

Because family reputation was so important, relatives played a major role in controlling the actions of their kin. People suffered personally from the reckless actions of relatives and therefore felt that they had a right to interfere. Senior relatives, in particular, were often the key force preventing potential plaintiffs from going to court. One wife wanted to sue for annulment on the grounds of her husband's impotence, but could not. Her grandparents "would not hear of a

---

[190] Suit No. 1 of 1927, 1924–8 Notebook, III: 61.

[191] See Chapter 7 at 291.

[192] "The Parsi Dispute. Another Defamation Suit," *WRTOS* (2 May 1914), 40.

[193] Suit No. 5 of 1893, 1893–1903 PCMC Notebook, I: 39.

[194] Suit No. 2 of 1941, 1937–41 PCMC Notebook, II: 196–8.

[195] "Parsi Defamation Suit. Mr. B. Cowasji's Evidence," *WRTOS* (25 July 1914), 41; "Interlocutory Proceedings and Orders. No. 82: Affidavit of S. Cowasji, one of the respondents, with a copy of Marriage Certificate attached. Rangoon, 18 January 1921," 838 in *Saklat v. Bella* JCPC case papers.

scandal being created. . . . As long as my grandfather and grandmother were alive nothing could be done."[196] In another case, a wife wanted to sue for divorce because her husband was living with his European mistress. The wife delayed under pressure from her husband's mother for the sake of the family reputation: "I filed my suit in January 1928, and not before because my mother-in-law implored me not to."[197]

Property could be wielded to increase the pressure. When senior relatives were creditors of junior members, their prohibitions had more force. One husband-plaintiff was convinced that his wife was bearing his brother's children and yet he delayed in filing suit. "My uncle said it would throw discredit on the family to go to law. I was ... indebted to him. He is dead now. He was most averse to my filing a suit. I could not oppose his wishes."[198] Another financial tool wielded by some senior relatives was the threat of disinheritance, a move made possible through the introduction of English legal principles. One mother-in-law threatened to disinherit her son's wife and other relatives if they testified in a particular case. The lawyer, aware of the threat, did not call on the daughter-in-law in court.[199]

For social rather than religious reasons, senior relatives often opposed going to court. Concern with the family name was a commonly expressed reason not to litigate. Even orthodox priestly families did not mention specifically religious reasons – whether doctrinal or institutional – for not going to court.[200] Despite the prohibition on oath-taking in Zoroastrian theology, few Parsis expressed reservations by the late colonial period about this aspect of coming to court.[201] Some plaintiffs told the court that they had delayed coming because there had been several deaths in the family: "as I was poor and [harassed] on account of the deaths of my father's brother and sister within two years I did not bring a suit."[202] Zoroastrian death ceremonies were elaborate and often costly, and they continued over an extended period.[203] Deaths in the family meant a sequence of religious ceremonies that could keep one's attention from litigation.

---

[196] Suit No. 3 of 1915, 1913–20 PCMC Notebook, II: 173.
[197] Suit No. 2 of 1928, 1928–9 PCMC Notebook, I: 15.
[198] Suit No. 5 of 1893, 1893–1903 PCMC Notebook, I: 39.
[199] Suit No. 4 of 1913, 1913–20 PCMC Notebook, I: 21.
[200] At least five of the cases between 1893 and 1947 involved orthodox Parsi parties. See Suit No. 7 of 1920, 1920–3 PCMC Notebook; Suit No. 3 of 1934, 1929–35 PCMC Notebook; and, in 1935–7 PCMC Notebook, Suits No. 3 of 1935, 11 of 1935, and 22 of 1936. In these cases, the statement "I am an orthodox Zoroastrian" was followed by descriptions of prayers and rituals performed, seclusion during menstruation, and other forms of adherence to the purity laws, usually relating to the consumption of food and water.
[201] See J. J. Modi, "Darab Hormazdyar's Rivâyat. A Few Notes on the Study of an Early Part of its Contents," *JKRCOI* 23 (1932), 139–42; Sharafi, "Bella's Case," 89, 253.
[202] Suit No. 2 of 1903, 1893–1903 PCMC Notebook, III: 54.
[203] See J. J. Modi, *The Religious Ceremonies and Customs of the Parsees* (Bombay: Society for the Promotion of Zoroastrian Religious Knowledge and Education, 1937), 49–82.

Using Law: Parsis Go to Court 69

This was a religious reason not to sue, but it was of a practical nature, not a principled one.

Because of the importance of family reputation and the sensitive nature of the facts in matrimonial suits, there were generous provisions for hearing matrimonial cases behind closed doors.[204] Parsi marital suits often took place in this way.[205] However, even proceedings *in camera* would not keep the details of matrimonial cases secret. Neither the press nor the public could attend these hearings. But the press could still report on the *outcome* of these cases – and it did. In one 1906 case, the judge commented that "it would have been better if no report had been published, but newspapers are entitled to publish the result of a case held in camera."[206] With so many community members involved as parties, witnesses, jurors, lawyers, and judges, there were many other opportunities for information about the proceedings to trickle out into the community.

If the desire to preserve the family reputation kept potential plaintiffs out of court before the scandal broke, everything changed once the story was out. Here, law did not cause further damage to reputation but enabled its repair. Plaintiffs in libel suits sued for precisely this reason. Sometimes litigants even pressed a weak case to protect the family reputation. As one plaintiff wrote to another in a trust case that was appealed to the Privy Council in the 1890s: "If we lose our case what of it. Why should we let go [of] the name of the family; I see no reason whatever to withdraw."[207]

Occasionally, defendants came to the Parsi matrimonial court to clear their name. In an attempt to sidestep fault requirements for divorce at the turn of the twentieth century, one husband allegedly offered to pay his wife Rs 500 if she would not appear when he sued her in court for divorce, alleging adultery. She refused. The wife not only came to court; she represented herself and won. As she asked her husband while cross-examining him in court: "Did I not write to you again that you might do what you like but I would not allow a stain on my character?"[208] In a more sinister attempt at collusion three decades later in 1935, a husband and wife agreed to frame a young female friend – an orphan who worked as a nurse – by pretending that the husband had committed adultery with the young woman. Both spouses told the woman not to come to court. But she did and defended herself so convincingly that the Parsi delegates affixed a final note to their findings: "there is no stain on Co-Defendant's

---

[204] A case would be heard behind closed doors at the request of any party. See PMDA 1865, s. 38 in Rana (1934), 93–4; Wadia and Katpitia, 124–5.

[205] For example, see "Parsee Chief Matrimonial Court. *Cawasjee Nowrojee Khajotia v. Sonabai and Perozshah Sheriadjee Bharoocha*," *TI* (9 August 1886), 3; "A Parsee Divorce Suit," *TI* (10 August 1891), 3.

[206] Suit No. 1 of 1906, 1903–13 PCMC Notebook, II: 81.

[207] "Record. No. 122. Exhibit F3: Translation of a Gujarati letter from Burjorji Jamshedji to Jamshedji Viccaji, dated 25 November 1896," 384 in *Pestonji Jeevanji v. Chinoy* JCPC case papers.

[208] Suit No. 1 of 1901, 1893–1903 PCMC Notebook, II: 138.

character."[209] A similar case of attempted manipulation occurred in the same year when a collusive couple tried to present a blameless young man as the Other Man. He, too, received an identical vindication from the delegates.[210]

Although some Parsis went to court to restore their reputations, others probably felt that their reputations were already so tarnished by rumor that further exposure was a price worth paying for divorce. The classic example was the cuckolded, estranged husband. Often, it was through gossip that he learned of his wife's actions in the first place. Two scenarios were the most common. In the first, a husband learned that his wife had become pregnant since their last meeting.[211] He might then confirm the rumor by confronting his wife with her newborn infant at the lying-in hospital, sending a photographer there to take a picture of his wife with her child, producing a birth register entry, or even reading an obituary of the child (when deceased) in a Parsi newspaper.[212] In a second scenario, a husband would discover that his wife had been living as a prostitute. This evidence was usually locational. For example, the husband claimed that his wife had been frequenting an area like Suklaji Street or Kamathipura, both known for their brothels.[213] One plaintiff-husband told the court, "I heard that she was behaving like a common prostitute. I believed this when I saw her afterwards in Suklaji Street. . . . Now I think the respondent is at Kamathipura."[214] Sometimes the evidence was gestural and dress-based. One husband claimed to have seen his wife sitting in front of a house "with three Mussalman women on each side just as prostitutes sit. . . . I say like a prostitute because she had a black sari on and nothing on her hair – draped like a Parsi but with no head dress."[215] It was not clear whether cuckolded husbands were the butt of jokes in colonial Bombay as they were in Shakespearean England.[216] Regardless, plaintiff-husbands expressed no concerns about the preservation of reputation once their wives' infidelity was the subject of rumor.

---

[209] Suit No. 3 of 1935, 1935–7 PCMC Notebook, I: 228.
[210] Suit No. 1 of 1935, 1935–7 PCMC Notebook, I: 273.
[211] See 60–1.
[212] See Suit No. 3 of 1914, 1913–20 PCMC Notebook, II: 17; Suit No. 1A of 1925, 1924–8 PCMC Notebook, II: 13; Suit No. 6 of 1926, 1924–8 PCMC Notebook, III: 22; 4 of 1903, 1903–13 PCMC Notebook, I: 33.
[213] On Kamathipura, see Tambe.
[214] Suit No. 1 of 1897, 1893–1903 PCMC Notebook, I: 241–2.
[215] Suit No. 4 of 1895, 1893–1903 PCMC Notebook, I: 202.
[216] The popularity of Shakespeare's plays in British India (in English, Gujarati, and Urdu) suggested that Parsi audiences were familiar with the Shakespearean figure of the ridiculed cuckold. See Somnath Gupt, *The Parsi Theatre*, trans. by Kathryn Hansen (Calcutta: Seagull, 2005), 41–2, 87–91, 137, 151; Kathryn Hansen, "Language, Community, and the Theatrical Public: Linguistic Pluralism and Change in the Nineteenth-century Parsi Theatre," in *India's Literary History: Essays on the Nineteenth Century*, eds. Stuart H. Blackburn and Vasudha Dalmia (Delhi: Permanent Black, 2004), 67.

Using Law: Parsis Go to Court

As already noted, senior relatives were the guardians of the family reputation. They acted as a brake on litigation when the initiation of a suit would create a scandal. Once a scandal had erupted, a marked reversal occurred: senior family members then acted as *catalysts* for litigation. Many plaintiffs told the matrimonial court that they began their suits because a senior relative pushed them to do so. In 1898, one party to a religious trust case told the court: "My mother begged of me not to withdraw from the suit for the sake of the name made by my ancestors at least." He cited maternal pressure as a significant factor that led him to go to court initially.[217] It was often a senior relative who took the plaintiff by the hand to a solicitor's office. In the 1920s, one plaintiff-wife heard rumors of her husband's adultery. She told the court: "One Mrs. Chichgar, a relative of [mine] asked me to take steps. ... She said she would take me to [Mr.] Wadia and he would advise me."[218] In a 1928 case, it was the plaintiff-wife's father-in-law who advised her to "take steps in the First class Magistrate's Court at Calicut for maintenance." It was unusual for a father to advise that legal action be taken against his own son, but standard nonetheless for a senior family member to urge a junior one to go to court.[219] In one 1932 case, a woman's mother took her to see a lawyer on learning that the woman's husband had brought his mistress to live in the marital home.[220] The maternal uncle was often the senior relative who initiated legal action, whether by accompanying the junior relative to the lawyer's office or even by going to see a lawyer alone.[221] Either way, family reputation was central to the strategizing of Parsi litigants.

EXPLAINING PARSI LEGALISM

Parsi disputants held back from court on occasion to protect their family reputation. But they made the opposite decision often enough to be frequent litigants, particularly against each other. Why was dispute resolution among Parsis so court-centric? Many modern Parsis have understood the Zoroastrian concept of *asha* (Av. *aṣa*) to refer to moral order and righteousness and to encourage intellectual independence, truth-telling, and a militant attitude toward right and wrong.[222] Dadabhai Naoroji

---

[217] "Witness No. 10 for Defendants: Pestonji, son of Jivanji" (12–12–1898), 222 in *Pestonji Jeevanji v. Chinoy* JCPC case papers.

[218] Suit No. 4 of 1925, 1924–8 PCMC Notebook, II: 41.

[219] Suit No. 9 of 1928, 1928–9 PCMC Notebook, II: 29.

[220] Suit No. 9 of 1932 in 1929–35 PCMC Notebook, IV: 60–2.

[221] See Suit No. 4 of 1930 in 1929–34 PCMC Notebook, I: 82–4; Suit No. 14 of 1937 in 1937–41 PCMC Notebook, II: 47.

[222] For instance, see Luhrmann, 100–1; "Truth and Tolerance," *Parsiana* (7 October 2012), 30–3. This popular understanding of *asha* represented only one part of the doctrine in its broader, more theological sense. See Boyce, *Zoroastrians*, 8; Prods Oktor Skjærvø, "Truth and Deception in Ancient Iran," in *Ātaš-e-dorun, The Fire Within: Jamshid Soroush Soroushian commemorative*

described the Zoroastrian idealization of truth-telling in his famous 1866 defense of South Asian religious value systems against accusations of Oriental mendacity.[223] *Hindi Punch* used ancient Persian martial images to depict the good Zoroastrian locked in combat against evil (Figure 1.2).[224] It also focused on priestly claims to being true to one's own conscience in intragroup conflicts. Resisting pressure from orthodox Parsis not to initiate the girl Bella into the religion, the High Priest of the Deccan declared in one cartoon caption from 1914, "I am an independent dastur" (Figure 1.3).[225] Could this value system have made Parsis particularly comfortable in the adversarial courtroom, where getting at truth required confrontation?

Much could happen between a religious doctrine's existence and its influence on everyday life, making institutional factors a better place to look. During the colonial period, the Parsis were notable for the weakness of their internal dispute resolution structures both at religious and community levels. At the time the British arrived in India, Zoroastrianism lacked a well developed or preserved tradition of religious law in South Asia. It differed from Islam and Judaism, traditions in which law was an elaborate and formalized subfield of religious knowledge in the substantive, procedural, and institutional sense. Having a well developed religious law was particularly useful when mobile. While living in polities that recognized the principle of personal law, Islamic and Jewish diasporas could reach for readymade religious law that permitted them to maintain a certain degree of religious continuity and autonomy.[226] Zoroastrians did not have the same ability.

The absence of religious law in Zoroastrianism (as it appeared in the colonial period) was partly a by-product of invasion and the destruction of texts in ancient Persia and of the migration of Zoroastrians to India. There was certainly law in ancient Persia that was informed by Zoroastrianism, the state-sponsored religion.[227] Institutions like temporary and next-of-kin marriage, along with a

---

volume, ed. Caro G. Cereti (n.p.: 1 Books Library, 2003), 407–16; Stausberg, *Zarathustra*, 27–8; Rose, *Zoroastrianism: A Guide*, 24.

[223] See Dadabhai Naoroji, "The European and Asiatic Races (27 March 1866, read before the Ethnological Society, London)," in *The Grand Little Man of India: Dadabhai Naoroji Speeches and Writings*, ed. A. M. Zaidi (Delhi: S. Chand and Co., 1984), I: 383.

[224] See "1284–5," *HP* (12 September 1915), 20–1. See also Hinnells, "War and Medicine," 294–5; and by Jamsheed K. Choksy, *Purity and Pollution*, 5 and "The Theme of Truth in Zoroastrian Mythology," in Godrej and Punthakey Mistree, 157–8.

[225] "I am an Independent Dastur" from "The Rangoon Romance (Bella and the Anjuman)," *HP* (7 June 1914), 14.

[226] On the importance of law (particularly purity laws) for mobile minorities, see Yuri Slezkine, *The Jewish Century* (Princeton: Princeton University Press, 2004), 13–16.

[227] Maria Macuch, "Law in Pre-Modern Zoroastrianism," in Stausberg and Vevaina.

Using Law: Parsis Go to Court

FIGURE 1.2. "Prince Hushang, the grandson of King Kaiomars, the first of the famous monarchs of Ancient Persia, waged war against the Spirit of Evil, overthrew him and tore him to pieces. – *Shah Nameh*."
Source: *HP* (8 Sept. 1912), 17. Courtesy of the British Library SV576.

trust-like device for pious foundations, were part of that legal tradition.[228] By Parsi accounts, much of the textual basis for this body of law was destroyed by

---

[228] On the trust-like device, see Janós Jany, "The Idea of Trust in Zoroastrian Law," *JLH* 25: 1 (2004), 271–6; Maria Macuch, "Die sasanidische Stiftung 'für die Seele' – Vorbild für den islamischen waqf?," in *Iranian and Indo-European Studies: Memorial Volume of Otakar Klima*, ed. Petr Vavroušek (Prague: Enigma, 1994), 163–80; Stausberg, *Zarathustra*, 77–8. On temporary and incestuous marriage, see Maria Macuch, "The Function of Temporary Marriage in the Context of Sasanian Family Law," *Societas Iranologica Europæa – Proceedings 2003*, I (Milan, 2005), 377–89; Prods Oktor Sjaervø, "Next-of-Kin Marriage in Zoroastrianism" in Yarshater. In the colonial period (as today), the validity of next-of-kin marriage in ancient Persian law was a topic of great controversy in the Parsi community. See, for instance, B. J. Billimoria, *A Warning Word to Parsees* (Bombay: Ardeshir and Co., 1900), 102–5.

FIGURE 1.3. "I am an independent dastur."
Source: *HP* (7 June 1914), 14. Courtesy of the British Library SV576.

Using Law: Parsis Go to Court

two waves of invaders to Persia: the forces of Alexander of Macedon and the Arab Muslims.[229]

With the migration of Zoroastrians from Persia to India, further religious knowledge was lost. This occurred primarily through the progressive loss of the ability of Zoroastrian priests in India to understand ancient and middle Persian languages.[230] When particularly difficult religious questions stumped communities in India, letters and delegations of Zoroastrians from India were sent to Persia to consult priestly authorities, particularly in the east-central Zoroastrian centers of Yazd and Kerman.[231] These question-and-answer dialogues were written down, forming a multilingual body of texts called the *rivayats* (Pers. *revāyat*) that interspersed archaic and modern forms of Persian with Gujarati. Further legal material was contained in texts like the *Digest of a Thousand Points of Law* and the *Vendidad*, a work best known for its coverage of the Zoroastrian purity laws. The legal richness of these texts was not recognized until late in the colonial period, a theme explored in Chapter 3. When the British arrived in India and promised Islamic law for Muslims and Hindu law for Hindus, Zoroastrians were presumably left out because they were regarded as not having a body of law in accessible textual form.

The Zoroastrian community lacked not only a written body of religious law, but also robust institutions for dispute resolution. Priestly roles and structures were central. First, the structure of the Zoroastrian priesthood was decentralized and lacked a single supreme authority. Within each of the five traditional dioceses or *panthaks* (Guj. *pañthak*) carved out of the Parsi heartland of Gujarat, there was a clear hierarchy of priestly authority. Between them, however, there was none.[232] The rise of Bombay, which was a small fishing village at the time the *panthaks* were created, further complicated lines of priestly authority.[233] There also existed no clear prohibition or penalty on taking disputes to outside authorities, in contrast to many Islamic, Hindu, and Jewish traditions.[234] Even in the precolonial setting and in the princely states, religious disputes between members of different *panthaks* were taken to local non-Parsi

---

[229] For instance, see Pestanji M. Ghadiali, "Preface," in *Zoroastrianism in the Light of Theosophy*, ed. N. F. Bilimoria (Madras: Blavatsky Lodge, Theosophical Society, 1898), xiv-xv.

[230] Kulke, 239; "Bombay: Mayor's Court Proceedings (14 September 1790–1790)," fol. 2633, 26 October1790 (IOR/P/148/1). I thank James Jaffe for sharing the IOR reference with me.

[231] Karaka, I: 215–17.

[232] See the agreement of approximately 1290 CE in H. D. K. Mirza, *Outlines of Parsi History* (Bombay: the author, 1987), 234–5; and of 6 June 1685 in R. B. Paymaster, *Early History of the Parsees in India from their landing in Sanjan to 1700* (Bombay: Zarthoshti Dharam Sambandhi Kelavni Apnari ane Dnyan Felavnari Mandli, 1954), 105–6. See also Hinnells, "Changing Perceptions," 102–13.

[233] See Hinnells, "Changing Perceptions," 109.

[234] S. T. Lokhandwalla, "Islamic Law and Ismaili Communities," *IESHR* 4: 2 (1967), 172; Shodhan, *Question*, 131–3; "Rabbinical Courts: Modern Day Solomons," *Colum. JL & Soc. Probs.* 6 (1970), 53–4; Lauren Benton, *Law and Colonial Cultures: Legal Regimes in World History* (Cambridge: Cambridge University Press, 2002), 113–14. See also Michael J. Broyde,

76   *Law and Identity in Colonial South Asia: Parsi Legal Culture*

rulers for resolution. For instance, disputes concerning the placing of the *padam* (Guj. *padām*) or ritual veil over the mouth of the dead and the crossing of the legs of corpses were taken to the ruling princes of Baroda, the Gaekwars.[235] Indeed, the absence of prohibitions on taking inside disputes to outside adjudicators may have been a cause as well as an effect of the priests' relative powerlessness.

Second, Zoroastrian priestly work focused on the performance of rituals. Since the colonial period, the study of religion among Anglophone scholars has been skewed by the Protestant assumption that belief, not ritual, lies at the heart of religion.[236] In colonial India, orthodox Parsis explained their religious identity in terms of their adherence to Zoroastrian purity laws and rituals.[237] The key job of Zoroastrian priests was to recite prayers and perform ceremonies. It was neither to provide advice or counseling (unlike Carol Greenhouse's Baptist pastors), nor to settle disputes (unlike the Bohri Muslims' religious leader, the *Da'i*).[238] Even before British rule, matrimonial disputes between Parsis in Surat were resolved by a nonreligious Parsi hereditary authority known as the Modi or Davar (Guj. *Dāvar*).[239] The Modi of Surat occasionally consulted Zoroastrian priests in deciding matrimonial cases, but it was he who was the final authority. The Modi lost his adjudicatory power with the passage of the Parsi Marriage and Divorce Act of 1865.[240] Although he tried to have inserted a special provision that would maintain his authority, the Modi saw his adjudicatory role replaced by the Parsi matrimonial courts and their new jury system. His description of the precolonial Modi's role suggested that, even before British

---

"Informing on Others for Violating American Law: A Jewish Law View" (accessed on 7 October 2012): http://www.jlaw.com/Articles/mesiralaw2.html.

[235] See Menant, "Social Evolution of the Parsis," *JIA*, 10: 5 (August 1921), 151; Paymaster, 99; Hinnells, "Changing Perceptions," 109.

[236] See, for instance, Will Sweetman, "'Hinduism' and the History of 'Religion': Protestant Presuppositions in the Critique of the Concept of Hinduism," *Method and Theory in the Study of Religion* 15 (2003), 334.

[237] See note 200.

[238] Carol Greenhouse, *Praying for Justice: Faith, Order, and Community in an American Town* (Ithaca: Cornell University Press, 1986); Lokhandwalla. Some practice of legal consultation does seem to have existed. Daniel Sheffield notes that some Zoroastrian priests wrote *fatwa*s (Pers. *fatvā*, from Arabic), but their interpretation of whether Zoroastrian customs or purity laws had been violated were often slanted in favor of the wealthy patron who had commissioned the opinion. See Daniel Sheffield, "This Town isn't big enough for the two of us: Struggles for the High Priestship of Bombay, 1830–1900," 39 Annual Conference on South Asia (Madison, 16 October 2010). On traditions of legal consultation in South Asia, see Donald R. Davis, Jr., "Responsa in Hindu Law," paper presented at Legal History and Religion Workshop, University of Wisconsin Law School (Madison, 24 September 2010).

[239] The Modi also represented the Parsi community in interactions with local rulers. See Karaka, II: 19–21.

[240] Wadia and Katpitia's treatise on the PMDA 1936 was dedicated to "the ancient Modi family of Surat whose ancestors as Davars or Heads of the Surat Parsi Community, had, for a long series of years, before the Parsi Marriage and Divorce Act XV of 1865 was enacted, given their services gratuitously in the exercise of Matrimonial Jurisdiction over the Surat Parsis...." (Dedication in Wadia and Katpitia).

Using Law: Parsis Go to Court

rule, Zoroastrian priests did not have the power of adjudication over matrimonial disputes. In many other communities, religious authorities would have resolved these cases by applying religious law.[241]

A final important feature of the Zoroastrian priesthood in British India was its poverty. In many religious traditions, priests enjoyed power, status, and relative financial prosperity vis-à-vis the laity. During the colonial period, the hereditary priestly class of Zoroastrians was generally underprivileged. It was not unusual, for instance, for priests to support themselves through a mix of ritual and menial labor. One priest from Lahore testified in a religious trust suit that he supported himself by working as a priest and a cook, for instance.[242] Case records from Privy Council appeals attested to the economic disparity between poor priests and the wealthy Parsis who endowed and managed religious trust funds. The latter employed the former and asserted their dominant position in multiple ways. Privy Council papers included multiple accounts of wealthy Parsis pressuring Zoroastrian priests to perform ceremonies the former desired, including ceremonies that were religiously unorthodox.[243] The bottom line was that the priests were on the payroll of elite laity and were vulnerable because of it. "All dasturs [high priests] are our servants," declared one Parsi whose family had financed the construction of a tower of silence or *dakhma* in Secunderabad. "If I wish it that the dastur should be turned out from office, it could be done like fun."[244] European-led Christian proselytizing in the mid-nineteenth century triggered a backlash among affluent Parsis, who set up charitable funds and institutions that would better educate and provide for priests.[245] Even so,

---

[241] See "Appendix C: Minute by Mr. Rustomjee Khoorshedji Dawur, or Modee of Surat, with reference to the proposed report to Government of a majority of the Parsee Law Commission" (with supporting documents), 9–50 in "1862–3 Government of India Bill to amend law for Parsees"; "Proposed Legislation regarding the Parsee Community – Mr. Rustomjee Khoorshedjee's Memorial. No. 29. To His Excellency the Hon'ble Sir H. B. E. Frere, K.C.B. ... Governor in Council, Bombay. The Humble Memorial of Rustomjee Khoorshedjee, Davur or head of the Parsee community of Surat," *Proceedings of the Government of India, Home Department. Legislative. November 1864* (Calcutta: Home Secretariat, 1864), 669–77. I am grateful to James Jaffe for this latter reference.

[242] For example, see "Witness No. 15 for Plaintiffs. Sorabji Rustomji. 9–8–1897," 122 in "Record: No. 15. Plaintiff's Evidence," *Pestonji Jeevanji v. Chinoy* JCPC case papers.

[243] In *Pestonji Jeevanji v. Chinoy* JCPC case papers, see "Record. No. 23. Exhibit F. Letter from Jamasp Edulji Dastur to Viccaji Meherji" (1 May 1838), 293 and "Record. No. 24. Letter from Viccaji Meherji to Dastur Jamaspji Edulji," 295. In the *Saklat v. Bella* JCPC case papers, see "Exhibit RP: Letter, B. Cowasjee to Unwalla, Rangoon, 18 August 1915," 69; "Exhibit RQ. Translation of Letter from B. B. Unwalla to B. Cowasjee. Rangoon, 21 August 1915," 71–2; "Exhibit RR: Letter from B. Cowasjee to B. B. Unwalla, Rangoon, 3 September 1915," 75–6; "Exhibit RF: Letter from B. B. Unwalla to B. Cowasjee. Rangoon, 10 September 1915," 80.

[244] "Witness No. 9 for Plaintiffs. Kaikhusru Jivanji. 8–7–1897," 99–100 in "Record: No. 15. Plaintiff's Evidence," *Pestonji Jeevanji v. Chinoy* JCPC case papers.

[245] See Palsetia, *Parsis*, 163–4; Christine Dobbin, "The Growth of Urban Leadership in Western India, with Special Reference to Bombay City, 1840–85" (D.Phil dissertation, Oxford University, 1967), 113–15.

78 *Law and Identity in Colonial South Asia: Parsi Legal Culture*

around the turn of the twentieth century, orthodox Parsis still complained that priests could be hired to perform any ceremony (including the initiation of ethnic outsiders) if paid enough.[246] The charge hinted at the economic desperation of the priesthood.[247]

With so little adjudicative authority, money, and status – and with no body of religious law to apply – Zoroastrian priests failed to offer colonial Parsis a viable forum for the resolution of their disputes. But "inside" alternatives to the courts need not have been religious. What about community bodies like the Bombay Parsi Panchayat?[248] *Panchayats* were councils of elders that existed in many religious, caste, and village communities.[249] They were promoted by the British during the Company period as a forum for alternative dispute resolution, both lightening the colonial courts' case load and allowing South Asian norms to be applied in an economical and efficient way.[250] The Bombay Parsi Panchayat was in many ways created and supported under British patronage. In the 1670s and again in 1787 under a reconstitution scheme, between five and twelve male heads of the Parsi community were appointed in response to a call from government to form the *panchayat*. Its purpose was to adjudicate social and religious disputes among Parsis and to provide for the social welfare of the community.[251] The Parsi Panchayat decided most cases between Bombay Parsis in the early colonial period.[252] As the British observer Maria Dundas Graham Calcott noted in 1813, "This little council decides all questions of property, subject, however, to the Recorder's Court; but an appeal seldom happens, as the panchaït is jealous of its authority, and is consequently cautious in its decisions. It superintends all marriages and adoptions, and inquires into the state of every individual of the community."[253]

The *panchayat's* sanctions were predominantly social.[254] Those who violated a resolution or *bandobast* (Guj. *bandobast*) were effectively excommunicated from the community. They would be excluded from fire temples. Their bodies would not be consigned to the *dakhmas* for exposure to vultures after death. They would be barred from attending marriage and funeral ceremonies or

---

[246] See "The Parsis and Proselytism," *TI* (13 August 1904), 7; "The Parsi Panchayat Case," *HP* (27 December 1908), 20; "Defendant's Evidence. No. 27: Evidence of Jamshedji Dadabhoy Nadirshaw taken on Commission. In the Court of Small Causes, Bombay," 426–7 in *Saklat v. Bella* JCPC case papers.

[247] See *Udvāḍā Īrānshāh Ātaśbeherām Kesno Cukādo*, 13, 100.

[248] See generally Stausberg, *Die Religion*, II: 34–44; Kulke, 61–7.

[249] See Delphine Menant, *Les Parsis: Histoire des Communautés Zoroastriennes de l'Inde* (Paris: Ernest Leroux, 1898), 236; Shodhan, *Question*.

[250] James A. Jaffe, "Arbitration and Panchayats in Early Colonial Bombay," *JKRCOI* (2012), 41–58.

[251] Desai, *History*, 2, 5; Karaka, I: 223.

[252] Q. in the Corner, I: 3. See also Palsetia, *Parsis*, 75–95.

[253] Maria Dundas Graham Callcott, *Journal of a Residence in India* (Edinburgh: Archibald Constable, 1813), 41.

[254] See Kulke, 63 at note 10.

Using Law: Parsis Go to Court 79

community feasts (*ghambars*), and priests would refuse to perform religious ceremonies for them. There were also financial, physical, and shame-based punishments meted out by the *panchayat*. These included forcing violators to beat themselves with a shoe; forcing them to wear a halter around their neck and to beg for the *panchayat*'s pardon; making them undergo ritual purification; obliging them to pay a fine, compensation for any financial loss caused, or a wife's continuing maintenance; and confining women who left their homes unescorted after dark in the *nasakhana* (Guj. *nasākhānū*) or building where the ritually polluted hereditary corpse bearers known as *nasasalars* resided and prepared the dead for exposure.[255] "So great," wrote the Parsi historian Karaka, "was the penalty of excommunication that the Parsis seldom failed to accept without demur the decision of their governing body."[256] Between the late seventeenth and early nineteenth century, then, disputes among Parsis in Bombay were typically handled by the city's Parsi Panchayat.[257]

By the 1820s–30s, this situation had changed. The *panchayat* lost its near monopoly on adjudication within the community, and disputes between Parsis appeared in court with increasing regularity. Writing in 1821, a group of British magistrates noted how often Parsis frequented the Recorder's Court, a Company court in Bombay:[258] "They are ... litigious, and are proud to shew their independence by battling for what they consider their legal rights in the Court of the Recorder. The old Punchayets [that] governed by maxims and an indirect influence are nearly obsolete. It would be difficult to enact an unexceptional body of regulations for the conduct of their Punchayets, and unless that were done, there would be food for eternal lawsuits. ... The Recorder's Court is their favorite Punchayet. The spirit that would have made them submit in preference to their own heads of Caste when they were a humble body struggling for subsistence is gone and cannot be reversed."[259]

The Company courts would occasionally refer a question on a point of custom to the *panchayat*.[260] However, this practice diminished as the traffic of Parsi lawsuits increased and a body of usable precedents developed.[261] By the mid-nineteenth century, the Bombay Parsi Panchayat had shed its former role as adjudicator. It was now a body that controlled charitable funds and properties

---

[255] Q. in the Corner, I: 9, 11; Menant, *Les Parsis*, 245–6; Desai, *History*, 4, 7; Sohrab P. Davar, *The History of the Parsi Punchayet* (Bombay: New Book Company, 1949), 31.

[256] Karaka, I: 218.

[257] Davar, *History*, 32.

[258] See Vachha, 19–27.

[259] "Extract from Judicial Letter from Bombay, 16 May 1821," 3–4 in "Report of the Bombay Police Magistrates on the decline of the influence exercised by upper class Parsees over their lower class brethren and on the internal relationships of the various Hindu castes" (IOR/F/4/767/20869).

[260] For an example from 1839, see *Burjorjee Bheemjee v. F. Dhunjeeshaw* 1 SDA Reports Bombay 206 (1820–40).

[261] On the colonial courts' reliance on case law in the determination of Parsi custom in 1856, see *Hormusjee v. Cooverbhaee* 173, reproducing 6 MIA 460.

and that itself was occasionally taken to court.[262] This shift was consistent with a broad transformation taking place across the common-law world in the mid-nineteenth century. Between the 1830s and 1860s, courts in India, Australia, and the United States ceased to regard colonized people's collective bodies as sovereign authorities operating their own legal systems and instead brought them within the jurisdiction of the courts.[263]

Several factors contributed to the change in the Parsi Panchayat's role.[264] The 1826 death of the respected *panchayat* leader Hormusji Bomanji Wadia was one.[265] Similarly damaging were conflicts about polygamy, class, and cronyism in the 1830s.[266] The Panchayat was accused of disciplining poor men who took second wives while tolerating the practice among wealthier men, many of whom had close ties to *panchayat* leaders.[267] There was also dissatisfaction because the heads of the *panchayat* were no longer elected by the *Anjuman* (Guj. *Añjuman*) or local Parsi community through its general meetings.[268] Instead, trusteeship had become hereditary.[269] A series of letters published in 1844–5 in the *Bombay Times and Journal of Commerce* by one "Q. in the Corner" – the judge and lobbyist Manekjee Cursetjee – summarized these criticisms and others and did serious damage to the reputation of the *panchayat*.[270] More generally, there was the rise of Parsi *nouveaux riches*, a population that did not accept the traditional authority of the *panchayat*.[271] As the British magistrates remarked in 1821, "the number of rich Parsis is very great, and they are of an independent turn of mind ... they are bold, blustering and purseproud."[272] Echoing the magistrates' report a decade later, a retired official named Francis Warden wrote in 1832 that the newer group of rich Parsis "wish to live and expend their money as they please, without troubling or being troubled by Punchayets." Warden observed the slide from *panchayat* to court: "Among a rich and numerous people,

---

[262] Karaka, I: 240–1; Chintamini, 128; Hinnells, "Changing Perceptions of Authority," 101. For examples, see Desai, *History*, 44–9, 129–49, 171–3.

[263] Shodhan, *Question*; Lisa Ford, *Settler Sovereignty: Jurisdiction and Indigenous People in America and Australia, 1788–1836* (Cambridge, MA: Harvard University Press, 2010). See also Paul G. McHugh, *Aboriginal Societies and the Common Law: A History of Sovereignty, Status, and Self-Determination* (Oxford: Oxford University Press, 2004), 117–214.

[264] See Kulke, 65–7.

[265] Desai, *History*, 10; Davar, *History*, 39; Hinnells, "Bombay Parsi Panchayat"; Palsetia, *Parsis*, 76–7.

[266] Menant, *Les Parsis*, 244–5; Susan Stiles Maneck, *The Death of Ahriman: Culture, Identity and Theological Change among the Parsis of India* (Bombay: K. R. Cama Oriental Institute, 1987), 171–5. See generally Davar, *History*, 44–9.

[267] See Palsetia, *Parsis*, 97; Hinnells, "Changing Perceptions of Authority," 101.

[268] See Desai, *History*, 174–82.

[269] Ibid., 7.

[270] See Q. in the Corner, I: 1–32. For an attack on Q's letters, see B. P. M., "A Poor Attempt," *BTJC* (30 April 1845), 286.

[271] See Ringer, *Pious Citizens*, 35.

[272] "Extract from Judicial Letter from Bombay, 16 May 1821," 2 in "Report of the Bombay Police Magistrates."

Using Law: Parsis Go to Court

who have lost their habits of personal attachment and obedience [to the *panchayat*], law must complete the submission which opinions and habits no longer command."[273]

The final blow to the Parsi Panchayat's adjudicatory role came in 1865, with the passage of the Parsi Marriage and Divorce Act. Initially, draftsmen proposed that Parsi *panchayats* across India would resolve marital disputes by applying the rules of the new statute. But reformists protested.[274] In addition, H. B. Harrington, a member of the Governor General's Council in Delhi, argued that the *panchayat* had the potential to become "an irresponsible tribunal," neither answerable to the Parsi population nor to colonial law.[275] The *panchayat* was replaced with a new set of institutions for dispute resolution: the Parsi matrimonial courts. These courts would employ a jury of Parsis and would be overseen by a judge from the colonial courts. In the words of the Parsi lobbyist S. S. Bengalee, "they would be presided over by Judges, and be subject to the checks and safeguards of established legal procedure, while the presence of the Parsee Jury, to determine all questions of fact, would secure the confidence and approval of the Parsee community."[276] Not only did the Bombay Parsi Panchayat look nothing like a community court by the turn of the twentieth century; it found *itself* in court when disputes arose among or against its trustees and even in the routine administration of its trust funds, which occasionally required judicial approval.[277] During the nineteenth century, caste and community bodies across India came to be structured by the common-law device of the trust.[278] Parsi Panchayat funds became trust funds by 1851, making *panchayat* heads trustees.[279]

There were alternative sources of authority within the Parsi community, but none asserted a consistent adjudicatory role in the late colonial period. After 1865, the Modi of Surat was no longer empowered to resolve matrimonial suits among the Parsis of Surat. The Parsi merchant Sir Jamsetjee Jeejeebhoy) and his descendants were regarded as the unofficial heads of Bombay's Parsi community for much of the period from the mid-nineteenth century, when the first "Sir JJ" was awarded a knighthood and hereditary baronetcy, until the 1920s.[280] However, the authority of any given Jamsetjee Jeejeebhoy rose and

---

[273] Francis Warden (30 August 1832) quoted in Desai, *History*, 9.

[274] Christine Dobbin, "The Parsi Panchayat in Bombay City in the Nineteenth Century," *MAS* 4: 2 (1970), 154–5.

[275] Davar, *History*, 76–7.

[276] Sorabjee Shapoorjee Bengalee, ed., *The Parsee Marriage and Divorce Act 1865 (Act No. XV of 1865), The Parsee Chattels Real Act (Act No. IX of 1837), The Parsee Succession Act (Act No. XXI of 1865), with an Appendix and Guzerattee Translation* (Bombay: Parsee Law Association, 1868), 233.

[277] See *Petit v. Jijibhai*; Sharafi, "Judging Conversion."

[278] See Appadurai, 173–4.

[279] Desai, *History*, 10–11.

[280] By Palsetia, see *Parsis of India*, 54–7, 130–8; and "Merchant Charity," 197–217.

82   *Law and Identity in Colonial South Asia: Parsi Legal Culture*

fell with the reputation of that particular individual. Sir Jamsetjee Jeejeebhoy II, for instance, showed greater enthusiasm for the purchase of horses, carriages, cigars, and alcohol than for community affairs.[281] As John Hinnells has observed, lines of authority within the Parsi community were chaotic and shifting in the late colonial period. Everyone accepted that, at the abstract level, the Anjuman or general Parsi community in any particular place was the ultimate source of social authority. It was less clear, though, what this meant in an applied sense. The power of the Sir JJs to call Anjuman meetings was contested, particularly as the status of other Parsi families like the Adenwalas and Readymoneys grew in the twentieth century.[282] As respected Parsi *shethia* (Guj. *seṭhiyā*), the heads of the Jijibhai family would have occasionally acted as informal mediators in Parsi disputes. They were frequently elected as delegates of the PCMC and, by the other delegates, as the foremen who spoke on behalf of the jury.[283] However, their adjudicatory role was no more formal or independent than this. The Parsi arbitration bodies already discussed did exist, but only from the 1930s and after at least one false start. Neither priestly nor community authorities provided robust, centralized, and long-lasting forums for dispute resolution among the Parsis. The colonial courts filled the gap.

CONCLUSION

In 1897, a husband told the Parsi matrimonial court that he would have taken back his estranged wife even after she had worked as a prostitute. "I was willing to take her back," he said, "to save the reputation of the community."[284] The statement was illuminating at several levels. It expressed a common mode of articulating community boundaries in the late colonial period: through sexual activity. Prostitution was problematic not just because of its violation of the double standard that equated female chastity (but not its male equivalent) with social respectability.[285] It was also troubling to staunch defenders of communal boundaries because it brought people of different communities into intimate contact with each other.[286]

---

[281] Hinnells, "Changing Perceptions," 113–14.

[282] Ibid., 102, 113–14.

[283] See Suit No. 5 of 1898, II: 44 and Suit No. 1 of 1903, III: 48; both in 1893–1903 PCMC Notebook.

[284] Suit No. 1 of 1897, 1893–1903 PCMC Notebook, I: 237.

[285] The Parsi community prided itself on having neither beggars nor prostitutes among its numbers. See Karaka, I: 99; *Petit v. Jijibhai*, 551; "XXI. September 7, 1910. Mr. Vimadalal and the "Juddin" Question. Letter from J. J. Vimadalal" in *Mr. Vimadalal and the Juddin Question: a Series of Articles reprinted from "The Oriental Review"* (Bombay: Crown Press, 1910), 52.

[286] The Parsi prostitute crisis of 1870 highlighted anxieties over intercommunity sex. See "Morality among the Parsees," *TI* (29 June 1870), 3; *KH* (28 July 1918), cited in Patel and Paymaster, V: 441 at note 1, trans. Homi D. Patel; "Letter from K.R. Cama of 3 July 1870, Bombay" in "Defendant's Exhibit 2: Report of the results of a meeting of the entire large and small

Concern with community reputation was not unusual in the context of sexual activity. By contrast, Parsis did not refer to community reputation when asked about their attitudes toward litigation. When explaining to the court why they had delayed in bringing suit, none of the matrimonial court plaintiffs said that they wanted to protect the community's reputation. Family reputation was central to the court avoidance narratives of many, but community reputation was not. In *Petit v. Jijibhai*, the judge F. C. O. Beaman remarked that the case had exposed much of the community's "dirty linen" to public view.[287] He was probably referring to his colleague Davar's excursus on lower caste servant mistresses among the Parsis of Surat.[288] Beaman's comment was striking because it was a sentiment so rarely expressed by Parsis themselves.[289]

How should the absence of communal reflexivity be understood? It was not as if Parsis failed to see themselves as a group. Fierce resistance to the admission of ethnic outsiders through religious conversion, and equally the desire that Zoroastrians who converted out be kept out, signaled a strong sense of community boundaries in this period.[290] The simple explanation may have been that Parsis did not regard the colonial legal system as an outside forum. Legal pluralism and legal consciousness intersected in the decision to move from the realm of social negotiations into court. Non-state spaces for Parsi dispute resolution were entirely populated by Parsis but even in the state realm, there were many Parsis, too. The presence of these figures may have contributed to the high comfort levels of Parsi disputants in the courts. With so many Parsi lawyers, judges, law clerks, and court officials, the colonial courts must have felt like home. The complement to the phenomenon of frequent Parsi law users was Parsis in the legal profession. It is to these lawyers and judges, along with their lobbying and legislating co-religionists, that we now turn.

Zoroastrian Anjuman, filed before Commissioner (in translation), 1870," 137 in *Saklat v. Bella* JCPC case papers. For testimony against intercommunity mixing in a case in which a young Parsi wife was alleged to have committed adultery with an older Muslim man, see Suit No. 7 of 1920, 1920–3 PCMC Notebook, I: 50–1, II: 36.

[287] *Petit v. Jijibhai*, 576.

[288] *Parsi Punchayet Case*, 38.

[289] For an unusual exception, see "Parsi Marriage Laws," *TI* (11 July 1932), 14.

[290] See Introduction at 22–3. On the desire to exclude Parsis who had converted to other religions, see *Jiwaji Dinshaw Ghandy and others v. Bomanji Ardeshir Wadia and others* 5 Bom LR 655 (1903); PMDA 1936, ss. 25, 32(j) in Wadia and Katpitia, 52, 69, 84–5; "M. B. Sanjana, MA, LLB, President, Surat Borough Municipality... to the Collector of Surat... 6 November 1934," 21 in "Paper No. I. Opinions on the Parsi Marriage and Divorce Bill" in "The Parsi Marriage and Divorce Act 1936 (16 August 1934–23 July 1936)" (IOR/L/PJ/7/716).

2

Making Law

Two Patterns

In an 1892 trial at the Old Bailey, a young Parsi named Pallonjee Munchergee was charged with obtaining money by false pretenses from three London solicitors' firms. He had gone to the senior partners asking for loans. Munchergee claimed to be the son of a Parsi solicitor or managing clerk from well-known Parsi law firms in Bombay or Singapore. In each case, he told the British lawyers that he had been in Europe for work or study and needed just enough money to survive until his ship arrived, when he would return to Asia. His father would repay the loans. The British solicitors did not recognize the name of the young man's father, but were probably too embarrassed to admit it. He provided forged letters of introduction from the India and Colonial Offices, and the lawyers gave him the money. The fraud was only revealed because a partner from the actual Singapore firm happened to meet with one of the duped solicitors in London.[1] Pallonjee Munchergee's ploy failed in the end, but it worked initially because he was Parsi. Not only were Parsis hearty consumers of law as regular litigants in the colonial courts. They were also involved in the production of colonial law. Pallonjee's story was plausible because the Parsi lawyer was a familiar figure in the British Empire.

Parsis made law by two routes. One was a collective and deliberate strategy aimed at changing the law that applied to the Parsi population. From the 1830s, Parsis organized themselves into lobby groups that drafted and pushed for the passage of legislation pertaining to Parsi marriage and inheritance. These statutes replaced doctrines of English law with rules that reflected the values of colonial Parsis. The legislation came into force in the century between 1837 and 1940 and created Parsi personal law. It lifted Parsis out of their early colonial

---

[1] "Charge against a Parsee," *The Globe* (21 July 1892) in "Pallonjee Munchergee, a Parsee, charged at Bow Street with obtaining money by false pretences," 30 May 1892 (IOR/L/PJ/6/323, file 1080).

84

Making Law: Two Patterns 85

situation, in which English law applied in blanket fashion, and put them in a position parallel to Hindus and Muslims, to whom Anglo-Hindu and -Islamic law had applied since the eighteenth century.

From the 1860s, Parsis also helped make colonial law by a second path whose collective benefits were less clearly foreseen or even intended: they went into law as a profession. Being a lawyer offered the obvious personal rewards of income and status. It enabled upward mobility for poorer Parsis in a way that few other occupations did. But although personal self-interest made a legal career appealing, there were also collective benefits from going into law. As Parsi lawyers advanced in their careers, some took up judicial appointments. Both as lawyers and as judges, these figures were often involved in litigation involving their co-religionists, a theme of Chapter 6. Indeed, the sizeable presence of Parsis in the legal profession may have increased the volume of intragroup litigation. Parsis have been portrayed as quintessential middlemen in early colonial trade between Indian and British merchants, but the work of colonial intermediaries extended beyond the mercantile world.[2] Legal professionals from colonized populations were intellectual and cultural middlemen, a phenomenon underestimated by Gregory Kozlowski in his examination of Muslims in the legal profession.[3] Parsis in law communicated the needs of their co-religionists to the colonial legal system and the mechanics of colonial law to their community members. For Parsi judges, especially, membership in the community could not but inform their rulings, particularly when the case turned on Parsi religious or social norms. As such, they were key players in the creation of an ethnographically informed jurisprudence of the Parsi community.

The two complementary pathways of lobbying and the legal profession also cross-fertilized, perpetuating the *habitus* at the heart of Parsi legal culture. Some of the earliest Parsi lobbyists were lower-ranking officials in the East India Company's courts. They were also some of the first to send their sons to London to become barristers at the Inns of Court in the 1860s–1870s. Being a barrister was a standard precondition (although not an essential one) for becoming a judge. Equally, once the legal profession opened its upper levels to South Asians, Parsis trained as lawyers often led lobbying efforts to pass legislation on Parsi personal law. It would be going too far to suggest that these occasionally intersecting lines of legal activity were planned in a coherent and conscious manner. Their effects at the collective level, however, were overwhelming.

LOBBYING

There were historically two phases to the lobby-and-legislate strategy. Minority groups initially pressed for exemption from existing legislation. Across the

---

[2] For example, see Preeti Chopra, *A Joint Enterprise: Indian Elites and the Making of British Bombay* (Minneapolis: University of Minnesota Press, 2011), 73–115.

[3] Kozlowski, 117–18, 121–2. See also Sharafi, "A New History."

86 *Law and Identity in Colonial South Asia: Parsi Legal Culture*

English-speaking world, the Quakers, Jews, and Amish found considerable success following this route.[4] Some of the earliest lobbying campaigns by colonial Parsis sought exemption from existing legal regimes. In 1835, a Parsi son provoked uproar by successfully arguing that he ought to inherit the whole of his father's real estate under the English rule of primogeniture. According to the primogeniture principle, the eldest son inherited all real estate to the exclusion of other siblings. Parsis campaigned to change the applicable law. They argued that primogeniture was an alien concept that violated Parsi inheritance norms. The result was the Succession to Parsees Immoveable Property Act (IX of 1837). By a circuitous route described in Chapter 3, the statute exempted Parsis from the application of primogeniture.

Fifty years later, Parsi lobbying produced another legal exemption. The Administrator General's Act of 1874 required that the colonial official known as the Administrator General be closely involved in the administration of real estate left by people who died without a valid will, known as *intestates*. The Act was designed with Europeans in mind. Those who died without family in India lacked a relative to manage the administration of their estates.[5] Although Hindus, Muslims, and Buddhists were exempt, the statute applied to Europeans, Indian Christians, and Parsis. It was Parsis in the *mofussil*, rather than their more urban co-religionists in Bombay City, who led the campaign for community exemption from the Administrator General's Act. In a memorial to government, the Parsis of Surat observed that the majority of Parsis in the *mofussil* were "steeped in poverty," but that many owned small houses and therefore were affected by the statute:

---

[4] Quakers obtained exemptions from a wide variety of laws in the British imperial world, including the obligation to comply with marriage ceremony procedures, swear oaths, perform military service, or pay tithes and war taxes. See E. W. Kirby, "The Quakers' Efforts to Secure Civil and Religious Liberty, 1660–96," *J. Mod. Hist.* 7:4 (1935), 411–21; E. B. Greene, "The Anglican Outlook on the American Colonies in the Early Eighteenth Century," *AHR* 20:1 (1914), 77. See also John Bergin, "The Quaker Lobby and Its Influence on Irish Legislation, 1692–1705," *Eighteenth-Century Ireland* 19 (2004), 9–36. Jews obtained exemption from the prohibition on uncle–niece marriage in Rhode Island, and from matrimonial, burial, and animal slaughter regulations in Britain. See "An Act Regulating Marriage and Divorce" (1798), s. 1, in *Public Laws of the State of Rhode-Island and Providence Plantations* (Providence, NH: Knowles and Vose, 1844), 263; Benjamin H. Hartogensis, "Rhode Island and Consanguineous Jewish Marriages," *Publ. Am. Jewish Hist. Soc.* 20 (1911), 137–46; *Goldsmid v. Bromer* 161 Eng. Rep. 568 (1752–1865); Sebastian Poulter, *Ethnicity, Law and Human Rights: The English Experience* (Oxford: Clarendon Press, 1998), 132–3. See also British legislation including the Burial Act 1853 (16 and 17 Vict. 134), s. 2; Slaughter of Poultry Act 1967 (c.24), s. 2; Slaughterhouse Act 1974 (c.3), ss. 36(3) and 40(1)a. On the Amish, see Marc A. Olshan, "The National Amish Steering Committee," in *The Amish and the State*, ed. Donald B. Kraybill (Baltimore: Johns Hopkins University Press, 2003), 68–76; R. L. Kidder and J. A. Hostetler, "Managing Ideologies: Harmony as Ideology in Amish and Japanese Societies," *LSR* 24 (1990), 909–13.

[5] "Statement of Objects and Reasons. By W. Stokes, 19 June 1880" (unpaginated) in "Act No. IX of 1881: An Act to Amend the Administrator General's Act 1874," file 578 (IOR/L/PJ/6/37).

Making Law: Two Patterns

To force such poor individuals ... living as they do scattered and at wide distances from Bombay and other station-towns – ignorant as they are of the law, its intricacies, its formalities, its procedures – to go to the heavy expenses, troubles and annoyances necessarily incident to such proceedings in order to procure a useless paper called a certificate for permission to manage their own undisputed and partly ancestral estates from an Administrator General having his office in Bombay, or even through the District Courts, acting as his agents, would be, your memorialists humbly and respectfully submit, a totally needless, vexatious and impolitic interference of the law, not warranted by any requirements of their society and utterly repugnant to its condition.[6]

Their efforts led to the passage of a statute that would exempt Parsis from the 1874 Act, "to the same extent as Hindus, Muhammadans and Buddhists."[7] Referring to the Parsis, the statute's draftsman Whitley Stokes commented that the earlier Act was "oppressive and burdensome to them and repugnant to their social and religious customs." The Parsis were not foreigners like the Europeans, for whom the 1874 Act was intended. They were "distinctly Asiatics with an Indian domicile." As a result, Parsis always had relatives or friends willing to oversee the administration of their property after death. A final line asserted a concern for community privacy that would be utterly lacking in Parsi legal history both before and after. Stokes noted "the repugnance with which Parsis regard such an exposure of their family affairs and resources as would some-times result if the Act were enforced in their case."[8] Stokes may have believed what the *mofussil* Parsis were telling him, or perhaps *mofussil* Parsis felt a greater sense of community privacy than their Bombay co-religionists who would dominate Parsi legal history for the rest of the colonial period. Either way, the claim worked, helping Parsis achieve an exit from a burdensome set of obligations.

The most famous instance of exemption-oriented lobbying bore fruit in 1882, when the Parsis used their close ties with the British to secure a tax exemption for the Zoroastrians of Persia.[9] The Parsis migrated to India after the seventh-century Muslim conquest of Persia, but other Zoroastrians remained in Persia, where they continued to practice their religion. The two groups had sporadic

---

[6] "Memorial of Davar Rustomji Khurshedji Modi and the Parsi Community of Surat, dated 15 September 1880, Surat," 2 in "Bill to exempt Parsis from certain provisions of the Administrator General's Act 1874," file 312 (14 February 1881; IOR/L/PJ/6/33).

[7] Preamble to "Act No.IX of 1881. An Act to Amend the Administrator General's Act 1874," 1 in "Act No.IX of 1881," file 578 (21 March 1881).

[8] W. Stokes, "Statement of Objects and Reasons" (unpaginated) in "Act No. IX of 1881" in "Act No. IX of 1881: Annexure."

[9] Karaka, I: 61–82; Stausberg, *Die Religion*, II: 154–64; Jamsheed K. Choksy,"Despite Shāhs and Mollās: Minority Sociopolitics in Premodern and Modern Iran," *JAH* 40:2 (2006), 143–4; Palsetia, *Parsis*, 170; Monica Ringer, "Reform Transplanted: Parsi Agents of Change amongst Zoroastrians in Nineteenth-Century Iran," *Iranian Studies* 42:4 (2009), 553–5 and her *Pious Citizens*, 147–9; Reza Zia-Ebrahimi, "An Emissary of the Golden Age: Manekji Limji Hataria and the Charisma of the Archaic in Pre-Nationalist Iran," *Studies in Ethnicity and Nationalism* 10:3 (2010), 377–90; Green, 121.

contact over the centuries, particularly on religious questions. The last delegation of Parsis consulted Zoroastrian religious authorities in central Persia in the eighteenth century, producing the *Ithoter rivayat*.[10] By the next century, the shift in affluence and influence was visible. The Persian Zoroastrians' impoverishment contrasted starkly with the power and wealth of elite Parsis.[11] Many Parsis felt that the Persian Zoroastrians' poverty was largely attributable to the tax known as the *jazieh* (Pers. *jezīeh*).[12] Under Islamic law and rule, this tax was imposed upon all non-Muslims.[13] Parsis sent charitable aid to cover the marriage expenses of poor Zoroastrian girls in Persia.[14] They created charities like the Society for the Amelioration of Conditions in Iran, through which they built charitable dispensaries and poorhouses.[15] They traveled to Persia to explore investment opportunities and to promote religious education among Zoroastrians.[16] And they used their good relations with the colonial administration to apply British diplomatic pressure in the Persian royal court. In 1882, Zoroastrians in Persia were officially exempted from the *jazieh* because of the Parsi campaign. Parsi lobbying, in other words, worked *across* Eurasian polities – from the British to the Persian – as well as within them.

A second, more ambitious approach aimed for something beyond exemptions. From the 1830s, Parsis began to press for an entirely new and comprehensive legal regime governing their community alone in the domains of marriage and inheritance. This aspiration held real viability in a personal law system like India's. Religious affiliation was not just a spiritual and social matter in South Asia; it was also a jurisdictional one. The personal law system was a necessary precondition for Parsi legislative success on the scale that it was achieved: a group like the Parsis could lobby for their own special legal regime because the legal system recognized separate, community-specific bodies of

---

[10] See Paymaster, 66–84; Mario Vitalone, *The Persian Revayat "Ithoter": Zoroastrian Rituals in the Eighteenth Century* (Napoli: Istituto Universitario Orientale Dipartimento Di Studi Asiatici, Series Minor, XLIX, 1996); Ringer, "Reform Transplanted," 550–1.

[11] See Chapter 7 at note 196.

[12] J. J. Modi, *Papers Read before the Bombay Branch of the Royal Asiatic Society*, Part Four (Bombay: Times of India Press, 1929), 79; Karaka, I: 61–2.

[13] Majid Khadduri and Herbert J. Liebesny, eds., *Law in the Middle East. Vol. 1: Origin and Development of Islamic Law* (Clark, NJ: Lawbook Exchange, 2008), 335. See also Mark R. Cohen, *Poverty and Charity in the Jewish Community of Medieval Egypt* (Princeton, NJ: Princeton University Press, 2005), 130–8; S. D. Goitein, *A Mediterranean Society. An Abridgment in One Volume*, ed. Jacob Lassner (Berkeley: University of California Press, 1999), 182–8; Halil Inalcik, *An Economic and Social History of the Ottoman Empire, Vol.1: 1300–1600* (Cambridge: Cambridge University Press, 1994); N. J. Coulson, *A History of Islamic Law* (Edinburgh: Edinburgh University Press, 1964), 27.

[14] Karaka, I: 84.

[15] Ibid., I: 55. See also Talinn Grigor, "Parsi Patronage of the *Urheimat*," *Getty Res. J.* 2 (2010), 56.

[16] Karaka, I: 82–5; Green, 120–1; Ringer, "Reform Transplanted," 552–3; R. P. Masani, "With Dinshah Irani in New Iran" in *Dinshah Irani Memorial Volume: Papers on Zoroastrian and Iranian Subjects in Honour of the Late Mr Dinshah Jijibhai Irani, BA, LLB, Solicitor, Nishan-I Elmi (Iran)* (Bombay: Dinshah J. Irani Memorial Fund Committee, 1943), xv–xxiv.

Making Law: Two Patterns

89

state-applied religious law. Lobbying for change in the personal law system had its own special mechanics. Lobbying for something that would affect one's own group alone could elicit jealousy from other groups, a sentiment not unknown to Parsis in law generally.[17] But it also created opportunities to enshrine greater religio-cultural autonomy, diversity, and specificity in law. Beyond inspiring a pique of envy, Parsi personal law would not affect non-Parsis in a very concrete way. Equally, non-Parsis may have recognized that if they permitted Parsis to do what they wanted with Parsi law, a principle of mutual non-interference between South Asian communities could benefit their own communities in the future. The distinction, in other words, between lobbying in a unified or a segmented field was an important one. The sinister effects of divide-and-rule policies have received much scholarly attention, but this other aspect of the community-differentiated principle was equally part of colonial politics.[18] Having different rules for different communities meant that, by the late colonial period, legally savvy colonized elites could lobby for change affecting their own community more easily than they would have been able to in a purely territorial legal system. Later in India's history, lobbying for legal change that would affect everyone elicited greater resistance from other groups. Lobbyists in a unified field faced huge hurdles when proposing legal change – whether in the Constitution-framing discussions of the Constituent Assembly (1947–50) or in the deadlocked debates since 1947 over the proposed replacement of the personal law system with a Uniform Civil Code.[19]

With few exceptions, the statutes that created Parsi personal law were drafted by elite Parsi men in Bombay. Many were lawyers by training. In the late colonial period, these statutes were carried through the legislative process by Parsi legislators, particularly when passed in the Bombay Presidency legislature in Poona. The community's pattern of success with legislation began in 1835, with a Parsi petition submitted to government, then the East India Company. The first Indian Law Commission had been created earlier that year. Its job was to revise and condense the codes of law applicable to India.[20] A group of eighteen Parsi men in Bombay took the opportunity to ask one newly appointed Law

---

[17] See 102–3.

[18] On divide-and-rule policies, see Shabnum Tejani, *Indian Secularism: A Social and Intellectual History, 1890–1950* (Bloomington: Indiana University Press, 2008), 113–43; Matthew Groves, "Law, Religion and Public Order in Colonial India: Contextualising the 1887 Allahabad High Court Case on 'Sacred' Cows," *South Asia: J. South Asian Stud.* 33:1 (2010), 98–100.

[19] See Rohit De, "The Republic of Writs: Litigious Citizens and the Rule of Law in the Indian Republic (1947–1964)" (PhD dissertation, Princeton University, 2013); Flavia Agnes, "The Supreme Court, the Media, and the Uniform Civil Code Debate in India" in *The Crisis of Secularism in India*, eds. Anuradha Dingwaney Needham and Rajeswari Sunder Rajan (Durham, NC: Duke University Press, 2007), 294–315.

[20] See Jain, *Outlines*, 474–89. The "most constructive and significant contribution" of the First Law Commission was its draft of the Indian Penal Code (Jain, *Outlines*, 475–6).

Commissioner for a written code of law.[21] A few colonial administrators had favored the idea since the late 1820s. Both Henry Borradaile and Bombay Supreme Court Chief Justice Herbert Compton felt that the Parsis needed their own written law because the void was producing chaos in the courts.[22] The 1835 Parsi petition to the Law Commissioner referred to this view: "you are aware that we have no fixed or written laws or even a good record of the past proceedings of the caste where serious and important questions have been involved and that therefore we cannot in coming to decisions draw even upon the wisdom of our ancestors."[23] It emphasized that "the usages of the tribe of Parsees are very peculiar." The petitioners proposed that they themselves would produce the text of a Parsi legal code.[24] Company officials agreed.[25]

Nothing happened for twenty years, despite prodding from the Chief Justice of the Supreme Court of Bombay, Erskine Perry.[26] The Parsis who had promised to deliver a code undoubtedly felt paralyzed by the enormity of the task. However, the 1850s and '60s saw a flurry of legislative activity.[27] A younger generation of lobbyists led by Nowrozjee Furdoonjee and Sorabji Shapurji Bengalee began work, having obtained financial backing for the project from the Bombay Parsi Panchayat.[28] The result was the passage of two all-India Acts in 1865. The Parsi Marriage and Divorce Act (XV of 1865) and the Parsi Intestate Succession Act (XXI of 1865) marked the official birth of Parsi personal law.[29] This project progressed in two stages. First, a body called the Parsi Law Association was created in 1855 as a result of mass meetings within the Parsi community. As one British newspaper commented after the initiation of the campaign to create the Parsi Acts of 1865, "The Parsees act under no European instigation, for no European has any personal interest in the question. They have benefited by no European guidance, for no European knew anything of the matter in hand. They did their own work by themselves. They used their own language to express their own thoughts. They appointed a Committee entirely of their own race, and their speeches were, for the most part, the free

---

[21] "Address from leaders of the Parsee community of Bombay to George William Anderson, regarding the formation of a code of laws to embody and determine the customs and usages of the Parsee community (with associated correspondence)" (April–August 1835) 1 (IOR/F/4/1555/63508).

[22] See Menant, *Les Parsis*, 274; Desai, *History*, 35.

[23] "[Extract] from certain respectable inhabitants of Bombay to George William Anderson, Bombay, 2 April 1835," 4 in "Address from leaders of the Parsee community of Bombay."

[24] "Extract of a Letter to the Hon. The Court of Directors in the Legislative Department dated 24 August 1835," 1 in "Address from leaders of the Parsee community of Bombay."

[25] Reply to "Extract from certain respectable inhabitants of Bombay to George William Anderson, Bombay, 2 April 1845," 14 in "Address from leaders of the Parsee community of Bombay."

[26] Desai, *History*, 35.

[27] See generally Agnes, *Family Law*, I: 79.

[28] Desai, *History*, 36.

[29] For a succinct overview, see Kulke, 67–9.

Making Law: Two Patterns

expression of Parsee ideas. *In short, they originated instead of merely imitating.*"[30]

The Parsi Law Association drafted the text of the two bills and presented them to the colonial government in 1859. Government officials recognized that there was internal disagreement between Parsis in Bombay and in the *mofussil*, particularly over the right of Parsi women to inherit. The state created the Parsi Law Commission, a group of two British officials and two Parsi men. One of the two Parsis represented Bombay and the other, the *mofussil*. On most divisive points, the Parsi Law Commission favored the Bombay Parsi perspective. They pointed to the concentration of the Parsi population in the presidency capital: the majority of Parsis lived in Bombay.[31]

Two Bombay Parsis prominent in the lobbying process, Nowrozjee Furdoonjee and Manekjee Cursetjee, brought their knowledge of colonial law to the project.[32] One was an official in the colonial courts, whereas the other was a *vakil*. Arguably, it was through their day jobs that both acquired the skills and confidence to manage the earliest legislative project to codify matrimonial law in British India. Their paid work exposed them to the mechanics of the colonial legal system, knowledge which they took home and harnessed in the service of their community. Nowrozjee Furdoonjee was a court interpreter in the Bombay High Court.[33] In an 1862 letter he wrote to the Parsi Law Commission, he noted that he had been an officer of the Supreme Court of Bombay (first under the East India Company and then under the Raj) for seventeen years.[34] Manekjee Cursetjee was a *vakil* in the East India Company's civil court for Bombay Presidency, the Sudder Dewanny Adawlut (Pers. *Ṣadr Dīvānī 'Adālat*).[35] Later, he became a judge in the Bombay Court of Small Causes.[36] Both men would play a central role in the legislative process that led to the passage of the 1865 Acts, and the 1865 legislation created the model for a collective strategy that Parsi elites would repeat again and again (Figure 2.1). Nowrozjee Furdoonjee was a leader of the Parsi Law Association and pushed hard to disapply English inheritance law to Parsis. Manekjee Cursetjee responded vigorously to the marriage bill, submitting written feedback and authoring a pamphlet that became central to the Parsi Law Commissioners' discussion of child

---

[30] *The Friend of India* (undated), cited in Palsetia, *Parsis*, 210. Italics added.

[31] "Report into the usages recognized as laws by the Parsee Community of India," 9 in "1862–3 Government of India Bill."

[32] The future legislator Dadabhai Naoroji was also very involved in the lobbying efforts of the 1850s–60s (Parekh, 3).

[33] Darukhanawala, *Parsi Lustre*, I: 138; Mistry, *Reminiscences* [1911], 70.

[34] Letter from Nowrozjee Furdoonjee to Kaikhusrow Hormusjee, Secretary to the Parsee Law Commission, Bombay, 28 April 1862, 14 in "1862–3 Government of India Bill." Furdoonjee went on to become a major "public man" in Bombay and British India. See D. E. Wacha, *Rise and Growth of Bombay Municipal Government* (Madras: Natesan, [1913]), 138–40; Bayly, 240–1 (where "Furdoonjee Nowrozjee" should read Nowrozjee Furdoonjee).

[35] Darukhanawala, *Parsi Lustre*, I: 333.

[36] Bengalee, 231.

THE

AMENDED BILL;

WITH A

MEMORANDUM

OF

ALTERATIONS, ADDITIONS, AND OMISSIONS

SUGGESTED IN THE

DRAFT CODE OF LAWS FOR THE PARSEES.

FIGURE 2.1. Draft text of what would become the Parsi Marriage and Divorce Act and the Parsi Intestate Succession Act, both of 1865.
Source: 1862–3 Government of India bill to amend law for Parsees. © The British Library Board IOR/L/PJ/5/400.

Making Law: Two Patterns

marriage. He was also instrumental in having the Parsi Panchayat replaced by the new Parsi matrimonial courts as adjudicator of matrimonial disputes in 1865.

Seventy years after the 1865 Acts came the second major wave of Parsi lobbying at the all-India level.[37] Between 1936 and 1940, significant changes were made to the Parsi Marriage and Divorce Act of 1865. The new version was passed in two parts: the main Parsi Marriage and Divorce Act of 1936 was followed by a short amending statute on divorced wives' alimony, the Parsi Marriage and Divorce (Amendment) Act (XIV of 1940).[38] The Parsi Intestate Succession Act of 1865 was also reworked and passed as part of the Indian Succession Act (XXXIX of 1925). As in the 1860s, elite male Parsis from Bombay initiated and drafted these changes. People like Bombay businessman Sir Cowasji Jehangir presided over the Parsi Central Association, the 1930s equivalent of the earlier Parsi Law Association.[39] Both bodies initiated the creation of Parsi-specific statutes and undertook the drafting of the text. Other central figures in the flurry of 1930s Parsi statutory activity included business-men like Sir Phiroze C. Sethna and solicitors like F. A. Vakeel.[40]

This second wave differed from the first in several ways. In the 1850s–'60s, Parsis had designed and lobbied for a special statutory regime. They had con-sulted internally with Parsi groups from Bombay and the *mofussil* and had received feedback from Parsi individuals and groups.[41] In the 1930s, all of the same processes took place, but on an amplified scale. Consultation processes extended to Parsi groups in China and Persia and to corners of India with Parsi populations three families large.[42] More importantly, in the seventy years since the first push for Parsi legislation, Parsis had become well entrenched in the courts and legislature. Figures like the Bombay High Court judge B. J. Wadia and the jurist and Privy Council judge D. F. Mulla contributed their views on the legislation.[43] In the 1850s and '60s, Parsis in such positions of power did not exist. Parsis had also become important legislators. With reforms like the

---

[37] See Agnes, *Family Law*, I: 81–2.

[38] On the 1940 Act, see "The Parsi Marriage and Divorce (Amendment) Act 1940, 2 March 1939–15 August 1940" (IOR/L/PJ/7/2502); Sharafi, "Law and Modern Zoroastrians."

[39] On the Parsi Central Association, see Kulke, 213–14.

[40] On Sethna, see Darukhanawala, *Parsi Lustre*, I: 139–41; Sanjana, *Ancient Persia*, 597–8.

[41] See Desai, *History*, 36. There had been little consultation of the Parsi community by the Parsi elite (led by Jamsetjee Jeejeebhoy) that negotiated the passage of the 1837 intestacy legislation. See "Correspondence on the subject of the law of inheritance among the Parsees between Manockjee Cursetjee and some of the prominent members of the Parsee Community at Bombay and others in 1837–1838 and 1859" in Q. in the Corner, 6–7, 12–13, 16–21.

[42] "Extract from the Council of State Debates, Vol. 1, No. 9" (Delhi, 13 March 1936), 3; and "No. 7 – Coorg," "No. 8 – Madras," "No. 15 – United Province," and "No. 16 – Bihar and Orissa" in "Paper No. 1: Opinions on the Parsi Marriage and Divorce Bill. Opinions Nos. 1–19," 37, 40, 52, 56 (respectively); all in "The Parsi Marriage and Divorce Act 1936 (16 August 1934–23 July 1936)." See also Desai, *History*, 41.

[43] "Extract" (13 March 1936), 3 in "The Parsi Marriage and Divorce Act 1936."

94   *Law and Identity in Colonial South Asia: Parsi Legal Culture*

Morley-Minto legislation of 1909, increased representation for South Asians in government meant that more Parsis could be elected to legislative bodies at the presidency and all–India level.[44] Occupying a non-Muslim seat for the Bombay Presidency, Phiroze Sethna led the new Parsi Marriage and Divorce bill through the legislative process in Delhi and Simla in 1934–5.[45] He was a leading Bombay businessman, as well as a Justice of the Peace and honorary magistrate.[46] Sethna noted the new presence of Parsi legislators: "I will admit that in or about 1865 no members of the Parsi community were members of the Supreme Legislature whereas we have today Parsis as Members of both Houses of the Central Legislature."[47] Sethna obtained special permission from the Council to create a Select Committee that included members of both Houses; normally, a Select Committee of lower house members alone would have considered the bill. He did so to maximize the number of Parsi legislators influencing the bill.[48] As a result, the Select Committee included the two people who had steered the project through the Parsi community (Sir Cowasji Jehangir, heading the Parsi Central Association) and legislature (Sir Phiroze Sethna), along with Parsi legislators such as physician Nasarvanji Choksy and the legally trained businessman H. P. Mody.[49]

The existence of Parsi legislators in the 1930s allowed Parsi lobbying to become vertically integrated, both in Bombay Presidency and at the all-India level.[50] In 1936, the Parsi Public Trusts Registration Act (Bombay XXIII of 1936) became law in Bombay Presidency. The statute brought Parsi trusts under closer supervision by the state by requiring the registration of all charitable trusts. Its sponsor was Parsi physician-legislator Dr. M. D. Gilder.[51] Parsis constituted approximately half of the Select Committee members who assessed the bill.[52] Gilder promoted the bill by arguing for greater accountability in the

---

[44] See Heather Frazer, "Morley-Minto Reforms," in *Historical Dictionary of the British Empire*, eds. James S. Olson and Robert Shadle (Westport, CT: Greenport Press, 1996), II: 759–60.

[45] Under the Morley-Minto reforms (Indian Councils Act 1909) and the Government of India Act 1919, separate "Muhammadan" and "Non-Muhammadan" seats were created for South Asian representatives. See Frazer; Arnold Kaminsky, "Government of India Act of 1919," in *Historical Dictionary of European Imperialism*, ed. James S. Olson (Westport, CT: Greenwood Press, 1991), 257–8.

[46] Darukhanawala, *Parsi Lustre*, I: 140.

[47] "Extract from the Council of State Debates, Vol. I, No. 9," 13 March 1936, 2 in "The Parsi Marriage and Divorce Act 1936."

[48] "Extract from the Council of State Debates, Vol. I, No. 9," 27 February 1935, 2 in "The Parsi Marriage and Divorce Act 1936."

[49] See entries on H. P. Mody and Cowasji Jehangir in Thomas Peters, ed., *Famous Business Houses and Who's Who in India and Pakistan* (Bombay: Modern Press and Publicity, [1949]), 74, 370 (respectively); Kali H. Mody and Alice Pastakia, "Sir Homi Mody and Piloo Mody: Lasting Influence," 126–40 in Mody, *Enduring Legacy*, I.

[50] See Desai, *History*, 116–7.

[51] See entry on Gilder in Peters, 354–5; Nawaz B. Mody, "Dr. Manchersha D. Gilder: Healer Politician," in *Enduring Legacy*, ed. Mody, I: 104–11.

[52] "Bombay Legislative Proceedings. 23 March 1936. Dr. M. D. Gilder," 1–4 in "Parsi Public Trusts Registration Act 1936 (1 August 1935–29 April 1937)" (IOR/L/PJ/7/920).

Making Law: Two Patterns

95

administration of trust-based Parsi charitable funds. He claimed that preventable poverty existed among Parsis because charitable funds were not well organized. In many cases, their existence was unknown to potential beneficiaries. In others, their purposes overlapped, with trustees unaware of this fact. The community's legal expertise permeated these legislative debates. Gilder boasted that the bill had been "through the hands of two Parsis who have acted as Advocates General."[53] A Muslim representative, Moulvi Sir Rafiuddin Ahmad, noted that the Parsi community included top lawyers, some of whom were members of the legislature. If some *mofussil* Parsis did not like the phrasing of certain clauses, he recommended they give the text to their co-religionists. Parsi lawyers, said Ahmad, had the skills to "remodel the whole bill" in-house.[54]

The details of trust administration were not the most interesting aspect of these debates. At the broader conceptual level, some members of Bombay's Legislative Council questioned the personal law principle itself. Parsi legislators may have disagreed among themselves on the contents of the trusts regulation statute. All agreed, though, that their community needed its own special legislation. "We do not want to come under the general law," declared K. B. Vakil.[55] Against them were a number of Hindu legislators who commented that having special statutes for Parsis was inefficient and unjustifiable. After all, the Parsi population was miniscule. Acts regulating Hindu and Muslim religious endowments had recently been passed.[56] Surely it would have been simpler, argued Hindu legislator L. R. Gokhale, for Parsis to bring themselves under the Hindu Act, with exemptions from any specifically Hindu provisions. "I am expecting tomorrow a separate bill from the Goanese Christian community and another separate bill for the East Indian Christian community and so on, and then one for Jains," he complained. "How many bills are we going to have to govern charities?" He also noted that the procedures followed in passing Parsi legislation gave them special privileges. When the Hindu charities bill was being considered, Hindu public opinion was not polled in the thorough way that it was done for the Parsis.[57] In the same vein, Dr. M. K. Dixit also criticized the personal law principle, foreshadowing debates in independent India over the proposed replacement of the system with a Uniform Civil Code: "it is a pity we have been enacting separate laws for the different communities in this Presidency ... I wish that only one common law existed for all the people in

---

[53] "Bombay Legislative Proceedings. 10 October 1935. Dr. M. D. Gilder (Bombay City, North)," 16 in "Parsi Public Trusts Registration Act."

[54] "Bombay Legislative Proceedings. 23 March 1936. Moulvi Sir Rafiuddin Ahmad," 16 in "Parsi Public Trusts Registration Act."

[55] "Bombay Legislative Proceedings. 23 March 1936. K. B. Vakil," 12 in "Parsi Public Trusts Registration Act."

[56] C. A. [Turnbridge], "The Mahomedan Wakfs Act and the Hindu Trusts Registration Act Were Both Passed in 1936–7," 22 April 1937, unnumbered in "Parsi Public Trusts Registration Act."

[57] "Bombay Legislative Proceedings. 10 October 1935. L. R. Gokhale," 11–13 in "Parsi Public Trusts Registration Act."

96   *Law and Identity in Colonial South Asia: Parsi Legal Culture*

this Presidency, as a matter of fact for the whole country."[58] As in independent India, the leading proponents of a single, territorial law for India were members of the Hindu majority.

Parsi supporters of the bill disagreed, clinging to the principle of community-specific rules. Hindus and Muslims had their own special statutes, and Parsis deserved one, too. No one would suggest that Muslims be brought under the Hindu Act, argued Parsi legislator A. E. Servai.[59] By the same logic, Parsis deserved their own legal regime, differing as they did from Hindus in crucial ways. The bill's sponsor, Gilder, noted that the law pertaining to Hindu religious endowments recognized Hindu deities as legal persons so that they could own temple property.[60] Gilder stressed the monotheism of his religion. "We worship a God who we believe has created the whole world, and there is no necessity for the ownership of any temporary property for Him."[61] Hindu legislator S. T. Kambli noted that the Hindu Act was designed for a largely illiterate population of trust managers. This was not the case in "an enlightened community like the Parsis" whose high rates of literacy permitted different types of accounting and reporting procedures.[62]

Some Parsi legislators worried that their community's interests would be neglected by the Hindu majority as India moved toward independence. They may have realized that minority group rights would not necessarily be better protected in a majoritarian polity than by the colonial state. Servai predicted that under the "reformed constitution," "electorates will be very much enlarged and it is likely ... that there may be no Parsi member sitting in this House, because there is no separate electorate for the Parsi community."[63] If Parsi trusts were folded into a larger Hindu Act, even with exemptions made at the outset, later changes to the Hindu Act could apply in blanket fashion. Without the presence of a Parsi legislator working to protect the community's interests, provisions

---

[58] "Bombay Legislative Proceedings. 10 October 1935. M. K. Dixit," 14 in "Parsi Public Trusts Registration Act."

[59] "Bombay Legislative Proceedings. 10 October 1935. A. E. Servai," 4 in "Parsi Public Trusts Registration Act."

[60] See the Privy Council case of *P. N. Mullick v. P. K. Mullick* (1925) LR 52 IA 245; P. W. Duff, "The Personality of an Idol," *Cam LJ* 3 (1927–9) 42–9; and Richard H. Davis, "Temples, Deities and the Law" in *Hinduism and Law: An Introduction*, eds. Timothy Lubin, Donald R. Davis, Jr., and Jayanth Krishnan (Cambridge: Cambridge University Press, 2010), 204–6.

[61] "Bombay Legislative Proceedings. 10 October 1935. Dr. M. D. Gilder," 4 in "Parsi Public Trusts Registration Act." See also Introduction at 15.

[62] "Bombay Legislative Proceedings. 14 September 1936. S. T. Kambli," 33 in "Parsi Public Trusts Registration Act."

[63] "Bombay Legislative Proceedings. 10 October 1935. A. E. Servai," 4 in "The Parsi Public Trusts Registration Act 1936." Servai's prediction was quite accurate. In the 1949 Bombay Legislative Assembly, only two of 170 representatives were Parsi, namely Dr. Gilder (as before) and Rustomji Pardiwala. Both represented areas of Bombay with Parsi concentrations (Turner, 25–7). Servai's mention of a "reformed constitution" related to the Government of India Act of 1935, which inched India toward dominion status. See Arnold P. Kaminsky, "Government of India Act 1935" in Olson, 258–9.

Making Law: Two Patterns

appropriate for Hindus but unsuited to Zoroastrians might be applied inadvertently to Parsi trusts. The Bombay High Court judge M. P. Khareghat was even more direct in his lack of enthusiasm for the majoritarian future. He told the presidency legislature: "I deplore the mentality that is opposed to Government because it is supposed to be a foreign Government. That foreign Government has done a great deal of good for India and it is still capable of doing more good. But you are going to have a Swaraj Government very soon."[64] The same logic pushed another Bombay High Court denizen, M. A. Jinnah, to press for a separate state for Muslims: the future Pakistan. Khareghat and Jinnah were animated by a special concern for minorities under majority rule. Khareghat predicted the erosion of the neat chain of command that Parsis had created by the late colonial period. During this window of opportunity – when South Asians had a greater role in government but before independence and Hindu-majority rule – the legislative process could be carried by Parsis almost to the top.

The Parsi legislative lobby began modestly in the mid-1830s with the aim of securing exemptions from a particular rule of English law. Its ambitions quickly expanded. In 1835, leaders of the Parsi lobby expressed the desire to create a separate body of family law for Parsis alone. From 1835 until Indian independence in 1947, elite Parsis perfected the practice of drafting and eventually helping to pass the legislation that created Parsi personal law. The process consisted of an accumulation of expertise and influence. Parsi control over the process increased vis-à-vis Britons over the course of a century. Over time, the Parsis dominating the legislative lobby were elites in Bombay City, rather than their *mofussil* counterparts.

Parsi lobbying also occurred on a third plane. Around the same time as Parsi lobbyists started pressing for a Parsi-only regime of family law, they also began intervening in the development of general legislation that would affect them adversely. The most famous instance involved the Special Marriages Act (III of 1872). This statute created a religiously neutral, civil marriage regime that would allow couples (where neither party was Christian) to marry outside of the personal law system, an option ideally suited to couples marrying across religious lines.[65] Notoriously, the statute required any person marrying under its provisions to renounce his or her religion under oath. This requirement prevented many people from marrying under the Act and was progressively eliminated when the statute was revised in 1923 and 1954.[66] The rule was the work of Parsi lobbyists, who were animated by the orthodox desire to minimize

---

[64] "Bombay Legislative Proceedings. 14 September 1936. M. P. Khareghat," 8 in "Parsi Public Trusts Registration Act."

[65] The Indian Christian Marriage Act 1872 applied to couples in which only one party was Christian (s. 4). [S. Krishnamurthi Aiyar, *Law and Practice Relating to Marriages in India and Burma* (Lahore: University Book Agency Law Publishers, 1937), 75–6.]

[66] Hindus, Buddhists, Sikhs, and Jains alone were exempted from the renunciation clause under the Special Marriage (Amendment) Act (XXX of 1923). See Perveez Mody, *The Intimate State: Love-Marriage and the Law in Delhi* (Delhi: Routledge, 2008), 91–2; Aiyar, 56 at note (w).

98   *Law and Identity in Colonial South Asia: Parsi Legal Culture*

intermarriage between Parsis and non-Parsis. More precisely, the renunciation requirement made it clear that any Parsi who married under the Special Marriages Act could not claim to be Parsi for other purposes, including consignment to the *dakhmas* after death or benefiting from religious trust funds.[67] There were other instances in which Parsi influence shaped the general, territorial law of India.[68] All reflected a keen appreciation for the power of lobbying.

THE LEGAL PROFESSION

The process of lobbying for the passage of legislation was an organized and deliberate strategy for increasing group autonomy. The second mode of Parsi law making – the pursuit of law as a profession – could not be construed as equally intentional or collective in its aims. Nonetheless, this pattern created a notable degree of control. The Parsi community produced a disproportionate number of lawyers and judges, both in the Bombay High Court (where many cases involved Parsis) and in the Parsi Chief Matrimonial Court (where all cases involved Parsis). Parsi legal professionals also maintained a solid presence in Bombay's subordinate courts, such as the Court of Small Causes, the Insolvency Courts, and the Police Courts.[69] Although Parsis constituted just 6 percent of the population of Bombay in the early twentieth century, between a third and a half of all lawyers (including Europeans) and roughly one sixth of High Court judges in Bombay were Parsi.[70] Describing the legal profession in Bombay, the Parsi law firm clerk A. J. C. Mistry wrote in 1911 that "the Parsees are the life and soul of litigation in Bombay and in one shape or the other they are connected with the majority of the suits in [the] High Court."[71] From the late nineteenth century, much of the litigation between Parsis came to be managed by their own lawyers and judges. The pattern was historically unusual. Even when 60–80 percent of the lawyers in Berlin and Vienna were Jewish in the 1930s, it was not clear that Jews used the state courts for settling intragroup disputes in the way that the Parsis did.[72] Unlike Parsis, Jews had a well developed body of

---

[67] Desai, *History*, 96. The required declaration read: "I do not profess the Christian, Jewish, Hindu, Muhammadan, Parsi, Buddhist, Sikh or Jaina religion." [Special Marriages Act 1872 (Second Schedule) in Aiyar, 56–7.] See also Perveez Mody, "Love and the Law: Love-Marriage in Delhi," *MAS* 36:1 (2002), 232–40.

[68] See, for instance, Desai, *History*, 115.

[69] For example, see Patel and Paymaster, III: 825–8; Mistry, *Reminiscences* [1911], 66; "Mahomedans in the High Court," *TI* (13 April 1926), 13.

[70] In 1908, 61 out of the 124 solicitors practicing in the High Court of Bombay (or 49 percent) were Parsi. In 1924, 116 out of 278 (41.7 percent) were Parsi. Thirty-six percent of the names on a 1925 list of Bombay advocates (68 of 189) were Parsi. [Mistry, *Forty Years' Reminiscences of the High Court of Judicature at Bombay* (Bombay: Author, 1925), 47, 60–3.] See also note 169 and Chapter 1 at note 8.

[71] Mistry, *Reminiscences* [1911], 72.

[72] Ingo Müller, *Hitler's Justice: The Courts of the Third Reich* (London: Tauris, 1991), 60.

Making Law: Two Patterns

religious law and institutions to resolve inside disputes, as well as clear prohibitions on taking Jewish disputes to non-Jewish adjudicators.[73]

At the individual level, becoming a lawyer appealed for a number of reasons. The most obvious were income and status. By the turn of the twentieth century, many South Asian lawyers made a good living in the presidency capitals, with the top "nabobs of law" commanding fees that allowed them to live like princes.[74] *Hindi Punch* never missed an opportunity to satirize the profit motive in colonial lawyering. In one scene of South Asian lawyers and litigants, a plaintiff tugged on a cow's horns while a defendant pulled on its tail. The cow, a complicated choice of animal in the Indian context, represented the property at stake in the suit. Two lawyers chatted while a third busily milked the animal (Figure 2.2).[75] In 1908, two protracted religious cases were being heard by the Bombay High Court at the same time: the famous *Petit v. Jijibhai* case and an equally well-known suit about authority structures among the Khoja followers of the Aga Khan.[76] A *Hindi Punch* cartoon placed two geese on a judge's chair with their backsides facing the reader, each representing one of the suits (Figure 2.3). These geese were laying not eggs but gold mohurs, the traditional unit of currency through which lawyers' fees were expressed.[77] Two grinning lawyers in robes and bands happily held open a sack labeled "Law Charges – Counsel's Fees" to catch the coins. The caption noted that the costs in the Parsi case would total several hundred thousand rupees and that the Aga Khan case would also be "extraordinarily heavy." Although the racial identity of the illustrated lawyers was ambiguous, many of the lawyers in the two cases were South Asian, and Parsis had a particular presence in *Petit v. Jijibhai.*

It was not just the promise of wealth that drew large numbers of young South Asian men to law in the late colonial period. Law offered special opportunities for social mobility. Legal careers were accessible to young Parsi men coming from poorer backgrounds in ways that business careers were not.[78] Most major business concerns among Parsis were family-run; one typically had to be born into the family to be eligible for its upper corporate ranks. Law, by contrast, could be an individual endeavor. This was not to say that it usually was. Lawyerly lineages soon developed among Parsis, as in other South Asian

---

[73] See "Rabbinical Courts"; Broyde.

[74] Macleod, "Reminiscences" (1894–1914), 78; Samuel Schmitthener, "A Sketch of the Development of the Legal Profession in India," *LSR* 3:2/3 (1968), 369–72.

[75] "A Milch-Cow, a Plaintiff, a Defendant and Lawyers," *HP* (3 Dec. 1916), 19. See also Pamela G. Price, "Ideology and Ethnicity under British Imperial Rule: 'Brahmans,' Lawyers and Kin-Caste Rules in Madras Presidency," *MAS* 23:1 (1999), 174.

[76] *Haji Bibi v. H. H. Sir Sultan Mahomed Shah, the Aga Khan* 11 Bom LR 409 (1911).

[77] "The Gold Mohur," *Bom LJ* 2 (1924–5), 13–15.

[78] See D. D. Davar, *Hints to Young Lawyers, Being an Address Delivered by the Hon. Mr. Justice D. D. Davar to the Students of the Government Law School, Bombay, on 15th Feb. 1911* (Bombay: Tripathi and Co., 1911), 13. Also conversation with R. P. Vachha (Mumbai, 22 February 2004).

FIGURE 2.2. "A Milch-Cow, a Plaintiff, a Defendant and Lawyers."
Source: *HP* (3 Dec. 1916), 19. Courtesy of the British Library SV576.

communities that converted social and family capital into legal capital.[79] The pleader Manekshah Jehangirshah Taleyarkhan, for example, was the leading Parsi lawyer to appear for Parsi litigants from the 1870s until the 1890s.[80] His son, K. M. Taleyarkan, became a barrister who occupied a series of important positions at the High Court, including Official Assignee, Administrator General, and Receiver. In turn, Manekshah's grandson N. H. C. Coyajee would become a judge of the Bombay High Court (1943–57).[81] Coyajee came from legal stock through the paternal line, too. His own father, H. C. Coyajee, was a High Court judge in the 1920s.[82] Mentoring and referrals from other lawyers were crucial early in one's career, and legal families could provide these instantly. Even so, encouragement and informal apprenticeship also emanated from nonfamilial sources, both Parsi and British. A number of top Parsi legal figures in Bombay City emerged from nonelite and provincial backgrounds with the help of such

---

[79] By A. J. C. Mistry, see *Forty Years' Reminiscences of the High Court*, 45, 48–9; *Forty Years' Reminiscences of the Firm of Messrs. Wadia Ghandy and Co.* (Bombay: Author, 1925), 2. See also Yves Dezalay and Bryant G. Garth, eds., *Asian Legal Revivals: Lawyers in the Shadow of Empire* (Chicago: University of Chicago Press, 2010), 3.

[80] For examples, see "Parsee Chief Matrimonial Court," *TI* (4 February 1878), 3; "A Parsee Divorce Case," *TI* (21 November 1879), 3; *Ardesir Jehangir Framji Banaji v. Secretary of State for India in Council* ILR 6 Bom 398 (1882); *Queen-Empress v. Gustadji Barjorji* ILR 10 Bom 181 (1886); "A Parsee Divorce Suit. *Furdoonjee Pallonjee Desai v. Kharshedbai*," *TI* (30 November 1887), 3; "The Parsee Chief Matrimonial Court," *TI* (19 July 1892), 3. See also Vachha, 169–70; Darukhanawala, *Parsi Lustre*, I: 151.

[81] Vachha, 170.

[82] "Death of Mr. Justice Coyajee," *TI* (24 December 1955), 11.

Making Law: Two Patterns

FIGURE 2.3. "The Geese with the Gold Mohurs."
Source: HP (19 April 1908), 13. Courtesy of the British Library SV576.

lines of support. D. F. Mulla was the eldest son of a struggling schoolteacher.[83] He began his career as a solicitor, but then took the unusual step of also qualifying as an advocate at the urging of the Bombay Chief Justice, Sir Lawrence Jenkins, after the judge took an interest in the young lawyer.[84]

[83] Darukhanawala, *Parsi Lustre*, I: 148; Patel and Paymaster, VII: 174-5.
[84] See "Famous Indian Jurist Dead: Life Sketch of Sir D. F. Mulla," *TI* (27 April 1934), 10.

Vikaji Fardunji Taraporewala was a pleader then barrister from Rajkot, a small princely state in western India's Kathiawar peninsula. He struggled to establish himself in Bombay during "the difficult period of the first World War," but then rather quickly became successful after attracting the attention of the British judge F. C. O. Beaman. Beaman would later claim that he "had a hand" in launching Taraporewala's career.[85] The Parsi judge Sir Nusserwanji Phirozshah Engineer followed in Mulla's footsteps in many ways. Coming from a humble background and receiving his early schooling at a Parsi charitable school, he first joined Mulla's law firm but then switched to the Bar in 1922, with the encouragement of then Advocate General Sir Thomas Strangman and Parsi businessman F. E. Dinshaw. Engineer became a judge of the Bombay High Court in 1936, Advocate General of Bombay in 1942, and Advocate General of India in 1945.[86]

Legal training also gave South Asians special opportunities vis-à-vis the colonial state. On the one hand, legal credentials opened up the possibility of securing government posts, particularly in the courts, as well as in the Revenue and Judicial Departments. This route was taken by South Asian lawyers in the 1870s–'80s especially, when their small numbers among High Court practitioners struggled to break into European socioprofessional networks.[87] Parsis excelled by this route, occasionally incurring the resentment of others.[88] As one *Times of India* reader observed of the Bombay High Court in 1926, it was "a common remark that the High Court is run by the Parsis . . . the Parsis at present have more of the plums of the High Court appointments than the Hindus, Musalmans and all the other communities combined."[89] Why should this tiny minority get "most of the fat posts," asked others, suggesting that Parsis were unfairly privileged while Muslims and Christians were underrepresented.[90] Against them, Parsi respondents protested that such appointments were based on merit or seniority, praising "an alien Government" for not yet beginning "the communal Swaraj."[91] A perpetual issue hovering above the phenomenon of Parsi legalism was the possibility of other communities' envy. Here was a

---

[85] Vachha, 157–8; *Records of Lincoln's Inn*, II: 49 (admitted to Lincoln's Inn on 7 May 1903); Ronald Roxburgh, ed., *The Records of the Honourable Society of Lincoln's Inn. The Black Books, Vol. V. AD 1845–1914* (London: Lincoln's Inn, 1968), 435 (called to the Bar on 17 June 1906).

[86] "Late Sir Nusserwanji Phirozshah Engineer," *Mah LJ* (1970), 132–6.

[87] Christine Dobbin, *Urban Leadership in Western India: Politics and Communities in Bombay City 1840–1885* (Oxford: Oxford University Press, 1972), 166–70.

[88] On Parsi officials in the Bombay High Court, see Mistry, *Forty Years' Reminiscences of the High Court*, 11–21.

[89] "To the Editor of 'The Times of India,'" *TI* (14 April 1926), 15.

[90] "Mahomedans in the High Court," *TI* (26 March 1926), 12; (6 April 1926), 13; (5 May 1926), 15.

[91] "Mahomedans in the High Court," *TI* (13 April 1926), 13. See also "Ultimus Romanorum," *KH* (3 May 1931), 22 and "An English Judge," *Jam-e Jamshed* (4 May 1926), n.p., both in "Press Cuttings, 1915–40" (HRA/D63/A6) in Macleod of Cadboll Papers.

Making Law: Two Patterns

moment, striking for its rarity, when comparisons were made explicitly and in writing. There is little evidence that such criticism induced any sort of change: the Parsi proclivity to secure law-related government positions continued until the end of British rule and arguably beyond.

Law was also a good choice if one wanted a job that was independent of the colonial state. A career in private practice was ideal for lawyers like the future nationalist politician, Khurshed Framji Nariman.[92] In a 1928 suit, he was acquitted of criminal libel charges after accusing a British official of corruption.[93] A Parsi supporter noted that Nariman could expose "the scandalous doings of Government departments" because of his profession, "which does not for its living depend upon Government patronage or the truckling of high placed officials."[94] The case itself epitomized the Parsi penetration of the legal establishment on all sides. The Advocate General representing the government in the case was also Parsi – none other than D. F. Mulla.[95] In the late colonial period, legal training offered Parsis both the opportunity to join *or* critique the state, according to their taste.[96]

One reason why late colonial Parsis were able to populate the legal profession at disproportionately high rates was because so many were fluent and literate in English.[97] More than Bombay's other mercantile communities, Parsis began educating their sons (and some daughters) in English from the 1830s–'40s. Leading English-medium institutions, such as Elphinstone College in Bombay, had a large and steady contingent of elite Parsi students, as well as benefactors, during the nineteenth century.[98]

Equally important was the fact that Parsis lived in a colonial jurisdiction where non-Europeans lawyers were permitted to practice and, speaking relatively, to prosper. In the white settler colonies (later dominions) of South Africa, Canada, Australia, and New Zealand, race-based barriers – often tied to voting rights or a knowledge of Latin – prevented colonized people from developing a significant presence in the legal profession.[99] The relative size of the white

---

[92] For a photograph of Nariman, see S. M. Surveyor, ed., *Harvey-Nariman Libel Case* (Bombay: Minerva Press, 1927–8), frontispiece.

[93] See Y. D. Phadke, "Khurshed Framji Nariman: Man of Many Causes," 112–25 in Mody, *Enduring Legacy*, I.

[94] Surveyor, v.

[95] "A Verdict for Fair Play," *TI* (17 May 1928), 12. See also Tehmtan R. Andhyarujina, "The Bombay High Court and the Office of the Advocate General," 153, 156 in *The Bombay High Court: The Story of the Building – 1878–2003*, eds. Rahul Mehrotra and Sharada Dwivedi (Mumbai: Eminence Designs, 2004).

[96] Dobbin, *Urban Leadership*, 170.

[97] See John R. Hinnells, "Parsis and British Education, 1820–1880," 141–73 in Hinnells, *Zoroastrian and Parsi Studies*.

[98] Palsetia, *Parsis*, 133–40; Ringer, *Pious Citizens*, 37–40.

[99] See Sharafi, "A New History," 1079.

104 Law and Identity in Colonial South Asia: Parsi Legal Culture

population, along with its intention to stay, made all the difference.[100] Contrast the proportion of the 1901 population that was white in New South Wales (99 percent) or New Zealand (95 percent) with the figures for India or the Gold Coast in West Africa (both 0.07 percent).[101] Decolonization was particularly fraught in the white settler colonies, when it happened at all.[102] In territories with a sufficiently large European population, legal skills could be provided by whites for whites. The demographics of race permitted the "luxury" of racial exclusivity.

From surprisingly early in the colonial occupation of the nonsettler colonies, the British recognized that they would not stay forever.[103] From the mid-nineteenth century in India and the West African colonies, remarkably large numbers of non-Europeans became lawyers and judges while racial restrictions were becoming more and more exclusionary in the settler colonies.[104] When Gandhi tried to gain admission as an advocate of the Supreme Court in Natal, he was outraged by the race-based obstacles put in his path – obstacles that had no equivalent in British India.[105] From the 1860s on, a stream of South Asian and West African students were admitted to the Inns of Court in London in order to become barristers.[106] At their peak around 1930, South Asians constituted between a third and half of all students being admitted to the Inns, particularly Middle Temple and Lincoln's Inn.[107] There was at least one joke on the subject.

---

[100] West Africa in particular was considered unsuitable for permanent European settlement because of its climate, even after the development of quinine in the mid-nineteenth century. The region had been dubbed "the White Man's Grave" since the onset of the Atlantic slave trade. See Philip D. Curtin, *The Atlantic Slave Trade: A Census* (Madison: University of Wisconsin Press, 1969), 282; Colin Palmer, "The Slave Trade, African Slavers, and the Demography of the Caribbean to 1750," in *General History of the Caribbean. Vol. III: The Slave Societies of the Caribbean*, ed. Frank Knight (London: UNESCO Publishing, 1997), 23.

[101] *Census of the British Empire, 1901. Report with summary and detailed tables for the several colonies...* (London: H. M. Stationery Office, by Darling and Son, 1906), 144–5, 215, 262; *Statistical Abstract Relating to British India from 1894–5 to 1903–4* (London: H. M. S. O., by Wyman and Sons, 1905), tables no. 1 and 9. See also Frederick Pollock, *English Opportunities and Duties in the Historical and Comparative Study of Law* (London: Macmillan, 1883), 19.

[102] Compare decolonization conflict in Kenya and Southern Rhodesia (the future Zimbabwe), with the comparatively easy British departure from the Gold Coast and other West African colonies. See P. J. Marshall, ed., *The Cambridge Illustrated History of the British Empire* (Cambridge: Cambridge University Press, 1996), 102–5.

[103] For instance, see Charles Metcalfe (1829) in Roderick Cavaliero, *Strangers in the Land: The Rise and Decline of the British Empire* (London: I. B. Tauris, 2002), 108.

[104] On West African students at the Inns, see Omoniyi Adewoye, *The Judicial System in Southern Nigeria, 1854–1954: Law and Justice in a Dependency* (Atlantic Highlands, NJ: Humanities Press, 1977), 110–12; Sharafi, "A New History," 1069.

[105] Gandhi, 54–7. On the "Natal model" of Asian exclusion across the British Empire, see R. A. Huttenback, "The British Empire as a 'White Man's Country' – Racial Attitudes and Immigration Legislation in the Colonies of White Settlement," *J. Brit. Stud.* 13:1 (1973), 108–37.

[106] On South Asian students at the Inns, see Schmitthener, 365–9.

[107] Over the 1926–31 period, between 32 and 54 percent of the students admitted to Lincoln's Inn each year were South Asian. [*Records of Lincoln's Inn.*, III.]

Making Law: Two Patterns

A European lawyer entered the Lincoln's Inn library and encountered a sea of non-white faces, but spotted one lone Briton in the corner. Replaying the famous episode in which Henry M. Stanley found the British explorer among African tribesmen after months of searching, the new arrival approached the other white man and enquired dryly, "Dr. Livingstone, I presume?"[108]

The legal profession in British India had not always been open to South Asians. Until the 1860s, the upper ranks of the profession were almost exclusively British, particularly in the presidency capitals of Calcutta, Bombay, and Madras.[109] With the 1858 transfer of power from the East India Company to the British Crown came a restructuring of the courts. The Company's separate system of Supreme Courts for presidency capitals and *mofussil* courts outside of these cities was replaced by a single system of High Courts in the presidency capitals, into which appeals from the *mofussil*'s lower courts flowed. The rules of legal practice were also rewritten, and South Asian *vakils* were admitted to practice alongside British barristers in the High Courts. This change was contested. The commissioners in charge of designing the new court system had recommended that only London-trained barristers and Europeans (usually synonymous in this period) be permitted to practice in the High Courts. But opponents, such as Madras governor Charles Trevelyan, protested, and their view prevailed.[110] In Trevelyan's words, excluding Indians would deprive the public of the "service of the ablest men, preventing wholesome competitions, and unduly exalting some without reference to their personal merits and depressing others."[111] In Bombay, High Court judge Joseph Arnould agreed, calling the new fused legal profession "a great change for the better."[112] The rise of South Asians in the legal profession in the first few decades of the new courts was gradual, initially.[113] By the turn of the twentieth century, though, the legal profession in the presidency capitals had been racially transformed.[114]

In many ways, white racial prejudice against South Asians intensified under the Raj.[115] It was certainly not unknown to South Asian lawyers, particularly in the first few decades after the creation of the new High Courts. In addition to race-based snubs in law offices, there was the challenge of getting business from

---

[108] John Aye (pseud. of John Atkinson), *Humour Among the Lawyers* (London: Universal Press, 1931), 73. I am grateful to Marc Galanter for this account. See also "Gleanings. The Bar of England," *Bom LR* (journal), 6 (1904), 24.

[109] Vachha, 31.

[110] See Paul, 45–50.

[111] Trevelyan in Schmitthener, 356. See also "Reply to the Address of the Trade Association," *BTJC* (27 April 1859), 268.

[112] Untitled editorial, *TI* (10 March 1886), 4.

[113] See Dobbin, *Urban Leadership*, 169.

[114] See Mistry, *Forty Years' Reminiscences of the High Court*; Price.

[115] See, for example, Kenneth Ballhatchet, *Race, Sex and Class under the Raj: Imperial Attitudes and Policies and their Critics, 1793–1905* (New York: St. Martin's, 1980), 144.

the largely European solicitors' firms.[116] According to the early Parsi barrister C. M. Cursetji, European solicitors would not refer courtroom work to South Asian barristers in the 1860s and '70s, a situation he claimed had changed by the 1890s.[117] Many colonial clubs, which were a hub of social activity in legal circles, admitted white members only. The Byculla Club was one; it was a favorite haunt of Bombay High Court judges.[118] For some elite Indians, this pattern simply extended the logic of South Asian caste and community boundaries. It was as if Europeans were just another of India's many communities, with similarly exclusive rules of membership.[119] There were clubs that only admitted Parsis as members, for instance.[120] But others were more critical of the white racism that permeated the legal profession. Early Congress leaders such as Dadabhai Naoroji complained that Indian judges were not being appointed in large enough numbers.[121] In 1873, his colleague Pherozeshah Mehta was chastised by the Bombay Bar for publishing articles in *The Indian Statesman* stressing salary disparities between British and Indian advocates.[122]

South Asians in the colonial legal profession did feel racial prejudice around them, particularly in the first few decades after the High Court bar was technically opened to them. However, their situation was very different from that of non-Europeans aspiring to be lawyers in the white settler colonies. As judge D. D. Davar told a class of Indian law students in Bombay in 1911, "Let it encourage you to keep the fact in your mind that whatever else an Indian may be unfitted for ... it is conceded by all in high authority that in the practice and administration of law an Indian is considered worthy of all confidence. The highest position in the judicial administration of this country is always open to an Indian."[123]

---

[116] See Zaidi, I: 404; D. J. Ferreira, "Reminiscences," 263 and R. A. Gagrat, "Reminiscences," 265–7, both in *The Bombay Incorporated Law Society Centenary* (Mumbai: Bombay Incorporated Law Society, 1995); "The Bombay Beucle as constituted 29 April 1884" (HRA/D63/A1) in Macleod of Cadboll Papers; letter from D. E. Wacha to Dadabhai Naoroji (21 March 1896) in R. P. Patwardhan, ed., *Dadabhai Naoroji Correspondence* (Bombay: Allied Publishers, 1977), II: 2, 483; F. C. O. Beaman, "Eheu Fugaces!! Guzerat and Guzeratis," *Bom LJ* 3:11 (1925), 511. I am grateful to Sohrab Morris of Mumbai for generously giving me a copy of the Bombay Law Society's centennial volume.

[117] Letter from C. M. Cursetji to S. W. Edgerley, Bombay (1 January 1894), C-301, pp. 1–3, Dadabhai Naoroji Papers, National Archives of India (Delhi). I owe this reference to Dinyar Patel and thank him for sharing this excerpt with me.

[118] Darukhanawala, *Parsi Lustre*, I: 323; Macleod, "Reminiscences" (1894–1914), 3, 18, 33, 38; F. C. O. Beaman, "Eheu Fugaces!" *Bom LJ* 3 (1925–6), 6–7. See also Nariman, 39–40.

[119] Conversation with Pestonji P. Ginwala (Mumbai, 5 February 2006). See also Dana Lightstone, "Caste and Legislation in Colonial India, 1772–1883" (PhD. Dissertation, University of Wisconsin–Madison, 2009), 112–50; Kolsky, *Colonial Justice*, 95–6.

[120] Since its creation in 1884, Bombay's Ripon Club has admitted only Parsis as members. See Palsetia, *Parsis*, 306.

[121] Zaidi, II: 280–1.

[122] Vachha, 135–6.

[123] Davar, *Hints*, 36.

Making Law: Two Patterns

Davar was hardly naïve. He was famous for fighting for the equal rights of Indian lawyers vis-à-vis their European colleagues.[124] But he also realized that the number of South Asians in the legal profession had increased significantly since the late nineteenth century. The clerk A. J. C. Mistry documented the surge. In 1884, there were twenty-eight European and twenty-four South Asian solicitors in Bombay. By 1908, there were sixteen Europeans and 108 non-Europeans in the business.[125] In 1884, there were thirteen law firms in Bombay with exclusively British partners. Another two had a mix of European and South Asian partners, and sixteen had South Asian partners only. In 1908, only four all-European partnerships remained, with two being mixed, and forty firms headed by South Asian solicitors. "This list," declared Mistry, "shows the proportion in which the natives are ousting the European firms."[126] "The Europeans have found it hard to compete with the Natives who have secured almost the whole of the native public for their clients."[127] In the early twentieth century, junior Britons on the bench deferred to more senior South Asian judges.[128] It was not unknown for European lawyers who made disparaging remarks about Indian culture or religion to be taken to task by Indian judges.[129] Compare this to British Columbia, where aspiring lawyers of indigenous and Asian origin were barred from practicing until they gained the right to vote in provincial elections in 1949.[130] In Australia, the first aboriginal lawyer was admitted to practice in 1976.[131] For colonized peoples, the opportunity to have a legal career existed in British India in ways in which it did not in the white settler colonies. Without this background condition, the pursuit of law by so many Parsis would have been impossible.

As we have seen, Parsis worked in the legal profession in the early colonial period of Company rule but at subordinate and provincial levels. They surfaced here and there in the early records as agents who represented clients in the lower courts (*vakils*), civil judges of the lowest grade (*moonsifs;* Pers. *monṣef*), and court registrars (*sheristadars;* Pers. *sarreshtehdār*).[132] They did not appear as

---

[124] Darukhanawala, *Parsi Lustre*, I: 149–50.

[125] Mistry, *Reminiscences* [1911], 75. See also Gagrat, 31–3.

[126] Mistry, *Reminiscences* [1911], 76.

[127] Ibid., 73–4.

[128] See Sharafi, "Judging Conversion," 159–80.

[129] For example, see Ferreira, 261–2 (on BHC judge Chandavarkar); Kumud Prasanna, "Tyabji, Badruddin (1844–1906)," in *Dictionary of National Biography*, ed. S. P. Sen (Calcutta: Institute of Historical Studies, 1974), IV: 366.

[130] Constance Backhouse, "Gender and Race in the Construction of 'Legal Professionalism': Historical Perspectives," Colloquium of the Chief Justice of Ontario's Advisory Committee on Professionalism (London, Canada; 20 October 2003), 8–9.

[131] Roberta Sykes, *Murawina: Australian Women of High Achievement* (Sydney: Doubleday, 1993), 68–73.

[132] See *Treekumdass Bhekhareedas v. Byramjee Eduljee and Framjee Khoorsedjee* Reports of Civil Cases determined in the Court of Sudder Dewanee Adawlut (1840–8) 78–9; "First Report from the Select Committee on Indian Territories," 322–5 (IOR/V/4/1852–3/27); Vachha, 169.

108   *Law and Identity in Colonial South Asia: Parsi Legal Culture*

lawyers or judges in the superior courts until the later nineteenth century, led by figures like M. J. Taleyarkhan.[133] From the mid-nineteenth century, Parsis began to occupy official positions in the court bureaucracy of Bombay Presidency. Most common were the Parsi court interpreters who translated from Gujarati into English.[134] (Most European lawyers and judges, particularly those trained as barristers, had poor Indian language skills.[135]) Few of these figures were lawyers. However, they were of key importance to the Parsi acquisition of legal fluency. Lobbyist Nowrozjee Furdoonjee was a court interpreter, as already noted. Other Parsis in the court bureaucracy were among the first South Asians to send their sons to London to become barristers at the Inns of Court from the 1860s on.[136] In the 1920s, there may have been as many as fifteen Parsis at the Inns at any one time.[137] The law-related flow of young Parsis to London bore all the signs of chain migration. Particularly in the early period, many of these Parsi law students were related to each other.[138] By the 1890s, many were the children of Parsi barristers who had come to the same Inns a generation before.[139] Male students outnumbered female by a large factor during this period, but nonetheless, a handful of young Parsi women came to London to study at the Inns.[140]

---

[133] See note 80.

[134] For example, see Suit No. 1 of 1895, 1893–1903 PCMC Notebook, I: 154; "Thana Parsi Judge to Retire. Mr. N. N. Master's Career," *TI* (6 August 1934), 14. See also 91 and 116.

[135] Norman Macleod, "Reminiscences of the Bombay Bar (1890–1926)," *Bom LJ* 23 (1945), 403. See also "First Report...on Indian Territories," 227, 236, 239–40, 288, 371, 374–5, 460; Beaman, "Eheu Fugaces!! Guzerat," 511–12.

[136] See, for example, Cursetjee Manockjee Cursetjee, admitted to Lincoln's Inn on 19 May 1866 (*Records of Lincoln's Inn*, II: 321); Maneckji Byramji Dadabhoy, admitted to Middle Temple on 8 April 1884 (H. A. C. Sturgess, *Register of Admissions to the Hon. Society of the Middle Temple. From the Fifteenth Century to the Year 1944* (London: Butterworth and Co., 1949), II: 643.

[137] Across the Middle Temple, Inner Temple, and Lincoln's Inn, there were approximately four or five Parsis admitted each year in the 1920s, with each student's stay usually lasting three years. Admission records for Gray's Inn are unavailable, but this fourth Inn may also have had Parsi students. [Sturgess; *Records of Lincoln's Inn*, III; *Inner Temple Archives: Alphabetical Index of Members (1851–1929), showing dates of Admission and Call* (London: n.p., 1997).]

[138] For example, brothers Nasarvanji P. Cama and Navroji P. Cama were both admitted to Middle Temple on 15 November 1873. (Sturgess, II: 588.)

[139] See, for instance, *Records of Lincoln's Inn* III: 2, 71, 79 (Bhownaggree, Boyce, Mehta); Sturgess, II: 643 (Dadabhoy). Miss Goolbanoo Nanabhai Cowasjee (1930) was the daughter of the Rangoon barrister N. M. Cowasjee and the granddaughter of Merwanji Cowasji Captain, who led the case against Bella in *Saklat v. Bella* (*Records of Lincoln's Inn*, III: 229).

[140] For examples, see *Records of ... Lincoln's Inn*, III: 141, 159, 194, 213, 221, 232, 364; and P. V. Baker, ed., *The Records of the Honorable Society of Lincoln's Inn. The Black Books. Vol. VI: AD 1914–AD 1965* (London: Lincoln's Inn, 2001), 754–5, 761–2 (Tata, Sorabji, Saklatvala, Kooka, Bahadurji, Mehta, Mody). See also Mistry, *Forty Years' Reminiscences of the High Court*, 44–5; Patel and Paymaster, VI: 397 (Dantra); Lam; Sanjana, *Ancient Persia*, 590; Cornelia Sorabji Papers (MSS Eur F165) (APAC); Chandani Lokugé. ed., *India Calling: The Memories of Cornelia Sorabji, India's First Woman Barrister* (Delhi: Oxford University Press, 2001); Mossman, *The First Women Lawyers*, 191–237 and her "Gender and Professionalism in

Making Law: Two Patterns

Parsi law students boarded with British families in the same neighborhoods or even in the same homes.[141] Senior Parsis in law, like the former Bombay Small Causes Court judge Ratanji Dadachanji, sometimes settled in London for work or retirement. They played an informal supervisory role over Parsi law students, who were often related to friends back in Bombay.[142] Dadabhai Naoroji, "the Grand Old Man of India," was in London for many years as a Member of Parliament.[143] He received many letters of introduction from his co-religionists in Bombay and helped Parsi law students adjust to their new surroundings.[144] The Inns of Court were one more piece of the Parsi pathway for gaining legal expertise. This route was reinforced by intracommunity philanthropy. Some of the first Parsis to study at the Inns were funded by wealthy Parsi philanthropists who created scholarships for Zoroastrians to study law in England.[145]

In the Bombay High Court, the legal profession was divided into two main groups: solicitors (or attorneys) and advocates. Only advocates had full rights of audience in the Bombay courts, but it was solicitors who enjoyed greater financial security and prestige. Solicitors managed all aspects of a case except for court appearances, for which they hired advocates.[146] They had to pass a notoriously difficult exam. Solicitors worked in firms, where they had at their disposal small armies of "peons," copyists and articled clerks (solicitors in training), as well as extensive law libraries.[147] By 1908, there were no fewer than sixty-one Parsi solicitors in Bombay, compared to sixteen Europeans.[148] The orthodox solicitor J. J. Vimadalal was one.[149] He made his mark in libel and religious trust suits, opposing the admission of ethnic outsiders into the Parsi community.[150] Mistry noted that "the Parsees have gone headlong in the line,"

Law," 19–34; Anil Chandra Banerjee, *English Law in India* (Delhi: Shakti Malik Abhinav Publications, 1984), 116–49. For a case in which the lawyer leading each side was a Parsi woman, see untitled entry, Patel and Paymaster, VII: 317. Contrast "Cousin Tehmi and Sorab Talk," *HP* (9 February 1908), 21.

[141] See Sturgess, II: 619, 626, 631, 683.

[142] Conversations with R. P. Vachha (Mumbai, 22 February 2004–8 March 2004). Dadachanji also oversaw the Bombay commission established to collect evidence in *Saklat v. Bella.*

[143] See Introduction at note 88.

[144] Letter from D. E. Wacha to Dadabhai Naoroji (8 October 1898) in Patwardhan, II: 650; "Pherozeshah M. Mehta" in C. L. Parekh, *Eminent Indians in Indian Politics* (1892), reprinted in Chintamini, ii.

[145] "P. M. Mehta" in Chintamini, ii; Schmitthener, 365–6; John R. Hinnells, *Zoroastrians in Britain. The Ratanbai Katrak Lectures, University of Oxford 1985* (Oxford: Clarendon Press, 1996), 82.

[146] On the division of labor between solicitors and advocates in Bombay, see S. P. Bharucha, "As I Remember It" in *Bombay Inc. Law Society Centenary*, 248.

[147] See Mistry, *Reminiscences* [1911] and *Forty Years' Reminiscences of Wadia Ghandy*; "The Reminiscences of a Solicitor," 18–22.

[148] Mistry, *Reminiscences*, [1911] 75.

[149] See Patel and Paymaster, VII: 19–20, trans. Homi D. Patel.

[150] See Sharafi, "Judging Conversion," 170.

producing more solicitors than any single community.[151] Among their firms were some that continue to operate today, like Wadia Ghandy and Co. and Mulla and Mulla. With them in the law reports of late colonial Bombay were others no longer in existence, such as Jehangir, Gulabhai and Bilimoria; Merwanji, Kola and Co.; and Ardeshir, Hormasji and Dinsha.[152]

By contrast, advocates were self-employed.[153] Most had no office; they sat in court libraries when not arguing in court. One could attain the rank of advocate in the Bombay High Court by becoming a barrister in Britain, which required spending three years at one of the four Inns of Court (namely, Inner or Middle Temple, Lincoln's or Gray's Inn), passing a set of exams, and attending a number of formal dinners.[154] In line with Macaulay's aspiration to create an elite body of Anglicized Indians, the Inns of Court were as much a socialization device as one delivering legal education.[155] An alternative route was to obtain a Bachelor of Law degree at the University of Bombay, attend the sittings of the Original and Appellate Sides of the court for one year each, and pass the advocates' exams. Aspiring Parsi advocates often used the PCMC as a training ground, along with the Court of Small Causes and the Police Courts, before advancing to a full career on the Original Side of the Bombay High Court.[156]

Another type of courtroom lawyer did exist. *Vakils* or pleaders were of lower status than advocates.[157] Unlike advocates, they did not have to be hired through solicitors, but could deal directly with litigants.[158] In the early twentieth century, one could become a *vakil* by matriculating at an Indian university, passing the *vakils'* exams, attending court sessions, and proving proficiency in English and an Indian language.[159] Their positions were vestiges of a precolonial body of agents who were marginalized by the British forms of solicitor and

---

[151] Mistry, *Reminiscences* [1911], 76.

[152] See, for instance, Patel and Paymaster, III: 847; *Shirinbai v. Ratanbai and others* ILR 43 Bom 845 (1919); *Kaikhushroo M. Talyarkhan and Bai Gulab* ILR 53 Bom 408 (1929); *Ardeshir Dadabhoy Baria v. Dadabhoy Rustomjee Baria* ILR 69 Bom 493 (1945); Mistry, *Forty Years' Reminiscences of Wadia Ghandy*, iv–vii.

[153] On Parsi advocates generally, see Fredun E. DeVitre, "Eminent Lawyers: Advocating Justice" in Mody, II: 358–68.

[154] See C. E. A. Bedwell, "Conditions of Admission to the Legal Profession throughout the British Empire," *JSCL* (new series) 12: 2 (1912), 210; Guenther, "Syed Mahmood," 53–4. From the early twentieth century, candidates had to obtain a BA before joining the Inns (Mistry, *Forty Years' Reminiscences of the High Court*, 42).

[155] On the perceived value of the dining requirement, see Raymond Cocks, *Foundations of the Modern Bar* (London: Sweet and Maxwell, 1983), 96.

[156] On the early independence period, see Nariman, *Before Memory Fades*, 45.

[157] Rather than using the terms "pleader" and *vakil* synonymously, Schmitthener ranks *vakils* above pleaders and associated the latter with the lower courts (Schmitthener, 358). In favor of equivalence, though, see C. E. A. Bedwell, "Conditions of Admission to the Legal Profession throughout the British Empire," *JSCL* (new series) 13:1 (1912), 130 at note 2.

[158] "Creation of an Indian Bar," 324.

[159] Bedwell, 13:1, 130–1; "Creation of an Indian Bar," 253–72.

Making Law: Two Patterns

advocate.[160] By the early twentieth century, *vakils* began to complain about the many inequalities between themselves and these newer species of lawyer – particularly barristers.[161] Barristers were the more elite courtroom lawyers, but in fact, *vakils*' examinations in India were more difficult than the barristers' equivalent in London and took six years' preparation, rather than three.[162] Cynics suggested that it was South Asians with money more than aptitude who became barristers rather than *vakils*.[163]

Young advocates typically began their careers through an informal English system of mentoring known as "devilling," whereby juniors appeared with or in the place of senior advocates in court, often preparing the case together beforehand.[164] Jamshedji B. Kanga, "the grand old man of the Bombay bar," was a leading advocate, additional judge of the High Court (1919–22), and the first South Asian Advocate General of Bombay (between 1922 and 1935, although not continuously) (Figure 2.4).[165] He mentored several generations of young advocates who served as his "devils." These juniors included Parsi lawyers such as H. M. Seervai, Nani Palkhivala, Soli Sorabji, and Fali Nariman, who would go on to become some of independent India's top litigators on constitutional matters especially.[166]

Being an advocate opened the path to a possible judicial career. With some exceptions, Indian judges at the Indian High Courts were selected from this part of the profession.[167] Parsi barristers like Dinshah Dhanjibhai Davar went on to

---

[160] See "Creation of an Indian Bar," *Bom LJ* 1 (1923), 271; Benton, *Law and Colonial Cultures*, 138.

[161] For example, see "Vakils' Dress,'" *TI* (4 April 1908), 13; "Barring the Door!" *HP* (26 November 1916), 23.

[162] "Indians in England," *TL* (19 November 1906), 5; "Indian Students and Legal Education," *TL* (26 September 1908), 4; Mistry, *Reminiscences* [1911], 78; Daniel Duman, *The English and Colonial Bars in the Nineteenth Century* (London: Croom Helm, 1983), 131.

[163] "Creation of an Indian Bar," 253, 313; Phiroze R. Vakil, "I Remember, I Remember," 173 in Mehrotra and Dwivedi.

[164] See B. Lentin, "Between Bench and Bar: A Memoir," 177 in Mehrotra and Dwivedi; Nariman, 56 at note 2.

[165] See *Who's Who in India, Burma and Ceylon* (Poona: Sun Publishing House, 1937), 177; Umrīgar and Pāṭhak, 158–9; "Large Gathering at Funeral of J. B. Kanga," *TI* (24 March 1969), 5; "High Court Pays Homage to Kanga," *TI* (25 March 1969), 5; Seervai, *Seervai Legacy*, 170–3; Nariman, *Before Memory Fades*, 31–44. I am also grateful to R. P. Vachha for sharing with me memories of J. B. Kanga and his legacy (Mumbai, 22 February 2004).

[166] Seervai, *Seervai Legacy*, 171–2; Nariman, *Before Memory Fades*, 51–6; Mehrotra and Dwivedi, 136, 138–9, 141, 156–7 (memoirs by S. P. Bharucha, Soli J. Sorabjee, Tehmtan R. Andhyarujina).

[167] Among Parsi judges, the exception was D. F. Mulla, who was a solicitor. See 114. Although less common (and less prestigious), it was also possible to come to the bench via the Indian Civil Service, rather than the Bar (see Sharafi, "Judging Conversion," 162). The first Parsi judge in any Indian High Court followed this route: Cursetjee Rustomjee Wadia was an acting judge of the Allahabad High Court in 1906 [ILR 28 All (1906), n.p. (list of judges); Mistry, *Reminiscences* [1911], 60].

FIGURE 2.4 J. B. Kanga in advocate's dress and priestly turban.
Source: private collection. Courtesy of Navroz H. Seervai.

Making Law: Two Patterns

113

become judges.[168] Between his appointment in 1906 and Indian independence in 1947, a sixth of the judges appointed to the Bombay High Court bench were Parsi.[169] The French historian Delphine Menant noted that the Parsi was no longer "the broker or *dubash* of the European" as he had been in the Company period, but now sat next to the Briton on the High Court bench.[170]

Parsi judges officiated in other courts, too. Those who were part of the Indian Civil Service could be stationed almost anywhere in India and probably accounted for a good part of the Parsi "educated persons" in remote outposts who submitted responses to draft legislation in the 1930s.[171] There were many Parsi magistrates, too.[172] Two of Bombay's best known magistrates were D. F. Karaka (in the 1880s) and D. N. D. Khandalavala (in the 1930s).[173] Magistrates E. D. Mehta and C. H. Rustomjee commented on all-India draft legislation from Ajmer and Calcutta in the 1930s.[174] In Bombay, presidency magistrates Phiroze Hoshang Dastur and one "Mr. Khambatta" heard their fair share of privately prosecuted criminal suits between Parsis in the 1890s and 1940s, respectively.[175] In 1935, a list of Parsi magistrates included 107 names for Bombay and western India.[176] Parsis were prominent as judges of the Bombay Small Causes Court, too.[177]

Parsis also wrote about law. Legal treatises mattered because, in the absence of settled case law or clear legislation, judges relied on these publications in their

---

[168] See S. Radhakrishnan, "Illustrious Judges: Legal Luminaries" in Mody, II: 340–3.

[169] Twelve of seventy judges (17 percent) were Parsi, namely: H. C. Coyajee and his son N. H. C. Coyajee, Dinshah D. Davar and his son Jehangir D. Davar, N. P. Engineer, Jamshedji B. Kanga, Muncherji Pestanji Khareghat, Dinshah F. Mulla, F. S. Taleyarkhan, Vicaji F. Taraporewala, B. J. Wadia, and N. J. Wadia.

[170] Menant, "Zoroastrianism and the Parsis," 136.

[171] See "No. 15 – United Provinces" and "No. 16 – Bihar and Orissa" in "Paper No. 1," 56, 62 in "The Parsi Marriage and Divorce Act 1936." See also K. F. Rustamji and Jamsheed G. Kanga, "The Administrative Services. Guardians of Integrity," 419–30 in Mody, *Enduring Legacy*, II; Arudra Burra, "The ICS and the Raj: 1919–50," 27–9 (unpublished paper).

[172] See, for instance, *Jehangir M. Cursetji v. Secretary of State for India in Council* ILR 27 Bom 189 (1903).

[173] On Karaka, see Mistry, *Reminiscences* [1911], 65; Patel and Paymaster, V: 137; "Administering Intoxicating Drug" (7 July 1880), 3 and "The Police Courts" (11 January 1887), 3, both in *TI*. See also Ringer, *Pious Citizens*, 76–8. On Khandalavala, see "Press Manager Fined. Factory Act Offence," *TI* (10 February 1938), 20; Patel and Paymaster, VII: 346, 364.

[174] "No. 12 [Bengal]" and "No. 19 – Ajmer-Merwara," in "Paper No. 1," 49, 59 in "The Parsi Marriage and Divorce Act 1936."

[175] See Suit No. 3 of 1895, 1893–1903 PCMC Notebook, I: 176; Suit No. 1097 of 1946: *Kaikhushroo Sorabji Joshi v. Shahiar Khodaram Irani* (13 March 1947), "Hon. Justice N. H. C. Coyajee. Typed Notes of Evidence (4 December 1946–23 April 1949)," 1–3 (both BHC). See also Desai, *History*, 211.

[176] List of Parsi Bombay honorary presidency magistrates (1935), Patel and Paymaster, VII: 272–3.

[177] See, for instance, "Head Clerk to the Prothonotary," *TI* (19 February 1876), 3 (J. M. Shroff); "Hormusji Dadabhoy (Late Judge Small Causes Court of Bombay)," *Bom LR* (journal) 4 (1902), 292; "Lucky Dog!," *HP* (20 September 1908), 21 (R. M. Patel); Mistry, *Reminiscences* [1911], 66 (R. M. Patel, C. M. Cursetji, B. E. and J. E. Mody).

114   *Law and Identity in Colonial South Asia: Parsi Legal Culture*

decisions. These summaries of different areas of law were especially important in the empire, where it was harder to stock law libraries than in the metropole – at least with books from England.[178] The greatest of Parsi treatise writers was Dinshah Fardunji Mulla.[179] Mulla was perhaps the quintessential example of the Parsi self-made man in law. He was "born to humble parents and nurtured in poverty," but became a solicitor in Bombay and founded, with his brother, the law firm of Mulla and Mulla.[180] Mulla subsequently became a Bombay High Court judge (1922–4), the first Parsi to become Law Member of the Governor General's Council (1928), and ultimately, the first Parsi judge of the Judicial Committee of the Privy Council (1930–4).[181] Although not a barrister, Mulla was named an honorary bencher of Lincoln's Inn following his elevation to the Privy Council. Mulla's sixteen textbooks were published in multiple editions and covered everything from Hindu and Muslim personal law to contract and insolvency law.[182] Mulla co-authored a work on Indian Contract Law with the English legal author Sir Frederick Pollock. In a comment that reflected the racial dynamics of the day, Pollock remarked, upon Mulla's death, that "[o]ne could discuss authorities with him exactly as one would with an English learned friend, and with the like profit."[183] There were many other Parsi treatise writers. Framjee A. Rana wrote the definitive treatise on Parsi law before 1936, along with works on Hindu and Muslim personal law, equity, and law in the princely states of western India.[184] A compiler of the famous Parsi almanac *Parsi Prakash* was also an advocate and legal treatise writer. R. B. Paymaster published works on landlord–tenant relations, caste and law, charitable trusts, Parsis and law in

---

[178] See Christopher Tomlins, "Affairs of Scale: Toward a History of the Literature of Law" in *Law Books in Action: Essays on the Anglo-American Legal Treatise*, eds. Angela Fernandez and Markus D. Dubber (Oxford: Hart, 2012), 220–42. Publishers in British India, such as Thacker Spink and Co., produced a huge number of treatises on Indian law.

[179] "Our Bar VI. Dinshah F. Mulla," *Bom LJ* 5 (1927–8), 305–8; "Sir Dinshah Mulla," *Bom LR* (journal) (1934), 57–62; Vachha, 158–9. See also Nariman, *Before Memory Fades*, 25; note 84. For a photograph of Mulla, see Sanjana, 602.

[180] Darukhanawala, *Parsi Lustre*, I: 148. See also "Sir Dinshah Mulla," *Mad LJ* 60 (1931), 18; "In Memoriam: The Right Hon'ble Sir Dinshah Fardunji Mulla," *Bom LJ* 11(1934), 459–62.

[181] On Mulla's influence on legislation, see Patel and Paymaster, VII: 68. On his JCPC decisions, see S. G. Velinker, "Rt. Hon'ble Sir Dinshaw Mulla's Work in the Privy Council," *Bom LJ* 12 (1934), 27–8.

[182] "Sir Dinshah Fardunji Mulla," *Bombay Inc. Law Society Centenary*, 157; "Sir Dinshah Mulla. Work on the Judicial Committee," *TL* (27 April 1934), 16. See also "Memorial to Sir Dinshah Mulla," *Bom LJ* 15 (1937–8), 296–7.

[183] "Sir Dinshah Mulla," *TL* (28 April 1934), 14.

[184] Titles by F. A. Rana included *Parsi Law* (1902, 1934), *Pārsī Dhārā* (1910), *Kathiawar Agency Circulars* (1912), and *Directory of Porebunder and Dhrangadhra State* (n.d.). He co-authored *An Epitome of Hindu Law* (1894), *An Epitome of Mahomedan Law* (1897, 1903), and *Epitomes of the Principles of Equity* (n.d.). See also review probably written by P. B. Vachha entitled "Parsi Law," *TI* (13 July 1934), 7.

Making Law: Two Patterns

the princely states, and the restitution of conjugal rights.[185] Others produced legal textbooks for audiences from students to magistrates and on topics from medical jurisprudence to club law.[186] Collectively, these Parsi lawyers synthesized the contents of vast swathes of Indian law.

Parsis were key players in other facets of legal publishing, too. Sohrab R. Davar, barrister, was an editor of the *Bombay Law Journal*.[187] J. S. Khergamvala and P. B. Vachha were editors of the *Indian Law Reports Bombay series*, the official law reports for the presidency. K. S. Shavaksha and A. J. Poonawala were law reporters for the same series.[188] Being a law reporter was an alternate way of earning income as a young, "briefless barrister." Law reporters sat in court and took notes on cases. When a case was recommended by the judge for publication, these notes would form the basis for the reported version of a case, usually in conjunction with the text of the judgment itself.[189] The selection and publication of particular judgments, like the slant given to the case through the potted summary or "headnote" at the beginning of the published report, had huge influence on future interpretations of the case. The government was not above bullying law reporters to publish a particular account of a case.[190] Parsi involvement with law books also extended to their physical production. D. B. Taraporevala and Sons was a Parsi-run publishing house and bookstore in Bombay that sold legal treatises and government publications on law, including legislation.[191] Parsi bookbinders like Eduljee Furdoonjee and Company bound judges' notebooks for the Bombay High Court in the 1920s and '30s.[192]

---

[185] See "Publications of Mr. R. B. Paymaster, B. A., LL. B." in Patel and Paymaster, VII: unnumbered page facing 1.

[186] For example, see Patel and Paymaster, II: 248 (title by Kotwal), VII: 74, 111, 162, 278–9 (titles by Davar, Daver, Jeejeebhoy, Jhabvala, Khambata, Patuck, Pirozshaw, Shavaksha, and Turner). For further titles by Rustomji and Shavaksha, see endpages of "Hon. Mr. Justice Coyajee's Typed Notes of Evidence" (9 January 1945–27 August 1945) (BHC). See also Jehangeer Merwanjee's work on libel and slander, noted in "Death of Mr. Jehangeer Merwanjee, Pleader."

[187] See cover page of *Bom LJ* V: 11 (1928).

[188] See cover page of *ILR Bom*, vols. 52–4 (1928–30) and for 1947.

[189] For the form used by judges to identify cases to be reported, see "Hon. Justice J. D. Davar. Judgments" (11 January 1927–13 April 1927), inserted at 77 (BHC).

[190] Letter from P. E. Percival, Office of the Remembrancer of Legal Affairs, to the editors of the *Bombay Law Reporter* (14 February 1914), 373–5; letter from Messrs Ratanlal and Dhirajlal, *Bombay Law Reporter* to Legal Remembrancer, Mahableshwar (20 April 1914), 379; both in *Merwanji Muncherji Cama and another v. Secretary of State for India in Council*, B-1/1 of 1907–10: serial no. 253 of compilation 1910, suit no. 63 of 1910 in the High Court of Bombay, Legal Dept. Records (MSA).

[191] Taraporevala and Sons published titles like S. R. Davar's *Elements of Indian Mercantile Law* (1928), P. S. Sivaswamy Aiyer's *Indian Constitutional Problems* (1928); R. S. Singh's *The Indian States under the Government of India Act 1935* [1938]. See also "List of Agents from Whom Government of India Publications Are Available" (no page number) in "Indian Succession (Amendment) Act 1939 (26 November 1938–8 August 1939)" (IOR/L/PJ/7/2493).

[192] See, for instance, the notebooks of J. D. Davar, 1927–35 (BHC).

116   *Law and Identity in Colonial South Asia: Parsi Legal Culture*

There were many Parsis in the legal profession who were not necessarily lawyers or judges. It would be easy to overlook these figures, but they constituted an important layer of the Parsi legal pyramid. Many Parsis acted as translators, clerks, bailiffs, and oath-administering officials in the courts and jails.[193] The majority of official translators working in the Bombay High Court from the 1880s until 1911 were Parsi.[194] Outside of Bombay, legal translators like G. K. Nariman and M. C. Forbes made their mark on Parsi law. Nariman was the official Gujarati-to-English translator at the Chief Court of Lower Burma around 1912. As an orthodox Parsi opposed to admitting ethnic outsiders into the community, he became personally involved in *Saklat v. Bella* and was even a defendant in a spin-off libel suit related to the case.[195] Forbes was the Gujarati translator, as well as the Commissioner for Oaths and Checking Accounts, at the Madras High Court in the 1930s. He submitted feedback on all of the Parsi-related draft legislation of his day.[196] K. B. Pudumjee was Registrar of the Court of Small Causes in Poona in 1906. Producing the father–son career path noted earlier, his son became a barrister at Middle Temple in London.[197] The professional experience of Nariman, Forbes, and Pudumjee spilled into their personal and community lives, either helping to set the legal contours of major social and religious institutions within the Parsi community or positioning offspring to do so.

One would expect Parsis working lower down in law firms and the courts to be largely invisible in the colonial archive. Nonelites usually were, leaving few written records. But, around 1911 and again in 1925, Ardeshir Jamshedji Chanji Mistry, a "managing clerk" at the Parsi-run solicitors' firm Wadia Ghandy and Co., wrote memoirs of his time in legal Bombay.[198] Mistry described the everyday lives of the men who worked as bookkeepers, bill clerks, court clerks,

---

[193] For instance, see "Notification," *TI* (12 July 1877), 2 (Cursetjee); "Witness No. 9 for the Defendants: Edulji, Son of Sorabji," 219 and "Record. No. 99. Exhibit D5: Bill for Religious Work Done for the House of Jivanji Pestonji," 367 (Sanjana), both in *Pestonji Jeevanji v. Chinoy* JCPC case papers; Mistry, *Reminiscences* [1911], 51, 62, 64, 69–70 (Sethna, Banaji, Gagrat, Motiwalla, Daruwalla, Wadia, Master, Furdoonji, Thanawalla, Registrar); Patel and Paymaster, V: 111 (Panthaki); "Parsi Defamation Suit. Mr. B. Cowasji's Evidence," *WRTOS* (25 July 1914), 42 (Hormusji); and "Bombay Government Gazette. Civil Appointments," *TI* (12 July 1918), 4 (Khandalawalla, Davar, Chinoy); Suit No. 6 of 1924, 1924–8 PCMC Notebook, I: 6.

[194] Mistry, *Reminiscences* [1911], 69.

[195] See Chapter 7 at text accompanying notes 74–94.

[196] "No. 8: Madras" in "Paper No. I: Opinions on the Parsi Marriage and Divorce Bill," 38 in "Parsi Marriage and Divorce Act 1936"; "No. 5: Madras" in "Paper No. I: Opinions on the Indian Succession (Amendment) Bill," 5 in "Indian Succession (Amendment) Act 1939"; "No. 16: Madras" in "Paper No. I: Opinions on the Parsi and Divorce (Amendment) Bill," 21 in "Parsi Marriage and Divorce (Amendment) Act 1940."

[197] Sturgess, II: 756.

[198] By Mistry, see *Reminiscences* [1911]; *Forty Years' Reminiscences of Wadia Ghandy; Forty Years' Reminiscences of the High Court.* See also Lentin, 177, in Mehrotra and Dwivedi; Mitra Sharafi, "Two Lives in Law: The Reminiscences of A. J. C. Mistry and Sir Norman Macleod, 1884–1926," in *A Heritage of Judging: The Bombay High Court through*

Making Law: Two Patterns

shorthand writers, typists, sheriffs, bailiffs, servants, and guards. He noted who was sociable and who was not, who gambled at the races, who succumbed to bubonic plague, and who was a stylish dresser.[199] Mistry also reported that 36 percent of the eighty-nine clerks at Wadia Ghandy were Parsi and that many had been employed through family or community connections.[200]

Parsis were everywhere in the legal world, acting as translators, clerks, and pleaders in the early days, then also as barristers and solicitors, and ultimately as judges and treatise writers in India and the empire. We cannot forget about this army of Parsis in the legal profession when asking why Parsis were such heavy intragroup users of colonial law. Together, these two phenomena presented a chicken-or-egg conundrum: did Parsis go into law as a profession because there was such a demand for legal expertise within their own community? Or did Parsis start using law more because they were surrounded by lawyers? The answer was probably a bit of both. No doubt Parsi litigants and lawyers fed each others' appetites for law. But if there was a premium on being Parsi *and* a lawyer, vis-à-vis a Parsi clientele, many non-Parsi clients also found the combination useful. As leading practitioners along the Indian Ocean littoral – from Zanzibar and Ceylon to Burma and Singapore – Parsis served as a species of universal lawyer within the empire.[201] Legal education, evidence-gathering commissions, and appeals required colonial lawyers and their document bundles to criss-cross the empire. Parsi lawyers often represented non-white client populations in these processes. They were occasionally employed by the imperial state, too. During a British attack on the Sultanate of Zanzibar in 1897, military authorities turned to a Parsi lawyer based in Zanzibar for legal advice on the slave trade. "His services were much appreciated," noted the *Times of India* at the lawyer's death.[202] Parsi lawyers were also enlisted to set up legal systems in new corners of empire. In 1919, one British official noted the work of "the capable Indian staff, a dozen members in all, who made the Courts" in Iraq, a newly acquired British territory under the League of Nations mandate system.

---

150 Years, eds. Dhananjaya Y. Chandrachud, Anoop V. Mohta, and Roshan S. Dalvi (Mumbai: Maharashtra Judicial Academy, 2012), 258–83.

[199] Mistry, *Reminiscences* [1911], 12–32, 82–91.

[200] Ibid., 23, 25, 28–31, 88.

[201] The Parsi Talati brothers bought and ran the formerly English law firm of Wiggins and Stevens in colonial Zanzibar [personal correspondence with Asad Talati of Toronto (9 and 17 December 2006)]. On Parsi lawyers in Zanzibar, see Hoshang Kased, "Parsis in Zanzibar: the Emerald Isle" (unpublished manuscript), 46, 63, 68, 83, 95–8, 108, A8–10. I am grateful to John R. Hinnells and Michael Stausberg for sharing with me this source or their knowledge of it. In Ceylon, the Choksy family produced a number of leading lawyers [Jamsheed K. Choksy, "Iranians and Indians on the Shores of Serendib (Sri Lanka)," 190–2 in Hinnells and Williams]. On Parsi lawyers in Burma, see "Parsi Defamation Suit. Bombay Editors Charged," *WRTOS* (6 June 1914), 47; "The Parsi Dispute. Another Defamation Suit," 40; N. R. Chakravarti, *The Indian Minority in Burma: The Rise and Decline of an Immigrant Community* (London: Oxford University Press, 1971), 115. On Singapore, see R. B. Krishnan, *Indians in Malaya: A Pageant of Greater India* (Singapore: Malayan Publishers, 1936), 33.

[202] "Ahmedabad Bar's Loss. Mr. H. B. Vakil Dead," *TI* (16 March 1938).

"They have done excellent work for Basrah and, I hope, much for the new administration because of the sound training these Indians, *notably the Parsis*, have given to their Arab subordinates, who will now presumably replace them."[203] Parsi lawyers were not only agents for the pursuit of their own community's legal autonomy and identity. They also helped consolidate an empire of common law.

Yuri Slezkine has developed the notion of "service nomads," describing the historically common specialization in trade and money lending among diasporic minority groups like Jews, Armenians, and Parsis.[204] Being *legal* service nomads may have suited Parsis because of what they were not. Parsi lawyers were neither Hindu nor Muslim, neither European nor (by some accounts) Indian. These characteristics may have made Parsi lawyers acceptable to litigants of many backgrounds. In western India, Indian Jewish and Muslim communities failed to produce enough elite lawyers to represent their own members in the superior courts. A small circle of Muslim lawyers from Bombay's Gujarati-speaking communities were some of the earliest and most successful Indian lawyers and judges. The High Court judge Badruddin Tyabji and barrister Mohammad Ali Jinnah were among them.[205] But what this group enjoyed in stature, it lacked in numbers. Only 14 percent of advocates and 6 percent of High Court judges were Muslim in Bombay between the High Court's creation in 1861 and independence in 1947.[206] Just three of 103 solicitors' firms in the city in 1924 had Muslim

---

[203] Emphasis added. "Report of the Administration on Civil and Criminal Justice in the Basrah Vilayet by the Courts established under the Iraq Occupied Territories Code during the Year 1918" (PRO CO 696) (National Archives, UK). I owe this reference to Binyamin Blum, with gratitude.

[204] Slezkine, 4–39. For an overview of the diaspora literature, see Robin Cohen, *Global Diasporas: An Introduction* (Seattle: University of Washington, 1997). For a sample of works on particular historical diasporas, see Paul Gilroy, *The Black Atlantic: Modernity and Double Consciousness* (Cambridge, MA: Harvard University Press, 1993); Dobbin, *Asian Entrepreneurial Minorities*; Sarah Abrevaya Stein, *Plumes: Ostrich Feathers, Jews, and a Lost World of Global Commerce* (New Haven, CT: Yale University Press, 2008); Francesca Trivellato, *The Familiarity of Strangers: The Sephardic Diaspora, Livorno, and Cross-Cultural Trade in the Early Modern Period* (New Haven, CT: Yale University Press, 2009). See also William Safran, "Concepts, theories and challenges of diaspora: a panoptic approach," paper presented at the workshop on "Dispersione, 'globalizzazione' e costruzione dell'alterità: diaspore et migrazioni nel bacino del Mediterraneo et oltre (XIX–XX secc.)," sponsored by the University of Pisa (Marsala, Italy; 18 September 2007; accessed on 1 October 2012): www.sissco.it/index.php?id=1311

[205] N. K. Jain, *Muslims in India: A Biographical Dictionary* Delhi: Manohar, 1983), I: 229–40; II: 195–7; Vallabhjī Suñdarjī Puñjābhāī, *Muṁbaīna Mahāśyo* (Kathiawad: Author, 1920), 354–7; Kozlowski, 179. Mahomedbhoy Alladinbhoy Somjee, who became a High Court judge in the late 1930s, was another example. See "Death of Bombay Judge. Mr. Justice M.A. Somjee," *TI* (15 June 1942), 7. Somjee and Jinnah were members of the Khoja community, whereas Tyabji was Bohra.

[206] There were seven Muslim judges out of a total of 121 judges (5.8 percent) on the High Court bench between 1861 and 1947, namely: Mohammedali Currim Chagla, Abdeally Mahomedally Kajiji, Mirza Ali Akbar Khan, Mahomed Alladinbhoy Somjee and his brother Kasambhoy Alladinbhoy Somjee, and Badruddin Tyabji and his son Faiz B. Tyabji. There were twenty-six

Making Law: Two Patterns

partners.[207] At the time, Muslims were approximately a fifth of the population of Bombay City and Presidency.[208] There were even fewer Indian Jews in law. In 1924, there were only three Jewish solicitors and no Jewish advocates in Bombay.[209] There were no Indian Jewish judges at the Bombay High Court under the Raj.[210] That said, the Jewish population was also tiny – just 0.7 percent of the population of Bombay City.[211] The result was that Muslim and Jewish litigants often hired Parsi lawyers.[212] Kozlowski has argued that the community affiliation of lawyers played no role in attracting clients, that lawyers were hired guns willing to make any argument, and that their clients' only interest was in the lawyers' records of wins and losses.[213] Kozlwoski's description may have been reasonable at the uppermost levels, among the top dozen litigators at the High Court bar. But among most High Court advocates and their clients, community and perhaps vernacular did play some role. Especially with Partition looming large in the late 1940s, Muslim parties in Bombay seem to have avoided Hindu lawyers and hired Parsis instead.[214]

At least some Parsi lawyers and judges fed the pattern by not showing favoritism toward Parsi parties in mixed suits. In 1927, J. D. Davar reserved some of his most vituperative comments for a Parsi defendant (with a Parsi lawyer) whom he found to have swindled an impoverished Jewish quarry contractor. After calling the defendant a pompous tax evader and forger of evidence, Davar called him a liar: "I do not believe a single word of his evidence."[215] Davar demonstrated the same tendency in other mixed cases, implicitly promoting the idea that Parsi judges did not favor their own co-religionists.[216] Parsi legal professionals, in other words, may not simply have been useful to their own

---

Muslims out of 189 advocates admitted to the Bombay Bar, 1872–1922. (Mistry, *Forty Years' Reminiscences of the High Court*, 10, 60–3.)

[207] Mistry, *Forty Years' Reminiscences of the High Court*, 50.

[208] In the census of 1911, Muslims constituted 18.3 percent of the population of Bombay City and 20.5 percent of Bombay Presidency. [*Statistical Abstract Relating to British India from 1910–11 to 1919–20* (London: His Majesty's Stationary Office, 1922), 4, 6.]

[209] Mistry, *Forty Years' Reminiscences of the High Court*, 50, 60–6 (Solomon Moses Vakrulkar, Moses Samson Ezekiel, Ellis Jacob Judah).

[210] An ICS judge named "G. Jacob" (or J. Jacob) was appointed an acting High Court judge sometime in 1903–4. He was probably British and may or may not have been Jewish. I am grateful to Joan Roland, Sifra Lentin, and Mitch Numark for their thoughts on this point.

[211] The population of Jews in Bombay in the 1901 census was just 5,357 out of a total of 776,006. (*Gazetteer of Bombay City and Island*, I: 273).

[212] For example, see Suit No. 3415 of 1925, "Hon. Justice J.D. Davar, Short Causes and Motions (6 January 1927–14 April 1927)," I: 63 (BHC); *Rachel Benjamin v. Benjamin Solomon Benjamin* ILR 50 Bom 369 (1926).

[213] Kozlowski, 122.

[214] See Suits No. 1236 of 1944, 1262 of 1945, and 701 of 1947; all in "Hon. Justice N. H. C. Coyajee. Typed Notes of Evidence (4 December 1946–23 April 1949)" (BHC).

[215] Suit No. 3415 of 1925 in "J. D. Davar, Judgments (11 January 1927–13 April 1927)," 7–9 (BHC).

[216] Suit No. 3099 of 1924 in J. D. Davar's Judgments 1927, 51–4, 60–8; Suit No. 1120 of 1925 in "J. D. Davar, Judgments (17 June 1931 to 31 August 1931)," 333, 338 (BHC).

co-religionists for the resolution of intragroup disputes. Their skills and community identity may equally have held appeal for non-Parsi litigants, giving Parsi lawyers special social currency in the British Empire.

CONCLUSION

There were other South Asian communities whose members pursued legal careers with special zeal. Upper caste Hindus were the leading examples across India.[217] In Madras Presidency, Tamil-speaking Brahmins dominated the Bar from the late nineteenth century on. Many of the legal luminaries of South India were Aiyangars and Aiyars, including the founders of India's earliest law journal, the *Madras Law Journal*.[218] In Bombay, 40 percent of law students in the late 1870s were Brahmin, an even larger proportion than Parsis at 27 percent.[219] Parsi and Brahmin populations in Bombay were roughly the same size during the late colonial period, constituting between 4.5 and 6 percent of the city.[220] Gujarati-speaking Vanias (Guj. *Vāṇiyo*) or Banias joined their Brahmin colleagues in increasing numbers during the first few decades of the twentieth century, an unsurprising phenomenon given the caste dynamics of the region.[221] By 1925, Mistry observed that the Vanias dominated among Bombay's 122 Hindu solicitors, who represented 44 percent of all solicitors in Bombay. (At the time, 42 percent of Bombay's solicitors were Parsi.[222]) Across the subcontinent, Hindu lawyers played a critical and fascinating role – both as lawyers and judges – in their own and other Hindu communities' intragroup lawsuits, particularly in disputes over religious endowments and the partition of the joint family.[223] The full richness of these connections awaits future scholars.

[217] Lloyd I. Rudolph and Susanne Hoeber Rudolph, "Barristers and Brahmans in India: Legal Cultures and Social Change," *CSSH* 8:1 (1965), 35.

[218] Price, "Ideology and Ethnicity." 163–72.

[219] Dobbin, *Urban Leadership*, 169.

[220] In the 1860s, 4.9 percent of the population of Bombay City was Brahmin (39,604 of 816,562). [*Statistical Abstract Relating to British India from 1860 to 1869* (London: George E. Eyre and William Spottiswoode, 1870), 4.] In 1911, Brahmins constituted 4.6 percent of British India and the princely states (14,598,708 of 315,156,396). [*Statistical Abstract Relating to British India from 1903–4 to 1912–13* (London: H.M.S.O., 1915), 1, 14.] For Parsi population figures, see Chapter 1 at note 8.

[221] As the government ethnographer R. E. Enthoven observed, "[p]ractically a plutocracy has arisen in Gujarát and the Vánia is often socially more important than the Bráhman." [R. E. Enthoven, *Tribes and Castes of Bombay* (Bombay: Government of Bombay, 1920), III: 423.]

[222] Mistry, *Forty Years' Reminiscences of the High Court*, 46–7. Vanias represented 1.9 percent of the population of Bombay Presidency in the 1901 Census. [Enthoven, III: 412; *Statistical Abstract Relating to British India from 1894–95 to 1903–04*, 1.]

[223] See Price, "Ideology and Ethnicity," 173–4; Mytheli Sreenivas, "Conjugality and Capital: Gender, Families, and Property under Colonial Law in India," *JAS* 63:4 (2004), 937; Appadurai, 183–5; Sturman, 146–95. For a list of Hindu judges knowledgeable of *dharmaśāstra*, see Derrett, "Administration," 38 at notes 115–17 and accompanying text.

Making Law: Two Patterns

More work has been done on Muslim lawyers and judges in late colonial India. There were certainly individuals with dazzling legal acumen and influence. Muslim judges like Syed Mahmood at the Allahabad High Court, Syed Ameer Ali at the Calcutta High Court, and Faiz B. Tyabji in Bombay produced judgments and treatises that altered the shape of Anglo-Islamic law.[224] Mohammad Ali Jinnah was not only one of the most sought-after barristers for decades at the Bombay High Court. He also relocated to London for several years in the 1930s to represent Indian clients in Privy Council appeals, contributing to the representation of Indian communities (including Muslims) at the highest level of imperial case law.[225] We know less about volume and breadth. It did not seem that the *number* of Muslims pursuing law as a profession ever rose beyond low levels, at least not in Bombay Presidency.[226] The question, then, would be whether Muslim lawyering was fundamentally an elite phenomenon concentrated in the leading metropolitan centers of British India or whether it had deeper penetration within its own community, as was the case among Parsis.

Populations other than the Parsis also lobbied for legislation.[227] From the late 1870s, some of western India's Muslim communities adopted a law-centered approach to reform.[228] The Khoja Law Commission failed to produce the legislation it desired in the 1870s and '80s, but the legalistic model would prove successful several decades later, led by the Khoja lawyer Jinnah, among others.[229] In the first half of the twentieth century, Muslim-led campaigns for legislation enabled the passage of the Mussalman Wakf Validating Act (VI of 1913), the Muslim Personal Law (Shariat) Application Act (XXVI of 1937), and the Dissolution of Muslim Marriages Act (VIII of 1939). This legislation changed the way colonial law applied to Muslims.[230] Hindu legislative

---

[224] Kozlowski, 111–23; Scott Alan Kugle, "Framed, Blamed and Renamed: The Recasting of Islamic Jurisprudence in Colonial South Asia," *MAS* 35:2 (2001), 301–11; Guenther, "Syed Mahmood"; Avril A. Powell, "Islamic Modernism and Women's Status: The Influence of Syed Ameer Ali" in *Rhetoric and Reality: Gender and the Colonial Experience in South Asia*, eds. Avril A. Powell and Siobhan Lambert-Hurley (Oxford: Oxford University Press, 2006), 282–317; Beverley, 164–73.

[225] Vachha, 149–51. For a sample of Jinnah's JCPC cases, see *Bibi Aesha v. Mohammad Abdul Kabir* AIR 1931 PC 310; *Abdul Majid Khan v. Sharaswatibai* AIR 1934 PC 4.

[226] See text accompanying notes 205–14.

[227] See Sturman, 27.

[228] See David S. Powers, "Orientalism, Colonialism and Legal History: The Attack on Muslim Family Endowments in Algeria and India," *CSSH* 31:3 (1989), 557–63.

[229] See "The Khoja Succession Bill," *TI* (17 July 1884), 6; untitled editorial, *TI* (19 July 1884), 4; Sturman, 204–5. The Cutchee Memons (another Muslim trading community from western India) proposed a similar statute on the model of the Khoja bill. Both bills seem to have failed due to intracommunity dissent. See "The Cutchee Maimon Bill," *TI* (29 October 1885), 6; "The Cutchee Memon Bill," *TI* (9 January 1886), 3.

[230] See Kozlowski, 111–23, 178–91; Sturman, 210–18; as well as Kashi Prasad Saksena, *Muslim Law as Administered in British India* (Allahabad: Rai Sahib Ram Dayal Agarwala, 1938), 157b; Asaf A. A. Fyzee, *Outlines of Muhammadan Law* (Oxford: Oxford University Press, 1974), 468–70; Janaki Nair, *Women and Law in Colonial India: A Social History* (Delhi: Kali for

122 Law and Identity in Colonial South Asia: Parsi Legal Culture

mobilization began slightly later. There were Indian reformers involved in the nineteenth-century campaigns that led to the passage of the Bengal Sati Regulation (XVII of 1829), the Widow Remarriage Act (XV of 1856), and the Age of Consent Acts (incorporated into XLV of 1860; X of 1891). However, Europeans (including missionaries and women) played a major role in those campaigns.[231] It was not until the twentieth century that a Hindu-led movement to reform large portions of Hindu personal law developed. This push gained adherents by the 1920s, when communities like the Marwaris and Jains were also developing lobbying strategies.[232] It culminated in the creation of the Hindu Code bill that passed as a series of statutes on Hindu marriage and inheritance in independent India during the 1950s.[233] Legislative lobbying by Sikh community leaders in 1920s Punjab produced the Sikh Gurdwaras Act (Punjab Act VIII of 1925). In a similar way to the creation of the Parsi matrimonial courts with their Parsi-only juries in 1865, the Sikh statute introduced a new system of adjudication controlled by members of the community. In addition to creating a system of Sikh-elected boards that would directly manage Sikh temples or *gurdwaras* (Punj. *gurduārā*), the Act instituted a system of "judicial commissions" consisting of three Sikh lawyers or judges who would resolve disputes relating to *gurdwaras* and the religious trusts that governed them.[234]

Women, 1996), 192–5; Gail Minault, "Women, Legal Reform and Muslim Identity in South Asia," *Jura Gentium: J. Philos. Internat. L. Glob. Pol. I* (2005), text accompanying notes 21–43. By Eleanor Newbigin, see "The Codification of Personal Law and Secular Citizenship: Revisiting the History of Law Reform in late colonial India," *IESHR* 46:1 (2009), 83–104; "Personal Law and Citizenship in India's Transition to Independence," *MAS* 45:1 (2011), 7–32. By Rohit De, see "Mumtaz Bibi's Broken Heart: The Many Lives of the Dissolution of Muslim Marriages Act," *IESHR* 46:1 (2009), 105–30; "The Two Husbands of Vero Tiscenko: Apostasy, Conversion and Divorce in Late Colonial India," *LHR* 28:4 (2010), 1011–41.

[231] See Agnes, *Family Law*, I: 14–18; Barbara N. Ramusack, "Cultural Missionaries, Maternal Imperialists, Feminist Allies: British Women Activists in India, 1865–1945" in *Western Women and Imperialism: Complicity and Resistance*, eds. Nupur Chaudhuri and Margaret Strobel (Bloomington: Indiana University Press, 1992), 120–34. See also Anand A. Yang, "Whose Sati? Widow Burning in Early Nineteenth-Century India," 21–52 and Lata Mani, "Production of an Official Discourse on Sati in Early Nineteenth-Century Bengal," 53–82, both in *Women and Social Reform in Modern India: A Reader*, eds. Sumit Sarkar and Tanika Sarkar (Ranikhet: Permanent Black, 2007), vol. 1. See also Chapters 3 at note 151 and 4 at note 73.

[232] See Ritu Birla, *Stages of Capital: Law, Culture, and Market Governance in Late Colonial India* (Durham, NC: Duke University Press, 2009), 199–231. By Peter Flügel, see "A Short History," 8–9; "Jaina Law," in Stanley N. Katz, ed., *The Oxford International Encyclopedia of Legal History* (Oxford: Oxford University Press, 2009).

[233] See Harold Lewis Levy, "Lawyer-Scholars, Lawyer-Politicians and the Hindu Code Bill, 1921–1956," *LSR* 3:2/3 (1969), 303–16; Rina Verma Williams, *Postcolonial Politics and Personal Laws: Colonial Legal Legacies and the Indian State* (Oxford: Oxford University Press, 2006), 96–124; Newbigin, "Codification"; Narendra Subramanian, "Making Family and Nation: Hindu Marriage Law in Early Postcolonial India," *JAS* 69:3 (2010), 771–98; Agnes, *Family Law*, I: 18–23.

[234] Sikh Gurdwaras Act, s. 70 in Des Raj Narang, *The Sikh Gurdwaras Act (Act VIII of 1925)* (Lahore: Puri Brothers, 1926), 40. I am grateful to M. S. Gill (Minister of Youth Affairs and

Making Law: Two Patterns

Parsi legal mobilization predated its Muslim, Hindu, Jain, and Sikh counterparts, beginning in the 1830s and achieving major success with the matrimonial and inheritance statutes of 1865. Indeed, it would be tempting to suggest lines of influence between these various legal awakenings. Eleanor Newbigin has suggested that Muslim legislative lobbying stimulated the development of a similar movement among Hindus.[235] In turn, the Parsi lobbying tradition may have provided a model for the Muslim campaign of the early twentieth century. Jinnah was a close friend of the leading Parsi advocate, Dinshaw Petit – at least until Jinnah married Petit's only daughter, Ratanbai, in 1918 and caused an uproar among Parsis over intercommunity marriage.[236] One can only wonder whether Jinnah observed the Parsi mode of legislative lobbying and used it to perpetuate similar methods in his own community.

Parsis were not the only South Asians to effect legal change through lobbying and the pursuit of law as a profession. However, these patterns were unusually clear and strong among them. Furthermore, legal mobilization occurred earlier among Parsis than among Muslims, Hindus, Jains, or Sikhs and on a more expansive scale, enabling the passage of legislation at an all-India level that created the rules for an entire corpus of personal law. As the next chapter suggests, the early application of English law to the Parsis created a strong external incentive to organize for legal change. Equally, the small size and geographic concentration of this "compact race," as well as its elite's fluency and literacy in English, probably facilitated the establishment and perpetuation of its legal culture.[237] Both lobbying and the development of a critical mass in the legal profession must have been enabled through the imitation, mentorship, and support that resulted from close social contact and communication in western India. Although Parsis' involvement in the production of law was not unique, in other words, differences of degree and timing set them apart from other South Asian populations. Arguably, they were British India's quintessential legalistic community.

Sports, Government of India) for introducing me to the 1925 Act and the history of Sikh legislative lobbying.

[235] Newbigin, "Codification," 86, 100; and her "Personal Law," 19–21.

[236] Ratanbai converted to Islam, and the couple married under Anglo-Islamic law. See "Mahomedan-Parsi Wedding," *TI* (20 April 1918), 10; "Mr Punch's Fancy Portraits. Best Orthodox in Excelsis," *HP* (28 July 1918), 21; "Parsi Alien Marriage Question," *Bombay Chronicle* (29 July 1918), 5; "Parsi Anjuman Meeting," *TI* (30 July 1918), 10.

[237] I borrow the phrase from a discussion of the Parsi community in another context. ["Degeneration of Parsis. High Mortality," *TI* (15 November 1929), 13.]

PART 2

THE CREATION OF PARSI PERSONAL LAW

3

The Limits of English Law

The Inheritance Acts

The legislation that created Parsi matrimonial and inheritance law was an assertion of independence in multiple ways. Its contents bore little resemblance to the law of the ancient Zoroastrians.[1] It also failed to replicate the customary norms of Parsis in the *mofussil*.[2] To be sure, English statutes served as a template for the Parsi Acts' basic framework, and in some ways, the Parsi statutes mirrored developments in English legislation.[3] In other ways, though, the Parsi statutes rejected the law of the imperial metropole. The Parsi legislation created something new. Its framers considered it modern, but not English. If Tanya Luhrmann and others have characterized colonial Parsis as the ultimate mimic men, that mimicry – in the field of law, at least – was limited to the simple acquisition of skills.[4] These skills were quickly put to work reversing substantive English law. The phenomenon was clearest in the law of inheritance and particularly, in the law of intestate succession, the default rules of distribution that applied in the absence of a valid will.[5]

The law of inheritance highlighted the relationship between Parsis and English law. By standard accounts, Indian law Anglicized over the colonial period. Legislation was the key vehicle for this transformation.[6] Most change

---

[1] See Macuch, "Law."

[2] See Palsetia, *Parsis*, 211–26.

[3] See Agnes, *Family Law*, I: 79–80.

[4] Luhrmann, 1–26; Feroza Jussawalla, "'Hybridity,' Our Ancestral Heritage: Minority 'Indian' Writers Speak of their Diversity," in *Hybridity and Postcolonialism: Twentieth-century Indian Literature*, ed. Monika Fludernik (Tuebingen: Stauffenburg Verlag, 1998), 210, 216.

[5] For a useful overview of Parsi intestacy legislation, see Phiroze K. Irani, "The Personal Law of the Parsis of India," in *Family Law in Asia and Africa*, ed. J. N. D. Anderson (New York: Frederick A. Praeger, 1967), 296–7.

[6] Michael R. Anderson, "Islamic Law and the Colonial Encounter in British India," in *Institutions and Ideologies: A SOAS South Asia Reader*, eds. David Arnold and Peter Robb (Richmond, UK: Curzon, 1993), 169–70; Fali S. Nariman, *India's Legal System: Can It Be Saved?* (Delhi: Penguin, 2006), 20–1; Jain, *Outlines*, 541. See also Banerjee, *English Law*, 166–99.

occurred during the legislative bulge of the long 1860s. The Codes of Civil Procedure (VIII of 1859) and of Criminal Procedure (XXV of 1861), the Indian Penal Code (XLV of 1860), the Indian Evidence Act (I of 1872) and the Indian Contract Act (IX of 1872) became law within thirteen short years.[7] However, legislation would equally be a site for the expression of culturally distinct values. The Parsi law of intestacy moved in the opposite direction from the legislated Anglicization of most other areas of law. In other words, although legislation was often a tool for Anglicization, it could equally be mobilized by legally skilled populations to distance themselves from English law ways.

Parsi lobbyists refashioned inheritance law to reflect their own vision of the Parsi family. The net result differed from its English counterpart in significant ways. In particular, the Parsis rejected English doctrines that concentrated wealth in a single person or small cluster of people. The English principle of primogeniture, for instance, entitled the eldest son to inherit all of his father's real estate. Parsi lobbyists rejected it, insisting that all male children receive equal shares. The English doctrine of coverture or unity also had ramifications for inheritance law. It recognized husband and wife as a single legal person, making the man (upon marriage) the sole legal owner of what was formerly the woman's property. A husband's control over his wife's property through coverture meant that, on her death, the property continued to be his. Parsi lobbyists made coverture inapplicable to Parsis. English law concentrated wealth at other points, too. In English intestacy law post-1925, intestates' property could devolve to a comparatively small list of relatives and was unlikely to be split among them. The Parsi regime of 1939 distributed an intestate's property in smaller pieces to a much larger circle of relatives, including the intestate's parents and the widows of the intestate's descendants. Perhaps surprisingly, a community with major family business interests did not seek to concentrate family wealth, whether through the kind of patterns reflected in English law or through a model akin to the Hindu joint family, in which many family members held property as co-parcenors.[8] On the contrary, Parsi lobbyists enshrined in law a default vision of the family that recognized a broad web of social bonds *despite* the inevitable dilution of control over family assets. English intestacy rules were winner-take-all. Parsi law spread the wealth.

---

[7] See Jain, 499–502; Mantena, 90–2; Thomas R. Metcalf, *Imperial Connections: India in the Indian Ocean Arena, 1860–1920* (Berkeley: University of California Press, 2007), 18–19. On the Criminal Procedure Code, see Kolsky, "Codification." On the Indian Contract Act, Evidence Act, and Penal Code, see George Claus Rankin, *Background to Indian Law* (Cambridge: Cambridge University Press, 1946), 88–134, 197–217.

[8] See Sturman; Leigh Denault, "Partition and the Politics of the Joint Family in Nineteenth-century North India," *IESHR* 46:1 (2009), 27–55. Some scholars have attributed the financial success of wealthy mercantile communities to personal law systems that concentrated assets. Colonial-era Parsis were an example to the contrary. For an example of the former view, see Anantdeep Singh, "The Divergence of the Economic Fortunes of Hindus and Muslims in British India: A Comparative Institutional Analysis" (PhD dissertation, University of Southern California, 2008); Timur Kuran and Anantdeep Singh, "Economic Modernization in Late British India: Hindu-Muslim Differences" (accessed on 13 October 2012): http://www.econ.yale.edu/~egcenter/Kuran_SinghPaper.pdf.

The Inheritance Acts

Over time, Parsi intestacy statutes provided larger and larger shares for women (both widows and daughters) in relation to sons. English law did, too – but at a different tempo and by a different route. It would be tempting to focus on the gender-based theme when charting the development of Parsi intestacy law. Gender was a central site of conflict between English and Parsi legal values, a point made clear by Jesse Palsetia on the 1850s–60s and Flavia Agnes on the 1930s.[9] However, assessing inheritance law both Parsi and English over the century from the 1830s until the 1930s, we see that gender-based movements became less clear over time and that other differences in values also emerged. Fluctuations in English law, the imperial baseline, revealed that English law did not consistently lead on the path to equality between the sexes. In 1865, it was Parsi law that recognized married women's property rights, discarding the English doctrine of coverture. English law sloughed off coverture (or most of it) between 1870 and 1882.[10] In 1925, English legislation equalized the entitlement of male and female heirs, whether those females were offspring or spouses. Only then did Parsi law give wives and daughters less, in comparison. The 1939 statute covering Parsi intestacy granted the intestate's widow and son equal shares and daughters a half-share each. The English legal developments of 1925 would have been very much in the minds of Parsi law reformers in 1939. But arguably, the Parsi failure to grant equal shares to daughters (vis-à-vis sons) had as much to do with a heightened sense of duty to the extended family as with their notion of gender roles. Inheritance law was the site of cultural clash, and a fundamental disagreement between Parsi and English law over the nineteenth and twentieth centuries turned on the degree to which wealth ought to be concentrated. Disagreements over women's entitlements undoubtedly ran parallel to the concentration issue. But Parsis and Britons took turns championing women's inheritance rights, making it hard to argue that Parsi law consistently lagged behind English law on gender equality.

PERSONAL LAW, BUT NOT FOR YOU: THE FATE OF THE SMALLER MINORITIES

The personal law system was standard among the great Islamic empires of the early modern period. The Ottomans, Safavids, and Mughals allowed religious minorities to settle disputes among their members.[11] Under the Ottoman *millet* system, community bodies enjoyed wide authority in resolving internal

---

[9] Palsetia, *Parsis*, 197–226; Agnes, *Family Law*, I: 81–2.

[10] See Lee Holcombe, *Wives and Property: Reform of the Married Women's Property Law in Nineteenth-Century England* (Toronto: University of Toronto Press, 1983), 166–205; Mary Lyndon Shanley, *Feminism, Marriage and the Law in Victorian England, 1850–1895* (Princeton: Princeton University Press, 1989), 49–78, 103–30.

[11] Kugle, 263; C. E. Bosworth, "The Concept of *Dhimma* in Early Islam," in *Christians and Jews in the Ottoman Empire: The Functioning of a Plural Society*, eds. Benjamin Braude and Bernard Lewis (New York: Holmes and Meier, 1982), 45, 49.

disputes.[12] A similar system operated in early modern India.[13] The East India Company adopted this system from the Mughals and made two major changes.[14] First, the adjudicators of personal law were no longer community authorities but the colonial courts themselves. British judges decided what Islamic and Hindu law said, a process permeated by cross-cultural mistrust and problematic translations.[15] From the late eighteenth century until 1864, these judges relied on South Asian experts in religious law: *muftis* (Pers. *maftī*), *maulvis* (Pers. *mulavī*), and *qadis* (Pers. *qāżī*) for Islamic law and *pandits* (Sanskr. *paṇḍita*) for Hindu law.[16] From the early nineteenth century and particularly after the mid-century abolition of native law officers, colonial judges turned to Orientalists' translations of classical Hindu and Islamic legal texts, a body of government-commissioned treatises that reduced the judicial reliance on Indian experts.[17] The second change to the Mughal system was to limit personal law to Hindus and Muslims alone.[18] India was home to Buddhists, Sikhs, Jains, Jews, Christians, and Zoroastrians when Warren Hastings made his personal

---

[12] See Karen Barkey, "Aspects of Legal Pluralism in the Ottoman Empire: A Relational Field of Religious Differentiation," Symposium on New Perspectives on Legal Pluralism, Newberry Library, Chicago, 23 April 2010; Taş, 67–75.

[13] Banerjee, 267; Ibn Hasan, *The Central Structure of the Mughal Empire* (Lahore: Oxford University Press, Pakistan branch, 1967), 309–10, 340; Ram Sharma, *The Religious Policy of the Mughal Emperors* (New York: Asia Publishing House, 1972), 219, 221; Derrett, "Administration," 17; Jadunath Sarkar, *The Mughal Administration: Six Lectures* (Patna: Government Printing, 1920), 10; K. M. Yusuf, "The Judiciary in India under the Sultans of Delhi and the Mughal Emperors," *Indo-Iranica* XVIII: 4 (1965), 4, 8. See also Richard M. Eaton, *The Rise of Islam and the Bengal Frontier, 1204–1760* (Berkeley: University of California Press, 1993), 179–83.

[14] Asaf A. A. Fyzee, "Muhammadan Law in India," *CSSH* 5: 4 (July 1963), 414. On the role of the "Mughal constitution" in Company governance during the late eighteenth century, see Travers.

[15] See S. R. Kulkarni, "Widow in a Joint Hindu Family," *Bom LR* (journal) 37 (1935), 35–7; Anderson, "Islamic Law," 170–6; Banerjee, *English Law*, 30–5, 42–6; Kugle, 272; Thomas R. Metcalf, *Ideologies of the Raj* (Cambridge: Cambridge University Press, 1995), 23–4; Anver Emon, "Islamic Law and the Canadian Mosaic: Politics, Jurisprudence and Multicultural Accommodation," University of Toronto Legal Studies Research Paper No. 947149, 10–12 (accessed on 3 February 2013): http://papers.ssrn.com/sol3/papers.cfm?abstract_id=947149.

[16] Jain, 581–4; B. B. Misra, *The Indian Middle Classes: Their Growth in Modern Times* (London: Oxford University Press, 1961), 174–5; Anderson, "Islamic Law," 173–4.

[17] On the legal Orientalists' compilation and translation projects, see Nandini Bhattacharyya-Panda, *Appropriation and Invention of Tradition: The East India Company and Hindu Law in Early Colonial Bengal* (Delhi: Oxford University Press, 2008); Kugle, 257–313; Metcalf, *Ideologies*, 12–13; David Ibbetson, "Sir William Jones as Comparative Lawyer," in *Sir William Jones, 1746–1794: A Commemoration*, ed. Alexander Murray (Oxford: Oxford University Press, on behalf of University College Oxford, 1998), 17–42; Anderson, "Islamic Law"; Derrett, *Religion*, 269–73; Bernard S. Cohn, "Law and the Colonial State in India," in *Colonialism*, ed. Cohn, 57–75; Rosane Rocher, "The Creation of Anglo-Hindu Law" in Lubin, Davis, and Krishnan, 78–88; Richard W. Lariviere, "Justices and Paṇḍitas: Some Ironies in Contemporary Readings of the Hindu Legal Past," *JAS* 48:4 (1989), 757–63; Anderson, "Islamic Law," 173–6; Banerjee, *English Law*, 42–6; Travers, 124–6.

[18] Rankin, 3–7.

The Inheritance Acts   131

law promise to Muslims and Hindus in 1772.[19] In western India, the promise was reiterated in the 1823 Charter that replaced the Recorder's Court with the Supreme Court of Bombay.[20]

Why were the smaller religious groups left out? Hastings's 1772 Plan emerged in the context of two important conversations. In the early 1770s, a parliamentary committee in England considered requiring the Company to apply English law in India. This body operated with the assumption that under the Mughals' despotic rule, India had no law. Hastings responded by educating influential members of Parliament and the Company on the richness of Hindu law.[21] By Robert Travers's account, an exchange between the Company and the Mughal deputy *diwan*, one Muhammad Reza Khan, was equally important. Responding to a Company proposal to resolve civil disputes between Indians through arbitration, Reza Khan insisted that Islamic law continue to apply. Hastings' plan incorporated the idea that, in civil disputes, Islamic law would apply to Muslims. Against Reza Khan's protests, though, it added that Hindu law would apply to Hindus.[22] The Company's promise of personal law, in other words, was extended in the context of two heated debates about Islamic and Hindu law. Company officials may not have been thinking beyond the bounds of these discussions.

Other scholars have proposed additional reasons for the failure to include non-Muslims and -Hindus. M. P. Jain has suggested that religious minorities' small numbers made the translation and compilation of their religious legal texts a low priority for the Company in the late eighteenth century.[23] It was true that Sikh and Buddhist populations in British India were negligible until the British victory in the Anglo-Sikh Wars of the 1840s and the complete annexation of Burma in the 1880s. But, in the late eighteenth century, powerful merchants and financiers who traded closely with the British were Parsi, Jewish, and Armenian Christian. This was particularly true in port cities like Bombay and Calcutta, precisely the locations where English law applied to these populations.[24] These communities' networks stretched across Eurasia and the Indian Ocean littoral. They dominated the trade of commodities crucial to British rule in India, including opium.[25] As late as the early nineteenth century, company records

---

[19] "A Plan for the Administration of Justice, Extracted from the Proceedings of the Committee of Circuit, 15 August, 1772," in *Readings in the Constitutional History of India, 1757–1947*, ed. S. V. Desika Char (Delhi, 1983), 106; Erskine Perry in Vachha, 34. On the 1772 Plan generally, see Travers, 104–7, 124–6; Derrett, *Religion*, 232–7.

[20] "Report into the usages recognized as laws by the Parsee Community of India," 1 in "1862–3 Government of India Bill."

[21] Cohn, *Colonialism*, 65–6. See generally Derrett, "Administration," 51–2.

[22] Travers, 119–23, 129–30. Travers doubts the claim that under Mughal rule, Islamic law governed Hindu disputes (Travers, 121–2).

[23] Jain, 460.

[24] See Chapter 1 at 45.

[25] See Introduction at note 79.

132   *Law and Identity in Colonial South Asia: Parsi Legal Culture*

reflected British awe – at times, even fear – of these diasporic trading minorities, making it unlikely that the Company would jeopardize relations for reasons of administrative convenience.[26]

Rather than denying personal law to the smaller minorities on the basis of numbers, the colonial authorities' omission may have been rooted in a set of views about religious legal traditions. If the omission was an oversight in 1772, it may have been justified in subsequent decades on the basis of these views. By adopting the personal law principle, the colonial legal system became one of the most extensive experiments ever in the state-administered application of religious law. British Indian law was not only a playground for utilitarians, in other words: it was also one for religious-law comparativists.[27] Non-Muslims and -Hindus may have been left out of the personal law promise because the British believed these populations had no religious law. Many Britons were convinced that groups like the Jains, Buddhists, and Armenian Christians had never developed a general body of religious law that applied to their followers, ascetics aside. A related view was that some communities (arguably Zoroastrians and again Buddhists) had a body of textual religious law historically, but that most of those texts had been subsequently lost or destroyed.

The British assumed that the Jains had no proper legal texts – that there was no such thing as Jain (or Jaina) law.[28] Werner Menski has suggested that the Jains deliberately concealed their scriptures from British legal officials to keep the texts from being defiled. One Jain author described the pollution inherent in engagement with the colonial legal system: "the court officials generally employ the saliva of their mouth for turning over the leaves of the books, which must cause pain to a devout heart."[29] Strict adherents to Jain purity laws generally avoided the courts, again because coming to court was polluting. According to Menski, "pollution-conscious mendicants would not as readily engage with the polluting environment of the British courts as Hindu *pundits*."[30] By contrast, the judge J. L. Jaini attributed the paucity of English-language Jain legal texts by the

---

[26] For example, see "Extract from Judicial Letter from Bombay, 16 May 1821," 13 in "Report of the Bombay Police Magistrates."

[27] See Stokes; Andrew Huxley, "Positivists and Buddhists: The Rise and Fall of Anglo-Burmese Ecclesiastical Law," *LSI* 26:1 (2001), 113–42. For an overview of the comparative study of religious law, see in Andrew Huxley, ed., *Religion, Law and Tradition: Comparative Studies in Religious Law* (London: Routledge Curzon, 2002): Andrew Huxley, "Introduction," 1–19; "Religious Law: A Discussion," 148–56; Jacques Vanderlinden, "Religious Laws as Systems of Law – A Comparativist's View," 165–82.

[28] Menski, "Jaina Law," 428.

[29] C. R. Jain, *Jaina Law* (1921) quoted in Menski, "Jaina Law," 428.

[30] Menski, "Jaina Law," 428.

The Inheritance Acts

early twentieth century to the community's prior "backward and disorganized state." He began the work of recovering and translating Jain legal texts, like many other Indian legal middlemen, declaring that a "world of work yet awaits doing at the hands of Jaina Pandits and Lawyers."[31]

Among Buddhists and Armenian Christians, some Britons believed that religious law – as a body of norms applicable to all followers – simply did not exist. Both traditions had elaborate bodies of ecclesiastical law applicable to monastic orders. But, by some accounts, both lacked a sophisticated body of law applicable to the general follower, in contrast to Islamic and Judaic traditions, which rejected asceticism.[32] Before the annexation of Burma in the 1850s–'80s, Buddhist populations skimmed the edges of British India – in Tibet, to the north, and in Ceylon, to the south.[33] It was only because of the ambition to absorb majority-Buddhist Burma into British India that the translation of a corpus of Buddhist legal texts became a colonial priority.[34] As Andrew Huxley has argued, it was no accident that a wave of interest in Burmese Buddhist law immediately preceded the British annexation of Burma in 1886. The portrayal by legal Orientalists John Jardine and Em Forchhammer of Burmese Buddhist law as undeveloped set up one justification for the invasion: the British would bring good government and the rule of law to the Burmese people who had hitherto been deprived of it.[35] According to Huxley, their work was tainted by strained logic, poor linguistic skills, and ignorance of huge bodies of texts.[36] Despite all this, Jardine and Forchhammer had huge influence on the colonial judges who came after them.

Both Jardine and Forchhammer disregarded texts and publications from as late as the 1870s that gave Burmese Buddhist law a more substantial character.[37]

---

[31] J. L. Jaini, *Jaina Law. "Bhadrabahu Samhita"* (Arrah: K. D. Prasad, [1916]), x, 95.

[32] On Buddhism, see Alan Gledhill, "Community of Property in the Marriage Law of Burma," in Anderson, *Family Law* 205.

[33] Ceylon became a British crown colony in 1802. It had been briefly under the control of Madras Presidency. Subsequently, it was administered from a different imperial center than British India, namely the Colonial Office, rather than the India Office. See Goonesekere, 194–5. On the paucity of Buddhist legal texts in Ceylon, see Andrew Huxley, "Studying Theravada Legal Literature," *J. Internat. Assoc. Buddhist Stud.* 20 (1997), 65–8.

[34] By Andrew Huxley, see "Positivists and Buddhists," 120–1, 129–30; "Legal Transplants as Historical Data: Exemplum Birmanicum," *J. Imperial Commonwealth Hist.* 37:2 (2009), 167–82. One exceptionally early work was D. Richardson, *The Damathat, or the Laws of Menoo, Translated from the Burmese* (Maulmein: American Baptist Mission Press, 1847). In Ceylon, Buddhist legal texts did not survive into the period of European colonial rule. Sinhalese customary law, known as Kandyan law, was applied in colonial courts. (Roshan de Silva Wijeyeratne, Biswajit Chandra, and Prakash Shah, "South Asian Law" in Katz.)

[35] Equally, these legal Orientalists argued that Burmese Buddhist law was derived from Hindu law. If Burma had once been a Hindu colony under Indian influence, making it part of British India would simply be a return to the old model. See Huxley, "Legal Transplants"; Gledhill, "Community of Property," 205–6.

[36] See Huxley, "Legal Transplants."

[37] See Andrew Huxley, "Is Burmese Law Burmese? John Jardine, Em Forchhammer, and Legal Orientalism," *Austral. J. Asian L.* 10:2 (2008), 191–2, 197–9.

Jardine explained that his interest in the subject was triggered by complaints about the ambiguity of Buddhist law.[38] "At present the Judges are in a position like a blind man feeling his way with his staff and taking the way that is best," he wrote.[39] Jardine published his *Notes on Buddhist Law* in 1883, about a century after Orientalist translations of Hindu and Islamic legal texts had been commissioned by the state. In the *Notes*, he asserted that the vast majority of religious legal texts, written on fragile palm leaves, had not survived over the centuries.[40] Forchhammer claimed that Buddhist law had never existed as a comprehensive body of religious law. In his introduction to Jardine's book, he complained that the "Buddhist law" of marriage and inheritance was a misnomer. "Buddhist law" consisted of rules applicable within the Buddhist monastic tradition only, he wrote. It was contained in texts like the *Vinayapitakam* or Code of Monastic Discipline, and had no effect on lay people. According to Forchhammer, what colonial judges called Buddhist law for marital and inheritance disputes was simply the customary practices of Burmese people who happened to be Buddhist.[41] Other works followed those of Jardine and Forchhammer, including U Gaung's translation of the central surviving texts of Buddhist law, the *Dhammathats* (1898–1902) and collections on Burmese Buddhist law by Chan Toon (1899), Lahiri (1925), and Mootham (1939).[42] Despite these publications, the general sense among British judges remained that Buddhist law was thin by nature and that it was better to rely on the growing case law than on scriptural sources.[43] By the 1930s, judges were referring to the *Dhammathats* not as strictly religious texts, but as records of the customs and rulings of Burmese kings who were incidentally Buddhist.[44]

To a greater extent than the Burmese Buddhists, the Armenian Christians were deemed not to have their own body of religious law. From Bombay to Calcutta, colonial South Asia was home to this mercantile diaspora with extensive links across Eurasia, particularly in the silk trade emanating from the Isfahan suburb of New Julfa in Persia.[45] The former Chief Justice of Bengal,

---

[38] See Hilary McGeachy, "The Invention of Burmese Buddhist Law: A Case Study in Legal Orientalism," *Austral. J. Asian L.* 4 (2002), 34.

[39] John Jardine, *Notes on Buddhist Law* (Rangoon: Government Press, 1883), 1.

[40] Jardine, *Notes*, i–iii.

[41] E. Forchhammer, "Introductory Remarks" in Jardine, *Notes*, viii–ix.

[42] U Gaung, *A Digest of the Burmese Buddhist Law Concerning Inheritance and Marriage: Being a Collection of Texts from Thirty-six Dhammathats* (Rangoon: Superintendent, Government Printing, Burma, 1898–1902); Sisira-Chandra Lahiri, *Principles of Modern Burmese Buddhist Law* (Rangoon: n.p., 1925); O.H. Mootham, *Burmese Buddhist Law* (London: Humphrey Milford, Oxford University Press, 1939).

[43] See Andrew Huxley, "Three Nineteenth-Century Law Book Lists: Burmese Legal History from the Inside," *J. Burma Stud.* 13 (2009), 95–6.

[44] See, for example, *Ma Hnin Zan v. Ma Myaing* AIR 1936 Rang31 at 34.

[45] See Sebouh Aslanian, "Trade Diaspora versus Colonial State: Armenian Merchants, the English East India Company, and the High Court of Admiralty in London, 1748–1752," *Diaspora* 13:1 (2004), 37–100; Ina Baghdiantz McCabe, "Global Trading Ambitions in Diaspora: The

The Inheritance Acts

George Rankin, characterized the Armenians (along with the Parsis) as "persons of whose country of origin the laws could not be ascertained."[46] Two old Armenian law codes had been spoken of in the *mofussil*, but neither was ever produced.[47] One judge named Jackson went further in the Armenian matrimonial case of *Aratoon v. Aratoon* (1868). Jeremy Bentham had commented that Christian scripture, unlike its Islamic counterpart, was vague and unsatisfying as a source of legal rules, being "completely silent on many material points of morality and legislation."[48] Jackson, perhaps a utilitarian like so many other colonial officials of the time, was similarly convinced that Armenians (like other Christians) did not have religious law in the same way that Muslims and Hindus did:

> From the precedents, it appears to have been the practice of this Court to refer to Armenian priests for an exposition of their usages; but this practice is open to many objections. I know of no reason for referring to priests as expounders of civil law. *Among the Mahomedans and Hindoos, the ritual and civil law are so mixed together as to be undistinguishable, and the priests are consequently the persons most able to explain either. But this is not the case with Christians: with them religion is altogether independent of civil law; and I see no reason for placing Armenian Christians in civil matters under the authority of their priests, who are probably as unfit to decide a question of civil law as those of our own Protestant church.* Indeed, many of the Armenian priests, on a requisition from this Court, refused to give an opinion on a point of this description, alleging not only that they were priests, and not jurists, but that it was contrary to the principles of their religion, and to the practice of their priesthood, to meddle with temporal concerns.[49]

Aratoon followed a line of cases that applied English law to Armenians.[50]

Armenians and Their Eurasian Silk Trade, 1530–1750," 27–50 and Sushil Chaudhury, "Trading Networks in a Traditional Diaspora: Armenians in India, c.1600–1800," 51–72, both in *Diaspora Entrepreneurial Networks: Four Centuries of History*, eds. Ina Baghdiantz McCabe, Gelina Harlagtis and Ioanna Peplasis Minoglou (Oxford: Berg, 2005).

[46] Rankin, 25.

[47] Charles Hay Cameron (14 April 1853) in "First Report from the Select Committee on Indian Territories," in *The Sessional Papers ... in the Session 1852–3 (16 & 17 Victoriae) ... Vol. XLI: Reports from Select Committees of the House of Commons, and Evidence: Indian Territories* (London: House of Commons, 1853), 258. These codes may have been the Armenian law codes created between the fourteenth and seventeenth centuries. See Rodolphe Dareste, *Études d'Histoire du Droit* (Paris: Librairie de la Société du Receuil J.-B. Sirey et du Journal du Palais, 1908), I: 126–9.

[48] Bentham in J. Steintrager, "Language and Politics: Bentham on Religion" in Bhikhu Parekh, ed., *Jeremy Bentham: Critical Assessments. Vol. II: Philosophy, Psychology, Religion and Ethics* (London: Routledge, 1993), 97.

[49] *Aratoon Harapiet Aratoon v. Catherina Aratoon* (1856) in William H. Morley, *An Analytical Digest of All the Reported Cases Decided in the Supreme Courts of Judicature in India, in the Courts of the Hon. East-India Co., and on Appeal from India, by Her Majesty in Council. New Series. Vol.1: Containing the cases to the end of the year 1850* (London: Allen, 1852), 182–3 (italics added).

[50] See *Jacob Joseph v. Rowand Ronald* Ind. Dec. (O.S.) I: 68 (1818) and *Emin v. Emin* cited in *Stephen v. Hume* Ind. Dec. (OS), I: 778; both in Jain, *Outlines*, 418. See also Mallampalli, *Race*, 227–8.

Similarly, colonial administrators felt that there was no such thing as religious law in the Zoroastrian tradition. They disagreed over whether this was because of an absence of law from the beginning or a later loss of material. In a letter to the Parsis of Bombay and Surat in 1828, colonial administrator Harry Borradaile commented that the Parsis had "no ancient book of laws which all their tribe accept," "no record of their ancient usages," and "no regular Code of laws."[51] He noted three years earlier, in 1825, that "[t]he Parsis have no laws, for such books as they had before they emigrated from Persia were at that time all lost."[52] Fifteen years later, the Bombay judge Erskine Perry wrote a similar missive, supporting a campaign to create a Parsi code of law: "a very cursory inquiry into your ancient books, laws, and customs satisfies me . . . that you have no such undeviating rules as could at once be adopted into law." To complicate matters, "your people are not agreed amongst themselves as to what the law ought to be."[53]

Zoroastrians did not always have "no law."[54] Particularly before the conquest of Persia by Arab Muslims, Zoroastrian law was a comprehensive body of knowledge, encompassing everything from trusts and contracts to criminal and family law.[55] By the late eighteenth century, after repeated cycles of invasion and migration, knowledge of most ancient Zoroastrian law had been lost in India.[56] A large part of the unique manuscript of the seventh-century *Digest of a Thousand Points of Law* (Pahl. *Mādayān ī Hazār Dādestān*) was obtained in Persia and bequeathed to Parsi institutions in India by Manekji Limji Hataria after his death in 1890. This text was the only exclusively legal work to have survived from pre-Islamic Persia.[57] Hataria was in Persia on behalf of the Society for the Amelioration of the Conditions of the Zoroastrians of Persia.[58] He acquired this text, among others, through preservation efforts.[59] His segment

---

[51] Borradaile cited in "Report into the Usages," 2 in "1862–3 Government of India Bill."

[52] Borradaile cited in *Mithiba'i v. Bana'ji* ILR 5 Bom 506 (1881) at 523.

[53] Letter from Erskine Perry to Bomanjee Hormusjee (Bombay, 21 August 1843), 18 in "1862–3 Government of India Bill."

[54] See Chapter 1 at 72–3.

[55] See Macuch, "Law"; János Jany, "Criminal Justice in Sasanian Persia," *Iranica Antiqua* 42 (2007), 347–86. There is debate as to whether ancient Persian law may be treated as distinctly Zoroastrian religious law, in the style of Islamic or Jewish law, or whether it was the law of a society that happened to be Zoroastrian. Compare Bodil Hjerrild, *Studies in Zoroastrian Family Law: A Comparative Analysis* (Copenhagen: Museum Tusculanum Press, 2002), 9; Maria Macuch, "Mādigān ī Hazār Dādestān (Book of a Thousand Judgments), Pahlavi Law Book from the late Sasanian period (first half of the seventh century)" in Yarshater.

[56] See Introduction at 16–17.

[57] Hjerrild, 9; Macuch, "Mādigān" in Yarshater. I thank Daniel Sheffield for sharing with me his knowledge of the history of this text.

[58] Hataria was instrumental in the lifting of the *jazieh* in 1882. See Chapter 2 at 88. On Hataria, see Pheroza J. Godrej, "Faces from the Mists of Time: Parsi Portraits of Western India (1750–1900)," in Godrej and Punthakey Mistree, 650–2.

[59] "Manekji Limji Hataria, A Parsi Mission to Iran. An English Translation of Manekji's Travel Report (1865)" (accessed on 7 April 2012): http://www.fravahr.org/spip.php?article61.

The Inheritance Acts

of the manuscript became part of the M. N. Hataria library in Poona before that library was moved to the Anjuman Atash Behram and finally the K. R. Cama Oriental Institute (both in Bombay). Another piece of the manuscript was sold to Tehmuras Dinshah Anklesaria in Persia around 1872.[60] This portion was also brought to India by its new owner. During the first quarter of the twentieth century, parts of the *Digest* were published in facsimile edition in its original Pahlavi (1901–12) or translated into German by Christian Bartholomae (1910– 23).[61] In either language, the text remained inaccessible to most Parsis and Britons in colonial India. English translations had been in progress since the late nineteenth century, but none was published until the 1930s.[62] By this time, Parsi personal law had been codified once with another round of revisions nearing completion. L. Bogdanov published English versions of the German translations in 1931–6.[63] The first edition of Sohrab Jamshedji Bulsara's more extensive English translation appeared in 1937. Bulsara's work had been commissioned by the Parsi Panchayat through a competitive process some time between 1910 and 1912, and it took decades to complete.[64] Colonial lawyers would regard it as the leading text on ancient Zoroastrian law, although it would not be as well received by later scholars.[65] Bulsara prefaced his translation by trumpeting the text's resurrection: "It has been assumed by previous writers, without proper reason, that the Sasanian Persians had no codified law! This was a surprising assumption by scholars who knew that the ancient Iranians possessed codified laws from the most primitive times, and that seven of their

---

[60] See T. D. Anklesaria, *The Social Code of the Parsis in Sasanian Times or Mādigān i Hazār Dādistān, Part II* (Bombay: Fort Printing Press, 1912), 3; Sohrab J. Bulsara, *The Laws of the Ancient Persians* (Mumbai: K. R. Cama Oriental Institute, 1999; reprint of 1937 ed.), 10–11.

[61] J. J. Modi, ed., *Mādigān-i-Hazār Dādistān. A Photozincographed Facsimile of a MS belonging to the Mānockji Limji Hoshang Hātariā Library in the Zarthoshti Anjuman Ātashbeharām* (Poona: Government Photozingraphic Department, 1901); Anklesaria. By Christian Bartholomae, see *Über ein sasanidisches Rechtsbuch* (Heidelberg: Winter, 1910); "Beiträge zur Kenntnis des Sasanidischen Rechts," Mitteliranische Studien IV, *Wiener Zeitschrift für die Kunde des Morgenlandes* Separat-Abdruck aus Band 27 [1913], 347–74; *Zum sasanidischen Recht I–V* (Heidelberg: Winter, 1918–23).

[62] See Modi, "Introduction" and letter to T. D. Anklesaria from E. W. West (Munich, 5 October 1887) in Anklesaria, 18–24.

[63] The following translations by L. Bogdanov appeared in the *JKRCOI*: "Notes on Sasanian Law from the German of Prof. Ch. Bartholomae (Heidelberg)," 18 (1931), i–vii, 1–59; the introductory "Notes on a Sasanian Law-Book," 21 (1932), i–v, 1–40; "Notes on Sasanian Law: Part II," 26 (1934), 1–80; "Notes on Sasanian Law. Part III," 30 (1936), 1–103.

[64] Modi, "Introduction" in Anklesaria, 15–16; Bulsara, 9–10.

[65] See Jamshedji Kanga cited in letter from Muhammad Zafrulla Khan to Rabbi Yitzhak (Isaac) ha-Levi Herzog (Delhi, 26 November 1945) in Amihai Radzyner, "Between Scholar and Jurist: The Controversy over the Research of Jewish Law using Comparative Methods at the Early Time of the Field," *J. Law Religion* 23 (2007–8), 247. I am grateful to Nathan Brun for bringing this work to my attention. For criticisms of the quality of Bulsara's translation, see Macuch, "Mādigān" in Yarshater; Hjerrild, 10.

138   *Law and Identity in Colonial South Asia: Parsi Legal Culture*

twenty-one holy books, treated of a huge field of law which covered much more domains than the laws of other nations did."

Bulsara acknowledged that there were huge gaps in the manuscript he had translated, even with the Hataria and Anklesaria portions united.[66] The *Digest* also referred to major works that had not survived, among them "a great work of codified law which is named Dâtastân Nâmak or Book of Laws," along with "other legal treatises and codes," and "statutes and decrees passed by the Imperial legislature" of the Persian empire.[67]

There were other Zoroastrian texts containing religio-legal material. The leading surviving text on ritual purity was the *Vendidad* (Av. *Vīdaēuuō.dāta*, Pahl. *Wīdēwdād*); it contained elements of civil and criminal law.[68] The *rivayats* documented exchanges between Zoroastrians in early modern Persia and India on doctrinal dilemmas.[69] These occasionally described the type of disputes that would be framed as religious trust suits later in the colonial courts.[70] Colonial case law contained a few fleeting references to these texts.[71] But in general, neither the *Vendidad* nor the *rivayats* were mined by Parsi law makers as they might have been. Here was a suggestion that the reinvention of Parsi law was a creative process because its makers wished it to be so and not simply because of the declared thinness of ancient texts.[72] In this way, the construction of Parsi law in British India differed sharply from the text-dependent processes that forged Anglo-Hindu and -Islamic law.

---

[66] Bulsara, 10–12.

[67] Ibid., 20.

[68] Although German and French translations of the *Vendidad* were available by the early nineteenth century, it was not until 1864 that the Avestan text (with Pahlavi additions) was published in Gujarati and English translations. See K. E. Kanga, *Vañdīdādanī pehelī tathā bījī paragaraṭ no Gujarātī tarajumo (darek śabdnā vyākaraṇ tathā kholosā sāthe (Vendidad translated into Gujerati with grammatical and explanatory notes)* (Bombay: Duftur Ashkara Pres, 1864); Arthur Henry Bleeck, *Avesta: The Religious Books of the Parsees; from Professor Spiegel's German Translation of the Original Manuscripts. Vol. 1: Vendidad* (London: Bernard Quaritch, 1864). See also Pestanji Kuvarji Motiwala, "The Criminal Law of Ancient Iran," 183–99 in J. J. Modi, ed., *The K. R. Cama Memorial Volume: Essays on Iranian Subjects* (Bombay: Fort Printing Press, 1900; reprinted Mumbai: K. R. Cama Oriental Institute, 2005); William W. Malandra, "Vendīdād" in Yarshater; Stausberg, *Zarathustra*, 42–6.

[69] The most thorough overview of the *rivayats* is Paymaster, 66–84. See also Writer, 120; Stiles Maneck, 34–8; Rose, *Zoroastrianism: An Introduction*, 174–5. For the *rivayats* themselves, see Manockji R. Unvala, ed. *Darab Hormazyar's Rivayat* (Bombay: British India Press, 1922); B. N. Dhabhar, *The Persian Rivayats of Hormazyar Framarz and Others* (Bombay: Cama Institute, 1932), 347–57; Vitalone.

[70] See, for instance, the Surat *dakhma* dispute in Paymaster, 79–81.

[71] For instance, see *Meherwanjee Nuoshirwanjee v. Awan Baee* 2 Borradaile's Reports 209 (1825) at 220; "Exhibit H: Letter from Jamasp Edulji Dastur Poona to Viccaji Meherjibhai," 296 in *Pestonji Jeevanji v. Chinoy* JCPC case papers; "Beaman. Notes in Parsi *Panchayat* Case," 24, 45–8.

[72] Contrast J. J. Modi's "Introduction" to Anklesaria, 13.

The Inheritance Acts

Although a surprising array of Zoroastrian texts were not considered usable in the refashioning of Parsi personal law, law firms like Wadia Ghandy and Co. kept a selection of Zoroastrian religious and historical works (in English or Gujarati translation) on their shelves.[73] Why keep such books at all? From 1865 on, the Parsi law of marriage and inheritance was determined by statutes that made no reference to Zoroastrian sacred texts. By the late nineteenth century, most other areas of law were governed by legislation, which usually applied to everyone in India. However, the Zoroastrian books in solicitors' law libraries were consulted not on legal points, but on theological and historical questions arising in religious trust suits. Although governed by the quasi-territorial law of trusts, these suits were the real point of entry for the Zoroastrian religion into law.

Colonial judges came to the rescue of some of the smaller religious minorities. The courts ushered Sikhs and Jains under the personal law umbrella through the legal fiction that they were Hindu subsects, framing derogations from Hindu law as special customs.[74] Jews were eventually entitled to their own personal law for matrimonial and inheritance cases under the Colonial Letters Patent Act of 1863.[75] For Zoroastrians, a series of judicial pronouncements starting with *Naoroji v. Rogers* (1866–7) firmly established that English law was the default for Zoroastrians living in presidency towns like Bombay.[76] As the Parsi advocate and Persianist P. B. Vachha commented in 1934, "If possible, the Parsis are more law-laden than other Indian communities. They are not only subject to all the British-Indian Statutes of general application, but the early English judges, finding that the Bombay Parsis had no special systems of law of their own, with mistaken benevolence dumped on their loyal and devoted heads the whole of the uncertain and amorphous Common Law of England."[77] Parsis took the law into their own hands in a technical sense, developing the legal skills to push through legislation that would loosen the grip of English law. The 1865 matrimonial and inheritance statutes came almost a century after Hastings's 1772 promise of personal law for Hindus and Muslims. But because Parsis had to do it

---

[73] For the holdings of the Wadia Ghandy law library circa 1911, see Mistry, *Reminiscences* [1911], 92–111 (accessed on 10 November 2012): http://hosted.law.wisc.edu/wordpress/sharafi/law-library-of-a-colonial-bombay-firm/.

[74] See *Chotay Lall v. Chunnoo Lall* 6 IA 15 (1878) (Jains); *Rani Bhagwan Koer v. Jogendra Chandra Bose* 30 IA 249 (1903) (Sikhs).

[75] Compare *Musleah v. Musleah* Ind. Dec. (OS) I: 894 (1844) with *Rachel Benjamin v. Benjamin Solomon Benjamin* ILR 50 Bom 369 (1926). It is hard to understand why Indian Jews were left out of Hastings's 1772 promise of personal law. Company officials would have known of Jewish law from Europe. M. P. Jain has speculated that the Company may not have realized that there were Jews in India (Jain, 420). See generally Joan G. Roland, *The Jewish Communities of India: Identity in a Colonial Era* (New Brunswick, NJ: Transaction, 1998).

[76] *Naoroji Beramji v. Henry Rogers* 4 Bom HC Rep 1 (1866–7); cited in *Peshotam Hormasji Dustoor v. Meherba'i* ILR 13 Bom 302 (1889) at 305–6; *Bai Shirinbai v. Kharshedji Nasarvanji Masalavala* ILR 22 Bom 430 (1896) at 435. See also Rana (1934), 2–3, 131–2.

[77] P. B. V., "Parsi Law. By F. A. Rana," *TI* (13 July 1934), 7.

140   *Law and Identity in Colonial South Asia: Parsi Legal Culture*

themselves, they developed skills that neither Hindu nor Muslim communities gained en masse until later and in response to different stimuli.

USING WILLS

In common-law jurisdictions, inheritance law operated along two tracks. Where there was a valid will, the law of testamentary succession applied. If there was no will or if the will was invalid, the law of intestate succession determined the default distribution of property among heirs. The Parsi fight to pull away from English law took place in the latter realm: the Parsi Acts applied only to intestacy. What happened in the law of wills? The English law of testamentary disposition shifted the architecture of family life not only among Parsis, but among Hindus and Muslims, too. Property holders received new powers that were utterly foreign and especially contrary to the foundational principles of Hindu law.[78] English law (and its influence) gave testators the unfettered freedom to write a will in favor of anyone. Maximizing testators' powers made property, especially land, more alienable and maneuverable. It reinforced the hard-edged free-market ideology in vogue among colonial administrators, themselves intellectual progeny of the Scottish Enlightenment and utilitarianism.[79] It also undermined the family unit, inviting senior family members to support certain relatives instead of others or not to support family members at all.[80] From a colonial perspective, the power of testamentary disposition was an attempt to speed South Asians through the purported stages of historical development, pushing them "from status to contract."[81] According to the early Henry Maine, strong ties to the collectivity into which one was born – whether the extended family, caste, or community – were oppressive and restrictive.[82] He failed to see that these same affiliations lay at the heart of South Asian social identities and economic interactions, a point illuminated by the work of Ritu Birla.[83]

---

[78] See Radhabinod Pal, *The History of the Law of Primogeniture with Special Reference to India, Ancient and Modern. Tagore Law Lectures, 1925* (Calcutta: University of Calcutta, 1929), 487.

[79] See Karuna Mantena, *Alibis of Empire: Henry Maine and the Ends of Liberal Imperialism* (Princeton, NJ: Princeton University Press, 2010), 160–5. On the maximization of property's alienability under colonial law, see Lloyd I. Rudolph and Susanne Hoeber Rudolph, *The Modernity of Tradition: Political Development in India* (Chicago: University of Chicago Press, 1967), 288–90.

[80] On the duty of support owed by the head of the Hindu joint family under classical Hindu law, see Donald R. Davis, *The Spirit of Hindu Law* (Cambridge: Cambridge University Press, 2000), 84–5, 95.

[81] Henry Sumner Maine, *Ancient Law: Its Connection with the Early History of Society and Its Relation to Modern Ideas* (London: John Murray, 1887), 168–70. See also Mantena, 73–82.

[82] See Henderson at note 85. See also David Washbrook, "Law, State, and Agrarian Society in Colonial India," *MAS* 15:3 (1981), 649–721.

[83] Birla, *Stages of Capital*.

The Inheritance Acts

Anglo-Hindu law was drastically affected by the introduction of the power to write a will. There were Hindu populations that did not follow the joint or Hindu undivided family (HUF) system.[84] However, in the classical tradition of those who did structure themselves through the HUF, wills were unknown. In its archetypal form, the HUF consisted of a husband and wife, along with their adult sons, and the sons' wives and children. The HUF was a living arrangement: this group typically lived together under one roof. It was also a property-holding device. In the joint family, it was not the individual who owned most property, but the HUF. The property held by the HUF was deemed "ancestral," as distinct from the self-acquired property earned by an adult male through his own individual efforts.[85] From the early eighteenth century, the power of testamentary disposition for self-acquired *and* ancestral property was gradually introduced through the courts and then by the legislatures.[86] In a complementary development solidified during the 1860s–'80s, the courts further eroded the Hindu joint family by facilitating partition, the process through which a member of the joint family could break away, taking a share of the family's collective property with him.[87] Later, protection for the joint family came in the form of special tax status for the HUF with the development of income tax legislation.[88] But it came late – in the 1920s – and without touching the power of testamentary disposition or partition, by then firmly entrenched in law.

The colonial courts tried to maximize testamentary powers among Muslims, too. The Hanafite school of legal interpretation (from which Anglo-Islamic law drew) permitted property holders to bequeath up to one third of their property by will without the consent of their heirs. The other two thirds devolved to prescribed family members in set proportions.[89] Judges did their best to loosen the one-third rule. In many cases, they did so by defining consent expansively.

---

[84] Tarapada Mukherjee and J. C. Wright, "An Early Testamentary Document in Sanskrit," *Bull. Sch. Orient. Afr. Stud.* 42:2 (1979), 320. I thank Donald R. Davis Jr. for this reference.

[85] This distinction existed in the Mitakshara school of Hindu law that effectively governed Hindus in most of India, but not in the Dayabhaga school (governing Bengal). See Ram Charan Mitra, *The Law of Joint Property and Partition in British India. Tagore Law Lecture 1895* (Calcutta: Thacker Spink and Co., 1897), 12, 178.

[86] *Nagalutchmee Ummal v. Gopoo Nadaraja Chetty* 6 MIA 309 (1854–7); G. S. Henderson, *The Law of Testamentary Devise as Administered in India* (Calcutta: Thacker Spink and Co., 1889), 19–60; Arun Mohan, *Princely States and the Reform in Hindu Law* (Bombay: N. M. Tripathi, 1990), 201–20. The power to make a will was granted to Hindus in Bombay in 1726 (*Mancharji Pestanji v. Narayan Lakshumanji* 1 Bom H Ct Reps 77 at 82). On legislation, see Rankin, 52–5.

[87] See the 1866 case of *Appovier alias Seetarameir v. Rama Subba Aiyan and others* 20 Eng. Rep. 173, reproducing 11 MIA 75; Mitra, *Law of Joint Property*, 299–308; Debendra Nath Datta, *Law and Practice Relating to Partition in British India* (Calcutta: Butterworth and Co., 1928), 1–3, 162–3; H. S. Gour, "Law of Partition," *Bom LR* (journal) 4 (1902), 221–43, 248–68; Sturman, 116–24.

[88] See Eleanor Newbigin, *The Hindu Family and the Emergence of Modern India: Law, Citizenship and Community* (Cambridge: Cambridge University Press, 2013), chapter 2.

[89] Neil B. E. Baillie, *A Digest of Moohummudan Law on the Subjects to Which It Is Usually Applied by British Courts of Justice in India* (London: Smith, Elder and Co., 1887), 233.

The colonial courts capitalized on the notion of implied or constructive consent: the heirs did not need to *explicitly* consent to having more than a third of the estate willed away. Through their acts or omissions, heirs may have inadvertently consented to the testator's derogation from the one-third rule. When they did so, more than a third of the estate could be diverted from Islamic law's set distribution scheme.[90]

Across South Asia, colonized populations were startled by the vast powers of testamentary disposition granted by colonial law. In Ceylon, all bodies of precolonial personal law imposed on estates a duty of maintenance for dependents. But the colonial Wills Ordinance of 1844 introduced complete testamentary freedom, with the result that many family members were cut off from support.[91] For Parsis, the colonial courts quickly established that testators had the right to disinherit close family members, including sons, brothers, and nephews.[92] In the words of one Privy Council judgment, "there is no restraint upon the testamentary power of disposition by a Parsi."[93] English-style testamentary freedom seemed to have been unknown in precolonial Zoroastrian society. Under the Sasanians in Persia, the power of testamentary disposition applied only to particular types of property in an estate. Property received as a gift (one type of Av. *xwēšīh* property) and property bequeathed for charitable or religious purposes (Av. *ruwān dāštan* and *ahlawdād* property) could be willed away, although the latter could not constitute more than a third of a person's estate.[94] The bulk of most estates belonged to the joint family (Av. *xwāstagdārīh* property). The head of the family was merely the possessor of this property: he had the right to dispose of the income produced by this property, but not of the property itself.[95] Furthermore, a father could not disinherit his son under Sasanian law. If an heir misbehaved, a father could require that his future estate be placed under the rough equivalent of a trust, ensuring the supervision of the property's management and use.[96]

---

[90] *Daulatram Khushalchand v. Abdul Kayum Nurudin* ILR 26 Bom 497 (1902). See also *Mussamut Hurmut-ool-Nissa Begum v. Allahdia Khan and Hajee Hidayat* 17 Suth. WR 108 (1892); *Sharifa Bibi v. Gulam Mahomed Dastagir Khan* ILR 16 Mad 43 (1893); *Musammat Fakhr Jahan Begam v. Muhammad Abdul Ghani Khan and another, Muhammad Hamid Ullah Khan and others* 5 Oudh LJ 49 at 66 (1918); *Abdul Rahiman v. Uthumansa* AIR 1925 Mad 997 at 999–1001; *Mohammad Ali Khan v. Nisar Ali Khan* AIR 1928 Oudh 67 at 71, 76–7; *Mahomed Hussein Haji Gulam Mahomet Ajam v. Aishabai* ILR 1935 Bom 84 at 90; *Ma Khatoon v. Ma Mya* ILR 1936 Rang 448 at 452.

[91] Savitri Goonesekere, "Colonial Legislation and Sri Lanka Family Law: The Legacy of History," in *Asian Panorama*, eds. K. M. de Silva et al. (Delhi: Vikas Pub. House, 1990), 201.

[92] *Meherwanji v. Poojeeabhai* 1 Borr. 141 (1825); *Hormusjee v. Cooverbhaee.*

[93] *Hormusjee v. Cooverbhaee* 168.

[94] Maria Macuch, "Inheritance. I. Sasanian Period" in Yarshater (accessed on 29 July 2010): http://www.iranica.com/articles/inheritance-i.

[95] Ibid.

[96] Bulsara, 54.

The Inheritance Acts

Inheritance practices among Parsis during the millennium between their arrival in India and colonial rule were unclear. However, we can say that at least during the eighteenth and the first half of the nineteenth century (and probably before), a weak version of the joint family existed, particularly in wealthy mercantile circles.[97] Being part of a Parsi joint family (a term never used explicitly) did not necessarily mean living under the same roof, but it did mean eating, trading, and observing certain religious ceremonies together.[98] On death, a man's wealth went to his sons collectively. They could choose to "live separately," a decision that would dissolve or partition the joint family. In such an event, each son inherited an equal share of the property. Here was the custom held up by the antiprimogeniture petitioners whose campaign led to the first Parsi statute in 1837.

An 1856 Privy Council suit revealed vestiges of the joint family's structure.[99] A Parsi in Surat named Modee Rustomjee Hormusjee died in 1849 without any male heirs. He left a will that bequeathed his property to his wife and daughters. His brother challenged this distribution of property, arguing that, by the custom of Surat's Parsis, the property of a man who had no sons went to his brothers or nephews, not to the man's wife or daughters. Presumably, the brother was referring to a situation in which the testator and his brothers were part of a joint family, such that the property was held by several co-parcenors (in common-law language). In the case, the testator's wife, daughters, and grand-daughter acknowledged that the challenger's description of the custom was correct – but only while the joint family remained intact. They reminded the brother that, in 1823, he and the testator had "divided the little property of their father between them, and having executed releases to each other respectively, they separated, and they took their meals separate [sic], and traded separately. Therefore, according to the custom of the world, and the rules of their caste, they, the wife and daughters of the deceased ... were [the testator's] heir-esses."[100] In a Privy Council case decided in 1837, another wealthy Parsi merchant from Surat had used his will to urge his sons to remain together, along with their wives and children. He allowed for the dissolution of the joint family, but regarded it as a fall from grace: "And if they cannot live together and they do not agree, *as this is a bad world*, then they may live separately; and, according as it is written, each shall receive for his own expenses, and they shall eat separately."[101] The Privy Councillors suspected this will to be forged.[102]

---

[97] See, for example, Q. in the Corner, II: 4; "A Parsee Deed of Partition More than 150 Years Old: A form of slavery referred to therein," in *Anthropological Papers*, ed. J. J. Modi (Bombay: [British India Press, 1912]), 167–72.

[98] See 1837 case of *Khoorshed-jee Manik-jee v. Mehrwan-jee Khoorshed-jee and Dada-bhaee Khoorshed-jee* 18 Eng. Rep. 173 (1809–1865) at 174–5, reproducing 1 MIA 431 (1836–7) at 433–6.

[99] *Hormusjee v. Cooverbhaee.*

[100] Ibid., 451.

[101] *Khoorshed-jee Manik-jee v. Mehrwan-jee*, 435. Italics added.

[102] Ibid., 440.

144   *Law and Identity in Colonial South Asia: Parsi Legal Culture*

Even so, the text's sentiments were plausible, reflecting typical social arrangements of the era among Parsi elites in the *mofussil*.

By the later nineteenth century, the Parsi joint family ceased to be standard in Bombay and the *mofussil*. It received no mention in the 1862–3 talks that led to the passage of the Parsi Intestate Succession Act of 1865, and parties to inheritance cases no longer mentioned brothers' families eating, trading, or living together. The widespread use of wills among the wealthy, encouraged by the courts' willingness to enforce these at the expense of preexisting customary norms, may have helped undermine the joint family.[103] Before the 1837 Act, individual Parsis used wills to protect themselves against primogeniture, using one English device to undermine another. These wills adopted as their starting point the equal distribution of property among the testator's sons, in conformity with the Parsi mode of effecting partition of the joint family.[104] However, wealthy Parsis quickly realized that wills could do more than just shield an estate from primogeniture. The power of testamentary disposition could be wielded to induce particular types of behavior in family members. Testators began adding conditions that would trigger an unequal distribution between sons if one son disobeyed his father's wishes.

One of the earliest cases reflecting this use of wills was *Mihirwanjee Ruttonjee v. His brothers Poonjeea Bhaee and Dada Bhaee* (1815). Translating from the Gujarati, the judgment reproduced the full text of the Parsi will in question, a practice that would become rare in subsequent case law.[105] Ruttonjee Manukjee was a wealthy Parsi merchant in Surat. His will, written in 1808, began with a cosmic preamble that referred to Zoroastrian eschatology and the fragility of human life: "In the name of the Omniscient being, the Almighty Dispenser of benefits to mankind, the Fountain Head of Wisdom, by whose permission this writing is written. Whosoever is born in this world most assuredly shall appear before the Throne of Truth. There is no reliance to be placed on the Life of man. He is momentarily subject to annihilation. Revolution succeeds revolution, nothing on earth is permanent."[106] The will then described the father's troubled relationship with his son, the future plaintiff: "My son Mihirwanjee is an exceeding dissolute character. He will not attend to my advice. He has spent

---

[103] See *Hormusjee v. Cooverbhaee* 449, 460–1, 463.

[104] See, for example, the will written some time before 1857 in *Frámji Kávasji Marker v. Hormasji Kávasji Marker* 1 Bom. HCt Rep. 220 (1862–5).

[105] For a similar early judgment that included the full text of a Parsi will, see the 1837 case of *Manik-jee v. Mehrwan-jee*, 432–8 9. Compare to a late colonial case like *Kaikhushro Bezonji Capadia v. Shirinbai Bezonji Capadia* ILR 43 Bom 88 (1919).

[106] From the 1815 case of *Mihirwanjee Ruttunjee v. his brothers Poonjeea Bhaee and Dada Bhaee, sons of Ruttunjee Manukjee Paruk* 1 Borradaile's Reports 141 (1800–20) at 142–3. For other similar references to Zoroastrian divine forces, see *Manik-jee v. Mehrwan-jee*, 432 (alleged will of 1815); *Shirinbai v. Ratanbai and others* ILR 43 Bom 845 at 847 (will of 1872).

The Inheritance Acts

sums of money on vicious pursuits and given himself up to dissolute habits. . . . Great is the uneasiness I suffer on his account."[107]

Earlier, the father had paid a large debt on Mihirwanjee's behalf on the condition that Mihirwanjee would agree, in writing, to "renounce his wickedness and live a sober and virtuous life" or lose much of his inheritance.[108] Mihirwanjee continued living recklessly, and the father's will entrusted management of his business warehouse to his other two sons, the defendants in the case. The will also gave Mihirwanjee one last chance: "Should Mihirwanjee attend to his Brothers' admonition, abjure his vicious habits, no longer disgrace my name, and conduct himself as his two brothers do, then my property is to be equally divided between them, neither shall one Brother's share exceed that of another; but if he will not attend to their advice, nor forsake his evil propensities, and should wish to have his share of my property separate, then the House purchased from Hajee Hoossain, Rupees 2,000 in Cash, and a proportion of the Cooking Utensils being given to him, he must separate himself from my House and Family, and has no further claim whatsoever to any property of mine."[109]

In court, Mihirwanjee's brothers insisted that they were only carrying out their father's wishes: Mihirwanjee had not changed his ways after his father's death. Mihirwanjee protested that the will must be a forgery or that it was written when his father was not of sound mind "because his Father, who knew the world well, *could not have made [a will] at variance with the Laws of every Sect, whether Hindoo, Moohummudan, or Parsee.*"[110] The case moved through three levels of court. Each court took the predictably English approach. On the first appeal, the Provincial Council found it perfectly reasonable for a father to use his will to induce good behavior from a son. "His being cut off with so small a Portion was the natural and proper consequence of his own misconduct," declared the judges.[111] One level up, the Sudder Dewanny Adawlut agreed. Under the terms of his father's will, Mihirwanjee was entitled to the house, money, and cooking pots alone. Rejecting the new system that gave wealthy Parsi fathers more power within their own families, the son refused to accept a thing. He left the court and his natal family without taking a rupee.[112]

Even as Parsi merchants began to use wills in the first half of the nineteenth century, testamentary freedom was not clearly accepted by community authorities. In an 1843 case, the Parsi Panchayat of Surat vacillated on the question of whether testamentary disposition was legal according to "caste usage," issuing at least one negative report on consultation by the colonial courts.[113] However, as the Company ceded power to the British Crown in mid-century, the practice

---

[107] *Mihirwanjee Ruttonjee v. his brothers*, 143.
[108] Ibid., 145.
[109] Ibid., 143–4.
[110] Ibid., 142. Italics added.
[111] Ibid., 146.
[112] Ibid., 147.
[113] *Burjorjee Bheemjee v. Ferozshaw Dhunjeeshaw* 1 SDA Bom 206 (1820–40).

146 Law and Identity in Colonial South Asia: Parsi Legal Culture

of consulting community authorities faded. Amrita Shodhan has documented this pattern in Hindu and Muslim intracommunity suits of the 1860s.[114] Parsi cases reflected the same tendency even before the onset of the Raj.[115] By 1856, when the Privy Council confirmed the unrestricted right of testamentary disposition among Parsis, the power was firmly established in case law, making community opposition irrelevant.[116]

From the mid-nineteenth century, those who wished to have Parsi wills invalidated no longer tried to pit the power of testamentary disposition against Parsi custom. Instead, they made arguments that promoted the connected colonial ideals of the autonomous, liberal subject and the easy circulation of property in the market. A line of cases in the early twentieth century documented relatives' attempts to have wills set aside on the basis of the testator's mental incapacity or because he (or she) was under the undue influence of another.[117] The ability to exercise free will was, of course, an essential feature of the liberal subject. Late colonial courts were also partial to the free-market argument that the dead ought not to put excessive restraints on what the living could do with inherited property.[118] The property in question usually included a mix of real estate (especially "bungalows," meaning sizeable houses), investments (especially "Government Paper" or promissory loan notes of the government of India), businesses, and cash.[119] Jewelry and formal saris were often family heirlooms and part of Parsi estates, too.[120] In a line of protracted late colonial suits, wills that attempted to create trusts to fund Zoroastrian ceremonies were contested by

[114] Shodhan, *Question*, 82, 192.

[115] See Chapter 5 at 197; *Hormusjee v. Cooverbhaee*, 460.

[116] *Hormusjee v. Cooverbhaee*, 458–62.

[117] In the judgment notebooks of D. D. Davar, see *Byramji Jehangirji v. Cooverbai* (Suit No. 3 of 1907) in "Judgments (5 January 1909–7 October 1909)," 1–51; *Bapuji Nusserwanji Vatchagandy v. Sorabji Ardeshir Vatchagandy* (Suit No. 17 of 1909) in "Judgments (22 July 1910–24 December 1910)," 1–152; *Bai Jaiji Nusserwanji Kathoke v. Bai Soonabai* (Suit No. 657 of 1912) in "Judgments (11 January 1912–25 July 1912)," 1–14; *Jerbai H. Warden v. Bai Ratanji J. A. Wadia* (Suit No. 18 of 1913) in "Judgments (1914)," 1–22 (BHC).

[118] *Bapuji Rustomji Kerawalla v. Haji Esmail Haji Ahmed* ILR 46 Bom 694 (1922).

[119] For example, see *Merbai and Ratanji Jivanji v. Perozbai* ILR 5 Bom. 269 (1881); *Mithiba'i v. Bana'ji; Dossibai Framji Marker v. Cooverbai Hormusji Marker* ILR 32 Bom. 575 (1908); *Sirdar Nowroji Pudumji v. Putlibai, wife of Nadershaw Bomanji Vakil* (Suit No. 1248 of 1912), 1–24; *Merwanji Jehangir Vakil v. Manaji Cooverji Rajeshirke* (Suit No. 1201 of 1912), 1–43; all in D. D. Davar Judgments (14 January 1913–18 December 1913; BHC). See also *Jamsetji Nassarwanji Ginwalla v. Hirjibhai Naoroji Anklesaria* ILR 37 Bom. 158 (1913).

[120] The will of Rustom Vakil of Ahmedabad discussed jewelry at length: "In order that no misunderstanding of any kind may arise, I confidently assert that my wife has not the slightest right to any of my ornaments, and no right whatever of hers prevails over the same. I have not presented any of my ornaments or jewelry to my wife. All the ornaments used to be given to her only for wearing. Therefore my wife has no right whatever to my ornaments or jewelry." Nonetheless, the family chronicler noted that when the will was read, the testator's wife "dropped all pretenses of mourning and threw an almighty tantrum, whereupon her eldest son Jehangir placated her by allowing her to keep whatever jewels she wanted. . . . She never gave up the jewels, and after her death at the age of 80, willed it all to her youngest daughter-in-law."

The Inheritance Acts

relatives who stood to inherit the portion intended for religious purposes. These litigants tried to harness classical principles of English trust law, such as the rule that noncharitable trusts could not exist in perpetuity.[121] This rule, too, was reinforced by the desire to maximize the circulation of property in the market.

By the late colonial period, the use of wills was deeply entrenched in Parsi life, particularly among the wealthy. English law triumphed because it appealed to these elites' personal self-interest vis-à-vis close family members. Wills gave parents (especially fathers) a powerful tool for controlling their offspring (especially sons). As Dinshah Davar declared in one 1910 case in which a son, "possibly one of nature's failures," had been disinherited in his mother's will: "A son has no right to behave as an undutiful son and then expect parents to leave him fortunes or shares in fortunes."[122] And yet, critical voices did exist. One fascinating attack on the concept of broad testators' powers emerged in 1938, as Parsi intestacy law was being revised. Delegates of the Parsi Chief Matrimonial Court submitted a collective response to the bill that would become the Indian Succession (Amendment) Act of 1939. Kaikhosru K. Dadachanji was a Parsi physician and delegate of the matrimonial court, as well as a former expert witness in that court.[123] He added his own individual comments to the delegates' collective statement, going beyond the issue of intestacy and proposing restrictions on the freedom of Parsi testamentary disposition. Dadachanji wrote that the ability to dispose of one's property by will was an "absolute and arbitrary power" that was "dangerous in itself, looking at the facts of human nature." If the rules of intestate succession reflected the prevailing public opinion of the Parsi community, why apply them to the property of intestates alone? "[N]o individual should be allowed the absolute power to dispose of his property by Will in such a manner as to defeat the objects of the law of intestate succession and flout public opinion." In other words, permitting people to sidestep their obligations to family members was contrary to "justice, equity and good conscience," that favorite standard of colonial Indian law.[124]

[Jehangir Vakil, "A Brief History of the Vakil Family of Ahmedabad," 16–17; I am grateful to Jehangir Vakil for sharing this unpublished manuscript with me.] See also Pheroza Punthakey Mistree and Pheroze J. Godrej, "Style and Elegance: Parsi Costumes in the 18th and 19th Century" in their edited volume, 609, 614.

[121] See Chapter 6 at 264–8.

[122] *Rustomji Edjulji Laher v. Jehangir Edulji Laher* (Suit No. 4 of 1910) in "D. D. Davar, Judgments (22 July 1910–24 December 1910)," 1–2 (BHC).

[123] Dadachanji's name appeared in lists of delegates involved in PCMC cases, 1940–44 ["Registrar's Minute Book from 15 October 1937 to 10 February 1948," I: 490, II: 201, 232, 257, 282 (BHC).] He gave expert medical testimony in Suits No. 1 of 1930 (I: 51–2) and 3 of 1930 (I: 69–70), both in PCMC Notebook 1929–35. See also Puñjābhāī, 387.

[124] "Further additions to the Bill, proposed by Mr. K. K. Dadachanji," in "Bombay. No.14 – From the Secretary to the Government of Bombay, Home Department, No. 9944/3-B, dated the 1 February, 1938, and enclosures" in "Paper No. II: Opinions on the Indian Succession (Amendment) Bill," 28 in "The Indian Succession (Amendment) Act 1939 (26 November 1938–8 August 1939)." Similarly, see Q. in the Corner, II: 8. See also Chapter 1 at note 56.

Dadachanji proposed the Islamic "one-third" rule for Zoroastrians. The text of his proposed section gave Parsi testators the freedom to bequeath up to a third of their property to anyone by will. The other two thirds would be distributed according to the rules developed for intestates. Dadachanji presented his plan as a return to ancient Persian law at a time when Parsis were identifying with Persianness in newly pronounced, scientized ways: "As a matter of fact, the existing Mahomedan Law of Testamentary and Intestate Succession has been actually based upon the ancient Persian law of the Parsis which prevailed during the Sasanian Empire." Inverting lines of provenance and gratitude, Dadachanji suggested that it was not Parsis who owed thanks to Muslims for the sensible one-third principle, but Muslims who ought to thank Parsis. Furthermore, the unbridled English power of testamentary disposition was not only pernicious, but also anomalous, even by Western standards. In "the civilized world" (meaning Europe and America), an unfettered power of testamentary disposition existed only among the "Anglo-Saxon races." In Scottish law, the "Law of Legatim" restricted the arbitrary power of testators. France and other continental jurisdictions had similar controls. Dadabhanji claimed that the Parsis had staged public protests when the full power of testamentary disposition was first applied to them but that they had been unable to reverse the rule.[125]

Dadachanji's critique was too radical to be taken up. By the late 1930s, wide powers of testamentary disposition for Parsis were deeply entrenched in legislation and case law and had been exercised by Parsi property owners for more than a century. Like other South Asian communities, the Parsis bowed to the influence of English law on wills. Intestacy was different. First, the Parsis successfully rejected the English rule of primogeniture as it applied to Parsis who died without valid wills. Second, they also reversed the application of coverture, the infamous English doctrine dictating that married women had no independent legal personality. When a Parsi married woman died intestate, her entire property would go solely to her husband – in fact, it would be co-owned by him in the first place – if coverture applied. Third, they created a scheme for the distribution of property that looked very different from that of English law, giving legal shape to a distinctively Parsi vision of the family. What Parsis yielded on wills, they clawed back on intestacy.

One wonders why Parsis were able to oust English legal influence in the one area but not in the other. The answer was probably a confluence of the self-interest of elite Parsis, on the one hand, and the colonial ideal of the autonomous liberal subject, on the other. For those with a certain degree of wealth, wills provided senior family members with new leverage in relation to their heirs. Simultaneously, the fact that wills created *choice* rather than any set distribution of property fed perfectly into the status-to-contract pedagogical project. Intestacy, by contrast, was not about options. One fell into the regime of intestate succession by default, whether because one had no will or because

---

[125] "Further additions ... proposed by Dadachanji," 28.

The Inheritance Acts

one's will was invalid. There was greater objection to primogeniture than to wills among Parsis, in part, perhaps, because Parsi elites found the allure of wills irresistible. But equally, colonial liberal ideology aimed to maximize the voluntary determination of one's obligations and entitlements. From the colonizers' perspective, it may have been that the realm of intestate succession – a regime that applied involuntarily – was a domain worth sacrificing to placate Parsi elites. More pragmatically, it was also possible that colonial administrators thought Parsi lobbyists' fragmented model of intestate property distribution would increase the circulation of property in the market.

REJECTING PRIMOGENITURE AND COVERTURE

In 1835, the eldest son of a Parsi intestate came to the Supreme Court of Bombay claiming to be the sole heir to his father's property. At the point of partition of the Parsi joint family, the custom was to divide a father's property equally among sons. According to the English law of primogeniture, however, the eldest son of a man without a valid will inherited all of his father's real estate. English law applied to Parsis in the city of Bombay. In protest, Parsis in the presidency towns sent a petition to the East India Council's Legislative Council, "praying to be protected against this threatened application of the English law." This was not the first time Parsis had expressed outrage over an intestacy case in the colonial courts. In what was known as the "Gheestas" case (1811), the Recorder's Court granted the property of a Parsi intestate to the man's extramarital son because the latter had been initiated into the Zoroastrian religion. Parsis protested that this decision contradicted their customary norms, which required heirs to be born within marriage. It was hastily reversed on appeal.[126] Two decades later, officials at the Legislative Department were receptive to Parsi demands for a larger solution. They commented that "though the national usages of the Parsees, were not, like the Hindoo and Mahometan rules of Inheritance, Marriage and Succession, recognized by law; yet the Parsees who were in possession of land, within the jurisdiction of the Supreme Courts, which they have inherited according to their national usages and with the acquiescence of all interested parties, ought not to be disturbed in that possession ... [this appears to be] one of those cases in which the strict enforcement of law would defeat the end for which laws are made, would render property insecure, and would shake the confidence of the people in the Institutions under which they live."[127]

Half a century earlier, the application of primogeniture to Muslims and Hindus had been discontinued for similar reasons: it was repugnant to both

---

[126] Q. in the Corner, II: 27–8; Davar *History*, 46, 56, 71; Desai, *History*, 34–5; Menant, *Les Parsis*, 273.

[127] Resolution of the Legislative Department quoted in "Report into the usages," 2 in "1862–3 Government of India Bill."

traditions, denying many relatives a share in the estate or even maintenance.[128] For the Parsis, relief came with the Succession to Parsees Immovable Property Act of 1837. This was the first statute for which Parsis lobbied, and the last that was not drafted predominantly by them. The Act exempted Parsis from the operation of primogeniture, but by an odd route. On the death and intestacy of a Parsi, his immovable property would be treated as if it were "chattels real" (immovable property governed by leasehold interests), rather than real estate governed by freehold.[129] The English law of chattels real was governed by the 1670 Statute of Distribution, according to which an intestate's widow inherited one-third of his chattels real, with his children splitting the rest equally among themselves.[130] The Parsi custom (at partition) had been to divide the estate among sons, with daughters and widows getting maintenance only. In other words, the new Act replaced one English rule with another. Both differed significantly from Parsi practice. A year after the 1837 Act came into operation, the Parsis petitioned the colonial state again. They documented their customary norms and requested a regulation that would embrace "the rights of Inheritance and Succession that are acknowledged by the Parsee nation."[131]

The 1837 Act was ultimately remedied through the Parsi Intestate Succession Act (PISA) of 1865. The PISA was a statute drafted by the Parsi body, the Parsi Law Association. Among other things, it abolished the earlier English distinctions between types of property (i.e., chattels real, leasehold, freehold, realty, personalty) and made all property of Parsi intestates subject to the same general rules of distribution.[132] Of special interest were the documents sent to government administrators during the lobbying process. One petition of 1838 protested against the 1837 regime, under which widows took a third of their husbands' estates, and sons and daughters split the remainder among themselves equally. This was not primogeniture, but it was equally English – and equally inappropriate. "Every day is bringing forth stronger proofs of the necessity of something being done for us, as, in the event of parties dying intestate, their property is liable to the operation of the English Law, which is quite at variance with our customs and usages."[133] The petitioners and others asserted that the new rule gave too much property to women. They complained that women who married men two months before the husbands' deaths were walking away with a

---

[128] S.1 of Regulation XI of 1793 in Rankin, 7.

[129] "Act IX of 1837. Passed by the Right Honourable Governor General of India in Council, on 15 May 1837," "India Acts 1834–40" (IOR/V/8/31). See also Karaka, II: 297; Desai, *History*, 35; Palsetia, *Parsis*, 201–3.

[130] An Act for the Better Settling of Intestates' Estates 1670 (22 & 23 Car. II, Ch. 10), s. III in John Raithby, ed., *The Statutes of the Realm Vol. V: 1625–80* ([London: G. Eyre and A. Strahan, 1819]), 720.

[131] "Report into the usages," 3 in "1862–3 Government of India Bill." See also Palsetia, *Parsis*, 203–4.

[132] Rana (1934), 131.

[133] Petition of 1838 quoted in "Report into the usages," 3 in "1862–3 Government of India Bill."

The Inheritance Acts

third of the estate, depriving the men's sons from prior marriages of their much larger traditional entitlement.[134] Customarily, widows would receive maintenance only or, at most, an eighth of the estate. But Parsi critics claimed that, between daughters and sons, the new rule deprived sons of the means with which to maintain the family name, carry out ritual duties for the larger family, and support other family members, as they were traditionally obliged to do.[135] Making an argument that would recur in other times and places, equal shares for men and women meant depriving men of their ability to support a family, while increasing women's pocket money (which they were allegedly too naïve to manage).[136]

It would be misleading to construe the 1838 discussion as a simple disagreement in which English law stood for gender equality and Parsi custom for gender inequality. The rules being applied to all Parsi property under the 1837 Act only affected chattels real (roughly leasehold interests) under English law. Primogeniture still governed freehold real estate in English law, handing all of the land to the eldest son.[137] A string of relatives lined up behind the eldest son, but the intestate's widow was nowhere on the list.[138] More importantly, the differences between Parsi custom and English law extended beyond the comparative size of inherited shares between women and men. In 1838, critical Parsis wanted women to inherit less than English law was giving them. But they also insisted that Parsi women deserved more *during* marriage: there was no such thing as coverture among Parsis.

The common-law doctrine of unity or coverture deprived a married woman of independent legal personality. Paraphrasing Blackstone, the man and woman became one legal person upon marriage, and that person was the man.[139] Married women could not enter into contracts, own property, or write a will.

---

[134] "Mr. Nowrozjee Furdoonjee's Letter to the Parsee Law Commission with Petition of Calcutta Parsee Inhabitants to the Legislative Council of India," 9–10 in "1862–3 Government of India Bill."

[135] "Report into the usages," 10 in "1862–3 Government of India Bill."

[136] Ibid., 3.; Bengalee, 157–8; "Opinion of Sir Sorabji B. Mehta, Nagpur" in "Paper No. 1: Opinions of the Indian Succession (Amendment) Bill," 2 in "The Indian Succession (Amendment) Act 1939 (26 November 1938–8 August 1939)."

[137] On primogeniture in English legal history, see Frederick Pollock and Frederic William Maitland, *The History of English Law before the Time of Edward I* (Cambridge: Cambridge University Press, 1899), II: 262–356; J. H. Baker, *An Introduction to English Legal History* (London: Butterworths, 1990), 303–7; Eileen Spring, *Law, Land, and Family: Aristocratic Inheritance in England, 1300 to 1800* (Chapel Hill: University of North Carolina Press, 1993), 66–91.

[138] If the eldest son was dead, the real estate went to the eldest son's issue, or to the younger sons (in order of seniority), followed by daughters (sharing equally). If the intestate had no children at all, or if the children and their issue were dead, the property reverted to the intestate's brothers (in order of seniority), followed by his sisters (sharing equally). [John Wade, *The Cabinet Lawyer: A Popular Digest of the Laws of England* (London: printed for Longman, Rees, Orme, Brown, Green, and Longman, 1837), 238–9.]

[139] William Blackstone, *Commentaries on the Laws of England in Four Books* (Philadelphia: George T. Bisel Co., 1922), 397–418 (Book 1, ch. XV). See also Baker, 550–7.

152 *Law and Identity in Colonial South Asia: Parsi Legal Culture*

English women from affluent natal families sidestepped the effects of coverture through the use of marriage settlements or trusts set up by their fathers.[140] But, in general, coverture was a harsh and vilified principle across the English-speaking world.[141] In representations to government, Parsi lobbyists used Joseph Story's explanation of coverture:

> In respect to property in England, the husband by the marriage, independent of any marriage settlement, becomes *ipso facto* entitled to all her personal or moveable property of every description . . . and may dispose of it at his pleasure. He has also a freehold in [i.e., owns] her real estate during their joint lives, and if he has issue by her, and survives her, he has a freehold also during his own life in her real estate, and an exclusive right to the whole profits of it during the same period. There is not any community between them in regard to property as in the French law. Upon his death, she is simply entitled to a dower of one-third of his real estate during her life, and he may at his pleasure, by a testamentary disposition, deprive her of all right and interest in his personal or movable estate, although the whole of it came to him from her by the marriage. During the coverture she is also incapable of changing, transferring, or in any manner disposing of her real estate except with his concurrence, and she is incapable of making an effectual will or testament.[142]

An extensive literature has examined coverture in English and American legal history.[143] Coverture's colonial history has been less well investigated, particularly in its application to non-European populations.[144] Sally Engle Merry and Savitri Goonesekere have documented the extension of coverture to indigenous

[140] Cretney, 92; Hazel D. Lord, "Husband and Wife: English Marriage Law from 1750: A Bibliographic Essay," *S. Cal. Rev. L. Women's Stud.* 11 (2001–2), 31–5; Spring, 119–21. See also Frances E. Dolan, *Marriage and Violence: The Early Modern Legacy* (Philadelphia: University of Pennsylvania Press, 2008), 77–9. Compare Susan Moller Okin, "Patriarchy and Married Women's Property in England: Questions on Some Current Views," *Eighteenth-Century Studies* 17: 2 (1983–4), 121–38.

[141] Holcombe, 18–36; Shanley, 8; Joanne Bailey, "Favoured or Oppressed? Married Women, Property and 'Coverture' in England, 1660–1800," *Continuity and Change* 17:3 (2002), 352; Elizabeth B. Clark, "Matrimonial Bonds: Slavery and Divorce in Nineteenth-Century America," *LHR* 8 (1990), 30–34. Compare Margot Finn, "Women, Consumption and Coverture in England, c. 1760–1860," *Hist. J.* 39:3 (1996), 703–22; Bailey, 351–72. On the American context, see Nancy F. Cott, *Public Vows: A History of Marriage and the Nation* (Cambridge, MA: Harvard University Press, 2000), 64.

[142] Story's *Conflict of Laws* quoted in "Mr. Nowrozjee Furdoonjee's Letter to the Parsee Law Commission" (Bombay, 28 April 1862), 10 in "1862–3 Government of India Bill."

[143] For a sample of the scholarship on English law, see Holcombe; Danaya C. Wright, "'Well Behaved Women Don't Make History': Rethinking English Family, Law, and History," *Wisc. Women's LJ* 19 (2004), 231–43, 256–8; Amy Louise Erickson, "Coverture and Capitalism," *Hist. Worksh. J.* 59 (2005), 1–16; Lord, 27–41; Cretney, 90–141; Bailey, 353–4; Okin; Shanley. On the US, see Hartog, *Man*, 93–135.

[144] On white populations in colonial contexts, see the following in *LHR*: Constance B. Backhouse, "Married Women's Property Law in Nineteenth-Century Canada" 6: 2 (year), 211–17; Hilary Golder and Diane Kirkby, "Mrs. Mayne and Her Boxing Kangaroo: A Married Woman Tests Her Property Rights in Colonial New South Wales" 21:3 (2003), 585–605. See also Kercher, 49–51, 141–3.

The Inheritance Acts 153

peoples in newly American Hawaii and to Sinhalese and Tamil peoples in colonial Ceylon, respectively. In these cases, coverture replaced non-European norms that recognized the separate legal status and property of women.[145] The Parsi episode ended differently. Parsi lobbyists' reversal of coverture destabilized the favorite British contrast between empowered Western women and oppressed Eastern ones.[146]

In precolonial India, Parsi wives were not stripped of their property rights. In 1862, the court interpreter Nowrozjee Furdoonjee offered a catalogue of miseries that had arisen from the application of coverture to Parsis in Bombay City. Prime among them were cases in which unscrupulous husbands claimed for themselves property customarily regarded as wives' separate property. This included property that wives had inherited and property they owned at the time of marriage. In one case, a wealthy Parsi named Furdoonjee Sorabjee Parekh bequeathed to each of his four granddaughters a legacy free from the control of their husbands. Two granddaughters received their intended shares. The other two did not. Their stories served as cautionary tales. The husband of one was insolvent. He successfully claimed his wife's inheritance through coverture and promptly saw it pass to his creditors. The other granddaughter died, after which time her husband also obtained her inheritance through coverture. In the process, he excluded their son, "who did not get a single rupee out of the large fortune to which his mother was entitled."[147] In two other cases, husbands sued in court to claim their wives' inheritance while their wives were alive. These women opposed the men in court and lost. The legal fees for all sides came out of the women's inheritance, consuming a major part of it.[148] Several similar cases were pending in the Bombay Supreme Court when Nowrozjee Furdoonjee submitted his letter. The Parsi community regarded these cases as unjust and contrary to their norms, he wrote. "They consider it wrong to allow a husband or his creditors to recover and make away with any portion of his wife's separate property, fortune, or inheritance."[149]

The Parsi Law Commission was won over by Nowrozjee Furdoonjee's examples. In a tirade against English law, the commissioners noted that coverture was a bizarre anomaly, even by European standards. It had only persisted in England because of the "cumbrous device of marriage settlements, an expedient, as is well known, almost always resorted to where there is any property or expectation of property on the lady's side." The Commissioners huffed: "if the English nation

---

[145] Sally Engle Merry, *Colonizing Hawai'i: The Cultural Power of Law* (Princeton, NJ: Princeton University Press, 2000), 95–97; Goonesekere, 201–2.

[146] In Bentham's words, "Women in Europe are accustomed to enjoy liberty, and even a sort of domestic empire; women in Asia are prepared by their education for the imprisonment of the seraglio, and even for servitude." [Jeremy Bentham, *Bentham's Theory of Legislation*, trans. and ed. Charles Milner Atkinson and Étienne Dumont (London: H. Milford, 1914), II: 61.]

[147] "Mr. Nowrozjee Furdoonjee's Letter," 11–12 in "1862–3 Government of India Bill."

[148] Ibid., 11.

[149] Ibid., 12.

can ever acquire for itself a Code of substantive Civil Law, one of the most welcome modifications of the existing common law would be, the exchange for a more civilized system of the barbarous and feudal rule of the common law by which the wife, for all purposes of property, is merged in the Husband, or to use language both historically and technically more correct – by which the *Feme* is *Coverte* by the *Baron*."[150]

Parsi lobbyists had convinced even the British commissioners of the backwardness of English law. The conversation about coverture was an important episode in colonial gender debates. Colonial reform campaigns against Hindu widow immolation or sati (Sanskr. *sati*), female infanticide, dowry death, child marriage, and a form of female seclusion known as living in *purdah* (Pers. *pardeh*) were framed as being emancipatory for women.[151] And yet, there were also colonial efforts to stop South Asian matriliny, polyandry, and modes of dress deemed immodest, like toplessness among tribal women, nakedness among female Hindu ascetics, and ritual nudity during fertility, rain, and mother goddess rites.[152] The automatic application of coverture to populations like the Parsis fit into this latter policy stream. Understood collectively, these movements were not about the promotion of women's rights as much as they were about making South Asian women more like European ones.

According to Parsi customary norms, wives held their own separate property. This property did not usually accrue from women's own earnings, but through two channels linked to their natal families: bridal presents and inheritance.[153] Women received gifts, particularly jewelry, from their own family and their

---

[150] "Report into the usages," 10 in "1862–3 Government of India Bill." See also Menant, *Les Parsis*, 282.

[151] See Lata Mani, "Contentious Traditions: The Debate on Sati in Colonial India," in *Recasting Women: Essays in Indian Colonial History*, eds. Kumkum Sangari and Sudesh Vaid (New Brunswick, NJ: Rutgers University Press, 1990), 88–126; Veena Talwar Oldenburg, *Dowry Murder: The Imperial Origins of a Cultural Crime* (Oxford: Oxford University Press, 2002), 41–72; Gayatri Chakravorty Spivak, "Can the Subaltern Speak?," in *Marxism and the Interpretation of Culture*, eds. Cary Nelson and Lawrence Grossberg (Urbana and Chicago: University of Illinois Press, 1988), 297–308; Mrinalini Sinha, *Colonial Masculinity: The "Manly Englishman" and the "Effeminate Bengali" in the Late Nineteenth Century* (Manchester: Manchester University Press, 1995), 138–80; Jörg Fisch, "Dying for the Dead: Sati in Universal Context," *J. World Hist.* 16:3 (2005), 293–325.

[152] See G. Arunima, *There Comes Papa: Colonialism and the Transformation of Matriliny in Kerala, Malabar, c. 1850–1940* (Delhi: Orient Longman, 2003); Y.S. Parmar, *Polyandry in the Himalayas* (Delhi: Vikas, 1975), 172–3; W. Crooke, "Nudity in India in Custom and Ritual," *JRAI GB Ireland* 49 (July–December 1919), 237–51.

[153] Domestic service aside, salaried jobs were unusual before Parsi women started to become nurses and teachers in the 1930s. On nursing jobs, see Suits No. 8 of 1932, IV: 13 and No. 5 of 1933, IV: 124–5, both in 1929–35 PCMC Notebook; Suit No. 3 of 1935, I: 209; and No. 7 of 1936, I: 373, both in 1935–7 PCMC Notebook; and Suit No. 28 of 1941, 1941–8 PCMC Notebook, I: 254–5. For an unusually early case, see Suit No. 1 of 1915, 1913–20 PCMC Notebook, II: 89. For examples of Parsi women working as teachers or principals in schools, see Suit No. 16 of 1936, 1935–7 PCMC Notebook, I: 376.

The Inheritance Acts

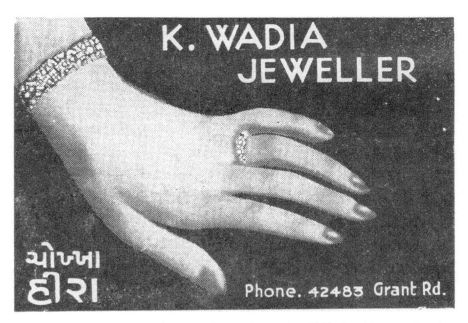

FIGURE 3.1. Advertisement for "pure diamonds" (Guj. *cokhkhā hīrā*) in 1940s Bombay from Parsi jeweler K. Wadia (est. 1902).
Source: Umrīgar and Pāṭhak, 258. Courtesy of K. Wadia & Co., Jewellers.

fiancés upon engagement and marriage. These "ornaments" were often handed down from previous generations, whether in their original form or with gemstones remounted in fashionable new settings by contemporary jewelers (Figure 3.1).[154] Jewels given to the bride by her husband's side were deemed the joint property of the couple. Jewels given to the woman by her family were customarily her own separate property. The point was contested in later colonial case law, when judges occasionally found that all of a woman's jewelry belonged to her and her husband jointly.[155] Nonetheless, in social practice, women and their natal families continued to assert control over jewelry gifted from their side. When treated as the wife's separate property, these jewels functioned as dower did among Muslims and *stridhan* (Sanskr. *strīdhana*) among Hindus, providing a wife with a financial safety net if the marriage broke down through discord or

---

[154] Suit No. 1 of 1933, 1929–35 PCMC Notebook, IV: 164. See also Pheroza J. Godrej and Firoza Punthakey Mistree, "Parsis of Western India: A Panorama," in Godrej and Punthakey Mistree, 700–1.
[155] See Rana (1934), 105–7.

death.[156] Jewels could be worth huge sums, and the Parsi Chief Matrimonial Court regularly called in merchants to testify on fluctuations in the market value of gems and precious metals in divorce suits between affluent couples.[157]

Because jewels were both portable and valuable, their custody could be a source of conflict in wealthy families. Wives wore jewels for special occasions, like formal dinners and weddings. The rest of the time, the proper place for jewels given to the wife by her side was with her natal family. This generally meant that the jewels would be left with the wife's parents for safekeeping.[158] In the 1930s, affluent wives started storing their jewels in their own safety deposit boxes in banks, sometimes surreptitiously.[159] However, husbands and their parents occasionally gained control of the bridal ornaments granted by the wife's side. Typically, they convinced the wives that the jewels would be both more secure and readily available to the wife if kept in the marital home, which was occasionally shared with the husband's parents.[160] In fact, husbands and their natal families realized that a woman's ornaments represented emergency resources if she ever chose to leave. The husband's family could reduce the likelihood of her departure by gaining control of the jewels. Wives complained to the Parsi Chief Matrimonial Court that their husbands and in-laws not only controlled the ornaments, but also prevented the wives from wearing them on legitimate occasions like weddings.[161] In one 1936 case, a mother-in-law prevented a wife from having access to the younger woman's own jewels, especially when the wife was going to see her own parents. Audaciously, the mother-in-law wore the jewels herself. She also wore her daughter-in-law's best silk saris, which were also under the older woman's control.[162] In another case from the 1930s, a wife alleged that her husband and father-in-law forced her to hand over her jewels, then kept her locked in a room while the husband was at work.[163] Women who left their husbands tried to take their ornaments with them.[164] Those who failed had little chance of recovering their jewels after they had moved out of the marital home. As one plaintiff-wife's mother told the matrimonial court in 1902: "My daughter never went to [her] husband's house [after

---

[156] On the role of dower in Anglo-Islamic law, see Sharafi, ""Semi-Autonomous Judge," 67–72. On *stridhan*, see W. H. Macnaghten, *Principles of Hindu and Mohammadan Law*, ed. H. H. Wilson (London: Williams and Norgate, 1873), 40–44.

[157] For example, see Suit No. 1 of 1933, 1929–35 PCMC Notebook, IV: 158.

[158] Suit No. 3 of 1930, 1929–35 PCMC Notebook. I: 78, 87. See also *Shapurji Bezonjee Motiwalla v. Dossabhoy Bezonjee Motiwalla* ILR 30 Bom 359 (1906).

[159] Suit No. 6 of 1936, 1935–7 PCMC Notebook, II: 257–8.

[160] Suit No. 23 of 1936, 1935–7 PCMC Notebook, II: 242–3; Suit No. 1 of 1933, 1929–35 PCMC Notebook, IV: 153.

[161] Suit No. 4 of 1913, 1913–20 PCMC Notebook, I: 20; Suit No. 21 of 1938, 1937–41 PCMC Notebook, II: 184–5.

[162] Suit No. 23 of 1936, 1935–7 PCMC Notebook, II; 242–3, 247–9.

[163] Suit No. 3 of 1930, 1941–8 PCMC Notebook, I: 72–3.

[164] Suit No. 1 of 1927, 1924–8 PCMC Notebook, III: 47. For an exceptional case, see Suit No. 2 of 1920, 1920–3 PCMC Notebook, I: 11.

The Inheritance Acts 157

moving out] except on one occasion for ornaments ... [the] defendant said he would not give the ornaments."[165]

Judges in the city of Bombay dutifully applied the doctrine of coverture to Parsi wives before the 1865 legislation abolished it.[166] Outside of the presidency towns, though, colonial courts were instructed not to apply English law even before 1865. Instead, their default standard was the amorphous formula, "justice, equity and good conscience."[167] By the mid-nineteenth century, this phrase often served as a proxy for English legal sensibilities. In the earlier period, it was often understood to mean customary norms – where not repugnant to European values.[168] At that time, judges in the *mofussil* sided with wives when husbands tried to claim ownership of the women's separate property. In *Kaoosji Ruttonji v. Awanbaee* (1817), a provincial court ordered a husband to deliver his wives' clothes and jewels to her: they were her separate property.[169] In *Meherwanji Nosherwanji v. Awanbaee* (1822), a husband failed in his attempt to claim his wife's dower. The property was not "in its nature subject to the control of her husband," and the claim was "foreign to general practice and usage, and wholly unsupported by precedent, custom, or rule of caste."[170]

In their report recommending the 1865 draft legislation, the Parsi Law Commissioners acknowledged that Parsi wives customarily had property rights "over the joys and jewels given them on marriage *by their father's family*."[171] They also noted that wives could inherit property and that husbands had no claim to it. Inheritance was the second route by which women acquired separate property. The records of the matrimonial court documented the inheritance of property by wives after the abolition of coverture in 1865. This pathway often allowed women to delay or avoid getting a divorce: they could afford to live apart from their husbands without the men's financial support and did not need court-ordered maintenance to survive.[172] In turn, married women could also pass on property by will and (like Parsi men) could disinherit close family members.[173]

Interestingly, Parsi custom included a quasi-matrilineal tradition running between female family members. When the custom was documented in the 1860s, it applied where a Parsi woman had left no valid will. The custom varied somewhat by region, but across western India, a larger share of an intestate's property passed to daughters when the deceased was female. Among the Parsis of Surat, the whole of a female intestate's property descended to her female

---

[165] Suit No. 3 of 1902, 1893–1903 PCMC Notebook, III: 30.
[166] See Q. in the Corner, II: 8–9.
[167] See *Mithiba'i v. Bana'ji*, 506. See also Chapter 1 at note 56.
[168] Jain, *Outlines*, 437–40; *Motiwalla v. Motiwalla*.
[169] *Kaoosji Ruttonji v. Awanbaee* (1817) described in Rana (1934), 107.
[170] *Meherwanji Nosherwanji v. Awanbaee* (1822) described in Rana (1934), 107.
[171] "Report into the usages," 9 in "1862–3 Government of India Bill." Italics original.
[172] PCMC Suit No. 6 of 1936, 1935–7 PCMC Notebook, II: 166.
[173] PCMC Suit No. 3 of 1936, 1937–41 PCMC Notebook, II: 4.

offspring, "to the exclusion of her husband and her sons; the husband, being entitled only to the jewels, ornaments, or other property presented by him and his parents."[174] The female intestate's property was divided equally among sons and daughters (among others). By contrast, for every share of a male intestate's property that went to a son, only an eighth went to a daughter, at best. Some *mofussil* Parsis argued that daughters were customarily entitled to maintenance alone when their father died intestate. In the final version of the Parsi Intestate Succession Act, the children of a female intestate inherited equal shares, regardless of their gender.[175]

This final version of the 1865 Act was curt in its abolition of coverture: "No person shall by marriage acquire any interest in the property of the person whom he or she marries, nor become incapable of doing any act in respect of his or her own property, which he or she could have done if unmarried."[176] An earlier, more baroque version of the bill reflected Parsi resistance in full bloom:

All property ... which shall be given, granted, conveyed, or bequeathed to, or which shall in any way be acquired by any woman, whether married or single, excepting only the joys, jewels, ornaments, or paraphernalia given to the wife by her husband or his relatives in contemplation of and during her marriage, which shall revert to her husband in case of her death, *shall ... be taken to be her sole and separate property; and she shall have and exercise the same absolute control over the disposal and use thereof notwithstanding any marriage which she may contract, and may enter into any contracts relating to the disposition and use thereof, and give as effectual acquittances and receipts in respect thereto, and sue and be sued in any action or suit in respect thereof touching the same as if she were a* feme sole.[177]

In the imperial metropole, by contrast, coverture lingered on. The most important Married Women's Property Acts became law in England in 1870 and 1882.[178] In 1893, 1935, and beyond, they were followed by subsequent statutes that continued to eliminate the lasting effects of coverture.[179] From a Parsi vantage point, this was not the well-trodden imperial story of the colonies "catching up" to the metropole, but the reverse. Over the longer period, though, Parsi lobbyists would not consistently promote gender equality in the personal law that they forged. The larger pattern revealed other priorities, like the broad distribution of wealth (in intestacy) and the strategic reconfiguration of patriarchal privilege (in marriage).

[174] "Mr. Nowrozjee Furdoonjee's Letter," 6 in "1862–3 Government of India Bill."
[175] PISA 1865, ss. 51, 53 in Rana (1934), 137–8.
[176] PISA 1865, s. 20 in Rana (1934), 119.
[177] "The Amended Bill; with a Memorandum of alterations, additions, and omissions suggested in the Draft Code of Laws for the Parsees," 7 in "1862–3 Government of India Bill."
[178] See Vivienne Ullrich, "The Reform of Matrimonial Property Law in England during the Nineteenth Century," *Victoria U. Wellington Law Rev.* 13 (1977–8), 13–35.
[179] On the Married Women's Property Act 1893, the Law Reform (Married Women and Tortfeasors) Act 1935, and the Law Reform (Husband and Wife) Act 1962, see Lord, 31; Cretney, 102–41.

The Inheritance Acts

REJECTING CONCENTRATION

In the interim between Parsi intestacy statutes of 1865 and 1939, English law transformed itself. The Married Women's Property Acts of the 1870s–'80s abolished most of the effects of coverture in England. In 1925, new legislation revolutionized property law.[180] The Law of Property Act of 1925 created a new English property regime that would govern for the rest of the twentieth century. The Administration of Estates Act of 1925 shaved off the vestigial bits left by medieval intestacy law, including "tenancy by the curtesy," dower, and free-bench.[181] It also effectively abolished primogeniture.[182] In the place of these doctrines, the English statute created an intestacy regime that was gender blind: husbands and wives inherited in identical ways, as did sons and daughters.[183]

For Parsis, the 1837 and 1865 Parsi Acts achieved the real break from English law. Nevertheless, English law continued to linger in the background, the imperial standard against which Parsi law (like other systems across the empire) was measured.[184] The most obvious feature of the Parsi Acts was the gradual approach toward gender equality. For every share inherited by a son, the 1865 Act gave widows a half share and daughters a quarter share. The 1939 Parsi statute changed the math in favor of women. For every full share granted to a son, widows received an equal share and daughters a half-share.[185] At first glance, one could interpret the Parsi Acts as lagging behind English law on gender equality. But this would ignore the preceding rejection of coverture back when Parsi norms gave women more than did English law. Because of these fluctuations, the codification of gender equality was not a straight path. Greater entitlements to women may have been provided by Parsi law in the early period and by English law in the later one. But, in addition to gender, there was an equally important and long-standing difference between English and Parsi law: the Parsi preference for the division of property and the English for concentration. In the 1930s, Parsi law prioritized provision for a wider range of family members than did English law, including parents and widows of

---

[180] Duncan Campbell Lee, 'Recent Changes in the English Law of Property," *Annual Report of the American Bar Association, 49th meeting* (1926), 329–43. See also W. S. Holdsworth, "The Reform of the Land Law: An Historical Retrospect," *LQR* 42 (1926) 158–83; Percy Bordwell, "Property Reform in England," *Iowa LR* 11:1 (1925) 1–27.

[181] Administration of Estates Act 1925 (15 Geo. 5 Ch. 23), s. 45(1) in *The Law Reports. The Public General Statutes passed in the fifteenth and sixteenth years of the reign of His Majesty King George the Fifth. 1925* (London: Council of Law Reporting, 1925), I: 916. On "curtesy," dower, and freebench, see Lord, 29–32; A. S. Oppé, *Wharton's Law Lexicon* (Delhi: Universal Law Publishing, 2003), 291, 437; Spring, 121.

[182] Administration of Estates Act 1925, s. 45(1); Lee, 336–7; Bordwell, 24.

[183] Administration of Estates Act 1925, ss. 45–52 in *Public General Statutes 1925*, I: 916–23.

[184] For instance, see F. P. Walton, "Introduction," *JCLIL* 3 series, 13 (1931), xxvii.

[185] The shares of male and female heirs were not fully equalized until the Indian Succession (Amendment) Act of 1991, when each spouse and child was granted equal shares of the estate, regardless of gender. See Flavia Agnes, "Parsi Law" in Katz.

160   *Law and Identity in Colonial South Asia: Parsi Legal Culture*

descendants. In the century preceding, Parsi law rejected the concentration of wealth in the eldest son or husband. The turn away from English law's concentrating tendencies reflected a different vision of familial relations, and one that was particularly Parsi.

Under the English statutory regime of 1925, intestates' chattels went to their spouses. Spouses were entitled to the first thousand pounds of the estate.[186] Beyond that, a spouse had a life interest in the residue. Typically, this meant that the widow (or widower) had a right to live in the family house, but not to sell it. Absolute ownership of the real estate went to someone else: first, the children, but if there were none, then (in order of priority) the intestate's parents, siblings, grandparents, aunts, uncles, or first cousins.[187] If the first available layer of living relations consisted of more than one person at equal proximity to the intestate, the property would be divided among them. Otherwise, the closer person would inherit all of the real estate to the exclusion of others. The 1925 scheme divided real estate more than primogeniture had done previously. There could be only one eldest son, after all. But it stood in stark contrast to the Parsi regime that would become law fifteen years later.

Under the Parsi provisions of the Indian Succession (Amendment) Act of 1939, each son and the intestate's widow took equal shares of the estate, with daughters taking a half-share each.[188] If the intestate was female, her widower and each child (regardless of gender) received an equal share.[189] Unlike English law, there was no concept of a life interest for surviving spouses. English law's spousal life interest kept real estate in a single block and underscored the priority of blood relations over marital ones. It was certain under Parsi law that a spouse would receive a share of the estate. However, the spouse would get a slice, never the whole pie.

If they were alive, the parents of male Parsi intestates also received a share of the estate: the intestate's father received a half-share (half of what each son received), and the intestate's mother received a quarter-share (half of what each daughter received). The granting of any share to the intestate's parents was a source of controversy, violating as it did the canonical principle of English inheritance law that property would devolve upward only if it could not move downward.[190] Parsis such as Kavasji Jamshedji Petigara, the Deputy Commissioner of the Bombay Police, opposed parental inheritance. He and

---

[186] Cretney, 480–1; Bordwell, 24.

[187] See note 203.

[188] IS(A) Act 1939, s. 51 (available as "A Bill to amend the Indian Succession Act, 1925, as respects intestate succession among Parsis" as passed by the Indian Legislature) in "The Indian Succession (Amendment) Act 1939."

[189] IS(A) Act 1939, s. 52.

[190] William Draper Lewis, *Commentaries on the Laws of England in Four Books by Sir William Blackstone* (Philadelphia: George T. Bisel, 1922), Book II, Ch. II: 208 (p. 674), 210 (p. 678). See also Judicial Secretary, 25 January 1938 in "No. 13: Bihar," "Paper No. 1: Opinions," 11; Secretary of the Bombay Incorporated Law Society, 17 December 1937 in "No. 14: Bombay,"

The Inheritance Acts   161

others argued that it was unfair for the intestate's parents' share to diminish that of the intestate's widow and children. After all, the parents might only have a few years left to live.[191] These critics lost the debate.[192] The final statute cut in half the parental share proposed in the draft bill. The earlier version had granted to the intestate's father a share equal to that of the intestate's son. It gave the intestate's mother a share equal to that of the intestate's daughter.[193] But by retaining any share for the intestate's parents, the legislation reflected the view that adult Parsis had a financial duty to their parents that was almost as important as their duty to their wives and children.

Providing for parents was the first of two important differences between English and Parsi law in the 1920s–'30s. The other concerned widows and widowers. The Parsi statute of 1939 gave a share of the estate to the spouses of dead lineal descendants – in other words, to the spouses of the intestate's dead children or grandchildren. It was generous. These individuals could receive a share equal to the share of the intestate's own spouse. The intestate's spouse and the spouse of lineal descendants would get a third of the estate each. (If there was more than one spouse of deceased lineal descendants, they would share a third of the estate among them.)[194] This too triggered debate. Some, like B. D. Mehta of the Advocates' Association of Western India, argued that the intestate's own spouse deserved a larger share than the widows or widowers of descendants.[195] He was in the minority. Most contributors to the discussion felt that Parsis had a duty to support their relations, including relations through marriage.[196] Many voiced concern at the thought that widows of lineal descendants could remarry and still inherit a one-third share.[197] This scenario was explicitly blocked by the

11; Collector of Kaira, 23 December 1937 in "No. 14: Bombay," 19; all in "The Indian Succession (Amendment) Act 1939."

[191] Y. Taraporavala, 31 December 1937 in "No. 13: Bihar," "Paper No. 1: Opinions," 1; Kavasji J. Petigara, 21 December 1937 in "No. 14: Bombay," 23; both in "The Indian Succession (Amendment) Act 1939."

[192] M. N. Dalal, 23 March 1939 in "Extract from the Council of State Debates, Vol. 1, No. 17" in "The Indian Succession (Amendment) Act 1939."

[193] Compare "A Bill to amend the Indian Succession Act 1925, as respects intestate succession among Parsis (as passed by the Indian Legislature)," s. 51(2); and the bill by the same name, "to be introduced in the Council of State," s. 51(c); both in "The Indian Succession (Amendment) Act 1939."

[194] IS(A) Act 1939, s. 54(b) in "A Bill to amend the Indian Succession Act 1925, as respects intestate succession among Parsis (as passed by the Indian Legislature)," in "Indian Succession (Amendment) Act 1939."

[195] Secretary of the Advocates' Association of Western India, 23 December 1937, 18. For a similar view from a non-Parsi contributor (one M. A. Bhave), see the District Judge of Thana, 14 January 1938, 25. Both in "No. 14: Bombay," "Paper No. 1: Opinions" in "The Indian Succession (Amendment) Act 1939."

[196] IS(A) Act 1939, s. 54(b).

[197] District Judge of Thana, 14 January 1938 in "No. 14: Bombay," 25; District Officer, Jalaun, 3 February 1938 in "No. 15: United Provinces," 28; both in "Paper No. 1: Opinions"; and "A Comparative Statement showing the present Law of Intestate Succession amongst Parsis, along with the Law as proposed to be amended by the bill introduced in the Council of State and the

1939 Act: it prohibited a widow of a lineal descendant who had remarried during the intestate's lifetime from inheriting anything.[198] This preoccupation was undoubtedly a reaction to ongoing debates in Hindu communities over whether widows who remarried should be permitted to retain property inherited from their first husbands.[199] Interestingly, there was a gender-based double standard: Parsi widowers who remarried were entitled to inherit from their previous wives' intestate parents, a point established by the 1887 case of *Surti v. Perozbai.*[200]

Finally, the breadth of relations named as potential heirs also distinguished Parsi from English law. If there was no issue, half to two-thirds of the estate would be taken by the intestate's own widow and any widows or widowers of the intestate's lineal descendants. What remained of the estate then went to the first living individual of a long list of relations. The list started with the intestate's parents and extended all the way to descendants of the intestate's paternal great-grandparents.[201] Again a critic, Deputy Police Commissioner Petigara complained of the absence of provision for relatives on the intestate's mother's side (except where the intestate had no spouse, issue, or spouses of dead issue).[202] The final Act retained this preference for agnates over cognates, highlighting the historically patrilineal nature of Parsi family structure. By contrast, English intestacy law cast a narrow net: if the intestate had no issue or living parents, potential heirs were limited to the intestate's siblings, grandparents, aunts or uncles, or first cousins, with no distinction made between paternal or maternal relations.[203] Relatives more remote than first cousins were excluded in English law.[204] In the absence of any of these relations, the real estate went to the spouse absolutely. If there was no living spouse, it went to the Crown.[205] No final default to the state existed in Parsi law. Even for a population as close to the state as the Parsis, this was an unsurprising feature in the context of empire.

Draft suggested by the Bombay Bar Association," proposed s. 49B; all in "The Indian Succession (Amendment) Act 1939."

[198] IS(A) Act 1939, s. 50(c).

[199] See Kulkarni, 33–46; "Forfeiture of Widow's Estate on Re-Marriage," *Trav. LJ* 26 (1936) 117–24. On the property rights of Hindu widows generally in this period, see Mytheli Sreenivas, *Wives, Widows and Concubines: The Conjugal Family Ideal in Colonial India* (Bloomington: Indiana University Press, 2008), 59–65.

[200] *Jehangir Dhanjibhai Surti v. Perozbai* ILR 11 Bom 1 (1887); Patel and Paymaster, III: 842.

[201] IS(A) Act 1939, s. 54 and Schedule II, Part I.

[202] IS(A) Act 1939, s. 55 and Schedule II, Part II; Kavasji J. Petigara, 21 December 1937 in "No. 14: Bombay," 23 in "The Indian Succession (Amendment) Act 1939."

[203] Administration of Estates Act 1925, s. 46 in *The Public General Statutes* 1925, I: 917–19. On first cousins, see Bordwell, 24; R. R. A. Walker, "The English Property Legislation of 1922–6," *JCLIL* (3 series), 10:4 (1928), 181.

[204] Lee, 338.

[205] Administration of Estates Act 1925, s.46 (v–vi).

The Inheritance Acts

163

CONCLUSION

In the background to the formation of Parsi intestacy law lay the debate over imperial legal transplants.[206] The nineteenth-century utilitarian push for codification in India understood law – through legislation – to be modular and exportable.[207] In his "Essay on the Influence of Time and Place in Matters of Legislation," Jeremy Bentham acknowledged that differences in culture and climate mattered. Nonetheless, he remained convinced that with proper information about these differences, a legislator could tweak good legislation from England and enact it in Bengal.[208] His successors in the empire showed little interest in making changes even to this degree. The result in places like Upper Burma, where utilitarian legal transplants hit fast and hard, was that the British "did the most damage" in the empire "in the shortest time," "adopting the most rigorous form of direct rule."[209]

A competing model of legal philosophy understood law to be a cultural artifact, a unique product of the *Volksgeist* of a community, its history, and belief systems. Followers of the German Historical School founded by Friedrich Karl von Savigny in the first half of the nineteenth century regarded large-scale codification as reckless and culturally inappropriate.[210] Savigny had huge influence across the English-speaking world.[211] In places like New York, his followers helped foil attempts to create a civil code.[212] In the colonial context, the position became less clear. Henry Maine was probably the leading proponent of the Historical School in British India. Yet, as Karuna Mantena and others have reminded us, his position on legislation differed from Savigny's.[213] Maine was responsible for the passage of more than 200 statutes during his time as Law Member to the Viceroy's Council (1862–9) and was even accused of overlegislating. He embraced the use of legislation in India because he considered it a lesser evil to the haphazard development of law through case law in a context

---

[206] For a useful review of the literature, see Margit Cohn, "Legal Transplant Chronicles: The Evolution of Unreasonableness and Proportionality Review of the Administration in the United Kingdom," *Am. J. Comp. L.* 58 (2010), 586–90. See also *Theoretical Inquiries in Law* 10:2 (2009) ("Histories of Legal Transplantations" special issue).

[207] See Stokes; Banerjee, *English Law*, 168–70.

[208] Jeremy Bentham, "Essay on the Influence of Time and Place in Matters of Legislation," in *The Works of Jeremy Bentham*, ed. John Bowring (Edinburgh: William Tait, 1843), I: 169–94. See also Jennifer Pitts, *A Turn to Empire: The Rise of Imperial Liberalism in Britain and France* (Princeton, NJ: Princeton University Press, 2005), 115–21.

[209] Huxley, "Positivists and Buddhists," 122–3, 139.

[210] Hermann Kantorowicz, "Savigny and the Historical School of Law," *LQR* 53 (1937), 332–3; Mantena, 100–1.

[211] Michael H. Hoeflich, "Savigny and His Anglo-American Disciples," *Am. J. Comp. L.* 37 (1989), 17–37.

[212] Mathias Reimann, "The Historical School against Codification: Savigny, Carter, and the Defeat of the New York Civil Code," *Am. J. Comp. L.* 37 (1989), 95–119.

[213] Mantena, 101–2; Kantorowicz, 33.

where the natural evolution of custom had been interrupted by colonial rule.[214] Maine felt that India needed legislation because the colonial courts had created such a chaotic jumble – "undigested masses of English law," in which "fragments of English law joust against shreds of native custom." In India, judicial legislation was "legislation by foreigners, who are under the thraldom of precedents and analogies belonging to a foreign law, developed thousands of miles away, under a different climate, and for a different civilization."[215]

Leaving to one side the complexities of Maine's position, one could imagine more Savigny-like proponents of the Historical School sympathizing with Parsi opponents of English law.[216] Writing in 1888 under the name "Mansukh," the Parsi polemicist Muncherjee Cowasjee Lungra railed – with Historical School sensibilities – against the application of English law to Parsis: "It appears upon a comparison of the code of the Chinese with that of the Hebrews, that Laws naturally follow the manners of the people who make them. If vultures and doves had laws, they would undoubtedly be of a very different character."[217] In this spirit, the cultural clash over intestacy was an instance of distinct cultural priorities being expressed through legislation. Instead of keeping property in a single block and passing it to a member of the close nuclear family, Parsi law reflected a sense of financial obligation to a wider group of relations, defined through blood *and* marriage, and prioritized the potentially vulnerable among them, particularly parents and widows in the family. Like their Hindu and Muslim counterparts, Parsi elites did not prevent the power of testamentary disposition from taking hold. The adoption of wills probably had as much to do with these elites' self-interest as with the ideological priorities of colonial administrators. But in the realm of intestacy, Parsi elites shook off the hypnotic pull of English law. By reversing primogeniture and coverture and in avoiding the focusing tendencies of the 1925 English intestacy regime, Parsi lawmakers rejected the Anglo value of concentration in the intergenerational transmission of wealth.

[214] Mantena, 89–118, especially at 101–13. See also Grant Duff, 24–5.
[215] Maine in Mantena, 112.
[216] See generally "The German Historical School of Jurisprudence," *Am. Jurist and Law Mag.* 14 (1835), 52–60; Rudolph and Rudolph, *The Modernity of Tradition*, 255.
[217] Mansukh (or Muncherjee Cowasjee [Lungra]), *Pārsī Dhārā Parnī Nuktecīnī* (Bombay: "Satya Mitra" Office, 1888), 83; see also 84–88.

4

Reconfiguring Male Privilege

The Matrimonial Acts

In the 1850s and '60s, Zoroastrian lobbyists identified the ways in which Parsi values differed from those of English law. In the 1920s–'30s, their successors returned to consider how Parsi values had changed since 1865. These two generations engaged in the exercise of colonial summarizing: they selectively melded descriptions of custom with aspirational visions of community life for an imperial audience.[1] Their disagreements with the preexisting English rules were more than isolated critiques of specific points of law. The regime they created produced a distinctive vision of the family, and one that many elite male Parsis in Bombay, in particular, regarded as an embodiment of the community's core values. Law making, in other words, was a vehicle for the expression of collective identity, particularly for one subset of the Parsi population. In the law of inheritance, the privileged model of the Parsi family included the creation of default rules that spread the wealth among an extended group of relatives. In matrimonial law, the powers and privileges of Parsi husbands and fathers were crystallized and reconfigured in ways that sustained certain kinds of control over wives and children while curtailing legal opportunities for sex with multiple partners. Combined, these two planes of personal law created a prescriptive picture of the male head of the family. He had a duty to provide for a wide circle of relatives – both senior and junior to himself, through blood and marriage – and equally, the privilege to choose his children's spouses (in the nineteenth century) and to discipline his wife violently (into the twentieth). Parsi matrimonial law also instituted a distinctive mechanism for dispute resolution: the Parsi matrimonial jury. It gave the elite Parsi men who served as delegates an unusual form of intragroup control: the power to discipline errant husbands, often working class, by dissolving their marriages. Here was yet another type of

---

[1] On the importance of an imperial audience in the context of legislation, see Likhovski, 84–105.

165

power ensconced in law through the efforts of lobbyists, albeit one that accrued only to elite Parsi patriarchs.

Patriarchy, the socioeconomic system in which adult females and minors derived their social status and financial support from adult males, acquired a particular shape through the Parsi Marriage and Divorce Acts of 1865 and 1936.[2] During the colonial period, these statutes were celebrated as symbols of the voluntary relinquishment of patriarchal power. The 1865 Act criminalized polygamy among Parsis. Men, more than women, had been accused of taking second spouses prior to 1865.[3] The 1936 Act made the grounds for divorce the same for wives and husbands. Until 1865, it had been easier for husbands to divorce their wives than vice versa. In particular, the 1936 statute eliminated the prostitution exception under which a Parsi husband's sex with a prostitute did not constitute adultery, a partial ground for divorce.

The cleavage between Parsi factions vying for control over trust and libel law usually fell along the orthodox–reformist axis, a line in community politics that was defined in the early twentieth century through disagreement over religious controversies like *juddin* admission and appropriate death rites. In matrimonial law, the divisions were less clear. Disagreement congealed around the theme of women's rights but without the self-proclaimed labels and well-known alliances of the orthodox–reformist rivalry. Conservatives were often both religiously orthodox *and* opposed to equal rights for women, but it was not always so. Equally, proponents of one type of women's rights could be opponents of another type. But although idiosyncratic arguments made it hard to group players conceptually, these disputants had much in common demographically. The makers of Parsi matrimonial law were almost entirely male, socially and economically privileged, and Bombay-based, particularly as the colonial period wore on.

Parsi male elites disagreed over the proper balance between their own self-interest as husbands and fathers, on the one hand, and what could be called the "civilizing" mileage that could be gained by promoting women's rights, on the other. Champions of the Acts' gender-equalizing provisions declared the Parsis to be the most advanced and enlightened people of Asia because of their treatment of women. However, the Parsi statutes' curtailment of patriarchal power was uneven. Although certain powers were relinquished, others were maintained or amplified. Overall, Parsi male elites ceded their legal entitlement to have multiple sexual partners but guarded their control over wives and children. The 1865 Act was notably soft on child marriage: Zoroastrian members of the Parsi Law Commission resisted British pressure to criminalize the practice. The right to arrange the marriage of one's offspring constituted a patriarchal prerogative, allowing fathers to forge important social and economic alliances with

---

[2] I borrow from Yngvesson and Gordon in Hartog, *Man*, 318–19 at note 7.

[3] See "List of Cases of Bigamy (so far as ascertained)" (unpaginated) in "1862–3 Government of India Bill."

The Matrimonial Acts

each other – and the most reliable form of arranged marriage was child marriage. The 1936 Act strengthened the husband's ability to inflict violence on his wife. Even certain types of criminal assault would not constitute grounds for divorce. Eleanor Newbigin has described twentieth-century Hindu and Muslim personal law reform as the "propping up" of "particular formations of patriarchal power."[4] Her phrase is equally apt in describing the formation and revision of Parsi matrimonial law.

GENDER IN COLONIAL PARSI HISTORY

Both the criminalization of polygamy and the elimination of the prostitution exception among Parsis were part of a long and volatile public discussion about gender inequality and British rule in India. During the extended last century of colonial rule, a series of politically charged reform movements focused on practices affecting South Asian women.[5] The burning of Hindu widows on their dead husbands' funeral pyres (*sati*), framed by its defenders as a form of voluntary martyrdom, was criminalized in 1829.[6] The campaign to permit and destigmatize the remarriage of Hindu widows led to the (Hindu) Widow Remarriage Act 1856, followed by a continuing campaign to change social mores.[7] Colonial officials' wives held "purdah parties" in an effort to draw elite Hindu and Muslim women living in seclusion out of the inner quarters of their homes.[8] There was also a movement against the dedication of girls to Hindu temples, a practice that allegedly led to sacral prostitution.[9] Europeans were generally in favor of reform, regarding the South Asian practices as uncivilized. Indian reformists joined them. Other South Asians opposed reform, defending the practices under attack by coupling endorsement of the practice with resistance to imperial cultural domination generally. Debates about gender

---

[4] Newbigin, "Codification," 101.

[5] For an overview, see "Child-Marriage and Enforced Widowhood in India," *TL* (13 September 1890), 8; (20 September 1890), 8; (7 October 1890), 8.

[6] See Chapter 3 at note 151.

[7] See Sturman, 187–94; Lucy Carroll, "Law, Custom and Statutory Social Reform: The Hindu Widows' Remarriage Act of 1856," in *Women in Colonial India: Essays in Survival, Work and the State*, ed. J. Krishnamurty (Delhi: Oxford University Press, 1989), 1–26.

[8] Between 1900 and 1939, 253 stories about purdah parties appeared in the *Times of India* alone. For a sample, see "Purdah Party at Government House" (8 January 1915), 8 and (7 February 1918), 9; "Simla Purdah Party" (2 October 1920), 15; "Purdah Party at Mahableshwar" (23 May 1928), 12. For an account of a purdah party held by the wife of the BHC Chief Justice, see Norman Macleod, "Letters from India" (17 December 1921), 33A (HRA/D63/A1) in Macleod of Cadboll Papers. An attempt by Parsi women to claim that they were "purdah women" and should not be compelled to appear in court was rejected by the Parsi Chief Matrimonial Court: the practice was not recognized among Parsis. [Suit No. 9 of 1868, "Parsi Chief Matrimonial Court at Bombay. Record of Proceedings. No. 2 (8 September 1868–22 Dec.1869)," 42–3.]

[9] See Sturman, 173–82; Kunal Parker, "'A Corporation of Superior Prostitutes': Anglo-Indian Legal Conceptions of Temple Dancing Girls, 1800–1914," *MAS* 32:3 (1998), 559–633.

were inescapably debates about colonialism, a point made expansively by Rachel Sturman's study of these reform movements.[10] Attacking South Asian gender practices was an implicit way of justifying colonial rule. The civilizing mission drew not only on the Christianizing missionary project, but also on the promotion of women's rights. Few scholars have situated discussions about gender in the Parsi community in this larger context. But the political mileage gained by Parsi elites for rejecting polygamy (1865) and making sex with prostitutes a basis for divorce (1936) was a direct product of the social movements swirling around gender in the late colonial period.

The key players in gender-related reform debates were rarely, if ever, women. As Lata Mani has observed, women were objects or symbols being fought over by competing groups of men.[11] Parsi women were held up as the most liberated of South Asian women after the passage of the 1865 and 1936 statutes. And yet, in discussions over the Parsi Acts, very few women were involved in any visible way: the written record reflected very little female input. There was change over time. Women were more involved in the passage of matrimonial legislation in 1936–40 than for the 1865 legislation. But even in the later period, only a small proportion of the documented feedback responding to draft bills came from individual women or women's groups.[12] Discussions leading to the Parsi Matrimonial Acts followed the same pattern as gender-related debates in other communities, in other words. They were largely about women, but they hardly involved women.

Finally, a word on the historiography of colonial Parsi women (Figure 4.1). With the exceptions of Jennifer Rose and Ketayun Gould, few scholars writing about Parsis under British rule have made gender a major focus of their work.[13] Primary sources by and about Parsi men were more detailed and voluminous

---

[10] See Sturman.

[11] See Mani.

[12] The only female voices to contribute to the debate over the 1936 draft Act were the Stree Zarthosti Mandal (Bombay), which simply endorsed the Parsi Panchayat's statement, and the Women's Indian Association (Madras), which was probably not a Parsi organization. ["Joint opinion of the Trustees of the Parsee Panchayet Funds and Properties and 20 other Parsi Associations of Bombay," 22–3; "Copy of letter from the Honorary General Secretary, Women's Indian Association, Pantheon Gardens, Egmore, Madras, dated 18 Dec. 1934," 43; both in "Paper No. 1: Opinions on the Parsi Marriage and Divorce Bill," "Parsi Marriage and Divorce Act 1936"]. See also Mithan J. Lam, *Autumn Leaves* (Mumbai: K. R. Cama Oriental Institute, 2009), 23. For female contributions to the Parsi Marriage and Divorce (Amendment) Act 1940, see comments by Miss T. A. Boga of Amritsar, "No. 8 – Punjab," 14; by Honorary General Secretary, Women's Indian Association, Mylapore, Madras, "No. 16 – Madras," 21; both in "Paper No. 1: Opinions on the Parsi Marriage and Divorce (Amendment) Bill" in "Parsi Marriage and Divorce (Amendment) Act 1940."

[13] Jennifer Rose, "The Traditional Role of Women in the Iranian and Indian (Parsi) Zoroastrian Communities from the Nineteenth to the Twentieth Centuries," *JKRCOI* 56 (1989), 17–24; Jenny Rose, "Gender" in Stausberg and Vevaina; Ketayun Gould, "Outside the Discipline, Inside the Experience: Women in Zoroastrianism," in *Religion and Women*, ed. Arvind Sharma (New York: SUNY Press, 1994), 167–74, 177.

FIGURE 4.1. Portrait of a Parsi woman taken in Bombay during the early twentieth century.
Source: Private collection. Courtesy of the author.

Law and Identity in Colonial South Asia: Parsi Legal Culture

than those written by and about women, but the latter did exist. Elite women, particularly wealthy widows, appeared in the colonial case law in inheritance and trust-based suits and in newspapers and the society columns of magazines for their social work and philanthropic giving.[14] Famous female figures of Parsi background left written records of their lives and work. They included memorialist Dosebai Cowasjee Jessawalla; the revolutionary in exile, Madame Bhicaiji Cama; lawyers Cornelia Sorabji and Mithan Lam (née Tata); and social worker Soonamai Desai of Naosari.[15] The records of the Parsi Chief Matrimonial Court contain a wealth of testimony describing the everyday lives of poorer Parsi women. The history of matrimonial legislation itself, though, is notably thin on the female perspective. Because the debates among lobbyists were so male-dominated, the conversations leading to the passage of the Parsi Acts said more about the way Parsi men conceptualized their own role in the nuclear family than about Parsi women's views. The longer history of colonial matrimonial legislation, building on Palsetia's account of the 1865 Act, revealed the shifting shape of patriarchal powers as defined by Parsi male elites themselves.[16]

POLYGAMY

Colonial Parsis spoke of polygamy when referring more specifically to polygyny – marriage involving one man and multiple women. Its inversion, polyandry (one woman and multiple men) and similar matrilocal relationships existed in South Asia, particularly among the Nayars of Kerala and in certain

---

[14] See, for instance, *Homabaee, widow of Dosabhaee v. Punjeabhaee Dosabhaee* 5 Suth. WR 102 (1866); *Tarachand v. Soonabai; Capadia v. Capadia.* For a case of one Parsi widow suing another, see *Bai Meherbai, widow and administratrix of J. D. Mistry v. Bai Maherbai, widow and administratrix of M. S. Katrak* (Suit No. 769 of 1925), "Hon. Mr. Justice J. D. Davar. Judgments. 17 June 1931–31 August 1931," 23–8 (BHC). See also the social column by Shirin Maneckjee in *The Parsi* (for example, 1: 1, 29–30, 32; 1: 2, 66–8; 1: 4, 190; 1: 9, 325, all of 1905); Hinnells, "Flowering," in his *Zoroastrian and Parsi Studies*, 228.

[15] See Dosebai Cowasjee Jessawalla, *The Story of My Life* (Bombay: Times Press, 1911). On Madame Cama, see Introduction at note 87. On Cornelia Sorabji, see Chapter 2 at note 140. Cornelia Sorabji was of Parsi background on her paternal side, but was Christian by religion. On Lam and Desai, see Lam; Aban Mukherji and Vera Desai, eds., *Soonamai Desai of Naovsari: A Biographical and Autobiographical Sketch* (Mumbai: K. R. Cama Oriental Institute, 2007). On notable women of Parsi background, see Eunice de Souza and Lindsay Pereira, eds., *Women's Voices: Selections from Nineteenth and Early Twentieth-Century Indian Writing in English* (Delhi: Oxford University Press, 2002), 1–16, 76–103, 127–40, 195–208.

[16] See Palsetia, *Parsis*, 205–26. For overviews of the PMDA 1936, see Irani, 288–92; Agnes, "Parsi Law."

The Matrimonial Acts

Himalayan societies.[17] Polyandry baffled British administrators.[18] They regarded the marriage of one woman to more than one man as a curiosity, but as a statistically unusual practice. Polygyny horrified them. They believed it to be more widely practiced than polyandry and to exemplify the barbarism and backwardness of Eastern societies that put women in a position akin to slaves. Judges across the Anglosphere linked images of Mormon and South Asian polygyny when conjuring up visions of excessive religious toleration and moral relativism.[19] From the early twentieth century, British women were warned against marrying Indian men visiting or studying in Britain: these naïve young girls would return to India to discover that their husbands had other wives.[20] Although polygamy existed among both Muslim and Hindu populations in India, it was most clearly associated with Muslim populations. Islamic polygamy fed into the stereotype of Muslims in colonial India as particularly backward.[21]

Under the Indian Penal Code, bigamy was a crime for everyone except Muslim and Hindu males.[22] Hindu polygamy would only be officially prohibited in 1955 under the Hindu Marriage Act.[23] Polygyny was permitted under Muslim personal law throughout the colonial period (as today).[24] The 1865 Parsi Act prohibited the taking of a second spouse during the lifetime of the first in the absence of divorce.[25] Although the Penal Code became law several years before the Parsi Act, the Penal Code's prohibition of bigamy was not applicable to Parsis until the Parsi Act made it so. The criminal penalty for

---

[17] On Kerala, see Lewis Moore, *Malabar Law and Custom* (Madras: Higginbotham and Company, 1905), 68–9; Praveena Kodoth, "Courting Legitimacy or Delegitimizing Custom? Sexuality, Sambandham, and Marriage Reform in Late Nineteenth-Century Malabar," *MAS* 35:2 (2001), 349–84.

[18] On colonial efforts to curb polyandry, see Y. S. Parmar, *Polyandry in the Himalayas* (Delhi: Vikas, 1975), 172–3.

[19] See *George Reynolds, pl. in err. v. United States* 98 US (1879) 166; "Is Polygamy a Crime? Arguments in the United States Supreme Court in the Case of a Convicted Mormon," *NYT* (15 November 1878), 4.

[20] "Mixed Marriages in India. The Legal Position," *TL* (12 May 1913), 5; Gail Savage, "More than One Mrs. Mir Anwaruddin: Islamic Divorce and Christian Marriage in Early Twentieth-Century London," *J. Brit. Stud.* 47 (2008), 348–74.

[21] See W. W. Hunter, *The Indian Musulmans* (London: Trübner and Co., 1872).

[22] IPC, s. 494 in Ranchhoddas and Thakore, *IPC*, 435–40. See also "Polygamy in Hindu Law," *All LJ* 42 (1944), 49–50.

[23] Hindu Marriage Act (25 of 1955), s. 5. See also Subramanian, 776.

[24] The legality of polygyny in Muslim personal law has subtended the debate over the Uniform Civil Code since independence. See Archana Parashar, *Women and Family Law Reform in India: Uniform Civil Code and Gender Equality* (Delhi: Sage, 1992); Gerald James Larson, ed., *Religion and Personal Law in Secular India: A Call to Judgment* (Bloomington: Indiana University Press, 2001); Werner F. Menski, *Modern Indian Family Law* (Richmond, UK: 2001), 139–230, 345–402; Agnes, "The Supreme Court," 294–315; Jeffrey A. Redding, "Slicing the American Pie: Federalism and Personal Law," *N.Y.U. J. Int'l L. & Pol.* 40:4 (2008), 961–72.

[25] PMDA 1865, s. 5 in Rana (1934), 28–9.

violation, under the Indian Penal Code, was a fine and up to seven or ten years' imprisonment, depending on whether the new spouse was aware of the bigamy.[26] The Parsi Act added harsh sanctions against any Zoroastrian priest who performed a second marriage that turned out to be bigamous. He could be punished with a fine or imprisonment for up to six months, or both.[27]

The fact that polygamy was prohibited for Parsis *by Parsis* at a comparatively early date was politically important. Although the British drafters of the Indian Penal Code would have liked to criminalize polygyny for Hindus and Muslims in 1837, they would not dream of "attacking, by law, an evil so deeply rooted in the manners of the people of this country as polygamy." Instead, they would "leave it to the slow" but certain operation of "education and time."[28] Almost three decades later, the Parsis declared themselves pioneers among India's communities. The 1865 Act laid out a whole new legal regime for marriage among Parsis, but the prohibition of polygamy was its single most publicized achievement. Parsis celebrated the new rules as proof of the enlightened status of the community. S. S. Bengalee, the honorary secretary of the Parsi Law Association that drafted the statute, declared the Parsis to be Asia's most civilized people. They were "the first of Oriental peoples who, by legally defining her individual marital rights, have raised woman to a definitively higher social position on the basis of her own personal claims as a reasonable and responsible being."[29] Bengalee published an account of the passage of the Parsi Acts and reminded his readers of the comments of William Muir, a member of the Governor General's Council in Delhi. According to Bengalee, Muir considered the Parsis to be more advanced than India's other communities, a point made "evident from the fact that no other class of Native society would venture to propose that the penalties of the Criminal Code for bigamy should be made applicable to them."[30] Writing sixty years later, a Parsi lawyer named A. F. G. Chinoy called the Act "the Magna Charta of the rights and privileges of woman," who until then was considered "as a mere plaything to be thrown away at will" with her husband's taking of a second wife considered "as no offence against her."[31]

In fact, polygamy was not clearly accepted among Parsis even before 1865. The Parsi Panchayat issued a ban in 1791. By the 1830s, the *panchayat*'s authority was crumbling and the practice of polygamy was slowly gaining adherents.[32] Parsi reformers claimed that a clear triggering moment when polygamy increased was the Privy Council's ruling in the famous matrimonial

[26] IPC 1860, ss. 494–5.
[27] PMDA 1865, s. 9 in Rana (1934), 32–3.
[28] T. B. Macaulay et al., *The Indian Penal Code as originally framed in 1837* (Madras: Higginbotham and Co., 1888), 175.
[29] Bengalee, vii.
[30] Ibid., 205.
[31] A. F. G. Chinoy, "Stray Thoughts on the Parsi Marriage and Divorce Act of 1865," *Bom LJ* 1 (1923–4), 538.
[32] Palsetia, 76–7. See also Jessawalla, 10–11.

The Matrimonial Acts

suit of *Ardaseer Cursetjee v. Perozeboye.*[33] The wife, who was the original plaintiff, sued her husband for the restitution of conjugal rights and for maintenance. Her husband had abandoned her and married another woman. The case had been filed under the ecclesiastical jurisdiction of the Supreme Court of Bombay. The Privy Council suggested the Bombay court did not have jurisdiction *on its ecclesiastical side* over marriages between Parsis. The judges were optimistic that in its civil, nonecclesiastial jurisdiction, the Supreme Court may have been able to handle such cases.[34] But Parsi reformers ignored this aspect of the judgment and panicked. They claimed that the ruling plunged Parsis into a lawless vacuum, allowing unscrupulous spouses to marry a second time with impunity during the lifetime of their first spouses.

Polygamy conjured up a particular stereotype in the imperial imagination. Under the harem model of polygyny, multiple wives cohabited in *purdah*, competing for their husband's fancy both sexually and with regard to their offspring's inheritance. The polygamy that followed in the wake of *Cursetjee v. Perozeboye* looked different. In many of the twenty-six documented cases of polygamy among Bombay Parsis in 1860–1, the couple had informally separated before one spouse entered into a second marriage. In other words, what was technically polygamy was, in practice, serial monogamy. Parsi polygamy looked more like the nineteenth-century American "Wild West" model, in which a husband would take a second wife in the West after leaving his first wife in the East, than the seraglio fantasies of imperial critics.[35] This distinction was not emphasized by Parsi lobbyists as they pressed for polygamy's criminalization in the 1850s–'60s. Abolition brought greater rewards when it tapped into Orientalist visions of simultaneous, rather than consecutive, multiple spouses.

PROSTITUTION

With the first wave of matrimonial legislation, Parsi husbands lost the right to take more than one wife (if such a right even existed before 1865). However, they retained the right to sexual diversity in another form. The 1865 Act explicitly protected the right of Parsi husbands to have sex with prostitutes. Specifically, a man's extramarital sexual relations constituted adultery, a partial ground for divorce, *unless* the other woman was a prostitute. The Parsi Law Commission explained its thinking. "Illicit intercourse with courtesans carried on casually and beyond the precincts of the conjugal residence" was not enough to dissolve a marriage. The prostitution exception ended at the threshold of the matrimonial home: "the gross and flagrant violation of the feelings of a wife

---

[33] *Ardaseer Cursetjee v. Perozeboye* 6 MIA 348 (1854–7). See also "Foreign and Colonial," *Spectator* 16:806 (9 December 1843), 1159. I thank James Jaffe for the *Spectator* reference.

[34] *Ardaseer Cursetjee v. Perozeboye*, 391.

[35] See Hartog, *Man*, 259–62; Bluma Goldstein, *Enforced Marginality: Jewish Narratives on Abandoned Wives* (Berkeley: University of California Press, 2007), 99–100.

involved in the establishment of a kept mistress *under the marital roof* ought not to be regarded as falling within the just limits of the exception."[36] It was not the *extramarital* nature of the sexual intercourse that was problematic, but the lack of discretion surrounding it. Combined, the prostitution exception and the ban on polygamy suggested that some degree of sexual diversity was a patriarchal privilege. A clear hierarchy existed among the married man's female partners. There could be other women, namely prostitutes, but they could not be placed on an open and equal legal footing with one's wife. The 1865 Act gave the Parsi wife a bundle of legal entitlements, but her husband's sexual fidelity was not one of them.

The prostitution exception did not exist in the divorce law of the imperial metropole. Under English law, adultery by a husband was defined as the act of sexual intercourse with any woman not his wife, prostitutes included.[37] That Parsi law diverged from English law on prostitution reflected a deliberate choice made in the mid-nineteenth century. It was one more example of the ways in which Parsi lawmakers did not replicate English law, but pulled away from it at points that mattered. The prostitution exception was also striking because of the movement toward the increased regulation of prostitution in this period. The campaign to reduce prostitution and the spread of venereal disease targeted female prostitutes, not their male clients.[38] Furthermore, colonial legislation that regulated prostitution left untouched the relations of elite Indian men with their mistresses.[39] Parsi matrimonial law's protection of husbands in their pursuit of paid sexual services fit neatly alongside these other class- and gender-based exceptions. Together, they blunted the effects of the antiprostitution campaign. They were presumably a price colonial administrators were willing to pay to maintain the support of South Asian male elites.

The prostitution exception was not eliminated until the second wave of Parsi marital legislation in 1936. In the intervening seven decades, husbands tried to defeat their wives' divorce suits by arguing that the Other Woman was a prostitute.[40] The rule was not without its Parsi critics. In a scathing attack in 1888, the Parsi writer known as Mansukh lambasted the Act for protecting husbands' right to have sex with prostitutes (Figure 4.2). Travel allowed Parsi husbands to frequent Chinese brothels in China and visit European "Madames" in England. The transgressions took place in a spirit of fun and merriment. When questioned by their wives, Parsi husbands responded that their actions were

---

[36] Italics added. "Report into the usages recognized as laws by the Parsee Community of India," 13 in "1862–3 Government of India Bill."

[37] W. J. Dixon, *Law and Practice in Divorce and Other Matrimonial Causes* (London, 1900), 17, 150–1. See also the 1828 case of *Astley v. Astley* 162 ER 728 (1752–1865).

[38] See Tambe; Philippa Levine, "Sexuality, Gender and Empire," in *Gender and Empire*, ed. P. Levine (Oxford: Oxford University Press, 2004), 144–5.

[39] Tambe, 39.

[40] For examples, see "Parsee Chief Matrimonial Court," *TI* (4 September 1880), 3; Suit No. 5 of 1895, 1893–1903 PCMC Notebook, I: 215.

FIGURE 4.2. Title page from Mansukh's book (1888) criticizing Parsi matrimonial law. *Source*: Mansukh. ©The British Library Board 14146.e.25.

perfectly legal. Mansukh complained that the legislation had been passed with the assumption that Parsi gentlemen would feel duty bound not to frequent prostitutes even if it posed no legal threat to their marriages. Philandering Parsi husbands, however, aligned moral standards with legal ones, using their awareness of state law to legitimize the double standard on extramarital sex. According to the writer, Parsi law invited men to live like the Hindu king, Raja Gopichand, who was legendary for his immense harem (albeit of wives, not concubines).[41]

Mansukh lamented the indifference of Parsi priests and leaders toward the purchase of sexual services by Parsi men.[42] His position was echoed regularly for the next fifty years. Early Zoroastrian leaders of the Congress movement complained that Parsi men occasionally depleted their finances this way. "They gamble and whore and indulge in other vices," grumbled Dinsha Wacha to Dadabhai Naoroji in 1904.[43] In 1923, another Parsi critic made a eugenics-based argument against prostitution. Mysore barrister and philosophy professor A. R. Wadia described the effects of prostitution on wives and their children. He noted that a campaign to abolish the prostitution exception was growing among Parsis.[44] Wadia's argument was hardly driven by an acknowledgment of the rights of women (whether wives or prostitutes). His work, at least during the 1920s, was antifeminist in important ways.[45] Rather, eugenics animated Wadia's thought.[46] Like other Parsi lawyers, including J. J. Vimadalal in Bombay, Wadia was an adherent to the race science that would enjoy global favor from the later nineteenth century until World War II. His opposition to prostitution was also tied to another obsession of his age: the link between prostitution and the spread of venereal disease.[47] Colonial efforts to control venereal disease, particularly among the lower ranks of the military, took the form of antiprostitution statutes and the creation of lock hospitals, where prostitutes were ordered to register and remain if infected.[48] Wadia considered prostitution "the greatest social problem of the age," in part because it encouraged the spread of venereal disease – not just to husbands, but also to innocent parties like wives and the children they bore.[49] The infection of wives and babies were situations occasionally alleged in the Parsi Chief Matrimonial

[41] Mansukh, 73–4, 78. Raja Gopichand was the subject of several films in the 1920s–'30s. See, for instance, "Saraswati's 'Gopichand,'" *TI* (19 August 1938), 7.

[42] Mansukh, 79.

[43] Letter from D. E. Wacha to Dadabhai Naoroji (6 August 1904) in Patwardhan, II: 2, 869.

[44] Ardeshir Ruttonji Wadia, *Ethics of Feminism* (orig. pub. 1923) in *Anti-Feminism in Edwardian Literature*, eds. Lucy Delap and Ann Heilmann (London and Tokyo: Thoemmes and Edition Synapse, 2006), III: 236.

[45] See Wadia, *Ethics;* Lucy Delap and Ann Heilmann, "Introduction" in Delap and Heilmann, I: xxxiii–xxxviii.

[46] See Wadia, *Ethics,* 188–209.

[47] Ibid., 127–34.

[48] Tambe, 26–51; see also note 38.

[49] Wadia, *Ethics,* 134; see also 199–200.

The Matrimonial Acts

Court.[50] Wadia blamed prostitution for damaging the population's constitution and eugenic stock by this route.

In the process of equalizing grounds for divorce between husbands and wives, the 1936 Parsi Marriage and Divorce Act abolished the prostitution exception. The Act became famous for eliminating the double standard between husbands and wives. Under the 1865 Act, a Parsi wife had to prove worse behavior on the part of her husband than a husband had to prove to divorce his wife. The 1936 Act made uniform the grounds for divorce between husbands and wives. From then on, it was irrelevant whether a wife was seeking a divorce from her husband or a husband from his wife. Furthermore, a husband's adultery was no longer defined as extramarital sex with a married or unmarried women "not being a prostitute."[51] Parsi commentators on the draft bill recommended the quiet deletion of this qualifying phrase.[52]

Like its 1865 predecessor, the 1936 Act was celebrated for its gender equality. Legal officials, Bar Councils, Parsi Anjumans, and Panchayats expressed their support across South Asia. They approved explicitly of the equalization of grounds for divorce and, less directly, of the abolition of the prostitution exception.[53] Treating the sexes equally was "a blessing to an advanced nation" like the Parsis, wrote one observer.[54] The Parsi advocate K. J. Khambata raved about the Act's equalization of grounds for divorce in ways reminiscent of his predecessors' celebration of the ban on polygamy in 1865. Writing in *The Times of India*, he noted that the statute "makes the Parsis the first community in India to place men and women on an exactly equal footing so far as matrimonial causes are concerned; and that it makes the Parsi community the first in the East to put its divorce law on a more rational, humane and equitable basis."[55]

The Act eliminated this patriarchal privilege in theory more than in action. Both before and after 1936, Parsi wives accused their husbands in court of visiting prostitutes and keeping mistresses.[56] One Parsi memorialist who grew

---

[50] For a case of an infected baby who may have died of gonorrhea, see Suit No. 11 of 1933, 1929–35 PCMC Notebook, IV: 170–1. For cases in which wives claimed that their husbands had given them syphilis or gonorrhea, see Chapter 5 at note 169.

[51] See Wadia and Katpitia, 67.

[52] "Amendments suggested by the Zoroastrian Brotherhood in the Parsi Marriage and Divorce Act Amendment Bill," 12 in "The Parsi Marriage and Divorce Act 1936."

[53] E. D. Mehta, City Magistrate, First Class, Ajmer, "Paper No. 1: Opinions on the Parsi Marriage and Divorce Bill," 60, in "The Parsi Marriage and Divorce Act 1936."

[54] "S. H. Sui, Esq., Colliery Manager, the Central Bank of India, Ltd., P. O. Jharia, to the Senior Deputy Collector in charge, Dhanbad, dated Jharia, 25 December 1934" in "Paper No. 1: Opinions on the Parsi Marriage and Divorce Bill (introduced by the Hon. Sir Phiroze C. Sethna)," 58 in "The Parsi Marriage and Divorce Act 1936."

[55] K. J. Khambata, "New Law of Marriage and Divorce among Parsis: A Progressive Measure," *TI* (17 July 1936), 14.

[56] For a sample, see Suit No. 3 of 1899, 1893–1903 PCMC Notebook, II: 68, 75; Suit No. 8 of 1914, 1913–20 PCMC Notebook, II: 72; Suit No. 4 of 1925, 1924–8 PCMC Notebook, II: 48; Suit No. 3 of 1927, 1928–9 PCMC Notebook, II: 43; Suit No. 9 of 1932, 1929–35 Notebook, IV: 60; Suit

up in the 1920s and '30s argued for the legalization of prostitution by appealing to marital etiquette: it was better for a man to take a mistress or visit prostitutes than to pester his wife when she was not interested.[57] Nonetheless, the 1936 Act meant that previously open activity was forced underground. The Act may explain why one husband, lured by his wife's detective into a street brawl as he left a brothel in 1941, panicked as a crowd of potential witnesses gathered around him.[58]

The patriarchal entitlement to sexual diversity within marriage shrank in two steps. The earlier generation of Parsi lobbyists criminalized polygamy, itself of dubious legal and social status even before 1865. In the 1930s, the later generation eliminated the exception carved out of the 1865 definition of adultery that permitted husbands to have sex with prostitutes. Both moves were important politically, although the first received greater publicity. The promotion of women's rights was a key plank in the civilizing mission that justified colonialism. In the words of one wife whose husband demanded to know where she was going, "This is British rule under which husbands have no right to ask such questions."[59] While promoting reforms perceived to better the status of women, Parsis declared themselves the most progressive of Asian communities. However, while relinquishing one type of patriarchal privilege, lobbyists were reinforcing others, namely the paterfamilias's control over his children's marriage alliances and his right to beat his wife.

CHILD MARRIAGE

The 1865 matrimonial legislation became famous for its stance against bigamy. However, another issue received equal publicity during negotiations and went discreetly unmentioned later. Child or "infant marriage" triggered lengthy debate among members of the Parsi Law Commission. The commission consisted of two British judges of the Bombay High Court, Joseph Arnould and H. Newton, and two Parsis, namely the Modi of Surat (Rustomjee Khorshedjee) and Framjee Nasserwanjee of Bombay. Child marriage divided the commission along ethnic lines. The British commissioners opposed the practice. The Parsis argued that it was too ingrained to ban and even that it ought to be fortified.

The child marriage debate was intriguing for its intercommunity valences. One would expect it to have nothing to do with Hindus: the discussants were Parsi and European. However, critics of Parsi child marriage made Hindu

No. 5 of 1933, 1929–35 PCMC Notebook, IV: 124, 126; Suit No. 11 of 1933, 1929–35 PCMC Notebook, IV: 171; Suit No. 9 of 1935, 1935–7 PCMC Notebook, I: 239–40; Suit No. 13 of 1938, 1937–41 PCMC Notebook, II: 112; Suit No. 26 of 1941, 1941–8 PCMC Notebook, IA: 4–5, 14.

[57] P. P. Ginwala, "Prostitution" in his collection of unpublished essays, "Dog's Eye View: Take Nothing on Trust, but Sniff All Round It First. Views and Vitae Curriculum of a Heretic" (Mumbai, 2007). I thank the author (now deceased) for sharing this collection with me.

[58] See Chapter 1 at 60.

[59] Suit No. 3 of 1914, 1913–20 PCMC Notebook 1913–20, I: 97.

The Matrimonial Acts

influence a centerpiece of the discussion. Equally, the ancient Persians had a spectral presence at the negotiating table. The two were linked. Reformists dismissed many Parsi social practices as inauthentic, claiming that they were adoptions of Hindu customs.[60] Parsi critics of colonial modernity also used ancient Persia as a Utopian foil against which to attack undesirable aspects of contemporary social life.[61] The two-part move discrediting Parsi practices (particularly those in the *mofussil*) was, first, to blame Hindu custom and, second, to contrast the practice with those of the ancient Persians. This rhetorical sequence encouraged Parsis to reform their practices by claiming that they were returning to true Zoroastrian ways. It also served a political function, drawing Parsi reformers closer to the British who were encouraging the reform. It permitted Parsis, like Europeans, to contrast "authentic" practices (i.e., those of ancient Persia) with "barbaric" Hindu customs. This line of argument also served British purposes: it created divisions between South Asian communities in classic divide-and-rule manner.[62] Intriguingly, the same type of argument emerged from reform campaigns targeting Muslim *and* Hindu customs. Muslim customs deemed uncivilized were blamed on Hindu influence. Undesirable Hindu customs were blamed on precolonial Muslim rule.[63]

British commissioners couched their criticism of Parsi child marriage in terms that flattered the Zoroasrtrian collective ego, characterizing the Parsis as a community that was distinct from and more civilized than the Hindu majority. Arnould and Newton claimed that child marriage was "a practice plainly derived from the Hindoos and not in any way sanctioned by Zoroastrian Scripture or ancient Zoroastrian usage."[64] Despite the relative lack of knowledge of ancient Zoroastrian law in the colonial period, reform was often presented as a return to ancient Persian ways. This type of neo-retro argument was particularly common when a proposed reform furthered the rights of women. Colonial Parsis regarded ancient Persian society and Zoroastrian scripture as an ideal model of gender equality, a characterization doubted by later scholars of ancient Zoroastrianism.[65] By joining in the glorification of ancient Persian law and custom, the European commissioners were inviting Parsis to reform without looking Westernized or losing face.

---

[60] See Rana (1934), 14.

[61] See, for example, Dadabhai Naoroji in Parekh, 13–15.

[62] See Chapter 2 at note 18.

[63] See Minault, text accompanying notes 32–3 (on reform debates over child marriage among Muslims); "Child-Marriage and Enforced Widowhood in India."

[64] "Report into the usages recognized as laws by the Parsee Community of India," 13 in "1862–3 Government of India Bill."

[65] See Dosabhoy Framjee, *The Parsees. Their History, Manners, Customs and Religion* (Delhi: Asian Educational Services, 2003; orig. pub. 1858), 73; Darab Dastur Peshotan Sanjana, *The Position of Zoroastrian Women in Remote Antiquity* (Bombay: Education Society's Steam Press, 1892); Zaidi, I, 394. For a current scholarly view of ancient Persian gender relations, see Gould, 147–57; Macuch, "Law"; Rose, "Gender."

The British commissioners also avoided framing the debate as a Parsi-versus-European conflict by relying on the writings of the Parsi lobbyist and judge, Manekjee Cursetjee, an outspoken critic of child marriage.[66] "There have been instances," wrote Cursetjee in an 1844 letter to the *Bombay Times and Journal of Commerce*, "where nuptial ceremonies of infants have been performed while [sitting] on their mothers' laps, having sugar plums administered to them in order to keep them quiet and from crying during the performance of the ceremony by their priests!"[67] Like the two British commissioners, Manekjee Cursetjee drew on the idea of Hindu contagion, blaming the Parsi practice of child marriage on the Hindus around them. "This is one of the many barbarous and cruel rites and customs which the Parsees have borrowed and adopted from the Hindoos and which is productive of incalculable mischief among them."[68] Parsi and European critics alike would have read the writings of Parsi magistrate and historian, Dossabhoy Framjee Karaka.[69] In 1858, Karaka wrote that child marriage was one of the many Hindu customs that the Parsis had imitated. According to Karaka, Hindus were enjoined by their scriptures to have their daughters married by the age of nine and felt great shame if they did not. Parsi parents had imitated the Hindu approach.[70] Karaka noted that ancient Zoroastrian law set the minimum age of marriage at fifteen, a point adopted in the child marriage case law.[71]

The British members of the Parsi Law Commission relied on Manekjee Cursetjee in stressing the social and medical costs of child marriage. Their report included the following excerpt from his writings: "The extent of domestic discord and family derangement caused by infant marriages and betrothals among the natives of India, few if any foreigners can have any adequate conception of – Little babes and children are *quasi* sold and bartered but by another name miscalled marriage which ... saps the foundation of their domestic comforts, ruins and destroys their health, and obstructs the development of their mental faculties."[72] Allusion to the damaging effects of sex and pregnancy on young couples foreshadowed the age of consent debates that swept across India during the 1880s and early 1890s, and again in the 1920s.[73]

---

[66] Bengalee, 231.

[67] "The Parsee Punchyat – its Rise, its Fall and the Causes that led to the same," *BTJC* (25 Dec. 1844), 828.

[68] Manekjee Cursetjee quoted in "Report into the usages recognized as laws by the Parsee Community of India," 14 in "1862–3 Government of India Bill." See also Q. in the Corner, I: 13, 17–19; II: 22.

[69] See Chapter 2 at note 173.

[70] For a similar account, see Jessawalla, 58–9.

[71] Karaka, I, 170; *Dustoor v. Meherba'i* 311.

[72] Manekjee Cursetjee quoted in "Report," 14 in "1862–3 Government of India Bill."

[73] Sinha, 138–180; Padma Anagol-McGinn, "The Age of Consent Act (1891) Reconsidered: Women's Perspectives and Participation in the Child-Marriage Controversy in India," *SAR* 12:2 (1992), 100–18; Birla, *Stages of Capital*, 216–22, 227–31; Ishita Pande, *Medicine, Race and Liberalism in British Bengal: Symptoms of Empire* (London: Routledge, 2009), 160–70.

The Matrimonial Acts

By contrast, the Parsi commissioners wanted child marriage to be tolerated. Although neither claimed to endorse the practice personally, the Modi of Surat said he represented *mofussil* Parsis who did. He did not give reasons for his constituents' views, but there were presumably two. The practice allowed fathers to use their children's marriages to forge important social and economic alliances. For a diasporic trading community like the Parsis, strategic marriages could be essential in reinforcing networks of trust and trade across long distances. Child marriage also reduced the likelihood of premarital pregnancy, which was socially stigmatized and economically problematic in colonial Parsi social life.[74] On both rationales, child marriage gave the *paterfamilias* control over his children – both over their choice of marriage partner and over their potential to embarrass the family socially and burden it financially through premarital pregnancy.

Not only did the Modi want the 1865 Act *not* to prohibit child marriage; he also wanted it to strengthen the institution by punishing the *breach* of child marriage contracts. Where two families had agreed to marriage between their children, the Modi complained that one side could withdraw with impunity. The ability to sue the breaching party through a civil suit would be useful. But criminal sanctions would be better, especially where the victims of the breach were poor and unable to fund a civil action. In a conflation of two key themes of the 1865 Act – polygamy and child marriage – the Modi argued that enforcing child marriage contracts would also prevent bigamy.[75] When one side breached a child marriage contract and then entered into a marriage with a third party, the result was technically bigamy:

> The temptation for the commission of such breaches [is] great and often irresistible, and the door would be opened for the commission of the crime of bigamy if the views of my [European] colleagues in this respect were carried out in their entirety. Where a husband or his relations were the reverse of influential and wealthy, the inconvenience, delay and expense to which they would be subjected by a resort to civil proceedings would frequently prevent them from seeking any redress at all, and compel them silently to submit to injustice as only a misfortune; whereas the dread of criminal penalties from the comparative promptitude of their imposition, and the disgrace attaching to them (the further institution of civil proceedings not being thereby barred, but left optional with the party wronged) would prove an effectual check.[76]

The European commissioners tried to distance child marriage from the Parsis by blaming it on Hindu influence. By contrast, the Modi looked to Zoroastrian

---

[74] *Doodhpiti* (Guj. *dūdhpītī*), an expression loosely translated as "making an infant drink milk," referred to the drowning of an unwanted baby in a basin of milk. See Mukherji and Desai, 12.

[75] The French historian Delphine Menant also blamed Parsi polygamy on child marriage, although she did not favor harsher penalties for breach of child marriage contracts. See Menant, *Les Parsis*, 284–5.

[76] "Appendix B. Minute by Modee Rustomjee Khoorshedjee," 8–9 in "1862–3 Government of India Bill."

182 *Law and Identity in Colonial South Asia: Parsi Legal Culture*

scripture for support: "In the 4th chapter of the [*Vendidad*], the breach by the father, and constructively by the guardian, of contracts of the marriage of children, is shown to render the offending party or parties amenable to a very heavy punishment . . ."[77]

The Modi claimed not to support child marriage personally but to tolerate it because it was "so deeply rooted among the Parsees."[78] His disavowal was unconvincing, following as it did on his lengthy plea for criminal sanctions against the breach of child marriage contracts. The other Parsi commissioner, however, made the point more plausibly. Framjee Nasserwanjee represented Parsis in Bombay City. He accepted that the introduction of criminal sanctions for breach of contract was unlikely. But he wanted parties who were victims of a breach to be able to sue in court for civil redress. "I am no advocate of the practice of infant marriage which prevails extensively amongst my co-religionists, yet I feel convinced that it cannot be put down by legislative restriction or discouragement."[79]

The final Act represented a compromise, but one that leaned in favor of child marriage. The Parsi commissioners failed to have penalties for the breach of child marriage contracts included in the statute, a point unmentioned in Palsetia's account.[80] This was a concession to the Europeans. As the Governor wrote in response to the Parsi Law Commission's report, "The British Government cannot justly be called on, when legislating for the assertion of Parsee rights, to recognize customs which it deems injurious, and which have no sanction from the religious law of the Parsees, but which have been insensibly adopted from the Hindoos around them."[81] But equally, and against British wishes, the Act did not prohibit child marriage. The only provision of the Act that did address the issue was ambiguous – a reflection, no doubt, of the uncomfortable compromise between Parsi and European commissioners. The statute did not invalidate child marriage contracts but simply prevented parties from suing for enforcement of these contracts while the wife was under the age of fourteen or the husband under sixteen.[82]

As early as 1858, Karaka claimed that child marriage was dying out among Zoroastrians, particularly in Bombay.[83] The Bombay Parsi Panchayat had tried to excommunicate parents who engineered child marriages in 1777 but with

---

[77] Ibid., 9. See also *Vendidad*, Fargard IV, IId: 16 (51), IIe: 44 (118) in *The Vendîdâd* trans. James Darmesteter (Oxford: Clarendon Press, 1880), 38–9, 45 (Vol. IV of Friedrich Max Müller, ed., *Sacred Books of the East*).

[78] "Appendix B. Minute by Modee Rustomjee Khoorshedjee," 9 in "1862–3 Government of India Bill."

[79] "Appendix A: Minute by Mr. Framjee Nasserwanjee," 3 in "1862–3 Government of India Bill."

[80] Palsetia, *Parsis of India*, 222–3.

[81] "Resolution by the Honourable Board, dated 20 October 1863," 2 in "1862–3 Government of India Bill."

[82] PMDA 1865, s.37 in Rana (1934), 90.

[83] Framjee, 77–8.

The Matrimonial Acts

little effect.[84] By 1881, an attempt by an elderly priest to have his grandchildren married in a group "infant marriage" ceremony raised the "cry of indignation" in the Parsi press.[85] If social views were changing, though, they were not reflected in court rulings. Courts in the 1880s–'90s confirmed the validity of unconsummated child marriages. The leading case was *Peshotam Hormasji Dustoor v. Meherba'i* (1889), in which the adult plaintiff-husband argued that his 1868 marriage was invalid: he was seven at the time of wedding, whereas his bride was six. The parties had not consummated the relationship, although they had lived under the same roof with the husband's parents. The Bombay High Court judge, a Briton named Scott, repeated the arguments of the European members of the Parsi Law Commission and added some. Citing Karaka, Scott noted that ancient Persian law did not allow marriage before the age of fifteen. He also indicated that, in the seventeenth century, Persian Zoroastrians had been consulted by Indian Zoroastrians on the minimum age for marriage. According to the Persians, boys had to be at least fourteen and girls ten. Despite these age limits, though, a custom to the contrary had developed among the Parsis. Like the critics of child marriage in the 1860s, the judge blamed regressive Parsi practices on Hindu influence: "When the Parsis settled in Western India eleven hundred and sixty years ago they probably brought with them a system, both of law and custom, from Persia. But it was all unwritten, and gradually fell into desuetude, and this mere handful of Persian strangers gradually and naturally adopted much of the law and usage that obtained in the Hindu community in whose midst they were forced to dwell. There is no doubt they adopted, amongst other things, the injurious practice of infant marriage."[86]

Intriguingly, Scott failed to apply the very stringent legal test required to prove the existence of a custom. To be recognized by law, a custom had to be ancient, invariable, and not repugnant to the general law (which often meant British sensibilities). Few attempts to prove a custom according to this test succeeded in court, which was perhaps why the test was sidestepped in other Parsi cases, too.[87] In 1908, Dinshah Davar recognized as customary the practice of not accepting converts to Zoroastrianism and of regarding the children of Parsi men and non-Parsi women as eligible for initiation into the religion.[88] He, too, failed to apply the technical test for custom – no doubt because he realized that the test was hard to pass.[89]

---

[84] Karaka, I: 173.

[85] Ibid., I, 172.

[86] *Dustoor v. Meherba'i*, 311. See also Mistry, *Reminiscences* [1911], 60–1.

[87] For failed attempts, see *Rahimatbai v. Hirbai* ILR 3 Bom 34 (1879) and *Bachebi v. Makhan Lal* ILR 3 All 55 (1881), discussed in Chandra Mallampalli, "Escaping the Grip of Personal Law in Colonial India: Proving Custom, Negotiating Hindu-ness," *LHR* 28: 4 (2010), 1058–9, 1061–2; *Joao Mariano Lopes v. Francisco Lopes* 5 Bom HCR 172 (1867–8). See also Sturman, 151–8.

[88] *Judgments:* Petit v. Jeejeebhoy *1908*, 64, 68–9. See also "The Parsi Panchayat Case," *HP* (27 December 1908), 19.

[89] For example, see *Nugender Narain v. Rughoonath Narain Dey* Suth. WR 20 (1864).

184 Law and Identity in Colonial South Asia: Parsi Legal Culture

Dustoor v. Meherbai set a precedent that subsequent judges followed. *Bai Shirinbai v. Kharsedji N. Masalavala* (1898) was an extreme case in which a marriage had been contracted when the bride was less than three years old.[90] At the age of twenty-four, she came to court asking for the unconsummated marriage to be invalidated. Meherbai argued that a toddler could not consent to marriage, but she lost. The court recognized that the practice of child marriage was less popular than it had been earlier. It may not even have been a legally binding custom in 1890, when the suit was filed. However, at the time of bride's marriage in 1869, the custom was apparently recognized by the lower courts. Again, the legal test for custom was quietly avoided – this time, through reliance on unidentified precedents.[91]

Despite Karaka's prediction that child marriage among Parsis would be dead by 1880, the practice continued well into the twentieth century (Figure 4.3 and 4.4).[92] In many cases before the Parsi Chief Matrimonial Court, the parties had married as young teenagers.[93] Cohabitation was normally delayed for several years.[94] The Parsi priest M. N. Dhalla, for instance, recounted in his autobiography that he was married in 1881 at age six to a "five-year-old delicate beauty," but that he did not live with his wife until both were nineteen or twenty years old.[95] By the 1930s, child marriage seems to have died out among Parsis. The practice had even subsided among *mofussil* Parsis, a shift perhaps influenced by the pan-Indian discussion about child marriage since the age of consent controversy of the late nineteenth century. Intriguingly, a leading opponent of child

[90] *Bai Shirinbai v. Kharshedji Nasarvanji Masalavala* ILR 22 Bom 430 (1898).
[91] Ibid., 437–8.
[92] See note 83.
[93] The most common age of marriage for Parsi girls who married as minors was about thirteen. Their husbands tended to be two to six years older. See, for example, Suit No. 5 of 1895, 1893–1903 PCMC Notebook, I: 212 (bride twelve to thirteen, groom eighteen to nineteen); Suit No. 9 of 1926, 1924–8 PCMC Notebook, III: 23 (bride eleven to twelve, groom thirteen to fourteen). For cases of earlier marriage, see the following in the *TI*: "A Parsee Divorce Suit. *Furdoonjee Pallonjee Desai v. Kharshedbai*" (30 November 1887), 3 (both about eight years old at marriage); "A Suit for the Restitution of Conjugal Rights. *Dinbai v. Jehangeer Rustomjee Sodawaterwalla*" (23 June 1890), 3 (bride nine, groom ten). See also Suit No. 4 of 1896, 1893–1903 PCMC Notebook, I: 227 (bride seven, groom nine); Suit No. 9 of 1926, 1924–8 PCMC Notebook, III: 23 (bride eleven to twelve, groom thirteen to fourteen); Suit No. 3 of 1932, 1929–35 PCMC Notebook, IV: 6 (bride eight, groom ten); Suit No. 18 of 1941, 1941–8 PCMC Notebook, I: 278 (bride nine, groom fifteen).
[94] See Suit No. 5 of 1898, 1893–1903 PCMC Notebook, II: 45 (no cohabitation immediately after marriage because bride was "very young"; groom was nineteen); Suit No. 4 of 1902, 1893–1903 PCMC Notebook, III: 38 (bride nine, groom fifteen; cohabitation began three to four years after the wedding); Suit No. 7 of 1914, 1913–20 PCMC Notebook, II: 98 (wife married at age seven; no cohabitation when husband died five or six years later); Suit No. 18 of 1941, 1941–8 PCMC Notebook, I: 278 (bride nine, husband fifteen; no cohabitation until eight years later).
[95] M. N. Dhalla, *Dastur Dhalla: The Saga of a Soul. An Autobiography of Shams-ul-Ulama Dastur Dr. Maneckji Nusserwanji Dhalla, High Priest of the Parsis of Pakistan* (Karachi: Dastur Dr. Dhalla Memorial Institute, 1975), 45. On Dhalla, see Stausberg, *Die Religion*, II, 109–11; Ringer, *Pious Citizens*, 126–34.

FIGURE 4.3. Portrait of a Parsi girl taken in Bombay during the early twentieth century. *Source*: Private collection. Courtesy of the author.

FIGURE 4.4. Portrait of a Parsi boy taken in Bombay during the early twentieth century. *Source*: Private collection. Courtesy of the author.

The Matrimonial Acts

marriage among Hindus in the 1880s was Behramji Malabari, a Parsi criticized for impolitic interference as a non-Hindu.[96]

The compromise provisions of the 1865 Act remained a part of the revised Parsi legislation of 1936.[97] By then, the passage of the all-India Child Marriage Restraint Act (XIX of 1929) had prohibited child marriage, defined as marriage in which the bride was under the age of fourteen or the groom under eighteen.[98] Conservative Parsis continued to push for influence over their children's marriages, but in the 1920s–'30s, their desired form of legal control took a very different shape. Parsis of this later period tried to prevent their children themselves from contracting love marriages as teenagers. This generation of lobbyists wanted parental consent to be required for the marriage of individuals between the ages of eighteen and twenty-one to prevent their teenaged children from eloping. As Parsi advocate M. M. Bhesania wrote in 1928–9, requiring parental consent until the age of twenty-one would prevent the risk of "impulsive or rash union in the heat of youth which can ordinarily be expected to be moved by considerations other than those of permanent conjugal and domestic consistency and harmony."[99] Bhesania's allies also wanted provisions invalidating any attempts by their children to convert to another religion – like Islam – in order to sidestep the requirement of parental consent.[100] The power to marry young was no longer a patriarchal prerogative. It had come to be associated with teenagers, not children, and with the follies of youth, rather than strategic alliances between parents. Nonetheless, in trying to *prevent* marriage among teenagers, conservative Parsis in the 1920s–'30s still wanted control over their children's marriages. In this way, their priorities were consistent with those of their predecessors in the 1850s–'60s who fought to protect child marriage as a privilege of the *paterfamilias*.

MARITAL VIOLENCE

If the 1865 Act tolerated one form of patriarchal control over nuclear family members (the ability to contract child marriages), the 1936 Act represented a more emphatic protection of another: the right to use violence against one's

---

[96] Sturman, 184.

[97] PMDA 1936, s. 38 in Wadia and Katpitia, 112–13.

[98] Child Marriage Restraint Act 1929, s. 2(a), noted in Wadia and Katpitia, 22.

[99] M. M. Bhesania, "Revision of Parsi Laws," *Bom LJ* 4 (1928–9) 174.

[100] PMDA 1936, s.3(c) in Wadia and Katpitia, 20; "Opinion of the members of the Managing Committee, Parsee Anjuman, Agra, to the Collector, Agra, dated 16 November 1934" in "Paper No. 1: Opinions on the Parsi Marriage and Divorce Bill," 56 in "The Parsi Marriage and Divorce Act 1936." On alleged forum shopping through conversion to Islam, see PCMC Suit No. 2 of 1883 in Patel and Paymaster, III, 840; "The Parsee Chief Matrimonial Court ... *Awabai v. Peroshaw Framjee and Ashabai*," *TI* (3 July 1883), 3; PCMC Suit No. 5 of 1895, 1893–1903 PCMC Notebook, I: 214; *Dhunbai Sorabji Palkhiwalla v. Sorabji Ardeshir Palkhiwalla* 39 Bom LR (journal) 1143 (1937). See also De, "Two Husbands," 1011–4.

188   *Law and Identity in Colonial South Asia: Parsi Legal Culture*

spouse. Both powers were protected while married men's legal right to sexual diversity shrank away. Under the 1936 Act, one Parsi spouse could file for divorce if she (as it usually was) suffered from "grievous hurt" inflicted by the other.[101] The 1865 Act had made cruelty the basis for judicial separation, but not by itself for divorce.[102] If the later Act seemed to take a sterner view of marital violence by upgrading it from a ground for judicial separation to one for divorce, it was only in appearance. The key question was: what constituted grievous hurt? Out of this discussion came a newly precise and permissive standard enabling husbands to inflict a notable degree of violence on their wives. It was as if the 1936 Act represented a quiet trade-off, only the first part of which was publicized.[103] Parsi married men gave up the right to have sex with prostitutes but found fortified their right to beat their wives.

The concept most closely resembling grievous hurt in the 1865 Parsi legislation was cruelty. Under the 1865 rules, "cruelty or personal violence" could function as the basis for a wife's suit for judicial separation, as could "reasonable grounds for apprehending danger to life or serious personal injury."[104] Coupled with adultery, cruelty could serve as the basis for a divorce claim.[105] It could also block a husband's suit for the restitution of conjugal rights.[106] The Indian courts, including the Parsi Chief Matrimonial Court, adopted the definition of cruelty in English case law: "there must be actual violence of such a character as to endanger personal health or safety, or there must be a reasonable apprehension of it."[107] But the insistence on "actual violence" was unraveled by the finding that personal health included mental health and that a continuing course of conduct could amount to cruelty without the occurrence of assault.[108] Although "cruelty" was undefined in the 1865 Act and unsettled in the case law, it was broad enough to include psychological trauma and types of physical injury that would be removed from the concept of "grievous hurt" in the 1930s.

The Indian Penal Code (IPC) defined any of the following as "grievous hurt": emasculation; blinding of an eye or deprivation of hearing in an ear; privation, destruction, or permanent impairing of any member or joint; permanent disfiguration of the head or face; fracture or dislocation of a bone or tooth; or "any hurt which endangers life or which causes the sufferer to be, during the space of twenty days, in severe bodily pain, or unable to follow his ordinary

---

[101] PMDA 1936, s. 32(e) in Wadia and Katpitia, 68, 77.

[102] PMDA 1865, ss. 30–1 in Rana (1934), 50–1, 60–3.

[103] See, for instance, K. J. Khambata's misleading summary of the Act's definition of "grievous hurt": Khambata, 14.

[104] PMDA 1865, s. 31.

[105] Ibid., s. 30.

[106] Ibid., s. 36 in Rana (1934), 86–7.

[107] See the 1867 Privy Council case of *Moonshee Buzloor Raheem v. Shumsoonnissa Begam* 20 Eng. Rep. 208 (1809–65), reproducing 11 MIA 611. See also Rana (1934), 51, 87.

[108] *Florence Amelia Thompson v. George S. Thompson* and *George S. Thompson v. Florence Amelia Thompson and another* (joined cases) ILR 39 Cal 395 (1912); Rana (1934), 50–1, 87.

The Matrimonial Acts

pursuits."[109] Early versions of the 1936 bill imported this list wholesale: grievous hurt in Parsi divorce law would be the same as grievous hurt in Indian criminal law. But Parsi organizations and individuals objected. Submitting written critiques, some argued that "grievous hurt" ought to act as a basis for judicial separation only, not divorce.[110] Others insisted that a certain degree of violence was an acceptable and everyday part of marriage. Two parts of the IPC definition came under attack: the fracture or dislocation of a bone or tooth and any hurt that caused severe bodily pain for twenty days or that prevented the victim from following her ordinary pursuits.[111] Organizations like the Dadar-Matunga Zoroastrian Association and the conservative Zoroastrian Brotherhood wanted both items removed from the Parsi Act's definition of grievous hurt.[112] The Grant Road Parsi Association, whose matrimonial arbitration services were well known in the 1930s, went further. In addition to the two parts just mentioned, it also wanted a third part of the IPC definition removed: "the destruction or permanent impairing of the powers of any member or joint."[113] A series of newspaper articles appearing in the leading Parsi newspaper, *Jam-e-Jamshed*, took a similar view. The *Jam-e-Jamshed*'s defense of marital violence was unabashed: "if a husband, at some provocation from his wife, were to slap her and this caused a decayed tooth to drop out, it would be a good ground for divorce! Again a chastisement which may not cause much pain to a robust woman may keep an ailing or weak woman in pain for twenty days! *Having experience as worldly men, that husbands are rather too free with their hands, notwithstanding the provisions of the penal Code, would it be safe to dissolve marriage at every violent quarrel between a husband and wife?*"[114]

---

[109] IPC s. 320 in Ranchhoddas and Thakore, *IPC*, 83–5.

[110] "Opinion of Sardar Davar T. K. Modi" in "Opinion No. 2 – Bombay," 20; "Copy of letter dated 17 November 1934, from the President and Secretary, Parsi Committee, Sialkot Cantonment, to the Executive Officer, Sialkot" in "Opinion No. 10 – Punjab," 47; "From M. B. Sanjana, Esq., MA, LLB, President, Surat Borough Municipality, Surat, to the Collector of Surat, Surat, dated Surat, the 6 November, 1934" in "Opinion No. 2 – Bombay," 21; all in "Paper No. I: Opinions of the Parsi Marriage and Divorce Bill" in "Parsi Marriage and Divorce Act 1936."

[111] On broken teeth and grievous hurt under the IPC, see W. D. Sutherland, "Teeth-Blows in their Medico-Legal Aspect," *Ind. Med. Gaz.* 34 (July 1899), 241–2.

[112] "From the Joint Honorary Secretaries, Dadar-Matunga Zoroastrian Association, to the Secretary to the Government of Bombay, Home Department Secretariat, Bombay, dated Bombay, the 17 November 1934" in "Opinion No. 2 – Bombay,"15 in "Paper No. I: Opinions on the Parsi Marriage and Divorce Bill"; "Paper No. IV. Opinion No. 23 – Bombay. The Zoroastrian Brotherhood, Bombay, 8 June 1935 to the Hon. Pres. and Members of the Council of State and of the Legislative Assembly, New Delhi," 73; both in "Parsi Marriage and Divorce Act 1936."

[113] "Appendix A: Alterations or amendments as suggested by individuals and Associations in the Bill to amend the Parsee Marriage and Divorce Act of 1865," 69 in "Parsi Marriage and Divorce Act 1936." See also Chapter 1 at 43.

[114] "Parsi Marriage and Divorce Bill: III," *Jam-e-Jamshed* (7 January 1935) in "Paper No. VII: Opinions on the Parsi Marriage and Divorce Bill. Opinion No. 23 – From the Honorary

It was not only in Bombay that elite Parsi men regarded violence as a husband's privilege. From Surat, a High Priest suggested that the bill was too hard on husbands who acted under a momentary loss of self-control or who were provoked by their wives.[115] Parsis trained as lawyers, such as the Collector of Surat, T. K. Modi and the president of the Surat Borough Municipality, M. B. Sanjana agreed. They insisted that it was "absurd to grant divorce for one single instance of grievous hurt."[116] The Collector was himself the successor of the Modi of Surat who had exercised jurisdiction over Parsi matrimonial suits in Surat before 1865. He was also a juror or delegate of Surat's Parsi Matrimonial Court, a trustee of several Parsi fire temples in Surat, a Member of the Bombay Legislative Council, a major land owner, director of a bank and corporation, and professor of law at the Sarvajanik Law College in Surat – in short, a leading member of the provincial elite.[117]

Permissive voices like these prevailed. Certain parts of the definition of grievous hurt in criminal law were removed from the 1936 Act.[118] Specifically, the fracture or dislocation of a bone or tooth would not constitute grievous hurt in Parsi matrimonial law, although it would continue to do so under Indian criminal law. Any injury that caused the wife to be in "severe bodily pain" for twenty days or unable to follow her ordinary pursuits would also not constitute a ground for divorce. Similarly, the permanent impairing of any member or joint, if it fell short of "privation" of that member or joint, would not count for the purposes of Parsi law. The message was clear: a notable degree of violence was a standard part of married life. Almost all of the formal commentators were male, but it was not only men who took this view. It was not unusual for female relatives to tell battered wives that they should return to their husbands, that the wives had provoked the assault, or that they must tolerate the attacks despite being blameless. In one mother-in-law's words, "all men and husbands do this."[119] One wife told the matrimonial court that her husband's assaults, communication of gonorrhea and syphilis, and threats to take a mistress drove her to attempt suicide by drinking poison. She had told her mother that the husband beat her and locked her inside their home when he went out. The mother "remonstrated with me and said such things must take place if [one]

Secretary, the Zoroastrian Brotherhood, Bombay, dated the 8 June, 1935, with enclosures," 79 in "Parsi Marriage and Divorce Act 1936." Italics added.

[115] "From Dastur Jamshed Dastur Sorab Coomana, High Priest, Surat, to the Collector of Surat, Surat, dated the 29 October 1934," 21 in "Parsi Marriage and Divorce Act 1936."

[116] "Opinion of Sardar Davar T. K. Modi" in "From Sardar Davar T. K. Modi, Collector of Surat, Surat, dated the 3 November 1934," 20; "Opinion" in "From M. B. Sanjana, Esq., MA, LLB, President, Surat Borough Municipality, Surat, to the Collector of Surat, Surat, dated Surat, the 6 November, 1934," 21; both in "Parsi Marriage and Divorce Act 1936."

[117] "Modi, Sardar Davar T. K." in, Who's Who in India, Burma and Ceylon, 541–2; Darukhanawala, Parsi Lustre, I, 370–1.

[118] See PMDA 1936, s. 2(4) in Wadia and Katpitia, 11, 13.

[119] Suit No. 2 of 1929, 1929–35 PCMC Notebook, I: 23.

The Matrimonial Acts

lived with a husband."[120] Such comments between women were oral and informal. They were made during unguarded moments in the family home. By contrast, the discussion of domestic violence leading to the 1936 Act was probably the most formal, precise, and public discussion of Parsi marital violence of the colonial period. It was breathtakingly bold: elite male Parsis acknowledged and defended their right to "moderately" assault their wives, claiming entitlement to use forms of violence that constituted criminal offenses. Civil wrongs not rising to the level of criminal acts were common enough phenomena, but the inverse phenomenon – criminal acts that somehow did not constitute civil wrongs – was legally bizarre. Even so, organized community efforts ensured that the final Act protected and even amplified this form of patriarchal privilege. An 1898 Parsi matrimonial court case had established the concept of reasonable marital violence: striking one's wife three times with a cane was fine, whereas threatening her with a knife was not.[121] Three decades later, these views seemed to persist among the most vocal and organized of Parsi bodies, in Bombay as much as in the more conservative *mofussil*.[122] In the same way that Parsi legislation protected patriarchal control over children's marriages in the 1860s, it similarly preserved and expanded husbands' power to assault wives in the 1930s.

CONCLUSION

Parsi marital legislation was celebrated for promoting the rights of women. The criminalization of polygamy occurred in 1865. In 1936, the grounds for divorce were equalized between the sexes, eliminating the prostitution exception. For the first time, a husband's relations with prostitutes would count as adultery and a basis for divorce. These were the aspects of the statutes heralded as signs of Parsi advancement, in the language of the day. The promotion of women's rights offered maximum political value in Parsi–British relations, and the disproportionate emphasis placed on the ban on polygamy, especially, reflected this dynamic. However, a more complicated renegotiation of Parsi values occurred through the creation and amendment of the matrimonial statutes. As the colonial period progressed, legislative processes were increasingly controlled by elite Parsi men from Bombay, and British officials acknowledged implicitly that the legislation was an internal matter. Across the two major waves of legislating activity, senior Parsi males redefined their own patriarchal powers and

---

[120] Suit No. 3 of 1903, 1903–13 PCMC Notebook, I: 2.
[121] Suit No. 2 of 1898, 1893–1903 PCMC Notebook, II: 20–1.
[122] The Bombay Parsi Panchayat's statement represented itself and twenty other Parsi organizations. It, too, wanted the IPC definition of grievous hurt truncated in the PMDA 1936, although not to the degree advocated by some other bodies. See "Joint Opinion of the Trustees of the Parsee Panchayet Funds and Properties and 20 other Parsi Associations of Bombay" in "Paper No. I: Opinions on the Parsi Marriage and Divorce Bill," 22–3 in "Parsi Marriage and Divorce Act 1936."

entitlements. They gave up the legal right to enjoy multiple sexual partners while married, renouncing the power to take more than one wife (1865) and to have sex with prostitutes (1936). But they were careful to retain other privileges, especially particular types of control over wives and children. The 1865 Act took a notably soft touch on child marriage, permitting Parsi family heads to continue to determine their offspring's marital alliances until well into the twentieth century. The 1936 Act preserved and even expanded Parsi husbands' right to inflict a level of violence on their wives that constituted crimes. For Parsi lawmakers, control over immediate family members was more precious than a formalized right to sexual diversity. The Parsi Marriage and Divorce Acts represented the reshaping of patriarchal power in Parsi life, but it was more a reconfiguration than a steady curtailing of male privilege.

5

The Jury and Intragroup Control
The Parsi Chief Matrimonial Court

From 1865, matrimonial disputes among Parsis were decided by what was effectively a jury of co-religionists (Figure 5.1). The Parsi jury was an anomaly. No other South Asian community had the right to a jury in marital cases – nor, for that matter, did Europeans living in British India. Although personal law governed most other religious communities in matrimonial disputes, colonial judges (typically European) applied these bodies of law. Furthermore, the jury was not used in any other area of civil law.[1] Juries were employed in particular types of criminal trials, having been introduced in piecemeal and ambivalent fashion at the local level. Debates over the value of using Indian jurors highlighted colonial anxieties: many Europeans worried that the jury gave South Asians too much power. The existence of the Parsi jury reflected the community's reputation for loyalty to British rule. One colonial administrator declared himself "no friend of exceptional legislation for the creeds and classes of India," but regarded the Parsis as special due to their "unwavering loyalty, integrity and public spirit.[2] In the words of Sir Jamsetjee Jeejeebhoy, "the Government of India evinced a wise and benign consideration for the special position of the Parsee community in India" in approving the creation of the Parsi matrimonial courts.[3] One could speculate that the court's existence exemplified classic divide-and-rule strategy.[4] Equally, though, the creation of the matrimonial jury system reflected the skill of Parsi lobbyists. This unique, community-specific civil jury

---

[1] Sorab P. N. Wadia, *The Institution of Trial by Jury in India* (Bombay: "Fort" Printing Press, 1897), 17–18; Syed Ameer Ali and John George Woodroffe, *The Law of Evidence Applicable to British India* (Calcutta: Thacker, Spink and Co., 1907), 797; S. Srinivasa Rajagopalachariar, "The System of Trial by Jury – A Retrospect and an Analysis," *Mad LJ* 70 (1936), 88, 94. I thank Kalyani Ramnath for introducing me to Wadia's book.

[2] D. Cowie in Bengalee, 204.

[3] "Address to the Hon'ble Mr. Justice Melvill," *TI* (5 March 1883), 7.

[4] See chapter 2 at note 18.

193

FIGURE 5.1 A representation of the Parsi Chief Matrimonial Court of Bombay, with delegates (and possibly a litigant) at center and right before presiding judge, 1888. *Source*: Mansukh, end pages. © The British Library Board 14146.e.25.

The Parsi Chief Matrimonial Court

was introduced by the Parsi Marriage and Divorce Act of 1865, which was drafted by the Parsi Law Association. If the community's colonial legal history suggested Parsi exceptionalism in the legal domain (how Parsis differed from other communities in British India), it did so most clearly through the existence of the Parsi matrimonial jury.

The British model of the personal law system disempowered South Asian male elites: juryless courts, not community bodies, applied personal law. The Parsi jury was the exception, effectively creating an Ottoman-style *millet* system for the Parsis alone. The delegates of the Parsi matrimonial court had the opportunity to replicate and reinforce their social influence in the community in ways denied to the senior men of other communities. Those who ran for election may have been motivated by a charitable impulse to perform a much needed service for their community; they were not paid for serving as delegates. They may equally have been driven by prurience. Most of all, however, the desire to exercise intragroup influence probably drew them to the job. A distinct dynamic developed between the Parsi jury and matrimonial litigants. The former were almost exclusively senior Parsi men, drawn from Bombay's mercantile, professional, and intellectual elites. Plaintiffs, by contrast, were disproportionately women. In divorce suits, female plaintiffs outnumbered male by a factor of two or three.[5] Many of these women were working-class, and they usually won their suits. In the vast majority of cases, the jury of senior elite males released poorer females from their marriages, disciplining these women's husbands, invariably nonelite men. The pattern was particularly pronounced in cases of arranged marriage induced by fraud. Once Parsis became judges in the Bombay High Court, the cultural autonomy of the Parsi matrimonial court increased. It became customary that any Parsi judge on the Bombay High Court bench would also be named the presiding judge of the Parsi Chief Matrimonial Court.[6] With such appointments, even the pretense of supervision by an outsider disappeared.

THE JURY IN COLONIAL INDIA

In a colony in which there was one Briton for every 1,400 South Asians circa 1900, it was hardly surprising that the British needed the help of the colonized in running the legal system.[7] This was the case in nonsettler colonies across the British Empire. In South Asia, the need for "native" involvement was particularly acute, running high into the upper courts because of the personal law system and the diversity of religious and linguistic traditions. The colonial administration experimented with a series of practices that would allow legal administrators to harness the cultural, religious, and linguistic knowledge of

[5] See notes 175–6.
[6] See note 119.
[7] See 104; Jain, 205.

196   *Law and Identity in Colonial South Asia: Parsi Legal Culture*

South Asians, making the system both practicable for the British and better accepted among Indians, but without ceding too much power. The jury had a long and vexed history in this context. It was one of several models of South Asian participation with which the colonial state dabbled.

One of the earliest experiments was the employment of "native law officers." In the early period of colonial rule, these experts were brought into court and consulted by colonial judges for their opinion on particular points of Hindu and Islamic law.[8] What was missing was trust. Figures like the Orientalist scholar and Calcutta High Court judge William Jones and treatise author W.H. Macnaghten famously suspected that the native law officers were misleading European judges to further their own interests.[9] This view played a role in the abolition of the native law officers' positions in 1864. They could be removed because they had been replaced with something else: English translations of classical Hindu and Islamic legal texts.[10] From the late eighteenth century on, the colonial state commissioned a flurry of translation and compilation, hiring European Orientalist scholars and colonial administrators, in collaboration with Indian translators and religious law authorities, to translate classical texts of Hindu law from Sanskrit and of Islamic law from Arabic and Persian.[11] The selection of texts was haphazard.[12] Many translations were messy and their application misleading.[13] Infamously, some texts of Islamic law were not translated directly into English, but from Arabic into Persian, and then from Persian into English.[14] It was on these problematic texts that the colonial courts relied in applying Anglo-Hindu and Anglo-Islamic law, particularly after 1864.[15]

---

[8] See "No. 218: Report of the Commission appointed to consider and report on certain questions connected with trial by jury in Bengal," 230 in "Report on the System of Trial by Jury in Courts of Session in the Mofassal during the year[s]1890–97" (IOR/V/23/75, No. 366); Jörg Fisch, *Cheap Lives and Dear Limbs: The British Transformation of the Bengal Criminal Law 1769–1817* (Wiesbaden: Franz Steiner Verlag, 1983), 108–17; Anderson, "Islamic Law," 173–4; Radhika Singha, *A Despotism of Law: Crime and Justice in Early Colonial India* (Delhi: Oxford University Press, 1998), 49–51, 294–6; Mallampalli, *Race*, 197–9; Travers, 185 at note 15.

[9] Jain, 582; Rudolph and Rudolph, *Modernity*, 283–4; D. H. A. Kolff, "The Indian and the British Law Machines: Some Remarks on Law and Society in British India," in *European Expansion and Law: The Encounter of European and Indigenous Law in 19th- and 20th-Century Africa and Asia*, eds. W. J. Mommsen and J. A. De Moor (Oxford: Berg, 1992), 213; R. Rocher, 81–3; Travers, 197–9, 201–5.

[10] Jain, 583; Rudolph and Rudolph, *Modernity of Tradition*, 284.

[11] See Bernard S. Cohn, "Law," 57–75.

[12] See Emon, 10–12.

[13] Derrett, "Administration," 34–7; Rudolph and Rudolph, *Modernity of Tradition*, 284; Nicholas B. Dirks, "From Little King to Landlord: Property, Law, and the Gift under the Madras Permanent Settlement," *CSSH* 28:2 (1986), 321; R. Rocher, 79–80; Emon, 10.

[14] Anderson, "Islamic Law," 174.

[15] For examples, see the 1867 joined cases of *Moonshee Buzloor Ruheem v. Shumsoonnissa Begum* and *Jodonath Bose v. Shumsoonnissa Begum* 11 MIA 551; *Badarannissa Bibi v. Mafiattala* 7 Beng. LR 442 (1871); *Sharifa Bibi v. Gulam Mahomed Dastagir Khan and others* ILR 16 Mad 43 (1893). See also L. Rocher, 420.

The Parsi Chief Matrimonial Court

There was another way in which the early colonial courts tried to capture Indian legal knowledge. On customary norms (themselves distinct from religious law), the East India Company's courts referred questions to the village, caste, or community councils known as *panchayats*.[16] In the Parsi context, this pattern revealed itself in the earliest published case law of the late eighteenth century.[17] The practice of consulting *panchayats* did not survive the transfer of power from the East India Company to the British Crown in 1858. The early colonial state had been hopeful that *panchayats* could be an integral part of colonial adjudication.[18] However, colonial administrators seemed to lose interest in promoting *panchayats* by the 1830s. Only in the 1920s did a series of statutes attempt to reintegrate *panchayats* into the legal system as an alternative to adjudication by the lower courts.[19] In the same way that the consultation of living experts was replaced with textual sources in the application of Anglo-Hindu and -Islamic law, so consultation with the *panchayats* was arguably replaced with written descriptions of customs in particular parts of India, a process discussed shortly.

A third experiment involved assessors. Assessors were Indian officials who sat, usually two or three at a time, with a colonial judge. Modeled on the nautical assessors used in Admiralty cases in England, assessors in India, in theory, were to be consulted by the judge, making recommendations to help him reach an informed decision.[20] In practice, assessors were a pale shadow of both the native law officers and the jury: their views were not binding.[21] Judges could and did ignore assessors' recommendations.[22] Writing in 1897, the Parsi commentator Sorab P. N. Wadia fumed that the assessor system was a sham: "Why then should the system be at all suffered to exist! And why should the Government encourage ridicule of persons whom it calls upon to sacrifice their time and energy for the administration of justice! In some places the Assessors are paid

---

[16] "No. 218: Report of the Commission appointed to consider and report on certain questions connected with trial by jury in Bengal," 230 in "Report on the System of Trial by Jury."

[17] See the 1839 case of *Burjorjee Bheemjee v. Ferozshaw Dhunjeeshaw* 1 SDA Bom 206; the 1854 case of *Baee Dhunbaee and Sonabaee, represented by Homjeebhaee v. Sorabjee Wacha Ghandy* 1 SDA Reports 3. In addition to consulting the Parsi Panchayat of Surat, the court also consulted the Modi of Surat in *Bomanjee Rustomjee v. Pestonjee* 2 SDA 114 (1855) at 116–17.

[18] See James A. Jaffe, "Arbitration and Panchayats in Early Colonial Bombay," K. R. Cama Oriental Institute, Mumbai (3 December 2009).

[19] Upendra Baxi and Marc Galanter, "Panchayat Justice: An Indian Experiment in Legal Access" (1979), text accompanying notes 13–17 (accessed on 1 March 2011): http://marcgalanter.net/ Documents/papers/scannedpdf/panchayatjustice.pdf.

[20] Satya Chandra Mukerji, ""Trial by Jury and with the Aid of Assessors in the United Provinces," *All LJ* II: 7 (1905), 116–8; Rajagopalachariar, 88.

[21] Rajagopalachariar, 88; Mukerji, 113.

[22] See *The Code of Indian Criminal Procedure being Act No. X of 1872* (London: William H. Allen and Co., 1872), 66–7 (Code of Criminal Procedure, ss. 261–2). See also "No. 7: From H.R. Farmer, Sessions Judge, Vizagapatam, to the Chief Secretary to the Government of Madras, No. 575, 12 August 1890," 4; "No. 8: From R. S. Benson, Sessions Judge of South Arcot, to the Chief Secretary to the Government of Madras, No. 74, 12 August 1890," 5; both in "Report on the System of Trial by Jury."

fees, but to what purpose when their verdict is liable to be ignored and defied! The system becomes farcical and unmaintainable."[23] In 1905, Satya Chandra Mukherji similarly described the whole system as "a solemn farce," with assessors, who often lacked the education to follow the details of the case, passing "from the listening into the somnolent attitude."[24] Across the British Empire, assessors were conveniently impotent. They made the legal process appear to incorporate native views and norms, but, in fact, they exercised no real influence on judicial outcomes. The use of assessors was particularly widespread in Britain's African colonies.[25] In many parts of India, they were used in the majority of criminal trials.[26] Britons hostile to the jury as an institution wanted it replaced with assessors.[27]

Finally, there was the jury.[28] In trials before the High Courts in the presidency capitals, the jury consisted of nine people. In the lower Courts of Session, an uneven number between three and nine was required. Unanimity was not required of juries in India, unlike in England. Jurors in India ruled on points of fact, not law, although the judge could direct them on the weight, value, and materiality of evidence.[29] The jury was introduced in piecemeal fashion across the three presidencies of Bengal, Bombay, and Madras, as well as in territories that sat outside of the presidencies, such as the Northwest Frontier Province.[30]

---

[23] Wadia, *Institution*, 81–2.

[24] Mukerji, 114.

[25] See A. N. Allott, "The Judicial Ascertainment of Customary Law in British Africa," *MLR* 20:3 (1957), 249–51; and by J. H. Jearey, "The Structure, Composition and Jurisdiction of Courts and Authorities Enforcing the Criminal Law in British African Territories," *ICLQ* 9:3 (1960), 396–414; along with his "Trial by Jury and Trial with the Aid of Assessors in the Superior Courts of British African Territories," *J. Afr. L.* 4:3 (1960), 133–46 (part 1); 5: 1 (1961), 36–47 (part 2); 5: 2 (1961), 82–98 (part 3). I am grateful to Rohit De for alerting me to Jearey's work.

[26] Mukerji, 113; "No. 26: From S. Hammick, Sessions Judge, Surat," 26 and "No. 33: From G. M. Macpherson, Judicial Commissioner in Sind" (including comments from S. Hammick, Sessions Judge, Ahmednagar), 35–6, both in "Report on the System of Trial by Jury."

[27] "No. 4: From C. J. Lyall, Secretary to the Government of India, to the Registrar of the High Court of Judicature at Fort William in Bengal" (including comments from H. R. Farmer, Sessions Judge, Vizagapatam), 4; "No. 8: R. S. Benson, Sessions Judge, Madras Presidency," 5; "No. 32: from E. Hosking, Sessions Judge, Karachi," 34; all in "Report on the System of Trial by Jury."

[28] See generally Kalyani Ramnath, "The Colonial Difference between Law and Fact: Notes on the Criminal Jury in India," 50 (July 2013) *IESHR*, 341–63. Under Company rule, the grand jury was used to indict criminal defendants, while the petit or common jury (using fewer jurors) acted as trial jury. Under the Raj, the grand jury was abolished by the High Courts' Criminal Procedure Amendment Act (XIII of 1865). See Henry Maine, "Abolition of Grand Juries (18 November 1864)" in Grant Duff, 179–92.

[29] Hasanat, 26. See generally Wadia, *Institution*, 22, 68–83.

[30] See "Trial by Jury in India," *The Saturday Review* (7 January 1893), 4. On the history of the jury during the Company period, see Wadia, *Institution*, 15–55; Kolsky, *Colonial Justice*, 217–21; Singha, 301; Fraas, "'They Have Travailed,'" especially 174–8; Mitch Fraas, "Primary Sources at a Distance: Researching Indian Colonial Law," *Focus on Global Resources (Center for Research Libraries Global Resources Network)* 32:1 (fall 2012), 9–11.

The Parsi Chief Matrimonial Court

From 1861, local governments could extend the right to jury trial to any type of criminal trial in any district.[31] Judges equally had the power to use a special jury, upon request by one party, in important cases in which they felt it necessary for jurors to have "superior qualifications in respect of property, character or education."[32] Unlike the normal jurors' list, the list of eligible special jurors in Bombay was heavily European. The decision to use a special jury in a case with a South Asian defendant increased the likelihood that the majority of jurors would be white.[33]

When the defendant was white, a majority of jurors had to be European or American if the accused requested it (as he or she usually did).[34] If the accused was South Asian, the majority of jurors would be, too.[35] In her portrait of the early colonial jury, Elizabeth Kolsky has shown that, almost from the beginning, British critics railed against the use of Indian jurors even for Indian defendants. European notions of Oriental mendacity combined with assumptions that the average Indian juror was too culturally backward and politically childlike to be fit for the job.[36] The colonizers' ambivalence toward the jury stretched across the nonsettler colonies of the British Empire. The jury was a fraught institution in these territories because it exacerbated racial divisions between colonizer and colonized. In colonial India and Africa, the jury was a particularly volatile element in criminal suits involving people of different races – where the non-white defendant had allegedly committed a crime against a white victim or where a white defendant was accused of victimizing a member of the colonized population.[37] Across the empire, majority-white juries often acquitted white

---

[31] See Ranganadhaiyar, 752–5 (Crim. Proc. Code s. 269); Mukerji, 113.

[32] See Ranganadhaiyar, 765–9, 1365 (Crim. Proc. Code ss. 276, 325); Wadia, *Institution*, 13–14; N. C. Kelkar, ed., *Full and Authentic Report of the Tilak Trial (1908)* (Bombay: N. K. Kelkar at the Indu-Prakash Steam Press, 1908), 21. To be included on the special jurors' list for Bombay City, a man eligible for normal jury duty had to state the reasons why he felt he was also qualified to serve on a special jury. The Bombay High Court's Clerk of the Crown assessed these reasons and considered adding the person, provided there was a spot available on the 400-person list. (Wadia, *Institution*, 17 at note.) On the use of the special jury in criminal libel trials, see Chapter 7 at 278.

[33] In the nationalist leader B. G. Tilak's 1908 trial for seditious libel, his lawyer argued against the use of a special jury by pointing out that the common jury list included 569 Europeans and 1,673 South Asians, whereas the special jurors' list consisted of 242 Europeans but only 156 South Asians. A majority-white jury would almost surely convict Tilak. Justice Davar disagreed and approved the request for a special jury (Kelkar, 20–22).

[34] Mukerji, 115.

[35] Kolsky, *Colonial Justice*, 219.

[36] Ibid., 217–21. On Oriental mendacity, see Wendie Schneider, "'Enfeebling the Arm of Justice': Perjury and Colonial Administration under the East India Company," in *Modern Histories of Crime and Punishment*, eds. Markus Dirk Dubber and Lindsay Farmer (Palo Alto: Stanford University Press, 2007), 299–327.

[37] Richard Vogler, "The International Development of the Jury: The Role of the British Empire," *Int'l. Rev. Penal L.* 72 (2001), 538–9, 541–3.

200 Law and Identity in Colonial South Asia: Parsi Legal Culture

defendants against the evidence, a phenomenon observed by Kolsky, Chanock, and others.[38]

Debates over the viability of the jury filled the pages of magazines and law journals in late colonial India. A government-commissioned report on the jury in the *mofussil* documented the views of several hundred colonial officials from across the subcontinent during the 1890s.[39] What emerged from these sources was a general clustering of opinion along racial lines. There were Britons who defended the jury in India and Indians who argued for its abolition.[40] Most Britons, however, were critical of the jury and wanted its use restricted in India. South Asians joined these discussions as they rose among the ranks of lawyers, judges, and civil servants. They generally defended the jury system.[41] This racial divide was striking because it persisted despite the phenomenon so clearly documented by Kolsky: the consistent acquittal by white juries of white defendants accused of killing South Asians, especially in the contexts of alleged hunting accidents and labor-related conflicts on tea plantations.[42]

A common criticism of the jury was that Indian jurors allowed communal and caste dynamics to taint their findings.[43] Writing in 1938, one of the few Indians to oppose the jury referred to the "now-prevailing communal spirit" between Hindus and Muslims: "there have been cases and cases in which the jury [has] divided communally."[44] An older complaint, and one more commonly made by Britons, related to caste: Brahmin defendants were treated with undue leniency by Hindu jurors, who acquitted them regardless of the evidence.[45] Lower caste jurors were especially susceptible to being pressured, particularly when the defendant came from an influential family, and it was almost impossible to get upper caste Hindus to agree to do jury service.[46] In turn, lower caste defendants

---

[38] Kolsky, *Colonial Justice*, 26, 185–228; Martin Chanock, *The Making of South African Legal Culture 1902–1936: Fear, Favor and Prejudice* (Cambridge: Cambridge University Press, 2001), 120. See also Mukerji, 115–6; letter from D. E. Wacha to D. Naoroji (3 June 1899) in Patwardhan, II: 702.

[39] "Report on the System of Trial by Jury."

[40] See C. D. Field, "Trial by Jury in Bengal," *IAQROCR* V: 9–10 (1893), 309–23; Rajagopalachariar, 81–94; Abul Hasanat, "Trial by Jury," *Crim. LJ of India* 39 (1938), 25–29. Jeremy Bentham proposed a model for the jury in colonial India. See Pitts, 119–21.

[41] For one of the most extensive defenses of the jury, see Wadia, *Institution*.

[42] Kolsky, *Colonial Justice*, 142–228.

[43] "No. 38: From Dr. A. D. Pollen, Sessions Judge, Belgaum, to the Secretary to the Government of Bombay, Judicial Dept. No. 1317, 23 July 1890," 45 in "Report on the System of Trial by Jury."

[44] Hasanat, 27.

[45] J. Jardine, "Indian Official Opinions on Trial by Jury," *IAQROCR* V: 9–10 (1893), 302–3; "Trial by Jury," *Saturday Review*, 4; "No. 7: From H.R. Farmer," 3 in "Report on the System of Trial by Jury."

[46] "No. 42: H. F. Matthews, Officiating Sessions Judge of Burdwan, to the Chief Secretary to the Government of Bengal, No. 1606, 7 July 1890," 51; "Nos. 47–8. J. Tweedie, Judge of Patna, to the Officiating Under Secretary to the Government of Bengal. No. Sct. 197, 21 July 1890," 56–7; both in "Report on the System of Trial by Jury."

The Parsi Chief Matrimonial Court

were more likely to be convicted by Indian jurors, particularly if they were deemed members of the "criminal classes."[47]

A related and recurring point of debate pertained to the death penalty: critics of the jury argued that Hindu, Jain, and Buddhist jurors were likely to acquit in capital cases because of their religious objections to causing death.[48] A British judge based in Assam complained of the phenomenon in his district. Many of his jurors were Marwari and either religiously Jain or Vaishnavite Hindu. Apparently without irony, he observed that it was "one of the marks of a very advanced stage of civilization, that people grow too humane to tolerate capital punishment."[49] Regional differences in the model of jury adopted were relevant on this point. By the 1890s, the jury system was generally limited to property crimes in Madras Presidency and the Northwest Frontier Province. Most British discussants admitted that this model had enjoyed limited success.[50] In Bombay Presidency, by contrast, the model was the opposite: the jury was used for the most serious crimes, including potentially capital crimes like murder. In the Ahmedabad and Surat districts of western India, this model had proven disastrous from the British perspective: Gujarati-speaking Hindu jurors showed the strongest opposition to the death penalty and consistently acquitted defendants in capital cases when the evidence supported conviction.[51]

Critics also complained that jury lists were poorly drawn up, particularly in the *mofussil*. The Code of Criminal Procedure did not limit juror eligibility to men with certain amounts of property or education. All men between the ages of twenty-one and sixty could be called for jury duty, except for upper ranking civil servants, legislators, judges, members of the military or police, practicing physicians, and lawyers.[52] The local police, Collector, or village officers drew up the list of potential jurors through an opaque process once a year, and these officials were accused of paying no attention to the literacy or education levels of the people selected.[53] The result, argued many British judges, was that jurors often

---

[47] "No. 8: From R. S. Benson," 5 in "Report on the System of Trial by Jury."

[48] Jardine, "Indian Official Opinions," 303–4; "No. 43–46. F. F. Handley, Sessions Judge of Nadia to the Secretary to the Government of Bengal, Judicial Department, No. 477, 19 July 1890," 52 in "Report on the System of Trial by Jury."

[49] "No. 114. H. Luttman-Johnson, Judge of the Assam Valley Districts, to the Secretary of the Chief Commissioner of Assam. No. 1271, 17 November 1890," 152 in "Report on the System of Trial by Jury."

[50] Jardine, "Indian Official Opinions," 298.

[51] Ibid., 296–7.

[52] Ranganadhaiyar, 1361–3 (Crim. Proc. Code ss. 319–20). However, the High Courts could impose their own additional eligibility criteria. In the city of Bombay, potential jurors needed a minimum monthly income of Rs 70 and the ability to understand English (Wadia, *Institution*, 17 at note).

[53] "No. 43–46. F. F. Handley," 53 in "Report on the System of Trial by Jury." Compare to Ranganadhaiyar, 1363–5 (Crim. Proc. Code ss. 321–24); Wadia, *Institution*, 20–1.

202   *Law and Identity in Colonial South Asia: Parsi Legal Culture*

lacked the education to comprehend the subtleties of colonial law, particularly on points of criminal procedure.[54]

Against these criticisms, South Asian writers rose to the defense of Indian jurors. When juries made poor decisions, the fault usually lay with the judge for giving improper instructions.[55] It took a firm and experienced judge to manage a jury, but many of the British sessions court judges sent to the *mofussil* were young and ignorant of local conditions.[56] Although Indian Civil Service judicial officers were required to study multiple Indian languages, few spoke them well enough to deliver a careful and precise set of instructions to the jury; interpreters were not used at lower criminal courts in the *mofussil*.[57] It was precisely because of these shortcomings that the Indian jury was so valuable, argued proponents like Sorab P. N. Wadia: "For a Jury of the country ... can alone well understand ... the shades of evidence, the characters of witnesses, and their moral standard, and assist the Judge, – quite a stranger to the people – in his office."[58] From Bengal, Syama Churn Haldar insisted that jurors could better weigh evidence and determine the facts than could British judges who were ignorant of local customs and manners.[59] The future nationalist leader P. Ananda Charlu noted that the Indian jury was in a unique position to assess vernacular witness testimony, not just by its members' fluency with the languages in use, but also because of their cultural knowledge: "The transient hesitation, the coughing, the taking more time than is necessary before giving the answer, the gestures, looks, furtive or side glances and even the tone of voice and the very twang – all these small minutiae, as the straw shows how the wind blows, show the bent and the bias of the native witness which natives alone could know best. All these make a strong and serviceable impression on the jury and determine the trustworthiness or otherwise of a witness or witnesses, while they must be wholly lost to the Judge, who must needs be busy taking down the

[54] "No. 29: Dr. A. D. Pollen, Sessions Judge, Belgaum, to the Registrar, High Court, Bombay. No. 699, 17 April 1890," 29; "No. 205: Letter from C. G. W. Macpherson, Sessions Judge, Belgaum, to the District Magistrate, Belgaum. No. 2491, 19 December 1892," 221–2; both in "Report on the System of Trial by Jury."

[55] Views of Calcutta High Court judges Ghose and Bannerjee, referred to in Field, 320; P. Ananda Charlu, 222; "The Jury System," *Mad LJ* 12 (1902), 296.

[56] "No. 43–46.B. Babu Rajendra Lal Lahiri, Secretary to the Bar Library, Kishnaghur, to the Sessions Judge of Nadia, 19 July 1890," 54–5; "No. 145: The Humble Memorial, dated 23 December 1892, of the Inhabitants of Calcutta and its Suburbs, in Public Meeting assembled, to Her Majesty's Secretary of State for India in Council," 172; both in "Report on the System of Trial by Jury."

[57] Field, 320; Charlu, 220. On the cultural and linguistic ignorance of British ICS judges generally, see J. R. B. Jeejeebhoy, ed., *Some Unpublished and Later Speeches and Writings of the Hon. Sir Pherozeshah Mehta* (Bombay: Commercial Press, 1918), 359, 381, 391–2.

[58] Wadia, *Institution*, 58.

[59] Babu Syama Churn Haldar, Mukhtear, Hooghly, to the District and Sessions Judge of Hooghly in "No. 54–57. J. Crawford, Officiating Sessions Judge of Hooghly, to the Chief Secretary to the Government of Bengal. No. 1334, 23 September 1890," 72 in "Report on the System of Trial by Jury."

The Parsi Chief Matrimonial Court

evidence."[60] Indian commentators observed that even in the upper courts where court interpreters were used, important information got lost in the translation of testimony.[61]

Some Britons argued that the jury was a distinctly English institution inappropriately transplanted into India.[62] The jury was "altogether external and foreign to native ideas," and it was dangerous for "rash experimentalist[s]" to try to convert Hindus and Muslims into "genuine Anglo Saxons." Britain could lose India through "premature experiments" like the jury, warned the *Saturday Review*.[63] Using a popular metaphor of the late colonial period, others called the Indian jury "a sickly exotic plant."[64] Many Indians disagreed emphatically. The Bombay High Court judge Jardine noted that "many of our Indian subjects admire the jury because of a supposed likeness to the indigenous Punchayet or Arbitration of five."[65] "The people in general liken it to trial by punchayet," wrote the Madras High Court judge Muttasami Aiyar.[66] P. Ananda Charlu commented that both the *panchayat* system and South Asian modes of arbitration had arisen out of the formula that was "immemorially on the lips of a Hindu culprit," namely "that he would abide by what four men would decide." This "faith in the verdict of the four" (or often six) was the indigenous trunk onto which the jury system had been grafted.[67] In Calcutta, Indians in favor of the jury noted that it had been a success in Ceylon since 1812.[68] It had also worked in Bengal, the early administrators who introduced it being "guided by their experience of one of the most ancient, most useful, and most valued institutions of the people of India – the settlement of disputes by a *punchayet* (council of five). It is beyond question that the knowledge of the people of the *punchayet* removed from the jury system in the eyes of the community all appearance of unfamiliarity with an institution so prized in England, and disposed them strongly in its favor."[69]

In Assam, honorary magistrate Jagannath Barua described a regional variant of the *panchayat* system, known as the *mel*. He reported that the population liked the jury because it was so "perfectly in consonance with the genius of the

---

[60] P. Ananda Charlu, 220.

[61] Ibid., 220–1.

[62] On legal transplants, see Chapter 3 at 163–4.

[63] "Trial by Jury," *Saturday Review*, 4.

[64] Ibid.; Kolsky, *Colonial Justice*, 220.

[65] Jardine, "Indian Official Opinions," 308.

[66] Muttasami Aiyar cited in "No. 12: H. W. Foster, Officiating Registrar of the High Court of Judicature, Appellate Side, Madras, to the Chief Secretary to the Government of Madras, No. 2543, 5 November 1890," 10 in "Report on the System of Trial by Jury."

[67] P. Ananda Charlu, "Trial by Jury," *Mad. Rev.* 2 (May 1896), 223. See also Jaffe, "Arbitration and Panchayats," 48–9.

[68] On the jury in Ceylon, see T. Nadaraja, *The Legal System of Ceylon in Its Historical Setting* (Leiden: Brill, 1972), 62; H. W. Tambiah, *The Judicature of Sri Lanka in Its Historical Setting* (Colombo: Gunasena, 1977), 67–8.

[69] "No. 145: The Humble Memorial," 171 in "Report on the System of Trial by Jury."

people of Assam. In religious and social matters the people hold a trial called '*mel*' on the same principal as the trial of legal crimes, and in case the defendant is pronounced guilty, the *Pandit* or the *Gossain* passes the sentence prescribed by the 'Dharma Shastras.' Such a procedure in respect of religious and social offences has been in practice since time [immemorial]."[70] A British judge in Assam commented that his best jurymen had, in fact, been men with little formal education who presided over the village *mel*.[71] Thus, the jury was hardly a new or alien institution in colonial India. It bore a family resemblance to South Asian modes of dispute resolution.

According to certain Britons, the jury served a pedagogical function within the civilizing mission that justified colonial rule. Bombay High Court Justice Birdwood described the introduction of the jury as "a step in the political education of the people."[72] The jury taught Indians to advance into political adulthood by forcing them to take a greater role in the workings of public institutions.[73] As W. Lee-Warner of the Bombay Judicial Department reported to the Government of India, "The jurymen themselves receive and carry away a true idea of legal principles. They learn that the Judges are acute, wise, and impartial, and see how really difficult a task adjudication is. They diffuse these experiences and the consequent regard for law and the judicial administration throughout society."[74]

A related argument flipped the power dynamic. The jury was a "bulwark of liberty" that had not been pushed on Indians from above but demanded by them from below. Indian elites valued the jury and fought to keep it.[75] In 1892, Indians in Calcutta protested against a sudden reduction in the use of the jury mandated by an executive order of the local government. They passed resolutions asserting that the move would "disturb the trust of the people in the Government." It would "take away one of the greatest safeguards of liberty." The people looked on trial by jury and the High Court as "the only two safeguards for their lives and liberties and their only protection against the despotic and arbitrary power in the hands of the executive."[76] The jury counteracted India's "ignorant police and untrained judiciary, having at best but a

---

[70] Babu Jagannath Barua cited in "No. 114. H. Luttman-Johnson," 127 in "Report on the System of Trial by Jury."

[71] "No. 114. H. Luttman-Johnson," 131 in "Report on the System of Trial by Jury."

[72] "Minute by the Hon. Mr. Justice Birdwood," 15 in "Report on the System of Trial by Jury."

[73] Jardine, "Indian Official Opinions," 306; "Trial by Jury," *Mad. Rev.* 4; "No. 218: Report of the Commission," 233–4 in "Report on the System of Trial by Jury."

[74] "From W. Lee-Warner, Secretary to the Government of Bombay, Judicial Department, to the Secretary to the Government of India, Home Department, No. 7105, 19 December 1890," 14 in "Report on the System of Trial by Jury."

[75] Jardine, "Indian Official Opinions," 300.

[76] "No. 151: The humble Memorial of the Committee appointed by the inhabitants of Calcutta and its Suburbs in Public Meeting assembled on the 20 December 1892," 190 in "Report on the System of Trial by Jury."

The Parsi Chief Matrimonial Court

limited knowledge of the complicated conditions of native society."[77] In 1893, the former Calcutta High Court judge C. D. Field noted that the people of Bengal regarded trial by jury as a privilege.[78] Indian honorary magistrates reported that the people of Assam felt the same way.[79] Indeed, extension of the jury system was generally "a plank in the platform of all native associations" in the 1890s, including the Indian National Congress.[80]

Once the jury had been introduced in India, even British critics realized that taking it away would be impolitic. Some commentators noted snidely that it had been introduced for political reasons in the first place, allowing "the odium of apparently harsh decisions [to be] taken off from the shoulders of the official class."[81] The most feasible solution was to quietly undermine the institution through the power of reference. In 1872 and 1882, amended versions of the Criminal Procedure Code expanded the power of the judge to refer jury verdicts to the upper courts for potential reversal. When the lower court judge disagreed "so completely that he considers it necessary for the ends of justice to submit the case to the High Court, he shall submit the case accordingly, recording the grounds of his opinion."[82] The power applied equally to jury acquittals and convictions. However, the real problem (from a British perspective) was the situation in which the jury had acquitted the accused against the evidence. From the late nineteenth century on, much of the debate on the jury focused on this question: should the upper courts' power to overturn jury verdicts be narrowly or widely construed?[83]

The use of the criminal jury in India invited questions about its absence in the civil context, particularly on points of custom. Around the mid-nineteenth century, colonial administrators realized that many of the populations to whom personal law was being applied did not actually follow the rules described in classical religious texts. Instead, they followed their own customary norms. The courts were empowered to uphold a custom that ran contrary to the personal law.[84] In the same way that the colonial administration replaced native law officers with written sources in translation, here, too, it attempted to minimize reliance on Indians, whether as individuals or in groups, by writing

---

[77] Field, 321–2; "No. 145: Humble Memorial," 172 in "Report on the System of Trial by Jury." Similarly, see Wadia, *Institution*, 58–9.

[78] Field, 323.

[79] Maulvi Rahamat Ali and Babu Jagannath Barua cited in "No. 114. H. Luttman-Johnson," 126 in "Report on the System of Trial by Jury."

[80] "Nos. 19–21: Minute by the Hon. Mr. Justice Candy," Ibid., 20.

[81] Rajagopalachariar, 86–7; Jardine, "Indian Official Opinions," 307.

[82] Field, 314. See also Ranganadhaiyar, 1323–47 (Crim Proc Code s. 307); Rajagopalachariar, 87–8.

[83] See, for instance, Jardine, "Indian Official Opinions," 294, 298–9; P. Ananda Charlu, 222; D. B. B., "Criminal Revision and Appeals from Jury Trials," *Bom LR* (journal) 17 (1915), 105–9, 121–5; V. B. Raju, "References against Jury Verdicts," *Bom LR* (journal) 49 (1947), 24–7.

[84] See Chapter 4 at 183.

206 Law and Identity in Colonial South Asia: Parsi Legal Culture

down descriptions of customs.[85] The prime laboratory was Punjab.[86] Charles L. Tupper and others created multivolume works describing customary practice in Punjab.[87] Similar projects took place along the Malabar coast in southwest India and, earlier in the nineteenth century, in Bombay Presidency.[88] Naturally, turning customary norms into written text fixed them and invalidated local variations that escaped the attention of the compilers.[89] In English legal history, juries were especially well employed when they consisted of members of a group – typically mercantile – that followed their own customary practices, from financiers to fishmongers.[90] The development of the notion of custom in common-law jurisprudence migrated from the mercantile to the imperial ethnographic context. Why did the jury not follow? Its use would seem to be the single most effective way to capture local customary norms.

In England, critics of the jury urged its abolition in civil cases, arguing that the complexity of many civil trials made them better suited to adjudication by judges alone.[91] This sentiment probably existed in British India, too. But mistrust of the colonized population also loomed larger. For the same reason that colonial administrators were deeply uncomfortable with the criminal jury, they avoided using the civil jury to process customary claims: doing so would confer too much power on South Asians. The point was admittedly speculative in the civil context. Late colonial officials spilled little ink debating the merits of the civil jury because, by the era of Crown rule, it was deemed extinct in British India.[92]

---

[85] On Madras Presidency, see Mallampalli, *Race*, 245.

[86] See Kolff, 228–33; Anderson, "Islamic Law," 176–8. By David Gilmartin, see *Empire and Islam: Punjab and the Making of Pakistan* (London: Tauris, 1988), 13–18; "Customary Law and Shariat in British Punjab," *Shariat and Ambiguity in South Asian Islam*, ed. Katherine P. Ewing (Berkeley: University of California Press, 1988), 43–62.

[87] C.A. Boulnois and W.H. Rattigan, *Notes on Customary Law as Administered in the Courts of Punjab* (London: W. Clowes and Sons, 1878); C.L. Tupper, *Punjab Customary Law* (Simla: Office of the Superintendent of Government Printing, 1881); T.P. Ellis, *Notes on Punjab Custom* (Lahore: Civil and Military Gazette Press, 1921); Kaikhosru J. Rustomji, *A Treatise on Customary Law in the Punjab* (Lahore: University Book Agency, 1936); W.H. Rattigan, *A Digest of Civil Law for the Punjab. Chiefly Based on the Customary Law* (Lahore: Law Publishers, 1938).

[88] See Lewis Moore and Herbert Wigram, *Malabar Law and Custom* (Madras: Higginbotham, 1905); Borradaile and Nathoobhoy; Arthur Steele, *The Law and Custom of Hindoo Castes within the Dekhun Provinces subject to the Presidency of Bombay, chiefly affecting Civil Suits* (London: William H. Allen and Co., 1868; orig. pub. 1827). I am grateful to Amrita Shodhan for introducing me to the early documentation of custom in Gujarat. See her "Caste," 32–49; *Question*. See also Derrett, "Administration," 29; Hiroyuki Kotani, "The 'Caste Autonomy' Policy in the Nineteenth-Century Bombay Presidency," in his *Western India in Historical Transition: Seventeenth to Early Twentieth Centuries* (Delhi: Manohar, 2002), 94.

[89] See Mantena, 109.

[90] James Oldham, "The English Origins of the Special Jury" and "Special Juries in England: Nineteenth-Century Usage and Reform," both in his *Trial by Jury: The Seventh Amendment and Anglo-American Special Juries* (New York: New York University Press, 2006), 127–73.

[91] Conor Hanly, "The Decline of the Civil Jury Trial in Nineteenth-century England," *JLH* 26:3 (2005), 259–66.

[92] See notes 1 and 97.

The Parsi Chief Matrimonial Court

However, many of their concerns over the criminal jury would have been equally applicable in the civil context.

From the period of Company rule, British administrators were nervous about "giving power to native jurors" (in criminal cases) with which "they could not be safely entrusted."[93] In the 1890s, a British judge in Patna named J. Tweedie detailed the ways in which the criminal jury system allowed Indians to subvert colonial law. Many Indians objected to "much of our law," taking issue with the law of joint liability for crime and the de-emphasis in criminal procedure on eyewitness accounts, which had been central in Islamic criminal law. Many jurors felt "downright sympathy" with crimes like perjury and forgery, complained Tweedie. Aside from the fact that the colonial "law of documents" was far too complex for most Indian jurors, "the native has his own ideas of offences relating to documents" and "cares not about Ch.18 of the Penal Code," which covered forgery.[94] It was not socially taboo to return a false verdict or give false testimony, and Indians even felt that it was good and generous to help a guilty man escape, wrote Tweedie.[95] If Tweedie's observations were correct, one could speculate that anti-imperial sentiment had created an inverse morality. Could Indian jurors have committed "perverse" jury acquittals as a form of resistance to British rule? If so, the ever-growing power of reference of jury verdicts to the higher courts was no surprise. Judges in England had ways to undermine criminal jury verdicts, but they had no clear equivalent to the power of reference that was adopted in British India.[96]

Against the backdrop of European ambivalence toward the jury, the Parsi jury stood out. This community-specific civil jury elicited no mention in debates over the criminal jury and seems to have been a blind spot in the Raj-era consensus that the civil jury no longer existed in India.[97] In part, the Parsi jury avoided controversy by hiding behind a different label. Parsi jurors were officially called "delegates" of the PCMC, but they were commonly regarded as a

---

[93] "No. 218: Report of the Commission," 231 in "Report on the System of Trial by Jury."

[94] See Ranchhoddas and Thakore, *IPC*, 403–34.

[95] "Nos. 47–8: J. Tweedie," 56–8 in "Report on System of Trial by Jury."

[96] Judgment of the Chief Justice in Criminal Reference 166 of 1889, *Imperatrix v. Bai Jiba et al.*, cited in "Nos. 19–21: Minute by the Honorable Mr. Justice Candy," 21; "No. 218: Report of the Commission," 232; both in "Report on the System of Trial by Jury." Compare John H. Langbein, Renée Lettow Lerner, and Bruce P. Smith, *History of the Common Law: The Development of Anglo-American Legal Institutions* (Austin: Wolters Kluwer, 2009), 416–46; "Forum: From the Twelve Judges to the Court for Crown Cases Reserved," *LHR* 29 (2011), 181–302.

[97] See note 1. There was one other exception. Under Regulation VI of 1832, juries could be resorted to in civil cases in courts specially empowered to employ them. ["No. 145: "The Humble Memorial, 23 December 1892, of the Inhabitants of Calcutta and its Suburbs, in Public Meeting assembled, to Her Majesty's Secretary of State for India in Council," 172 in "Report on the System of Trial by Jury."] However, law reports from the late nineteenth century onward suggested that juries were not often empowered in this way or that judges chose not to take advantage of the power (where granted). The 1832 regulation may have been repealed some time in the late nineteenth century.

FIGURE 5.2 Three candidates running for the position of delegate of the Parsi Chief Matrimonial Court of Bombay.
Source: "A Tug and Pull. Three dogs fighting for a bone," *HP* (19 March 1916), 20. Courtesy of the British Library SV576.

jury.[98] Depicting one election for a delegate's seat, *Hindi Punch* represented three Parsi candidates as dogs. All were tugging energetically on the same bone, whose twisted shape spelled "P. J. Vote" for Parsi Jury Vote (Figure 5.2).[99] In a Parsi matrimonial court case appealed to the local colonial court, the Nagpur Assistant Judicial Commissioner commented that delegates to the Parsi court were essentially jurors.[100]

The Parsi matrimonial jury was the only place in British Indian civil law where the full sociocultural potential of the jury was harnessed. The colonial judge Fulton alluded to it in the 1900 case of *Hirabai v. Dhunjibhai*. Discussing the fact–law division of labor between jury and judge, he noted that

The statutory law must doubtless be pointed out by the Court [i.e., the judge], but the customary law is a matter, like other matters of fact, within the cognizance of the delegates. That the custom binding on the conscience of the Parsis, and as such forming the law subject to which the status of marriage is entered into, is to be ascertained as a question of fact, like any other customary law peculiar to a particular community, needs little support from authority, as it is a principle which is universally recognized by the

---

[98] See "The Parsee Divorce Law," *TI* (14 September 1885), 5.
[99] See "Parsi Matrimonial Court," *TI* (13 March 1916), 6.
[100] *Dinbai v. Framroz and Shawock* 43 IC 71 (1918) at 72.

The Parsi Chief Matrimonial Court

Courts. But if authority is desired reference may be made to *Shirinbai v. Kharshedji . . .* in which this Court treated as a question of fact, not open to second appeal, the finding as to the existence of a custom binding amongst Parsis sanctioning infant marriages.[101]

The fact that, for Muslims and Hindus, such a question would have been a question of law to be decided by a judge "afford[ed] no argument" affecting a "special community such as the Parsis" with their unique system.[102] In comparative community context, the Parsi matrimonial jury represented an alternate world. It offered a model of how custom claims might have been dealt with for India's other communities. Why then was it only the Parsis who enjoyed the privilege? Undoubtedly, the jury system was a reward for the stereotypical loyalty of the Parsis toward British rule.[103] *Hindi Punch* regularly graced its pages with pictures of the plump and jovial Mr. Hindi Punch (occasionally named Parsi Punch) wishing health and longevity to the British monarch and showing gratitude for British rule.[104]

Equally, though, the existence of the Parsi jury reflected the ability of Parsi lobbyists to shape legislation. The Parsi jury was a late addition to the Parsi-drafted Marriage and Divorce Act of 1865. According to early drafts of the legislation, Parsi *panchayats* would adjudicate Parsi matrimonial disputes. Only late in the deliberating phase were the *panchayats* replaced with the idea of the Parsi matrimonial courts, a wholly new set of institutions. The alteration occurred, moreover, during a period when Henry Maine, the Law Member of the Viceroy's Legislative Council in Calcutta, prevented the matrimonial jury – an option in English divorce law – from being imported into the matrimonial law for Christians in India.[105] The Parsi change was initiated by reformists who doubted the Bombay Parsi Panchayat's legitimacy. The judge and lobbyist Manekjee Cursetjee played a key role. In 1844–5, he wrote an important series of letters published in the *Bombay Times and Journal of Commerce* using the pseudonym "Q. in the Corner" that stressed the Parsi population's loss of respect for the Bombay Parsi Panchayat. The Parsi Panchayat had once exercised great authority over Parsis, who obeyed its resolutions or *bundobasts "because the parties knew them to have been passed by the Punchyat* at their *general assembly, and to have been* CONSCIENTIOUSLY given." *Bundobasts* in that period applied equally to rich and poor, wrote Cursetjee, alluding to the accusation that the Panchayat in his own time tolerated polygyny among the rich.[106] Furthermore, the Parsi Panchayat no longer worked to curtail the escalating

---

[101] *Hirabai v. Dhanjibhai* 2 Bom LR 845 (1900) at 848.
[102] Ibid.
[103] See untitled, *TI* (11 March 1885), 5.
[104] See "The Flag of Peace: A New Year's Gift," *HP* (8 September 1912), 22–23. This figure was a Parsi version of the amiable hunch-backed figure featured in the London original, *Punch*. See Chapter 7 at 278–9.
[105] Maine, "Divorce" in Grant Duff, 97–8.
[106] Q. in the Corner, I: 12; as well as I: 2, 9, 21–1, 32; II: 25. Emphasis original.

Law and Identity in Colonial South Asia: Parsi Legal Culture

expense and ostentation of Parsi ceremonial life, particularly rites commemorating death and child marriage.[107] Cursetjee's letters proved instrumental in having the Bombay Parsi Panchayat replaced by the new Parsi matrimonial courts as adjudicator of matrimonial disputes in 1865.

In 1883, a Bombay High Court judge named Melvill addressed the Parsi jury after presiding over the PCMC of Bombay for the previous decade. "We English are accustomed to think that no court can adjudicate so well on the merits of a case as that which consists of a Judge and a jury." The Parsi matrimonial court system was even better than a jury (as it appeared in many Indian criminal contexts) because its members were not selected at random but were appointed "from the elite of the Parsee community, for their education, intelligence, and status in their community." In fact, the delegate system resembled "the model of your old Punchayet."[108] Melvill's comments foreshadowed a number of future patterns and public discussions. Even as criticism would be heaped on the Indian criminal jury in the decades to come, the Parsi matrimonial jury was regarded as a success. It was different and unproblematic from the perspective of colonial administrators – a fitting reward for the collective fidelity of so many Parsis to British rule. And it was populated by the leaders of its community, in sharp contrast to most Indian criminal juries whose members were distinctly nonelite.

THE PARSI JURY AND ITS COURT

Since their creation in 1865, the Parsi matrimonial courts were the only bodies able to dissolve marriages between Parsis in British India. Mirroring Parsi population patterns, the densest concentration of these courts was in western India. Surat, Broach, Ahmedabad, Karachi, and Poona each had its own Parsi district matrimonial court.[109] The flagship court was the PCMC in Bombay.[110] A web of Parsi matrimonial courts stretched beyond western India into regions with sufficient Parsi populations. Madras, Calcutta, Berar, and Rangoon each had one.[111] The Parsi matrimonial courts were not organized hierarchically among themselves: rulings of the Parsi district court in Surat were not appealed to the PCMC in Bombay, for instance. Their judgments could, however, be appealed to the general colonial courts. Occasionally, they were.[112] These appeals were notably different from criminal jury referrals sent to the higher

---

[107] See Q. in the Corner, I: 13–17.

[108] "Address to the Hon'ble Mr. Justice Melvill," 7.

[109] PMDA 1865, s. 17 in Rana (1934), 36; Menant, *Les Parsis*, 289–90 at note 1.

[110] For a photograph of PCMC delegates in 1895 with presiding BHC judge (Justice John Jardine), see Darukhanawala, *Parsi Lustre*, I: 146.

[111] PMDA 1865, ss. 15–19 and PMDA 1936 ss. 18–22 in Wadia and Katpitia, 44–50. See also Rana (1934), 34–7. For lists of delegates from across India and Burma (1910–20), see "Annex 7: Parsi Matrimonial Court Delegates," Patel and Paymaster, V: 533–4.

[112] PMDA 1865, s. 42 in Rana (1934), 97–8; PMDA 1936, s. 47 in Wadia and Katpitia, 129–31. See *Darukhanawala v. Motibai*; Patel and Paymaster, III: 846.

The Parsi Chief Matrimonial Court

courts. Judges of the Bombay High Court usually refused to interfere with the PCMC's rulings, construing the Parsi court's jurisdiction widely and restricting their own.[113] As one High Court judge named Fulton described it while presiding over the matrimonial court, a wide discretion was given to delegates who were appointed to act as "the Conscience of the Community."[114] Arguably, this was yet another difference in treatment between Parsis and other South Asian populations. At the same time, it could equally be construed as a difference between civil and criminal contexts: the latter deserved closer scrutiny because more was at stake.

There was another way in which the colonial courts interacted with the Parsi courts. A judge from the colonial court system presided over each Parsi court.[115] As in a common-law court with jury, the judge decided on points of law, whereas the jury ruled on points of fact.[116] The judge gave instructions to the jury, establishing the correct legal test to be applied. The jury delivered its findings, without reasons, on each of the issues. Its conclusions were by simple majority.[117] Close votes were often recorded. And, as in the common-law court setting, the jury occasionally ignored the judge's clear leanings in the case.[118] As Parsis rose within the legal profession, the Bombay High Court judge assigned to the PCMC was Parsi himself.[119] In fact, it became customary that if there was a Parsi judge on the High Court bench, he would also preside over the Parsi matrimonial court.[120] If the Indian criminal jury allowed colonial administrators to avoid taking responsibility for difficult rulings, the Parsi matrimonial courts similarly allowed the British to wash their hands of anything these courts might do. What could be construed as empowering the Parsi community – drawing not only the jurors but also the judge from its ranks – could also be seen as a convenient disavowal of responsibility by the British. But, if so, it was a delegation of duty that no other South Asian community had the privilege to enjoy.

---

[113] See "High Court – Appellate Side (Before Sir Charles Sargent, Chief Justice, and the Hon. Mr. Justice Candy). A Matrimonial Suit. *Hirabai Dhunjibhoy Kalfati v. Dhunjibhoy Bomanjee Kalfati*," TI (14 October 1892), 3; *Goolbai Behramsha Harver v. Behramsha D. Harver* ILR 38 Bom 615 (1914); *Manekbai, formerly wife of Nadirshaw Jamshedji Vachha and at present wife of Rustomji M. Kapadia v. Nadirshaw Jamshedji Vachha* ILR 60 Bom 868 (1936).

[114] Suit No. 4 of 1899, 1893–1903 PCMC Notebook, II: 104.

[115] PMDA 1865, ss. 16–17 and PMDA 1936, ss. 19–20 in Wadia and Katpitia, 47–8. See also Rana (1934), 35–6.

[116] PMDA 1865, s. 41 in Rana (1934), 96–7.

[117] PMDA 1865, s. 41 in Rana (1934), 97.

[118] For example, see Suit No. 2 of 1898, 1893–1903 PCMC Notebook, II: 21.

[119] At least six Parsi judges presided over the PCMC between the 1910s and 1947 (in chronological order): Dinshah D. Davar, his son Jehangir D. Davar, F. S. Taleyarkhan, B. J. Wadia, N. J. Wadia, and N. H. C. Coyajee.

[120] Conversations with Rustom P. Vachha, Mumbai (24 February–8 March 2004) and personal communication (23 September 2010). See also Mancerjī Hośañgji Jāgoś, *Ānarebal Sar Dīnshāh Dhanjībhāī Dāvar, Nāīṭ, Hāī Kōrṭnā Nāmdār Jaḍjnū Ṭukū Janm Caritr* (*A Short Sketch of the Life of the Hon. Justice Sir Dinshaw Dhanjibhoy Davar Kt.*) (Bombay: Author, 1912), 4.

212   Law and Identity in Colonial South Asia: Parsi Legal Culture

In Bombay, the Parsi matrimonial court operated with a jury of eleven delegates. They were selected in rotation from the full pool of thirty. The delegates were appointed by the local colonial government, but the government generally acted on the recommendation of the local Parsi community.[121] In Bombay, this recommendation was the product of an election held among the Parsi justices of the peace (JPs), themselves a body of elite Parsi men who were ineligible to run as delegates.[122] The Parsi JPs were generally merchants, bankers, professionals, and intellectuals who were appointed by the colonial state. Along with other JPs, they constituted the municipal legislative body of Bombay.[123] In other words, one group of elite Parsi men elected another.

The social importance of a Parsi delegate's position came out during moments of crisis. At multiple points, there were complaints in the press that prospective delegates canvassed for votes too openly – even at the funeral of one delegate whose position lay vacant.[124] "The office of a delegate," noted the *Jam-e-Jamshed*, "requires not merely birth and lineage," but also "social position, character, large experience of the world, intimate knowledge of human nature, and, above all, a close insight into the conditions of social life in the various strata of the Parsi community."[125] In the 1920s and '30s, Parsis disagreed over the qualities that should disqualify a delegate. The Parsi Marriage and Divorce Act 1936 introduced a new rule. In addition to the earlier one that a criminal conviction would trigger the removal of a delegate, delegates would also be replaced if they became insolvent or ceased to follow the Zoroastrian religion. This latter addition reflected the anxiety of the period over the conversion of Parsis to other religions, particularly Christianity and Islam.[126] The 1936 Act also changed the position of a delegate from a lifetime appointment to a ten-year term, reflecting an awareness that each seat was precious.[127]

---

[121] PMDA 1865, ss. 21–2 and PMDA 1936, ss. 24–5 in Wadia and Katpitia, 50–2. See also Rana (1934), 37; "Opinion on the Report of the Parsee Laws Revision Rule Sub-Committee" in letter from Kavasji Barjorji Vakil, President, Parsi Panchayat Board, Surat, to V. B. Mardhekar, Collector of Surat (17 May 1932), part of "Opinion No. 2: Bombay. From the Secretary to Government of Bombay, Home Dept., No. 5377/3-II-B, dated 28 December 1934, with enclosures" in "Paper No. 1: Opinions on the Parsi Marriage and Divorce Bill," 17–18 in "Parsi Marriage and Divorce Act 1936."

[122] See Karaka, II: 264 at note 1; "The Parsee Chief Matrimonial Court," *TI* (19 July 1892), 3; "A Tug and Pull," 10.

[123] See D. E. Wacha, *Rise and Growth of Bombay Municipal Government* (Madras: Natesan, [1913]), 17–18.

[124] Untitled," *TI* (11 March 1885), 5. See also "Parsi Chief Matrimonial Court. Qualifications of a Delegate" in Jeejeebhoy, 19.

[125] "Parsi Matrimonial Court," *TI* (29 January 1916), 12. See also "Letter to the Editor: Parsee Delegates," *TI* (13 August 1895), 4.

[126] See Karaka, II: 291–5; Palsetia, *Parsis*, 105–27; PMDA 1936, ss. 3(c), 25 and 32(j) in Wadia and Katpitia, 16–17, 20, 51–2, 66–9, 84; by Sharafi, "Bella's Case," 159 at note 526 and "The Marital Patchwork," 983 at note 12. See also Chapter 4 at 187.

[127] PMDA 1865, s. 22 and PMDA 1936, s. 25 in Wadia and Katpitia, 51–2. See also Rana (1934), 38; "Letter to the Editor: Parsi Matrimonial Courts," *TI* (9 April 1932), 14.

The Parsi Chief Matrimonial Court

The roster of 104 delegates to the PCMC of Bombay between 1893 and 1947 included many of the community's most elite men.[128] From among Bombay's "merchant princes" of traders, financiers, and industrialists came eight members from each of the Jijibhai (or Jeejeebhoy) and Wadia families, including the hereditary baronet, Sir Jamsetjee Jeejeebhoy III.[129] There were delegates from the illustrious Petit family and from the Cowasji Dinshaw (or Adenwala) family that helped build Aden, the most important port along the Bombay–Marseilles shipping route.[130] The dynast of the Tata corporate empire, J. N. Tata, was a delegate.[131] There were intellectual and religious leaders, too. K. R. Cama, the renowned linguist, religious studies scholar, and educator, was a delegate of the PCMC.[132] So, too, was the leading Zoroastrian priestly scholar and expert witness of the nineteenth and twentieth centuries, Sir J. J. Modi.[133] More than one high priest (Guj. *dastur*) from the Sanjana family was a delegate, including head priests of the Wadiajee Fire Temple in Bombay and scholars of Zoroastrian religious studies, some of whom had been involved in the famous Parsi Priest defamation case of 1869.[134] The social reformer and compiler of one of the earliest English-Gujarati dictionaries, N. R. Ranina, served as a delegate.[135] Editor and owner of the Gujarati-language daily newspaper *Kaiser-i-Hind*, Erachshaw R. Heerjibehedin, was a delegate.[136] The leading Bombay architect and community leader Vicaji Ardeshir Taraporewala was a Parsi juror, as was

---

[128] List of PCMC delegates compiled from PCMC Notebooks 1893–1947.

[129] See R. A. Wadia, *Scions of Lowjee Wadia* (Bombay: Author, 1964); Zafar Hai's film, *Merchant Princes of Bombay*. For another delegate from a famous Parsi mercantile family, see "The Late Mr. Dadabhoy Rustomjee Banajee," *TI* (15 March 1890), 3. See also Chapter 1 at 81–2.

[130] See Darukhanawala, *Parsi Lustre*, I: 92, 100, 401, 431; Karaka, II: 260–1 at note 1; Stausberg, *Die Religion*, II: 25–6.

[131] R. P. Karkaria, "A Great Parsi. The Late Mr Jamshedji N. Tata. An Appreciation," *The Parsi* I: 1 (January 1905), 10–13; Darukhanawala, *Parsi Lustre*, I: 432–3; F. R. Harris, *Jamsetji Nusserwanji Tata: A Chronicle of his Life* (London: Oxford University Press, Humphrey Milford, 1925), 280; Amalendu Guha, "More about the Parsi Seths: Their Roots, Entrepreneurship, and Comprador Role, 1650–1918" in *Business Communities of India: A Historical Perspective*, ed. Dwijendra Tripathi (Delhi: Manohar, 1984), 143; Godrej, "Faces," in Godrej and Punthakey Mistree, 654–5; R. M. Lala, "Jamsetji Nusserwanji Tata: The Man and His Vision" in Mody, *Enduring Legacy*, I: 186–93.

[132] See "The Late Mr. K. R. Cama; A Scholar and Reformer," *TI* (21 August 1909), 7.

[133] See Sharafi, "Judging Conversion," 165–70; Ringer, *Pious Citizens*, 116–19; Godrej, "Faces," in Godrej and Punthakey Mistree, 652; Marzban J. Giara, *Shams-ul-Ulama Dr. Sir Ervad Jivanji Jamshedji Modi* ((Mumbai: Author, 2001); Chapter 6 at note 144. For a list of Modi's publications in English and Gujarati, see Modi, *Anthropological Papers*, i–iv.

[134] On P. B. Sanjana and his son, D. P. Sanjana, see Darukhanawala, *Parsi Lustre*, I: 63, 65. On the defamation case, see Chapter 7 at 284–5.

[135] N. R. Ranina, *A Manual of English-Gujarati Dictionary*, ed. Rustam R. Ranina (Delhi: Asian Educational Services, 2003, orig. pub. 1910); H. A. K., *A Sketch of the Life and Writings of Nanabhai Rustamji Ranina, written for his comprehensive English-Gujarati Dictionary* (Bombay: Union Press, 1908), 19–32.

[136] "Parsi Chief Matrimonial Court," *TI* (27 July 1921), 7.

214 *Law and Identity in Colonial South Asia: Parsi Legal Culture*

the lobbyist-philanthropist who funded many large-scale charitable constructions in Bombay and London, Sir Cowasji Jehangir.[137] There were physicians on the Parsi jury, among them Dr. K. K. Dadachanji, the critic of English inheritance law.[138] And there were insurance agents and honorary magistrates like Major Sorab R. Bamji, who played an important role in the Parsi arbitration movement of the 1930s.[139]

With one exception, the Parsi jurors were always men. Mrs. Bapsi A. Sabavala was the first and only female delegate to sit during the colonial period, although others had been candidates for a seat.[140] From 1936, litigants had the right to have up to three delegates replaced by request at the start of a case. No reasons were required.[141] By this process, Mrs. Sabavala seems to have been excluded from the jury more frequently than her male counterparts.[142] It was not clear why. She may have had many social connections to litigants, or it might have been that her gender played a role. One case from which Mrs. Sabavala was excluded involved allegations of homosexuality, coercive sexual relations with servants, and blackmail, all in a leading business family.[143] It was possible that litigants and their lawyers felt it inappropriate to expose a Parsi lady to certain indelicate matters – although Mrs. Sabavala herself was known for being hard-nosed in outlook. The reasons most commonly cited for the exclusion of male delegates were illness, a death in the family, or social ties to one party.[144]

The net result was a jury that resembled two other dispute resolution models. First, the Parsi jury looked rather like the older English jury of experts, the "special jury." As described by James Oldham, the concept behind the special jury was to create a group of experts with special knowledge of the customary norms in question. In England, the institution was particularly cherished for use among commercial communities. It was a favorite in Lord Mansfield's eighteenth-century court for banking and insurance cases.[145] In the four centuries before, there were special juries of cooks in cases on bad food sales, of booksellers and printers in libel suits, of farmers in disputes over improvements

---

[137] Darukhanawala, *Parsi Lustre*, I: 99, 214–16. See also Chapter 2 at 93.

[138] See Chapter 3 at 147–8.

[139] See *Who's Who in India, Burma and Ceylon*, 276–7; Suit No. 1 of 1935, 1935–7 PCMC Notebook, I: 242, 249–50.

[140] On Sabavala, see "Parsi Chief Matrimonial Court," *TI* (24 November 1936), 3; "The Cry of the Poor Parsi," *HP* (11 October 1925), 21. On other female candidates like Miss Dhun Desai, see "Parsi Chief Matrimonial Court," *TI* (22 February 1938), 3. See also letter to the editor by Dinshaw M. Mehta, "Parsi Matrimonial Courts," *TI* (14 April 1932), 7.

[141] PMDA 1936, s. 27 in Wadia and Katpitia, 54.

[142] For instance, Suit No. 12 of 1939, I: 490; No. 11 of 1941, II: 143; both in "PCMC Registrar's Minute Book (15 October 1937–10 February 1948)"(BHC). See also Suit No. 14 of 1939, 1937–48 Registrar's Minute Book, II: 105.

[143] See Suit No. 14 of 1939, 1937–41 PCMC Notebook, III: 117–55, 164.

[144] For instance, Registrar's Minute Book 1937–48, I: 343; II: 389.

[145] Oldham, "Special Juries in England,"154–5.

The Parsi Chief Matrimonial Court

to land, and of law clerks and attorneys in suits on the falsification of writs.[146] This model of the jury was the exact opposite of the model that prevailed in the United States, particularly in the twentieth century: the jury of one's peers or, more usually, of the putative average person. The modern American jury model rejected the idea of prior, specific knowledge about community norms and sought the opposite: a mental blank slate, a lack of any prior connection to the setting involved.[147] The second obvious comparison was with the *panchayat*. Although Parsis rejected the Parsi *panchayats* as arbiters of matrimonial cases, the jury system that they created in its place was reminiscent of the *panchayat*.[148] The delegates, like the *panchayat* trustees, were among the most elite senior males of the community. The Parsi jury was hardly a sample of "average" members of the Parsi community. Its structure replicated and even amplified the preexisting social hierarchies within the community.

The courts' earliest years have remained obscure due to a paucity of source material.[149] Between 1873 and 1883, the court heard a very small number of cases – on average, just 3.1 cases per year.[150] Between 1893 and 1947, there were references to 537 cases in the court's records, averaging ten cases per year before the passage of the 1936 matrimonial legislation and twenty-nine cases per year thereafter.[151] Usable case records for approximately 350 cases – almost two-thirds of the court's cases – existed in the form of notebooks containing witness testimony and delegates' findings. Early colonial British observers speculated that the Parsis were so litigious among themselves because the law governing them was so thin – because there was no Parsi law.[152] The surge in matrimonial cases following the 1936 Act in fact suggested the opposite. The greater precision and volume of applicable legal provisions spawned more litigation. New grounds for divorce, particularly desertion, either responded to preexisting unmet needs or created new legal tastes and expectations, a phenomenon observed by Lawrence Friedman and Marc Galanter in other settings.[153]

---

[146] Oldham, "The English Origins of the Special Jury," 141.

[147] James Oldham, "Special Juries in the US and Modern Jury Formation Procedures" in his *Trial by Jury*, 174–212.

[148] See "Address to the Hon'ble Mr. Justice Melvill," 7.

[149] On the 1860s, see Patel and Paymaster, II: 164, 211, 229, 261–2, 284. For cases from the 1870s, see press coverage in the *Bombay Gazette*: "Parsee Matrimonial Court" (5 July 1870), 3; (20 July 1870), 2; (13 December 1870), 2; and in the *TI*: "The Parsee Chief Matrimonial Court," (11 May 1871), 3; (4 February 1878), 3; (4 September 1880), 3. (I owe all *Bombay Gazette* references to Simin Patel, with thanks.) Most importantly, PCMC notebooks for 1865–7 and 1870–93 were unavailable at the Bombay High Court.

[150] "Address to the Hon'ble Mr. Justice Melvill," 7.

[151] These averages are somewhat artificial: for unknown reasons, there were dry spells and low periods. For instance, there were no cases in 1904–5, 1907–9, or 1923. There were only four cases in 1934.

[152] See Introduction at 25.

[153] See Lawrence Friedman, "Legal Culture and the Welfare State," in *Law in Action: A Socio-Legal Reader*, eds. Stewart Macaulay, Lawrence M. Friedman, and Elizabeth Mertz (New York:

216 Law and Identity in Colonial South Asia: Parsi Legal Culture

Four causes of action fell within the court's jurisdiction. Annulment was the cancellation of a marriage *ab initio*. Divorce was the dissolution of a marriage in midstream. Judicial separation was a cause of action available until 1936 to wives only. It resulted in legal separation with maintenance payments to the wife but no right to remarry for either spouse.[154] Finally, the restitution of conjugal rights was a cause of action deriving from English ecclesiastical law whereby one spouse asked the court to make the other spouse return.[155] Roughly three-quarters of cases were for divorce. Annulment suits constituted approximately a tenth of the cases heard. Cases for judicial separation and the restitution of conjugal rights together constituted another tenth.[156] Husbands' suits for the restitution of conjugal rights were commonly coupled with wives' countersuits for judicial separation.[157] Before the 1936 matrimonial statute, wives seeking divorce had to prove greater fault by husbands than husbands had to prove of wives. Under the 1865 Act, husbands only had to prove that their wives had been adulterous. Wives had to prove that their husbands had committed adultery (or fornication) plus cruelty, bigamy, or desertion (for at least two years), or that they had committed rape (against someone other than their wives) or an unnatural offense.[158] Most wives seeking divorce asserted adultery and cruelty.[159] After the 1936 Act, the dominant argument became desertion, a euphemistic ground that allowed a couple to get a divorce without proving fault once they had lived apart for three years.[160] Custody issues became more involved and prevalent as the colonial period wore on: as desertion became the leading ground for divorce, fault was shuffled from the divorce to the custody phase of family rearrangements.[161] There were notable bulges of particular types of cases as the two

Foundation Press, 2007), 261; Marc Galanter, "Law Abounding: Legalisation around the North Atlantic," *MLR* 55:1 (1992), 1–24 (especially at 7–11).

[154] The grounds for judicial separation were expanded (and made available to husbands) under the s. 34 of the PMDA 1936. However, because the grounds for divorce were simultaneously expanded (PMDA 1936, s. 32), parties who may have sued for judicial separation before the 1936 Act usually sued for divorce after it. Judicial separation was only rarely pursued after 1936. For two instances, see Suit No. 21 of 1936, 1935–7 PCMC Notebook, I: 379, II: 1–2; Suit No. 25 of 1938, 1937–41 PCMC Notebook, II: 157, 181–3.

[155] See Sharafi, "Marital Patchwork," 993–5; Sturman, 140–2.

[156] Of about 350 cases, roughly 265 were for divorce, forty for annulment, twenty for the restitution of conjugal rights, and sixteen for judicial separation (PCMC Notebooks, 1893–1947). Illegible and fragmentary records make these figures approximate.

[157] For a sample, see Suit No. 3 of 1903, 1893–1903 PCMC Notebook, III: 64–75 and 1903–13 PCMC Notebook, I: 1–31; Suit No. 5 of 1920, 1920–3 PCMC Notebook, I: 4–5, 26, 36–38, IV:54–5; Suit No. 9 of 1920, 1920–3 PCMC Notebook, III: 9–25, 30–59, IV:2–3.

[158] PMDA 1865, s. 30 in Rana (1934), 45–56. On rape and unnatural offenses (IPC ss. 375 and 377, respectively), see Ranchhodas and Thakore, *IPC*, 321–3.

[159] For example, see Suit No. 5 of 1913, 1913–20 PCMC Notebook, I: 35–48; Suit No. 8 of 1933, 1929–35 PCMC Notebook, IV:131–4.

[160] PMDA 1936, s. 32(g) in Wadia and Katpitia, 68, 79–83. For example, see Suit No. 17 of 1936, 1935–7 PCMC Notebook, I: 377, II: 24–5; Suit No. 17 of 1942, 1941–8 PCMC Notebook, I: 327, 343–5.

[161] For example, see Suit No. 2 of 1937, 1935–7 PCMC Notebook, II: 260–7.

The Parsi Chief Matrimonial Court

World Wars ended.[162] A wave of annulment suits moved through the court as World War I ended, as did a similar group of restitution-of-conjugal-rights cases at the close of World War II.[163] Although these spikes may have been attributable to changes in local personnel or policy, they also raised questions about the relationship between war (or global crisis) and litigation.[164]

That the Parsi delegates usually ruled in favor of female plaintiffs did not necessarily reflect a feminist agenda. Parsi marriage entailed duties and responsibilities that were by no means symmetrical between the sexes. Husbands could have sex with prostitutes (until 1936) and "moderately" beat their wives without risking divorce. The PCMC records were replete with stories of terrible domestic violence.[165] One husband allegedly beat his wife with a hammer, threatening to douse her with kerosene and set her on fire. He also vowed to kill their young son by drowning him or throwing him on the train tracks.[166] Another was accused of throwing wine bottles at and pouring boiling water on his wife, children, and in-laws and of stabbing his wife in the stomach with a knife.[167] Still another was accused of beating his wife so badly (with the help of his natal family) as to cause permanent hearing loss.[168] It was also not unusual for husbands to communicate venereal disease to their wives, suggesting that many men maintained active extramarital sex lives.[169]

Married women, by contrast, had to be faithful to their husbands. When detected, wives' extramarital pregnancies triggered the delegates' swift dissolution of their marriages.[170] Husbands occasionally had extramarital children whom

---

[162] South Asian involvement in both world wars was significant. See Visram, *Asians*, 169–95, 341–53. PCMC cases involving parties who served in World War I included Suit No. 3 of 1916, 1913–20 PCMC Notebook, III: 40; No. 3 of 1919, 1913–20 PCMC Notebook, III: 169; No. 27 of 1941, 1942–4 PCMC Notes of Evidence, I: 77.

[163] On annulment at the end of World War I, see Suit No. 1 of 1917, III: 48–50, 61; 1 of 1918, III: 63–5; 7 of 1919, III: 92, 97–9; all in 1913–20 PCMC Notebook. On the restitution of conjugal rights at the end of World War II, see Suits No. 3, 11, 16, 20, 21, 22, 30, 33 of 1945 and Suits No. 20, 33, 34 of 1946; all in 1941–8 PCMC Notebook, I: 403, 407, 413, II: 302, 343 and in 1937–48 PCMC Registrar's Minute Book, II: 339–42, 379, 399.

[164] See John Stookey, "Trials and Tribulations: Crises, Litigation, and Legal Change," *LSR*, 24:2 (1990), 497–520.

[165] For a sample, see Suit No. 21 of 1938, PCMC Notebook 1937–41, II: 184–200, III: 1–5; No. 16 of 1940, PCMC Notebook 1937–41, III: 198–200; Suit No. 24 of 1941, PCMC Notebook 1941–8, I: 318–22. See also "Parsee Chief Matrimonial Court. *Jamasjee Jamsetjee Pawri v. Buchoobai*," *TI* (24 April 1882), 3; "Custody of a Minor," *TI* (25 February 1918), 10.

[166] Suit No. 10 of 1935, 1935–7 PCMC Notebook, I: 298–330, 332–48, II: 13–14.

[167] Suit No. 11 of 1935, 1935–7 PCMC Notebook, I: 274–97, 360.

[168] Suit No. 13 of 1936, 1935–7 PCMC Notebook, II: 120–48, 252.

[169] On syphilis and gonorrhea, see Suit No. 4 of 1903, 1903–13 PCMC Notebook, I: 1–40, II: 31; in 1929–35 PCMC Notebook, Suit No. 3 of 1930, I: 68–81, 86–95 and Suit No. 1 of 1932, III: 96, IV: 14–15, 17–45.

[170] There were at least thirteen such cases between 1893 and 1947, and more in which there were allegations of extramarital pregnancy. For a sample, see Suit No. 3 of 1896, 1893–1903 PCMC Notebook, I: 211, 222–4; Suit No. 4 of 1896, 1893–1903 PCMC Notebook, I: 225–30; Suit No.

218   Law and Identity in Colonial South Asia: Parsi Legal Culture

they quietly maintained or even adopted, pretending to be charitable toward an orphan or a servant's child.[171] At the heart of the Rangoon *navjote* case, the little girl Bella was presented as an unrelated orphan taken in by her adoptive parents as an act of random kindness. In fact, she was probably the extramarital child of her adoptive father's younger brother, himself a married man.[172] Similarly, Dinshah Davar ridiculed the testimony of a Parsi hospital worker from the princely state of Cambay who claimed to have adopted an orphaned Hindu child named Sonabai. The man had shown her unusual generosity and devotion despite his very limited means. Davar and Beaman were convinced that she was the man's biological child.[173] It was perhaps because the inequalities within Parsi marriage were so pronounced that the Parsi jury strictly policed fraud against wives, in particular, at the point of entry. The emphasis on free and voluntary consent also suggested lines of colonial influence: liberalism in India aspired to replace status with contract, maximizing choice and individual free will.[174] The Parsi jury may have been driven by a desire to flag abuses within the arranged marriage system the better to defend it implicitly against European disapproval.

THE PLAINTIFFS

It was Parsi wives, more than husbands, who came to the Parsi jury for relief. Suits for divorce or judicial separation dominated the docket. In these cases, female plaintiffs outnumbered male by a factor of two to one.[175] From the late 1920s, the ratio became three to one.[176] Because a surprising number of these wives were underprivileged and because plaintiffs usually won their cases, the PCMC of Bombay was effectively a court for poor wives.[177] However, it was not all kinds of poor Parsi women who came to the court for help. The PCMC records captured a particular slice of poor Parsi women: those whose families were too poor to support them, but who could raise the money to go to court. These women were moderately poor, but not abjectly so. Parsi women in bad

---

    1A of 1925, 1924–8 PCMC Notebook, II: 12–14, 53; Suit No. 6 of 1926, 1924–8 PCMC Notebook, III: 19–22; Suit No. 5 of 1937, 1935–7 PCMC Notebook, II: 224–6. For a case in which the wife of a prominent Parsi police officer went mad after being divorced for an extramarital pregnancy, see Patel and Paymaster, III: 843.

[171] On the euphemistic use of adoption elsewhere in the Anglosphere, see William H. Whitmore, *The Law of Adoption in the United States, and Especially in Massachusetts* (Albany: Joel Munsell, 1876), 75.

[172] See Sharafi, "Bella's Case," 32–45.

[173] *Petit v. Jijibhai* 575–6; *Judgments: Petit v. Jeejeebhoy 1908*, 71–4. See also Beaman, "Notes in Parsi Panchayat Case," 22–3, 27.

[174] See Chapter 3 at 140.

[175] Between 1893 and 1929, roughly 65 percent of the divorce or judicial separation cases with usable records had female plaintiffs, whereas only 35 percent were initiated by husbands.

[176] Between 1929 and 1947, approximately three-quarters of divorce or judicial separation cases with usable records had female plaintiffs, whereas a quarter had male ones.

[177] Plaintiffs won in approximately 88 percent of PCMC cases with usable records (1893–1947).

The Parsi Chief Matrimonial Court 219

marriages regarded litigation as a solution, in other words, when the options of de facto separation and long-term financial support from their natal families were unavailable. The diminished presence of both very affluent *and* very poor women suggested that law was a solution for Parsi wives of the middling working class, a finding that has been replicated in studies of divorce courts in other times and places.[178] Elite Parsi couples typically avoided divorce when their marriages fell apart.[179] If the wife's natal family was wealthy enough to support her, she simply returned to live there. Long-term informal separation was not unusual in privileged Parsi circles, as among elite British couples in the same period.[180] The property-related consequences of divorce, along with the publicity of a court case, may have explained elite avoidance of the matrimonial court.[181]

If a woman's natal family was too poor to support her, she might be forced to return to the troubled marital home. In one 1903 case, the mother of a battered woman explained why she had sent her daughter back to an abusive husband: "As I was poor I could not afford to keep her with me."[182] Other women came to court when their natal families could not support them. When it was the husband who had left the home and was not supporting his wife, some wives sued for maintenance in the magistrate's court.[183] When wives wanted to end cohabitation permanently, they sued for divorce or judicial separation in the Parsi matrimonial courts: permanent alimony usually accompanied both types of suits.[184] One woman had been supported by a male relative since her departure from the marital home after her husband's adultery. When that relative died, the woman came to the court: "there was no one to support me."[185] In a similar case, a wife left the marital home following her husband's affair and lived with her brother and his wife. She told the court, "I did not think of filing the suit but now they are in bad circumstances so I am forced to take action."[186]

Coming to court was expensive for plaintiffs and defendants alike. When he retired from overseeing the court in 1883, Justice Melvill claimed that the Parsi matrimonial court's fees were reasonable and that a person representing him- or herself could spend much less than the cost of a suit in the Small Causes Court.[187] However, it was unusual for parties to represent themselves in the

---

[178] See Merry, *Getting Justice*, 59, 178; Margaret Woo, "Shaping Citizenship: Chinese Family Law and Women," *Yale J.L. & Feminism* 15 (2003), 99–134.
[179] A famous instance was the Indian revolutionary Bhikhaiji Cama. Madame Cama lived in exile in Paris, separated from her Bombay-based husband, a lawyer named Rustom K. R. Cama. (Nath and Vithalani, 50.) See Introduction at note 87.
[180] See, for example, *Kaikhasru v. Jerba'i*, 538.
[181] On publicity, see Chapter 1 at 69.
[182] Suit No. 3 of 1903, 1893–1903 PCMC Notebook, I: 21.
[183] For example, see Suit No. 12 of 1920, 1920–3 Notebook, IV: 9.
[184] See PMDA 1865, s. 34 in Rana (1934), 78–82.
[185] Suit No. 4 of 1902, 1893–1903 PCMC Notebook, III: 39.
[186] Suit No. 4 of 1925, 1924–8 PCMC Notebook, II: 42.
[187] "Address to the Hon'ble Mr. Justice Melvill," 7.

220   *Law and Identity in Colonial South Asia: Parsi Legal Culture*

matrimonial court, particularly after Melvill's time. Of the approximately 350 cases with usable records heard between 1893 and 1947, people represented themselves in only twelve cases (3 percent).[188] Most litigants hired a team of lawyers consisting of a solicitor, a senior advocate, and his junior. According to Rana's table of fees for 1900–34, a lawyer could charge Rs 30–75 for each appearance in the matrimonial court. Arranging for translations and expert witnesses, taking oaths, and submitting documents each involved an additional fee.[189] A husband in one 1930 case allegedly earned Rs 80 per month as a hospital typist, giving him a solid working-class salary.[190] His wife filed for divorce. She convinced the delegates that her husband was having an affair with her older sister. The wife did not want maintenance or alimony, but she did want her husband to pay her legal costs. Given the husband's earnings, his lawyer asked the judge to cap the maximum payable for her costs at Rs 300. But the judge increased the maximum to Rs 500.[191] What this meant was that court fees for one side alone could amount to six months' income on a working-class salary. For a woman, salaried positions were less common. Parsi women only started becoming nurses and teachers in the 1930s, and, even then, such jobs were unusual.[192]

It often took years for poor parties to raise the necessary funds. Because unreasonable delay nullified a suit, working-class plaintiffs explained that they had saved over a long period or traveled from Bombay to the *mofussil* to borrow from relatives.[193] At other times, a relative agreed to lend the plaintiff money – or died, leaving the plaintiff an estate.[194] One battered wife suing for divorce raised funds by public subscription through a Parsi newspaper.[195] From the mid-1930s, it was also possible to sue as a pauper.[196] Defendants also struggled to raise funds. The mother of one female defendant sold her jewelry to pay for her daughter's legal expenses.[197]

---

[188] See Suits No. 2 of 1898, 2 of 1900, 1 of 1901, 2 of 1901 (1893–1903 PCMC Notebook, II: 6, 107, 121, 133); 1 of 1906 (1903–13 Notebook, II: 52); 1 of 1913, 1 of 1914, 7 of 1914 (1913–20 PCMC Notebook, I: 10, 38, II: 61); 1 of 1930 (1929–35 PCMC Notebook, IV: 177); 6 of 1937, 10 of 1938, 2 of 1939 (1937–41 PCMC Notebook, II: 13, 126, III: 70).

[189] Rana (1934), 113.

[190] Between 1927 and 1939, the court was told that a Parsi tram inspector made Rs 70 per month; a clerk working at the docks, Rs 80; and a storekeeper for the Great Indian Peninsular Railway, Rs 88. (Suit No. 3 of 1927, 1928–9 PCMC Notebook, II: 135; Suit No. 24 of 1936, 1935–7 PCMC Notebook, II: 272; Suit No. 4 of 1939, 1937–41 PCMC Notebook, III: 36–7, respectively.)

[191] Suit No. 6 of 1930, 1929–35 PCMC Notebook, III: 1–6.

[192] See Chapter 3 at note 153.

[193] For instance, see Suit 2 of 1920, 1920–3 PCMC Notebook, I: 10.

[194] For example, Suit No. 2 of 1920, 1920–3 PCMC Notebook, I: 10; Suit No. 4 of 1902, 1893–1903 PCMC Notebook, III: 42.

[195] Suit No. 4 of 1899, 1893–1903 PCMC Notebook, II: 101.

[196] Coming to court *in forma pauperis* required its own approval process. Pauper suits began appearing in the PCMC from the mid-1930s. For the first such suits, see Suit 1 of 1935, I: 251, 273; Suit 13 of 1936, I: 372, II: 148; both in the 1935–7 PCMC Notebook.

[197] Suit 24 of 1936, 1935–7 PCMC Notebook, II: 276.

The Parsi Chief Matrimonial Court

How do we know that many plaintiff-wives were working class? Occasional statements about husbands' and fathers' incomes suggested that many women did not come from affluent backgrounds, at least by their own accounts.[198] Some of these women also told the court that they were illiterate.[199] The female education movement had enjoyed great support and success among Parsis from the mid-nineteenth century on, such that illiteracy implied nonelite status.[200] Although some of the wives testifying in the PCMC had servants, others did not.[201] Some worked as servants themselves.[202] Still others both worked as servants *and* occasionally hired their own.[203] The range of status and cost within the domestic labor pool, along with the low wages of the lowest paid servants, meant that having servants was potentially an option for members of the middling working class. Many of the parties and their families lived in low-rent one-room *chawl* housing, in which residents on each floor shared a common toilet and bath.[204] Finally, many plaintiff-wives received charitable aid.[205] One had her marriage expenses (and perhaps her dowry) paid by a charitable fund established for poor Parsi women.[206] Another received meals from a kindly neighbor.[207] Combined,

---

[198] Male salaries noted included a watch repairman (Rs 30–65 per month in 1898), employee at Pallonji Plumbers (Rs 35 in 1915), carpenter (Rs 60 in 1915), office worker (Rs 75 in 1893), clerk in the Police Commissioner's Office (Rs 75 per month in 1914), and head ticket collector at a major Bombay train station (Rs 80 in 1928). (Suit No. 2 of 1898, 1893–1903 PCMC Notebook, II: 17; Suit No. 1 of 1915, 1913–20 PCMC Notebook, II: 93; Suit No. 1 of 1915, 1913–20 PCMC Notebook, II: 89; Suit No. 4 of 1893, 1893–1903 PCMC Notebook, I: 4; Suit No. 3 of 1914, 1913–20 PCMC Notebook, II: 6; Suit No. 6 of 1928, 1928–9 PCMC Notebook, I: 75, respectively). To put these figures into perspective, the 1895 salary of a judge in the Small Causes Court of Bombay was Rs 900 per month [Macleod, "Reminiscences" (1894–1914), 17.] An Indian sepoy or soldier in the colonial army made Rs 7 per month circa 1884, whereas "a Parsi in the lowest employment that he can enter upon – namely that of a cook or domestic servant – earns nearly double the sum which is paid to the sepoy" (Karaka, I: 103).

[199] See Suit No. 4 of 1902, 1893–1903 Notebook, III: 39; Suit No. 6 of 1919, 1920–3 PCMC Notebook, I: 17.

[200] See Shirin Maneckjee's "The Ladies' Page," *The Parsi* I: 1 (January 1905), 29–31; "Indian Affairs. Parsee Exclusiveness," *TI* (23 May 1905), 4. See also John R. Hinnells, "Parsis and British Education, 1820–1880" in Hinnells, *Zoroastrian and Parsi Studies*, 157–61; Gould, 170.

[201] On women without servants, see Suit No. 4 of 1893, 1893–1903 PCMC Notebook, I: 19; Suit No. 9 of 1920, 1920–3 PCMC Notebook, III: 33.

[202] See, for example, Suit No. 1 of 1890, 1893–1903 PCMC Notebook, I: 154; Suit No. 1 of 1901, 1893–1902 PCMC Notebook, II: 143, 145; Suit No. 3 of 1910, 1903–13 PCMC Notebook, II: 132.

[203] For example, Suit No. 1 of 1901, 1893–1903 PCMC Notebook, II: 141–3.

[204] See Suit No. 3 of 1903, 1893–1903 PCMC Notebook, III: 68; Suit No. 4 of 1903, 1903–13 PCMC Notebook, I: 1.

[205] For example, see Suit No. 7 of 1920, 1920–3 PCMC Notebook, II: 33; Suit No. 3 of 1927, 1928–9 PCMC Notebook, II: 135.

[206] Suit No. 4 of 1903, I: 1. See also Sapur Faredun Desai, *Parsis and Eugenics* (Bombay: Author, 1940), 86.

[207] Suit No. 3 of 1927, 1928–9 PCMC Notebook, II: 135.

222   *Law and Identity in Colonial South Asia: Parsi Legal Culture*

these indicators suggested moderate levels of poverty among a good number of plaintiff-wives.[208]

COUNTERING FRAUD

One social scenario appeared occasionally before the Parsi jury: marriage arranged through force or fraud. Force was more common than fraud.[209] Although – or perhaps because – many Parsis married late or not at all, it was not uncommon for Parsi families to pressure their junior members to marry.[210] The Parsi jury was especially likely to release spouses from such marriages, acting as a social corrective to potential abuses within the system of arranged marriage. Involuntary marriage often lurked in the background of divorce cases. Some men forced into marriages showed their resentment by being cruel to their wives; others had extramarital relationships. If a man was both cruel and adulterous, his wife could ask the court for a divorce.[211] If he was cruel but not adulterous, she could request a judicial separation. If he simply left, his wife could sue for divorce after three years (desertion became a ground for divorce in 1936).[212] Women forced into marriages had similar ways out. Some had affairs, giving their husbands grounds for divorce. Others left the marital home, giving their husbands two legal options: to sue for the restitution of conjugal rights or, after 1936, to sue for divorce on the basis of desertion.[213] When the husband sued for the restitution of conjugal rights, the wife often countersued for judicial separation. When she could show that she had married involuntarily, she usually won.[214] Whether it was the man or the woman who had allegedly been forced into the marriage, the Parsi jury generally dissolved the marriage.

Arranged marriage was commonly practiced among Parsis in the early twentieth century. Perhaps reflecting the new distinction between arranged and non-arranged marriages observed by Rochona Majumdar in late colonial India, "love marriages" were occasionally noted explicitly by parties in the court.[215]

---

[208] There are also many statements from wives and their witnesses claiming that the wives or their natal families were poor. For example, see Suit No. 7 of 1927, 1928–9 PCMC Notebook, I: 88; Suit No. 3 of 1927, 1928–9 PCMC Notebook, II: 37. As both husbands and wives had obvious reasons to overstate such claims, I have sought added contextual corroboration.

[209] For comparative purposes, see R. H. Helmholz, *Marriage Litigation in Medieval England* (Cambridge: Cambridge University Press, 1974), 90–4.

[210] See Chapter 6 at note 12.

[211] For example, see Suit No. 1 of 1931, 1929–35 PCMC Notebook, III: 22.

[212] For example, see Suit No. 14 of 1937, 1937–41 PCMC Notebook, II: 29.

[213] For example, see Suit No. 1 of 1938, 1937–41 PCMC Notebook, II: 79–81.

[214] For example, see Suit No. 4 of 1893, 1893–1903 PCMC Notebook, I: 1–35.

[215] Rochona Majumdar, *Marriage and Modernity: Family Values in Colonial Bengal* (Durham, NC: Duke University Press, 2009); Suit No. 9 of 1920, 1920–3 PCMC Notebook, III: 42; Suits No. 6 and 7 of 1924, 1924–8 PCMC Notebook, I: 3. For examples of arranged marriages, see Mukerji and Desai, 41–3.

The Parsi Chief Matrimonial Court

But equally, the practice of child marriage – the quintessential form of arranged marriage – continued into the late colonial period.[216] During the battle over child marriage in the 1860s, Parsi commissioners clung to the institution. They were right to note the widespread nature of child marriage in their community. These marriages especially were dissolved by the Parsi jury when one side claimed involuntariness.[217]

The most common cases of nonconsensual marriages were forced marriages that were consummated and that then foundered. These arrived before the Parsi jury as divorce suits. There were also cases in which a spouse claimed to have been tricked into getting married through fraud. These marriages were often unconsummated and took the form of annulment suits. These cases illustrated most clearly the gender- and class-based dynamic that developed between the Parsi jury and its litigants. Senior elite males released nonelite females alleging fraud during the arrangement of their marriages. When nonelite males attempted to make the same argument, they were less successful.

A number of annulment cases filed by wives suggested that information about their husbands was withheld at the time the marriage was arranged. The problem was usually mental illness or impotence.[218] Many of these suits existed because of the view that marriage could cure young men of their mental or sexual ailments. Such optimism was probably what inspired one family to withhold information and negotiate a marriage for a son who was both mentally ill and impotent. Like so many other cases before the matrimonial court, Suit No. 2 of 1895 involved working-class Parsis, originally from the *mofussil*.[219] The bride's father was a farmer. The groom was a fitter or turner, a type of mechanic's aid who assisted engineers in menial work. On the bride's side, the marriage was arranged through a female relative. Although the groom's family members knew of his mental condition, they kept it from the bride's relatives. Acquaintances of the groom's family knew of the groom's troubles, too, but did not get involved. "I did not know the present state of his mind. I did not know if they knew. I was not asked," protested one witness who had said nothing. The bride was fourteen and the groom twenty-one. She had seen him for fifteen minutes about six months before the wedding but had not noticed that he was gradually going "out of his senses," in the words of the acquaintance.[220]

---

[216] See Chapter 4 at 184.

[217] See, for example, Suit No. 2 of 1902, 1893–1903 PCMC Notebook, III: 20. See also Sharafi, "Marital Patchwork," 1001.

[218] A Parsi spouse could sue for nullity of marriage due to the partner's mental unsoundness at the time of marriage [PMDA 1865, s. 27 in Rana (1934), 40–2]. Under the 1936 legislation, this ground for annulment was changed into a ground for divorce [PMDA 1936, s. 32(b) in Wadia and Katpitia, 66–7, 71–2]. Annulment was available when consummation was "from natural causes impossible" [PMDA 1865, s. 28 in Rana (1934), 42–3; PMDA 1936, s. 30 in Wadia and Katpitia, 60–4].

[219] Suit No. 2 of 1895, 1893–1903 PCMC Notebook, I: 144–5, 169–74, 207–8.

[220] Ibid., I: 172.

224   *Law and Identity in Colonial South Asia: Parsi Legal Culture*

"He was selected as a husband for me by my relative and I simply said yes," the wife told the court.[221]

Several years later, the wife sued for annulment. By this time, her husband had been diagnosed with chronic dementia and admitted to the Colaba Lunatic Asylum in south Bombay. The physician in charge of the asylum, one Dr. Boyd, testified that the husband had initially suffered from delusions. The husband spoke in a wild, excited, and irrational manner, and "thought the Hindus had put him under a spell and would assault him." On a subsequent admission, the husband was convinced that his father was trying to poison him. The man had been violent initially, but by the time of trial, "this violen[t] mania with its excitement and assertiveness has disappeared and it is now dementia." The patient's mind had degenerated and become "silly." He shuddered to himself and was solitary in his habits. He did not understand that he was married. According to Dr. Boyd, the patient's sexual organs had also atrophied, one testicle shrinking to the size of a pea. "He seems to have no sexual inclination whatever."[222]

The bride's father realized that his side had been tricked. He blamed his relative and the groom's family: "*I repented at being brought through ignorance into a snare.* Before marriage, I had no reason to believe he was mad . . . I trusted a relative Bai Putli of Khetvadi to select plaintiff a husband. . . . I don't know why she did not find out that Defendant was mad."[223] The bride's brother was married on the same day as the bride. Their father did not attend his daughter's wedding, which was in a different place, and only learned of his new son-in-law's problems once it was too late. The husband had been violent and delusional toward his new wife on their wedding night. He had not attempted to consummate the marriage. The wife had returned to her parents and lived with them since that night. Like many of the plaintiffs in the Parsi matrimonial courts, she avoided coming to court for several years: "I delayed bringing this suit, hoping he might recover from his madness."[224] But her husband did not get better. The delegates unanimously granted an annulment on grounds of insanity and impotence.[225]

Impotence was the most common allegation made against husbands in annulment suits. The Parsi matrimonial court in Bombay dealt with approximately forty cases of alleged impotence between 1893 and 1947. In other times and places, impotence could be a made-up and collusive claim. It implied the use of annulment where fault-based divorce schemes made exit difficult or where the law did not recognize divorce at all.[226] Unless the testimony of medical experts

---

[221] Ibid., I: 171.
[222] Ibid., I: 169–70.
[223] Ibid., I: 172. Emphasis added.
[224] Suit No. 2 of 1895, 1893–1903 PCMC Notebook, I: 171.
[225] Ibid., I: 174.
[226] For example, see Helmholz, 88.

The Parsi Chief Matrimonial Court

was suspect, though, most allegations of impotence in the Parsi court seem to have been genuine. There were elaborate discussions surrounding the medical examination of the parties, and physicians on each side occasionally disagreed with each others' interpretations. Medical experts were usually Parsi or British men trained as physicians in Bombay, England, or Scotland.[227] On a rare occasion, a female physician or midwife gave expert testimony.[228]

These experts usually examined both spouses. They checked that wives' hymens were intact to confirm that the women were virgins. The analysis of the hymen was not always straightforward. Medical experts acknowledged that the hymen could be ruptured by causes other than sexual intercourse. For instance, treatment for painful menstruation often included the insertion of sharp instruments into the vaginal canal.[229] Some experts also testified that it was possible (although not common) for an elastic hymen to remain intact after sex. As Dr. Framroze Navroji Kapadia claimed: "An intact hymen is not a sign of virginity. Prostitutes even may have the hymen intact. But it would break at childbirth."[230] The same medical experts employed a variety of methods to determine whether men were impotent. These included ill-defined "physical and electrical tests" that induced erections.[231] Kaikhusroo Sorabji Engineer, an assistant surgeon in the Bombay Medical Service, explained to the court in 1894 that one husband suffered from palsy of the penis: "The muscles would not respond to the electric current so I think the case incurable."[232] In only one case did a female plaintiff lose her annulment suit, and it was on the basis of the medical expert's opinion that her hymen was ruptured and her husband potent. The delegates suspected that the wife had fabricated the accusation and convinced her relatives to lie in court on her behalf because she wanted to marry her husband's nephew.[233]

Although most impotence claims seemed to have been genuine, there was also a creative widening of the doctrine that produced an exit route for couples who would have sought a divorce by mutual consent had it been available. Like English and canon law courts, the Parsi court accepted the concept of *relative*

---

[227] For example, Suit No. 2 of 1906, 1903–1913 PCMC Notebook, II: 59–60 (Dr. Eduljee Nusserwanjee); Suit No. 3 of 1913, 1913–20 PCMC Notebook, I: 6 (Dr. Ardeshir Dhunjisha Contractor); Suit No. 3 of 1915, 1913–20 PCMC Notebook, II: 171 (Dr. Temulji Bhicaji Nariman); Suit No. 3 of 1919, 1913–20 PCMC Notebook, I: 7 (Dr. Framroze Nowroji Kapadia); Suit No. 6 of 1933, 1929–35 PCMC Notebook, IV: 118–19 (Dr. William Collis Spackman).

[228] For example, Suit No. 3 of 1898, 1893–1903 PCMC Notebook, II: 27 (midwife Maria O'Neill).

[229] Suit No. 3 of 1933, 1929–35 PCMC Notebook, IV: 106.

[230] Suit No. 4 of 1938, 1937–41 PCMC Notebook, I: 55.

[231] The use of electricity in medical treatment was in vogue at the turn of the twentieth century. See Sharafi, "Two Lives," 264.

[232] Suit No. 3 of 1894, 1893–1903 PCMC Notebook, I: 89.

[233] Suit No. 3 of 1902, 1893–1903 PCMC Notebook, III: 24–36.

226   *Law and Identity in Colonial South Asia: Parsi Legal Culture*

impotence.[234] Intriguingly, a man could be deemed impotent in relation to one woman (his wife) but not in relation to others.[235] From the late 1920s, an increasing number of husbands accused of impotence admitted to relative impotence as a way of saving face *and* obtaining an annulment, no matter how they fared during the medical exam.[236] The idea of relative impotence could theoretically be applied to a woman, too. But in only one case did a husband obtain an annulment because of his wife's relative impotence, the product of her "great repugnance" for him.[237]

Fraud and impotence sometimes traveled together in the matrimonial court. In Suit No. 2 of 1900, a wife asked the Parsi jury for an annulment. Her marriage had gone unconsummated for fourteen years.[238] She and her husband had married at the ages of sixteen and eighteen, respectively. They were first cousins, and it appeared that their families had arranged the marriage. He was a copyist at the post office. According to one Dr. Gillespie, the husband was impotent due to "weakened condition of the brain."[239] The husband was aware of his problem before the marriage and told the court that he had married under pressure. He told his wife after the marriage, "I have not virility in me and I am a hermit."[240] He told Dr. Gillespie that he had no sexual desire or experience, that he felt no affection for his wife, and that he had no desire to remarry. The husband had been forced into the marriage and had committed fraud by withholding the truth during negotiations. The delegates voted unanimously for an annulment.[241]

In the 1900 case, it was not clear whether the husband's family knew about his impotence. There were other cases in which the family was probably aware. In Suit No. 3 of 1919, the wife of a World War I soldier came to the matrimonial court requesting an annulment.[242] Her husband admitted to an intermediary that he had known he was impotent before their marriage but had allowed the match to be arranged anyway. His mother allegedly knew about her son's problem. As the wife told the court, "My mother-in-law was in league with my husband and knew that he was impotent."[243] The mother probably believed that

---

[234] *S. (the wife) v. B. (the husband)* ILR 16 Bom 639 (1892) and in Patel and Paymaster, III: 844; *Proceedings between the Lady Frances Howard, Countess of Essex, and Robert Earl of Essex, her husband* 2 Howell's State Trials 786 (1613); A. Esmein, *Le Mariage en Droit Canonique* (Paris: Larose and Forcel, 1891), I: 247–8.

[235] Suit No. 2 of 1900, 1893–1903 PCMC Notebook, II: 115.

[236] In 1929–35 PCMC Notebook, see Suit No. 6 of 1929, III: 16–17; Suit No. 2 of 1930, I: 59; Suit No. 7 of 1933, IV: 143.

[237] Suit No. 3 of 1932, 1929–35 PCMC Notebook, IV: 7–8.

[238] Suit No. 2 of 1900, PCMC Notebook 1893–1903, II: 107–17.

[239] Ibid., II: 115.

[240] Ibid., II: 113.

[241] Ibid., II: 117.

[242] Suit No. 3 of 1919, 1913–20 PCMC Notebook, III: 91, 169; 1920–3 PCMC Notebook, I: 1, 5–9, III: 2.

[243] Suit No. 3 of 1919, 1920–3 PCMC Notebook, I: 7.

The Parsi Chief Matrimonial Court

marriage would cure her son. For a couple of weeks, the husband had attempted to consummate the union. "He told me he was sorry he could not do it and that he had made a great mistake in marrying me."[244] He then left his wife and went to East Africa. Through the network of informal Parsi connections that stretched across the Indian Ocean, the wife made enquiries. A Parsi named Mr. Engineer told the court: "I am in Postal Service at Dar-es-Salaam in East Africa. In 1918, the Petitioner wrote to me. I did not know her then. I made enquiries about her husband. I met him at Dar-es-Salaam. We discussed his marriage. He told me that he oughtn't to have married as he was physically unfit. He said he was impotent."[245] The wife was declared a virgin following a medical exam, and the delegates granted the annulment.[246] The husband in this scenario was both a victim of his own family's pressure and, in yielding to that pressure, a perpetrator of fraud against his wife. At the same time, the view that impotence was curable through Western methods like electrical treatment or through *vaids* and *hakims* practicing traditional Indian medicine complicated the notion of fraud: its edges shaded into hope-infused denial and rationalization.[247] But although the delegates of the matrimonial court could not know the mental state of the former soldier and his mother on the day of the wedding, they did not hesitate to dissolve the marriage. The wife was a medically certified virgin. That was enough to prove relative impotence, at very least.

In most annulment cases involving fraud, the plaintiff was female. With the one exception noted, the Parsi jury sided with these women.[248] Husbands in the same situation were both less numerous and less successful in court. The 1916 case of *Dinbai v. Erachsha D. Toddyvala*, which was covered by the press, was an ideal illustration.[249] In that case, the husband alleged fraud on the part of a marriage broker in her representations about the woman he married. Erachsha D. Toddyvala asserted fraud not while suing for an annulment, but as a defense to his wife's suit for the restitution of conjugal rights. Like more than a million other South Asian men, Toddyvala was a soldier in World War I.[250] Soon after returning from Flanders and Egypt, he forced his wife out of the marital home.[251] She asked the Parsi jury to bring them back together. He claimed that he had been tricked into their marriage and that it was invalid under Parsi

---

[244] Ibid., I: 6.

[245] Ibid., I: 7.

[246] Ibid., I: 8.

[247] For examples of such treatment, see Suit No. 3 of 1902, 1893–1903 PCMC Notebook, III: 33 (*hakim*); Suit No. 6 of 1929, 1929–35 PCMC Notebook, III: 7 (electrical treatment).

[248] See 225.

[249] In the *TI*, see "Parsi Chief Matrimonial Court of Bombay, Suit No. 3 of 1916. *Dinbai, wife of Erachsha Dossabhai Toddywalla (plaintiff) v. Erachsha Dossabhai Toddywalla (defendant),*" (31 October 1916), 9 and (2 November 1916), 5.

[250] Visram, 169. See also notes 162–3. On Parsis who fought in World War I, see Desai, *History*, 233, 401–2.

[251] Suit No. 3 of 1916, 1913–20 PCMC Notebook, III: 26; Suit No. 7 of 1927, PCMC Notebook 1928–9, I: 87.

228   *Law and Identity in Colonial South Asia: Parsi Legal Culture*

law. Unlike the female plaintiffs who claimed they had been manipulated, however, he lost.

The suit was one of several between the pair, exemplifying the litigiousness that was common among Parsis. Initially, the couple had gone to arbitrators after the husband threw his wife out of the marital home. The arbitrators sided with Mrs. Toddyvala, urging a reconciliation. When Mr. Toddyvala ignored their recommendation, his wife filed her 1916 suit for the restitution of conjugal rights. She won, whereupon her husband made an unconvincing attempt to cohabit with his wife. On his solicitor's advice, Mr. Toddyvala rented a house with two separate rooms separated by a staircase. "He lived in one [room], and I lived in the other," his wife testified later.[252] He slept at his family's home, only visiting the new house during the daytime once every four days: "he kept the key of the other room with himself. I was not allowed to enter that room. He did not cohabit with [me] in that house. He would not come near me. He said he was not willing to keep me. My meals were supplied from Irani['s] shop, twice in a day. He never dined with me. I was given no utensils [with which] to cook. He gave me Rs 5 once on the first day. He did not supply my [wants]. My cousins supplied me with necessities. This went on for four months. I protested repeatedly."[253] Finally, the wife left the new house and moved in with relatives, alternating between her cousin's and father's homes.

The next round began a few months later, when Mrs. Toddyvala sued her husband in the Court of Small Causes for the recovery of some furniture and a government promissory note. The court referred this dispute to arbitrators, who agreed to take on this case and other outstanding conflicts between the couple. The arbitrators sided with Mrs. Toddyvala once again. They ordered Mr. Toddyvala to pay his wife Rs 800 for her legal costs from the 1916 restitution suit, in addition to maintenance of Rs 25 per month. When he did not, she sued him in the Court of Small Causes for enforcement of the arbitrators' award. Mr. Toddyvala lost again but appealed the decision to the Bombay High Court, trying to make a jurisdictional argument that his wife ought to have sued him in the PCMC instead. The High Court rejected his argument. The Small Causes Court was the place to sue when there was a written agreement like the one produced by arbitration.[254] Even after this, Mrs. Toddyvala had difficulty getting her husband to pay her. He had applied for insolvency status and had been granted it. It was now 1920.

By this time, Mrs. Toddyvala, now a seasoned litigant, was used to temporary setbacks. Several years passed, then she learned that her husband was living with another Parsi woman and that this woman had borne Mr. Toddyvala a daughter in 1923. This fact, substantiated through the records of the Parsi Lying-In Hospital where the baby was born, gave Mrs. Toddyvala clear evidence of her

[252] Suit No. 7 of 1927, 1928–9 PCMC Notebook, I: 87.
[253] Ibid., I: 88.
[254] *Toddiwala v. Dinbai.*

The Parsi Chief Matrimonial Court

husband's adultery.[255] In 1927, she coupled it with the claim that her husband had deserted her for over two years. She asked the PCMC for a divorce. The delegates granted her request.[256] It was not clear whether she ever received any alimony. A representative of her husband's firm testified that Mr. Toddyvala earned Rs 180 per month as a traveling inspector in the petroleum business.[257] According to the case law, the judge could award Mrs. Toddyvala as much as a third of his monthly income as permanent alimony for life, a sum that could be reduced (at the judge's discretion) if the ex-wife remarried.[258] But the records ran dry before noting the sum set by the judge.

Although Mr. Toddyvala lost every single round of this decade-long conflict, he may have seen himself as the victor. Even if he did have to pay his ex-wife monthly for the rest of her life, the marriage was dissolved. This was what he had wanted since his return from the Great War. For observers of the matrimonial court, though, it was his failures that were more interesting, particularly his attempt to assert racial misrepresentation in 1916. The delegates were quick to agree when the woman claimed the man's side had lied about his mental problems or impotence. This was so despite the common view of the day that both conditions were potentially curable. When the genders were flipped, though, the delegates were much more skeptical. Their mistrust of Mr. Toddyvala was particularly interesting because of the presence of a third party whom the delegates could easily have blamed for the fraud: Dinbai's marriage broker.

The negotiators of most arranged marriages were family members of the bride or groom. However, a striking number of unrelated, paid marriage brokers acted as substitutes for family. These brokers were usually older Parsi women who received a commission for each marriage arranged.[259] The most extensive testimony from a paid matchmaker came from the sixty-eight-year-old widow named Hirabai Vaju. She had arranged the Toddyvala marriage: "I have been a matchmaker how long? I am not usually but since my husband's death have engaged in this business. My husband left nothing. I have to earn my living . . . [I] had a hard struggle. Q. How many marriages have you brought about? Two or four. Sometimes I get Rs 50, sometimes Rs 100." Hirabai was paid nothing when a match failed. She had made two fruitless attempts for Dinbai before she

---

[255] Suit No. 7 of 1927, 1928–9 PCMC Notebook, I: 92.

[256] Ibid., I: 87–95.

[257] Ibid., I: 90.

[258] *Darukhanawala v. Motibai*, 63. There was major debate over whether remarriage by a divorced Parsi woman ought to automatically block her entitlement to permanent alimony from her earlier husband. In Aden, Parsi lobbyists had legislation passed that cut off a woman's alimony completely. In India, legislation was passed that granted the judge the discretionary power to reduce her permanent alimony. The decision was to be made on a case-by-case basis. See *Manekbai v. Vachha*. For Aden, see "File 3/29: Acts and Regulations. The Parsi Marriage and Divorce Ordinance (30 June 1937–19 May 1939)"(IOR/R/20/B/44). For India, see "The Parsi Marriage and Divorce (Amendment) Act 1940."

[259] See also Suit No. 1097 of 1946 in N. H. C. Coyajee, Typed Notes of Evidence (1946–9), 7.

230   Law and Identity in Colonial South Asia: Parsi Legal Culture

arranged the marriage to Mr. Toddyvala.[260] Matchmakers had a financial incentive to make a match – and, in the short term, to massage the truth.

Occasionally, husbands told the court that their wives had engaged in premarital relationships and even been impregnated by other men and that this information had been concealed from the husbands until after the marriage.[261] In *Dinbai v. Toddyvala*, the alleged fraud pertained to something more unusual: claims about the bride's racial purity.[262] The bride Dinbai's father had been Parsi by ethnicity and Zoroastrian by religion. Her mother, though, was part African. There were references to Dinbai's mother being "Abyssinian." At the time, Abyssinia was shorthand for Africa generally. Dinbai's mother Mana had a Parsi father and a Malagasy mother.[263] Dinbai's father, a man named Jamshedjee Dadabhai Khajotia, did business in Madagascar in the 1880s.[264] During that time, the half-Parsi, half-Malagasy Mana was his mistress. Dinbai was born in Madagascar from their union. When Dinbai was a young child, her father sent her from Madagascar to India to be raised among Parsis by his cousin.[265] Dinbai's illegitimacy was an issue, but the larger problem was that Dinbai's mother was racially impure, according to Mr. Toddyvala.[266] He argued that Dinbai's part-Malagasy background made her ineligible to be initiated into the Zoroastrian religion – that one needed two Parsi parents to be eligible for the *navjote*, itself an unsettled point in the early twentieth century. Because Dinbai's mother was part Malagasy, Dinbai's initiation into the religious community was invalid, claimed Toddyvala. In turn, this made their

---

[260] Suit No. 3 of 1916, 1913–20 PCMC Notebook, III: 37.

[261] See Suit No. 4 of 1903, I: 1–2 and Suit No. 1 of 1906, II: 80, both in PCMC Notebook 1903–13; Suit No. 11 of 1935, PCMC Notebook 1935–7, I: 289. During discussions over the drafting of the Parsi Marriage and Divorce Act 1936, many worried that unscrupulous husbands could falsely accuse their wives of premarital pregnancy by other men. See "Paper No. I: Opinions on the Parsi Marriage and Divorce Act. Opinion No. 2: From the Secretary to Government of Bombay, Home Dept., No. 5377/3-II-B, dated 10 November 1934, with enclosures," 7 (N. J. Shaikh, District Judge, Surat), 14 (Zoroastrian Brotherhood), 18–19 (K. B. Vakil, President of the Parsi Panchayat, Surat); "Paper No. II: Opinions on the Parsi Marriage and Divorce Bill. Opinion No. 20: Bombay. From the Secretary to the Government of Bombay, Home Dept. to the Secretary to the Government of India, Legislative Department, No. 5377/3-II-B, dated Bombay Castle, 2 February 1935," 64 (Parsi Zoroastrian priests); "Paper No. IV. Opinions on the Parsi Marriage and Divorce Bill. Opinion No. 23: The Zoroastrian Brotherhood (8 June 1935)," 74. All in "Parsi Marriage and Divorce Act 1936."

[262] Suit No. 3 of 1916, 1913–20 PCMC Notebook, III: 21–2, 24–47; "Parsi Matrimonial Suit. *Dinbai, wife of Erachsha Dossabhai Toddywalla v. Erachsha Dossabhai Toddywalla*" (31 October 1916), 9 and (2 November 1916), 5, both in *TI*; "A Curious Parsi Matrimonial Case," *Indian Social Reformer* (12 November 1916), 123.

[263] "*Parsi Matrimonial Suit. Dinbai v. Toddywalla*," 9; "A Curious Parsi Matrimonial Case"; Suit No. 3 of 1916, 1913–20 PCMC Notebook, III: 27.

[264] "*Dinbai, wife of Erachsha Dossabhai Toddywalla v. Erachsha Dossabhai Toddywalla*," *TI* (31 October 1916), 9.

[265] Suit No. 3 of 1916, 1913–20 PCMC Notebook, III: 27.

[266] "Parsi Matrimonial Suit. *Dinbai v. Toddywalla*," 9.

The Parsi Chief Matrimonial Court 231

marriage void under Parsi law, which applied only to the marriage of two Zoroastrians.[267] Toddyvala claimed to have asked the matchmaker, Hirabai, about the girl's dark complexion during early negotiations. By his account, Hirabai had assured him that the high salt content in the local water of the girl's village of Vesu, near Surat, made Dinbai's skin dark. Her complexion was sure to lighten once she moved to Bombay.[268]

The matchmaker's two earlier attempts to arrange a marriage for Dinbai had failed after Hirabai had revealed the truth about Dinbai's parentage. Nevertheless, Hirabai told the Parsi jury that she had informed the Toddyvala family of the girl's family background. "I had already told Defendant and his people that plaintiff was born of an alien mother. I knew that as a fact. They said there was no objection."[269] She also insisted that a person needed only Parsi *paternity* to be eligible for initiation into the Zoroastrian religion.

About six months after the wedding, the husband claimed to have learned of his wife's racial background through a distant relative in the town of Bulsar. He told the Parsi jury: "I returned to Bombay and told my mother not to allow the girl in our house. This was because of the information I'd received. If I'd known I would not have married the girl because I am orthodox. My parents also are orthodox."[270] It was unthinkable for a woman with questionable status to join a religiously orthodox family, he argued. When Mr. Toddyvala confronted Hirabai, she criticized his concern with purity. "[I]s your wife a cucumber or watermelon to cut and see the inside of," exclaimed the matchmaker.[271] The Parsi delegates rejected the husband's claims by a majority of ten to one. They considered the marriage valid, and they granted the wife her request for the restitution of conjugal rights.[272]

The matrimonial delegates did not provide reasons for their findings. In part, their decision probably reflected their adherence to the older, patrilineal definition of what it meant to be Parsi – and their rejection of the newer, eugenics-inspired model of racial purity. The old logic was patrilineal: one could be initiated into the fold if one had Parsi lineage through the "seed" of a male Parsi. In other words, having a Parsi father was enough to permit initiation into the religion; one did not also need a Parsi mother. By contrast, the new, racialized test privileged "blood" over "seed." What mattered was the composite purity of an individual's blood, not the line of male progenitors to the exclusion of the female. To be eligible for initiation into the Zoroastrian religion, one needed two Parsi parents, not just Parsi paternity. The new test was egalitarian: mothers mattered. But, at the same time, it introduced a new eugenics-driven

---

[267] Suit No. 3 of 1916, 1913–20 PCMC Notebook, III: 40–3.
[268] Ibid., III: 40.
[269] Ibid., III: 37.
[270] Ibid., III: 41.
[271] Ibid., III: 42.
[272] "*Dinbai Erachsha Toddywalla (plaintiff) v. Eracha Dossabhai Toddywalla (defendant)*," TI (2 November 1916), 5.

concern with purity and exclusion. The delegates' rejection of Toddyvala's argument represented a temporary brake on the new, rising model of Parsi identity and community membership.[273]

Equally, though, the Toddyvala verdict may have reflected the broader class- and gender-based dynamics at work in the Parsi matrimonial court. In disciplining nonelite males, elite male delegates probably considered themselves to be aiding nonelite females. And, like parties in any court, female plaintiffs probably massaged their narratives to say what they thought the jury wanted to hear.[274] But assuming that such adjustments bore some relationship to provable social conditions, it was relevant that Dinbai described her own background as poor. When suing her husband for divorce a decade after the restitution suit, she told the court that she was unable to live with her half-brother. He made only Rs 3 per day and had a family. He could not afford to support an adult woman, as well. Dinbai's own elderly father had been a farmer since returning to India. He and his wife had only enough money for their own bare maintenance.[275] Dinbai was from the demographic group of poor women who used the Parsi matrimonial court the most: those too poor to be able to live indefinitely with their natal families, but who could raise the funds to get to court. She told the Parsi delegates: "I have no means of my own ... I am not educated enough to earn anything on my own. I have lived on the charity of cousins. All these years my husband has paid me nothing. My father is eighty years old."[276] The last of her lawsuits against her husband was for divorce, but perhaps more importantly, it was for alimony.[277]

Fraud was a structural risk inherent in any system of arranged marriage. When the duped party was female, the delegates' willingness to cancel the marriage may have served as a way of cleansing the system. At some level, they may have been preempting European disapproval, with its celebration of individual agency and its thunderbolt ideal of "love marriage." Parsi jurists may also have been policing the community's collective reputation. Simin Patel has documented the ways in which late nineteenth-century Parsi leaders appealed to their poorer co-religionists to abstain from general violence to preserve the community's good reputation with the British.[278] Five decades earlier, a report by British magistrates in Bombay noted that, among Parsis, the elite took a closer interest in the behavior of its less privileged members than was common in larger South Asian communities: "It is the spirit of all small and insulated castes, as well as of small sects, established in the midst of larger communities of a different

---

[273] See Sharafi, "Bella's Case," 328–41.
[274] Compare Hartog, Man, 154–5, 305.
[275] Suit No. 7 of 1927, 1928–9 PCMC Notebook, I: 89.
[276] Ibid., I: 88, 90.
[277] Suit No. 7 of 1927, 1928–9 PCMC Notebook, I: 87–95.
[278] Patel, "A Cosmopolitan Crisis." There was also concern that the Gheestas' case (1811) would damage the Parsi community's reputation vis-à-vis the British. See Q. in the Corner, II: 27–8; Chapter 3 at 149.

The Parsi Chief Matrimonial Court

nation, or religion, to consider themselves as more intimately connected with each other, and to take a more lively interest in the prosperity or good character of each member of their little community than is felt by the rest of the population to each other. They seem more like persons of one family."[279] The Parsi jury, it would seem, embodied this dynamic.

The position of delegate to the Parsi matrimonial court took time and energy away from one's work and family. The position was also unpaid. Even so, delegates' seats were eagerly sought. *Hindi Punch* described one election in 1919, referring to the old *shethia* ideal that combined eminence and affluence in the figure of the "merchant prince": "What an abundance of public spirit must there be among Parsis who find three gentlemen wrangling for the honor of filling one vacancy among Delegates of the Parsi Matrimonial Court – the Parsi peers – who try the social disputes of Parsis. Perhaps the tinge of the old idea of Shettiaship still remains coupled with the function, for of old it was the prerogative of the Panchayet Shettias to decide matrimonial disputes."[280] The elite Parsis who sat on the matrimonial jury probably did so for the same reasons that they indulged in large philanthropic gifts. Both activities combined the charitable impulse with the desire for intragroup control, incentivizing and discouraging certain patterns of behavior among less elite co-religionists. The Parsi jury and its litigants exemplified the point made by the subaltern studies movement – that colonial elite and nonelite interactions *among* South Asians deserve as much attention as those *between* South Asians and Europeans.[281]

CONCLUSION

Historians of South Asia and the Indian Ocean have occasionally suggested that the colonial state avoided interfering with family and religious life in British India. It was certainly true that the state's priorities were to maximize order and efficiency in areas that bit to the bone of the colonial project. Above all else, colonialism was an economic project focused on the extraction of profits, commodities, and labor from the colony for the benefit of the imperial metropole (and imperial elites in the colony). These priorities put commercial and criminal law at the center of the colonial state's efforts. It was no coincidence that comprehensive legislation was introduced in both areas during the codification frenzy of the mid-nineteenth century. However, neither the family nor religion lay beyond the reach of the colonial legal system, not least of all because it was impossible to separate business and property from religion and the family, a

---

[279] "Report of the Bombay Police Magistrates," 5–6.
[280] "A Tug and Pull," 10.
[281] See Ranajit Guha, ed., *A Subaltern Studies Reader, 1986–1995* (Minneapolis: University of Minnesota Press, 1997).

234   *Law and Identity in Colonial South Asia: Parsi Legal Culture*

point made by Ritu Birla's work on law and the Hindu joint family.[282] It would be a mistake to take statements like Queen Victoria's Proclamation of 1858 too literally.[283] To suggest, as Nile Green has done, that the state in British India adopted a laissez-faire policy and stayed out of religious affairs would be to overlook many areas of law, from libel to the vast swathes of religious life and charitable enterprise governed by the law of trusts, including *wakfs* (Pers. *vaqf*, from Arabic).[284] Religious endowments funded and structured the administration of temples, mosques, churches, and other shrines; cemeteries, *dakhmas*, and cremation grounds; sanitoria, hospitals, clinics, resthouses, orphanages, schools, public tanks, and drinking fountains; maintenance and insurance schemes for the poor; printing presses, farms, and other charitable institutions. When there was serious disagreement over how to manage these enterprises, disputants came to court.[285] Some scholars have implied that religious endowments only came into infrequent contact with the state through litigation.[286] But court decisions affected people other than the parties to the case through the ripple effect of precedent and the phenomenon of "bargaining in the shadow of the law."[287] Furthermore, it was not only when there was a dispute that religious trusts and the courts had to interact. From the late nineteenth century, many routine matters pertaining to religious trusts required judicial approval. For the trustees

[282] By Ritu Birla, see *Stages*; and "Vernacular Capitalists and the Modern Subject in India: Law, Cultural Politics, and Market Ethics," in *Ethical Life in South Asia*, eds. Anand Pandian and Daud Ali (Bloomington: Indiana University Press, 2010), 83–100.

[283] "We disclaim . . . the right and the desire to impose our convictions on any of our subjects. We declare it to be our royal will and pleasure that none be in any ways favoured, none molested or disquieted, by reason of their religious faith or observances, but that all shall alike enjoy the equal and impartial protection of the law; and we do strictly charge and enjoin from all interference with the religious belief or worship of any of our subjects on pain of our highest displeasure." (Victoria, "Proclamation of 1858" in Desika Char, 299.) See also S. Ghosh, "Nineteenth-century Colonial Ideology."

[284] Green, 7, 11–12. See, for example, P. R. Ganapathi Iyer, *The Law Relating to Hindu and Mahomedan Religious Endowments* (Madras: Graves, Cookson and Co., 1905), viii; D. F. Mulla, *Jurisdiction of Courts in matters relating to the rights and powers of Castes* (Bombay: Caxton Printing Works, 1901).

[285] Green has described the Religious Endowments Act (XX of 1863) as a statute that "formally banned the colonial government from direct support or control over religious institutions" (Green, 11–12). See similarly Nandini Chatterjee, *The Making of Indian Secularism: Empire, Law and Christianity, 1830–1960* (Basingstoke, UK: Palgrave Macmillan, 2011), 61–3. However, the Act shifted the branch of state that would be involved with religious endowments – from the revenue to the judicial branch [Religious Endowments Act (XX of 1863), ss. 5, 14–20 in William Fischer Agnew, *The Law of Trusts in British India* (Calcutta: Thacker, Spink and Co., 1882), 398–406.] By Carol Appadurai Breckenridge's account, this transfer produced an intensification of state involvement in religious affairs. Disputes relating to religious funds and properties only increased in number and intensity with the shift to the courts. See Carol Appadurai Breckenridge, "The Sri Minaksi Sundaresvarer Temple: Worship and Endowments in South India, 1833 to 1925" (PhD dissertation, University of Wisconsin-Madison, 1976), 348–68.

[286] Green, 173, 217; N. Chatterjee, 55.

[287] See Chapter 1 at note 51; Appadurai Breckenridge, 211.

The Parsi Chief Matrimonial Court 235

of Parsi charitable trusts, this fact made interaction with the legal system a common occurrence.

The colonial legal system also reached right into the heart of the Indian home and family through the personal law system. Partha Chatterjee's suggestion that the family sat beyond the reach of the colonial state may have reflected nationalist discourse.[288] It did not ring true for the workings of the courts. The suggestion that the colonial legal system actually stayed out of South Asian family life ignores the basic mechanics of the personal law system, along with its enormous case law.[289] The validity of marriage and divorce, child custody, the interpretation of wills, the application of the rules of intestacy, the partition of the joint family – these matters and more fell within the purview of the personal law administered by the colonial courts.

Below sporadic expressions of nonintervention from the upper administration lay a legal system that was comprehensive in scope. And although litigation was more easily accessible to elites, it affected nonelites, too. The latter were recipients of many of the trust funds whose workings were clarified in court. Furthermore, an array of courts below the High Courts processed the problems of people from across the social spectrum. State claims of non-interference were essentially rhetorical flourishes aimed at smoothing public relations. The colonial state made similar claims to neutrality between South Asia's various religious traditions, a related but separate ideal that shaped the postcolonial state's model of secularism.[290] As with non-interference, the application of the neutrality policy was doubtful in practice. The existence of the Parsi matrimonial jury, for instance, implied preferential treatment for one group. Beyond the narrative the state told about itself, neither the policy of neutrality nor that of non-interference lived a very plausible life in the legal history of British India.

Against a backdrop of state involvement in South Asian private life, the Parsi matrimonial courts were exceptional. They gave a handful of elite Parsi men an unusual degree of control over their co-religionists while maintaining a discreet distance from the controversial use of criminal juries in India. It was true that the matrimonial courts were overseen by a judge from the colonial legal system. But from 1906, at the flagship Bombay court, that judge himself was often Parsi. And it was the Parsi jury that ultimately ruled on the issues, ignoring the leanings of the judge if necessary. Senior male elites in other South Asian communities were disempowered by the British model of personal law whereby a judge without a

---

[288] Partha Chatterjee, *The Nation and Its Fragments: Colonial and Postcolonial Histories* (Princeton, NJ: Princeton University Press, 1993), 116–34.

[289] See Nair, 181; Sumit Guha, "The Family Feud as Political Resource in Eighteenth-century India," in *Unfamiliar Relations: Family and History in South Asia*, ed. Indrani Chatterjee (New Brunswick, NJ: Rutgers University Press, 2004), 91; Majumdar, 4, 286–7 at note 51.

[290] For a sample of the large literature on secularism in the South Asian context, see Tejani; N. Chatterjee. On the neutrality policy, see Ian Copland et al., *A History of State and Religion in India* (London: Routledge, 2012), 162–84.

jury ruled on matrimonial cases. By creating the matrimonial jury in 1865, Parsi lobbyists minimized this process of colonial emasculation in the domain of marriage. The Parsi jury allowed senior male elites to police intragroup conduct by disciplining less elite members. It enabled Parsi elites to exert social influence *as legal power* within their own community.

PART 3

BEYOND PERSONAL LAW

6

Entrusting the Faith

Religious Trusts and the Parsi Legal Profession

During the latter half of the nineteenth century, Parsi charitable trust suits relating to religious funds and properties started arriving in the upper courts. These conflicts were power struggles among the people controlling Zoroastrian fire temples, towers of silence, cemeteries, rest houses, sanitoria, and charitable funds.[1] Often, these disputes turned on intragroup differences over religious doctrine, power relations, and collective identity. Could ethnic outsiders be initiated into the religion? Did sea travel by high priests invalidate the religious ceremonies carried out after their arrival?[2] Did priests determine practical operating procedures within a fire temple or was this a privilege of the patrons who funded the temple? These questions were resolved not by priestly or community bodies, but in court.

Around the same time as religious trust suits became common, Parsis started flourishing in the colonial legal profession. They soon became judges in the upper courts. In 1906, the first Parsi was appointed to the Bombay High Court bench. By 1930, the first Parsi had become a Privy Council judge in London. Patterns in litigation and the legal profession converged: by a lucky confluence of factors, Parsi lawyers and judges managed many of the lawsuits among their co-religionists. Through law, these figures became intellectual middlemen in the negotiation of their own community's image and identity.

The micro- and macro-effects of intragroup litigation were in tension with each other. On the one hand, the frequency and vigor with which Parsis turned to the courts came at a terrible social price. As it does today, litigation between Parsis ripped apart families, friends, and entire communities.[3] Major lawsuits lasted for

---

[1] Parsi bodies were buried in Parsi-only cemeteries (or sections of cemeteries) in Rangoon, Colombo, London, Berlin, and elsewhere because the Parsi population was too small to justify maintaining a *dakhma*. In these situations, the usual prohibition on burial did not apply. See Patel and Paymaster, V: 196; Desai, *History*, 196–7; Sharafi, "Bella's Case," 50–8.

[2] See Hinnells, "Changing Perceptions," 112; Sharafi, "Bella's Case," 248–56.

[3] See Hinnells, *Zoroastrian Diaspora*, 234–5.

239

240 Law and Identity in Colonial South Asia: Parsi Legal Culture

years. They dragged litigants around the world on appeal and for the collection of evidence "on commission."[4] Intragroup litigation bankrupted, embittered, and aged its Parsi participants. By oral history accounts, the ugliest Parsi trust suits hastened the deaths of their more sensitive participants.[5] Despite the heartbreak, though, the repetition of a painful microprocess created something collectively productive. In a different colonial context, Steve Stern has suggested that intragroup litigation in colonial courts weakened the colonized community vis-à-vis the colonizers.[6] The British Indian setting reflected an alternative outcome. Among the Parsis, the ceaseless airing of dirty laundry in the general Anglosphere produced embarrassment. Arguably, familiarity with the legal forum exacerbated intragroup conflict. But it was also enabling. By the coincidence that a corps of Parsi lawyers and judges existed, intragroup lawsuits simultaneously became a source of legal power for the community. The figure that epitomized this phenomenon was Dinshah D. Davar, the first Parsi judge of the Bombay High Court. Between 1906 and 1916, a series of Zoroastrian trust suits landed in his court. He decided them in ways that reflected his religiously orthodox vision of Parsi identity. Davar's career showed that the ethnic and religious identity of colonial judges mattered. Through the production of usable precedents, South Asian judges and lawyers interpreted the culture of the colonized for the colonial legal system. Sometimes they described "cousin" communities.[7] At other times, they inserted themselves into controversies in their own communities. Either way, these judges put the force of colonial law behind one side of intragroup disputes. Davar epitomized this phenomenon in the context of Zoroastrian charitable trusts.

IN-FIGHTING

Fighting in court came at a cost. Niklas Luhmann has described the shift from social fighting to litigation as a move from one normative vocabulary to another.[8] With this shift came a certain trauma and irreversibility. Stewart Macaulay has emphasized the destructive quality of litigation to long-term contractual relationships. In an effort to avoid litigation, Macaulay observed that businesspeople who wanted to preserve good relations would not insist on their strict legal rights.[9] Going to court destroyed relationships, a result

[4] See Sharafi, "Bella's Case," 184–5, 360–2.
[5] See ibid., 409.
[6] Steve J. Stern, *Peru's Indian Peoples and the Challenge of Spanish Conquest: Huamanga to 1640* (Madison: University of Wisconsin Press, 1982), 115, 132.
[7] See Sharafi, "New History," 1072–9.
[8] See Niklas Luhmann, "Communication about Law in Interaction Systems," in *Advances in Social Theory and Methodology*, eds. Karin Knorr-Cetina and Aaron V. Cicourel (Boston: Routledge and Kegan Paul, 1981), 241–2; Stewart Macaulay's discussion of Luhmann in his "Organic Transactions: Contract, Frank Lloyd Wright and the Johnson Building," *Wisc. LR* (1996), 114–15.
[9] Stewart Macaulay, "Non-Contractual Relations in Business: A Preliminary Study," 75–90 in Macaulay, Friedman, and Mertz.

Religious Trusts and the Parsi Legal Profession

particularly difficult to bear in close, face-to-face communities where people could not melt anonymously into a mobile and shifting population.

As one of the world's great mercantile minorities, Parsis had networks of trust and trade spanning the globe. Persia was a motherland of one type.[10] Britain was another.[11] Parsis enjoyed high mobility but low anonymity along their global diasporic circuits. The process of making inquiries across national and imperial borders produced remarkably private information about Parsis overseas. With the rise of fears over group extinction, the community became even more tight-knit and self-aware. These anxieties were heightened by the advent of the census in 1871: rates of marriage and birth rates among Parsis were comparatively low, and the average age at marriage was high.[12] Occasionally, elite Parsi men also married European women. Orthodox Parsis wanted these couples' children to be ineligible for initiation into the Zoroastrian religion.[13] For those who subscribed to a notion of racial purity, this form of desired exclusion further diminished the total number of Parsis.

In other diasporic mercantile minorities, disputes were typically handled within the group.[14] Social sanctions and taboos kept inside fights out of court. But the Parsis lacked the community institutions and culture to contain their own intragroup disputes. The case law between them was a catalogue of conflicts between siblings, relatives, spouses, friends, neighbors, parents and children, landlords and tenants, and former co-litigants.[15] In *Petit v. Jijibhai*, the British judge F. C. O. Beaman suggested that "too much dirty linen" was being

---

[10] See Suit No. 1 of 1930, 1929–35 PCMC Notebook, I: 48, 51, IV: 177; Suits No. 6 of 1937 and 3 of 1938, 1937–41 PCMC Notebook, I: 31, II: 13–14, 62–3; Suits No. 8 and 9 of 1942, 1941–8 PCMC Notebook, I: 331–5. See also by Sharafi, "Bella's Case," 341–9; "Marital Patchwork," 1003–6.

[11] See, for instance, Suit No. 5 of 1913, 1913–20 PCMC Notebook, I: 43–44; Suit No. 10 of 1933, 1929–35 PCMC Notebook, IV: 138–41. See also Chapter 2 at 109.

[12] Desai, *Parsis*, 71. By Leela Visaria, see "Religious and Regional Differences in Mortality and Fertility in the Indian Subcontinent" (PhD dissertation, Dept. of Sociology, Princeton University, 1972), 139–74; "Demographic Transition among Parsis: 1881–1971, III–Fertility Trends," *EPW* 9:43 (1974), 1828–32.

[13] See Sharafi, "Judging Conversion"; "Bella's Case," 76–8, 149–70.

[14] For example, see Janet T. Landa, "A Theory of the Ethnically Homogeneous Middleman Group: An Institutional Alternative to Contract Law," *J. Legal Stud.* 10 (1981), 349–62; Barak D. Richman, "How Community Institutions Create Economic Advantage: Jewish Diamond Merchants in New York," *LSI* 31 (2006), 383–418.

[15] For a sample from the notebooks of D. D. Davar (BHC), see *In the Matter of the Indian Trustee Act No. 27 of [1866] and Indian Trust Act No. 2 of 1882. In the matter of the deed of Charity Settlement of 29 May 1888 made by Framji Covasji Marker*, "Judgments (7 January 1908–7 December 1908)," 1–5; *Dinsha Framji Marker v. Dossibai Framji Marker* in "Judgments (5 January 1909–7 October 1909)," 1–7; *Payne and Company v. Pirosha Nusserwanji Patell* in "Judgments (19 January 1911 to 17 July 1911)," 1–40; and *Sirdar Nowroji Pudumji v. Putlibai*, "Judgments (14 January 1913–18 December 1913)," 87–93. From case papers (BHC), see *Framji Shapurji Patuck and others v. F. E. Davar*, Suit No. 791 of 1904; *Bhai Bhicaji v. Perojshaw Jivanji Kerawalla*, Suit No. 1288 of 1914; *Manekji Rustomji Bharucha v. Nanabhai Cursetji Bharucha*, Suit No. 258 of 1928. See also "Recorder's Court. Before W.F. Agnew, Esq. Dissolution of

242   *Law and Identity in Colonial South Asia: Parsi Legal Culture*

aired. He had in mind the historical prevalence of lower caste servant mistresses and extramarital children among Surat's Parsi patriarchs.[16] In another Parsi trust case between members of one family, Davar remarked caustically: "It appears to me that the members of the family have no real occupation in life and they amuse themselves principally by carrying on acrimonious correspondence and litigating amongst themselves."[17] One judge commented that he had abandoned hope for a settlement in a Parsi trust suit "due to the feelings of the parties having become embittered during the progress of the suit." Each side accused the other of lying in court.[18] Other cases between Parsis involved accusations of addiction and imbecility.[19] Allegations of violence, venereal disease, and adultery all featured prominently in the Parsi Chief Matrimonial Court.[20] By suing their co-religionists, Parsi plaintiffs showed their willingness to reveal secrets in the colonial courtroom. The desire for victory or punitive litigating overrode any sense that disputes among Parsis ought to be kept off the public stage.[21] In many cases, the impulse to litigate also overshadowed the desire to preserve long-term relationships.

Two examples illustrated the phenomenon. The case of Bomanjee Byramjee Colah was born out of the breakdown of relations within one family. *Pestonji Jeevanji v. Chinoy*, by contrast, reflected the disintegration of civility within the Parsi community of Secunderabad, a British military cantonment sitting within the subcontinent's largest princely state of Hyderabad.[22] Both cases were unusual in that they moved far beyond South Asia. Colah's case arose in the New York Court of Common Pleas. The Secunderabad case was appealed to the Privy Council in London. Both exemplified the destructive effects of litigation on

---

Partnership," *Rangoon Gazette Weekly Budget* (31 January 1890), 9; *Mancherji Manokji Poonjiajee v. Framji Manockji Poonjiajee* 2 Bom LR 1026 (1900); *Shapurji Bezonjee Motiwalla v. D. B. Motiwalla* case papers, Suit No. 473 of 1905 (BHC) and *Motiwalla v. Motiwalla*; *Sorabji Hormusji Batlivala v. J. M. Wadia* ILR 38 Bom 552 (1914); *Jehangir Dadabhoy and B. Jehangiri v. Kaikhusru Kavasha re estate of Pallonji Dadabhoy Cooverbai and Kavasha Edulji* JCPC case papers, 1914: vol. 34, judgment no. 98 (PCO); *Rustomji Heejeebhoy v. C. Dadabhoy and others* ILR 48 Bom 348 (1924); *Bai Meherbai Sorabji Master v. Pherozshaw Sorabji Gazdar* ILR 51 Bom 885 (1927); "Parsi Brothers in Court. Wild Allegations," *TI* (9 October 1929), 15.

[16] *Petit v. Jijibhai*, 576.
[17] "In the Matter of the Indian Trustee Act No. 27 of 1866 and Indian Trust Act No. 2 of 1882. In the Matter of the Deed of Charity Settlement of 29 May 1888 made by Framji Covasji Marker" in D. D. Davar, Judgments (1908), 2.
[18] "No. 294: Judgment of the Judicial Commissioner in Regular Appeal No. 76 of 1901, 12–12–1901," 718 in *Pestonji Jeevanji v. Chinoy* JCPC case papers.
[19] For allegations of imbecility and addiction to morphine, opium, and alcohol, see *Vatchagandy v. Vatchagandy* in D. D. Davar, Judgments (1910).
[20] For some of the most extreme cases, see Suit No. 14 of 1939, 1937–41 PCMC Notebook, III: 117–55; Suit No. 16 of 1940, 1941–8 PCMC Notebook, III: 198–200. See also Chapter 5 at 217.
[21] For a probable case of punitive litigating among Parsis, see "Rangoon Defamation Case. Personal Attendance Necessary," *Poona Observer* (22 May 1914), 5.
[22] See Sharafi, "Marital Patchwork," 984.

Religious Trusts and the Parsi Legal Profession 243

Parsi relations. And both illustrated the degree to which this breakdown unleashed a flow of compromising information in the public arena.

The Parsi merchant B. B. Colah arrived in New York in 1870 carrying $100,000 in gold.[23] He had battled his two brothers in the Bombay courts for his share of their father's inheritance. Having succeeded, he left his wife and children in Bombay in order to make "a pleasure trip of the world."[24] He began in Calcutta then proceeded to Europe and continued west to New York. Financed by his portable inheritance, Colah went on "a long and reckless spree in this city, and his conduct became a matter of such public notoriety that he was taken into custody as a person of unsound mind." Colah's case arrived before the New York Court of Common Pleas because he was deemed a "wandering lunatic."[25] He was committed to one asylum after another and was examined by a string of New York psychiatrists.

The Court had to decide how to convey Colah back to Bombay and how to protect his gold. No other Parsis could be located in New York. However, an American army major named Alexander George Constable took an interest in the case. Constable had spent fourteen years in Bombay Presidency and claimed to have been well acquainted with the "habits, customs, language, characteristics and religious faith and practices of the Parsis."[26] The New York court noted that Colah refused to speak in English and that Constable was the only person with whom he would speak because Constable spoke "Mahratta."[27] The claim was curious: the Parsi language was Gujarati, not Marathi. "Mahratta" or "Maratha" was the name of a people and dynasty in early modern western India. It was possible that Constable and Colah were speaking different (though related) languages to each other, that Colah was fluent in Marathi, or simply that Constable was misleading the court. If the last option were true, it was only the start of the Major's trickery. Constable agreed to escort Colah back to Bombay, making the trip by steamer from New York to San Francisco and then to Hong Kong and Bombay.[28] Colah could not manage such a trip alone, and the court worried that he would not survive even if accompanied by Constable and a

---

[23] I owe all Colah case materials to Kathryn Burns-Howard, who discovered the case during her archival research on the New York Court of Common Pleas. I thank her for her exceptional generosity in sharing with me images of these primary sources.

[24] "Mr. Jarvis must pay up. Ordered to account for the Colah Estate," *NYT* (24 August 1886), 8.

[25] "Only a Pittance Left. Management of a Parsee Merchant's Fortune," *NYT* (18 February 1886), 2.

[26] "In the Court of Common Pleas. In the matter of Bomanjee Byramjee Colah, a Lunatic" (undated), 1 in "Incompetency Hearings, 1873–95, Court of Common Pleas for the City and County of New York," B. B. Colah Case Papers, Court of Common Pleas of New York County, Division of Old Records (New York County Clerk's Office).

[27] "Court of Common Pleas, for the City and County of New York. In the Matter of Bomanjee Byramjee Colah, a Lunatic" (23 October 1871), 3 in Colah case papers.

[28] Ibid., 17.

244 Law and Identity in Colonial South Asia: Parsi Legal Culture

personal physician.[29] Colah was suffering from "subacute mania" along with more physical ailments that made even walking around his asylum room "the utmost torture."[30] The court decided to send Constable with Colah and to reimburse the major for his expenses out of Colah's gold. Years later, the outlandish sums siphoned out of Colah's estate would be the subject of an investigation. Implausibly, Constable claimed that the trip had cost $25,000, a quarter of the value of Colah's gold.[31]

Constable's dishonesty was minor compared to the larger tale of fraud surrounding the vulnerable Parsi. Constable did escort Colah back to Bombay, but Colah's condition worsened there and he died a few years later.[32] One reason the New York court had wanted to send Colah back to India was out of concern for Zoroastrian death rites. New York had neither Zoroastrian priests nor facilities for exposure to vultures. Both Colah's father-in-law and Constable testified that Parsis could be buried if they died in a place without towers of silence. "[T]here are many Parsee merchants in Great Britain and in other countries foreign to their own, and ... when they die, they are buried like other people according to the usages of the country of their residence," Constable reported accurately.[33] Still, with the view that Colah would be better off with his family, the court decided to send him back to India.[34] His gold would stay in the United States. Partly on Constable's recommendation, the court retained custody of the gold. It was sold, and its proceeds were invested in a trust company in New York. The person put in charge of managing this money was a clerk of the Court of Common Pleas: one Nathaniel Jarvis, Junior. Sixteen years later, Jarvis was convicted of embezzling the money. A fund that was initially $100,000 in the early 1870s and ought to have grown by 6 percent per year totaled a paltry $33 in 1886. Jarvis blamed the disappearance of Colah's money on a bad investment, but his records were almost nonexistent, and the court found that he had stolen most of the money. Jarvis had sent $3,000 – a mere 3 percent of the original total – to Colah's widow and children in Bombay in the early days. By the time of Jarvis' trial, they were nearly destitute. The court ordered the errant clerk to pay approximately $76,000. The parties ultimately settled for $65,000.[35]

---

[29] "In the Court of Common Pleas. In the matter of Bomanjee Byramjee Colah," 4; "Court of Common Please.... In the Matter of Bomanjee Byramjee Colah, A Lunatic," 18–19; both in Colah case papers.

[30] "New York Common Pleas. In the matter of Bomanjee Byramjee Colah, a Lunatic," 1–2 in Colah case papers.

[31] "Only a Pittance Left," 2.

[32] "Mr. Jarvis must pay up," 8.

[33] "In the Court of Common Pleas. In the matter of Colah," 3. See also note 1.

[34] "Court of Common Pleas. In the matter of Colah" (23 October 1871), 6.

[35] In the *NYT*, see "Mr. Jarvis must pay up" (24 August 1886), 8; "The Parsee Merchant's Estate" (16 August 1889), 8; "Tracing Colah's Estate. Nathaniel Jarvis will now have to account for $75,000" (30 October 1889), 3; "Nathaniel Jarvis must pay up" (26 December 1889), 8. On other accusations made against Jarvis, see "May Go to the Grand Jury" (28 August 1889), 2.

Religious Trusts and the Parsi Legal Profession

The exploitation of Colah's estate by two unscrupulous Americans never would have happened had it not been for his own family's litigious in-fighting. Before the court decided to send Colah back to India with an exploitative stranger, Colah's own father-in-law had come to New York to collect him. Framjee Dosabhoy C. Wadia arrived in New York with power of attorney from Colah's wife Heerabai, "authorizing him on her behalf to take charge of the person and property of the lunatic and to bring him back to Bombay." Colah and his gold may have returned uneventfully to Bombay by this route but for the intervention of Colah's brothers. Colah and his brothers had emerged from an inheritance suit on terrible terms. His brothers probably regarded Colah's insanity as an opportunity to win back some of the estate. They convinced the British Vice Consul in New York to oppose the father-in-law's application, arguing that "Mr. Wadia was not a proper person with whom to entrust either the person or the property."[36] They succeeded. Major Constable was then able to argue that the money would be safest under the court's control. He testified that "in money matters the Parsees are a greedy people, that a prominent trait in their character is avarice, and speaking from his observation and from [k]nowledge acquired by him while he was a resident among them, and speaking also with response to the circumstances under which the said Colah acquired his said property and his relations with his brothers on account thereof, he verily believes that the pecuniary interests of the said Colah will be abundantly promoted by retaining the property of said Colah during his life, or during his lunacy, in the custody of this Court."[37] Constable's testimony was self-serving. In-fighting among Parsi families often led to the destruction of long-term relationships and to the creation of vulnerabilities that could be exploited by opportunists like the major and the court clerk.

The Secunderabad litigation exhibited many of the same qualities. It arose from the breakdown of relations within a particular Parsi community rather than a single family. Like so many other protracted lawsuits between Parsis, it was a religious trust case. The case exemplified Parsi litigiousness at its most extreme: every adult Parsi male in Secunderabad was a party to the suit.[38] The full case name alone occupied four pages: there were 130 appellants and 35 respondents.[39] The suit also traveled on appeal through three levels of court until it reached the Privy Council in London. Other major Zoroastrian trust cases had been decided by the Privy Council or had stopped just short of it.[40] But the

---

[36] "Court of Common Pleas. In the matter of Colah" (23 October 1871), 5.

[37] "In the Court of Common Pleas. In the matter of Colah," 5.

[38] "In the Privy Council. No. 10 of 1907. Case for the Respondents," 2 in *Pestonji Jeevanji v. Chinoy* JCPC case papers.

[39] "In the Privy Council. No. 10 of 1907. On appeal from the Court of the Judicial Commissioner Hyderabad Assigned Districts," 1–4 in *Pestonji Jeevanji v. Chinoy* JCPC case papers.

[40] Although many people expected *Petit v. Jijibhai* to be appealed to the Privy Council, it was not. See "The Butterflies and the Light," *HP* (27 December 1908), 17. The Udwada Iran Shah fire

246 Law and Identity in Colonial South Asia: Parsi Legal Culture

Secunderabad case best illustrated the way in which an entire Parsi community could be divided through the experience of litigation.

The Parsis of Secunderabad disagreed over whether to build a new *dakhma* close to their existing one. The dispute was about personalities more than theology. The legal question was this: had the land on which the towers old and new would stand been granted to the two brothers who had built the original tower of silence in 1837?[41] Or had it been granted to them *for the use and benefit of the entire Parsi community*, giving ownership to the entire community, including the priests? If the latter, victory went to the general Parsi community, which wanted to build a second tower. If the former, the descendants of the original brothers had the right to prevent further construction.

The dirty laundry in the New York case had included explicit descriptions of B. B. Colah's mental condition, sexual behavior, and physical ailments, along with the family inheritance dispute. These private matters were documented in the court proceedings and were partially reported in the press. The Secunderabad case also revealed damaging information about Parsis. As plaintiffs and Privy Council appellants, the brothers' descendants made an argument that could help win its case but that promulgated a negative characterization of Parsi customs generally. In other colonial contexts, scholars have observed the irresistible allure of colonial law when presented alongside other dispute resolution systems.[42] Even colonized subjects who opposed the exposure of sensitive community information in the abstract found themselves drawn to the colonial courts, tempted by the possibility of winning a particular dispute. Immediate, individual interests often overrode long-term, collective ones. The net result was the public display of controversial "inside" information.

Many Zoroastrian trust suits of the early twentieth century put sensitive religious rituals in the spotlight. Parsis used *nirang* (Guj. *nīrang*), the consecrated urine of the white bull, as a purifying agent for ingestion and external cleansing in religious ceremonies.[43] *Nirang* was discussed in detail and ridiculed by the Parsi parties on one side of *Saklat v. Bella*.[44] The nine-night purification ceremony known as *barashnum* was a major theme of inquiry during the

---

temple dispute was settled shortly before being appealed to the Privy Council. See *Navroji M. Wadia v. Dastur Kharsedji Mancherji*; *Udvāḍā*, 5, 7, 11–12, 84, 87. See also *Saklat v. Bella*.

[41] According to popular belief in the nineteenth century, individuals who financed the construction of *dakhmas* were often among the first to have their corpses consigned to them. "It is for this reason, that we find, that rich liberal Parsees of the older generations ... though rich enough to build Towers at their own individual expenses, did not like, or were not allowed, to do so." As a result, *dakhma* construction was usually a collective effort. The Secunderabad brothers evidently ignored this superstition. ("A Short Account of the Life of Ervad Tehmuras Dinshaw Anklesaria" in Anklesaria, *Social Code*, 29.)

[42] See, for instance, Stern, 114–37; Brian P. Owensby, *Empire of Law and Indian Justice in Colonial Mexico* (Stanford: Stanford University Press, 2008).

[43] Modi, *Religious Ceremonies*, 64–5.

[44] See Sharafi, "Bella's Case," 272–5.

Religious Trusts and the Parsi Legal Profession

Bombay evidence-collection phase of the same suit.[45] This ceremony required the recipient, even if female, to be naked in front of male priests. In *Petit v. Jijibhai*, Justice Beaman had exclaimed that only people "in the lowest stage of development" would agree to undergo such a rite.[46] European observers characterized both *nirang* and *barashnum* as uncivilized, with Parsi reformists soon joining in. The Secunderabad case touched on a Zoroastrian ritual that was an even bigger target for European critics: the exposure of the dead to vultures in the towers of silence.[47]

In the mid-nineteenth century, the Oxford professor of Sanskrit Monier Monier-Williams described the Zoroastrian death rites that he had partially observed in Bombay.[48] The body of a dead Parsi was carried into the towers and prepared for exposure by *nasasalars*, the hereditary corpse bearers who were ritually polluted by their interaction with dead matter.[49] *Nasasalars* chained the corpse to one circle of "open stone coffins" lining the outer edge of the tower. A group of vultures swooped down on the body. Minutes later, only a skeleton remained. The *nasasalars* used tong-like instruments to transfer the bones into the tower's central cavity. There, "the dust of whole generations of Parsees commingling [was] left undisturbed for centuries."[50]

Monier-Williams was initially disgusted. The "revolting sight of the gorged vultures" made him turn his back with "ill-concealed abhorrence." But he changed his mind on learning of the theological underpinnings of the practice – a prohibition on polluting fire or earth with dead matter through cremation or burial. Being eaten by vultures was not so different from being eaten by worms, mused the professor. And he was clearly captivated by the collective and egalitarian nature of Zoroastrian death rites. As his guide explained, "Here in these five towers rest the bones of all the Parsees that have lived in Bombay for the last 200 years. We form a united body in life, and we are united in death. Even our leader, Sir Jamsetjee, likes to feel that when he dies he will be reduced to perfect equality with the poorest and humblest of the Parsee community."[51] Monier-Williams' views were unusual among European observers. The nineteenth-century Florentine scholar Paolo Mantegazza wondered how Parsis could "observe without horror those fowls roosted on the tamarind trees without thinking that they might be digesting the tender flesh of [the Parsis'] own child, or the heart of [their] mother." Angelo De Gubernatis, another Italian scholar and traveler, was repulsed by the idea that "a part of your blood, of your flesh, of your beloved forms may be ignobly lost in the voracious jaws of greedy beasts

---

[45] See ibid., 276–8.

[46] *Parsi Panchayat Case*, xvi.

[47] See Sharafi, "Bella's Case," 246, 275–6.

[48] "The Towers of Silence," *TI* (18 February 1876), 3. I thank James Jaffe for bringing this article to my attention.

[49] See "Parsi Funerals," *TI* (29 September 1926), 10.

[50] Ibid.

[51] Ibid.

which shall soon digest the infamous meal perched on the roof of your own house."[52] At the beginning of the twentieth century, George Birdwood described the towers as "the gloomy platforms" where Parsis left their loved ones' corpses "to be torn by hungry vultures."[53]

Obliquely, the Secunderabad plaintiffs tried to harness this line of critique for their own benefit. They claimed that the construction of a new tower would be unsanitary. The view scientized the basic disgust with which many Europeans viewed exposure to vultures. It was a recurring argument in *dakhma*-related conflicts throughout the Parsi world.[54] The plaintiffs extended the conclusion of the Sanitary Inspector of the Cantonment, a Mr. Hill, who fifteen years earlier had found the existing tower objectionable on the basis of sanitation. The existing tower sat on a "lofty hill" and occasionally emitted "a most abominable stench from the putrefaction of bodies," particularly when the weather was hot and humid. The problem was that there were not enough vultures. Bombay did not have this difficulty. There, vultures could "strip off the soft parts in less than a minute, leaving the hard bones to take their natural course of decay." But the Secunderabad area suffered from a shortage of the birds. Building a second tower would only create "a double source of effluvia." With echoes of miasmic theories of contagion, the plaintiffs warned that there would "be no end to epidemics of cholera and typhoid fever." There were many houses immediately below the site. Aiming squarely at British priorities, the plaintiffs also noted the military regiment stationed nearby. To make matters worse, the Parsi population of Secunderabad had increased rapidly in recent years and was producing a growing number of corpses. Although this fact could *support* the need for another tower, the plaintiffs used it to amplify the British military concern with disease generally: "the Cantonment authorities will have to consider very seriously ... the matter of these Towers."[55]

The argument was ultimately peripheral. The Secunderabad plaintiffs won their case initially and before the Privy Council through a close textual interpretation of the original grants of land, not because building another tower was a bad idea. Nonetheless, the appearance of the sanitation argument spoke volumes about the interplay between intragroup litigation and external perceptions of the group. The plaintiffs were trying to harness European disgust for Zoroastrian death rites in the service of their own immediate self-interest: victory in one particular dispute. Ironically, the plaintiffs' sanitation argument worked against their own long-term interests – after all, they had created and controlled

---

[52] Paolo Mantegazza and Angelo De Gubernatis in C. G. Cereti, "Prejudice vs Reality: Zoroastrians and Their Rituals as seen by two Nineteenth-century Italian Travellers" in *Zoroastrian Rituals in Context*, ed. Michael Stausberg (Leiden: Brill, 2004), 470–1.

[53] George Birdwood, "Letter. The Phrase 'Towers of Silence.' From George Birdwood," *TL* (8 August 1905), 9.

[54] On an 1886 conflict over sanitation and *dakhma* construction in Zanzibar, see Kased, 66–7.

[55] "No. 178. Exhibit 44. Petition of Cawaji Jivanji to the Cantonment Committee" (undated), 456–7 in *Pestonji Jeevanji v. Chinoy* JCPC case papers.

Religious Trusts and the Parsi Legal Profession

the first tower of silence in Secunderabad. And it damaged the collective long-term interests of Parsis in South Asia generally, confirming negative stereotypes of Zoroastrian rites.

Externally, litigation among Parsis perpetuated negative images of Parsis before an audience of Europeans, Indians, and others. It promulgated the stereotype of the litigious Parsi. More specifically, these lawsuits revealed details about individual Parsis' private lives, including their mental health, family dynamics, and sexual relations. Collectively, Parsi trust suits subjected religious rituals to public scrutiny and ridicule. One side of the dispute usually succumbed to the temptation to repeat typically European critiques of Zoroastrian rites, believing that this would help them win.[56] But even so, a legal phenomenon that was so destructive at the individual psychosocial level was also productive in larger political ways.

JUDICIAL ETHNOGRAPHY AND THE PARSI LEGAL PROFESSION

The density of judicial ethnography in Indian case law has gone underappreciated until recently.[57] Even when not required to do so, colonial judges wrote opinions rich in ethnographically informed content that described the history, practices, and authority structures of Indian communities.[58] The barrister and Advocate General Thomas Strangman grumbled about a case in which "the judge, overcome by the attractiveness of the study, had composed a learned treatise on Khots" (the community involved in the case), neglecting the statutory analysis on which the case turned.[59] Like the state's more explicitly ethnographic projects, judgments like these were governmental interpretations of Indian communities past and present.[60]

---

[56] Many Parsi reformers took their cues from this tradition, rejecting Zoroastrian ritual practices like exposure to vultures and use of *nirang*. See, for instance, "Parsi Lady Baptized. Embraces the Christian Religion. Her Views about Zoroastrianism," *AI* (4 October 1913), 6.

[57] Recent work includes Shodhan, *Question* and "Caste"; Kasturi, 137–71. Ritu Birla's *Stages of Capital* may be understood as a legal history of the Marwari community, although it is not explicitly presented as such.

[58] For a sample, see *Advocate General of Bombay at the relation of Arran Jacob Awaskar v. David Haim Devaker* ILR 11 Bom 185 (1887); *Haji Bibi v. H. H. Sir Sultan Mahomed Shah, the Aga Khan* 11 Bom LR 409 (1911); *Jan Mahomed Abdulla Datu and another v. Datu Jaffer and others* ILR 38 Bom 449 (1914); *Rachel Benjamin v. Benjamin Solomon Benjamin* ILR 50 Bom 369 (1926). On *Abraham v. Abraham* 9 MIA 199 (1863), see Chandra Mallampalli, *Race*; "Meet the Abrahams: Colonial Law and a Mixed Race Family from Bellary, South India, 1810–63," *MAS* 41 (2007), 1–42. See also Purohit; Sturman, 199–209; Shodhan, *Question*, 82–188.

[59] Strangman, 50–1.

[60] See Bernard S. Cohn, "The Census, Social Structure and Objectification in South Asia" in his book, *An Anthropologist among the Historians and other essays* (Delhi: Oxford University Press, 1987), 224–54.

250   *Law and Identity in Colonial South Asia: Parsi Legal Culture*

As the ethnic composition of the legal profession transformed itself in the late nineteenth century, judicial ethnography changed with it. From the 1870s on, South Asian advocates like Nanabhai Haridas and Badruddin Tyabji became judges of the Bombay High Court.[61] With this change in personnel came a profound intellectual turn. Judges continued to produce ethnographic accounts, but they no longer did so exclusively as European outsiders. South Asian judges began describing their own and neighboring communities' structures and practices. In so doing, they reshaped the law governing these communities, often in ways that reflected their own values.

By going into law, individual Parsis were not only pursuing a livelihood and a route for upward mobility. They were also representing their own community to the colonizer by crafting the official story that colonial law would tell about the Parsis. Parsi litigants often hired Parsi lawyers. In the Parsi Chief Matrimonial Court of Bombay, many suits were entirely Parsi-populated – not only by Parsi litigants and jurors, but also by lawyers and the presiding judge. But the alignment of Parsi litigants, lawyers, and judges persisted even in the mainstream colonial courts.[62]

Parsi lawyers and Zoroastrian trust suits were inseparable. Not only did these cases involve large sums of money, such that their lawyers would be paid well. These suits also turned on controversial points of principle. One of the best examples pertained to the trust case from Rangoon, *Saklat v. Bella.* Bella's case arose in the tiny Parsi community of Rangoon, British Burma's busiest port city. A Rangoon court decided the case initially and on its first appeal.[63] The second (and final) appeal was decided in London.[64] Bombay was also involved as a site for the collection of evidence; the Chief Court of Lower Burma approved the creation of a judicial commission there. Judicial commissions were bodies established in other cities or countries to collect evidence, particularly oral testimony. They were time-consuming and expensive.[65] The Bombay commission in *Saklat v. Bella* was a massive endeavor. There were only some 300 Parsis in Rangoon, whereas Bombay was the unofficial Parsi capital of British India and the world.[66] What better place than Bombay to ask what it meant to be Parsi? The Bombay commission collected testimony from Parsi physicians and trustees, high priests

---

[61] See the judgment notebooks of Justice Tyabji (BHC).

[62] See, for instance, *Tarachand v. Soonabai*; Suit No. 316 of 1913: *Bai Hirabai v. B.F. Commissariatwalla* (31 March 1913), in D. D. Davar, Judgments (1913), 1–6; "Dispute over Dead Parsi's Property. Brother and Wife compromise," *TI* (24 August 1934), 16; Suit No. 195 of 1941: *Framroze Edulji Tawaria v. 1st Def. and Miss Meherhomji, 2nd Def.* (24 February 1944) and Suit No. 1208 of 1943: *Goolbai Bomanji Petit v. Dhanjibhoy Bomanji Petit and others* (5 June 1944), both in "Hon. Justice N. H. C. Coyajee. Typed Notes of Evidence (3 January 1944–8 January 1945)," 1–22 (BHC).

[63] See Sharafi, "Bella's Case," 15–60.

[64] See ibid., 355–95.

[65] See ibid., 184–5.

[66] "Letter to Delphine Menant from G. K. Nariman, Chief Court, Rangoon (18 March 1912)" in Delphine Menant Papers.

Religious Trusts and the Parsi Legal Profession

and hereditary corpse bearers, scholars and salesmen.[67] The result was a unique survey of sorts, asking the question: was being Parsi predominantly about race or religion?[68]

Bella's Bombay commission was managed by Parsi lawyers on opposite sides of the conversion debate. Each was personally and politically invested in his client's case. This was cause lawyering at its best.[69] Representing Bella was the Parsi reformist D. M. Madon, a pleader involved with organizations like the Zoroastrian Conference that were dedicated to the reform and modernization of Parsi practices. He was both a member of and legal adviser to the reformist Iranian Association. Tributes at Madon's death described him as suffering through years of abuse and vilification during debates over reform, humbly refusing to take credit although he had borne many of the burdens.[70] Madon was involved with Bella's case beyond the Bombay commission. He had sent telegrams urging the high priest who would perform Bella's initiation to carry out the ceremony. Parsis in Rangoon sued orthodox Parsi newspaper editors in Bombay over the papers' coverage of the Bella proceedings.[71] In these spin-off libel suits, the lawyer working against the newspapers was Madon. He single-handedly undertook the "almost Herculean task of sifting a voluminous record of newspaper articles, of hunting out the proper material, of translating an enormous body of material into English, of arranging it, of drawing up a case and of instructing counsel."[72] Both inside and outside the courtroom, Madon took every opportunity to support Bella's cause.

Against Bella was the formidable J. J. Vimadalal. The prominent solicitor was an orator and doyen of Parsi orthodoxy, as well as a prominent theosophist and devotee of the Zoroastrian mystical *Ilm-e-Khshnoom* movement. He was touted as "the leader of the orthodox section of the community." Vimadalal's influence acted as a "mighty brake on the headlong course of goahead reformers, who, if left to themselves unchecked and unhindered, would have proceeded from one excess to another, and precipitated the

---

[67] For a sample, see the following testimony from "Plaintiff's Evidence" in *Saklat v. Bella* JCPC case papers: "No. 8: Dinshaw Bomanji Master," 129–59 (physician, trustee); "No. 9: Nowroji Jehangir Gamadia," 161–85 (trustee); "No. 11: Darab Pesotan Sanjana," 227–96 (priest, scholar); "No. 14: Khadabux Byram Irani," 344–66 (scholar); "No. 16: Shavakshaw Burjorji Sakai," 375–9 (hereditary corpse bearer); "No. 18: Shavakshaw Pestonji Kuka," 382–5 (salesman). From "Defendant's Evidence" in the same papers, see: "No. 27: Jamshedji Dadabhoy Nadirshaw," 409–19 (scholar); "No. 28: Kaikhusru Dastur Jamaspji Jamaspasana," 519–36 (high priest); "No. 30: Dastur Aderbad Dastur Naoshirwan," 592–636 (high priest).

[68] For discussion of the Bombay commission, see Sharafi, "Bella's Case," 176–289.

[69] By Austin Sarat and Stuart Scheingold, eds., see *Cause Lawyering: Political Commitments and Professional Responsibilities* (New York: Oxford University Press, 1998); *Cause Lawyering and the State in a Global Era* (Oxford: Oxford University Press, 2001).

[70] "Mr. D. M. Madon," *JIA* V: 6 (September 1916), 236.

[71] See Sharafi, "Bella's Case," 290–354.

[72] "Mr. D. M. Madon," 236.

community headlong into the vortex of destruction."[73] He was involved in countless Parsi charities and organizations, particularly those with an orthodox or priestly bent (he came from a priestly family himself). The Parsi solicitor also wrote. Vimadalal adapted Euro-American writings on eugenics to the South Asian and Parsi context. As early as 1910, he published eugenics-based works alluding to the dangers of allowing outsiders into the fold.[74] Bella was simply the latest in a series of female outsiders to threaten Parsi racial purity. Vimadalal tried to discredit her Bombay witnesses with every tool at his disposal, including the race science of the day.

Parsi clients did not always hire Parsi solicitors, and Parsi solicitors did not always engage Parsi advocates for court appearances. Yet Zoroastrian lawyers and clients were linked often enough to appear frequently together in the published case law.[75] If these lawyers and litigants found each other through community channels, the other half of the picture was harder to track: how were Parsi judges assigned to Parsi trust suits? The mechanism that matched judges with cases was discretionary and confidential: the Chief Justice and his office made these decisions. Oral history suggested that a candidate's ethnoreligious community was paramount in the appointment of South Asian judges.[76] Given that the colonial state cared about the community identity of its Indian judges, it might similarly have favored the referral of intracommunity cases to a judge from the same community. This was certainly the pattern for the first Parsi judge of the Bombay High Court, Dinshah Dhanjibhai Davar. Davar presided from 1906 until his death in 1916. During his decade on the bench, he decided most important suits between Parsis in Bombay. For the colonial state, the channeling of community-specific case law was strategic in several ways. It allowed the administration to deflect criticism for the outcomes of such cases, putting responsibility on the shoulders of the judge himself. At the same time, it advertised the fact that South Asians – albeit those vetted for loyalty to British rule – were represented at high levels within the colonial state. For the community in question, the gains were also significant. Like the Parsi matrimonial jury, the match of Parsi cases with Parsi judges may have been a reward for collective loyalty to British rule. And, like the jury, it created a bubble of group autonomy within the colonial legal system.

---

[73] *Shet Jehangir Vemadalal Yadgari Granth* (Bombay, 1937), 137; cited in Kulke, 103 at note 47.
[74] *Mr. Vimadalal.*
[75] See Mistry, *Reminiscences* [1911], 3–6.
[76] Conversations with R. P. Vachha (Mumbai, 19 February 2004 and 13 December 2009). On the importance of ethnoreligious community in the appointment of legal officials from the colonial administration's perspective, see letter from John Morley of the India Office to Lord Minto (27 September 1910), 2 in Morley Collection, 1905–11 (MSS Eur D573) (APAC).

DAVAR AND ZOROASTRIAN TRUSTS

Nowhere was the intragroup power of South Asian judges more visible than in the career of D. D. Davar. He was aptly named. *Davar* referred to a category of high judicial officials in Achaemenian Persia. His surname was singularly appropriate for the first Parsi judge of the Bombay High Court, a post to which he was elevated on 27 October 1906.[77] Davar was trained as a barrister at the Middle Temple in London.[78] He made a name for himself as a formidable cross-examiner in the Small Causes Court and the Police Court of Bombay.[79] As a judge, he was fierce and intimidating.[80] His independence of mind and forceful personality combined with a loyalty to British rule that grew as his career advanced. Davar was best known for his unusually harsh 1908 sentencing of the nationalist leader, Bal Gangadhar Tilak. After a special jury found Tilak guilty of seditious libel for his writings against British rule, Davar imposed a six-year sentence of transportation and a Rs 1,000 fine. Tilak's request to appeal to the Privy Council was rejected.[81] He was sent to a prison settlement in Mandalay, Burma.[82] Davar's sentence and characterization of Tilak's mind as "diseased and perverted" invited public criticism and surprise: Davar had been one of Tilak's own lawyers in a similar case a decade earlier.[83] Even Davar's own son, the barrister and future judge J. D. Davar, refused to speak to his father for a period after the Tilak sentence.[84] When Gandhi received a similar six-year sentence in an Ahmedabad court in 1922, the judge said he was simply following the Tilak precedent.[85]

Davar was not only forceful in his disapproval of the extremist brand of nationalist activity. He was also outspoken in his views on the Zoroastrian religion.[86] As a witness in a 1915 defamation case between Parsi organizations,

---

[77] Darukhanawala, 368; entry on "Databara" in Yarshater (accessed on 7 February 2013): http://www.iranicaonline.org/articles/databara.

[78] Entry for Dinshah Dhanjibhai Davar (admitted on 2 November 1877, called to the Bar on 9 June 1880) in Sturgess, II: 606.

[79] "First Parsee Judge. Mr. D. D. Davur appointed," *TI* (27 October 1926), 9; "Justice Davar's Death. A Sketch of His Career," *TI* (31 July 1916), 8; Davar, *Hints*, 31–3. See also Sharafi, "Judging Conversion," 163.

[80] "Death of Sir Dinshah Davar," *AI* (29 July 1916), 7; "Justice Davar's Death. A Sketch of His Career," *TI* (31 July 1916), 8; Jāgoś, 5; Sharafi, "Judging Conversion," 171.

[81] *In re Bal Gangadhar Tilak* ILR 33 Bom 221 (1909). See also Chapter 5 at note 33.

[82] See Kelkar, 18–19 ("Verdict and Sentence"), 121–40 ("Press opinion in the Tilak case").

[83] Davar represented Tilak in *Queen-Empress v. Bal Gangadhar Tilak and Keshav Mahadev Bal* ILR 22 Bom 112 (1898). See Kelkar, 11–12. See also untitled article, *The Mahratta* (28 June 1914), 205–7; "On the release of Tilak," *The Mahratta* (21 June 1914), 193–4; Vachha, 262–71; A. I. Chicherov, "Tilak's Trial and the Bombay Political Strike of 1908" in I. M. Reisner, ed., *Tilak and the Struggle for Indian Freedom* (Delhi: People's Publishing House, 1966), 545–626.

[84] Conversation with R. P. Vachha (Mumbai, 13 December 2009).

[85] Strangman, 142.

[86] "Justice Davar's Death," 8; Jāgoś, 4.

he described his position on a range of controversies over religious reform. His views were orthodox on every issue. He regarded the proposal to curtail and simplify death commemoration ceremonies as "an insult to the dead" and "extremely irreligious and offensive." The idea of reforming the Zoroastrian calendar was a "childish matter" that had been "laughed out." Changing the language of the prayers from archaic Persian languages to Gujarati was impracticable. "Nobody took it seriously," scoffed Davar. Similarly, limiting offerings of sandalwood to the sacred fire would only create resentment. Reformists considered excess offerings a "superstitious belief" and a waste of money, but Davar disagreed. He also felt that the suggestion to cut down *ghambars* or community feasts would be opposed by those people (particularly the poor) who were regularly fed at these events.[87] Davar became increasingly orthodox over the course of his adult life. In 1897, he supported the invalidation of trusts funding Zoroastrian death commemoration ceremonies.[88] A decade later, it was his own ruling that protected these trusts, an episode explored shortly. He testified in the 1915 libel case that the ceremony "was a portion of the Zoroastrian ritual which must be observed and was binding on the community."[89]

Similarly, at the beginning of *Petit v. Jijibhai*, Davar was open to the idea of allowing ethnic outsiders to convert to Zoroastrianism and to benefit from Parsi trusts. He even encouraged the defendants' lawyers to accept compromise terms that he and Justice Beaman had drafted (Figure 6.1). It was only in the later phase of the case that Davar changed his mind, turning toward orthodoxy and opposing the idea of conversion completely.[90] Davar admitted to the court in 1915 that he smoked and "went bareheaded," neither of which an orthodox Parsi man was supposed to do. Overlooking this lapse, images of Davar from the period showed him with the traditional Parsi man's hat known as a *paghri* (Guj. *pāghḍī*) (Figure 6.2). On the bench, the judicial dress code of the era required him to wear a heavy, horse-hair wig.[91]

Davar was a leader of the orthodox camp. By popular accounts, he would take the long route home after presiding over *Petit v. Jijibhai* to greet crowds of supporters in orthodox neighborhoods.[92] Books by sympathizers proclaimed him "a true Parsee Hero" for saving the Parsis from "racial degeneration and extinction" through his decision in *Petit*.[93] After his death in 1916, *Hindi Punch*

---

[87] "'Jame' Defamation Case," *TI* (29 April 1915), 5.
[88] See Desai, *History*, 291.
[89] "'Jame' Defamation Case," *TI* (29 April 1915), 5.
[90] See Sharafi, "Judging Conversion."
[91] For an image, see Darukhanawala, *Parsi Lustre*, I: 149. Davar's wig has been preserved at the Bombay High Court. See Mehrotra and Dwivedi, 128.
[92] Conversation with Fali S. Nariman (Delhi, 8 March 2004).
[93] Dedication of Phiroze Shapurji Masani, *Zoroastrianism Ancient and Modern. Comprising a Review of Dr. Dhalla's Book of Zoroastrian Theology* (Bombay: Author, 1917). See similarly note 97.

Religious Trusts and the Parsi Legal Profession

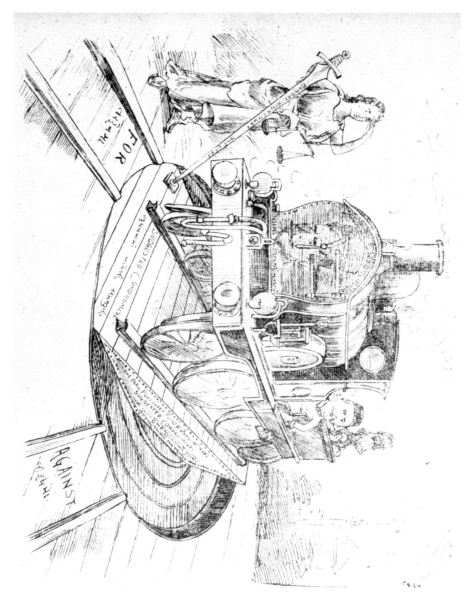

FIGURE 6.1. "On which track??? The Parsee Punchayet Funds and Juddin case ... has been postponed ... to allow the Trustees ... to lay before [the community] the suggested compromise ... "
Source: *HP* (15 March 1908), 10. Courtesy of the British Library SV576.

FIGURE 6.2. "Mr. Punch's Fancy Portrait" of Justice D. D. Davar in everyday dress. *Source*: *HP* (7 June 1908), 12. Courtesy of the British Library SV576.

Religious Trusts and the Parsi Legal Profession 257

commented that the "best orthodox section" had lost its "Din-shah." The weekly was punning on Dinshah Davar's first name to imply that he was king (Pers. *shāh*) of the faith (Pers. *dīn*). The orthodox continued to proclaim Davar "a pillar of the faith, the preserver and protector of the unity and solidarity of the community, which, alas! has split up into two bitter parties."[94]

Davar muted neither his strong personality nor his religious orthodoxy in the courtroom. On the bench, he drew on his knowledge of Parsi life, doubting representations placed before him if they contradicted his own personal knowledge.[95] His judgments also favored religiously orthodox outcomes.[96] The leading treatise on the 1865 Parsi matrimonial and inheritance legislation was dedicated to Davar, "whose zeal in the cause of the Zoroastrian religion will always be gratefully remembered by his co-religionists."[97] The judge's orthodox biographer, M. H. Jāgoś, repeated that Davar had done a great service to the Parsi community by accepting a judgeship: the move ensured that his own people's matters would be handled properly. In becoming a judge, Davar had accepted a significant drop in income by giving up his lucrative barrister's practice. He had done so, Jāgoś implied, because he recognized the importance *for the community* of having a Parsi on the bench.[98]

Some judges in colonial India refused to make public addresses outside of court or even to read newspapers or socialize widely.[99] Figures like M. R. Sausse, the first Chief Justice of Bombay, aimed for the ideal of the objective and disconnected judge.[100] This type of judge tried to minimize his own prior knowledge of the people and issues appearing in his courtroom. The ideal was a culturally rooted one. In many South Asian systems of dispute resolution, adjudicators were supposed to bring some knowledge of the social setting to the dispute.[101] The foundational concept in *panchayat*-based adjudication during the early colonial period in the Bombay Presidency, for instance, was to have an equal number of adjudicators chosen by each side. Fairness meant a balanced process of selecting the judges, not judicial ignorance of the controversy itself.[102] By contrast, the rule of law ideal required that decision makers have no connection to the parties or their social worlds. Justice in many non-state systems meant maximizing contextual information about the conflict, permitting the

---

[94] "1285–1286," *HP* (10 September 1916), 14.
[95] See Vachha, 91.
[96] See Sharafi, "Judging Conversion."
[97] Rana (1934), dedication page.
[98] Jāgoś, 1, 4–6.
[99] See D. J. Ferreira, "Reminiscences" in *Bombay Inc. Law Soc. Centenary*, 259.
[100] On Sausse, see Wacha, *Shells*, 250–1; Vachha, 59; Soli Sorabjee, "Traditions of Ethics and Learning," 115, and H. K. Chainani, "On the Occasion of the Centenary Celebrations," 8–9, both in the Bombay High Court's *Post-Centenary Silver Jubilee 1862–1987* (Bombay: Government Central Press, 1988).
[101] For example, see Desai, *History*, 7–8.
[102] Jaffe, 49–50.

judges to both decide the case and bring in a certain amount of evidence in the form of personal knowledge about the background context.[103] Justice in the rule of law universe meant a different notion of fairness – one entailing a carefully managed *lack* of information. Each model of judgeship had its own hazards. If the disconnected judge was wholly ignorant of the social setting, he could be vulnerable to manipulation.[104] But, equally, the connected judge's sociocultural knowledge could blur into bias.

The project of empire gained mileage from the model of the disconnected judge. Rule of law values threatened to turn European judges' ignorance of local languages and cultures into a perceived asset.[105] These judges' distance from the colonized population removed them from the intrigue and influence of factions within that population, enabling them to deliver fair and objective decisions. Or so the argument went. Spreading the rule of law was a classic justification for British rule.[106] The ideal of judicial distance was an important plank within the rule of law agenda. Mithi Mukhjerjee has documented the power of the ideal in India, applying it not just to individual judges, but also to courts. The Privy Council in faraway London embodied the figure of the objective and distant imperial adjudicator.[107] In the words of one judge of that court, "we sit there, perfectly impartial; we have no prejudices, either theological or otherwise."[108] Non-European judges, such as the orthodox Parsi Davar and his Hindu reform-ist colleague N. G. Chandavarkar lived a different ideal. They were embedded in the social life of their communities.[109] They appreciated the subtleties of South Asian languages, religions, and cultures. They had the local knowledge, and they used it – at times, in the service of their own vision of community identity.

In their simplest form, trusts were legal devices that required one person, the trustee, to control property on behalf of and for the benefit of another, the

---

[103] Rudolph and Rudolph, *Modernity*, 256–7.

[104] For example, Justice Jardine in *Bánáji v. Limbuwállá*. See also Sharafi, "Bella's Case," 127–8.

[105] See Chapter 5 at 202.

[106] See, for instance, Frederick Pollock, *English Opportunities and Duties in the Historical and Comparative Study of Law* (London: Macmillan, 1883), 20; William Wordsworth in Jeejeebhoy, 353 at note; Letter from E. S. Symes, Secretary to the Chief Commissioner, British Burma to the Secretary to the Government of India, Foreign Department (Rangoon, 16 October 1884), 3 in A. J. S. White Collection (ICS Burma, 1922–38), file 10, No. 1610 (MSS Eur. E356) (APAC). On rule of law values, see A. V. Dicey, *Introduction to the Study of the Law of the Constitution* (London: Macmillan, 1889), 189–90; Edward Jenks, *The Government of the British Empire* (Boston: Little, Brown and Co., 1919), 35; Rudolph and Rudolph, *Modernity*, 253.

[107] Mukherjee argues that newly independent India continued to project that role on to international bodies like the United Nations. See Mithi Mukherjee, *India in the Shadows of Empire: A Legal and Political History, 1774–1950* (Oxford: Oxford University Press, 2010).

[108] Haldane, 153.

[109] Both spoke extrajudicially often. See, for instance, Davar in Jeejeebhoy, 315 at note; Davar, *Hints*; L. V. Kaikini, ed., *The Speeches and Writings of Sir Narayen G. Chandavarkar, Kt.* (Bombay: Manoranjak Grantha Prasarak Mandali, 1911).

Religious Trusts and the Parsi Legal Profession

beneficiary.[110] By separating the enjoyment of property from its management, trusts helped provide for the vulnerable or those incapable of preserving the property in order to benefit from it. Trusts could be private, in which case they would be set up for the benefit of individuals or families "for private convenience and support." There were also public trusts, created for the benefit of the public or a significant subsection of it.[111] The latter, which were also known as charitable trusts, were governed by a different set of legal rules. Charitable trusts could be created to last indefinitely, for instance, unlike private trusts, which could not exist for longer than twenty-one years after the death of a particular person (or persons) living at the time the trust came into being. Charitable trusts were also tax-exempt and were supervised closely by legal authorities like the Attorney General and judiciary.[112]

The law of religious endowments was of ambiguous taxonomy during the Raj. As a subspecies of trust law (itself distinct from the personal law system), the law of religious endowments was a curious hybrid of personal and territorial law that leaned toward the latter.[113] Particular group-specific rules developed for Islamic *wakfs*, Hindu religious endowments, and trusts governing Sikh *gurdwaras*.[114] Nonetheless, the principles of English and Indian territorial trust law continued to subtend all religious endowments, regardless of religious affiliation.[115] Equally, treatise authors peppered their discussion of the general principles of India's charitable trust law with illustrations from the case law on both Hindu and Muslim religious endowments together, in distinction to the much clearer boundaries placed between Hindu, Muslim, and other bodies of family law.[116] In family law, the religiously neutral body of law created by the Special Marriages Acts was a latecomer and always a peripheral addition to the collection of the various bodies of religiously inspired law. In trust law, the relationship was the reverse: various carve-outs (mostly legislated) for particular religious groups remained rooted in a substrate of English trust law principles. The trust law that applied to Parsi charitable trusts remained territorial during the colonial period. Because the *content* of these trusts was often religious, trust law became a leading site for the production of judicial ethnography about India's many communities. Colonial case law was rich in disputes among

[110] See generally Simon Gardner, *An Introduction to the Law of Trusts* (Oxford: Clarendon Press, 1990).

[111] See Iyer, lxv–lxvi.

[112] W. H. Grimley, *An Income Tax Manual being Act II of 1886, with notes* (Calcutta: Thacker, Spink and Co., 1886), 8–10 [Income Tax Act 1886, s. 5(1)e]; ibid., lxxxiii–lxxxviii; Birla, *Stages*, 79, 108.

[113] Compare N. Chatterjee, 78.

[114] See Narang; Agnew, 380; Chapter 2 at text accompanying note 234.

[115] See, for instance, *Juggut Mohini Dossee and others v. Mussumat Sokheemoney Dossee and others* 20 Eng. Rep. PC 795 (1809–65), reproducing 14 MIA 289 (1871–2); *Mahomed v. Abdul Latif* 14 Bom LR 987 (1912); *T. P. Srinivasa Chariar v. C. N. Evalappa Mudaliar* ILR 45 Mad 565 (1922).

[116] For example, see Agnew, 364, 370.

260 Law and Identity in Colonial South Asia: Parsi Legal Culture

trustees of temples and other religious bodies.[117] Davar's Parsi trust cases were just one chapter in a broader history of trustlike devices and colonized peoples across the British Empire.[118]

Davar saw more than the average judge's share of Parsi trust litigation. It was as if Parsi disputants had been saving up their trust suits, waiting for a Parsi to appear on the High Court bench. Davar delivered his two most significant religious trust suits in *Jamshedji Cursetjee Tarachand v. Soonabai* (on death commemoration ceremonies) and *Petit v. Jijibhai* (on *juddin* admission). Both landed in Davar's court soon after his appointment in 1906. Both were highly publicized among Parsis and beyond. And both revealed the power of a judge in Davar's position to write the judicial ethnography of his own community. In so doing, Davar gave his vision of community identity the force of law.

Before and beyond big cases like these, Davar was busy with the daily business of administering Parsi trusts. These trusts often combined strictly religious purposes (like funding religious ceremonies) with other philanthropic efforts like education, poor relief, and medical care. All fell under the banner of charitable trusts. Parsi trusts of this kind required judicial approval at many points. For the appointment of a new trustee or any expenditure of trust funds that strayed from the literal purposes of the trust, judicial approval was often required. Trustees came to court asking for clarification on what they could and could not do, sometimes requesting changes to the original trust terms themselves. In one 1913 case, Davar deleted the trust term that prevented schools of the Parsi Girls' School Association from teaching in English. Religious education was part of the curriculum of these schools.[119] His role in the everyday administration of Parsi trusts also had a major effect on the distribution of trust-owned real estate in Bombay. In 1909, he approved the sale of land held by the Bombay Parsi Panchayat near the towers of silence, for instance.[120] He also shaped the purposes for which trust-held real estate would be used. In 1912, Davar approved the construction of *chawl* housing for poor Parsis by the N. M. Wadia Trust.[121] Perhaps because of this major housing project, he diverted funds the following year from another Parsi trust – from the proposed construction of more

[117] See Iyer; *Thackersey Dewra'j and others v. Hurbhum Nursey and others* ILR 8 Bom 432 (1884); Suit No. 1668 of 1932, "Hon. Justice J. D. Davar. Short Causes and Motions (1 August 1927–17 October 1935)," V: 3–7 (BHC).

[118] See Birla, *Stages*, 67–139; Kozlowski; Powers; Adam Hofri-Winogradow, "Zionist Settlers and the English Private Trust in Mandate Palestine," *LHR* 30:3 (2012), 813–64; Nurfadzilah Yahaya, "Courting Jurisdictions: Colonial Administration of Islamic Law pertaining to Arabs in the British Straits Settlements and the Netherlands East Indies, 1860–1941" (PhD dissertation, Princeton University, 2012), 164–203.

[119] "Parsi Girls' School. *Advocate-General of Bombay v. Nowroji Jehangir Gamadia and others,*" *TI* (5 August 1913), 5. See also "Parsi Girls' Schools. Report of the Association," *TI* (3 April 1914), 8.

[120] "Towers of Silence Land," *TI* (17 March 1909), 4. The sale was part of an exchange of land that may have related to a public road-widening project.

[121] "Habitations for Parsis," *TI* (20 March 1912), 4.

Religious Trusts and the Parsi Legal Profession   261

subsidized housing to the job of covering the everyday expenses of the Bomanji Petit Parsi General Hospital. Both options were presented by the parties to the 1913 case. It was Davar who made the choice.[122]

He was not overly constrained by a sense of judicial cautiousness. Like judges in so many other settings, Davar used legal doctrines as vehicles that would take him to his desired destination. At times, he applied opposite doctrinal approaches to similar fact patterns. Two contrasting trust administration matters that came to Davar in 1907 made this point nicely. In both, wealthy Parsis had left money to carry out charitable and religious projects for Parsis. It was allegedly impossible to follow their wishes because circumstances had changed since the time when the wills were written. A judge could approve the use of the money for a different charitable purpose. The determination of impossibility was for Davar to decide.

In the first case, a deceased Parsi named E. R. Soonawalla had donated a large piece of land in the Bombay neighborhood of Mahim. He had wanted an *agiary* (Guj. *agīārī*), a type of fire temple, to be built in honor of his dead wife, Soonabai. Two trustees came to court arguing that Soonabai's *agiary* would be impossible to build. The population of Parsis in Mahim had fallen too low to make the project viable: there were now just fifty families in the area. For these trustees, *impossible* meant *impracticable*. Judges had to balance fidelity to the testator's wishes against the best interests of the current population. The two trustees asked Davar to allow them instead to combine the funds with another fund left by the settlor; the second fund had been created to build a Parsi community hall. Davar refused. He adhered to the classic idea of upholding the intentions of the settlor, staying true to the desires expressed in the original text. Incidentally – and more to the point – he felt that it would be good to build a fire temple in Mahim, where there was currently none. He doubted the facts presented to him. Only fifty Parsi families in Mahim? "This I think can hardly be accurate."[123] The personal knowledge of this socially embedded judge hovered over every fact presented by the trustees' Parsi advocate. Showing great concern that the settlors' intentions be protected, Davar ordered the construction of a new fire temple. In this situation, literalist legal interpretation dovetailed with orthodox Parsi values.

Five months later, Davar came to the opposite conclusion in a similar case. A wealthy Parsi merchant named Hormusji Framji Warden had died in 1885, leaving money to build a community hall for Parsi marriages and dinners. The trustees came to Davar with the same impossibility argument: too many of these halls had been built since Warden wrote his will. Could the money instead be used to build an operating theater for Parsis in the Parsi General Hospital? This

---

[122] "The Dolimeherjee Charity. *Dhunjibhoy Sorabji Dolimeherji and another v. the Advocate-General of Bombay and others*," *TI* (22 September 1913), 8.

[123] *Byramji Edulji Soonawalla and another v. Jehangir Edulji Soonawalla and the Advocate General of Bombay*. Suit No. 158 of 1907 (11 March 1907) in D. D. Davar, Judgments (1906–7), 4.

262 *Law and Identity in Colonial South Asia: Parsi Legal Culture*

time, Davar agreed. In a forty-three-page unreported opinion, he explained why he was using the equitable *cy-près* doctrine to divert the money to another charitable purpose.[124] *Cy-près*, from the old legal French for "near here," allowed judges to authorize the use of trust funds for a purpose similar to but different from the settlor's original purpose when that purpose was "impossible."[125] *Cy-près* preserved the validity of the trust and responded to the present needs of the recipient community. It paid less heed to the intentions of the settlor. Sterner, more traditional judges would either require the original purpose to be followed or invalidate the term (or trust) entirely. In the Warden case, Davar's approval for the alternative scheme hinged on his loose definition of the word "impossible." To use *cy-près*, following the settlor's wishes had to be impossible. This time, Davar claimed that "impossible" did not mean physically impossible, but simply not possible under current circumstances – or even unsuitable or impracticable.[126] Without a word about his narrower, more traditional approach in the earlier Mahim case, he went through a long line of cases that reflected a generous recent use of *cy-près*.[127] Reading the Warden and Soonawalla decisions together, Davar looked less driven by legal doctrine than by his own views of current community needs.

Davar had consulted the acting Attorney General of Bombay, a Briton named E. B. Raikes, on the Warden medical proposal. Raikes argued for a narrow definition of "impossible." A wide definition would create a dangerous precedent. Would future Parsi philanthropists make similar bequests if they saw courts disregarding settlors' intentions? Raikes thought not. But on the contrary, insisted Davar, "right-minded charitably inclined people" would be *more* likely to leave money for charitable purposes if they knew it would not be wasted: "We are living in progressive times. Our surroundings, circumstances and modes of thought are undergoing changes. What may appear to be crying wants today may be useless superfluities in the future. ... [A donor] would in my opinion be more inclined to devote his property to charity if he felt that the Courts in India would be always alert to see that in the future under altered circumstances his funds would not be wasted on purposes that may become useless and cease to be beneficially employed."[128] Davar's willingness to disregard the donor's intentions was viewed with suspicion in some quarters, noted *Hindi Punch:* "after all, a donor's last wish must be respected" (Figure 6.3). The judge's reasoning

---

[124] *Re Hormusji Framji Warden, deceased. Hirjibhai Bomanji Warden and another, petitioners* (16 September 1907), "Hon. Justice Davar. Judgments (8 July 1907–19 December 1907)," 1–43 (BHC).

[125] See Oppé, 294–5; Agnew, 357–60. For the legal history of the *cy près* doctrine in another common-law context, see Lawrence M. Friedman, *Dead Hands: A Social History of Wills, Trusts, and Inheritance Law* (Palo Alto: Stanford University Press, 2009), 152–61.

[126] *Re Warden*, 12.

[127] The doctrine would be used often for Parsi trusts in the 1950s–'60s. See Desai, *History*, 141, 228.

[128] *Re Warden*, 36–7.

FIGURE 6.3. "Justitia: Here you are, sir! A good round sum – 82,000 odd. May it do you much good! [Parsi General Hospital] Fund: As many thanks as rupees, ma'am, and more than I can tell!"
Source: "Madame Justitia's Cheque," HP (29 Sept. 1907), 23. Courtesy of the British Library SV576.

privileged current social needs over fidelity to a particular legal doctrine – or even to a consistent model of judgeship.

Being Parsi was central to Davar's stance in both cases. It affected his acceptance of the facts presented to him. It also subtended his views of what the community needed. Non-Parsis around Davar deferred to him on this basis. At another point in the Warden case, Davar consulted the Attorney General at the time when the position was occupied by Basil Scott, a future High Court judge. Scott said he was not in a position to judge whether a Parsi community hall would be useless, given current Parsi needs. As Davar noted, this Attorney General was "good enough to remark that no one could be in a better position than this Court [i.e., Davar] to come to a conclusion upon the point which is likely to give satisfaction to the Parsi community."[129] The pattern repeated itself across Davar's case load. In *Petit v. Jijibhai*, Davar's British partner on the bench also made clear his deference on ethnoreligious grounds. Davar was a Parsi judge in a Parsi case. Beaman was not.[130] For European legal officials, Davar had unique authority in Zoroastrian trust cases. Unsurprisingly, Parsis felt the same

---

[129] *Re Warden*, 4.
[130] *Judgments*: Petit v. Jeejeebhoy *1908*, 193.

264   *Law and Identity in Colonial South Asia: Parsi Legal Culture*

way.[131] Davar was famous for being hot-tempered on the bench. His Parsi biographer noted that if he was not known for his circumspection, at least his cases were useful to the Parsi community. "Saheb's people" (meaning Parsis) and the government seemed to appreciate him equally.[132] Davar assumed the burden and privilege of judicial interference with South Asian religion. He alleviated Europeans of a politically charged job while maximizing his own community's autonomy in the courts.

DEATH AND CONVERSION

Judicial intervention cut deep into Zoroastrianism. Davar delivered his rulings in *Tarachand v. Soonabai* and *Petit v. Jijibhai* in 1906–8, during his first few years on the bench. Although both suits pitted one set of trustees against another, the first was best understood as a struggle against European ignorance of Zoroastrian practice. This gap was exploited by Parsi parties seeking to invalidate the trusts and inherit the property in question. The second was a principled intragroup struggle between reformists and orthodox Parsis over the same question that would later trigger *Saklat v. Bella*: was ethnicity (or race) an essential part of Parsi identity? Davar's ruling in *Tarachand* reached back, reversing a ruling that had frustrated the performance of death commemoration ceremonies for decades. His decision in *Petit* cast a long shadow forward: the Privy Council's 1925 decision in *Saklat v. Bella* deferred to Davar's *Petit* judgment.

Before there were any Parsi judges in the Bombay High Court, an important Parsi trust case was decided by the British judge John Jardine.[133] His 1887 ruling in *Limji Nowroji Bánáji v. Bápuji Ruttonji Limbuwállá* had a devastating effect on Zoroastrian death commemoration ceremonies for decades. *Muktad* ceremonies (Guj. *muktād*) were rites held during the last ten days of the Zoroastrian calendar to commemorate the death of particular Parsis (Figure 6.4).[134] Wealthy Parsis often left money in their wills for the creation of *muktad* trusts. This money would fund the performance of these ceremonies following the donors' own deaths. The trusts were supposed to last forever. The trouble was that this standard Parsi practice violated a rule of classical English trust law (and free-market economics): the rule against perpetuities.[135] Gregory Kozlowski, Ritu Birla, and Nurfadzilah Yahaya have documented the collision between this rule and traditional forms of giving in multiple parts of the British Empire.[136] A similar conflict occurred in the Parsi context. According to the rule against

---

[131] "First Parsee Judge"; Jāgoś, 3, 6.
[132] Jāgoś, 1, 4.
[133] See Vachha, 77–8.
[134] See Modi, 437–8; Sanjana, *Ancient Persia*, 623; Desai, *History*, 84.
[135] See Sharafi, "Bella's Case," 122–3.
[136] See Kozlowski, 148–9; Birla, *Stages*, 89–96; Yahaya, 183–191. See also Agnew, 370.

Religious Trusts and the Parsi Legal Profession 265

FIGURE 6.4. "In Praise of the Dead.... In the days of muktad, just ended with the advent of the New Year, the Parsees offer prayers and recite the good actions of their dead." *Source: HP* (19 Sept. 1909), 20. Courtesy of the British Library SV576.

perpetuities, trusts could not last indefinitely – in perpetuity – unless they were charitable, meaning that they were of public benefit.[137] The question for Jardine

[137] Over the centuries, the list of what constituted a charitable purpose evolved around the 1601 Elizabethan Statute of Charitable Uses' roster of acceptable categories. The Statute's charitable purposes included "the relief of aged, impotent and poor people; maintenance of sick and maimed soldiers and mariners; schools of learning, free schools and scholars in universities; repairs of bridges, ports, havens, causeways, churches, sea-banks and highways; education and

was whether the *muktad* trust before him would benefit a particular individual or a larger group instead. Even if the trust's purpose was to benefit the Parsi community alone, it would count as public. Jardine found that the ceremonies in question were for the benefit of the souls of particular dead Parsis. The benefit consisted of "consolation to the spirit of *certain* dead persons and comfort to *certain* living persons."[138] The words of the will did not point to benefits available to the entire Parsi community, according to Jardine.[139] The trust looked more like a gift to a private company than a charitable donation: there was no public benefit. As a result, the trust was invalid because it was framed to exist in perpetuity.

At least eight *muktad* trusts were challenged in the Bombay High Court after the *Limbuwállá* ruling. All were invalidated on the authority of Jardine's judgment.[140] Parsi lobbyists began to press for a statute that would validate *muktad* trusts for 60–80 years, if not forever. Their plans were foiled by dissent within the community. In response to lobbyists' petition, reformists sent the government a counter-requisition opposing the proposed bill. They argued, among other reasons, that a statute would only encourage ceremonial excess.[141] In 1908, another case presented itself. This time, it landed in Davar's court. The plaintiff was a Parsi barrister named J. K. Tarachand who represented himself. The defendants, pressing for the validation of the trusts, were backed by the Bombay Parsi Panchayat.[142] Although no one acknowledged it, the case had the whiff of a test case. Davar complimented Tarachand on his mature and conciliatory approach throughout the case, his willingness to lose (should the trust be upheld), his offer to waive his fees (and not recoup them from the trust funds), and his desire for clarification rather than financial gain (should the trust be void). Tarachand's own share of the trust was "so small that it would not have been worth his while troubling about it if his motive had been merely to share in the division of the funds."[143]

preferment of orphans; the relief, stock, or maintenance of houses of correction; marriages of poor maids; supportation, aid, and help of young tradesmen, handicraftsmen, and persons decayed; relief or redemption of prisoners or captives; and aid or ease of any poor inhabitants, concerning payments of fifteenths, setting out of soldiers, and other taxes." [Preamble to the Statute of Charitable Uses 1601 (43 Eliz. c.4).] This list lived on in colonial India. See Iyer, lxvii–lxviii; Desai, *History*, 397–8.

[138] *Bánáji v. Limbuwállá*, 447. Emphasis added.

[139] Ibid., 447.

[140] Six of these cases were unreported, namely *Dinbai v. Hormusji Dinsha Hodiwalla*, Suit No. 267 of 1890; *Dhunbaiji v. Nowroji Bomonji*, Suit No. 565 of 1889; *Cowasji Byramji Gorewalla v. Perrozbai*, Suit No. 281 of 1892; *Maneckji Edulji Allbless v. Sir Dinsha Maneckji Petit*, Suit No. 96 of 1892; *R. R. Dadina v. The Advocate General*, Suit No. 49 of 1895. The one reported case discussed by Davar was *Cowasji N. Pochkhanawalla v. R. D. Sethna* ILR 20 Bom 511 (1895). [*Tarachand v. Soonabai*, 153–62.] However, there were still other cases not mentioned by Davar. For example, see *Dady Nasserwanji Dady v. Acting Advocate General* 7 Bom LR 324 (1905).

[141] See Desai, *History*, 85–88, 282–93.

[142] Ibid., 88.

[143] *Tarachand v. Soonabai*, 211–12.

J. K. Tarachand gave Davar the chance to reverse *Limbuwállá*, an opportunity Davar seized. The Parsi judge was scathing in his account of Jardine's judgment. If Jardine was the distant, "objective" arbiter celebrated by rule of law ideals, he was also the ignorant Briton, utterly unfamiliar with the religious practices at issue and prone to being misled by opportunistic litigants. According to Davar, *Limbuwállá* had been a farce. It was a collusive suit manufactured by the parties. It only succeeded because a gullible British judge was ostensibly in control. The parties agreed to portray the trusts in a way that would produce invalidation. They could then share the spoils among themselves. Davar noted that the testimony of a single witness, the scholar-priest J. J. Modi, had been presented to Jardine.[144] Modi had been cross-examined for fifteen minutes and was not allowed to explain himself. Modi and the rest of the Parsi community were shocked to see Modi's testimony used to invalidate *muktad* trusts, an outcome he never would have supported.[145] The consultation of Zoroastrian texts in the post-*Limbuwállá* cases was virtually nonexistent, and when there was witness testimony, it was perfunctory. Davar retraced the process by which a single inept judgment had been mindlessly replicated, crushing what Davar regarded as a centuries-old practice.[146]

In *Tarachand v. Soonabai*, Davar ruled that *muktad* trusts were of public benefit, hence charitable and exempt from the rule against perpetuities. He offered a detailed reading of Zoroastrian theology and ritual practice. Davar explained that the *muktad* days were the holiest days of the year for Parsis and that undertaking the proper ceremonies was a religious duty.[147] These days fell on the last days of the Zoroastrian calendar. They were not tied to any particular individual's death date, unlike commemoration ceremonies held at particular intervals after a person's death.[148] Second, it was the Zoroastrian belief that, for three days after death, the soul hovered in the vicinity of the body. At dawn of the fourth day, the soul ascended to the mythical Chinvat Bridge, also known as the "Bridge of the Separator," for the final judgment by a team of divine powers. After the final judgment, the soul would be sent to the Zoroastrian equivalent of Heaven or Hell. "[T]he *Judgment is irrevocable*," insisted Davar. "There is nothing in the scriptures for the redemption of the soul after the final judgment

---

[144] For a chronology of Modi's life events (in Gujarati with some English), see Modi, *Religious Ceremonies*, 1–30 (terminal section). See also Stausberg, *Die Religion*, II: 106–8; Ringer, *Pious Citizens*, 116–19; Sharafi, "Judging Conversion," 165–70.

[145] *Tarachand v. Soonabai*, 149–51.

[146] Ibid., 153–62. The same snowball effect wreaked havoc on other Bombay communities. For an example affecting the Khojas, see *Jan Mahomed Abdulla Datu v. Jaffer*.

[147] *Tarachand v. Soonabai*, 174.

[148] Davar described individualized death commemoration ceremonies thus: "we have first, ceremonies performed for the benefit of the souls of the dead for the first three days, and on the fourth or Charum day. Then follow the Dasma, or the tenth-day ceremony, next the Massisa, or the thirtieth-day ceremony – next the Chhumsi, or the six-monthly day ceremony, and then the Varsi or the anniversary of the day of death." (*Tarachand v. Soonabai*, 176.)

of the fourth day."[149] Prayers would be of no use to a particular soul more than four days after death, so *muktad* ceremonies could not benefit any individual soul.[150] Third and most famously, Davar pointed out that the *muktad* ceremonies included prayers. Some were for the deceased and his or her family. Others were for the Parsi community. And there were even some for the well-being of all people.[151] Here was Davar's precious public benefit. Because *muktad* ceremonies included prayers for all of humanity, the trusts that funded them were for *public* benefit and could validly exist in perpetuity.

Davar made other less Zoroastrian-specific arguments. Drawing on recent case law addressing Catholics in Ireland, he pointed to the argument that a trust for religious purposes was *by definition* charitable. There was no need to show any additional, particular type of public benefit.[152] Furthermore, there had been much discussion in *Tarachand* of the benefit accruing to Parsi priests, who relied on *muktad* ceremonies for a good part of their meager incomes. The plaintiff Tarachand had argued that putting "money in the pockets of the priests" hardly constituted a public benefit. But the judges in the Irish case found that the trust for Masses was charitable in part because it helped support priests.[153]

Davar's judgment in *Tarachand* was a detailed investigation of Zoroastrian theology and ritual practice. His primary project was to discredit the view that *muktad* ceremonies produced private benefit alone. This was at the heart of Jardine's claim that the provision of benefit *to* and *from* specific individuals (or their souls) made the trust noncharitable and void. As reflected by his early work in trust administration, Davar was driven more by his perception of the community's social needs than by legal doctrine or a model of judicial restraint. In *Tarachand*, he waved precedent aside with breathtaking boldness. Davar claimed not to be bound by an earlier decision if it was based on scanty evidence. Davar had far richer evidence of Parsi custom and belief – not just from the evidence presented to him in court, but also undoubtedly from being Parsi himself. He pointed to the escape clause in Blackstone's definition of *stare decisis*: "this rule admits of *exception, where the former determination [i.e., judgment] is most evidently contrary to reason; much more if it be contrary to the divine law*."[154] For Davar, Jardine's view that *muktad* trusts were for private benefit alone was "*manifestly absurd or unjust*."[155] Davar's *Tarachand* ruling exemplified his willingness to strain conventional legal reasoning for the preservation of religious practice.

Davar's community identity and politics shone through in *Petit v. Jijibhai*, too.[156] The case involved a French woman named Suzanne Brière who had

[149] *Tarachand v. Soonabai*, 176.
[150] Ibid., 176.
[151] Ibid., 180.
[152] *O'Hanlon v. Logue* 1 IR 247 (1906) at 275; cited in *Tarachand v. Soonabai*, 207.
[153] *O'Hanlon v. Logue*, 271; cited in *Tarachand v. Soonabai*, 207.
[154] Blackstone's *Commentaries* (21st ed.) in *Tarachand v. Soonabai*, 147. Italics original.
[155] *Tarachand v. Soonabai*, 147. Italics original.
[156] See Introduction at note 98.

Religious Trusts and the Parsi Legal Profession

married into the illustrious Tata family of Parsi "merchant princes." She was married in a purportedly Zoroastrian ceremony and had been initiated into the religion through the *navjote* ceremony immediately before. Orthodox Zoroastrians challenged the validity of the *navjote* because Mrs. Tata did not have a Parsi father – a necessary precondition for eligibility, in their view. The lawsuit approached the issue of conversion obliquely rather than head on. Did the French Mrs. Tata have the right to benefit from the funds and properties of trusts created for Parsis? Even if Mrs. Tata had become a Zoroastrian (a question the judges avoided), could she be called a Parsi? This question presupposed a semantic distinction between the terms *Parsi* and *Zoroastrian*. Prior to Davar's judgment, the two terms had been used interchangeably.[157] For Davar, however, *Parsi* was a racial term (in the language of the day) whereas *Zoroastrian* was a religious one. His ruling in *Petit* separated the terms with the far-reaching effect that trust deeds framed for the benefit of *Parsis* came to be interpreted in the newly restricted, ethnic sense. The distinction seeped into the everyday speech of Parsis, reflecting the profound social influence of Davar's judgment.[158] Davar put the distinction simply. An English woman could marry a French man and convert to Catholicism, but she would remain English. In the same way, a Parsi could cease to be Zoroastrian by converting to another religion, but could not change the fact that he or she was ethnically Parsi.[159] It was Davar's 1908 judgment that formalized the contraction in the understanding of the term *Parsi*.

Davar made many other arguments in *Petit*. It was true that ancient Zoroastrian texts not only permitted conversion to Zoroastrianism, but encouraged it – a position that was only logical given that the religion must have gained adherents, by definition, when it began. Since their arrival in India, however, Parsis had not accepted converts into the fold. And customary practice trumped text, according to Davar.[160] He also made a floodgates argument: if ethnic outsiders were permitted to benefit from Parsi trust funds and properties, India's lower castes would convert in huge numbers to avail themselves of the Parsis' vast charitable funds. In crassly economic terms, they would deplete Parsi wealth.[161]

---

[157] See, for instance, the case of an alleged Parsi convert to Judaism: "Testimony of B. A. Wadia, taken on commission in London, given oath on the Old Testament" in "Return of Commission to take Evidence in London," 17–20 in *Ghandy v. Wadia*, Suit No. 52 of 1903 (BHC); reproduced in Sharafi, "Bella's Case," 420–8 and discussed at 159–60. See also *Ghandy v. Wadia*.

[158] See Writer, 148; "Second Accused's Statement," *WRTOS* (22 August 1914), 49. For instances of the general use of the term *Parsi Zoroastrian* after 1908, see coverage of three Parsi defamation cases by *WRTOS*: "The Parsi Dispute. Another Defamation Suit," 40; "The Parsi Dispute. Application in Revision" (23 May 1914), 44; "Parsi Defamation Case. The Community in Rangoon" (19 June 1914), 2; "Parsi Defamation Case. The Anjuman Meeting" (1 August 1914), 42.

[159] *Parsi Panchayat Case (Davar)*, 59–60.

[160] *Petit v. Jijibhai*, 532–3.

[161] Ibid., 551. See also Sharafi, "Bella's Case," 197–205.

270 *Law and Identity in Colonial South Asia: Parsi Legal Culture*

Together, the *Limbuwállá* and *Petit* cases epitomized the phenomenon that became possible as South Asians rose to the upper ranks of the colonial judiciary. Judges could rule in their own communities' intragroup disputes, shaping these groups' legal ethnography in the mold of the judges' own politics. Dinshah Davar revalidated trusts funding *muktad* ceremonies. He ruled against the entitlement of ethnic outsiders to enjoy trust property in the hugely divisive conversion debate. Even in his unreported work on the administration of trusts, he pushed certain types of developments over others, shaping the microprocesses of religious life at the local, spatial level. Nowhere did law more clearly meet Zoroastrian theology and ritual than in Davar's courtroom.

LITIGATION, TRUSTS, AND CHARITY

Charity was a theme that permeated these suits – and not just because the trusts themselves had charitable aims. The Parsi legal professionals who became involved often did so because they supported one side personally. Some even waived their fees.[162] Dinshah Davar may have accepted a judgeship despite the drop in income out of a charitable impulse toward his own community.[163] He was not the only one to combine law and charity. Parsi solicitors and magistrates gave up evenings and weekends to act as informal mediators among their co-religionists, particularly those in troubled marriages. Elite Parsis acted as delegates of the Parsi Chief Matrimonial Court on an unpaid basis. Given the large number of underprivileged female plaintiffs who approached that court, charity may have been an important motive.

Most Parsi lawyers were paid when they acted in Parsi–Parsi lawsuits. But this, too, had a potentially charitable twist. In Parsi trust suits, judges normally charged all sides' legal fees to the trust.[164] What this meant was that the parties, usually trustees, had no *personal* financial reason to stay out of court. Granted, they may have had to provide money up front for certain kinds of legal expenses. But they would normally be reimbursed later from the trust funds. In other words, the litigation would ultimately be free for the litigants as individuals. This fact was significant: fees in these suits could be staggering.[165]

The upshot was the diversion of charitable funds: instead of going to the neediest members of the community, large chunks of Parsi trust funds paid lawyers. A *Hindi Punch* cartoon depicted the phenomenon with alacrity during

---

[162] For example, see Mistry, *Reminiscences* [1911], 78.

[163] See 257. By contrast, when offered a judicial position with a salary of Rs 1,500 per month, then barrister Mohammad Ali Jinnah declined. He aimed to earn Rs 1,500 *per day*. [Nisar Ahmad Pannoun, *Jinnah the Lawyer* (Lahore: Mansoor Book House, 1976), vii.]

[164] See *Jijibhoy Muncherji Jijibhoy v. Byramji Jijibhoy* ILR 18 Bom 189 (1894); *Tarachand v. Soonabai*, 213; *Petit v. Jijibhai*, 557; untitled entry on 1913 Parsi trust suit decided by D. D. Davar in Patel and Paymaster, V: 178.

[165] See, for example, *Udvāḍā*, 11; *Petit v. Jijibhai*, 561; Desai, *History*, 26; Sharafi, "Bella's Case," 387–90.

FIGURE 6.5. "The Vultures."
Source: *HP* (13 Dec.1908), 21. Courtesy of the British Library SV576.

the proceedings in *Petit v. Jijibhai* (Figure 6.5). Two vultures – the agents of Zoroastrian death rites by exposure –appeared dressed as barristers in black gowns and white collar bands. Grinning and bespectacled, each had a bundle of papers tucked under his wing, one labeled "plaintiffs' costs" and the other "defendants' costs." The two were perched on a huge sack of coins representing the funds of the Parsi Panchayat. They were happily helping themselves. "Ha, ha, ha, ha! Jolly this, to feed on somebody else's sinews!" chortled one bird to the other. The caption declared that the judges in *Petit v. Jijibhai* had allowed both sides of the dispute to take their legal costs from the funds of the Parsi Panchayat. "This looks like fining a third party for the sins of the combatants."[166]

The illustrated weekly's cynicism was perhaps misplaced. The funds intended to help the neediest of Parsis were instead being spent on lawsuits. Parsi philanthropy was subsidizing Parsi litigation. But the fact that so many of the lawyers were Parsi themselves meant that much of the money never left the community. On the one hand, money intended to spawn cooperation and generosity between Parsis was funding conflict. But, on the other, it was diverted from one collective

---

[166] "The Vultures," *HP* (13 December 1908), 21.

aim – charitable aid to the neediest – to another: the acquisition of fluency in colonial law. Parsi familiarity with the structures and language of the colonial legal system brought increased autonomy and control. If the vulture barristers gorging themselves on *panchayat* funds could have stepped back, they may have observed that there were benefits more principled than the simple greed animating them. Of course, legal profiteering was not the only way to achieve the type of mobilization developed among Parsis. But self-interest helped produce a pool of Parsi lawyers large enough to further another perhaps coincidental and unanticipated aim: the creation of a bubble of semiautonomy within the courts and, with it, of a state-endorsed, Parsi-authored account of Parsi history and religion.

CONCLUSION

Parsi disputing behavior was oriented not toward exit from the state but rather toward infiltration of its institutions and assimilation of its methods. Unlike minorities that pursued separatism or that moved to a place at which they could become the majority, the Parsis stayed where they were, increasing their control over the legal processes that affected them through a two-pronged approach. The first prong was the pursuit of legislation by and for Parsis, creating a body of Parsi personal law governing marriage and inheritance. The second was semi-control of intragroup litigation by Parsis in the colonial courts. The first Parsis who lobbied for colonial legislation in the 1830s–'60s must have seen clearly what they needed to do and what benefits could result. The road to colonial legislation was sufficiently straight and clear, if not necessarily easy, that its pursuit could be described as a deliberate strategy.

The route to increased control of litigation was different. Particularly in the mainstream colonial courts (as opposed to the Parsi matrimonial courts), nobody could have known exactly where it would lead or if all the pieces would fit together in a productive way. And yet they did by a fortuitous intersection of conditions – both heavy intragroup litigation and a significant presence in the legal profession.[167] From the late nineteenth century on, disputes about the proper administration of Parsi charitable trusts began coming to court in growing numbers. From about the same time, Parsis started rising to the upper ranks of the legal profession in Bombay. With the appointment of the first Parsi

---

[167] For cases in which all of the advocates and solicitors' firms were Parsi (or in which the firms had at least one Parsi founding partner), see *Ardeshir Dadabhoy Baria and others v. Dadabhoy Rustomjee Baria and another* ILR 69 Bom 493 (1945); joined cases of *In re Shapurji Ratanji Tata and Pirojshah Ratanji Tata, insolvents, and Shapurji Ratanji Tata and another v. Byramji Muncherji Tata and another* ILR 1945 Bom 395. An all-Parsi cast was particularly common in the PCMC, where post-1906, a Parsi judge from the Bombay High Court was usually named presiding judge. See, for instance, *Cowasji Nusserwanji Patuck v. Shehra Cowasji Patuck* ILR 1938 Bom 75. The Bombay Parsi Panchayat frequently turned to Parsi lawyers for their professional advice. See Desai, *History*, 159–60, 222–5, 237–50, 299–301, 338–9, 376.

Religious Trusts and the Parsi Legal Profession 273

judge in the Bombay High Court, the pieces locked. Parsi trust suits and their Parsi lawyers found themselves in Dinshah Davar's court. Drawing on his own personal knowledge and an increasingly orthodox vision of Parsi identity, Davar crafted the judicial ethnography of his own community. He extended the Parsi *comprador* tradition from the world of trade into the world of law. South Asians had been acting as officials in the colonial legal system since the beginning of East India Company rule. However, it was only from Davar's period that they began acting in the same capacity as European judges and in the highest courts of India and the empire. Davar's work on the bench captured the potential of South Asian judges ruling on their own communities' religious affairs. There were other Parsi judges after him and other Zoroastrian trust suits that they decided.[168] But Davar's career best illuminated the magic moment that occurred for Parsis, even if it came with the inevitable pain and suffering of in-fighting on the public stage.

---

[168] See, for instance, Suit No. 243 of 1928: *Jalbhoy Rustomji and others v. Dinbai Jalbhoy and others* (20 February 1928) in "Hon. Justice J.D. Davar. Judgments (10 August 1927–5 April 1928)," 213–22; Suit No. 609 of 1946: *Major Ratan A. Bacha v. Def.* (16 April 1946), "Hon. Justice N.H. C. Coyajee. Short Causes and Motions (16 March 1943–3 October 1947)," 5–6; Suit No. 516 of 1943: *Ardeshir Bhicaji Malwa v. Kekobad Bhicaji Malwa* (11 August 1943), "Hon. Justice N.H. C. Coyajee. Judgments (2 March 1943–20 December 1944)" (all BHC).

7

Pure Parsi

Libel, Race, and Group Membership

"Do your people enjoy having arguments?" A London lawyer quizzed a Parsi witness named Spittama Cama during a 1929 libel suit between Parsis in England. The courtroom broke into laughter at Cama's reply: "Perhaps, in a friendly way, we may."[1] In fact, there was nothing friendly about the arguments that flared into lawsuits between Parsis. The initiation of legal action signaled the metamorphosis of personal relations, a rude push out of the social into the world of state law and sanctions. Nowhere was the transformation more jarring than in libel suits, which aimed to convert gossip – that glue of social life – into civil wrongs and crimes.[2] In many circles, gossip about group members flowed freely within the group but remained beyond reach to outsiders. The rich crop of libel suits between Parsis suggested a different reality among them. Some Parsi libel suits were simply the product of animosity between individuals. The more interesting cases married acidic personal relations with larger disagreements over principle, including the rules of membership in the community itself.[3] Like the most famous religious trust suits among Parsis, these libel suits turned on the question: "who is a Parsi?" In answer, some litigants drew on Parsi eugenics, a body of race theory popularized in the early twentieth century by the prominent Bombay solicitor and orthodox Zoroastrian, J.J. Vimadalal. They also reached for a newly amplified sense of Persianness.

---

[1] "Parsi Libel Suit in London," *TI* (27 July 1929), 11. I am grateful to John E. McLeod for bringing this case to my attention.

[2] See Max Gluckman, "Gossip and Scandal," *Current Anthropology* 4:3 (1963), 307–16.

[3] Legal scholars have observed that libel law is often about the articulation of the group membership principle. See Robert C. Post, "The Social Foundations of Defamation Law: Reputation and the Constitution," *California Law Review* 74:3 (1986), 691–742; Leora Bilsky, "The Habibi libel trial: Defamation and the Hidden-Community Basis of Criminal Law," *U. Toronto LJ.* 61:4 (2011), 617–55.

274

Pure Parsi: Libel, Race, and Group Membership 275

Across the Anglosphere, defamation suits turned on accusations of racial impurity. In the United States, individuals accused of being black sued to defend their reputation as white.[4] In colonial India and Burma, Parsis sued each other for the insinuation that some were not of pure Parsi stock but of mixed Asian lineage. Until the twentieth century, the patrilineal principle of group membership had applied among Parsis: to be eligible for religious initiation into the Zoroastrian religion, one needed to have a Parsi father. The ethnicity of one's mother did not matter. From the early twentieth century, a more restrictive and racialized conception of group membership took shape, requiring that one's mother also be ethnically Parsi. As litigants vied to have their preferred model of group identity endorsed by the state, libel law became a vehicle for the constriction of social rules. Like the most publicized trust suits between Parsis, these libel suits reflected the Parsi proclivity to take core questions about group membership – who was in and who was out – into the colonial courtroom.

The study of race and racial discourse in British India has concentrated on European perceptions of racial difference.[5] Until recently, historians of eugenics similarly made a staple of white people's understandings of racial purity and degeneration.[6] Libel suits between Parsis reflected racial self-perceptions from a South Asian perspective and revealed racial attitudes *between colonized*

---

[4] See *Morris v. State* 160 S.W. 387. In H. T. Catterall, ed. *Judicial Cases Concerning American Slavery and the Negro* (Shannon, Ireland: Irish University Press, 1968), see: *Eden v. Legare* (1791), II: 274; *King ads. Wood* (1818), II: 307; *Atkinson v. Hartley* (1821), II: 317; *Scott v. Peebles* (1844), III: 299; *Cauchoix v. Dupuy* (1831), III: 493; *Boullemet v. Philips* (1842), III: 546; *Dobard v. Nunez* (1851), III: 614; *Johnson v. Brown* (1832), IV: 187; *Linney v. Maton* (1855), V: 290. See also Ariela Gross, *What Blood Won't Tell: A History of Race on Trial in America* (Cambridge, MA: Harvard University Press, 2008), 64–70.

[5] For example, see Kolsky, *Colonial Justice*; Harald Fischer-Tiné, *Low and Licentious Europeans: Race, Class, and 'White subalternity' in Colonial India* (Delhi: Orient BlackSwan 2009); Ballhatchet; Peter Robb, ed. *The Concept of Race in South Asia* (Delhi: Oxford University Press, 1995); Mark Harrison, *Climates and Constitutions: Health, Race Environment and British Imperialism in India, 1600–1850* (Delhi: Oxford University Press, 1999).

[6] For example, see Mark B. Adams, ed., *The Well Born Science: Eugenics in Germany, France, Brazil and Russia* (New York: Oxford University Press, 1990); William Schneider, *Quality and Quantity: The Quest for Biological Regeneration in Twentieth-Century France* (Cambridge: Cambridge University Press, 1990); Marius Turda and Paul J. Weindling, eds., *"Blood and Homeland": Eugenics and Racial Nationalism in Central and Southeast Europe, 1900–1940* (Budapest: Central European University Press, 2007). For recent exceptions, see Ruth Rogaski, *Hygienic Modernity: Meanings of Health and Disease in Treaty-Port China* (Berkeley: University of California Press, 2004), 240–4; Cyrus Schayegh, *Who Is Knowledgeable, Is Strong: Science, Class and the Formation of Modern Iranian Society, 1900–1950* (Berkeley: University of California Press, 2009), 110–56; Sarah Hodges, "South Asia's Eugenic Past," in *The Oxford Handbook of Eugenics*, eds. Alison Bashford and Philippa Levine (Oxford: Oxford University Press, 2010), 228–42; Cyrus Schayegh, "Eugenics in Interwar Iran," in Bashford and Levine, 449–61; Gregory Michael Dorr and Angela Logan, "'Quantity, Not Mere Quantity, Counts': Black Eugenics and the NAACP Baby Contests," in *A Century of Eugenics in America: From the Indiana Experiment to the Human Genome Era*, ed. Paul A. Lombardo (Bloomington: Indiana University Press, 2011), 68–92.

populations as much as between colonizer and colonized. Whereas the last chapter asked how religious doctrine and practice were shaped in the colonial courtroom, this one shifts to the notions of racial purity and degeneration that lay at the heart of a cluster of libel suits linking Rangoon and Bombay during the 1910s. Despite the growing negative connotations associated with communalism during this period, orthodox Parsis pressed for strong community boundaries from the beginning of *Petit v. Jijibhai* in 1906 onward.[7] For many in this small minority, the dilution resulting from racial intermixing implied a kind of collective death. The trials reflected shifting notions of purity – from ritual to racial – and a new nostalgia for Persia as it was imagined by a community that had left many centuries before. Seeing themselves as Persian allowed Parsis to hold themselves at arm's length from the other Asians and Britons among whom they lived and mixed. It offered an origins narrative that was not just about religion and culture, but also about race, and that was equally sustainable both at the height of British rule and as Indian independence approached.

DEFAMATION PARSI STYLE

Speech-based wrongs came in four varieties under British Indian law: obscenity, seditious libel, criminal defamation, and civil defamation.[8] The first three were criminal offenses. Obscenity applied to acts, publications, and songs that "annoyed" others in public and had the tendency "to deprive and corrupt" those whose minds would be open to immoral influences.[9] A special exception was made for religious sculptures, paintings, and engravings, creating space for the occasional eroticism of Hindu temple art.[10] Seditious libel (the written variety of sedition) was the colonial state's favorite tool for suppressing nationalist newspapers at the turn of the twentieth century.[11] It carried a discretionary sentence of transportation for life.[12]

Civil defamation was a tort. It was part of the catchall category of civil wrongs that fell outside of the explicit obligations undertaken between individuals by contract. In other words, it was a violation of an implicit duty not to cause harm to others where no specific agreement had been made. Within civil

---

[7] On the evolution of communalism as a term, see Tejani, 22, 113–43.

[8] See IPC 1860, ss. 124A, 292–4, and 499–502 in Ranchhoddas and Thakore, *IPC*, 109–12, 238–9, 444–62; Ratanlal Ranchhoddas and Dhirajlal Keshavlal Thakore, *Law of Torts* (Bombay: Bombay Law Reporter Office, 1921), 170–221.

[9] IPC 1860, ss. 292–4 in Ranchhoddas and Thakore, *IPC*, 238–9. See also Deana Heath, *Purifying Empire: Obscenity and the Politics of Moral Regulation in Britain, India and Australia* (Cambridge: Cambridge University Press, 2010), 148–205.

[10] Ranchhoddas and Thakore, *IPC*, 239.

[11] See, for instance, *Queen-Empress v. Jogendra Chunder Bose* ILR 19 Cal 35 (1892); *Queen-Empress v. Bal Gangadhar Tilak and Keshav Mahadev Bal* ILR 22 Bom 112 (1897). See also 253.

[12] IPC 1860, s. 124A in Ranchhoddas and Thakore, *IPC*, 109–12.

Pure Parsi: Libel, Race, and Group Membership

defamation, there was slander (the oral form) and libel (the written). Libel was a false statement made in some form of writing that was "published" or communicated to a person other than the subject. It had to injure the reputation of the subject, bringing him or her "into hatred, contempt or ridicule," doing damage to his or her reputation in a profession or trade, or causing the person to be shunned by his or her neighbors.[13] The alleged defamer could protect him- or herself through a variety of defences. These included the claim that the statement was true ("justification") or a fair and bona fide comment on a matter of public interest; or that the context made the statement privileged, whether because it was uttered in a protected setting like a legislature or court ("absolute privilege") or because it was made out of a sense of social or moral duty, self-protection, or the protection of a common interest shared by alleged defamer and recipient ("qualified privilege").[14] Civil defamation was a cause of action entailing damages – monetary compensation for loss – rather than the fines, incarceration, or transportation of the criminal law.

Criminal defamation was a creation of the Indian Penal Code (IPC). Here, the offending statement could be spoken (criminal slander) or more commonly written (criminal libel). It could take the form of words, signs, or "visible representations."[15] Unlike civil defamation, the criminal variety required malice: the defamer had to intend to harm the reputation of the subject or have reason to believe that the statement would cause such harm. The IPC described harm to a person's reputation as an imputation that "directly or indirectly, in the estimation of others, lowers the moral or intellectual character of that person, or lowers the character of that person in respect of his caste or of his calling, or lowers the credit of the person, or causes it to be believed that the body of that person is in a loathsome state, or in a state generally considered disgraceful."[16]

A long list of exceptions provided the accused with defenses. These covered situations in which the statement was true and made for the public good. Equally, a bona fide statement would not constitute criminal defamation when it was expressed for the good of the accused or some other person or when the accused had lawful authority over the person targeted by the statement and was entitled to comment on the matter in question. It was also a defense to criminal defamation to show that the statement was made in good faith respecting any public question or performance or regarding the conduct of a public servant in the discharge of his official duties. The courtroom statements of judges and most advocates, reports of court proceedings that were substantially true, and fair comment made in good faith on any court case would also not constitute

---

[13] Ranchhoddas and Thakore, *Law of Torts*, 170; Nayan H. Pandia, "Defamation," *All LJ* 10 (1912), 58.

[14] Ranchhoddas and Thakore, *Law of Torts*, 191–218.

[15] IPC 1860, s. 499 in Ranchhoddas and Thakore, *IPC*, 444.

[16] Ibid.

278   *Law and Identity in Colonial South Asia: Parsi Legal Culture*

criminal defamation.[17] The maximum punishment for this offense was a prison term of up to two years, a fine, or both.[18] Private prosecutions were not uncommon in this period; they were the only way a criminal defamation suit could be launched.[19] Civil defamation was decided by a judge alone. By contrast, criminal defamation could be tried by a judge and special jury, whose members were generally more elite than normal jurors.[20]

Defamation suits were a risky business for the people who initiated them. If one claimed to be the target of defamation, the suit itself could draw more attention to the alleged slur than did the original statement.[21] At the same time, initiating a defamation suit sent a powerful signal, reflecting the purported victim's utter rejection of the statement. For some, the social value of showing outrage may have outweighed the risks of adding publicity or losing the case. There was also the fact that many plaintiffs seemed to want a public apology more than damages or a criminal sentence. Defamation suits often ended in out of court settlements, with published apologies at the heart of the negotiated deals. Together, these factors created an intriguing mixture of incentives to start, but not necessarily finish, a defamation suit in court. As a result, few libel suits between Parsis actually proceeded to judgment. But even these beginnings said important things about the construction of collective identity through law. Suits over reputation revealed the role of sexual behavior especially in defining community boundaries.

Most speech-related suits between Parsis were for libel. Typically, Parsis sued Gujarati-language Parsi-run newspapers and the people who published articles in them.[22] There were daily newspapers like *Jam-e-Jamshed, Bombay Samachar, Kaiser-i-Hind,* and *Sanj Vartaman* (Guj. *Sāñj Vartamān*).[23] There were weeklies like the *Satya Mitra* and *Rast Goftar* (Guj. *Rāst Gophtār*).[24] There were bilingual Anglo-Gujarati weeklies featuring political satirical cartoons, such as *Hindi Punch*. The newspaper, originally named *Parsee Punch* (Guj. *Pārsī Pañc*), was

---

[17] Ibid., 444–58 (IPC 1860, ss. 499–500).

[18] Ibid., 448–62 (IPC 1860, ss. 500–2).

[19] See Code of Criminal Procedure 1898, s. 198 in D. E. Cranenburgh, *The Code of Criminal Procedure being Act V of 1898 as Amended up to 1923* (Calcutta: Law-Publishing Press, 1924), 128–9. On a private prosecution for perjury originating in a Parsi matrimonial suit, see "The Police Courts. Alleged Perjury," *TI* (10 October 1891), 3.

[20] Compare *Nadirshaw H. Sukhia v. P. R. Ratnagar* 15 Bom LR 130 (1913) at 135, 139, 154, 159; "The Bhownugger Defamation Cases," *TI* (8 July 1890), 6. See also Chapter 5 at 199.

[21] On the amplification effect in British seditious libel cases, see Kathryn Temple, *Scandal Nation: Law and Authorship in Britain, 1750–1832* (Ithaca, NY: Cornell University Press, 2003), 198–9.

[22] See B. K. Karanjia, "Parsi Pioneers of the Press (1822–1915)," in Godrej and Punthakey Mistree, 479–82; Ratan Rustamji Marshal, *Gujarātī Patrakāritvano Itihās* (Surat: Sahitya Sangam, 2005).

[23] See Rasik Jhaverī, *Muṁbaī Samācār Doḍhso Varsni Tavārīkh* (*The Bombay Samachar 1822–1972*) (Bombay: Bombay Samachar, 1972) (Guj.).

[24] See Palsetia, *Parsis,* 190–1. The Gujarati transliteration of *Satya Mitra* and its Anglicized form were identical.

Pure Parsi: Libel, Race, and Group Membership

Parsi-edited and modeled itself upon London's legendary *Punch*. (Its name change to "Hindi" was an attempt to broaden its audience and reflected the usage of the day, in which "Hindi" meant Indian.[25]) Another favorite newspaper for comic relief was *Gup-Sup* (Guj. *Gapsap*), meaning chitchat or gossip.[26] Monthly newspapers like *Cherag* (Guj. *Cerāg*) were read by a predominantly Parsi audience. Elite Parsis also followed and contributed to the English-language press, including the nationalist *Bombay Chronicle* (created by the Parsi lawyer and early nationalist politician Pherozeshah Mehta); the conservative staple of Anglo-India, *The Times of India* (co-founded by a Parsi); and others like the *Bombay Gazette* and the more subversive *Advocate of India*.[27] It was against the Gujarati-language press, though, that most libel cases were filed. Some discussion of translation issues arose in court, particularly when British lawyers and judges were involved in a case and struggled to appreciate the full meaning of the original text.[28] When a Parsi judge like magistrate D. N. D. Khandalavala heard a libel case, he could appreciate the subtleties of Parsi Gujarati in its untranslated form.[29] Here was yet another way in which the assignment of Parsi cases to Parsi judges held appeal. In addition to the political incentives noted in the last chapter, the unofficial policy must have provided the colonial bureaucracy with a linguistic and cultural shortcut, facilitating greater institutional efficiency in a court system plagued by arrears and delays.[30]

Statements that formed the bases of Parsi defamation suits were typically about sex.[31] Some, like the one at the heart of *Karkaria v. Mistri* (1923), attacked the sexual reputation of Parsi women. Elsewhere in the English-speaking world, most defamation suits involving women in the nineteenth and early twentieth centuries turned on attacks on female chastity.[32] Parsi suits were

---

[25] See Ritu G. Khanduri, "Vernacular Punches: Cartoons and Politics in Colonial India," *History and Anthropology* 20:4 (2009), 470; Mushirul Hasan, *Wit and Wisdom: Pickings from the Parsee Punch* (Delhi: Niyogi Press, 2012). On Indian variants of *Punch*, see Khanduri, 459–86; Partha Mitter, *Art and Nationalism in Colonial India, 1850–1922* (Cambridge: Cambridge University Press, 1994); Elizabeth Lhost, "Political Cartooning – 1870–present (India)," in *Encyclopedia of Social Movement Media*, ed. John Downing (Thousand Oaks, CA: Sage, 2011), 405–6.

[26] See *Vatchagandy v. Vatchagandy*, 63–4.

[27] Framjee Cowasjee Banaji (1786–1851) was a founder of the *Bombay Times*, which later became the *Times of India*. (Darukhanawala, *Parsi Lustre*, I: 337.)

[28] See, for instance, "The Charge of Defamation on the Editor of the 'Parsee Punch,'" *TI* (8 January 1874), 3; "The Charge of Defamation against a Parsee Editor," *TI* (11 April 1882), 3.

[29] See suit against Pestanji Firozshah Kapadia and *Dadachanji v. Bharucha and Hirjibehdin* (both of 1937) in Patel and Paymaster, VII: 346 and 364, respectively.

[30] As Chief Justice of the Bombay High Court (1919–26), Norman Macleod's top priority was the reduction of case arrears. See Sharafi, "Two Lives," 269–70.

[31] On a similar intracommunity case in a non-Parsi context (the Maharaj libel case), see Shodhan, *Question*, 148–88; J. Barton Scott, "Libeled Subjects: Religious Selfhood in the Maharaj Libel Case," 40th Annual Conference on South Asia (Madison, 21 October 2011).

[32] See Lawrence M. Friedman, *Guarding Life's Dark Secrets: Legal and Social Controls over Reputation, Propriety, and Privacy* (Stanford, CA: Stanford University Press, 2007), 49–53;

FIGURE 7.1. Mrs. Mistry's future lawyer, Parsi advocate P. B. Vachha (center) with two Parsi associates circa 1909.
Source: Private collection. Courtesy of R. P. Vachha.

no different. When Dinshaw Edalji Karkaria accused his neighbor's wife, Mrs. Mistry, of having an affair with her husband's relative, Mr. Mistry initiated a criminal suit that led to Karkaria's conviction for defamation.[33] Mrs. Mistry herself then launched a successful civil suit against Karkaria for slander. She won damages of Rs 1,000, "a princely sum in 1926."[34] Many of the lawyers and judges in the case were Parsi, including Mrs. Mistry's advocate, the Persianist and legal historian, P. B. Vachha (Figure 7.1). He successfully argued that because adultery was a crime in India (unlike in England), the allegation of adultery was per se damaging and required no proof of the additional "special damage" that was required by English law.[35]

S. M. Waddams, *Sexual Slander in Nineteenth-Century England: Defamation in the Ecclesiastical Courts, 1815–1855* (Toronto: University of Toronto Press, 2000), 7.
[33] *Dinshaw Edalji Karkaria v. Jehangir Cowasji Mistri* ILR 47 Bom 15 (1923).
[34] Fali Nariman, "Legal Lessons," *Parsiana* 23:1 (2000), 152.
[35] *Hirabai Jehangir Mistry v. Dinshaw Edulji Karkaria* ILR 51 Bom 167 (1927). On the work of P. B. Vachha, see his *Famous Judges*; *Firdousi and the Shahnama: A Study of the Great Epic of the Homer of the East* (Delhi: Universal, 2011); *Prose and Verse* (Bombay: R. P. Vachha, 1970). See also *Jamshed A. Irani v. Banu J. Irani* 68 Bom LR (1966) 794 at 797–801.

Pure Parsi: Libel, Race, and Group Membership

Because female chastity was a central component of family reputation, insinuations about Parsi women were also attacks on the women's male family members – a phenomenon implied by the fact that it was Mr. Mistry, not his wife, who launched the first defamation suit against Karkaria. The 1882 case of *Kabraji v. Lungra*, a criminal suit between rival newspaper editors, was another classic instance of female sexual reputation acting as a proxy for male respectability.[36] Muncherjee Cowasjee Lungra was editor of the Gujarati-language weekly, *Satya Mitra*. He was also "Mansukh," the author of the 1888 book criticizing Parsi matrimonial law. Lungra had taken a disliking to Kaikhosro N. Kabrajee, who edited the daily Gujarati paper *Rast Goftar*. Lungra associated *Rast Goftar* with reformist, excessively Westernizing impulses. The magistrate, a Briton named Ryan, observed that Lungra had worked himself into "a state of unreasonable indignation" and that he came to regard Kabrajee as "A monster of such horrid mien, That to be hated needs but to be seen."[37]

Over a two-year period, Lungra published a series of attacks on Kabrajee in Lungra's own paper. Lungra suggested that Kabrajee encouraged Parsi women to give up the traditional white head covering known as the *mathabana* (Guj. *māthābānū*), and to sit in public among non-Parsi men (Figure 7.2). Kabrajee allegedly corrupted women and children, including his own daughters, by parading them on stage during musical recitals he organized.[38] Kabrajee found these practices immodest by orthodox standards.[39] Worse, though, was Kabrajee's insinuation that Lungra's unmarried seventeen-year-old daughter had fallen pregnant and been whisked out of Bombay to avoid disgracing the family.[40] The magistrate acknowledged the background context of journalistic rivalry and that a certain degree of verbal jousting had to be expected. Everyone in the case must have remembered a libel suit launched by Kabrajee himself against Nusserwanjee Dorabjee Apakhtyar, the founding editor of *Parsee Punch*, eight years earlier in 1874.[41] All the same, the magistrate felt that the statements went beyond the limits of fair criticism because they did not always address topics of public concern: "the law rigorously protects the sanctity of private life, and while allowing the fullest freedom of criticism of those things which call for public comment, will not allow any departure from it violating that privacy which is jealously cherished by society." He ruled in favor of Kabrajee, imposing a Rs 1,000 fine on Lungra, in default of which Lungra

---

[36] For another criminal libel suit between the families of two Parsi newspaper editors, see "Bombay Editor Sentenced," *TI* (1 July 1942), 7.

[37] "The Charge of Defamation against a Parsee Editor," *TI* (5 July 1882), 3. The judge was borrowing from Alexander Pope's description of vice. [Alexander Pope, *An Essay on Man*, ed. Mark Pattison (Oxford: Clarendon Press, 1881), 44 (lines 217–18).]

[38] "Charge of Defamation," *TI* (5 July 1882), 3.

[39] "The Charge of Defamation against a Parsee Editor," *TI* (28 March 1882), 3; (3 July 1882), 3.

[40] "The Charge of Defamation against a Parsee Editor" (11 April 1882).

[41] "The Charge of Defamation on the Editor of the 'Parsee Punch."

FIGURE 7.2. A domestic scene with a Parsi woman shown wearing the *mathabana* or traditional female head covering.
Source: *HP* (11 September 1910), 15. Courtesy of the British Library SV576.

would serve three months in prison. Lungra's supporters remained undaunted. The case concluded with cheers from his Parsi schoolboy supporters in the gallery.[42]

Although female chastity was an essential part of the reputation of male family members, it also played a role in the reputation of institutions, particularly sex-specific ones. In the early 1930s, Miss Phiroja Merwan Irani and her twin sister were expelled from their Parsi girls' school on the basis of allegations made against their chastity by a member of the Bombay branch of the Social Purity League. The League was an organization that existed across the English-speaking world to combat "social evils" like prostitution, alcoholism, and gambling.[43] The League had many Parsi members in Bombay and was the driving force behind a series of criminal prosecutions in the 1930s against Parsi adults for luring young Parsi women (including family members) into

---

[42] "Charge of Defamation," *TI* (5 July 1882), 3.
[43] "Social Purity League. Annual General Meeting," *TI* (17 March 1930), 5.

Pure Parsi: Libel, Race, and Group Membership

prostitution.[44] The defendant in the libel suit, a Parsi League worker named Bhikaji M. Karanjia, had been given the job of reporting to the League any "suspicious cases" that came to his notice.[45] He had initially urged the girls' school to have its students medically examined annually, presumably to confirm their virginity. The Lady Superintendent, a Parsi named Miss Kapadia, refused. The idea was "improper."[46] The defendant then volunteered information he claimed to have received in an anonymous letter about the twins' sexual behavior.[47] This time, the superintendent was more receptive. If the girls were not sent away, the school's reputation would suffer. On the basis of Karanjia's tip and under the influence of the secretary of the Social Purity League (another Parsi named Hormusjee Cursetji Giara), Miss Kapadia dismissed the twins and denied them good character certificates, a fact that would prevent any other school from admitting them.[48] She subsequently learned that there was no truth to the allegations and readmitted the sisters.[49] In court, Karanjia was convicted and fined Rs 500. He also apologized. The magistrate berated him for not attempting to discover whether there was any merit to the allegations before repeating them. Karanjia had also told the court that Giara, the head of the League, had engineered the whole episode in retaliation for Karanjia's identification of financial irregularities within the League.[50] The magistrate took no notice, emphasizing instead the persistence of the girls' mother, who pushed the case through court. But for her "brave action and conduct," her daughters' "future career" – their marriage prospects – "would have been completely ruined."[51]

Although many Parsi libel suits were about sex, not all turned on statements alleging female misconduct. Some were aimed at men. This cluster of cases was rooted in two features peculiar to the Parsi context: a heightened awareness among Parsis of their own shrinking minority status (understood in increasingly racial terms) and the necessity of ritual purity for Zoroastrian priests. The statements triggering the Rangoon libel suits were about racial impurity and

---

[44] In the *TI*, see "Parsi Youth in a Kidnapping Case. Story of Betrothal" (19 September 1931), 4; "Parsi Girl in Social Vice Court Case. Her Grandmother and Uncle Charged" (22 July 1932), 9; "Charge of Procuring Minor Girl for Immoral Purposes. Assignation at Victoria Terminus. Dramatic Arrest at Bombay Restaurant" (4 September 1931), 11; "'Miss A' in Bombay Social Vice Case. Girl's Name Not to be Mentioned. Huge Crowd of Parsis to Witness Sessions Trial of Accused" (14 October 1931), 11; "Living on Earnings of Prostitution. Girl Re-examined" (30 October 1931), 12.

[45] "Alleged Defamation of Schoolgirls. Purity League Case," *TI* (18 January 1934), 5.

[46] "Social Purity League Worker in Trouble. Charge of Defamation," *TI* (8 December 1933), 3.

[47] "Parsi Girl's Suit for Defamation. Social Purity League Ex-Official Examined," *TI* (25 January 1934), 11.

[48] "Social Purity League Worker," 3; "Parsi Girl's Suit for Defamation. Social Purity League Ex-Official Examined," *TI* (25 January 1934), 11.

[49] "Schoolgirl Files Suit for Defamation. Asked to Leave School," *TI* (21 December 1933), 4.

[50] "Purity League Case. 'Not Guilty' Please. Accused Denounces Former Secretary," *TI* (31 January 1934), 10.

[51] "Fined Rs. 500 for Defamation. Girl's Complaint," *TI* (21 February 1934), 11.

were grounded in rising disapproval of sex between Parsi men and non-Parsi women. Among Zoroastrian priests, in turn, the accusation of improper sexual behavior (usually extramarital intercommunity sex) was an effective way to damage a man's religious credibility and status. Priestly "fast living" caused ritual pollution, disqualifying priests from performing rituals and earning the accompanying fees. In both contexts, libel suits about male sexual impropriety channeled larger power struggles, whether among priestly clans or between orthodox and liberal Parsis who disagreed about the permissibility of conversion to Zoroastrianism.

The most famous priestly libel suit occurred in 1869, when factional strife between the Sunjana (or Sanjana) and Jamasp Asa priestly clans in Bombay resulted in a criminal libel trial before a special jury.[52] Male Parsis could only perform the ritual work of priests if they were born into priestly families and initiated into the priesthood. In addition, they must have undergone the requisite ritual purification to perform the ceremony in question. Not all Parsis in priestly families made their living as priests, but no Parsi born into a lay family could do so. In retaliation for a letter accusing one of their own members of marrying a non-Parsi woman, Jamsetjee Sorabjee Madun of the Jamasp Asa family published a letter in the *Sunday Review*. He accused Nowrojee Shapoorjee Sunjana, the brother of a high priest of the rival clan, of keeping a non-Parsi mistress – a Muslim courtesan named Papaji – while working as a timber merchant years earlier in a village called Wassind. The letter asserted that at least one child had been born to Sunjana and Papaji, and it insinuated that any daughter would become a prostitute like her mother. It also claimed that Sunjana had eaten food prepared by a Muslim cook, a violation of the Zoroastrian purity laws.[53] These allegations would ruin any priest professionally, and Nowrojee had been earning a living as a priest since leaving the timber trade. There were ways to purify a priest who had eaten food prepared by a non-Zoroastrian, but no ritual cleansing could purify him if the fornication claims were true.[54] The judge's instructions to the jury communicated clearly that he felt Papaji's testimony was a lie and that she had been bribed and coached by the rival Jamasp Asa clan.[55] The twelve-member jury, which included a single Parsi, took five minutes to convict

---

[52] For other criminal libel suits between priests, see in the *TI*: "Parsi Priest in Defamation Case" (1 December 1932), 3; "Defamation Charge Against Parsi Priest" (8 December 1932), 3; "Parsi Priest Charged with Defamation" (21 December 1932), 10; "Two Parsi Priests in Defamation Suit" (14 October 1933), 18; "Parsi Defamation Appeal (28 March 1934), 7; "Letter not in Good Faith" (29 March 1934), 4; "Dispute between Parsi Priests" (31 January 1935), 5.

[53] *The Parsee Priest Defamation Case. Full Report of the Trial of Jamsetjee Sorabjee Madun in Her Majesty's High Court at Bombay, for defaming Nowrojee Shapoorjee Sunjana* (Bombay: Dorabjee Eduljee Tata, 1870), 149. See also Daniel Sheffield, "This Town Isn't Big Enough for the Two of Us: Struggles for the High Priestship of Bombay, 1830–1900," 39th Annual Conference on South Asia (Madison, 16 October 2010). I am grateful to Daniel Sheffield for introducing me to this case and sharing this material with me.

[54] *Parsee Priest*, 41, 130–1.

[55] Ibid., 154–76.

Pure Parsi: Libel, Race, and Group Membership

on all counts.[56] The judge gave Madun a nine-month prison sentence and a fine of Rs 2,000, an unusually severe set of penalties.[57] The Sunjana family, noted commentator D. E. Tata, had not only cleared its name but had "earned a public reputation for purity of conduct in following their profession, and their claim upon the respect of their supporters is now greater than ever."[58]

LIBEL AND RACE

Like the priestly suit of 1869, a series of libel cases around the time of World War I focused on Parsi men's sexual behavior outside of the community. Purity was the dominant value underpinning both episodes, but the purity was of different kinds. In the 1860s, cosmopolitan sex by priests was problematic because it threatened their ritual purity. By the 1910s, cosmopolitan sex by all Parsi men was troubling because it threatened their racial purity. The Rangoon libel suits reflected the contest between the old, patrilineal principle and a newer, racialized model of group membership.

In 1914, the Zoroastrian High Priest of the Deccan Plateau came from western India to Burma to initiate a fourteen-year-old girl into the Zoroastrian religion by performing her *navjote*.[59] Bella had been informally adopted by a Parsi couple, Mr. and Mrs. Shapurji Cowasji Captain (Figure 7.3).[60] Bella's natural father was probably the successful and married Parsi lawyer, Bomanji Cowasji Captain. He was the younger brother of the man who adopted Bella. In other words, Bella's adoptive father (Shapurji) was probably her biological uncle, because her adoptive uncle (Bomanji) was probably her biological father. All of this was supposed to be a secret. For public purposes, Bella was presented as the biological child of an Indian Christian man, one Mr. Jones, and a woman who was probably also Indian and non-Parsi, one Mrs. Rebekah Jones.[61]

The Zoroastrian purity laws imposed conditions that made many religious ceremonies difficult if not impossible to perform outside of the Parsi heartland of

---

[56] Ibid., 6, 177. The special jury included seven Britons, one or two Goan Christians, and two Hindus.

[57] Ibid., 180.

[58] Ibid., vii–viii.

[59] See Sanjana, *Ancient Persia*, 612–15.

[60] As a legal device, adoption was controversial across the common-law world circa 1900. See 217–8. In English law, adoption only became legally recognized with the Adoption of Children Act of 1926. Informal adoption occurred before that date, but the parties were strangers in law. See Cretney, 596–8. On the United States, see Hendrik Hartog, "Someday All This Will Be Yours: Inheritance, Adoption, and Obligation in Capitalist America," *Indiana LJ* 79 (2004) 354. In India, adoption by Parsis was denied legal recognition through the lobbying efforts of orthodox Parsis in 1980–1. See Hinnells, *Zoroastrian Diaspora*, 123–4.

[61] See Mitra Sharafi, *Colonial Parsis and Law: A Cultural History. Government Research Fellowship Lectures 2009–2010* (Mumbai: K. R. Cama Oriental Institute, 2010), 67–70; "Bella's Case," 15–60.

FIGURE 7.3. "Bella, the waif."
Source: HP (7 June 1914), 13. Courtesy of the British Library SV576.

Pure Parsi: Libel, Race, and Group Membership

western India. When the high priest came to Lower Burma, Parsis other than Bella were also eager to take advantage of his presence. Mrs. Shapurji Cowasji Captain – Bella's adoptive mother – had her own initiation performed by Dastur Kaikobad. Mrs. and Mr. Captain also underwent the formal Zoroastrian marriage ceremony. Formerly, they had married by Burmese customary rites alone. Another Parsi family, the Contractors, arranged for the initiation of their child, a boy named Behram. None of these ceremonies had been available to the Parsis of Rangoon for decades, if ever.

However, the ritual validity of the Rangoon ceremonies was questionable. It was not clear that Zoroastrian initiation and marriage rites could be correctly performed in Burma by priests who came from India by sea. The priest performing the ceremonies had to be in the highest state of ritual purity, known as *barashnum*. *Barashnum* required that one undergo an elaborate nine-night sequence of purification ceremonies, including the drinking of consecrated bull's urine (*nirang*) and appearing naked before other priests.[62] Orthodox Parsis would contend that the ceremonies remained impossible in Rangoon: both the priest and the bull's urine (required equally for the ceremonies to come) lost their ritual purity on the trip over. Long-distance sea travel violated the Zoroastrian prohibition on polluting the elements: if the trip was long enough, the contents of the ship's toilets had to be dumped into the sea. The other difficulty was the near impossibility of fulfilling one's everyday ritual duties in confined and diversely populated shipboard spaces.[63] Together, the orthodox argued, these factors annulled the ritual purity of any priests and *nirang* crossing a large body of water. But there was no consensus across the orthodox–reformist divide. Perhaps because they recognized the difficulties of ritual life beyond India – in Zanzibar, Aden, Ceylon, and Burma – reformist Zoroastrians overlooked the issue of sea travel and accepted Dastur Kaikobad's Rangoon ceremonies.

Ritual validity was just one of several points on which orthodox and reformist Parsis clashed in Rangoon. The larger controversy centered on the relationship between race and religion. Bella's case was a family dispute, a fight among three brothers, as well as a community conflict. Her leading opponent was Merwanji Cowasji Captain, the elder brother of Bella's adoptive father and the most prominent Parsi in Burma. Popularly dubbed the "Grand Old Man of Burma," Merwanji was an unofficial member of the Provincial Council, a delegate to the Parsi Matrimonial Court in Rangoon, a First-Class Magistrate, a Municipal Commissioner, and the only Parsi from Burma selected to do

---

[62] See Modi, *Religious Ceremonies*, 97–157; Choksy, *Purity*.

[63] "Plaintiffs' Evidence. No. 11: Darab Pesotan Sanjana examined by Vimadalal, taken on Commission. In the Court of Small Causes, Bombay" (8 March [1916]), 230 and (22 March 1916), 287–8; "Defendant's Evidence. No. 30: Evidence of Dastur Kaikobad" (13 May 1916), 627; all in *Saklat v. Bella* JCPC case papers.

288   *Law and Identity in Colonial South Asia: Parsi Legal Culture*

homage to the King of England at the Durbar of 1911.[64] With other orthodox Parsis, including one Mr. Saklat, Merwanji asked the Chief Court of Lower Burma to stop Bella from entering the Rangoon fire temple again. *Saklat v. Bella* (1914–25) was ultimately decided by the Privy Council in London.[65] The plaintiffs' case was built on the Parsi concept of ritual privacy. Only members of the community could enter the temple and see the sacred fire. The presence of outsiders inside the temple would defile it, requiring huge expense and effort for reconsecration.[66] But who was a member of the community? Was it someone who was religiously Zoroastrian, or was it a person who was also ethnically Parsi through the paternal line? Merwanji and his associates argued for the latter. Because Bella was publically presented as the biological child of a non-Parsi father, they insisted that she desecrated the Rangoon fire temple by entering it. The irony, of course, was that Bella's actual paternity should have made the lawsuit unnecessary. For the sake of the family name, though, none of the Captain brothers was willing to acknowledge the affair through which Bella was conceived. And so the suit continued.

    The legal question was whether the trustees of the Rangoon Fire Temple Trust could bar Bella from entering the temple. Merwanji's side argued unsuccessfully that Bella had trespassed, a claim that failed for procedural reasons. Trespass had to be asserted by the trustee; at the time, the sole trustee was none other than Bella's purported uncle Bomanji. The man who was probably Bella's natural father was one of her chief backers throughout the litigation and had helped engineer her initial entry into the temple. Bella's orthodox opponents also asserted that she had violated their right of exclusive worship – the right to worship in the company of their own kind. In the court of first instance and on appeal, British judges in Burma found that although a right of exclusive worship may have existed for a religious group, it did not exist for a racial one. On appeal in London, the Privy Councillors agreed with the lower courts on both counts. However, they handed victory to Merwanji because they applied Dinshah Davar's interpretation of trust terms in *Petit v. Jijibhai*. Davar had distinguished the terms, *Zoroastrian* and *Parsi*, construing *Zoroastrian* as a religious label and *Parsi*, an ethnic or racial one. These definitions made trusts created for the benefit of Parsis (even those set up before Davar's definitions were accepted) racially restricted. The Privy Councillors interpreted the Rangoon Fire Temple trust to have been created for the benefit of ethnic Parsis who were also

---

[64] "Obituary: Merwanji Cowasji Captain," Patel and Paymaster, V: 382 (4 December 1917), trans. Homi D. Patel; "Parsi Defamation Suit. Mr. B. Cowasji's Evidence," *WRTOS* (25 July 1914), 41; "List appended to letter to Lord Hardinge from Lieut. Governor of Burma, Government House, Maymyo (Burma) (25 July 1911)" in Hardinge Papers, vol. 50 (Manuscripts and University Archives, Cambridge University Library). See also Chakravarti, 98.

[65] See Introduction at note 99.

[66] See Modi, *Religious Ceremonies*, 199–230; Mario Vitalone, "Fires and the Establishment of *Ātaš Bahrāms* in the Zoroastrian Tradition" in Stausberg, *Zoroastrian Rituals*, 425–7. The complexity of reconsecration rites varied according to the grade of fire housed inside the temple.

Pure Parsi: Libel, Race, and Group Membership

religiously Zoroastrian. Bella may have been the latter after her initiation ceremony was performed by the Parsi priest from India. But as long as her adoptive family insisted on the face-saving euphemism that she was a random orphan girl, she would not be considered ethnically Parsi. The Privy Council held that trustees were free to allow Bella into the temple at their discretion. However, Bella was not entitled *by right* to enter. It was Bella's bad luck that the trustees in power at the time of the judgment were against her. By the time of the London judgment, her sympathetic uncle Bomanji had been ousted as sole trustee in Rangoon. He was replaced by orthodox Parsis who disapproved of *juddins*.[67]

Parsis in Bombay were heavily involved in the case, both through the Bombay commission and because the Bombay press covered the Rangoon court proceedings in lurid detail. Parsi newspapers took sides (Figure 7.4). The most widely read Parsi daily, *Jam-e-Jamshed*, alleged that a conspiracy was afoot. Egged on by none other than Dinshah Davar (a friend of its editor), the newspaper suggested that a Bombay organization known as the Zoroastrian Conference was surreptitiously sponsored by the losing parties in the French Mrs. Tata's case.[68] These "Conferencias" had helped execute Bella's initiation to further their agenda of smuggling ethnic non-Parsis into the fold, a "lustful" idea driven by Parsi men's desire to marry white women. The newspaper likened Conference members to the ancient Zoroastrian heretics Mazdak and Mani.[69] Conference supporters, it argued, deserved to be treated like lepers, demons, vipers, and *Waghris*, a "low-class tribe" of bird-catchers. They were instigators of obscenity and sin "bent on bringing the Parsi community to hell and ruin."[70] The reformist press was not silent during this tirade. A more liberal newspaper called *The Parsi* printed pro-Conference articles, but it did not hurl abuse in the manner of *Jam-e-Jamshed*. The chairman and secretaries of the Zoroastrian Conference sued for criminal libel in Bombay and won. However, the fines imposed on the *Jam-e-Jamshed*'s editor and publisher were immediately paid by an orthodox supporter. The convicted defendants were greeted by cheers and flowers as they left the courtroom.[71]

A second set of libel suits flowed from press coverage of Bella's case, this time in the Rangoon courts. A cluster of orthodox newspapers in Bombay suggested that many of the recipients of the ceremonies performed in Burma by Dastur Kaikobad were "half-castes" of part Indian or Burmese background. They insinuated that certain members of the Rangoon Parsi community were less Parsi than others: infusions of Burmese or lower caste Hindu blood tainted the claim to being ethnically Parsi, even if these people were of Parsi paternity. Bella

---

[67] "Rangoon Parsis' Trusts," *TI* (26 September 1918), 9; *Saklat, Mehta v. Hormusjee*.

[68] "'Jame' Defamation Case," *TI* (29 April 1915), 5.

[69] See Pourshariati, 331–4, 344–7; Daryaee, 72–5, 86–91; Patricia Crone, "Kavād's Heresy and Mazdak's Revolt," *Iran* 29 (1991), 21–42.

[70] "'Jame' Defamation Case," *TI* (2 June 1915), 5; "'Jame' Defamation Case. The Judgment," *TI* (16 June 1915), 5.

[71] "'Jame' Defamation Case. The Judgment," 5.

FIGURE 7.4. "AN INKY SPORT!" "Indulged in [by] some of the Bombay Parsi dailies morning and evening, to the disgust of the sensible portion of the community."
Source: HP (19 April 1914), 12. Courtesy of the British Library SV576.

Pure Parsi: Libel, Race, and Group Membership

was born of "an iniquitous union of a low caste, low rank *juddin* father and a mean, renegade mother," alleged the *Jam-e-Jamshed*.[72] In the *Sanj Vartaman*, a letter by Bella's uncle Merwanji called Bella and her natural mother *ghatans* (Guj. *ghātaṇ*) or lower caste Hindu converts to Christianity.[73] An estranged friend of Bella's adoptive father also lashed out. The Chief Court translator G. K. Nariman wrote disparagingly of Bella's appearance in another letter to the *Sanj Vartaman*, implying that she was "so unlike a Parsi that no Parsi would accept her as a Parsi." He was talking about her complexion, implying that Bella was too dark to be Parsi.[74] The accusations extended to Bella's adoptive mother as well: she was Parsi on her father's side, but Burmese on her mother's. In print, Nariman and Bella's uncle Merwanji called Bella's adoptive mother a *juddin* and a "non-descript Indo-Burman."[75] The response from Rangoon was more litigation. Bella's adoptive father sued the newspapers for criminal libel.

The boy Behram Contractor's claim to be pure Parsi was also doubted. A small orthodox monthly called *Cherag* published an article that was reprinted in the *Sanj Vartaman*. The article reported that, in addition to performing the *navjote* of Bella and her adoptive mother, the high priest carried out a third initiation – a "half-caste *navjote*, that is, the *navjote* of an issue with mixed blood in it, or of a bastard."[76] Mr. Contractor claimed the statement could only refer to his son, the third person initiated by the high priest. Mrs. Contractor was of Parsi parentage on both sides. For Behram to be a bastard and of mixed blood, his father would have had to engage in an affair with a Burmese or other non-Parsi woman. Mr. Contractor sued both newspapers. His lawyers, a team of Parsis led by F. S. Doctor, tried to distance the Contractor case from the libel suits launched by Bella's adoptive father. They argued that the Contractor case had nothing to do with Shapurji Captain's case: Mrs. Shapurji Captain "was not a pure Zoroastrian" whereas Behram Contractor was "of a pure Parsi mother and father and therefore the libel was of the gravest nature." Mr. Contractor was the manager of Singer Manufacturing Company for the whole of Burma. He claimed to be a leading member of the community, known both in Rangoon and Bombay. He complained that he had been receiving letters from Bombay about the alleged interracial adultery. The statements were published with the intention of lowering Contractor in the eyes of everyone who knew him. If these claims were true, he would be effectively excommunicated from the Parsi community of Rangoon.[77]

---

[72] "The Parsi Dispute. Another Defamation Charge. The Jam-e-Jamshed Articles," *WRTOS* (16 May 1914), 32.

[73] "Parsi Defamation Suit. The Hearing Resumed" (4 July 1914), 32; "Parsis at Law. Alleged Defamatory Article. Charge against Mr. G. K. Nariman. The Recent *Navjote* Ceremony" (2 May 1914), 41; both in *WRTOS*.

[74] "Parsis at Law. Alleged Defamatory Article. Charge against Mr. G. K. Nariman. The Recent *Navjote* Ceremony," *WRTOS* (2 May 1914), 41.

[75] "Parsi Defamation Suit. The Hearing Resumed," *WRTOS* (4 July 1914), 32.

[76] "The Parsi Dispute. Another Defamation Suit," 40.

[77] Ibid.

Two of the three suits fizzled out before judgment, as happened so often with libel cases. In a lengthy published retraction, Nariman apologized to his former friend, Shapurji. He offered to donate Rs 500 to a charity of Shapurji's choice. *Sanj Vartaman* also apologized for what it had written about Shapurji's family. Shapurji withdrew all charges.[78] J. D. Contractor refused to accept an apology from *Sanj Vartaman*. For unknown reasons, the Rangoon press stopped covering the case after that.[79] Shapurji's case against *Jam-e-Jamshed* lived the longest, due largely to the tenacity of the defendants. The Marzbans, father and son, were used to being sued for libel. They were the defendants in the Bombay libel suits launched by the Zoroastrian Conference – and in many others.[80] Jehangir Behramji Marzban had spent decades in the wily world of Bombay journalism and Parsi community politics. The "father of Parsi journalism" and the Parsis' "Mark Twain" was a veteran of Bombay's libel wars.[81] His son, P. J. or "Pyjam" Marzban, was a well-known satirist with orthodox leanings.[82]

The Marzbans fought Shapurji until the final stages. They published two further articles that their lawyers held up as apologies. Shapurji's lawyers were unimpressed: these pieces only aggravated the initial libel and proved malice. The elder Marzban tried to claim ignorance. He insisted he was only the proprietor of the paper and had little knowledge or control over what was published, particularly when he spent half of every week at his country house in Matheran, a favorite Parsi hill station in the mountains east of Bombay.[83] He had been in Matheran when the statements in question were published and insisted that he had not seen the articles until reading them in print.[84] The claim was well rehearsed in the colonial courts. Being powerless and ignorant of the contents of one's newspaper, like being out of town at the time of publication, were familiar lines. Marzban senior was using the alibi presented by many editors before him.[85] It was particularly unlikely to work coming from one of the most experienced newspapermen in Bombay. Jehangir Marzban had managed three leading English dailies (the *Times of India, Advocate of India*, and the *Bombay Gazette*) and had edited the magazine *Noor-e Alam* (Guj. *Nure Elam*, from Pers.) before becoming sole owner and editor of the *Jam-e-Jamshed*.[86] Back in Bombay, the younger Marzban's correspondence suggested

---

[78] "Rangoon 'Navjote' Defamation Case. Mr. Nariman Tenders Apology," *Poona Observer* (21 May 1914), 5.

[79] "The Parsi Dispute. Application in Revision" (23 May 1914), 44; "The Parsi Dispute. Rangoon Navjot Ceremony. Dastur Kaikobad's Regrets," 44; both in *WRTOS*.

[80] See, for instance, *Nadirshaw Hormusji Sukhia v. Pirojshaw Ratanji Ratnagar* 15 Bom LR 130 (1913).

[81] Darukhanawala, *Parsi Lustre*, I: 298–300.

[82] Ibid., I: 300–1.

[83] See Strangman, 183–4; Mistry, *Reminiscences* [1911], 17–18, 54.

[84] "Parsi Defamation Case. Accused's Written Statement. An Expression of Regret," *Rangoon Times* (1 August 1914), 14.

[85] See, for example, *Ramasami v. Lokanada* ILR 9 Mad 387 (1885).

[86] "Obituary: J. B. Marzban," Patel and Paymaster, VI: 387–8, trans. Homi D. Patel.

Pure Parsi: Libel, Race, and Group Membership

that his father ruled the *Jam-e-Jamshed* with an iron grip. In a letter to a family member, the son once explained that he could not publish the relative's writing because "Pa would come down on my poor head like lightning and thunder."[87] And as Marzban senior told the Bombay High Court in another libel suit, "Whenever there is anything out of the common, it is a rule in the office to refer to me."[88]

The Marzbans' final tactic was to argue that the statements were true and made both in good faith and for the public good. They professed the intention of serving the community in a matter of great social and religious importance and not of causing harm to Shapurji and his family.[89] The magistrate was unconvinced, finding that the newspaper was "ready to try every dodge it could imagine to try to shirk responsibility for the scurrilous article it had published."[90] Finally, the Marzbans yielded and apologized before judgment was issued. Shapurji withdrew the charges.[91]

Despite the apology, both sides claimed victory. The reformist Iranian Association published a letter to Shapurji congratulating him on vindicating his family honor against "irresponsible journalism." It hoped the victory would bring home to those likely to "overstep the limits of decency in the public discussion of communal questions the need for greater caution and sobriety."[92] Shapurji thanked the association for its unflagging support. The *Jam-e-Jamshed* and *Sanj Vartaman* had been forced to withdraw all of their original statements, apologize, and cover Shapurji's legal costs.[93] Back in Rangoon, though, Merwanji held a meeting of Parsis to honor the editors of the two newspapers. Nariman was thanked publicly for his support on this "burning" community issue, and the younger Marzban was presented with a formal scroll.[94] More significant than the perceived outcomes of these cases was what they revealed about changing Parsi views. Why would it bring a Parsi into disrepute to have it known that his child or wife was part Indian or Burmese? Why did it suddenly matter if the non-Parsi influences were coming from the maternal side? These incidents only became lawsuits because Shapurji and Mr. Contractor felt injured by the suggestion that Parsi men were mixing in Burma.

---

[87] "Jame Jamshed Defamation Case. Full Text of Judgment," *JIA* IV: 4 (July 1915), 139.

[88] "'Jame' Defamation Case," *TI* (27 April 1915), 9.

[89] "Second Accused's Statement," *WRTOS* (22 August 1914), 49.

[90] "Parsi Defamation Suit. The Jam-e-Jamshed Article," *Rangoon Times* (6 June 1914), 13.

[91] "*Saklat v. Bella* and Related Defamation Cases," Patel and Paymaster, V: 210–1, trans. Homi D. Patel.

[92] "The Rangoon Navjot and Ourselves. Correspondence between this journal and Shapurjee Cowasjee. Letter from Iranian Association (H. J. Bhabha, President; P. A. Wadia and Byramji Hormusji, Joint Honorable Secretaries) to S. Cowasji, Rangoon. Bombay, 23 September 1914," *JIA* III: 8 (November 1914), 279.

[93] "The Rangoon Navjot and Ourselves," 280.

[94] *Jam-e-Jamshed* (21 September 1914) cited in "*Saklat v. Bella* and Related Defamation Cases," 210–1.

294   *Law and Identity in Colonial South Asia: Parsi Legal Culture*

As the work of Renisa Mawani has demonstrated, intermixing between non-white populations could be as complicated as couplings between white and non-white peoples in colonial contexts.[95] The Rangoon libel trials suggested that many Parsis disapproved of close interactions with Burmese people, particularly when sexual. The challenge of being doubly diasporic confronted Parsis from Shanghai to the Cape Colony; many worried that Parsi identity would fade the further Parsis moved from western India. In trade and the professions, it was crucial to be open and amiable in dealing with local populations. These were the easy cases: close links to local business associates did not yield progeny. Intimate relationships with local women were more difficult. In many places, they were not unknown, but nor were they acknowledged in polite society.

British rule was consolidated in Burma in the 1880s, later than in many other parts of South Asia. As Burma was absorbed into British India, it became the colony of a colony. More than a million Indians migrated to Burma to develop the rice and teak industries especially.[96] By the early twentieth century, over half of the population of Rangoon was Indian.[97] Most Parsis came to Burma as part of this late nineteenth-century influx.[98] In 1912, G. K. Nariman (of libel case fame) provided French historian Delphine Menant with a demographic sketch of the Parsi community in Burma. Rangoon had only four or five "indigenous families" in which Parsi men had married Burmese women. The Parsis of Rangoon totaled about 300 at the time.[99] But, in 1918, Bomanji Cowasji Captain pointed to an earlier pattern of intermarriage in Burma. He knew Parsi men who had married the offspring of intermarriage – women with Parsi fathers and Burmese mothers. Most of these women were no longer alive.[100] A specific example was a Parsi in Burma named Cowasjee Mancherjee. He had

---

[95] Renisa Mawani, *Colonial Proximities: Crossracial Encounters and Juridical Truths in British Columbia, 1871–1921* (Vancouver: University of British Columbia Press, 2009). See also Ann Laura Stoler, ed., *Haunted by Empire: Geographies of Intimacy in North American History* (Durham, NC: Duke University Press, 2006).

[96] Chakravarti, 30. On the rice and teak industries, see Cheng Siok-Hwa, *The Rice Industry of Burma (1852–1940)* (Kuala Lumpur: University of Malaya Press, 1968); W. S. Desai, *India and Burma* (Bombay: Orient Longmans, 1954), 25–9, 29; Joseph Dautremer, *Burma Under British Rule* (New York: Charles Scribner's Sons, 1913), 240–8; V. C. Scott O'Connor, *The Silken East: A Record of Life and Travel in Burma* (London: Hutchinson and Co., 1904), 751–832. See generally Michael Adas, *State, Market and Peasant in Colonial South and Southeast Asia* (Aldershot, UK: Ashgate, 1998).

[97] Desai, *India and Burma*, 31; Tin Maung Maung Than, "Some Aspects of Indians in Rangoon," in *Indian Communities in Southeast Asia*, eds. K. S. Sandhu and A. Mani (Singapore: Times Academic Press, 1993), 586.

[98] Above all, they came to seek their fortune. British Burma was a place where one could go from rags to riches, as did Bhikaji Dinyarji Unwalla. He lived in penury as a priest in Udwada before moving to Rangoon, where he prospered in business (*Udvāḍā*, 13, 100).

[99] Letter to Delphine Menant from G. K. Nariman, Chief Court, Rangoon (18 March 1912) in Menant Papers.

[100] "Defendant's Evidence. No. 34: Deposition of Shapurji Cowasji, the second defendant. In the Chief Court of Lower Burma," 710 in *Saklat v. Bella* JCPC case papers.

Pure Parsi: Libel, Race, and Group Membership

married the daughter of a Parsi man by a Burmese woman and done so by Burmese rites. Shapurji told the court that the brother of his own wife, who like Shapurji's wife would also have been a quarter Burmese, married one of Cowasjee Mancherjee's daughters. In other words, two quarter-Burmese Parsis married each other, with the result that their children would also have been a quarter Burmese.[101] An 1889 Parsi cemetery controversy in Rangoon had also turned on the issue of where to bury the bodies of Burmese wives – whether inside or outside of the Parsi section.[102] Parsi–Burmese intermarriage may have been rare at the time of Bella's case, but it had not always been so.

It was the Saklat in *Saklat v. Bella* who described Parsi attitudes toward intermixing with Burmese women. Dorabji R. Saklat was a fifty-five-year-old rice broker who had come to Rangoon from Bombay in 1890 after spending six years in Calcutta. He dealt with people of all races and creeds and mixed with them socially without restriction. "All Parsis mix similarly." In the same breath, he told the Chief Court of Lower Burma that it wounded his religious feelings to worship "my God in the presence of other worshippers of race other than mine." The reason was simple: the non-Parsi lacked Parsi *olad* (Guj. *olād*) or lineage.[103] Saklat captured the irony of Parsi trade and travel, or perhaps its antidote: the greater the cosmopolitanism, the greater the need for limits where the mixing would stop. For Saklat, this limit fell at the threshold of the fire temple. Here was what C. A. Bayly has called "the exclusivist cosmopolitanism of the Parsis."[104]

Saklat acknowledged that romance was trickier. Most Parsi–Burmese unions had occurred in the nineteenth century, when the number of Parsi men migrating to Burma outstripped the number of Parsi women. Sex imbalance during migration was the classic factor that triggered exogamy by South Asian populations.[105] Saklat's ambivalence was palpable. On the one hand, the children of Parsi men and Burmese women were fully entitled to membership in the Parsi community: "I know [a] good many Parsis in Rangoon and in other places of Burma who have married women of other races. These Parsis have never forfeited their position as Parsis and their children are recognized as Parsis if they are invested with *sudra* and *kusti*." But he uncomfortably acknowledged a certain stigma associated with Burmese wives themselves. In Rangoon, Burmese wives were not received socially by all Parsi families. Saklat himself may have been to the home of a Parsi with a Burmese wife, but strictly on business. He told the court that he had never invited the Burmese wife of a Parsi man into his own

---

[101] "Parsi Defamation Suit. Mr. B. Cowasjee's Evidence," *WRTOS* (25 July 1914), 41.

[102] "Untitled Statement by W. F. Agnew, Recorder, Rangoon," 177 in *Saklat v. Bella* JCPC case papers. See also Chapter 6 at note 1.

[103] "Plaintiffs' Evidence. No. 20: Evidence of Dorabji R. Saklat. In the Chief Court of Lower Burma," 389 in *Saklat v. Bella* JCPC case papers.

[104] Bayly, 236.

[105] See Ballhatchet, 145–55; Karen Leonard, *Making Ethnic Choices: California's Punjabi Mexican Americans* (Philadelphia: Temple University Press, 1992). Compare Stoler, 2.

296 Law and Identity in Colonial South Asia: Parsi Legal Culture

house. He was used to seeing Burmese women in the homes of Parsi gentlemen, but only for "entertainment" purposes.[106]

The basis for one of Shapurji's libel actions was the statement that Mrs. Shapurji Cowasji was part Burmese. It was true: her mother was Burmese. But her father was Parsi. And if the children of such unions were still accepted into the community as Saklat claimed, one would think that Shapurji would simply have acknowledged the truth of Nariman's statement or not responded at all. That Shapurji chose to sue was significant. His phraseology in court was also telling. Shapurji stated many times that his wife's father was Parsi, but he only acknowledged her mother's Burmese origins once.[107] Shapurji's own ambivalence toward his wife's Burmese background was a reflection of the flux in attitudes toward race and identity in Parsi society.

PARSIS AND EUGENICS

Shapurji was making a desperate appeal to the old Parsi paternity rule. If his wife had a Parsi father, she could be initiated into the fold. Both the judge Dinshah Davar and the Karachi high priest M. N. Dhalla noted that many Parsis had disapproved of this rule historically. Even so, it had effectively become the customary principle of access.[108] As the witness J. D. Nadirshaw told the court during the Bombay commission in *Saklat v. Bella*, there had been no problem admitting the children of Parsi fathers and alien mothers until the French Mrs. Tata's case began in 1906.[109] The Parsi Chief Matrimonial Court would also clearly endorse the customary rule in *Dinbai v. Toddyvala* (1916). The court confirmed that a woman of Parsi paternity whose mother was part Malagasy was herself Parsi. The Bombay commission in *Saklat v. Bella* gave the rule an older historical pedigree. "Aryan patrilinealism" was the view that Aryan peoples derived ethnic status through the paternal line alone. The retired High Court judge M. P. Khareghat told the commission: "the community is composed of families and ... families are to be derived only according to male descent, and this idea of patriarchal descent is common to most Aryan Nations as far as I know."[110] Witnesses considered the ancient Persians a branch of the Aryan race.[111]

---

[106] "Plaintiffs' Evidence. No. 20: Dorabji R. Saklat," 389–91 in *Saklat v. Bella* JCPC case papers.

[107] "Parsi Defamation Suit. The Hearing Resumed" (4 July 1914), 32; "Parsi Defamation Case. The Anjuman Meeting" (1 August 1914), 42; both in *WRTOS*.

[108] *Parsi Panchayat Case (Davar)*, 38–43; Dhalla, 386, 394, 704–5, 713.

[109] "No. 27: Evidence of J. D. Nadirshaw taken on Commission. In the Court of Small Causes, Bombay," 413 in *Saklat v. Bella* JCPC case papers. See also Dhalla, 387.

[110] "Plaintiffs' Evidence. No. 6: Muncherji Pestanji Khareghat," 26 in *Saklat v. Bella* JCPC case papers.

[111] "Plaintiffs' Evidence. No. 7: Evidence of Jehangir Cursetji Daji, Court of Small Causes, Bombay," 93–4 in *Saklat v. Bella* JCPC case papers.

Pure Parsi: Libel, Race, and Group Membership

There had been periodic attempts to overthrow the Parsi paternity rule. In 1836, a trustee of the Parsi Panchayat had resigned in protest over the practice of initiating the mixed offspring of Parsi men. A resolution had been passed condemning the religious initiation of these children without the *panchayat*'s permission. A similar resolution had been passed almost two decades earlier, in 1818.[112] Another would be issued in 1905.[113] This resolution was largely ignored even by orthodox Parsis like D. D. Davar.[114] But with the global rise of the eugenics movement, the notion of Parsi racial purity found new equipment with which to assert itself.

The new racial test privileged blood over seed. What mattered was the composite purity of an individual's blood, not the line of male progenitors to the exclusion of the female. With it came a new race-based exclusivity. Burmese wives – like their European and Hindu counterparts – became increasingly problematic. The new rule was conceptually dressed by the Parsi lawyer leading the case against Bella during the Bombay phase of *Saklat v. Bella*. Jehangir J. Vimadalal was an ardent eugenicist and published two books opposing the admission of outsiders on this basis.[115] Witnesses referred to his eugenicist views during the commission phase of Bella's case.[116] The Bombay solicitor drew on the writings of European race theorists like Gustave Le Bon and Houston Stewart Chamberlain and tailored the global eugenics movement to the Parsi colonial context. Vimadalal's work also provided the conceptual foundations for the later work of Parsi eugenicists like A. R. Wadia and Sapur Desai from the 1920s until the 1940s.[117]

Vimadalal's starting point was the generally accepted view among eugenicists that intermarriage between dissimilar races produced unhealthy children.[118] Mixed offspring tended to be a "low type of progeny" that suffered from atavism or "reversion," reviving pathological defects from the deep past.[119] The Eurasians of India, the mulatto "half-breeds" of America, and the *mestizos* of Peru and Paraguay were featured as unhappy crossbreeds in the work of

---

[112] Dhalla, 386.

[113] "The Recent Navjote Controversy. A Review of the Situation. II," *JIA* III: 7 (October 1914), 238–9.

[114] *Parsi Panchayat Case*, 38.

[115] *Mr. Vimadalal*; J. J. Vimadalal, *Racial Intermarriages: Their Scientific Aspect* (Bombay: The Times Press, 1922).

[116] For example, see "Defendant's Evidence. No. 27: Evidence of Jamshedji Dadabhoy Nadirshaw taken on Commission. In the Court of Small Causes, Bombay," 497–8 in *Saklat v. Bella* JCPC case papers.

[117] See Wadia, *Ethics*; Desai, *Parsis*.

[118] See Desai, *Parsis*, 47; "Race-crossing and Glands (Extracts from *The Eugenics Review*, April 1933)," 96 and Eldon Moore, "Mixed Marriages from the Genetical Standpoint," 344–5, both in *Marriage Hygiene* 1 (1934–5).

[119] "III. June 29, 1910. Is Zoroastrianism Evangelical? Mr. Vimadalal's Reply. To the Editor," 3 and "XVIII. August 31, 1910. Mr. Vimadalal and the Juddin Question. To the Editor, from Vimadalal," 45; both in *Mr. Vimadalal*.

Vimadalal and Chamberlain.[120] In the same vein, memorialists Max and Bertha Ferrars noted that the Indo-Burmese "*kala* half-breeds" or *Zerbadis*, like the "Euro-Burman half-breed," possessed "fewer good qualities" than any of the pure races. Chinese-Burmese "half-breeds," by contrast, had a promising future because they were a cross between such similar races.[121]

For Vimadalal, intermixing destroyed the character of a race. Borrowing from Chamberlain, he asserted that race lifted individuals above themselves, endowing them with "extraordinary" powers lacked by those springing from "the chaotic jumble of peoples drawn from all parts of the world." The person of pure race soared "heavenward like some strong and stately tree, nourished by thousands and thousands of roots – no solitary individual, but the living sum of untold souls striving for the same goal."[122] Purity of race acted like a magnet. It drew iron filings into a unified pattern, each at a slightly different angle but with a common center and cause. People of mixed race, by contrast, were barred by their own constitution "from all genuine community of life."[123] The mixed individual was unsuited to both parents' original environments.[124] Two of the strongest and most successful races of the time, the British and the Japanese, owed their power to the fact that they were "pure races." By living on islands effectively cut off from the rest of the world, they had been able to achieve purer "inbreeding."[125] Vimadalal argued that, for the Parsis, intermixing would destroy the distinctive constitution that had arisen over centuries of general endogamy: "It would disturb our physical and mental constitution, destroy our national character, loosen the hold of our common sentiments, interests and beliefs on our race and ultimately cause the disappearance of the Parsee race from the surface of the globe."[126]

Vimadalal acknowledged that some intermixing had resulted from Parsi trade and travel in East and Southeast Asia and in Africa. But it had been so small as to leave the general Parsi character intact, he wrote with a sense of relief.[127] It was this character in its most blatant physical terms that was joked about in the Rangoon courtroom during *Saklat v. Bella*. When asked to describe typical Parsi features, the lawyer Mr. Connell pointed to Mr. Hormasji and Mr. Patel, two of the Parsis in the room. To everyone's delight, the magistrate replied that he

---

[120] Vimadalal, 60; Chamberlain in Vimadalal, 87.
[121] Ferrars, 157, 161. The term *Zerbadi* was generally used to describe the children of Muslim Indian men and Burmese women. See Moshe Yegon, *The Muslims of Burma: A Study of a Minority Group* (Wiesbaden: Otto Harrassowitz, 1972), 33–5; Usha Mahajani, *The Role of Indian Minorities in Burma and Malaya* (Bombay: Vora and Co., 1960), 22–3, 29. On the Chinese-Burmese, see S. Vesey Fitzgerald, "India, Burma and Far Eastern Cases on the Conflict of Laws: 1935–1939," *JCLIL* 3rd series, 22:1 (1940), 68–9.
[122] Chamberlain in Vimadalal, 74.
[123] Ibid., 101–2.
[124] Vimadalal, 45.
[125] Chamberlain in Vimadalal, 76.
[126] Vimadalal, 59.
[127] Ibid., 64.

Pure Parsi: Libel, Race, and Group Membership

would not allow them to be put in as exhibits.[128] At a more serious level, it was Parsi features (both physical and mental) that constituted the "soul" of the Parsi community. Vimadalal did not provide a catalog of classically Parsi physical traits, but he did describe the hereditary mental element. "Parseeism" was a core of ethical precepts that represented goodness with the strength and independence to resist countervailing pressures. The collective Parsi "soul" had been shaped and reinforced over centuries through religious praxis – the "efficacy of the beautiful ritual" – and belief in the Zoroastrian ethical trio of good thoughts, good words, and good deeds. And it was this "noble bond of love, brotherliness, and unison" that made the Parsi feel that "the shame of any member of the community was his own shame" and rush to "repair" it.[129] Vimadalal failed to see the contradiction between descriptions like this and the phenomenon that provided a major part of his client base: Parsis suing Parsis.

Carefully engineered crossbreeding in animals and plants could produce exceptional results, according to the Bombay solicitor. But he accepted that human beings could not be matched in the same way.[130] Intermarriage would either have to be allowed completely or not at all. Certainly "free and continuous crossing" would destroy the Parsi character. "It is difficult to imagine what a shocking conglomeration of hybrids, mongrels, pariahs, half-castes and no-castes of all kinds we should have amidst us in a very short time if all restrictions against alien marriages be done away with at a stroke!"[131] In a critic's words, Vimadalal predicted the "pollution of blood" on a massive scale.[132] The Parsi solicitor shuddered at the thought "that the English and the French, the Italian and the German, the Chinaman and the Japanese, the Burman and the Sinhalese, the Negro and the Red Indian, the Bengali, Madrasi, Kathiawari and Sindhi, the Punjabi and the Sikh, Hindus of all castes and sub-castes, as well as Mahomedans of all grades, nay even Dubras, Bhils, Chamars and men of low caste may, if they so please, adopt Zoroastrianism and cross freely and continuously with the Parsee!"[133]

Vimadalal's inclusion of Europeans was significant. It was not "quality," but closeness of race that mattered.[134] Parsis and Europeans were both superior races for Vimadalal, but they were so dissimilar that intermixing would destroy the racial character of the Parsis. In fact, there existed no race close enough to the

---

[128] "Parsi Defamation Suit. Mr. B. Cowasjee's Evidence," *WRTOS* (25 July 1914), 42.

[129] "XXI. September 7, 1910. Mr. Vimadalal and the 'Juddin' Question. From Vimadalal" in *Mr. Vimadalal*, 52.

[130] Vimadalal, 35–6, 45. Compare Dhalla, 708.

[131] Vimadalal, 26, 35, 37. Compare Dhalla, 711.

[132] "VI. July 13, 1910. Mr. Vimadalal's Misrepresentations. A Crushing Reply. To the Editor, from 'D'," in *Mr. Vimadalal*, 11.

[133] Vimadalal, 36. Dubras, Bhils, and Chamars were lower castes in Bombay Presidency. See Enthoven, I: 151–78, 260–71, 341–7.

[134] "II. June 29, 1910. Is Zoroastrianism Evangelical? Mr. Vimadalal's Reply. To the Editor," in *Mr. Vimadalal*, 3.

300 *Law and Identity in Colonial South Asia: Parsi Legal Culture*

Parsis (with the exception of the Iranian Zoroastrians, who were arguably the same race) to provide a safe mix as close, for instance, as the English and Germans in America. Herbert Spencer had advised the Japanese, another "superior race," not to intermarry with Europeans for the same reason.[135]

Along with this main course of race theory came a side order of women's rights. The double standard between the sexes had long meant that Parsi men could marry out without being excluded from the community and that their children were also admitted into the fold. It had long been established that Parsi women who married non-Parsis, along with the offspring of these marriages, were unequivocally shut out. According to the Karachi priest Dhalla, men felt they could "hoodwink" aspects of their own behavior that they, in turn, suppressed "in the weaker sex." But with the arrival of sex-based egalitarianism, change was overdue: "if the Parsi Anjuman made up mainly of men, wish to resolve to stop their women marrying out of the community, they will have to agree to observe the same rule themselves also."[136] The argument was a claim for consistency, not exclusion. But, taken in tandem with Vimadalal's race science, it reinforced the narrowing of the group membership principle.

Two broad Parsi critiques of Vimadalal's views emerged. The first came from within a eugenicist framework. It served as a reminder that this body of thought was, in fact, available to both sides of the Parsi intermixing debate. An anonymous critic in the 1910 *Oriental Review* fumed that Vimadalal had gotten his eugenics all wrong.[137] No leading eugenicists' work showed that intermarriage between "higher races of mankind" caused degeneration. In most cases, sexual selection played its part in keeping the superior races from intermingling with the inferior ones: "the natural repulsion of civilized men to intermarry with lower races, like the negro, is a natural protection against such a result." But within the Indo-Aryan family, things were different. The Parsis, as one branch of this family, could surely intermix with other members of the same clan without detriment.[138] The writer was suggesting that marriage between Parsi men and European women was eugenically sound. This argument echoed fashionable notions of Aryanism in colonial India, which were used to emphasize the closeness of Britons and Indians of Aryan descent. In Thomas Trautmann's words, it was "the Aryan love story as family reunion."[139]

Others questioned Vimadalal's attack on exogamy. They insisted that it was in fact marriage *within* the community that was scientifically problematic.[140] As early as the 1880s, the Parsi magistrate and historian D. F. Karaka claimed that

---

[135] Vimadalal, 59–60.

[136] Dhalla, 388.

[137] "IV. July 6, 1910. (Anonymous) The Social Problems of the Parsees" in *Mr. Vimadalal*, 6.

[138] Ibid., 6.

[139] Thomas R. Trautmann, *Aryans and British India* (Berkeley: University of California Press, 1997), 15.

[140] For a postcolonial rendition of this argument, see Keki N. Daruwalla, "The Parsi Hell" in his book of poems, *The Keeper of the Dead* (Delhi: Oxford University Press, 1982), 44–5.

Pure Parsi: Libel, Race, and Group Membership

the Parsis were getting shorter due to inbreeding.[141] Two decades later, the *Times of India* attributed Parsi physical deterioration to endogamy, particularly in elite Bombay circles.[142] In the background was a recurring lament expressed since the late nineteenth century: the Parsi physique was deteriorating. The Prussian weightlifter Eugene Sandow commented in 1905 that the Parsis were turning into "a nation of weaklings." The number of "well-built, strong men and women" was very small, the majority being "small in stature and weak in limb." Elderly Parsis were all "stout and fatty" and suffered from indigestion. The young were "mostly weak-kneed, hollow-chested youths and maidens, whose kidneys and liver are all affected."[143] Sandow's words were self-serving. He helped spark the physical culture craze among Parsis and others worldwide and was soon the personal trainer to wealthy Parsi clients.[144] Trying to counter anxieties about physical degeneration, Parsis learned to "swordswing" and box on roller skates.[145] Ladies took jujitsu classes from Japanese instructors, and Parsi Physical Culture League members went on exchange between Karachi and Bombay to participate in joint bodybuilding "exhibitions."[146]

Vimadalal's eugenicist critics and their successors worried about more than physical deterioration. In 1910, one wrote that inbreeding exacerbated mental and neurological ailments in the Parsi population: "Think only of the nervous diathesis that must inevitably follow such a course; already signs are not wanting to show that the mental equilibrium of the Parsees is not what it ought to be."[147] Census findings of 1921 and 1931 revealed that of all communities in South Asia, the Parsis had the highest incidence of insanity.[148] The Director of Public Health for Bombay Presidency, a Parsi physician named Jamshed D. Munsiff, gave a lecture in 1929 in which he blamed "consanguineous" marriage (particularly between cousins) for the rise of mental illness and mortality among Parsis.[149] In response, bodies including the Parsi Federal Council and Parsi

---

[141] Karaka, I: 120.

[142] "Parsees and Proselytism," *TI* (22 April 1905), 13.

[143] Eugene Sandow, "The Physical Deterioration of the Parsis: A Word of Warning," *The Parsi* 1: 1 (January 1905), 15–16.

[144] For example, see "Death of Parsi Millionaire. Sir D. Bomanji," *TI* (2 April 1937), 3.

[145] "Physical Culture Exhibitions. Zoroastrian League Activities," *TI* (26 October 1922) 8; "Parsi Physical Culture," *TI* (19 November 1923), 10; H. D. Darukhanawala, *Parsis and Sports and Kindred Subjects* (Bombay: author, 1935), 307. For testimony from Parsis who worked as personal trainers at Bombay's Physical Culture Institute, see PCMC Suit No. 1 of 1935, 1935–37 PCMC Notebook, I: 250–2, 260–3.

[146] "A Peep into the Future – Physical Culture among Parsee Ladies in 1290," *HP* (12 September 1909), 34. See also letter from Norman C. Macleod to Torquil Macleod (Bombay, 23 March 1922), "Letters from India," 46A (HRA/D63/A1) in Macleod of Cadboll Papers.

[147] "IV. July 6, 1910. The Social Problems of the Parsees," 6. See also "XVI. August 24, 1910. The Question of Intermarriage. From 'New Reader," 42. Both in *Mr. Vimadalal*.

[148] Desai, *Parsis*, 100–1; Satyavrata Mukerjea, *Census of India, 1921. Vol. XVII: Baroda State. Part I: Report* (Bombay: Times Press, 1922), 305 (cited in Desai).

[149] "Are the Parsees degenerating? Conflicting views," *TI* (7 December 1929), 26; "Are the Parsees degenerating? A Bombay Lecture," *TI* (25 October 1930), 7.

Central Association planned to petition for a government inquiry into "the causes of racial degeneration" in their community.[150] The Federal Council created its own committee of physicians to examine the high incidence of insanity and suggested the opening of a special ward at the B. D. Petit Parsi General Hospital for incipient-stage patients. For unknown reasons, the plan was never enacted.[151] Medical specialists continued to press for curbs on endogamy, nonetheless. In 1934, the superintendent of the Ranchi Indian Mental Hospital lauded the inclusion of clear lists of prohibited degrees of consanguinity in Parsi matrimonial legislation. From what he had seen in his private practice as a psychiatrist among the Parsis, such limits would "help a lot in stamping out hereditary mental diseases, constitutional inferiority and other hereditary physical diseases within the community."[152] In the mid- to late 1930s, the Parsi judge B. J. Wadia adjudged a good number of Parsis to be lunatics for the purposes of civil law.[153] The ungenerous stereotype of the mentally imbalanced Parsi – from the eccentric to the insane – would become familiar in Hindi cinema after independence.[154]

The second reaction against Parsi eugenics, somewhat delayed, was the rejection of race as a meaningful category. As president of the Anthropological Society of Bombay, the Parsi journalist R. P. Masani made this argument in an address in 1932, two decades after the Rangoon libel trials.[155] The Anthropological Society worked to counter superstitious beliefs of the common people – human sacrifice, love and fertility potions, and the like. Equally, it strove against the "superstitions of the elite": race-based thinking. The nineteenth-century scientific study of race "according to the divergences of their cephalic index, their color, their facial angle, their height, their intellectual attainment and collective psychology, and other peculiarities and qualities" had contributed huge amounts of useful data for the study of humanity. But it also gave rise to "dire illusions and superstitions that have militated fatally against the peace and progress of the Human Family." It was no surprise that the "Science of White People" glorified whiteness. Had the Chinese or Egyptians been the architects of the dominant racial taxonomies, they would have put themselves at the top, too. Despite their differences in skin color, all people

---

[150] "Degeneration of Parsis. High Mortality. Inquiry into causes to be made," *TI* (15 November 1929), 13.

[151] Desai, *Parsis*, 99 at note 1.

[152] "From the Superintendent, Ranchi Indian Mental Hospital, to the Deputy Commissioner, Ranchi, No. 7702, dated Kanke, the 24 November, 1934" in "No. 16: Bihar and Orissa," 56 in "Paper No. 1: Opinions on the Parsi Marriage and Divorce Bill. Opinions No. 1–19" in "The Parsi Marriage and Divorce Act 1936."

[153] For example, see Lunacy Suits No. 2 of 1936, II: 155–7; unnumbered suit, II: 175–7; 6 of 1936, II: 192–4; 4 of 1939, III: 91–5; all in "Hon. Justice B. J. Wadia. Chamber Book (23 June 1931–17 April 1941)" (BHC).

[154] See Luhrmann, 50–1. For research on Parsi genetics (and perceptions thereof) since the 1940s, see Hinnells, *Zoroastrian Diaspora*, 87; Skjærvø, "Next-of-kin Marriage."

[155] Darukhanawala, *Parsi Lustre*, I: 374–7, 379.

Pure Parsi: Libel, Race, and Group Membership

seemed to be "equally susceptible to physical, moral or intellectual degradation." Once the principle of race-based inequality was rejected, the world would be free from "the nightmare of race prejudice." The "myopic vision of the unity of blood" would be corrected, the "right claimed by some to dominate others" would be eliminated, and the "puny gospel of hatred at home and hostility abroad" would be replaced by "inter-communal harmony and international comity."[156]

India was fraught with racialized thinking. Masani argued that Brahmins considered their blood pure vis-à-vis the lower castes, although caste was a relatively "modern" phenomenon dating from Buddhist times – around the fifth century BC. Hindus felt the same way relative to Muslims, forgetting that "Hindu blood courses through the veins of large sections of the Muhammadan community." In fact, the Hindu community had at one time consisted of a "wholesale admixture of aliens, not only the peoples inhabiting India but also Greeks and Persians." The Englishman, of course, still exhibited a "superstitious adherence" to racial paradigms. And the average Parsi was unable to "shake off his conceit of 'blue blood.'" Based on race, however, the concept of India as a nation could not work. The subcontinent was simply too diverse. To Masani, a nation was not a unity of blood but a set of common moral and material interests shared by a group of people living together.[157]

Masani's antiracialism was a brief and solitary flash. Vimadalal's mode of thought held stronger appeal in late colonial Bombay. Elaborating on his writings, his intellectual heirs built up the field of Parsi eugenics.[158] The most prominent was Sapur Desai. His 1940 book, *Parsis and Eugenics* appeared during World War II, as race science was teetering on the brink of its fall from worldwide favor. Like Vimadalal, Desai opposed intermarriage between Parsis and non-Parsis and side-stepped the eugenicist arguments against endogamy.[159] Like Parsi eugenicists of the 1920s, he favored the sterilization and even castration of "the feebleminded, the drunkards, the epileptic, the insane, the offenders against person and sex, paupers, criminals, [and] vagrants" among the Parsi population. Desai recognized, however, that the passage of sterilization legislation would not be politically feasible in 1940, unlike earlier in the century.[160] Instead, Desai proposed the systematic improvement of Parsi stock through the creation of a Eugenics Record Office and Research Laboratory (on the model of New York's Cold Spring Harbor complex) and a "Eugenical Marriage Association" that would encourage reproduction by eugenically sound couples

---

[156] R.P. Masani, "Presidential Address: A Survey of the Work Accomplished by the Anthropological Society of Bombay, with Suggestions for Extending the Sphere of its Activities and Influence," *J. Anthropol. Soc. Bombay* XV: 1 (1932), 38–42.

[157] Ibid.

[158] See, for instance, Wadia, *Ethics*, 188–209; "Eugenics and the Parsis," *TI* (25 May 1934), 14.

[159] Desai, *Parsis*, 47–8.

[160] Ibid., 102–5; compare Wadia, *Ethics*, 199–200.

304   *Law and Identity in Colonial South Asia: Parsi Legal Culture*

(on the German model).[161] What had started as a debate about intermarriage in the 1910s ended with proposals, a generation later, for the creation of institutions designed along eugenic principles.

PERSIANNESS

Inside and outside of the courtroom, discussions in the 1910s captured not just the impulse to look forward – toward a scientific, eugenically planned future – but also the urge to look back into the ancient Persian past. Vimadalal's writings helped erect the fence for the new Parsi identity, creating barriers to entry that were more conscious and secure than ever before. What lay inside the gates was the notion of Persianness. Luhrmann has perhaps overemphasized the Anglicization of colonial Parsis at the expense of their Persianness: "The good Parsi, the esteemed and ideal Parsi, was almost English."[162] It was true that many Parsis adopted English education, language, and dress. Many enjoyed harmonious relations with Europeans and the colonial state. But they drew the line at intermarriage. *Petit v. Jijibhai* documented the most famous attempt to keep the European wives of Parsi men out of the community. Beneath an outer layer of Anglophilia lay Persianness. Kathryn Hansen has made similar observations about Parsi theater in the late colonial period: there were Parsi productions of Shakespeare, but there were also renditions of Persian epics like the *Shah Nameh* (Pers. *Shāhnāmeh*) and others.[163]

"The Parsis are proud of what they call their blue blood," Vimadalal told the Bombay commission during his cross-examination of the reformist Nadirshaw in *Saklat v. Bella*. "Blue blood" meant descent from the ancient Persian Zoroastrians exclusively and "without contamination."[164] In 1916, the assertion of pure racial Persianness was a recent phenomenon – not more than about forty years old, according to Nadirshaw.[165] By his account, Parsis had only begun to glorify the achievements of the ancient Persians since 1800, following the first translation from Persian into Gujarati of the Persian epic, the *Shah Nameh*.[166] The Parsis' ancestors had taken pride in being the descendants of such heroes and "having Kiani blood in their veins," but they were also aware that much alien blood had been introduced through conversion to Zoroastrianism.[167] Very few of the Parsis' forefathers actually knew who their ancestors were beyond five or six generations, claimed the witness. The only

---

[161] Desai, *Parsis*, 126–36.
[162] See Luhrmann, 21, as well as 103–4 and 269 at note 22.
[163] Kathryn Hansen, "Languages on Stage: Linguistic Pluralism and Community Formation in the Nineteenth-Century Parsi Theatre," *MAS* 37:2 (2003), 388–93.
[164] "Defendant's Evidence. No. 27: Nadirshaw," 468 in *Saklat v. Bella* JCPC case papers. For similar references, see Karaka, I: 11; Dhalla, 706; "Hindus vs. Parsis," *HP* (19 December 1915), 19.
[165] "Defendant's Evidence. No. 27: Nadirshaw," 465–6 in *Saklat v. Bella* JCPC case papers.
[166] Ibid., 466.
[167] Ibid., 465.The Kiani or Kayanian dynasty was a family of ancient Persian kings.

Pure Parsi: Libel, Race, and Group Membership

exceptions were the priests, who could say they were of pure Persian stock. All sides agreed that it was impossible to become a priest by conversion.[168]

Vimadalal's cross-examination of P. A. Wadia, another reformist, confirmed these views. The solicitor asked if the Parsis were proud to have descended from Persian emigrants after the fall of the Sasanian empire in the seventh century. The exchange continued:

A. It is only after the agitation of Messrs Daji Vimadalal and Co. was started that the Parsis have begun to be proud of their alleged pure descent.

Q. Before that they were not proud of their descent and blood.

A. They did not take pride in their pure descent because they knew that there was an intermixture of Hindu and other alien blood.[169]

Reformists then argued that the Persian origin story was an invented tradition of relatively recent vintage.[170] The orthodox asserted a literal and ancient Persian genealogy.

The *Bella* testimony fit neatly into the larger cultural idealization of Persianness among Parsis in the early twentieth century.[171] Ancient Persian civilization was a constant focus of Parsi literature from the period. The priestly scholar J. J. Modi wrote a plethora of works on the ancient Iranians.[172] The Karachi priest, Dastur Dhalla proposed sending archeological missions to Persia for the collection of antiquities.[173] The weekly magazine, *The Parsi*, featured glowing accounts of ancient Persian educational and legal systems.[174] It urged the study of Persian for Parsi schoolchildren as a means of making themselves "worthy descendants of the ancient Persians."[175] The implicit value of ancient Persian civilization was that, aside from providing a narrative of origins for the Parsis, it compared so favorably to modern Bombay. Parsis claimed that women had been treated equally in ancient Persia. In modern Bombay, they had only recently come to be educated and permitted to drive their own carriages,

---

[168] Ibid., 465–6.

[169] "Defendant's Evidence. No. 32: Wadia," 675 in *Saklat v. Bella* JCPC case papers.

[170] See Eric Hobsbawm, "Introduction: Inventing Traditions," in *The Invention of Tradition*, eds. Eric Hobsbawm and Terence Ranger (Cambridge: Cambridge University Press, 1983), 1–14.

[171] See Stausberg, *Die Religion*, II: 68–71; Ringer, *Pious Citizens*, 154–62.

[172] For examples, see J. J. Modi, "Wine among the Ancient Persians: a lecture delivered before the Self-Improvement Association ... 1888" (Bombay: Bombay Gazette Steam Press, 1888); "Archery in Ancient Persia – A few extraordinary feats," *JBBRAS* XXV (1922), 175–86; "King Solomon's Temple and the Ancient Persians" (Bombay: Fort Printing Press, 1908). For a chronological list of Modi's works in Gujarati and English, see Modi, *Religious Ceremonies*, 1–40 (terminal section).

[173] "Chow-Chow," *HP* (28 March 1915), 13–14.

[174] In *The Parsi*, see J. J. Modi, "Education among the Ancient Iranians" I: 2 (February 1905), 53–5; Kaikobad B. Dastur, "Laws of the Ancient Persians" I: 3 (March 1905), 97–100 and I: 4 (April 1905), 138–40.

[175] "Our Persian Mother-Tongue," *The Parsi* I: 6 (June 1905), 212–3. See also "Mainly Parsi. If French, why not Persian?" *The Parsi* I: 12 (December 1905), 351.

306

unaccompanied by male family members.[176] Rebuffing the British picture of "Oriental mendacity," Parsis boasted that the ancient Persians glorified truth-telling long before Western societies ever did.[177]

By contrast, Persia's more recent history gave cause for regret. Persia had never regained its former glory after being converted to Islam following the seventh-century conquest by Arab Muslims.[178] "Enlightened Iran, the mother of the then world academies, was to be run over and strangled by a horde of mere barbarians."[179] Its Zoroastrian population had been oppressed and impoverished under Muslim rule.[180] However, there was a hidden Persia that served as a Utopian ideal. Followers of *Ilm-e Kshnoom* (Guj. *Ilme Kṣnūm*), the Parsi mystical movement that began in 1905 with the revelations of Behram Shroff, believed that a secret colony of Persian Zoroastrians lived inside Mount Damavand, a mountain in Iran to the northeast of Tehran.[181] Firdos was a self-sufficient vegetarian and environmental fantasy of clean air and water, green pastures, fresh fruit, vegetables, and grains. The animals in Firdos were treated humanely and were not killed for their meat.[182] Men and women enjoyed equal status, and no task was too low for any man or too "complex" for any women.[183] Daily life was athletic and austere. Education in the colony consisted of lessons in riding and archery, moral lessons in truth, mental independence, and the resistance of envy and greed, along with the development of the individual's capacity for telepathy and clairvoyance.[184] Honesty reigned, and colonists practiced the old Zoroastrian tradition of confession.[185] Firdos' colonists were in fact descendants of Sasanian royalty, and they preserved the treasures of Sasanian Persia (particularly its sacred texts) in the depths of the city.[186] Bombay was everything Firdos was not: a seething mass of capitalist greed, dishonesty,

---

[176] Karaka, I: xxvii; J. J. Modi, *K. R. Cama* (Bombay: Rustom J. J. Modi and J. M. Unvala, for the K. R. Cama Oriental Institute, [1932]), 174; Desai, *History*, 37.

[177] "The Ideal in Connection with the Parsis," *The Parsi* I: 3 (November 1905), 76–7. Contrast with F. C. O. Beaman, "Eheu! Fugaces!," *Bom LJ* III: 6 (November 1925), 209; and Macleod, "Reminiscences," 67 (HRA/D63/A5) in Macleod of Cadboll Papers.

[178] F. R. V., "To the Parsi Race," *The Parsi* I: 1 (January 1905), 7.

[179] Nanabhoy Framji Mama, *A Mazdaznan Mystic: Life-sketch of the late Behramshah Navroji Shroff, the 20th century exponent of Zarthoshti Elm-e-Khshnoom (i.e. Esotericism of Zoroastrianism)* (Bombay: Zarthushti Din Sahitya Mandal, 2001; orig. pub. 1944), 12.

[180] See Karaka, I: 53–90.

[181] See Sanjana, *Ancient Persia*, 6; Darukhanawala, *Parsi Lustre*, I: 607, 617; Almut Hintze, "New Religions, Sects and Alternative Spiritualities with Roots in Zoroastrianism" in Peter B. Clarke, ed., *Encyclopedia of New Religious Movements* (New York: Routledge, 2005), 146–56; Boyce, *Zoroastrians*, 205–6; Hinnells, "Parsi Attitudes," 208–9; Stausberg, *Die Religion*, II: 118–24.

[182] Mama, 32.

[183] Ibid., 25.

[184] Ibid., 34, 52. See also Pestanji M. Ghadiali, "Preface," in *Zoroastrianism in the light of Theosophy*, ed. Nasarvanji F. Bilimoria (Madras: Blavatsky Lodge, Theosophical Society, 1898), xvi.

[185] Mama, 33.

[186] Ibid., 27. See also Ghadiali, "Preface" in Bilimoria, xvi.

Pure Parsi: Libel, Race, and Group Membership

pollution, and sexism.[187] Parsi Khsnoomists were not alone in turning to a semi-fantastical world of ancient pedigree to critique the ills of colonial modernity. Firdos existed as a diasporic link with the homeland – in idealized and mythical form. In Tamil South India and among Theosophists, the lost continent of Lemuria (Tam. *Kumarināṭu*) functioned similarly as a former or secret "place of promise, plenitude and perfection" whose "wholeness, superior wisdom, well-being, peace, and harmony that once was in man's distant past" could be aspired to by all. For some, Lemuria continued to exist in a parallel mystical dimension or would reappear in the future as a site for "a universal human Utopia."[188]

There was also talk of creating a Parsi colony.[189] *The Parsi* toyed with several options in 1905.[190] The first of these was to start a colony in East Africa, where land for a Jewish homeland had been offered and declined.[191] Another possibility was Sind, in India's far west.[192] A Parsi writer named B. D. Patel published a scheme in two issues of the Parsi newspaper, *Rast Goftar*. His rationale for the colony was that, as content as the Parsis were in India at the moment, they were still aliens in India. If the British left India, the Parsis could suddenly become vulnerable. The creation of their own colony would allow them not to rely on any host's good favor for their well-being.[193] Another writer celebrated the "spirit of roving adventure" that was so Anglo-Saxon but also ancient Persian. A Parsi colony would allow for the "regeneration of the old Persian life with all its glorious features" and even perhaps lead to a new Persian nation in Asia.[194] The consensus was that the colony should be located as close to Persia as possible.[195] Such a plan would combine the desire to create a Parsi colony with the Parsi campaign to set a positive model for their less fortunate Iranian co-religionists.[196]

Finally, there were fantasies of return.[197] Between 1921 and 1926, a commander in the Persian army's Cossack Brigade named Reza Pahlavi ousted

---

[187] For a reformist attack on Kshnoomism, see Dhalla, 382.

[188] Sumathi Ramaswamy, *The Lost Land of Lemuria: Fabulous Geographies, Catastrophic Histories* (Berkeley: University of California Press, 2004), 85, 97.

[189] See Kulke, 110, 144–6; Stausberg, *Die Religion*, II: 71–2, 76.

[190] See "The Economic Aspect of the Proposed Parsi Colony out of India," *The Parsi* I: 2 (February 1905), 43–4.

[191] "East Africa for Parsis," *The Parsi* I: 12 (December 1905), 525.

[192] "The Colony Question," *The Parsi* I: 12 (December 1905), 534–5.

[193] B. D. Patel, "The Question of the Day. Do we need a Colony and can we found one?" *The Parsi* I: 6 (June 1905), 208–10 (referring to Patel's articles in *Rast Goftar*, 3–4 April 1904).

[194] "The Proposed Parsi Colony," *The Parsi* I: 7 (July 1905), 241–2.

[195] "East Africa for Parsis," *The Parsi* I: 12 (December 1905), 525.

[196] "Regeneration of Iran – Parsi Ambitions," *The Parsi* I: 4 (April 1905), 136. See also Armenius Vambéry, "A Parsi out of India," *The Parsi* I: 9 (September 1905), 346–7; Luhrmann, 102–3.

[197] Scholars of comparative diasporas seem to be unaware of the Parsis' continuing ties to Persia through philanthropy or colonial-era myths of return. By William Safran in *Diaspora: A Journal of Transnational Studies*, see "Diasporas in Modern Societies: Myths of Homeland and Return," 1:1 (1991), 89; "Comparing Diasporas: A Review Essay," 8: 3 (1999), 263. See also Cohen, *Global Diasporas*, 189.

308   *Law and Identity in Colonial South Asia: Parsi Legal Culture*

the Qajar (Pers. *Qājār*) dynasty and founded his own. The Pahlavis would rule Iran until the Islamic Revolution of 1979.[198] Reza Shah was an admirer of ancient Persia and encouraged Parsis to return to and invest in their historic motherland.[199] Many Parsis shared his enthusiasm.[200] *Hindi Punch* mused that leading Parsis might populate Reza Shah's cabinet and even occupy his throne should they move back (Figure 7.5).[201]

Two decades after the Rangoon suits, there was even a libel suit on the topic of the Parsi recolonization of Persia. Colonel Merwan S. Irani, the former Surgeon General of Bombay, sued a college student named Jehangir R. P. Mody for misconstruing the colonel's projects in Persia in a 1930 letter to the *Statesman*.[202] As his name suggested, the colonel was Irani: he came from the subgroup of Zoroastrians who migrated to India centuries after the Parsis and who were stereotyped as the Parsis' less sophisticated cousins.[203] The colonel's own parents had come from Persia. Irani was a member of a number of Parsi organizations in India that did charitable work in Persia for the benefit of Zoroastrians there.[204] The Iran League did this and more. During the trial, its efforts to recruit Parsis to work in railroad development in Iran came to light, as did its high-level visa negotiations with the Persian government on behalf of Parsis generally. Mody's letter commented on another project, the construction of a girls' school in Tehran. Because the school was not for Zoroastrian but Muslim girls, Mody suggested that the project was simply a "douceur" aimed at helping the Iran League facilitate a large-scale Parsi return to Persia. He implied that it was a bribe paid to the Persian government and a perversion of the Parsi donor's desire to fund a school for Zoroastrian girls in Tehran.[205] More generally, Mody's letter suggested that the idea of migration was gaining traction as Indian independence loomed. "This uncertainty concerning the future has led

---

[198] See Nikki R. Keddie, *Modern Iran: Roots and Results of Revolution* (New Haven, CT: Yale University Press, 2003), 80–104; Ali M. Ansari, *Modern Iran: The Pahlavis and After* (Harlow, UK: Pearson Longman, 2007), 20–211; Ervand Abrahamian, *A History of Modern Iran* (Cambridge: Cambridge University Press, 2008), 63–96; Michael Axworthy, *History of Iran: Empire of the Mind* (New York: Basic Books, 2010), 215–58.

[199] See R. P. Masani, "With Dinshah Irani in New Iran," in *Dinshah Irani Memorial Volume: Papers on Zoroastrian and Iranian Subjects in Honour of the late Mr Dinshah Jijibhai Irani, BA, LLB, Solicitor, Nishan-I Elmi (Iran)* (Bombay: Dinshah J. Irani Memorial Fund Committee, 1943), xv–xxiv; "Reza Shah of Persia – Ascending the Throne," Patel and Paymaster, VI: 232; "Reza Shah of Persia – Dr Jivanji J. Modi's Visit," Patel and Paymaster, VI: 235 (2 December 1925), both trans. Homi D. Patel. See also Abrahamian, 81–3.

[200] See Sanjana, *Ancient Persia*, front photos (Reza Shah and his son), 591, 605, photos facing 604–5 (Parsi philanthropists in Iran), 626.

[201] See "New Year Dreams" series (no. 1–5), *HP* (5 September 1925), 6, 24, 27.

[202] "Bombay Student in Defamation Charge. Early Trial Plea. Court's 'No' in Absence of Complainant," *TI* (23 December 1923), 5.

[203] See Sharafi, "Marital Patchwork," 1003–4.

[204] See Darukhanawala, *Parsi Lustre*, I: 357.

[205] "Alleged Defamation by Bombay Parsi. Col. Irani's Suit" (15 February 1933), 13; "Accused's Statement in Poona Libel Suit" (20 February 1933), 5; both in *TI*.

FIGURE 7.5. "When the Parsis regain Iran, their ancient Motherland, Sir Jamsetjee Jejeebhoy Baronet will be Shah-in-Shah Jamshid sitting on the Persian Throne of the Shahs of Persia."
Source: "New Year Dreams – No. 1," *HP* (6 September 1925), 6. © The British Library Board SV576.

310   *Law and Identity in Colonial South Asia: Parsi Legal Culture*

certain people to the absurdity of persuading the Parsis to re-colonize Persia," he wrote.[206] Irani claimed that this too was defamatory, despite the fact that the League had set up a special committee to consider a collective return to the motherland.[207] Eventually, Mody buckled under the pressure of the lawsuit and apologized for writing his letter, a common outcome for a libel suit. The Parsi magistrate, M. N. Mehta, acquitted him.[208] The magistrate's dismissive comment that Mody was "far too young to dabble in such matters" obscured the fact that the evidence supported Mody's general point: certain influential Parsis seriously considered a return to Persia.[209]

At celebrations for the Parsi New Year known as *Pateti*, a speech by the scholar K. R. Cama reflected many Parsis' sense of nostalgia for Persia around the turn of the twentieth century: "Breathed there a man in the assembly, who would not be rejoiced to say, Persia was his own, his native land. (Loud cheers.) They no doubt loved the land of their adoption, which was now to all intents and purposes their native country but the fire of their patriotism had not yet been extinguished in their hearts, which still yearned for their ancient home. (Loud cheers.)"[210] The idea of Persianness did useful work for a diaspora looking from hostland to homeland. It created an origins story, a racial identity, a Utopian foil against which to critique the social ills of late colonial modernity, and even a vehicle for the fantasy of return when India attained independence. It preserved Parsi self-respect and was politically strategic. The Anglicized Parsi ran the risk of being rejected by Britons on the basis of race. Like Homi Bhabha's mimicker, he could be perceived as "almost the same, but not white."[211] A strong Persian identity held Parsis far enough from the British both to insulate them from race-based snubs *and* to safeguard their future prospects in an independent India. Equally, it distanced Parsis from other South Asians enough to facilitate close relations with the British while colonialism lasted. Being Persian – neither British nor by some accounts Indian – had its uses.[212] In the Rangoon libel suits, Persianness teamed up with Parsi eugenics to ascribe a new offensiveness to racial mixing between Parsis and other populations in South and Southeast Asia.

---

[206] "Poona Defamation Charge," *TI* (10 February 1933), 14.

[207] Ibid.; "Iran League and 'Back to Persia' Movement," *TI* (1 March 1933), 7.

[208] See entry on Manekji Navroji Mehta in Umrīgar and Pāṭhak, 226.

[209] "College Student Apologises. Poona Defamation Case. Magistrate's Advice to Youth," *TI* (25 May 1933), 5.

[210] Cama delivered the speech some time before his death in 1909: "The Jamshedji Naoroz Dinner" (undated clipping from unidentified newspaper) in Menant Papers.

[211] Homi K. Bhabha, *The Location of Culture* (London and New York: Routledge, 1994), 89. An attack on the Parsi writer "Q. in the Corner" included the following passage: "Who is *Q in the Corner*? Is he a mannikin, half Parsee, half Policeman, who, because he knows a little English, imagines that, like the Frog in the Fable, he can become an Englishman by puffing himself out in size? Pooh, Pooh. The poor pigmy, he will never be more than a bull frog – let him puff and croak as he may . . . he is . . . not the ninth part of a Briton. . . .. If you, Mr. Editor, examine the matter, you will find *Q in the Corner* to be a nasty little black thing. . . .." (B. P. M., "A Poor Attempt.")

[212] For instance, see Ringer, *Pious Citizens*, 204–5.

Pure Parsi: Libel, Race, and Group Membership

Why may this hyperracialized identity have congealed in the late colonial period? Global faddishness was part of the answer: race theory was fashionable worldwide in the early twentieth century. But realigning the Rangoon cases of 1914–15 with the 1869 priestly libel suit, there may also have been a connection – specifically, an inverse relationship – between adherence to the Zoroastrian purity laws and endorsement of the new racial identity. An elaborate set of purity laws made problematic the consumption of food and water handled by non-Zoroastrians, smoking, the taking of oaths, long-distance sea travel, and the participation of menstruating women in social life.[213] Parsis could not adhere strictly to the purity laws if they wanted to take advantage of the educational, professional, and financial opportunities afforded by imperial subjecthood. Traveling to London for a legal education or to argue a case before the Privy Council; eating meals at clubs, restaurants, and British and Indian homes where food was not prepared by Zoroastrians; participating in the male smoking culture of the late imperial world; taking oaths in the colonial courtroom – each of these activities forced Parsis to choose between personal success and the purity laws.[214] So many chose the former, it seems, that they did not risk rejection by their own people for doing so.[215] But if being Parsi was no longer about following the Zoroastrian purity laws, what was it about? The obvious answer may have been race. A Persian racial identity may have arisen in tandem with and *even as a result of* the relaxation of adherence to the purity laws. The quest to prosper within the Anglicized circuits of the British Empire, in other words, may have contained within it the seeds of a hyperracialized sensibility. The new racial identity may have been a by-product of the fact that the Parsis did not wish to extricate themselves from imperial material culture.[216] In this way, Luhrmann's emphasis on Anglicization and the model of Persianness stressed here may have been related facets of Parsi identity more than mutually exclusive ones. The Rangoon libel suits provided a glimpse of these deeper processes.

---

[213] See *Parsi Panchayat Case*, 53; "Witness No. 2 [for the Defendants], Dastur Dorab Peshotan Sanjana, Examination in Chief, 4 April 1908" in Beaman, "Notes in Parsi Panchayat Case," 56; "Police Courts: Jam-e-Jamshed Defamation Case," *TI* (22 January 1915), 5; Modi, *Religious Ceremonies*, 160–8; Ibrahim Poure-Davoud, *The Conception of Truth in the Zoroastrian Religion* (Bombay: n.p., 1934), 13–14; Mirza, *Outlines*, 394–5; Paymaster, 47; Choksy, *Purity*, 18, 52, 97–100; Rose, "Traditional Role of Women," 19–25.

[214] On Parsis and smoking, see *The Parsi*: "For Parsi Smokers" and "The Tobacco Trade and Parsis," I: 2 (February 1905), 59; "Correspondence. Who is a Parsi? Letter from Rustom B. Paymaster, BA, LLB. Vakil, High Court," I: 3 (March 1905), 106; "To Parsi Smokers," I: 10 (October 1905), ix. See also "Parsis and Proselytism. Another lively meeting," *TI* (9 July 1904), 11; untitled ad by Parsi tobacco dealer, Hormusjee Aderji in B. N. Apakhtyar, *Cartoons from the 'Hindi Punch' for 1910* (Bombay: author, 1911), 16.

[215] See "A Short Account of the Life of ... Anklesaria," 49–50; Stausberg, *Die Religion*, II: 63–5; Ringer, *Pious Citizens*, 39–40.

[216] See Palsetia, *Parsis*, 154–7.

CONCLUSION

If "slander, libel, defamation, calumny, character assassination, mudslinging, scandalmongering, badmouthing and billingsgate" flourished in the world of late *ancien regime* France, the exchange of abuse was similarly energetic halfway around the world a century later.[217] Whereas Robert Darnton's French libelers saved their venom for the royal state, Parsi libel was inwardly turned. When a Parsi went to court over defamation, it was usually against another Parsi. Attacks from co-religionists alleging sexual and racial impurity especially pushed Parsis from the social register into the legal one.

The most divisive legal controversies among Parsis raged in areas that technically sat outside of Parsi personal law, namely trusts and libel. The two types of cases differed in constitution and longevity. If trust suits were the cockroaches of the colonial docket, libel suits were the butterflies. Trust suits lived on with tenacity and stamina. They were difficult to extinguish or divert from their march into the upper courts. They seemed to grow bigger and stronger the higher they climbed. By contrast, the color and flutter of libel suits were mesmerizing, but only for a moment. These cases usually expired before judgment. The Rangoon libel suits briefly flitted alongside *Saklat v. Bella* on the latter's relentless march to London. Yet even in their fragility, the libel cases documented a major cultural shift: the rise of a newly racialized sense of collective identity that glorified Persianness and stigmatized non-Parsi blood in the family, even at the fringes of the Indian Empire and through the female line. If maintaining ritual purity had once been a central part of being Parsi, the conditions of late imperial life forced the purity laws into a losing rivalry with material prosperity. The concept of racial purity filled the void, providing new content for Parsi identity in an age of eugenics.

---

[217] Robert Darnton, *The Devil in the Holy Water or the Art of Slander from Louis XIV to Napoleon* (Philadelphia: University of Pennsylvania Press, 2010), 439. Compare to "Gone Mad!," *HP* (26 March 1911), 20.

Conclusion

Law and Identity

In 1837, the judge and lobbyist Manekjee Cursetjee demanded that Parsi drafts-men reveal the sources on which they were relying in their proposed legislation. The inheritance bill that Sir Jamsetjee Jeejeebhoy and his associates were promoting did not appear to draw from Zoroastrian religious texts, nor was it based on "any settled national usages and customs sanctioned by their long observance among us." It was as if Jeejeebhoy and his camp were making it all up.[1]

The judge had a point not only for the 1830s but for the coming century, the period when Parsi legal mechanics worked themselves pure. Parsi law did reflect distinct models of the family and community, but these models did not have their roots in Zoroastrian antiquity. Parsi law emerged out of colonial culture clash, not from the ruins of Persepolis. The Bombay patriarchs who built Parsi legal infrastructure drew on their own aspirational visions of group life. In other words, what made Parsi law Parsi was not historically Zoroastrian content as much as it was *the fact that Parsis made it*. The identity politics of its genesis hitched law to community and community to law in special ways.

Persian heritage was notably absent in determining the content of Parsi law, but it lay at the core of how many Parsis saw themselves as a group. Colonial Parsis embodied both the model of the catastrophic or victim diaspora and the trade diaspora: they understood their migration as an escape from religious persecution, but probably circulated widely as merchants before and after this exodus. Like many others, this diaspora looked back to the homeland from the hostland and maintained ties with homeland co-religionists. With the rise of the Pahlavi dynasty

---

[1] "Correspondence on the subject of the law of inheritance among the Parsees between Manockjee Cursetjee and some of the prominent members of the Parsee community at Bombay and others in 1837–38 and 1859. No. 1: English version of a Guzratee Letter" (11 April 1837) in Q. in the Corner, 1–7.

313

314   *Conclusion*

in Persia, it also developed myths of return.[2] The thickening of a community identity among Raj-era Parsis enhanced the group's exclusivity and efficiency, pulling against the nascent Indian national identity that was also emerging in the last century of colonial rule. Exceptional figures like Congress pioneer Dadabhai Naoroji proclaimed that they were Indian first and Parsi second.[3] But more of Naoroji's co-religionists worked to fortify their separateness through law.

Law- and identity-making were closely connected processes. Most of this book has been devoted to the myriad ways in which Parsis' values shaped the state law that governed their social life. These visions of what it meant to be Parsi were contested in intragroup struggles over representation. All sides knew that the more one camp could capture the power of law, the more its model of the family and community would dominate.

Regardless of which side won in any particular contest, Parsi law became less Anglicized over time. In other areas of law, legislation and the assumptions of British officials infused South Asian law with Anglo values, shrinking the reach and depth of Indic legal traditions. Because Parsis took such an active role in the creation of their own personal law and because of their rising presence in the legal profession, their story was different. Parsi legal culture reflected a kind of agency limited by the bounds of a colonial system, but the semi-autonomy produced was powerful nonetheless.

The quest to brand law with Parsi values was clearest in disputes about the core principle of group membership. *Petit v. Jijibhai* and *Saklat v. Bella* were the most famous cases to harness law for this purpose, but there were also other, less successful attempts. In 1937–8, for instance, a group of orthodox Zoroastrian priests in Udwada proposed the Parsi Communal Constitution Act, a statute that would prevent "the penetration of non-Zoroastrian elements into the Zoroastrian fold." The bill would introduce a system of registration for the *navjote* ceremony and a tribunal with the power to investigate ritual offenses. The court would even be able to inquire into the conduct of any Parsi alleged "to be behaving in a manner detrimental to the social, religious, moral or economic interest of the community."[4] Had the bill become law, state law would have become the enforcer of ritual law and community leaders' diktats. The project failed because its priestly authors became mired in threatened litigation among themselves.[5] Still, the episode reflected a desire even in the priesthood – a

---

[2] See Cohen; by Safran, "Concepts" and "Diasporas"; Kim D. Butler, "Defining Diaspora, Refining a Discourse," *Diaspora: A Journal of Transnational Studies* 10:2 (2001), 189–219. See also Chapter 7 at note 197.

[3] "Inaugural Address by Dadabhai Naoroji, President of the Ninth Indian National Congress held at Lahore on 27 December 1903," in *Inaugural Addresses by Presidents of the Indian National Congress*, ed. Dinker Vishnu Gokhale (Bombay: Ripon Printing Press, 1895), 198.

[4] "The Parsi New Year. Problems before an Enterprising Community," *TI* (6 September 1938), 8.

[5] For example, see "Parsi Priests' Dispute. Legal Action Threatened," *TI* (20 January 1938), 16. Later efforts to pass a *navjote* registration bill in the 1940s also failed. See Desai, *History*, 40–3. On other litigation among priests, see Hinnells, "Changing Perceptions," 107–9.

Conclusion   315

stronghold against state authority in many other communities – to impress state law with a preferred model of group membership.

Neither priests nor laypeople could resist the opportunity to imprint Parsi values on law. But did law influence Parsi identity to the same degree? Tracing the social reception of legal outcomes is a "ticklish point," as speakers of the era would have put it. By itself, the fact that Parsis were heavily involved in the production and consumption of colonial law did not mean that they internalized colonial legal values. They obviously recognized the benefits of harnessing state power for their own ends. In the courtroom, for instance, Parsi litigants and lawyers may have tried any argument that would work. But they did not necessarily endorse these ideas outside of the legal forum. Given such instrumentalism, how can we know that influence flowed from law back into Parsi value systems? The possibility of the purely strategic use of law loomed over the colonial Parsi context, as it does for legal historians trying to yoke legal claims to larger social worlds in any time and place.

There are at least three potential responses to the instrumentalist critique. First, one could argue that to succeed, legal representations had to bear some resemblance to social perceptions of the same phenomenon. A legal claim that strayed too far from social realities would usually fail, in other words, because of the social knowledge of the players; it would be laughed out of court or legislature. This position may overestimate the ability of legal institutions to sift out the implausible. It may underestimate their susceptibility to manipulation. A second approach is the anthropological one. A scholar could note the social absorption of legal pronouncements in our own contemporary setting and use these to speculate that the same phenomenon occurred in the past. Many Parsis today are impressively conversant in the subtler points of *Petit v. Jijibhai*, for instance. And although they clash with each other on the interpretation of Davar's opinion, nobody says: "who cares? Why should a legal judgment have *social* weight among us?" But whereas anthropologists may commute happily between past and present, historians are less willing to do so.[6] Observations about the present do not necessarily tell us about the past, that proverbial foreign country. A third approach allows the legal historian to stay within the period of study and holds the most promise for this study. Rather than looking for ways in which *substantive* legal outcomes were absorbed socially, we may examine the social adoption of legal *processes*. It was not that colonial Parsis necessarily imbued Davar's courtroom views on religion and ethnicity with social value, in other words. Rather, it was the fact that, increasingly, Parsis turned to colonial courts and councils to address conflict within their own community. It was this general manner that best revealed law's influence on Parsi culture. As turning to law became a default mode of behavior repeated down the generations, legalism itself became a subcultural trait. Implicitly if not explicitly, using law became a part of what it meant to be Parsi – the reflexive pattern of behavior that came to

---

[6] For an example of the anthropological approach, see Luhrmann.

feel natural. Not only did Parsis make law, in other words. At the intersection of conflict, colonialism, and collective identity, *law also made the Parsis.*

And so a Raj-era stereotype developed. Its existence permits us to identify one flavor of the social internalization of law – a repeated turn to law's form – and lets us leave aside the unanswerable question of whether law's contents were ever "really" socially ingested by this population. Sometimes the association of Parsis with legal process was used to shame outliers. "You belong to a race," bellowed a British judge at a Parsi barrister convicted in a 1905 will forgery case, "that is famous on this side of India for obedience to law."[7] At other times, the association was martialed by community leaders to flatter themselves vis-à-vis other populations. When a London-based illustrated weekly published a graphic aerial photo of skeletons piled inside of Poona's towers of silence in 1923, the Bombay Parsi Panchayat protested. Airplanes were legally prohibited from flying over such sensitive religious sites.[8] The trustees flashed the Parsi legal stereotype in comparative terms, suggesting that the newspaper was lucky to be dealing with such a nonviolent community. "Our people are peaceful and law-abiding and so we limit ourselves to strictly constitutional action against such an offence but if it had been committed against some of the more excitable communities of India, one can well imagine the result."[9] But the nonviolent character of Parsi legalism was hardly the point. The Parsi approach was a highly conflictual mode of social interaction. The threat of legal action loitered just behind the trustees' thin request for an apology.

During the final century of colonial rule, Parsi law and identity formation became enmeshed. The more Parsi values shaped law through the work of Parsi lobbyists, judges, and litigants, the more Parsis sought legal solutions for their social problems, including core intragroup ones. Here was a minority population that enfleshed its collective sense of self not by avoiding the state, but by engaging so closely with state institutions as to become almost a part of them. Zoroastrians were not unique in taking this approach. But because the pattern was so strong, clear, and early, Parsi legal culture occupied a special place in the British Empire's traffic between law and community.

---

[7] "Bombay Criminal Sessions," *TI* (17 February 1905), 4.

[8] See "A Peep into a Tower of Silence," 278.

[9] Desai, *History*, 217. For a 1927 fictionalized account of this episode by Phiroshaw Jamsetjee Chaiwala (or Chevalier), see Gyan Prakash, *Mumbai Fables: A History of an Enchanted City* (Princeton, NJ: Princeton University Press, 2010), 1–2; Phiroshaw Jamsetjee Chevalier "Chaiwala," *The Tower of Silence*, ed. Gyan Prakash (Delhi: HarperCollins, 2013).

Appendix: Legislation

Below are key provisions or brief descriptions of colonial statutes affecting Parsis. All statutes applied across India unless otherwise indicated.

Sources: India Acts 1834–40 (IOR/V/8/31); Ranchhoddas and Thakore, *IPC*; Rana (1902, 1934); Wadia and Katpitia; Indian Succession (Amendment) Act 1939 (IOR/L/PJ/7/2493); Parsi Marriage and Divorce (Amendment) Act 1940 (IOR/L/PJ/7/2502)

SUCCESSION TO PARSEES IMMOVABLE PROPERTY ACT (IX OF 1837)

s. I: "It is hereby enacted, that...all immoveable Property, situated within the jurisdiction of any of the Courts established by His Majesty's Charter shall, as far as regards the transmission of such Property on the death and intestacy of any Parsee having a beneficial interest in the same, or by the last Will of any such Parsee, be taken to be and to have been of the nature of Chattels real and not of freehold."

INDIAN PENAL CODE (XLV OF 1860)

s. 320: "The following kinds of hurt only are designated as 'grievous':– Emasculation... Permanent privation of the sight of either eye...Permanent privation of the hearing of either ear...Privation of any member or joint...Destruction or permanent impairing of the powers of any member or joint...Permanent disfiguration of the head or face...Fracture or dislocation of a bone or tooth...Any hurt which endangers life or which causes the sufferer to be,

318   *Appendix: Legislation*

during the space of twenty days, in severe bodily pain, or unable to follow his ordinary pursuits."

s. 494: "Whoever, having a husband or wife living, marries in any case in which such marriage is void by reason of its taking place during the life of such husband or wife, shall be punished with imprisonment of either description [simple or rigorous] for a term which may extend to seven years, and shall also be liable to fine." (Act XV of 1865 made this section applicable to Parsis.)

s. 499: "Whoever by words either spoken or intended to be read, or by signs or by visible representations, makes or publishes any imputation concerning any person intending to harm, or knowing or having reason to believe that such imputation will harm, the reputation of such person, is said, except in the cases hereinafter excepted, to defame that person..."

PARSI MARRIAGE AND DIVORCE ACT (XV OF 1865)

s. 27: "If a Parsi, at the time of his or her marriage, was a lunatic or of habitually unsound mind, such marriage may, at the instance of his or her wife or husband, be declared null and void..."

s. 28: "In any case in which consummation of the marriage is, from natural causes, impossible, such marriage may, at the instance of either party thereto, be declared to be null and void."

s. 30: "Any husband may sue that his marriage may be dissolved, and a divorce granted, on the ground that his wife has, since the celebration thereof, been guilty of adultery; and any wife may sue that her marriage may be dissolved ... on the ground that, since the celebration thereof, her husband has been guilty of adultery with a married, or fornication with an unmarried woman not being a prostitute, or of bigamy coupled with adultery, or of adultery coupled with cruelty, or of adultery coupled with wilful desertion for two years or upwards, or of rape, or of an unnatural offence..."

PARSI INTESTATE SUCCESSION ACT (XXI OF 1865)

s. 1: "Where a Parsi dies leaving a widow and children, the property of which he shall have died intestate shall be divided among the widow and children, so that the share of each son shall be double the share of the widow, and that her share shall be double the share of each daughter."

s. 2: "Where a female Parsi dies leaving a widower and children, the property of which she shall have died intestate shall be divided among the widower and such children, so that his share shall be double the share of each of the children."

Appendix: Legislation

ADMINISTRATOR GENERAL'S ACT (IX OF 1881)

This Act exempted Parsis (like Hindus, Muslims, and Buddhists before them) from the Administrator General's Act (II of 1874), which imposed a regime of state control over the administration of intestates' estates.

INDIAN SUCCESSION ACT (XXXIX OF 1925)

This statute absorbed the PISA of 1865, making no changes to its text. The law of Parsi intestacy remained its own distinct body of law, but separate statutes for Parsi intestate succession would no longer be passed.

CHILD MARRIAGE RESTRAINT ACT (XIX OF 1929)

This statute criminalized marriages in which at least one party was a child, defined by s. 2(a) as a boy under eighteen or a girl under fourteen years of age.

PARSI MARRIAGE AND DIVORCE ACT (III OF 1936)

s. 2(4): "'Grievous hurt' means – (a) emasculation; (b) permanent privation of the sight of either eye; (c) permanent privation of the hearing of either ear; (d) privation of any member or joint; (e) destruction or permanent impairing of the powers of any member or joint; (f) permanent disfigurement of the head or face; or (g) any hurt which endangers life."

s. 30: "In any case in which consummation of the marriage is from natural causes impossible, such marriage may, at the instance of either party thereto, be declared to be null and void."

s. 32: "Any married person may sue for divorce on any one or more of the following grounds, namely:–(a) that the marriage has not been consummated within one year after its solemnization owing to the wilful refusal of the defendant to consummate it; (b) that the defendant at the time of the marriage was of unsound mind and has been habitually so up to the date of the suit. . .(c) that the defendant was at the time of marriage pregnant by some person other than the plaintiff. . .(d) that the defendant has since the marriage committed adultery or fornication or bigamy or rape or an unnatural offence. . .(e) that the defendant has since the marriage voluntarily caused grievous hurt to the plaintiff or has infected the plaintiff with venereal disease or, where the defendant is the husband, has compelled the wife to submit herself to prostitution. . .(f) that the defendant is undergoing a sentence of imprisonment for seven years or more for an offence as defined in the Indian Penal Code. . .(g) that the defendant has deserted the plaintiff for at least three years; (h) that a decree or order for judicial

320   *Appendix: Legislation*

separation has been passed against the defendant, or an order has been passed against the defendant by a Magistrate awarding separate maintenance to the plaintiff, and the parties have not had marital intercourse for three years or more since such decree or order; (i) that the defendant has failed to comply with a decree for restitution of conjugal rights for a year or more; and (j) that the defendant has ceased to be a Parsi..."

PARSI PUBLIC TRUSTS REGISTRATION ACT (BOMBAY ACT XXIII OF 1936)

This Act made compulsory the registration, publication, and inspection of audited accounts for charitable trusts created for the benefit of Parsis. Its aim was to create greater transparency and accountability in the administration of Parsi trusts.

INDIAN SUCCESSION (AMENDMENT) ACT (XVII OF 1939)

s. 51: "(1)...the property of which a male Parsi dies intestate shall be divided – (a) where he dies leaving a widow and children, among the widows and children, so that the share of each son and of the widow shall be double the share of each daughter, or (b) where he dies leaving children but no widow, among the children, so that the share of each son shall be double the share of each daughter. (2) Where a male Parsi dies leaving one or both parents in addition to children or a widow and children, the property of which he dies intestate shall be divided so that the father shall receive a share equal to half the share of a son and the mother shall receive a share equal to half the share of a daughter."

s. 52: "The property of which a female Parsi dies intestate shall be divided – (a) where she dies leaving a widower and children, among the widower and children so that the widower and each child receive equal shares, or (b) where she dies leaving children but no widower, among the children in equal shares."

PARSI MARRIAGE AND DIVORCE (AMENDMENT) ACT (XIV OF 1940)

s. 2(c): "Where an order for alimony or maintenance in favor of a wife has been made either under the provisions of the PMDA 1865, or under the provisions of this Act, the Court, if satisfied that the wife has remarried or has not remained chaste, shall vary or rescind the order."

Glossary

ābrū (Guj., from Pers.): reputation, credit, honor, or the good name of one's family

Adawlut court system (Pers. *'Adālat*): the East India Company's court system in the *mofussil*, outside of the presidency center of Bombay City

agiary (Guj. *agīārī*): general term for Zoroastrian fire temple, which houses a sacred fire

Ahura Mazda (Av. *Ahura Mazdā*, Pahl. *Ohrmazd*): the force of good in Zoroastrianism; the spirit of order, goodness, truth, fertility, life, and light

Angra Manyu (Av. *Aŋra Mainiiu*, Pahl. *Ahrimen*): the force of evil in Zoroastrianism; the spirit of deception, darkness, disorder, disease, death, and decay

Anjuman (Guj. *Añjuman*): the local Parsi community; its general meetings

asha (Av. *aṣa*): Zoroastrian principle of moral order, righteousness, and truth

Avesta (Pahl. *Abestāg*): the collection of Zoroastrian scriptures first put into writing between the fifth and tenth centuries CE after being transmitted orally for as long as two millennia

bandobast (Guj. *baṅdobast*): an order, management; in a Parsi context, a resolution of the Parsi Panchayat

barashnum (Pah. *baršnūm*): the highest state of Zoroastrian ritual purity; the ceremony that creates such a state

cause of action: the specific civil or criminal wrong pursued by the plaintiff (in a civil suit) or prosecution (in a criminal one); for example: slander, breach of contract, theft

chawl (Guj. *cāl*): poor tenement housing block usually with a single room per family and shared bath and toilet facilities

civil law: the body of law in common-law jurisdictions governing disputes between private parties (excluding privately prosecuted criminal suits)

322   *Glossary*

common law: the system of law originating in England (as compared to systems based on Roman law, Islamic law, etc.); introduced to most parts of the British Empire

coverture: common-law doctrine that a woman ceased to have independent legal personality upon marriage, from which point she would be represented by the legal person of her husband; also known as the *doctrine of unity*

criminal law: the body of law governing acts deemed to be offenses not only against particular individuals, but against society generally; with the exception of private prosecutions, the state initiates legal action against the accused

dakhmas (Guj. *dakhmā*): towers of silence where the bodies of deceased Zoroastrians are consigned to be exposed to vultures

dastur (Guj. *dastur*): a Zoroastrian high priest

Davar (Guj. *Dāvar*): nonreligious hereditary head of the Parsi community of Surat; also known as the Modi of Surat

Diwan (Pers. *Dīvān*): position of Prime Minister in many South Asian princely states

gurdwara (Punj. *gurduārā*): a Sikh temple

Ilm-e Kshnoom (Guj. *Ilme Kṣnūm*): Zoroastrian mystical movement based on the early twentieth-century revelations of Behram Shroff

fravahar (Pahl. *frawahr*): a winged, part-human figure encircled by a two-legged ring; the unofficial symbol of Zoroastrianism

ghambar (Guj. *ghāhambār*): a Zoroastrian collective religious feast

in camera proceedings: legal proceedings held behind closed doors

injunction: a type of civil remedy; a judicial order typically prohibiting a certain activity

intestacy: the default rules of distribution in inheritance law that apply in the absence of a valid will

Irani: Iranian Zoroastrians who migrated from Persia to South Asia generally between the eighteenth and twentieth centuries, following the Parsi migrations of earlier centuries

jazieh (Pers. *jezīeh*): tax paid by non-Muslim religious minorities under Islamic law

juddin (Guj. *juddīn*): ethnic outsider or non-Parsi

kusti (Guj. *kustī*): a cord tied around the waist over the *sudreh* and worn by devout Zoroastrians under their clothing

mofussil (Pers. *mafaṣal*): territory within a presidency of British India outside of the presidency's capital city; in Bombay Presidency, the region outside of Bombay City, including the traditional Parsi heartland of what is today southeastern Gujarat

muktad ceremonies (Guj. *muktād*): death commemoration rites held during the last ten days of the Zoroastrian calendar

nasasalar (Guj. *nasāsālār*): Zoroastrian hereditary corpse bearer who prepares bodies for consignment to the towers of silence

Glossary

navjote (Guj. *navjot*): ceremony of initiation into the Zoroastrian religion, investing the individual with the *sudreh* and *kusti*

nirang (Guj. *nīrang*): the consecrated urine of a white bull; used as a purifying agent for ingestion and external cleansing in Zoroastrian ceremonies

panchayat (Guj. pañcayāt): traditional South Asian caste or community council that may adjudicate disputes among members or (in the case of the Bombay Parsi Panchayat) manage charitable funds and properties

Parsi: since the early twentieth century, an ethnic or racial term describing the followers of the Zoroastrian religion who migrated from Persia to South Asia before the nineteenth century

primogeniture: traditional common-law principle that the eldest son inherits all real estate to the exclusion of other siblings

private prosecution: exceptional device in which the victim of an alleged crime (rather than the state) initiates a criminal suit against the accused; mandatory for certain offenses in British Indian law, including criminal defamation

purdah (Pers. *pardeh*): a form of female seclusion practiced by certain South Asian elites during the colonial period

rivayats (Pers. *revāyat*): texts documenting the discussion of doctrinal questions between Zoroastrians of India and Persia; dated to the period between the fifteenth and eighteenth centuries

special jury: jury in which jurors had special qualifications or technical knowledge relevant to the general context of a particular criminal case; lists of potential special jury members were maintained separately from normal jury lists in British India

Sudder Dewanny Adawlut (Pers. *Ṣadr Dīvānī 'Adālat*): the East India Company's highest civil court of appeal within a presidency for the *mofussil*; in Bombay Presidency, for cases originating outside of Bombay City

sudreh (Guj. *śudreh*): ritual undershirt of thin muslin worn with the *kusti* by devout Zoroastrians

Shah Nameh (Pers. *Shāhnāmeh*): epic by the Persian poet Ferdowsi of Tus depicting the pre-Islamic history of Persia; composed circa 1000 CE

shethia (Guj. *śethiyā*): honorific term describing respected senior men, typically merchants

tort: a category of civil wrongs falling outside of the explicit obligations undertaken between individuals by contract; a violation of an implicit duty not to cause harm to others where no specific agreement had been made between the parties

trust: a common-law device that separates the control and management of property, on the one hand, from its use and benefit, on the other; the trustee manages property on behalf and for the benefit of the beneficiary, who is often unable to manage his or her own affairs

vakil (Pers. *vakīl*): agent who represented clients in the lower courts

wakf (Pers. *vaqf*, from Arabic): under Islamic and British Indian law, religious endowment governing Muslim places of worship, institutions, or funds of an educational or charitable nature

Zoroastrianism: pre-Islamic, ancient Persian religion based on the teachings of the prophet Zarathustra

Selective Bibliography

PRIMARY SOURCES

Archives and Collections Consulted

Bombay High Court, Mumbai
Case papers (Original Civil Jurisdiction)
Petit, Sir Dinsha Manekji and others v. Sir Jamsetji Jijibhai and others (Suit No. 689 of 1906)
Tarachand, Jamshedji C. v. Soonabai (Suit No. 341 of 1907)
Judges' Notebooks
Chamber Books, Short Causes and Motions, Long Causes, Typed Notes of Evidence, Judgments, and Appeals of Justices F. C. O. Beaman, H. C. and N. H. C. Coyajee, D. D. and J. D. Davar, N. C. Macleod, B. J. Wadia (1906–47)
Parsi Chief Matrimonial Court Notebooks (1868–9, 1893–1947)

Highland Council Archives, Inverness, Scotland
Macleod of Cadboll Papers (1831–1983)

Asia, Pacific, and Africa Collections, British Library
India Office Records (IOR)
F: Board of Control Records (1784–1858)
L/PJ: India Office. Public and Judicial Department Records (1795–1950)
P: Proceedings and Consultations (1702–1945)
R/20: Records of the British Administrations in Aden (1837–1967)
V: India Office Records. Official Publications Series (1760–1957)

Maharashtra State Archives, Mumbai
Legal Dept. Suits B-1 to B-8 (1879–1928)

Musée Guimet, Paris
Delphine Menant Papers

325

326   *Selective Bibliography*

New York County Clerk's Office
B. B. Colah Case Papers, Court of Common Pleas of New York, Division of Old Records (courtesy of Kathryn Burns-Howard)

Privy Council Office, London
JCPC Appeal Case Papers
Jeevanji, Pestonji and others v. Shapurji Edulji Chinoy and others: JCPC Suit No. 10 of 1907, 1908: vol. 3, judgment 9
Saklat, Dorabjee Rustomjee, Sheriar Khodabux Irani and Jamsetji Burjorjee Sootaria v. Bella and Sapoorjee Cowasjee (since deceased): JCPC Suit No. 57 of 1924, 1925: vol. 24, judgment 88

For law reports, journals, and newspapers consulted, see "Note on Transliteration, Citation, and Abbreviation"

Printed Primary Sources

Anklesaria, T. D. *The Social Code of the Parsis in Sasanian Times or Mādigān i Hazār Dādistān, Part II.* Bombay: Fort Printing Press, 1912.

Baker, P. V., ed. *The Records of the Honorable Society of Lincoln's Inn. The Black Books. Vol. VI: AD 1914–AD 1965.* London: Lincoln's Inn, 2001.

Bengalee, Sorabjee Shapoorjee, ed. *The Parsee Marriage and Divorce Act 1865 (Act No. XV of 1865), The Parsee Chattels Real Act (Act No. IX of 1837), The Parsee Succession Act (Act No. XXI of 1865), with an Appendix and Guzerattee Translation.* Bombay: Parsee Law Association, 1868.

Bentwich, Norman. *The Practice of the Privy Council in Judicial Matters in Its Appeals from Courts of Civil, Criminal and Admiralty Jurisdiction and in Appeals from Ecclesiastical and Prize Courts with the Statutes, Rules and Forms of Procedure.* London: Sweet and Maxwell, 1912.

The Bombay Incorporated Law Society Centenary. Mumbai: Bombay Incorporated Law Society, 1995.

Bulsara, Sohrab J. *The Laws of the Ancient Persians.* Mumbai: K. R. Cama Oriental Institute, 1999 (reprint of 1937 ed.).

Chintamini, C. Y., ed. *Speeches and Writings of the Hon. Sir Pherozeshah M. Mehta.* Allahabad: The Indian Press, 1905.

Cowell, Herbert. *The History and Constitution of the Courts and Legislative Authorities in India (Tagore Law Lectures 1872).* Calcutta: Thacker, Spink and Co., 1872.

Cranenburgh, D. E. *The Code of Criminal Procedure being Act V of 1898 as Amended up to 1923.* Calcutta: Law-Publishing Press, 1924.

Darukhanawala, H. D. *Parsi Lustre on Indian Soil.* Bombay: G. Claridge and Co., 1939. 2 vols.

Davar, D. D. *Hints to Young Lawyers, being an Address delivered by the Hon. Mr. Justice D. D. Davar to the Students of the Government Law School, Bombay, on 15th Feb. 1911.* Bombay: Tripathi and Co., 1911.

Davar, Sohrab P. *The History of the Parsi Punchayet.* Bombay: New Book Company, 1949.

Selective Bibliography

Desai, Sapur Faredun. *History of the Bombay Parsi Punchayet, 1860–1960.* Bombay: Trustees of the Bombay Parsi Panchayat, [1977].

Parsis and Eugenics. Bombay: Author, 1940.

Desika Char, S. V. *Readings in the Constitutional History of India, 1757–1947.* Delhi: Oxford University Press, 1983.

Dhalla, M. N. *Dastur Dhalla: The Saga of a Soul. An Autobiography of Shams-ul-Ulama Dastur Dr. Maneckji Nusserwanji Dhalla, High Priest of the Parsis of Pakistan.* Trans. Gool and Behram Sohrab H. J. Rustomji. Karachi: Dastur Dr. Dhalla Memorial Institute, 1975.

Gandhi, M. K. *The Law and the Lawyers.* Ed. B. G. Kher. Ahmedabad: Navajivan Publishing House, 2004.

Inner Temple Archives: Alphabetical Index of Members (1851–1929), showing dates of Admission and Call. London: n.p., 1997.

Jāgoś, Mancerjī Hośañgji. *Ānarebal Sar Dīnshāh Dhanjībhāī Dāvar, Nāīṭ, Hāī Kōrṭnā Nāmdār Jaḍjnū Ṭukū Janm Caritr (A Short Sketch of the Life of the Hon. Justice Sir Dinshaw Dhanjibhoy Davar Kt.).* Bombay: author, 1912. (Gujarati)

Jardine, John. *Notes on Buddhist Law.* Rangoon: Government Press, 1883.

Jeejeebhoy, J. R. B., ed. *Some Unpublished and Later Speeches and Writings of the Hon. Sir Pherozeshah Mehta.* Bombay: Commercial Press, 1918.

Judgments: Petit v. Jeejeebhoy 1908 and Saklat v. Bella 1925. Mumbai: Parsiana Publications, 2005.

Karaka, Dosabhai Framji. *History of the Parsis Including Their Manners, Customs, Religion and Present Position.* London: Macmillan, 1884. 2 vols.

Mansukh (or Muncherjee Cowasjee [Lungra]). *Pārsī Dhārā Parnī Nuktecīnī.* Bombay: "Satya Mitra" Office, 1888. (Gujarati)

Menant, Delphine. *Les Parsis: histoire des communautés zoroastriennes de l'Inde. Première partie.* Paris: Ernest Leroux, 1898.

Mistry, Ardeshir Jamshedji Chanji. *Forty Years' Reminiscences of the Firm of Messrs. Wadia Ghandy and Co.* Bombay: Author, 1925.

Forty Years' Reminiscences of the High Court of Judicature at Bombay. Bombay: Author, 1925.

Reminiscences of the Office of Messrs Wadia Ghandy and Co. Bombay: Commercial Reporter's Press and the "Echo" Press, [1911].

Modi, J. J., ed. *Mādigān-i-Hazār Dādistān. A Photozincographed Facsimile of a MS belonging to the Mānockji Limji Hoshang Hātariā Library in the Zarthoshti Anjuman Ātashbeharām.* Poona: Government Photozingraphic Department, 1901.

The Religious Ceremonies and Customs of the Parsees. Bombay: Society for the Promotion of Zoroastrian Religious Knowledge and Education, Union Press, 1937.

Mr. Vimadalal and the Juddin Question: a Series of Articles reprinted from "The Oriental Review." Bombay: Crown Press, 1910.

Nariman, Fali S. *Before Memory Fades … An Autobiography.* Delhi: Hay House, 2010.

Oppé, A. S. *Wharton's Law Lexicon forming an epitome of the Laws of England … with select titles relating to the Civil, Scots, and Indian Law.* Delhi: Universal Law Publishing, 2003 (reprinting 14th ed., 1937).

Parekh, C. L., ed. *Essays, Speeches, Addresses and Writings (on Indian Politics) of the Honorable Dadabhai Naoroji.* Bombay: Caxton Printing Works, 1887.

328   *Selective Bibliography*

The Parsee Priest Defamation Case. Full Report of the Trial of Jamsetjee Sorabjee Madun in Her Majesty's High Court at Bombay, for defaming Nowrojee Shapoorjee Sunjana. Bombay: Dorabjee Eduljee Tata, 1870.

The Parsi Panchayat Case in the High Court of Judicature at Bombay (Suit No. 689 of 1906). Sir Dinsha Manockji Petit and others, plaintiffs v. Sir Jamsetjee Jeejeebhoy and others, defendants. Judgment of the Honourable Mr. Justice Davar delivered Friday, 27th November 1908; and Judgment of the Honourable Mr. Justice Beaman delivered Friday, 27th November 1908. Bombay: n.p., n.d.

Patel, Bomanjee Byhramjee and Rustam Barjorji Paymaster, eds. *Pārsī Prakāś (Parsi Prakash being a Record of Important Events in the Growth of the Parsee Community in Western India: chronologically arranged).* Bombay: Bombay Parsi Panchayat, 1878–1962, 10 vols. (Gujarati).

Patwardhan, R. P., ed. *Dadabhai Naoroji Correspondence.* Bombay: Allied Publishers, 1977.

Peters, Thomas, ed. *Famous Business Houses and Who's Who in India and Pakistan.* Bombay: Modern Press and Publicity, [1949].

Puñjābhāī, Vallabhjī Suñdarjī. *Mumbaīna Mahāśyo.* Kathiawad: author, 1920. (Gujarati)

Q. in the Corner [Manekjee Cursetjee]. *The Parsee Panchayet: its rise, its fall, and the causes that led to the same, being a series of letters in the Bombay Times of 1844–45.* Bombay: L. M.[D'Souza's] Press, 1860.

Rana, Framjee A. *Parsi Law containing the Law applicable to Parsis as regards succession and inheritance, marriage and divorce, etc.* Bombay: "Examiner Press," 1902.

Parsi Law embodying the Law of Marriage and Divorce and Inheritance and Succession applicable to Parsis in British India. Bombay: A. B. Dubash at the "Jam-e Jamshed" Printing Works, 1934.

Ranchhoddas, Ratanlal, and Dhirajlal Keshavlal Thakore. *The Indian Penal Code.* Bombay: Bombay Law Reporter Office, 1926.

Law of Torts. Bombay: Bombay Law Reporter Office, 1921.

Rankin, George Claus. *Background to Indian Law.* Cambridge: Cambridge University Press, 1946.

The Records of the Honorable Society of Lincoln's Inn. Vol. II–III: Admissions and Chapel Registers. London: Lincoln's Inn, 1896–1981.

Roxburgh, Ronald, ed., *The Records of the Honourable Society of Lincoln's Inn. The Black Books, Vol. V. AD 1845–1914.* London: Lincoln's Inn, 1968.

Sanjana, Jehangir Barjorji. *Ancient Persia and the Parsis. A Comprehensive History of the Parsis and their Religion from Primeval Times to Present Age.* Bombay: Hosang T. Anklesaria at the Fort Printing Press, 1935.

Shabbir, Mohammad, and S. C. Manchanda, *Parsi Law in India (as amended by Act of 1988).* Allahabad: Law Book Company, 1991.

Strangman, Thomas. *Indian Courts and Characters.* London: William Heinemann, 1931.

Sturgess, H. A C. *Register of Admissions to the Hon. Society of the Middle Temple. From the Fifteenth Century to the Year 1944.* London: Butterworth and Co., 1949. Vol. 2–3.

Surveyor, S. M., ed. *Harvey-Nariman Libel Case.* Bombay: Minerva Press, 1927–8.

Udvāḍā Īrānshāh Ātaśbeherām Kesno Cukādo. Rangoon: Bombay Burma Press, 1933. Unpublished trans. Homi D. Patel. (Gujarati)

Umrīgar, K. D., and M. J. Pāṭhak, eds., *Jāṇītī Pārsī Vyaktio (Parsi "Who's Who").* Jamnagar: Gujarati Who's Who Publishing Company, [194-]. (Gujarati)

Selective Bibliography

Vimadalal, J. J. *Racial Intermarriages: Their Scientific Aspect*. Bombay: The Times Press, 1922.

Wacha, D. E. *Shells from the Sands of Bombay, being my Recollections and Reminiscences – 1860–1875*. Bombay: Anklesaria, 1920.

Wadia, Ardeshir Ruttonji. *Ethics of Feminism* (orig. pub. 1923). In Lucy Delap and Ann Heilmann, eds. *Anti-Feminism in Edwardian Literature*. London: Thoemmes and Edition Synapse, 2006. Vol. 3.

Wadia, C. N., and S. B. Katpitia. *The Parsi Marriage and Divorce Act (India Act III of 1936)*. Surat: Jashvantsinh Gulabsinh Thakor at "Surat City" Printing Press, 1939.

Wadia, Sorab P. N. *The Institution of Trial by Jury in India*. Bombay: the "Fort" Printing Press, 1897.

Who's Who in India, Burma and Ceylon. Poona: Sun Publishing house, 1937.

Zaidi, A. M., ed. *The Grand Little Man of India: Dadabhai Naoroji Speeches and Writings*. Delhi: S. Chand and Co., 1984.

Secondary Sources

Agnes, Flavia. *Family Law. Vol. I: Family Laws and Constitutional Claims*. Delhi: Oxford University Press, 2011.

Anderson, J. N. D., ed. *Family Law in Asia and Africa*. New York: Frederick A. Praeger, 1967.

Anderson, Michael R. "Islamic Law and the Colonial Encounter in British India," 165–85. In David Arnold and Peter Robb, eds., *Institutions and Ideologies: A SOAS South Asia Reader*. Richmond, UK: Curzon, 1993.

Banerjee, Anil Chandra. *English Law in India*. Delhi: Shakti Malik Abhinav Publications, 1984.

Benton, Lauren. *Law and Colonial Cultures: Legal Regimes in World History*. Cambridge: Cambridge University Press, 2002.

Birla, Ritu. *Stages of Capital: Law, Culture, and Market Governance in Late Colonial India*. Durham, NC: Duke University Press, 2009.

Bourdieu, Pierre. *The Logic of Practice*. Trans. Richard Nice. Stanford, CA: Stanford University Press, 1980.

Boyce, Mary. *Zoroastrians: Their Religious Beliefs and Practices*. London: Routledge, 2001.

Boyce, Mary, and Frantz Grenet, *A History of Zoroastrianism. Vol. 3: Zoroastrianism under Macedonian and Roman Rule*. Leiden: E. J. Brill, 1991.

Chatterjee, Nandini. *The Making of Indian Secularism: Empire, Law and Christianity, 1830–1960*. Basingstoke, UK: Palgrave Macmillan, 2011.

Choksy, Jamsheed K. *Purity and Pollution in Zoroastrianism: Triumph over Evil*. Austin: University of Texas Press, 1989.

Chopra, Preeti. *A Joint Enterprise: Indian Elites and the Making of British Bombay*. Minneapolis: University of Minnesota Press, 2011.

Cohn, Bernard S. *An Anthropologist among the Historians and Other Essays*. Delhi: Oxford University Press, 1987.

    Colonialism and Its Forms of Knowledge: The British in India. Princeton, NJ: Princeton University Press, 1996.

330   *Selective Bibliography*

Cretney, Stephen Michael. *Family Law in the Twentieth Century: A History.* Oxford: Oxford University Press, 2003.

Derrett, J. D. M. *Religion, Law and the State in India.* Delhi: Oxford University Press, 1999.

Fisch, Jörg. *Cheap Lives and Dear Limbs: The British Transformation of the Bengal Criminal Law 1769–1817.* Wiesbaden: Franz Steiner Verlag, 1983.

Godrej, Pheroza J., and Firoza Punthakey Mistree, eds. *A Zoroastrian Tapestry: Art, Religion and Culture.* Ahmedabad: Mapin, 2002.

Green, Nile. *Bombay Islam: The Religious Economy of the Western Indian Ocean, 1840–1915.* Cambridge: Cambridge University Press, 2011

Hinnells, John R. *Zoroastrian and Parsi Studies: Selected Works by John R. Hinnells.* Aldershot, UK: Ashgate, 2000.

    The Zoroastrian Diaspora: Religion and Migration. Oxford: Oxford University Press, 2005.

    Zoroastrians in Britain. The Ratanbai Katrak Lectures, University of Oxford 1985. Oxford: Clarendon Press, 1996.

Hinnells, John R., and Alan Williams, eds. *Parsis in India and the Diaspora.* London: Routledge Curzon, 2007.

Irani, Phiroze K. "The Personal Law of the Parsis of India," 273–300. In Anderson, *Family Law.*

Jain, M. P. *Outlines of Indian Legal History.* Nagpur: Wadhwa, 2001.

Katz, Stanley N., ed. *Oxford International Encyclopedia of Legal History.* Oxford: Oxford University Press, 2009.

Kolsky, Elizabeth. *Colonial Justice in British India: White Violence and the Rule of Law.* Cambridge: Cambridge University Press, 2010.

Kozlowski, Gregory C. *Muslim Endowments and Society in British India.* Cambridge: Cambridge University Press, 1985.

Kulke, Eckehard. *The Parsees of India: A Minority as Agent of Social Change.* Delhi: Vikas Publishing House, 1974.

Likhovski, Assaf. *Law and Identity in Mandate Palestine.* Chapel Hill: University of North Carolina Press, 2006.

Lubin, Timothy, Donald R. Davis, Jr., and Jayanth Krishnan, eds. *Hinduism and Law: An Introduction.* Cambridge: Cambridge University Press, 2010.

Luhrmann, Tanya. *The Good Parsi: The Fate of a Colonial Elite in a Postcolonial Society.* Cambridge, MA: Harvard University Press, 1996.

Mallampalli, Chandra. *Race, Religion and Law in Colonial India: Trials of an Interracial Family.* Cambridge: Cambridge University Press, 2011.

Metcalf, Thomas R. *Ideologies of the Raj.* Cambridge: Cambridge University Press, 1995.

Mirza, Hormazdyar Dastur Kayoji. *Outlines of Parsi History.* Bombay: Author, 1987.

Mody, Nawaz B. ed. *Enduring Legacy: Parsis of the Twentieth Century.* Mumbai: Nawaz B. Mody, 2005.

Oldham, James. *Trial by Jury: The Seventh Amendment and Anglo-American Special Juries.* New York: New York University Press, 2006.

Palsetia, Jesse S. *The Parsis of India: Preservation of Identity in Bombay City.* Leiden: Brill, 2001.

Paymaster, R. B. *Early History of the Parsees in India from Their Landing in Sanjan to 1700.* Bombay: Zartoshti Dharam Sambandhi Kelavni Apnari ane Dnyan Felavnari Mandli, 1954.

Selective Bibliography

Price, Pamela. "Ideology and Ethnicity under British Imperial Rule: 'Brahmans,' Lawyers and Kin-Caste Rules in Madras Presidency." *MAS* 23, 1 (1999): 151–77.

Ringer, Monica M. *Pious Citizens: Reforming Zoroastrianism in India and Iran.* Syracuse, NY: Syracuse University Press, 2011.

Rose, Jenny. *Zoroastrianism: A Guide for the Perplexed.* London: Continuum, 2011.

Zoroastrianism: An Introduction. London: I. B. Tauris, 2011.

Rudolph, Lloyd I., and Susanne Hoeber Rudolph, *The Modernity of Tradition: Political Development in India.* Chicago: University of Chicago Press, 1967.

Schmitthener, Samuel. "A Sketch of the Development of the Legal Profession in India." *LSR* 3, 2/3 (1968): 337–82.

Sharafi, Mitra. "Bella's Case: Parsi Identity and the Law in Colonial Rangoon, Bombay and London, 1887–1925." PhD dissertation, Princeton University, 2006.

"The Marital Patchwork of Colonial South Asia: Forum Shopping from Britain to Baroda." *LHR* 28:4 (2010): 979–1009.

"A New History of Colonial Lawyering: Likhovski and Legal Identities in the British Empire." *LSI* 32, 4 (2007): 1059–94.

Shodhan, Amrita. *A Question of Community: Religious Groups and Colonial Law.* Calcutta: Samya, 2001.

Singha, Radhika. *A Despotism of Law: Crime and Justice in Early Colonial India.* Delhi: Oxford University Press, 1998.

Skjærvø, Prods Oktor. *The Spirit of Zoroastrianism.* New Haven, CT: Yale University Press, 2011.

Stausberg, Michael. *Die Religion Zarathustras. Geschichte-Gegenwart-Rituale.* Stuttgart: Verlag W. Kohlhammer, 2002. 2 vols.

Zarathustra and Zoroastrianism: A Short Introduction. Trans., Margret Preisler-Weller. London: Equinox, 2008.

Stausberg, Michael, and Yuhan Vevaina, eds. *Blackwell Companion to the Study of Zoroastrianism.* Malden, MA: Blackwell (in press).

Sturman, Rachel. *The Government of Social Life in Colonial India: Liberalism, Religious Law, and Women's Rights.* Cambridge: Cambridge University Press, 2012.

Subramanian, Narendra. "Making Family and Nation: Hindu Marriage Law in Early Postcolonial India," *JAS* 69, 3 (2010): 771–98.

Swinfen, David B. *Imperial Appeal: The Debate on the Appeal to the Privy Council, 1833–1986.* Manchester: Manchester University Press, 1987.

Tambe, Ashwini. *Codes of Misconduct: Regulating Prostitution in Law Colonial Bombay.* Minneapolis: University of Minnesota Press, 2009.

Tejani, Shabnum. *Indian Secularism: A Social and Intellectual History, 1890–1950.* Bloomington: Indiana University Press, 2008.

Travers, Robert. *Ideology and Empire in Eighteenth-Century India.* Cambridge: Cambridge University Press, 2007.

Vachha, P. B. *Famous Judges, Lawyers and Cases of Bombay: A Judicial History of Bombay during the British Period.* Delhi: Universal, 2011. First published in 1962 by N. M. Tripathi.

Visram, Rozina. *Asians in Britain: 400 Years of History.* London: Pluto, 2002.

Writer, Rashna. *Contemporary Zoroastrianism: An Unstructured Nation.* Lanham, MD: University Press of America, 1994.

Yarshater, Ehsan. *Encyclopedia Iranica.* London: Routledge and Kegan Paul, 1982–.

Index

Aden, 3, 42, 213, 229n258, 248n54
Administrator General's Act (IX of 1881), 86–7, 318
adoption, 218n171, 285n60. *See also Saklat v. Bella*
adultery, 173–8, 188, 216, 222, 242, 280, 284, 291–2. *See also* matrimonial law; sexuality
Advocate of India, 279, 292–3
Advocates' Association of Western India, 161
Africa, 103–5, 111–12, 198–200, 227, 307. *See also* Madagascar; Zanzibar
Age of Consent Acts, 122, 180, 184
Agnes, Flavia, 129
Ahmad, Rafiuddin, 95
Aiyar, Muttasami, 203
'Al-'Arif, 'Arif, 12
alcohol, 50, 53, 242n19, 282
Alexander of Macedon, 16, 75
Ali, Syed Ameer, 12, 121
Allahabad High Court, 121
Ananda Charlu, P., 202–3, 205n83
Angra, Dinsha, 48
annulments, 217, 223, 223n218, 224–7. *See also* matrimonial law
Anquetil-Duperron, Abraham-Hyacinthe, 20
Anthropological Society of Bombay, 302
Apakhtyar, Nusserwanjee Dorabjee, 281
Aratoon v. Aratoon, 135
arbitration, 41–4. *See also* families; law; panchayats
Ardeshir, Hormasji and Dinsha (firm), 110
Arnould, Joseph, 105, 178

Aryanism, 297–300, 305–12
asha (term), 71, 71n221
assessor system, 197–8
Aubert, Vilhelm, 58
Auerbach, Jerold, 5
Australia, 54, 80, 103–4, 107, 152n144
Avesta (text), 14
Avestan (language), 3, 14, 16, 21, 138n68

Bamji, Sorab R., 214
Banaji, Limji Naoroji, 62n163
Bánáji v. Limbuwállá, 264, 266–7, 270
Baroda, 19, 76, 301n148
Bartholomae, Christian, 137
Barua, Jagannath, 203
Bayly, C. A., 295
Beaman, F. C. O., 34, 83, 101, 241, 247, 254, 263
Behram, J. B. Boman, 44
Bella. *See* Captain, Bella
Bengalee, Sorabji Shapurji, 81, 90, 172
Bengal Sati Regulation (XVII of 1829), 122
Bentham, Jeremy, 135, 153n146, 163
Bhabha, Homi, 5, 310
Bhesania, M. M., 187
bigamy, 166, 171–2, 181, 216, 318–19
Birdwood, George, 204, 248
Birla, Ritu, 140, 234, 264
Blackstone, William, 151
Bogdanov, L., 137
Bombay Chronicle, 279
Bombay Dog riots, 29
Bombay Gazette, 215n149, 279

333

Index

Bombay High Court, 8–10, 29, 33, 45–59, 98–101, 109, 113–16, 228, 252, 273
Bombay Law Journal, 115
Bombay Samachar, 278
Bombay Supreme Court, 153
Bombay Times and Journal of Commerce, 80, 209
Borradaile, Henry, 25, 90, 136
Bourdieu, Pierre, 24
Breckendridge, Carol Appadurai, 234n285
Brière, Suzanne, 268–70. *See also Petit v. Jijibhai*
Britain: administration of India by, 47–56; colonial law of, 1–2, 9–12, 24, 75, 80–1, 105–7, 145–8, 165–74, 178–87, 193–211, 233–6, 276–85; legal training in, 4–5, 104–5, 108–9; Parsis' relation to, 19–20, 31, 39, 117–20, 127–40, 159–67, 178–88, 191–3, 209, 240, 304, 310; racial discourses and, 274–7. *See also* colonialism; India; law
British Columbia, 107
Buddhism, 131–4, 303
Bulsara, Sohrab Jamshedji, 137–8
Burjorjee D. Contractor v. J. K. Irani, 57n132
Burma, 22, 33, 55, 67, 131–3, 163, 250–2, 285–9, 291–2, 298–304
Burns-Howard, Kathryn, 243n23
Byculla Club, 106

Calcott, Maria Dundas Graham, 78
Calcutta High Court, 196
Cama, Bhikhaiji R., 19, 170, 219n179
Cama, K. R., 213, 310
Cama, Spittama, 274
Canada, 9n25, 54, 103, 152n144. *See also* British Columbia
Captain, Bella, 286. *See also Saklat v. Bella*
Captain, Bomanji Cowasji, 294. *See also Saklat v. Bella*
Captain, Merwanji Cowasji, 287–9, 291. *See also Saklat v. Bella*
Captain, Shapurji Cowasji, 285, 287, 292–5. *See also Saklat v. Bella*
cemeteries, 55, 239, 295. *See also* death rites (Zoroastrian); purity laws
Ceylon, 54, 117, 117n201, 133, 133n33, 142, 153, 203
Chamberlain, Houston Stewart, 297–8
Chandavarkar, Narayan G., 12, 258
Chanock, Martin, 200
charitable trusts, 20–3, 33, 76–80, 88, 94–5, 142–7, 234–40, 258–64

Chatterjee, Partha, 11, 235
Cherag (newspaper), 291
Child Marriage Restraint Act (XIX of 1929), 187, 319
child marriages, 30, 166–7, 184n93, 192, 223
China, 18, 93, 174. *See also* opium
Chinoy, A. F. G., 172
Choksy, Nasarvanji, 94
Christians, 14–15, 20, 31, 60, 77, 86, 95–102, 130–5, 168, 209–12; class: gender's intersections with, 167–73;inheritance law and, 145–7, 149; jury systems and, 200, 232–3; lobbying and, 85, 95, 97; marriage law and, 32–3, 170, 209, 218–23, 235
Code of Civil Procedure (VIII of 1859), 127
Code of Criminal Procedure (XXV of 1861), 127, 201
codification fallacy, 10, 25–6. *See also* law; Zoroastrianism
Colah, Bomanjee Byramjee, 242–6
colonialism: gender and, 32, 150–9, 234–6; judicial ethnography and, 249–52, 258–73, 313–16; juries and, 193–211; legal professionalism and, 4–9, 11, 46, 85, 97–9, 102–3, 106–7, 140–6, 252–64; liberal autonomy and, 143–9; mimicry and, 5, 53, 127, 310; minority politics and, 86–98, 120–40, 240, 274–7, 313–16; Parsis' relation to, 19–20, 44–58, 127–40, 146–50, 193, 210–36, 264–70, 313–16; racial doctrines and, 274–7, 293–304; settler-, 11, 103–7, 104n100, 198–9. *See also* Britain; India; law; Parsis
Colonial Letters Patent Act of 1863, 139
communalism, 25, 27, 82–3, 102, 200, 276, 303. *See also* India; Parsis; sexuality
Compton, Herbert, 90
Constable, Alexander George, 243–6
Constituent Assembly, 27, 89
Contractor, Behram, 291–2
Contractor, J. D., 67
Coroner's Court (Bombay), 51–2
cosmopolitanism, 23, 39–40, 285, 295
Court for the Relief of Insolvent Debtors (Bombay), 48–50
Court of Small Causes (Bombay), 47–8, 61, 91, 110, 113, 221n198, 228, 253
Courts of the Presidency Magistrates (Bombay). *See* Police Courts
coverture, 31, 128–9, 148, 151–9, 164
Coyajee, N. H. C., 100
Crawford (Arthur) case, 29

Index

cruelty (legal definition of), 188–9, 222
Cursetee v. Perozeboye, 173
Cursetjee, Manekjee, 80, 91, 93n41, 180, 209–10, 313
Cursetjee v. Perozeboye, 173
Cursetji, C. M., 106
cy-près doctrine, 261–2

Dadachanji, Kaikhosru, 147, 147n123, 148, 214
Dadachanji, Ratanji, 109
Dadar-Matunga Zoroastrian Association, 189
Danquah, Joseph Buaki, 11
Darmesteter, James, 20
Darnton, Robert, 312
Dastur, Hormuzdiar P., 43–4
Dastur, Phiroze Hoshang, 113
Dâtastân Nâmak, 138
Davar, Dinshah Dhanjibhai, 12, 31, 106–11, 240–2, 252–62, 256, 263, 264–73, 288–9, 296–7
Davar, J. D., 44, 119, 253
Davar, Rustomji Framji, 49
Davar, Sohrab R., 115
death rites (Zoroastrian), 15–16, 76–7, 244, 246–70, 267n148. *See also* cemeteries; *muktad* trusts; nasasalars (hereditary corpse bearers); purity laws; Towers of Silence (*dakhma*); Zoroastrianism
debtor suits, 47–50, 57
defamation suits, 29, 213, 274–85. *See also* libel suits; Parsis
De Ga case, 29
De Gubernatis, Angelo, 247
Derrett, J. D. M., 9–10
Desai, Sapur, 297, 303
Desai, Soonamai, 170
desertion (divorce grounds), 37, 215–16, 222, 228–9
detectives. *See* Ring, Charles Edward
devilling (legal profession), 111
Dhalla, Dastur M. N., 184, 300, 305
Dhammathats (texts), 134
Digest of a Thousand Points of Law (text), 75, 136–8
Dinbai v. Toddyvala, 43, 227–32, 296
Dinshaw, Cowasji, 213
Dinshaw, F. E., 101
Dissolution of Muslim Marriages Act (VIII of 1939), 121
divorce: arbitration and, 41–4; fault-based systems of, 58–63; gender and, 37–8, 41–2, 60–3, 67–70, 187–92, 195,

215–16, 218–36; Parsi juries and, 210–35; women's property and, 156–7. *See also* gender; matrimonial law
Dixit, M. K., 95
Doctor, F. S., 291
Dustoor v. Meherba'i, 139, 180, 183–4

East India Company, 18, 25–6, 45–6, 78, 85, 130–1, 145, 196–7, 207
Edalji (George) case, 29
Elphinstone College, 103
Engineer, Kaikhusroo Sorabji, 225
English law (in Britain): adoption and, 285n60; criminal-, 84; inheritances and, 31, 127–9, 140–6, 150–60; libel and, 274, 280; matrimonial-, 174
English law (in South Asia), 45, 127–9, 135, 139–42, 147–58, 163–4. *See also* Parsis
"Essay on the Influence of Time and Place in Matters of Legislation" (Bentham), 163
ethnography, 249–52, 258–73, 313–16
eugenics, 6, 33, 61, 176, 296–312

families: arranged marriages and, 222–36; child marriage and, 178–87; gender and, 129, 159–70, 173–8; inheritance law and, 6, 30–1, 140–6, 153–64; legal professionals and, 98–101, 117, 235; libel suits and, 65–6, 69, 240–6, 290–6; reputational concerns and, 30, 61–71, 82–3, 279–83. *See also* joint family
Federal Court of India, 55
Ferrars, Max and Bertha, 298
Field, C. D., 205
Forbes, M. C., 116
Forchhammer, Em, 133–4
forgery, 52, 84, 143, 145, 207, 316
fraud (in arranged marriage), 222–36
Friedman, Lawrence, 215–16
Furdoonjee, Nowrozjee, 90–1, 108, 153

Galanter, Marc, 215–16
Gamadia, Cuverjee Nowrojee, 50
gambling, 50, 117, 176, 282
Gandhi, M. K., 54, 104, 253
gender: child marriage and, 178–87, 184n93; inheritance law and, 129, 148, 150–3, 159–64; jury systems and, 214, 231–2; lobbying and, 93; masculinity and, 235–6; matrimonial law and, 30–2, 37, 41–2,

60–2, 93, 164, 173–92, 195, 216, 218–23;
Parsi family structure and, 8, 20–1, 129,
167–70, 234–6; sexual diversity and, 32,
82, 165–7, 173–8, 214, 280–3,
300. *See also* honor; legal profession
Ghosh, Subhasri, 47
Gilder, M. D., 94–6
Gokhale, L. R., 95
Goonesekere, Savitri, 152
Gould, Ketayun, 168
Gour, H. S., 54
Grant Road Parsi Association, 43, 189
Green, Nile, 234
Greenhouse, Carol, 76
Gujarati (language), 17, 21, 39, 65, 70n216, 75,
108, 116, 120, 138n68, 139, 144, 201,
213, 243, 254, 304. *See also* Parsis
Gup-Sup (newspaper), 279

Haldane of Clone (Viscount), 54
Haldar, Syama Churn, 202
Hanafite school of Islamic legal
interpretation, 141
Hansen, Kathryn, 304
Haridas, Nanabhai, 250
Harrington, H. B., 80–1
Hastings, Warren, 130–1, 139
Hataria, Manekji Limji, 136, 138
Haug, Martin, 20
Heerjibehedin, Erachshaw R., 213
Hindi Punch, 21, 41, 52, 99, 208, *208*, 209,
254–6, 262, 270–1, 278, 308; images in,
13, 73–4, 100–1, 255–6, 263, 265, 271,
282, 286, 290, 309. *See also Parsee Punch*
Hindu Marriage Act (25 of 1955), 171
Hindus: jury systems and, 196, 200–1, 209; as
legal professionals, 120, 122–3, 258;
litigation with Parsis of, 38–9, 289;
personal law and, 1–2, 6, 25–6, 30–2, 47,
75, 85, 87, 95–7, 114, 122, 127, 130,
139–41, 146, 149–50, 153, 162, 164, 167,
171, 178–9, 234; sex and marriage customs
of, 171, 178–9, 181–3, 187, 297. *See also*
joint family
Hinnells, John R., 117n201
Hirabai v. Dhunjibhai, 208
honor, 65–6. *See also* defamation suits; libel
suits; sexuality; violence
Hormarji, Hormarji A., 49
Hormusjee, Modee Rustomjee, 143
Huxley, Andrew, 133
Hyderabad, 61, 242

identity: British liberal autonomy and, 146,
148–9; race and eugenics and, 6, 21–3, 31,
33, 43, 61, 176, 230, 232, 297–312;
religious conversion and, 17, 22–3, 33,
87–98, 184, 187, 218, 230–1, 313; trust
suits and, 239–49
Ilm-e Kshnoom (mystical movement), 306–7
impotence, 224–7
India: case law in, 9–12, 138; colonial
administration of, 5, 45–8, 50–6,
145–6, 153–64, 167–70, 193–236; East
India Company's rule of, 8, 18, 25–6,
45–6, 78, 85, 105, 130–1, 145, 196–7,
198n28, 207; independence and
partitioning of, 5, 11, 24–6; territorial law
and, 95–6
Indian Contract Act (IX of 1872), 127
Indian Evidence Act (I of 1872), 127
Indian Law Commission, 89–90
Indian Law Reports Act (II of 1875), 46
Indian Law Reports Bombay series,
40, 115
Indian Penal Code (XLV of 1860), 127, 171–2,
188, 191n122, 277, 317–18
The Indian Statesman, 106
Indian Succession Act (XXXIX of 1925),
93, 319
Indian Succession (Amendment) Act (XVII of
1939), 147, 160–2, 171, 320
infanticide, 154, 181n74
inheritance law: family structure and, 6, 30–1,
67–8, 150–64; gender and, 129, 148,
150–64; Hindu personal law and, 140–1,
152–3, 155, 162, 164; intestacy and
testamentary concerns and, 127–9, 140–8,
158–61, 235, 261–4; intrafamilial litigation
and, 241–6; lobbying efforts and, 30–1,
86–7, 93–7, 149–59, 273; Muslim personal
law and, 141, 148, 152–3, 155, 164; Parsi
exceptionalism and, 6, 140–6, 149–59;
racial identity and, 31, 313; trusts and,
260–70, 265n137
Inns of Court, 85, 104, 108–10. *See also*
Lincoln's Inn; Middle Temple
intestacy (law of), 127, 129, 140–8, 157–8,
160–4, 235, 261–4
Iran. *See* Persia
Irani, Merwan S, 308
Irani, Phiroja Merwan, 282
Irani Anjuman, 43, 310
Iran League, 308
Ithoter rivayat (text), 87

Index

Jackson, A. V. Williams, 20
Jaffe, James, 247n48
Jāgos, M. H., 257
Jain, M. P., 131
Jaini, Jagmander Lal, 12, 131, 201
Jainism, 20, 95, 122–3, 130
Jains, 131–3
Jam-e-Jamshed (newspaper), 189, 212, 278, 289, 291–3
Jardine, John, 133–4, 203, 264–8
Jarvis, Nathaniel, Jr., 244
Jeejeebhoy, Jamsetjee, 81–2, 93n41, 193, 213, 309, 313
Jeevanji v. Chinoy, 242, 246–9
Jehangir, Cowasji, 93–4, 214
Jehangir, Gulabhai and Bilimoria (firm), 110
Jenkins, Lawrence, 101
Jessawalla, Dosebai Cowasjee, 41, 170
jewelry, 49, 146, 154–7, *155*, 220
Jews and Judaism, 14, 72, 75, 86, 98–9, 118–19, 130, 139, 269n157, 307
Jinnah, Mohammad Ali, 12, 50, 118, 121, 123
joint family (term), 31, 120, 128, 140n80, 141–4, 149, 234–5
Jones, William, 196
Joshi, Framroz Rustomji, 43
judicial ethnography, 249–52, 258–73, 313–16
judicial separation, 215–16, 216n154, 218n175, 222
jury systems, 32, 193–210

Kabrajee, Kaikhosro N., 281
Kaikobad, Dastur, 287, 289
Kaiser-i-Hind (newspaper), 213, 278
Kalyanwalla, Sorabji Framji, 50
Kambli, S. T., 96
Kanga, Jamshedji B., 111, *112*
Kaoosji Ruttonji v. Awanbaee, 157
Kapadia, Framroze Navroji, 225
Karaka, Dossabhoy Framjee, 79, 113, 180, 182–4, 300
Karanjia, Bhikaji M., 283
Karkaria, Dinshaw Edalji, 279–81
Karkaria v. Mistry, 279–80
Kasturi, Malavika, 65
Khajotia, Jamshedjee Dadabhai, 230
Khambata, K. J., 177
Khan, Muhammad Reza, 131
Khandalavala, D. N. D., 113, 279
Khareghat, M. P., 97, 296
Khergamvala, J. S., 115
Khoja Law Commission, 121

Khorshedjee, Rustomjee, 178
Kolsky, Elizabeth, 199–200
Kozlowski, Gregory, 85, 119, 264
K. R. Cama Oriental Institute, 137

Lam, Mithan (née Tata), 170
law: case-, 9–12, 25, 31, 46, 138, 146; civil-, 28–9, 208–35, 276; colonialism and, 11, 44–58, 75, 77–82, 103–4, 106–7, 159–73, 233–6, 249–64, 276–85; criminal-, 29, 37–8, 46, 50–3, 103, 113, 128, 136–8, 166–7, 171–3, 181–2, 190–1, 198–9, 201–2, 205, 207, 210–12, 233–6, 276–83, 289, 291, 317–19; customary and normative construals of, 6–7, 11–12, 171, 178–83, 187, 195–210, 214–15, 240, 252–70, 274–7, 313–16; intragroup litigation and, 5–6, 30, 37–58, 63–71, 82–3, 117, 129–40, 165–7, 182–3, 252–73, 296–304, 314; lobbying and, 30–1, 84–97, 122, 127, 149–59, 165–7, 180–7, 240, 273–7, 313–16; Parsis' de-Anglicization of, 5, 8–9, 24, 31, 98–123, 127–40, 159–78, 187–93, 195, 239–40, 249–52, 264–70, 310, 313–16; personal-, 1–2, 6, 25–6, 30–2, 47, 58–71, 75, 84–98, 114, 127–40, 127n8, 140–50, 153–62, 193–210, 222–36, 252, 258–9; professional positions in, 6–12, 30, 46, 85, 97–123, 140–6, 252–64; territorial-, 31–3, 47, 89, 95–8, 139, 259. *See also* colonialism; legal education; legal profession; Orientalism; Parsis; Zoroastrianism; *specific cases*
Law of Legatism (Scottish), 148
Law of Property Act (1925), 159
Le Bon, Gustave, 297
Lee-Warner, W., 204
legal consciousness (term), 58–63, 83
legal education, 103, 106, 120. *See also* Inns of Court; legal profession; Lincoln's Inn; Middle Temple
legal pluralism (term), 6–7, 11–12, 30, 41–4, 83
legal profession: barristers or advocates and, 5, 8, 11, 61–2, *100–1, 112*, 271, 280; in general, 98–120; judges and, 253–64; other court officials in, 91, 116–17, 153, 202–3, 291; solicitors or firms and, 44, 52n101, 63, 71, 84, 251–2, 272n167; women in, 108, 170. *See also* Advocates' Association of Western India; colonialism; devilling (legal profession); families; Hindus; law;

Mistry, A. J. C.; Muslims; Parsis; *vakils*;
specific firms and names
legal publishing, 113–15. *See also Bombay Law
Journal*; Indian Law Reports Act; *Indian
Law Reports Bombay series*; *Madras Law
Journal*
legislation, 7–10, 25–32, 39, 46–7, 51, 63,
85–98, 113–16, 121–3, 127–93, 209,
229n258, 313, 317–20. *See also* lobbying;
specific statutes
libel suits: family reputation and, 65–6, 69, 71;
religion and group representations and,
251–2, 274–7, 295–6, 302, 311–12,
315–16; sexual reputation and, 62–71,
116, 166, 295–6
Lincoln's Inn, 1–4, 2–4, 62n164,
104–5, 114
litigation: charitable or religious trusts and, 57–8,
72–3, 138, 146–7, 235, 240–9, 252–73;
defamation suits as, 29, 213, 274–85,
315–16; divorce suits as, 37, 58–63, 67–71,
93, 165–78, 187–92, 215–16, 222–36;
family reputation and, 65–71, 239–49,
290–6; inheritances and, 127–9, 140–7,
149–264; intercommunity suits and, 38–9,
289; racial and religious identity and,
251–2, 274–7, 283–96, 302, 311–16;
sexual reputation and, 62–71, 116, 166,
295–6. *See also specific cases*
lobbying: inheritance law and, 6, 25–6, 30–1,
84–7, 94–5, 127, 149–59, 273;
matrimonial law and, 6, 30–2, 84–5, 91–4,
122, 165–7, 180–3, 187, 273; minority
politics and, 85–98, 120–40, 240, 274–7,
313–16; Parsi jury system and, 193–4
London, 274. *See also* Inns of Court; Lincoln's
Inn; Middle Temple; Old Bailey
love marriage, 187, 222, 232
Luhmann, Niklas, 240, 304, 311
Luhrmann, Tanya, 127
Lungra, Muncherjee Cowasjee, 164,
281–2. *See also* Mansukh (writer)

Macaulay, Stewart, 240
Macaulay, Thomas Babington, 45–6, 110
Macleod, Norman, 279n30
Macnaghten, W. H., 196
Madagascar, 230, 296
Madon, D. M., 251
Madras High Court, 116, 203
Madras Law Journal, 120
Madun, Jamsetjee Sorabjee, 284–5

Mahmood, Syed, 121
Maine, Henry, 140, 163–4, 209
Majumdar, Rochona, 222
making enquiries (term), 59–61, 63, 227, 241
Mallal, Bashir Ahmad, 12
Mancherjee, Cowasjee, 295
Mansukh (writer), 174, *175*, 176. *See also*
Lungra, M. C.
Mantegazza, Paolo, 247
Mantena, Karuna, 163
marriage, 72–3. *See also* coverture; cruelty;
Hindus; matrimonial law; Muslims;
PCMC; polygamy; violence; *specific cases
and statutes*
Married Women's Property Acts (1870 and
1882), 158
Marzban, Jehangir Behramji, 292
Marzban, P. J., 292
Masani, R. P., 302–3
masculinity, 235–6
matchmaking. *See* families; Vaju, H.
matrimonial law: arbitration and, 41–4; child
marriages and, 30, 91, 93, 166–7, 178–87,
192, 223; class concerns and, 32–3; divorce
grounds and, 37, 58–63, 67–71,
93, 165–70, 173–8, 187–92, 215–16,
216n154, 218–36; family reputation and,
30, 61–71, 82; fraud and, 222–36;
inheritance and, 148, 150–64;
intercommunity marriages and, 285–304;
jury systems and, 32, 193, 208–36;
lobbying efforts and, 30–2, 94, 165–7,
180–3, 187, 273; Parsi exceptionalism and,
6, 27–8, 57, 193, 195, 208–10; religious
and racial differentiation
and, 120–2, 231; sexual behavior and,
59–62, 164–70, 188, 209, 223–5,
227. *See also* gender; Hindus; Muslims
Matsuda, Mari, 5
Mawani, Renisa, 294
Mazdaism. See Zoroastrianism
medical experts and evidence, 225–7,
302. *See also* Coroner's Court (Bombay);
pregnancy (extramarital); violence;
virginity
Mehta, B. D., 161
Mehta, M. N., 310
Mehta, Pherozeshah, 19, 106
Menant, Delphine, 113, 181n75, 294
Menski, Werner, 131
mental illness, 38, 223, 223n218, 224, 226–7,
243–6, 249, 301–2

Index

Merry, Sally Engle, 152
Merwanji, Jehangir, 44
Merwanji, Kola and Co. (firm), 110
Middle Temple, 116, 253. *See also* Inns of Court
millet system, 129–30, 195
mimicry, 5, 53, 127, 310
Mistry, Ardeshir Jamshedji Chanji, 98, 107, 116–17, 120
Mistry family, 64
Modi, J. J., 213, 267
Modi, T. K., 190
Mody, H. P., 94, 310
Mody, Jehangir R. P., 308
Monier-Williams, Monier, 247
Morley-Minto legislation, 94, 94n45
Moulton, J. H., 20
Mukherjee, Mithi, 258n107
Mukherji, Satya Chandra, 197–8
muktad trusts, 264–70, 265. *See also* death rites (Zoroastrian)
Mulla, Dinshah Fardunji, 3, 4, 93, 101, 103, 111n167, 114
Mulla and Mulla (firm), 110, 114
Munchergee, Pallonjee, 84
Munsiff, Jamshed D., 301
Muslim Personal Law (Shariat) Application Act (XXVI of 1937), 121
Muslims: colonial status of, 118–19, 303; conquests of, 72–5, 87, 136, 306; jury systems and, 200; legal codes of, 72, 207, 209; as legal professionals, 121–3; litigation with Parsis and, 38–9; as native law officers, 196; Parsi conversions and, 187, 212; personal law and, 1–2, 6, 25–6, 30–2, 47, 75, 85, 87–8, 95–6, 114, 129–41, 146, 148–50, 164, 167, 195; polygamy conventions and, 171, 171n24; Zoroastrianism and, 15, 63
Mussalman Wakf Validating Act, 121
mysticism. *See Ilm-e Kshnoom* (mystical movement); sufism

Nadirshaw, J. D., 296, 304
Naoroji, Dadabhai, 19, 71–2, 106, 109, 176, 314
Naoroji v. Rogers, 139
Nariman, Fali, 111
Nariman, G. K., 116, 291–2, 294, 296
Nariman, Khurshed Framji, 103
nasasalars (hereditary corpse bearers), 61, 79, 247

Nasserwanjee, Framjee, 178, 182
navjote (initiation ceremony), 21, 218, 285, 290, 291. *See also* Parsis; religion; Zoroastrianism
Newbigin, Eleanor, 123, 167
Newton, H., 178
New York Court of Common Pleas, 242–5
New Zealand, 103–4
nirang, 246–9, 249n56, 287
Noor-e Alam (newspaper), 292–3
Nosherwanji v. Awanabee, 157
Notes on Buddhist Law (Jardine), 134

oaths, 68, 86n4, 97, 116, 220, 269n157, 311
Old Bailey, 52n101, 84
Oldham, James, 214
opium, 18, 52, 131, 242n19
Orientalism: colonial administration and, 167–70, 197–9; legal-, 1–2, 19–20, 25–6, 71–2, 130–1, 133, 133n35, 134–6, 196, 203; religious-, 19–20, 246–8, 305–6; sexual-, 170–3, 178–87
"Oriental mendacity" (trope), 71–2, 199, 207, 306. *See also* forgery; oaths; perjury
Oriental Review, 300

Pahlavi (language). *See* Persian (languages)
Pahlavi, Reza, 307–8, 313–14
Palkhivala, Nani, 111
Palsetia, Jesse, 129, 182
panchayats, 77–81, 90–3, 137, 145, 168–72, 196–215, 257–60, 270–2
Parekh, Furdoonjee Sorabjee, 153
Parsee Punch, 278, 281. *See also Hindi Punch*
The Parsi, 289, 305, 307
Parsi Central Association, 6, 301–2
Parsi Communal Constitution Act, 314
Parsi Federal Council, 301
Parsi General Hospital, 261–3, 302
Parsi Girls' School Association, 260
Parsi Intestate Succession Act (XXI of 1865), 90, 92, 93, 143–4, 150–3, 158, 318
Parsi Law Association, 6, 91, 172, 195
Parsi Law Commission, 91, 157, 166, 173, 178, 181–3
Parsi League of Honor, 43, 283
Parsi Marriage and Divorce Act (III of 1936), 32, 59–62, 165–8, 187–92, 212–15, 319
Parsi Marriage and Divorce Act (XV of 1865), 32, 76–81, 90–3, 92, 93, 165–8, 187–9, 257, 318

Index

Parsi Marriage and Divorce (Amendment) Act (XIV of 1940), 93, 229n258, 320

Parsi personal law: absence of, 1–2, 136; creation of, 26, 30–1, 84–5, 89–90, 125–236. *See also* inheritance law; matrimonial law; religion; *specific cases and statutes*

Parsi Physical Culture League, 301

Parsi Prakash (Patel and Paymaster), 114

Parsi Public Trusts Registration Act (Bombay Act XXIII of 1936), 94–7, 320

Parsis: colonial law and politics and, 1–2, 4–5, 19–20, 24, 26, 31, 39, 84–5, 97, 127–40, 146–54, 157, 159–64, 187–92, 208–10, 240, 274–7, 304, 310, 313–16; cosmopolitanism of, 23, 39–40, 285, 295; diasporic histories of, 1–2, 16–17, 72, 75, 87–8, 118, 143, 295–6, 306–13; employment and, 42, 53, 62, 77, 83, 192, 214, 218, 221, 242; family structure and, 8, 30, 32, 41–4, 47, 57–71, 127, 142–6, 167–70; female-, 169, 185, 282; informal or familial dispute resolution and, 41–4, 76, 78–81, 241; inheritance law and, 6, 26, 89–90, 140–6, 150–64; journalism and, 19, 278–82, 289, 290, 292–3, 302; as judges and other legal professionals, 3–9, 11, 19, 27, 30, 39–40, 44–5, 59, 61–3, 77–85, 91, 98–123, 139, 195, 210–35, 239–40, 249–72; legal consciousness of, 58–63; litigation among, 5–6, 22–5, 28, 30, 33, 37–41, 44–58, 63–82, 85, 113, 213, 215, 222–36, 240–70, 274–85, 312; matrimonial law and, 6, 26–8, 89–91, 165–87, 209–35; nonviolence and, 316; panchayats and, 7, 137, 145, 168, 172, 182–3, 191n122, 209–10, 214–15, 257, 260, 266, 270–2; racial and religious identity of, 6, 17, 21, 31, 33, 43, 67, 109–10, 118–19, 183, 212, 218, 230–2, 249–52, 264–70, 274–7, 285–316. *See also* families; gender; inheritance law; law; legal education; legal profession; litigation; lobbying; matrimonial law; PCMC (Parsi Chief Matrimonial Court); trust suits; Zoroastrianism

Parsis and Eugenics (Desai), 303

Patel, B. D., 307

Patel, Simin, 215n149

Patel, Vallabhbhai, 27

paternity rule (of Zoroastrian descent), 231, 288–97

patriarchy, 166. *See also* colonialism; families; gender; inheritance law; matrimonial law

Paymaster, R. B., 114

PCMC (Parsi Chief Matrimonial Court), 10, 30–51, 58–63, 147, 167, 176–88, 193–5, 210–36; images of, 194, 208

perjury, 52, 199, 278n19. *See also* "Oriental mendacity" (trope)

perpetuities (rule against), 147, 264–8

Perry, Erskine, 90, 136

Persia, 306–10, 309, 313–14. *See also* Ilm-e Kshnoom; Pahlavi, R.; rivayats

Persian (languages), 14, 17–18, 20, 65, 75, 254. *See also* Avestan

Persian empire, 16, 87

Persianness, 304–12. *See also* eugenics; identity; Parsis; race; Zoroastrianism

personal law. *See* Buddhism; Hindus; inheritance law; Jainism; matrimonial law; Muslim Personal Law (Shariat) Application Act (XXVI of 1937); Muslims; Parsi personal law; religion

Petigara, Kavasji Jamshedji, 160, 162

Petit, Dinshaw, 123

Petit v. Jijibhai, 101, 255; community resources and, 270–2, 314; continuing awareness of, 315; family and community reputation and, 83, 241–2, 245n40; racial identity and, 22–3, 31, 33–4, 99, 183, 218, 247, 254, 260, 263–4, 268–70, 276, 288–9, 304, 314. *See also* families; Parsis; race

Phillimore, Robert Joseph and Walter George Frank, 55n116

Phirozshah, Nusserwanji, 101

Police Courts (Bombay), 29, 50–1, 110, 253

Pollock, Frederick, 114

polygamy, 167–74, 178, 181, 191, 209, 216. *See also* matrimonial law; sexuality

Poonawala, A. J., 115

Pope, Alexander, 281n37

pregnancy (extramarital), 217–18, 217n170, 230n261

primogeniture, 127, 143, 148–53, 151n138, 159–60, 164

princely states, 19, 102, 114–15, 218. *See also* Baroda; Hyderabad

Prince of Wales riots, 29

Prinseps, Henry Thoby, 2

private prosecutions, 29, 51, 277–8

Privy Council (Judicial Committee of), 3, 53–6, 77, 114, 121, 142–6, 172–3, 242–6, 288–9

Index

Proclamation of 1858 (Victoria), 234, 234n283
prostitutes and prostitution, 70, 82, 82n284, 167–70, 173–8, 192, 217, 225
Pudumjee, K. B., 116
purity laws (Zoroastrian), 52, 76, 285–9, 311

Quakers, 86, 86n4

race: colonialism and, 197–9, 202, 293–304; eugenics and, 6, 176, 296–304; libel suits and, 283–96, 311–12; Parsi identity and, 6, 33, 67, 99, 109–10, 231, 250–2, 274–7, 285–91, 304–12, 314. *See also* identity; Parsis
Raikes, E. B., 262
Rajabai Tower case, 29
Rana, Framjee A., 114
Rana, Jadi, 17
Ranade, Mahadev Govind, 12
Ranina, N. R., 213
Rankin, George, 134–5
Raphael, 1
Rast Goftar (newspaper), 278, 281, 307
reform movements (colonial), 122, 154, 167–8. *See also* Age of Consent Acts; Child Marriage Restraint Act (XIX of 1929); gender; Zoroastrianism
religion: conversions and, 17, 21, 31, 33, 183, 187, 212, 230–1, 268–70, 285–96, 304; gender and, 166; identity and, 6, 22–3, 63, 87–98, 109–10, 285–96; judicial ethnography and, 249–52, 258–73, 313–16; jury systems and, 32, 193, 210–36; personal law and, 1–2, 6, 25–32, 75, 80, 85–7, 95–9, 114, 122, 130, 139–53, 162–71, 178–9, 235, 258–9
reputation. *See* families; libel suits; litigation; matrimonial law; *Petit v. Jijibhai*; *Saklat v. Bella*; sexuality
restitution of conjugal rights, 216–17, 222
Reza Shah. *See* Pahlavi; Reza
Ring, Charles Edward, 60
rivayats (texts), 75, 88, 138
Rose, Jennifer, 168
Ruttonjee, Mihirwanjee, 144–5
Ruttonjee v. his brothers Poonjeea and Dada Bhaee, 144–5
Ruxton (Buck) case, 29

Saklat, Dorabji, 295–6
Saklat v. Bella: family reputation and, 67, 285–9, 291; libel suits and, 33, 116, 285–8,

290, 311–12; religious identity and, 22–3, 71–2, 246–7, 250–2, 264, 295–9, 304–5, 311, 314
Sandow, Eugene, 301
Sanj Vartaman (newspaper), 278, 291–3
Sarbah, John Mensah, 11
Sasanian law, 16, 137–8, 142, 148
Satya Mitra (newspaper), 278, 281
Savigny, Friedrich Karl von, 163–4
The School of Athens (Raphael), 1
Scotland, 148, 225. *See also* Wilson, John
Secunderabad case, 245–9
Seervai H. M. 111
Seervai, Kaikhushru 44
Servai, A. E., 96, 96n63
Sethna, Phiroze C., 93–4
sexuality: intercommunity sex and, 82n285, 291–6; Orientalism and, 170–3, 178–87, 248–9; racial purity and, 176, 285–304; reputational concerns and, 30, 61–71, 82–3, 279–84; sexual diversity and, 70, 82, 82n284, 165–70, 173–8, 188, 191–2, 209, 216–17, 300. *See also* families; gender; matrimonial law; religion
Shah Nameh (epic), 73, 304
Shakespeare, William, 70n215
Shavaksha, K. S., 115
Sheffield, Daniel, 17n75, 76n237
Shirinbai, Bai v. Masalavala, 139, 184, 209
Shodhan, Amrita, 146
Shroff, Behram, 306
Sidhwa, Rustom K., 27
Sikh Gurdwaras Act (Punjab Act VIII of 1925), 122–3
Sikhs, 122–3, 130, 139
Singapore, 3, 84, 117
Slezkine, Yuri, 118
smoking, 15, 311. *See also* purity laws
Social Purity League, 282
Soonawalla, E. R., 261–4
Sorabji, Cornelia, 170
Sorabji, Soli, 111
Special Marriages Act (III of 1872), 97–8, 259
Spencer, Herbert, 300
Spiegel, Friedrich, 20
spleen (defense of enlarged), 53
Stanley, Henry M., 105
Statesman, 308
Stausberg, Michael, 117n201
Stern, Steve, 240
Stokes, Whitley, 87

342   *Index*

Story, Joseph, 152
Strangman, Thomas, 51, 101, 249
Stree Zarthosti Mandal (Bombay), 168n12
Succession to Parsees Immovable Property Act
  (IX of 1837), 25, 86, 150, 317
Sudder Dewanny Adawlut, 45–6, 91, 145
sufism, 63
Sunjana, Nowrojee Shapoorjee, 284–5
Supreme Court of India, 54–5
Surti v. Perozbai, 162

Talati brothers, 117n201
Taleyarkhan, Manekshah Jehangirshah, 100,
  108
Tarachand, J. K., 266–7
Tarachand v. Soonabai, 58, 62, 170, 250, 260,
  264, 266–8, 270
Taraporevala, D. B., 115
Taraporewala, Vikaji Fardunji, 101, 213
Tata, D. E., 285
Tata, J. N., 213
Teland, Kasinath Trimbak, 12
Tilak, Bal Gangadhar, 253
Times of India, 38, 101, 117, 177, 279,
  292–3, 301
Toddyvala, Dinbai and Erachshaw, 43,
  227–32
towers of silence (*dakhmas*), 29, 246–9, 260,
  316. *See also* death rites (Zoroastrian)
Travers, Robert, 131, 131n22
Trevelyan, Charles, 105
trust suits, 57–8, 72–3, 138, 146–7, 235, 240–9,
  252–73
Tupper, Charles L., 206
Tweedie, J., 207
Tyabji, Badruddin, 12, 118, 250
Tyabji, Faiz B., 121

Uniform Civil Code, 89, 95–6, 171n24. *See also*
  India; personal law
United States, 5, 59n137, 80,
  171, 215, 218n171, 262n125, 275,
  285n60. *See also* New York Court of
  Common Pleas
Unwalla, Bhikaji Dinyarji, 294n98

Vachha, P. B., 115, 139, 280
Vaju, Hirabai, 229
Vakeel, F. A., 93
Vakil, K. B., 95
Vakil, Rustom, 146n120
vakils (or pleaders), 8, 91, 110–11

Vendidad (text), 75, 138, 138n68, 182
venereal disease, 176–7, 190, 217, 242
Victoria (Queen), 47
Vimadalal, Jehangir J., 33, 61, 109, 176, 251–2,
  297–9, 301, 304–5
Vinayapitakam (text), 134
violence, 41, 65, 187–92, 217, 219–20, 224,
  232, 242
virginity, 225, 227, 283. *See also* medical
  experts and evidence
vultures, 16, 60, 78, 244–9, 271. *See also* death
  rites (Zoroastrian); towers of silence
  (*dakhmas*)

Wacha, Dinshah, 19, 176
Wadia, A. R., 176–7, 297
Wadia, B. J., 93, 302
Wadia, Framjee Dosabhoy C., 245
Wadia, Hormusji, 80
Wadia, P. A., 305
Wadia, Sorab P. N., 197, 202
Wadia Ghandy and Co., 110, 117, 139
N. M. Wadia Trust, 260
Warden, Francis, 80
Warden, Hormusji Framji, 261–2
Watts, George Frederic, 1–3, *3*
Widow Remarriage Act (XV of 1856),
  122, 167
Wiggins and Stevens (firm), 117n201
Williams, Rina Verma, 47
wills, 31, 140–52, 157, 235, 264–6,
  316. *See also* cy-près doctrine; inheritance
  law; intestacy (law of); *muktad* trusts;
  perpetuities (rule against)
Wills Ordinance of 1844 (Ceylon), 142
Wilson, John, 20
Women's Indian Association, 168n12
World Wars I and II, 102, 176, 216–17,
  226–7, 303

Yahaya, Nurfadzilah, 264

Zanzibar, 42, 117
Zarathustra, 3, 12, *13*
Zerbadis, 298, 298n121
Zoroastrian Brotherhood, 189
Zoroastrian Conference, 251, 289, 292
Zoroastrianism: cosmology and theology of,
  14–15, 71–2, 267–8; legal codes of, 1,
  72–5, 136–8, 142; marriage and divorce
  law and, 63, 165–7, 180–3, 193,
  210–36; mysticism and, 306–12; priests'

Index

343

roles in, 15, 74, 75–6, 76n237, 77–8, 172, 283–5; racial and ethnic identity and, 12–23, 67, 230, 274–7, 285–8, 296–312; reformist and orthodox conflicts in, 21, 25, 166–8, 178–9, 218, 230, 240–9, 249n56, 252–70, 285–9, 304–12; religious orthodoxy in, 17, 68, 231, 254–7; religious trusts and, 28, 31, 72–3, 77–81, 96–7, 142–7, 239–49, 252–73. *See also* asha; families; law; Parsis; purity laws; religion; *specific cases*; *specific cases and texts*

For EU product safety concerns, contact us at Calle de José Abascal, 56–1°,
28003 Madrid, Spain or eugpsr@cambridge.org

www.ingramcontent.com/pod-product-compliance
Ingram Content Group UK Ltd.
Pitfield, Milton Keynes, MK11 3LW, UK
UKHW011325060825
461487UK00005B/354